Learning Constitutional Law

First Edition

Learning Constitutional Law

Leslie C. Griffin
University of Nevada, Las Vegas,
Boyd School of Law

Marci A. Hamilton
University of Pennsylvania

cognella
SAN DIEGO

Bassim Hamadeh, CEO and Publisher
Kristina Stolte, Senior Field Acquisitions Editor
Susana Christie, Deelopmental Editor
Michelle Piehl, Senior Project Editor
Jeanine Rees Production Editor
Kim Scott, Graphic Designer
Alexa Lucido, Licensing Manager
Natalie Piccotti, Director of Marketing
Kassie Graves, Vice President of Editorial
Jamie Giganti, Director of Academic Publishing

Printed in the United States of America.

cognella® | ACADEMIC PUBLISHING
3970 Sorrento Valley Blvd., Ste. 500, San Diego, CA 92121

Brief Contents

Detailed Contents

One

Article III: The Court

Introduction

This chapter introduces the Supreme Court's power to render the last word on the meaning of the Constitution and the limits on which cases it and the federal courts may decide. The Constitution creates a common law system, where federal courts are constrained to decide the case in front of them, which is distinct from the civil law countries, where the courts have the power to decide broad constitutional issues that extend beyond the particular case they are deciding. You will learn about (1) the requirement that federal cases must involve a case or controversy; (2) the requirement of standing as a prerequisite to file a case in the federal system; and (3) the political question doctrine, which is intended to remove the Court from political disputes. Each case in this chapter draws boundary lines between cases the federal courts may hear and those they may not.

What Justices currently serve on the Supreme Court of the United States? Beyond the Supreme Court, what other courts are in the federal system?

Read the following parts of Article III of the Constitution.

> Section 1.
>
> The judicial power of the United States, shall be vested in one Supreme Court, and in such inferior courts as the Congress may from time to time ordain and establish. The judges, both of the supreme and inferior courts, shall hold their offices during good behaviour, and shall, at stated times, receive for their services, a compensation, which shall not be diminished during their continuance in office.
>
> Section 2.
>
> The judicial power shall extend to all cases, in law and equity, arising under this Constitution, the laws of the United States, and treaties made, or which shall be made, under their authority; to all cases affecting ambassadors, other public ministers and consuls; to all cases of admiralty and maritime jurisdiction; to controversies to which the United States shall be a party; to controversies between two or more states; between

a state and citizens of another state; between citizens of different states; between citizens of the same state claiming lands under grants of different states, and between a state, or the citizens thereof, and foreign states, citizens or subjects.

In all cases affecting ambassadors, other public ministers and consuls, and those in which a state shall be party, the Supreme Court shall have original jurisdiction. In all the other cases before mentioned, the Supreme Court shall have appellate jurisdiction, both as to law and fact, with such exceptions, and under such regulations as the Congress shall make.

In these Sections, Article III is assigning and limiting jurisdiction for all federal courts. When can a federal court hear a case? What is a "case" as opposed to a "controversy"? When does a controversy begin and end? Based on the language of Article III Sections 1 and 2, can the Supreme Court hear the following cases? Why or why not? Consider these hypotheticals before you read *Marbury v. Madison* below. Which ones are appropriate for Supreme Court review and which aren't?

1. A pregnant woman brings a lawsuit to invoke her right to obtain an abortion, but the case gets to the Supreme Court after her pregnancy has ended. Yes_______ No_______
2. Plaintiffs ask for a judgment that a law limiting federal government employees' involvement in political campaigns is illegal because it might harm them in the future. Yes_______ No_______
3. Congress asks the Supreme Court to give them a ruling on whether a law they are considering is constitutional. Yes_______ No_______
4. Parents of Black public school children sue the Internal Revenue Service for its lax policies that are being employed to grant tax-exempt status to racially discriminatory private schools. Yes_______ No_______
5. Voters arguing over the result of an election allege that results are determined by district, not individual votes. So, one district with 1,000 voters counts the same as one district with 100,000 voters. Yes_______ No_______

A. The Court Hears Cases and Controversies

The following case, *Marbury v. Madison*, is remembered as the very famous proceeding in which the Supreme Court explained both why it had jurisdiction over cases *and* why it could declare some congressional legislation unconstitutional. In this case, President John Adams named justices of the peace to the District of Columbia courts before the next presidential election, which he lost to Thomas Jefferson. The Senate advised and consented to the appointments. Under typical practice, the judicial "commissions" had to be delivered by the Secretary of State. Secretary James Marshall, however, did not deliver all the commissions before Adams stepped down. As a result, William Marbury and other judges chosen by Adams did not take their Judicial seats. They sued the Jefferson administration, asking the Court to order the new Secretary of State Madison to give them their positions in a mandamus order. The lower courts had refused to order Madison to deliver the commissions.

A threshold question in this case was whether the Supreme Court could even interpret the Constitution and what a Supreme Court ruling meant. Do you agree with the Court's reasoning? Why or why not? Do you agree it is a very important case or think it is not very important? Why? Do you think this video gives a good presentation of the case's meaning? See Quimbee's presentation, *Marbury v. Madison* Case Brief Summary/Law Case Explained, Aug. 27, 2015, posted at https://www.youtube.com/watch?v=hjVAGF-N8oQ&list=PLsFE_Nvl6h_Y75KGR5pkGqcFisGvBnO9S&index=2.

Marbury v. Madison

SUPREME COURT OF THE UNITED STATES, 1803

1 Cranch 137, 5 U.S. 137

Mr. Chief Justice MARSHALL delivered the opinion of the Court.

...

In the order in which the court has viewed this subject, the following questions have been considered and decided.

1st. Has the applicant a right to the commission he demands?

2dly. If he has a right, and that right has been violated, do the laws of his country afford him a remedy?

3dly. If they do afford him a remedy, is it a *mandamus* issuing from this court?

The first object of inquiry is,

1st. Has the applicant a right to the commission he demands?

...

It is therefore decidedly the opinion of the court, that when a commission has been signed by the President, the appointment is made; and that the commission is complete, when the seal of the United States has been affixed to it by the secretary of state.

...

Mr. Marbury, then, since his commission was signed by the President, and sealed by the secretary of state, was appointed; and as the law creating the office, gave the officer a right to hold for five years, independent of the executive, the appointment was not revocable; but vested in the officer legal rights, which are protected by the laws of this country.

To withhold his commission, therefore, is an act deemed by the court not warranted by law, but violative of a vested legal right.

This brings us to the second inquiry; which is,

2dly. If he has a right, and that right has been violated, do the laws of this country afford him a remedy?

The very essence of civil liberty certainly consists in the right of every individual to claim the protection of the laws, whenever he receives an injury.

...

It follows then that the question, whether the legality of an act of the head of a department be examinable in a court of justice or not, must always depend on the nature of that act.

If some acts be examinable, and others not, there must be some rule of law to guide the court in the exercise of its jurisdiction.

In some instances there may be difficulty in applying the rule to particular cases; but there cannot, it is believed, be much difficulty in laying down the rule.

By the constitution of the United States, the President is invested with certain important political powers, in the exercise of which he is to use his own discretion, and is accountable only to his country in his political character, and to his own conscience. To aid him in the performance of these duties, he is authorized to appoint certain officers, who act by his authority and in conformity with his orders.

In such cases, their acts are his acts; and whatever opinion may be entertained of the manner in which executive discretion may be used, still there exists, and can exist, no power to control that discretion. The subjects are political. They respect the nation, not individual rights, and being entrusted to the executive, the decision of the executive is conclusive. The application of this remark will be perceived by adverting to the act of congress for establishing the department of foreign affairs. This officer, as his duties were prescribed by that act, is to conform precisely to the will of the President. He is the mere organ by whom that will is communicated. The acts of such an officer, as an officer, can never be examinable by the courts.

But when the legislature proceeds to impose on that officer other duties; when he is directed peremptorily to perform certain acts; when the rights of individuals are dependent on the performance of those acts; he is so far the officer of the law; is amenable to the laws for his conduct; and cannot at his discretion sport away the vested rights of others.

The conclusion from this reasoning is, that where the heads of departments are the political or confidential agents of the executive, merely to execute the will of the President, or rather to act in cases in which the executive possesses a constitutional or legal discretion, nothing can be more perfectly clear than that their acts are only politically examinable. But where a specific duty is assigned by law, and individual rights depend upon the performance of that duty, it seems equally clear that the individual who considers himself injured, has a right to resort to the laws of his country for a remedy.

If this be the rule, let us enquire how it applies to the case under the consideration of the court.

...

The question whether a right has vested or not, is, in its nature, judicial, and must be tried by the judicial authority. If, for example, Mr. Marbury had taken the oaths of a magistrate, and proceeded to act as one; in consequence of which a suit had been instituted against him, in which his defense had depended on his being a magistrate; the validity of his appointment must have been determined by judicial authority.

So, if he conceives that, by virtue of his appointment, he has a legal right, either to the commission which has been made out for him, or to a copy of that commission, it is equally a question examinable in a court, and the decision of the court upon it must depend on the opinion entertained of his appointment.

That question has been discussed, and the opinion is, that the latest point of time which can be taken as that at which the appointment was complete, and evidenced, was when, after the signature of the president, the seal of the United States was affixed to the commission.

It is then the opinion of the court,

1st. That by signing the commission of Mr. Marbury, the president of the United States appointed him a justice of peace, for the county of Washington in the district of Columbia; and that the seal of the United States, affixed thereto by the secretary of state, is conclusive testimony of the verity of the signature, and of the completion of the appointment; and that the appointment conferred on him a legal right to the office for the space of five years.

2dly. That, having this legal title to the office, he has a consequent right to the commission; a refusal to deliver which, is a plain violation of that right, for which the laws of his country afford him a remedy.

It remains to be inquired whether,

3dly. He is entitled to the remedy for which he applies. This depends on,

1st. The nature of the writ applied for, and,

2dly. The power of this court.

1st. The nature of the writ.

...

The doctrine, therefore, now advanced, is by no means a novel one.

It is true that the mandamus, now moved for, is not for the performance of an act expressly enjoined by statute.

It is to deliver a commission; on which subject the acts of Congress are silent. This difference is not considered as affecting the case. It has already been stated that the applicant has, to that commission, a vested legal right, of which the executive cannot deprive him. He has been appointed to an office, from which he is not removable, at the will of the executive; and being so appointed, he has a right to the commission which the secretary has received from the president for his use. The act of congress does not indeed order the secretary of state to send it to him, but it is placed in his hands for the person entitled to it; and cannot be more lawfully withheld by him, than by any other person.

...

This, then, is a plain case for a mandamus, either to deliver the commission, or a copy of it from the record; and it only remains to be inquired,

Whether it can issue from this court.

The act to establish the judicial courts of the United States authorizes the supreme court "to issue writs of mandamus, in cases warranted by the principles and usages of law, to any courts appointed, or persons holding office, under the authority of the United States."

The secretary of state, being a person holding an office under the authority of the United States, is precisely within the letter of the description; and if this court is not authorized to issue a writ of mandamus to such an officer, it must be because the law is unconstitutional, and therefore absolutely incapable of conferring the authority, and assigning the duties which its words purport to confer and assign.

The constitution vests the whole judicial power of the United States in one supreme court, and such inferior courts as congress shall, from time to time, ordain and establish. This power is expressly extended to all cases arising under the laws of the United States;

and consequently, in some form, may be exercised over the present case; because the right claimed is given by a law of the United States.

In the distribution of this power it is declared that "the supreme court shall have original jurisdiction in all cases affecting ambassadors, other public ministers and consuls, and those in which a state shall be a party. In all other cases, the supreme court shall have appellate jurisdiction."

It has been insisted, at the bar, that as the original grant of jurisdiction, to the supreme and inferior courts, is general, and the clause, assigning original jurisdiction to the supreme court, contains no negative or restrictive words; the power remains to the legislature, to assign original jurisdiction to that court in other cases than those specified in the article which has been recited; provided those cases belong to the judicial power of the United States.

If it had been intended to leave it in the discretion of the legislature to apportion the judicial power between the supreme and inferior courts according to the will of that body, it would certainly have been useless to have proceeded further than to have defined the judicial power, and the tribunals in which it should be vested. The subsequent part of the section is mere surplusage, is entirely without meaning, if such is to be the construction. If congress remains at liberty to give this court appellate jurisdiction, where the constitution has declared their jurisdiction shall be original; and original jurisdiction where the constitution has declared it shall be appellate; the distribution of jurisdiction, made in the constitution, is form without substance.

Affirmative words are often, in their operation, negative of other objects than those affirmed; and in this case, a negative or exclusive sense must be given to them or they have no operation at all.

It cannot be presumed that any clause in the constitution is intended to be without effect; and therefore such a construction is inadmissible, unless the words require it.

If the solicitude of the convention, respecting our peace with foreign powers, induced a provision that the supreme court should take original jurisdiction in cases which might be supposed to affect them; yet the clause would have proceeded no further than to provide for such cases, if no further restriction on the powers of congress had been intended. That they should have appellate jurisdiction in all other cases, with such exceptions as congress might make, is no restriction; unless the words be deemed exclusive of original jurisdiction.

When an instrument organizing fundamentally a judicial system, divides it into one supreme, and so many inferior courts as the legislature may ordain and establish; then enumerates its powers, and proceeds so far to distribute them, as to define the jurisdiction of the supreme court by declaring the cases in which it shall take original jurisdiction, and that in others it shall take appellate jurisdiction; the plain import of the words seems to be, that in one class of cases its jurisdiction is original, and not appellate; in the other it is appellate, and not original. If any other construction would render the clause inoperative, that is an additional reason for rejecting such other construction, and for adhering to their obvious meaning.

To enable this court then to issue a mandamus, it must be shewn to be an exercise of appellate jurisdiction, or to be necessary to enable them to exercise appellate jurisdiction.

It has been stated at the bar that the appellate jurisdiction may be exercised in a variety of forms, and that if it be the will of the legislature that a mandamus should be used for that purpose, that will must be obeyed. This is true, yet the jurisdiction must be appellate, not original.

It is the essential criterion of appellate jurisdiction, that it revises and corrects the proceedings in a cause already instituted, and does not create that cause. Although, therefore, a mandamus may be directed to courts, yet to issue such a writ to an officer for the delivery of a paper, is in effect the same as to sustain an original action for that paper, and therefore seems not to belong to appellate, but to original jurisdiction. Neither is it necessary in such a case as this, to enable the court to exercise its appellate jurisdiction.

The authority, therefore, given to the supreme court, by the act establishing the judicial courts of the United States, to issue writs of mandamus to public officers, appears not to be warranted by the constitution; and it becomes necessary to enquire whether a jurisdiction, so conferred, can be exercised.

The question, whether an act, repugnant to the constitution, can become the law of the land, is a question deeply interesting to the United States; but, happily, not of an intricacy proportioned to its interest. It seems only necessary to recognize certain principles, supposed to have been long and well established, to decide it.

That the people have an original right to establish, for their future government, such principles as, in their opinion, shall most conduce to their own happiness, is the basis, on which the whole American fabric has been erected. The exercise of this original right is a very great exertion; nor can it, nor ought it to be frequently repeated. The principles, therefore, so established, are deemed fundamental. And as the authority, from which they proceed, is supreme, and can seldom act, they are designed to be permanent.

This original and supreme will organizes the government, and assigns, to different departments, their respective powers. It may either stop here; or establish certain limits not to be transcended by those departments.

The government of the United States is of the latter description. The powers of the legislature are defined, and limited; and that those limits may not be mistaken, or forgotten, the constitution is written. To what purpose are powers limited, and to what purpose is that limitation committed to writing, if these limits may, at any time, be passed by those intended to be restrained? The distinction, between a government with limited and unlimited powers, is abolished, if those limits do not confine the persons on whom they are imposed, and if acts prohibited and acts allowed, are of equal obligation. It is a proposition too plain to be contested, that the constitution controls any legislative act repugnant to it; or, that the legislature may alter the constitution by an ordinary act.

Between these alternatives there is no middle ground. The constitution is either a superior, paramount law, unchangeable by ordinary means, or it is on a level with ordinary legislative acts, and like other acts, is alterable when the legislature shall please to alter it.

If the former part of the alternative be true, then a legislative act contrary to the constitution is not law: if the latter part be true, then written constitutions are absurd attempts, on the part of the people, to limit a power, in its own nature illimitable.

Certainly all those who have framed written constitutions contemplate them as forming the fundamental and paramount law of the nation, and consequently the theory of every such government must be, that an act of the legislature, repugnant to the constitution, is void.

This theory is essentially attached to a written constitution, and is consequently to be considered, by this court, as one of the fundamental principles of our society. It is not therefore to be lost sight of in the further consideration of this subject.

If an act of the legislature, repugnant to the constitution, is void, does it, notwithstanding its invalidity, bind the courts, and oblige them to give it effect? Or, in other words, though it be not law, does it constitute a rule as operative as if it was a law? This would be to overthrow in fact what was established in theory; and would seem, at first view, an absurdity too gross to be insisted on. It shall, however, receive a more attentive consideration.

It is emphatically the province and duty of the judicial department to say what the law is. Those who apply the rule to particular cases, must of necessity expound and interpret that rule. If two laws conflict with each other, the courts must decide on the operation of each.

So if a law be in opposition to the constitution; if both the law and the constitution apply to a particular case, so that the court must either decide that case conformably to the law, disregarding the constitution; or conformably to the constitution, disregarding the law; the court must determine which of these conflicting rules governs the case. This is of the very essence of judicial duty.

If then the courts are to regard the constitution; and the constitution is superior to any ordinary act of the legislature; the constitution, and not such ordinary act, must govern the case to which they both apply.

Those then who controvert the principle that the constitution is to be considered, in court, as a paramount law, are reduced to the necessity of maintaining that courts must close their eyes on the constitution, and see only the law.

This doctrine would subvert the very foundation of all written constitutions. It would declare that an act, which, according to the principles and theory of our government, is entirely void; is yet, in practice, completely obligatory. It would declare, that if the legislature shall do what is expressly forbidden, such act, notwithstanding the express prohibition, is in reality effectual. It would be giving to the legislature a practical and real omnipotence, with the same breath which professes to restrict their powers within narrow limits. It is prescribing limits, and declaring that those limits may be passed as pleasure.

That it thus reduces to nothing what we have deemed the greatest improvement on political institutions—a written constitution—would of itself be sufficient, in America, where written constitutions have been viewed with so much reverence, for rejecting the construction. But the peculiar expressions of the constitution of the United States furnish additional arguments in favour of its rejection.

The judicial power of the United States is extended to all cases arising under the constitution.

Could it be the intention of those who gave this power, to say that, in using it, the constitution should not be looked into? That a case arising under the constitution should be decided without examining the instrument under which it arises?

This is too extravagant to be maintained.

...

It is also not entirely unworthy of observation, that in declaring what shall be the *supreme* law of the land, the *constitution* itself is first mentioned; and not the laws of the United States generally, but those only which shall be made in *pursuance* of the constitution, have that rank.

Thus, the particular phraseology of the constitution of the United States confirms and strengthens the principle, supposed to be essential to all written constitutions, that a law repugnant to the constitution is void; and that *courts,* as well as other departments, are bound by that instrument.

The rule must be discharged.

Notes and Questions

1. *The power of the Court.* The Supreme Court has determined in *Marbury* that it has the power to interpret the Constitution and to be the last word on it. Is that a sheer power grab or required to separate power between the branches?
2. *How did you answer the following before you read* Marbury*?* Here is how the five issues listed before the case have been addressed by the courts. Which one(s) surprise you, if any?
   a. A pregnant woman brings a lawsuit to invoke her right to an abortion, but the case gets to the Supreme Court after her pregnancy has ended. "Moot" cases are dismissed when they are no longer an active case or controversy. The state argued that Jane Roe's case should be dismissed as moot because she was no longer pregnant. The Court allowed the case to proceed because the issue of pregnancy was "capable of repetition, yet evading review." *Roe v. Wade*, 410 U.S. 113 (1973).
   b. Plaintiffs ask for a judgment that a law limiting federal government employees' involvement in political campaigns is illegal because it might harm them in the future. Cases must be "*ripe*" if they are to be heard in court. If the injury has not yet occurred, the court may say the issue is not ripe for review. In a challenge to the Hatch Act, which prevents federal employees from participating in political campaigns, the employees argued that the law violated their First Amendment rights. The case could not proceed until the issue was ripe. *United Public Workers v. Mitchell*, 330 U.S. 75 (1947).
   c. Congress asks the Supreme Court to give them a ruling on whether a law it is considering is constitutional. The Court must hear live cases and controversies. It is not allowed to write essays about theoretical laws. Such an essay would be an *advisory opinion.* U.S. courts do not issue advisory opinions; they resolve cases.
   d. Parents of Black public school children sue the Internal Revenue Service for its lax policies that are being employed to grant tax-exempt status to racially discriminatory private schools. In this case, *Allen v. Wright,* 468 U.S. 737 (1984), the Court said that the plaintiff parents did not have "standing" to bring the case. You will see below that every person in court must have standing. Why do you think that is?
   e. Voters arguing over the result of an election allege that results are determined by district, not individual votes. So, one district with 1,000 voters counts the same as one district with

100,000 voters. Should this be viewed as a political question that the courts cannot hear or as a legal question that fits the jurisdiction of the federal courts? The Court heard this case, ruling the election must be decided by the count of individual voters, not by unequal district size vote. "One person, one vote" means the individuals' votes must be counted, and that unequal size districts could not get equal votes. *Reynolds v. Sims,* 377 U.S. 533 (1964).

3. *The first Chief Justice and his legacy.* Chief Justice John Marshall's name was removed from the law school at the University of Illinois at Chicago. A school task force concluded Marshall was a slave owner and a slave trader, and, therefore, it was inappropriate for a law school to bear his name. The school's name will change from UIC John Marshall Law School to UI-Chicago School of Law. The task force said despite Marshall's legacy "as one of the nation's most significant U.S. Supreme Court justices, the newly discovered research regarding his role as a slave trader, slave owner of hundreds of slaves, pro-slavery jurisprudence, and racist views render him a highly inappropriate namesake for the law school." AP Staff, UIC law school to drop John Marshall name, citing former chief justice's slaveholding, racist views, Chicago Tribune, May 24, 2021. What do you think of this decision? What does it tell you about John Marshall? Who is the audience for a law school's name?
4. *What about state court review of federal constitutional questions? Martin v. Hunter's Lessee,* 14 U.S. 304 (1816). Virginia residents and Virginia courts made decisions about property ownership, ruling that property owned by Loyalists to Britain should be returned to Virginia ownership. A federal treaty had different rules. Virginia argued that the Supreme Court should have nothing to say to them about this Virginia decision about Virginia law. The Supreme Court ruled that the federal courts have power to review state court decisions about federal law or the Constitution. Why?
5. *What about federal courts deciding cases involving state law? Cohens v. Virginia,* 19 U.S. 264 (1821). The Cohen brothers sold DC lottery tickets in the State of Virginia and violated Virginia criminal law. The state courts ruled they had the final authority over the Cohens's conviction. The Supreme Court unanimously ruled that the federal courts had power to review state criminal proceedings. They could review any state laws and constitutions and decide whether they violate the federal constitution. The Supreme Court upheld the rulings of the Virginia court. Why do you think the Court ruled that way?

B. Parties Need Standing to Get into Court

The Court has repeatedly explained that parties must have standing in order to have their cases heard in federal court. There are three factors that are *always* required for standing: 1) injury; 2) causation; and 3) redressability.

1. The Injury Needed to Justify Standing

Before you read the following opinion, read through the oral argument in the case, available on the case's website, https://www.oyez.org/cases/1983/81-757. What were the hardest questions asked by the Justices? Were there any easy questions? Which Justice was the best questioner?

The Court ruled that the plaintiffs did *not* have standing in the following case. Why not? Do you agree with the majority or with the dissent? Does the Court welcome too many people into court? Or too few? What role did racial justice play in the opinion? Does this video help you to understand the case? See Quimbee's *Allen v. Wright* Case Brief Summary/Law Case Explained, Mar. 2, 2016, posted at https://www.youtube.com/watch?v=AN93d-yD_p0&list=PLsFE_Nvl6h_Y75KGR5pkGqcFisGvBnO9S&index=6&t=3s.

Allen v. Wright

SUPREME COURT OF THE UNITED STATES, 1984

468 U.S. 737, 104 S.Ct. 3315

O'CONNOR, J., delivered the opinion of the Court, in which BURGER, C.J., and WHITE, POWELL, and REHNQUIST, JJ., joined. BRENNAN, J., filed a dissenting opinion. STEVENS, J., filed a dissenting opinion, in which BLACKMUN, J., joined. MARSHALL, J., took no part in the decision of the cases.

Justice O'CONNOR delivered the opinion of the Court.

Parents of black public school children allege in this nation-wide class action that the Internal Revenue Service (IRS) has not adopted sufficient standards and procedures to fulfill its obligation to deny tax-exempt status to racially discriminatory private schools. They assert that the IRS thereby harms them directly and interferes with the ability of their children to receive an education in desegregated public schools. The issue before us is whether plaintiffs have standing to bring this suit. We hold that they do not.

I

The IRS denied tax-exempt status ... hence eligibility to receive charitable contributions deductible from income taxes ... to racially discriminatory private schools.

...

Respondents allege in their complaint that many racially segregated private schools were created or expanded in their communities at the time the public schools were undergoing desegregation. According to the complaint, many such private schools, including 17 schools or school systems identified by name in the complaint (perhaps some 30 schools in all), receive tax exemptions either directly or through the tax-exempt status of "umbrella" organizations that operate or support the schools. Respondents allege that, despite the IRS policy of denying tax-exempt status to racially discriminatory private schools and despite the IRS guidelines and procedures for implementing that policy, some of the tax-exempt racially segregated private schools created or expanded in desegregating districts in fact have racially discriminatory policies. Respondents allege that the IRS grant of tax exemptions to such racially discriminatory schools is unlawful.

Respondents allege that the challenged Government conduct harms them in two ways. The challenged conduct

> "(a) constitutes tangible federal financial aid and other support for racially segregated educational institutions, and
>
> "(b) fosters and encourages the organization, operation and expansion of institutions providing racially segregated educational opportunities for white children avoiding attendance in desegregating public school districts and thereby interferes with the efforts of federal courts, HEW and local school authorities to desegregate public school districts which have been operating racially dual school systems."

Thus, respondents do not allege that their children have been the victims of discriminatory exclusion from the schools whose tax exemptions they challenge as unlawful. Indeed, they have not alleged at any stage of this litigation that their children have ever applied or would ever apply to any private school. Rather, respondents claim a direct injury from the mere fact of the challenged Government conduct and, as indicated by the restriction of the plaintiff class to parents of children in desegregating school districts, injury to their children's opportunity to receive a desegregated education. The latter injury is traceable to the IRS grant of tax exemptions to racially discriminatory schools, respondents allege, chiefly because contributions to such schools are deductible from income taxes and the "deductions facilitate the raising of funds to organize new schools and expand existing schools in order to accommodate white students avoiding attendance in desegregating public school districts."

Respondents request only prospective relief. They ask for a declaratory judgment that the challenged IRS tax-exemption practices are unlawful. They also ask for an injunction requiring the IRS to deny tax exemptions to a considerably broader class of private schools than the class of racially discriminatory private schools. Under the requested injunction, the IRS would have to deny tax-exempt status to all private schools "which have insubstantial or nonexistent minority enrollments, which are located in or serve desegregating public school districts, and which either—

> "(1) were established or expanded at or about the time the public school districts in which they are located or which they serve were desegregating;
>
> "(2) have been determined in adversary judicial or administrative proceedings to be racially segregated; or
>
> "(3) cannot demonstrate that they do not provide racially segregated educational opportunities for white children avoiding attendance in desegregating public school systems. ..."

Finally, respondents ask for an order directing the IRS to replace its 1975 guidelines with standards consistent with the requested injunction.

...

II

...

The case-or-controversy doctrines state fundamental limits on federal judicial power in our system of government.

...

Respondents' first claim of injury can be interpreted in two ways. It might be a claim simply to have the Government avoid the violation of law alleged in respondents' complaint. Alternatively, it might be a claim of stigmatic injury, or denigration, suffered by all members of a racial group when the Government discriminates on the basis of race. Under neither interpretation is this claim of injury judicially cognizable.

...

The consequences of recognizing respondents' standing on the basis of their first claim of injury illustrate why our cases plainly hold that such injury is not judicially cognizable. If the abstract stigmatic injury were cognizable, standing would extend nationwide to all members of the particular racial groups against which the Government was alleged to be discriminating by its grant of a tax exemption to a racially discriminatory school, regardless of the location of that school. All such persons could claim the same sort of abstract stigmatic injury respondents assert in their first claim of injury. A black person in Hawaii could challenge the grant of a tax exemption to a racially discriminatory school in Maine. Recognition of standing in such circumstances would transform the federal courts into "no more than a vehicle for the vindication of the value interests of concerned bystanders." Constitutional limits on the role of the federal courts preclude such a transformation.

...

The diminished ability of respondents' children to receive a desegregated education would be fairly traceable to unlawful IRS grants of tax exemptions only if there were enough racially discriminatory private schools receiving tax exemptions in respondents' communities for withdrawal of those exemptions to make an appreciable difference in public school integration. Respondents have made no such allegation. It is, first, uncertain how many racially discriminatory private schools are in fact receiving tax exemptions. Moreover, it is entirely speculative, as respondents themselves conceded whether withdrawal of a tax exemption from any particular school would lead the school to change its policies. It is just as speculative whether any given parent of a child attending such a private school would decide to transfer the child to public school as a result of any changes in educational or financial policy made by the private school once it was threatened with loss of tax-exempt status. It is also pure speculation whether, in a particular community, a large enough number of the numerous relevant school officials and parents would reach decisions that collectively would have a significant impact on the racial composition of the public schools.

The links in the chain of causation between the challenged Government conduct and the asserted injury are far too weak for the chain as a whole to sustain respondents' standing. In Simon v. Eastern Kentucky Welfare Rights Org., supra, the Court held that standing to challenge a Government grant of a tax exemption to hospitals could not be founded on the asserted connection between the grant of tax-exempt status and the hospitals' policy concerning the provision of medical services to indigents. The causal connection depended on the decisions hospitals would make in response to withdrawal of tax-exempt status, and those decisions were sufficiently uncertain to break the chain of causation between the plaintiffs' injury and the challenged Government action. The chain of causation is even weaker in this case. It involves numerous third parties (officials of racially discriminatory schools receiving tax exemptions and the parents of children attending such schools) who may not even exist in respondents' communities and whose independent decisions may not collectively have a significant effect on the ability of public school students to receive a desegregated education.

The idea of separation of powers that underlies standing doctrine explains why our cases preclude the conclusion that respondents' alleged injury "fairly can be traced to the challenged action" of the IRS. That conclusion would pave the way generally for suits challenging, not specifically identifiable Government violations of law, but the particular programs agencies establish to carry out their legal obligations. Such suits, even when premised on allegations of several instances of violations of law, are rarely if ever appropriate for federal-court adjudication.

"Carried to its logical end, [respondents'] approach would have the federal courts as virtually continuing monitors of the wisdom and soundness of Executive action; such a role is appropriate for the Congress acting through its committees and the 'power of the purse'; it is not the role of the judiciary, absent actual present or immediately threatened injury resulting from unlawful governmental action."

...

III

"The necessity that the plaintiff who seeks to invoke judicial power stand to profit in some personal interest remains an Art. III requirement. Respondents have not met this fundamental requirement. The judgment of the Court of Appeals is accordingly reversed, and the injunction issued by that court is vacated.

It is so ordered.

...

Justice BRENNAN, dissenting.

...

The Court's attempt to obscure the standing question must be seen, therefore, as no more than a cover for its failure to recognize the nature of the specific claims raised by the respondents in these cases. By relying on generalities concerning our tripartite system of government, the Court is able to conclude that the respondents lack standing to maintain this action without acknowledging the precise nature of the injuries they have alleged. In so doing, the Court displays a startling insensitivity to the historical role played by the federal courts in eradicating race discrimination from our Nation's schools—a role that has played a prominent part in this Court's decisions from Brown v. Board of Education through Bob Jones University v. United States. Because I cannot join in such misguided decisionmaking, I dissent.

...

Viewed in light of the injuries they claim, the respondents have alleged a direct causal relationship between the Government action they challenge and the injury they suffer: their inability to receive an education in a racially integrated school is directly and adversely affected by the tax-exempt status granted by the IRS to racially discriminatory schools in their respective school districts. Common sense alone would recognize that the elimination of tax-exempt status for racially discriminatory private schools would serve to lessen the impact that those institutions have in defeating efforts to desegregate the public schools.

...

More than one commentator has noted that the causation component of the Court's standing inquiry is no more than a poor disguise for the Court's view of the merits of the underlying claims.[10] The Court today does nothing to avoid that criticism. What is most disturbing about today's decision, therefore, is not the standing analysis applied, but the indifference evidenced by the Court to the detrimental effects that racially segregated schools, supported by tax-exempt status from the Federal Government, have on the respondents' attempt to obtain an education in a racially integrated school system. I cannot join such indifference, and would give the respondents a chance to prove their case on the merits.

...

Justice STEVENS, with whom Justice BLACKMUN joins, dissenting.

...

In short, I would deal with the question of the legal limitations on the IRS's enforcement discretion on its merits, rather than by making the untenable assumption that the granting of preferential tax treatment to segregated schools does not make those schools more attractive to white students and hence does not inhibit the process of desegregation. I respectfully dissent.

Notes and Questions

1. *Standing vs. the merits.* Court observers have long argued over the standing doctrine. Standing is supposed to be a question of "justiciability," which determines only whether courts have jurisdiction to hear a case. It is not a ruling on the merits of the case. Many people argue, however, that the Court is actually making a decision on the merits when it decides to dismiss a case for standing. Based on the written opinion, and not solely presuppositions divorced from the opinion, do you think that the *Allen* Court was using standing to avoid the substantive issues? Does the standing reasoning make sense in other contexts? How would you tell if a standing case was really about the merits?
2. *Injury.* What injury does a party need to have to get into the Court?

2. Standing vs. General Grievances

Justice Antonin Scalia cared a lot about standing. Scalia is the author of the following decision, *Lujan*. Can you anticipate the argument they would write from the discussion at the Court's oral argument, which you can read on the case's website, https://www.oyez.org/cases/1991/90-1424. As you can see from the list of Justices below, the Justices split on which sections of Scalia's opinion they would join. There are some Supreme Court decisions in which a chart showing who voted for what can be helpful:

TABLE 1.1

	Part I	Part II	Part III-A	Part III-B	Part IV
Harry Blackmun	✓				
Anthony Kennedy	✓	✓	✓		✓
Sandra Day O'Connor	✓				
William Rehnquist	✓	✓	✓	✓	✓
Antonin Scalia	✓	✓	✓	✓	✓
David Souter	✓	✓	✓		✓
John P. Stevens	✓	✓			✓
Clarence Thomas	✓	✓	✓	✓	✓
Byron White	✓	✓	✓	✓	✓

Why were there so many different perspectives in this opinion? Does the oral argument predict how the Justices would vote? Which opinion is the most persuasive? How much of the reasoning in the written opinions could you predict from the oral argument?

Lujan v. Defenders of Wildlife

SUPREME COURT OF THE UNITED STATES, 1992

504 U.S. 555

SCALIA, J., announced the judgment of the Court and delivered the opinion of the Court with respect to Parts I, II, III-A, and IV, in which REHNQUIST, C. J., and WHITE, KENNEDY, SOUTER, and THOMAS, JJ., joined, and an opinion with respect to Part III-B, in which REHNQUIST, C. J., and WHITE and

THOMAS, JJ., joined. KENNEDY, J., filed an opinion concurring in part and concurring in the judgment, in which SOUTER, J., joined. STEVENS, J., filed an opinion concurring in the judgment. BLACKMUN, J., filed a dissenting opinion, in which O'CONNOR, J., joined.

Justice SCALIA:

This case involves a challenge to a rule promulgated by the Secretary of the Interior interpreting § 7 of the Endangered Species Act of 1973 (ESA) in such fashion as to render it applicable only to actions within the United States or on the high seas. The preliminary issue, and the only one we reach, is whether respondents here, plaintiffs below, have standing to seek judicial review of the rule. ... respondents, organizations dedicated to wildlife conservation and other environmental causes, filed this action against the Secretary of the Interior, seeking a declaratory judgment that the new regulation is in error as to the geographic scope of § 7(a)(2) and an injunction requiring the Secretary to promulgate a new regulation restoring the initial interpretation. ...

II

...

Over the years, our cases have established that the irreducible constitutional minimum of standing contains three elements. First, the plaintiff must have suffered an "injury in fact"—an invasion of a legally protected interest which is (a) concrete and particularized, and (b) "actual or imminent, not 'conjectural' or 'hypothetical.'" Second, there must be a causal connection between the injury and the conduct complained of—the injury has to be "fairly ... trace[able] to the challenged action of the defendant, and not ... th[e] result [of] the independent action of some third party not before the court." Third, it must be "likely," as opposed to merely "speculative," that the injury will be "redressed by a favorable decision."

...

III [A]

...

To survive the Secretary's summary judgment motion, respondents had to submit affidavits or other evidence showing, through specific facts, not only that listed species were in fact being threatened by funded activities abroad, but also that one or more of respondents' members would thereby be "directly" affected apart from their "'special interest' in th[e] subject."

With respect to this aspect of the case, the Court of Appeals focused on the affidavits of two Defenders' members—Joyce Kelly and Amy Skilbred. Ms. Kelly stated that she traveled to Egypt in 1986 and "observed the traditional habitat of the endangered nile crocodile there and intend[s] to do so again, and hope[s] to observe the crocodile directly," and that she "will suffer harm in fact as the result of [the] American ... role ... in overseeing the rehabilitation of the Aswan High Dam on the Nile ... and [in] develop[ing] ... Egypt's ... Master Water Plan." App. 101. Ms. Skilbred averred that she traveled to Sri Lanka in 1981 and "observed th[e] habitat" of "endangered species such as the Asian elephant and the leopard" at what is now the site of the Mahaweli project funded by the Agency for International Development (AID), although she "was unable to see any of the endangered species"; "this development project," she continued, "will seriously reduce endangered, threatened, and endemic species habitat including areas that I visited ... [, which] may severely shorten the future of these species"; that threat, she concluded, harmed her because she "intend[s] to return to Sri Lanka in the future and hope[s] to be more fortunate in spotting at least the endangered elephant and leopard." When Ms. Skilbred was asked at a subsequent deposition if and when she had any plans to return to Sri Lanka, she reiterated that "I intend to go back to Sri Lanka," but confessed that she had no current plans: "I don't know [when]. There is a civil war going on right now. I don't know. Not next year, I will say. In the future."

We shall assume for the sake of argument that these affidavits contain facts showing that certain agency-funded projects threaten listed species—though that is questionable. They plainly contain no facts, however, showing how damage to the species will produce "imminent" injury to Mses. Kelly and Skilbred. ...

Besides relying upon the Kelly and Skilbred affidavits, respondents propose a series of novel standing theories. The first, inelegantly styled "ecosystem nexus," proposes that any person who uses *any part* of a "contiguous ecosystem" adversely affected by a funded activity has standing even if the activity is located a great distance away. ...

Respondents' other theories are called, alas, the "animal nexus" approach, whereby anyone who has an interest in studying or seeing the endangered animals anywhere on the globe has standing; and the "vocational nexus" approach, under which anyone with a professional interest in such animals can sue. Under these theories, anyone who goes to see Asian elephants in the Bronx Zoo, and anyone who is a keeper of Asian elephants in the Bronx Zoo, has standing to sue because the Director of the Agency for International Development (AID) did not consult with the Secretary regarding the AID-funded project in Sri Lanka. This is beyond all reason. Standing is not "an ingenious academic exercise in the conceivable." ...

III[B]

...

The most obvious problem in the present case is redressability. Since the agencies funding the projects were not parties to the case, the District Court could accord relief only against the Secretary: He could be ordered to revise his regulation to require consultation for foreign projects. But this would not remedy respondents' alleged injury unless the funding agencies were bound by the Secretary's regulation, which is very much an open question. ...

IV

The Court of Appeals found that respondents had standing for an additional reason: because they had suffered a "procedural injury." The so-called "citizen-suit" provision of the ESA provides, in pertinent part, that "any person may commence a civil suit on his own behalf (A) to enjoin any person, including the United States and any other governmental instrumentality or agency ... who is alleged to be in violation of any provision of this chapter." ...

We have consistently held that a plaintiff raising only a generally available grievance about government—claiming only harm to his and every citizen's interest in proper application of the Constitution and laws, and seeking relief that no more directly and tangibly benefits him than it does the public at large—does not state an Article III case or controversy. ...

Justice KENNEDY, with whom Justice SOUTER joins, concurring in part and concurring in the judgment.

... In light of the conclusion that respondents have not demonstrated a concrete injury here sufficient to support standing under our precedents, I would not reach the issue of redressability that is discussed by the plurality in Part III–B. ...

In exercising this power, however, Congress must at the very least identify the injury it seeks to vindicate and relate the injury to the class of persons entitled to bring suit. The citizen-suit provision of the Endangered Species Act does not meet these minimal requirements, because while the statute purports to confer a right on "any person ... to enjoin ... the United States and any other governmental instrumentality or agency ... who is alleged to be in violation of any provision of this chapter," it does not of its own force establish that there is an injury in "any person" by virtue of any "violation." ...

Justice STEVENS, concurring in the judgment.

Because I am not persuaded that Congress intended the consultation requirement in § 7(a)(2) of the Endangered Species Act of 1973 (ESA), to apply to activities in foreign countries, I concur in the judgment of reversal. I do not, however, agree with the Court's conclusion that respondents lack standing because the threatened injury to their interest in protecting the environment and studying endangered species is not "imminent." Nor do I agree with the plurality's additional conclusion that respondents' injury is not "redressable" in this litigation. ...

Justice BLACKMUN, with whom Justice O'CONNOR joins, dissenting.

I part company with the Court in this case in two respects. First, I believe that respondents have raised genuine issues of fact—sufficient to survive summary judgment—both as to injury and as to redressability. Second, I question the Court's breadth of language in rejecting standing for "procedural" injuries. I fear the Court seeks to impose fresh limitations on the constitutional authority of Congress to allow citizen suits in the federal courts for injuries deemed "procedural" in nature. I dissent. ...

By requiring a "description of concrete plans" or "specification of *when* the some day [for a return visit] will be," the Court, in my view, demands what is likely an empty formality. No substantial barriers prevent Kelly or Skilbred from simply purchasing plane tickets to return to the Aswan and Mahaweli projects. ...

In short, determining "injury" for Article III standing purposes is a fact-specific inquiry. "Typically

... the standing inquiry requires careful judicial examination of a complaint's allegations to ascertain whether the particular plaintiff is entitled to an adjudication of the particular claims asserted." There may be factual circumstances in which a congressionally imposed procedural requirement is so insubstantially connected to the prevention of a substantive harm that it cannot be said to work any conceivable injury to an individual litigant. But, as a general matter, the courts owe substantial deference to Congress' substantive purpose in imposing a certain procedural requirement. In all events, "[o]ur separation-of-powers analysis does not turn on the labeling of an activity as 'substantive' as opposed to 'procedural.'" There is no room for a *per se* rule or presumption excluding injuries labeled "procedural" in nature.

In conclusion, I cannot join the Court on what amounts to a slash-and-burn expedition through the law of environmental standing. In my view, "[t]he very essence of civil liberty certainly consists in the right of every individual to claim the protection of the laws, whenever he receives an injury." *Marbury v. Madison*, 1 Cranch 137, 163 (1803).

Notes and Questions

1. Marbury *and standing.* Why did Justice Blackmun cite *Marbury* at the end of his dissent? What does this case have to do with *Marbury?*
2. *What do you think of the Court's treatment of the travels of Kelly and Skilbred?* Do you agree with the majority that their future travels do not constitute real injuries? Or with the dissent that they do?
3. *What do you think of the ecosystem nexus, the animal nexus, and the vocational nexus?* Are they as imaginary or unrealistic as Justice Scalia suggests? Or could they provide the basis in some context for standing even under his reasoning?
4. *Video.* Does this video, Quimbee's *Lujan v. Defenders of Wildlife* Case Brief Summary/Law Case Explained, Mar. 2, 2021, posted at https://www.youtube.com/watch?v=LNFU0X-zpYw&list=PLsFE_Nvl6h_Y75KGR5pkGqcFisGvBnO9S&index=12, shed light on what happened in the case?

3. State Standing

Given the prior standing cases, the analysis in the next case, *Massachusetts v. EPA*, is different in that it involves a state that is seeking standing. How is a state's standing similar to an individual's standing? Or a corporation's standing? How are they different? Does the Court need a different test from *Allen* and *Lujan* to resolve questions about when a state has standing to get into court? The case also involves environmental questions. Are environmental questions particularly difficult for purposes of proving an injury?

Why do you think the Court reached a 5–4 outcome in the following case? Are you surprised that Justice Scalia, the author of *Lujan*, dissented in this case?

Read the oral argument in this proceeding on the case's website, https://www.oyez.org/cases/2006/05-1120. Which Justice did the best job of questioning? Which Justice did the worst? How do you decide which questions are good and which are not? Did all the Justices in the written opinion vote consistently with how they questioned the litigants in Court?

Massachusetts v. Environmental Protection Agency

SUPREME COURT OF THE UNITED STATES, 2007

549 U.S. 497, 127 S.Ct. 1438

STEVENS, J., delivered the opinion of the Court, in which KENNEDY, SOUTER, GINSBURG, and BREYER, JJ., joined. ROBERTS, C. J., filed a dissenting opinion, in which SCALIA, THOMAS, and ALITO, JJ., joined. SCALIA, J., filed a dissenting opinion, in which ROBERTS, C. J., and THOMAS and ALITO, JJ., joined.

Justice STEVENS delivered the opinion of the Court.

A well-documented rise in global temperatures has coincided with a significant increase in the concentration of carbon dioxide in the atmosphere. Respected scientists believe the two trends are related. For when carbon dioxide is released into the atmosphere, it acts like the ceiling of a greenhouse, trapping solar energy and retarding the escape of reflected heat. It is therefore a species—the most important species—of a "greenhouse gas."

Calling global warming "the most pressing environmental challenge of our time," a group of States, local governments, and private organizations alleged in a petition for certiorari that the Environmental Protection Agency (EPA) has abdicated its responsibility under the Clean Air Act to regulate the emissions of four greenhouse gases, including carbon dioxide. Specifically, petitioners asked us to answer two questions concerning the meaning of § 202(a)(1) of the Act: whether EPA has the statutory authority to regulate greenhouse gas emissions from new motor vehicles; and if so, whether its stated reasons for refusing to do so are consistent with the statute.

In response, EPA, supported by 10 intervening States and six trade associations, correctly argued that we may not address those two questions unless at least one petitioner has standing to invoke our jurisdiction under Article III of the Constitution. Notwithstanding the serious character of that jurisdictional argument and the absence of any conflicting decisions construing § 202(a)(1), the unusual importance of the underlying issue persuaded us to grant the writ.

...

II

On October 20, 1999, a group of 19 private organizations filed a rulemaking petition asking EPA to regulate "greenhouse gas emissions from new motor vehicles under § 202 of the Clean Air Act." ...

On September 8, 2003, EPA entered an order denying the rulemaking petition. The Agency gave two reasons for its decision: (1) that contrary to the opinions of its former general counsels, the Clean Air Act does not authorize EPA to issue mandatory regulations to address global climate change, and (2) that even if the Agency had the authority to set greenhouse gas emission standards, it would be unwise to do so at this time. ...

IV

Article III of the Constitution limits federal-court jurisdiction to "Cases" and "Controversies." Those two words confine "the business of federal courts to questions presented in an adversary context and in a form historically viewed as capable of resolution through the judicial process." It is therefore familiar learning that no justiciable "controversy" exists when parties seek adjudication of a political question, when they ask for an advisory opinion, or when the question sought to be adjudicated has been mooted by subsequent developments. This case suffers from none of these defects. ...

We stress here, as did Judge Tatel below, the special position and interest of Massachusetts. It is of considerable relevance that the party seeking review here is a sovereign State and not, as it was in *Lujan,* a private individual. ...

The Injury

The harms associated with climate change are serious and well recognized. Indeed, the NRC Report itself—which EPA regards as an "objective and independent assessment of the relevant science," identifies a number of environmental changes that have already inflicted significant harms, including "the global retreat of mountain glaciers, reduction in snow-cover extent, the earlier spring melting of ice on rivers and lakes, [and] the accelerated rate of rise of sea levels during the 20th century relative to the past few thousand years. ..."

Petitioners allege that this only hints at the environmental damage yet to come. According to the climate scientist Michael MacCracken, "qualified scientific experts involved in climate change research" have reached a "strong consensus" that global warming threatens (among other things) a precipitate rise in sea levels by the end of the century, "severe and irreversible changes to natural ecosystems," a "significant reduction in water storage in winter snowpack in mountainous regions with direct and important economic consequences," and an increase in the spread of disease. He also observes that rising ocean temperatures may contribute to the ferocity of hurricanes. ...

Because the Commonwealth "owns a substantial portion of the state's coastal property," it has alleged a particularized injury in its capacity as a landowner. The severity of that injury will only increase over the course of the next century: If sea levels continue to rise as predicted, one Massachusetts official believes that a significant fraction of coastal property will be "either permanently lost through inundation or temporarily lost through periodic storm surge and flooding events." Remediation costs alone, petitioners allege, could run well into the hundreds of millions of dollars.

Causation

... But EPA overstates its case. Its argument rests on the erroneous assumption that a small incremental step, because it is incremental, can never be attacked in a federal judicial forum. Yet accepting that premise would doom most challenges to regulatory action. Agencies, like legislatures, do not generally resolve massive problems in one fell regulatory swoop. ...

To put this in perspective: Considering just emissions from the transportation sector, which represent less than one-third of this country's total carbon dioxide emissions, the United States would still rank as the third-largest emitter of carbon dioxide in the world, outpaced only by the European Union and China. Judged by any standard, U.S. motor-vehicle emissions make a meaningful contribution to greenhouse gas concentrations and hence, according to petitioners, to global warming.

The Remedy

... A reduction in domestic emissions would slow the pace of global emissions increases, no matter what happens elsewhere. ...

In sum—at least according to petitioners' uncontested affidavits—the rise in sea levels associated with global warming has already harmed and will continue to harm Massachusetts. The risk of catastrophic harm, though remote, is nevertheless real. That risk would be reduced to some extent if petitioners received the relief they seek. We therefore hold that petitioners have standing to challenge EPA's denial of their rulemaking petition. ...

Chief Justice ROBERTS, with whom Justice SCALIA, THOMAS, and ALITO join, dissenting.

... This Court's standing jurisprudence simply recognizes that redress of grievances of the sort at issue here "is the function of Congress and the Chief Executive," not the federal courts. ...

I

...

Relaxing Article III standing requirements because asserted injuries are pressed by a State, however, has no basis in our jurisprudence, and support for any such "special solicitude" is conspicuously absent from the Court's opinion. The general judicial review provision cited by the Court, affords States no special rights or status. ...

On top of everything else, the Court overlooks the fact that our cases cast significant doubt on a State's standing to assert a quasi-sovereign interest—as opposed to a direct injury—against the Federal Government. ...

II

... Thus, aside from a single conclusory statement, there is nothing in petitioners' 43 standing declarations and accompanying exhibits to support an inference of actual loss of Massachusetts coastal land from 20th-century global sea level increases. It is pure conjecture. ...

III

... In light of the bit-part domestic new motor vehicle greenhouse gas emissions have played in what petitioners describe as a 150-year global phenomenon, and the myriad additional factors bearing on petitioners' alleged injury—the loss of Massachusetts coastal land—the connection is far too speculative to establish causation.

IV

Redressability is even more problematic. To the tenuous link between petitioners' alleged injury and the indeterminate fractional domestic emissions at issue here, add the fact that petitioners cannot meaningfully predict what will come of the 80 percent of global greenhouse gas emissions that originate outside the United States. ...

Justice SCALIA's dissent focused on the merits of the case.

Notes and Questions

1. *When should states get standing?* Did Justice Stevens's opinion accord states a different role from others in the law of standing? What did he say about states? Do you agree with him that states deserved standing here, or is the dissent better argued?
2. *The three elements of standing.* What are the injury, causation, and redressability in this case? Why do the majority and dissent disagree about what they are? Which is more persuasive?
3. *A unanimous standing decision.* In the earlier cases, the Justices disputed when standing was present, and the Court was frequently split on the outcome. Why was the decision unanimous in *Lexmark International v. Static Control Components,* 572 U.S. 118 (2014) where Justice Scalia delivered an opinion, joined by Roberts, Kennedy, Thomas Ginsburg, Breyer, Alito, Sotomayor and Kagan? Scalia was the author of *Lujan.* Does his reasoning change from *Lujan* to *Lexmark,* which is excerpted below?

...

IV. Application

Applying those principles to Static Control's false-advertising claim, we conclude that Static Control comes within the class of plaintiffs whom Congress authorized to sue under § 1125(a).

To begin, Static Control's alleged injuries—lost sales and damage to its business reputation—are injuries to precisely the sorts of commercial interests the Act protects. Static Control is suing not as a deceived consumer, but as a "perso[n] engaged in" "commerce within the control of Congress" whose position in the marketplace has been damaged by Lexmark's false advertising. § 1127. There is no doubt that it is within the zone of interests protected by the statute.

Static Control also sufficiently alleged that its injuries were proximately caused by Lexmark's misrepresentations. This case, it is true, does not present the "classic Lanham Act false-advertising claim" in which "'one competito[r] directly injur[es] another by making false statements about his own goods [or the competitor's goods] and thus inducing customers to switch.'" But although diversion of sales to a direct competitor may be the paradigmatic direct injury from false advertising, it is not the only type of injury cognizable under §1125(a). For at least two reasons, Static Control's allegations satisfy the requirement of proximate causation. ...

In addition, Static Control adequately alleged proximate causation by alleging that it designed, manufactured, and sold microchips that both (1) were necessary for, and (2) had no other use than, refurbishing Lexmark toner cartridges. It follows from that allegation that any false advertising that reduced the remanufacturers' business necessarily injured Static Control as well. Taking Static Control's assertions at face value, there is likely to be something very close to a 1:1 relationship between the number of refurbished Prebate cartridges sold (or not sold) by the remanufacturers and the number of Prebate microchips sold (or not sold) by Static Control. "Where the injury alleged is so integral an aspect of the [violation] alleged, there can be no question" that proximate cause is satisfied.

To be sure, on this view, the causal chain linking Static Control's injuries to consumer confusion is not direct, but includes the intervening link of injury to the remanufacturers. Static Control's allegations therefore might not support standing under a strict application of the "general tendency" not to stretch proximate causation "beyond the first step." But the reason for that general tendency is that there ordinarily is a "discontinuity" between the injury to the direct victim and the injury to the indirect victim, so that the latter is not surely attributable to the former (and thus also to the defendant's conduct), but might instead have resulted from "any number of [other] reasons." That is not the case here. Static Control's allegations suggest that if the remanufacturers sold 10,000 fewer refurbished cartridges because of Lexmark's false advertising, then it would follow more or less automatically that Static Control sold 10,000 fewer microchips for the same reason, without the need for any "speculative ... proceedings" or "intricate, uncertain inquiries." In these relatively unique circumstances, the remanufacturers are not "more immediate victim[s]" than Static Control.

Although we conclude that Static Control has *alleged* an adequate basis to proceed under § 1125(a) it cannot obtain relief without *evidence* of injury proximately caused by Lexmark's alleged misrepresentations. We hold only that Static Control is entitled to a chance to prove its case. ...

4. *A video analysis of the case.* Does this video help you understand the facts and significance of the case? See Quimbee's *Massachusetts v. Environmental Protection Agency* Case Brief Summary/Law Case Explained, May 26, 2016, posted at https://www.youtube.com/watch?v=LWJBGbQyHGE&list=PLsFE_Nvl6h_Y75KGR5pkGqcFisGvBnO9S&index=8.

C. The Political Question Cases

1. The Court Hears the Case

Review *Marbury* to see what the Court said a "political question" is. The Court has ruled that it does not hear political questions. The following case, *Baker v. Carr*, is a very significant case about political questions because it provides the test the Court will use to determine if something is a political question or not.

Read through the oral argument in this case, which is available on the case's website, listed in the website's upper left corner, https://www.oyez.org/cases/1960/6. As you read it, identify the hardest questions that the Justices were asked. Ask yourself if you disagree with any of the answers given by the lawyers. Now that you have read the argument, take note while reading this case whether this analysis was to be expected after oral argument. Do you agree with the majority or the dissent?

Baker v. Carr

SUPREME COURT OF THE UNITED STATES, 1962

369 U.S. 186, 82 S.Ct. 691

MR. JUSTICE BRENNAN delivered the opinion of the Court. [He was joined by Justices WARREN, BLACK, DOUGLAS, CLARK AND STEWART.]

This civil action was brought ... to redress the alleged deprivation of federal constitutional rights. The complaint, alleging that by means of a 1901 statute of Tennessee apportioning the members of the General Assembly among the State's 95 counties, 'these plaintiffs and others similarly situated, are denied the equal protection of the laws accorded them by the Fourteenth Amendment to the Constitution of the United States by virtue of the debasement of their votes.' ...

In light of the District Court's treatment of the case, we hold today only (a) that the court possessed jurisdiction of the subject matter; (b) that a justiciable cause of action is stated upon which appellants would be entitled to appropriate relief; and (c) because appellees raise the issue before this Court, that the appellants have standing to challenge the Tennessee apportionment statutes. Beyond noting that we have no cause at this stage to doubt the District Court will be able to fashion relief if violations of constitutional rights are found, it is improper now to consider what remedy would be most appropriate if appellants prevail at the trial. ...

We understand the District Court to have read the cited cases as compelling the conclusion that since the appellants sought to have a legislative apportionment held unconstitutional, their suit presented a 'political question' and was therefore nonjusticiable. We hold that this challenge to an apportionment presents no nonjusticiable 'political question.' The cited cases do not hold the contrary.

Of course the mere fact that the suit seeks protection of a political right does not mean it presents a political question. Such an objection 'is little more than a play upon words.' ...

It is apparent that several formulations which vary slightly according to the settings in which the questions arise may describe a political question, although each has one or more elements which identify it as essentially a function of the separation of powers. Prominent on the surface of any case held to involve a political question is found a textually demonstrable constitutional commitment of the issue to a coordinate political department; or a lack of judicially discoverable and manageable standards for resolving it; or the impossibility of deciding without an initial policy determination of a kind clearly for nonjudicial discretion; or the impossibility of a court's undertaking independent resolution without expressing lack of the respect due coordinate branches of government; or an unusual need for unquestioning adherence to a political decision already made; or the potentiality of embarrassment from multifarious pronouncements by various departments on one question.

Unless one of these formulations is inextricable from the case at bar, there should be no dismissal for non-justiciability on the ground of a political question's presence. The doctrine of which we treat is one of 'political questions,' not one of 'political cases.' The courts cannot reject as 'no law suit' a bona fide controversy as to whether some action denominated 'political' exceeds constitutional authority. The cases we have reviewed show the necessity for discriminating inquiry into the precise facts and posture of the particular case, and the impossibility of resolution by any semantic cataloguing. ...

Mr. Justice CLARK, concurring.

...

As is admitted, there is a wide disparity of voting strength between the large and small counties. Some samples are: Moore County has a total representation of two with a population (2,340) of only one-eleventh of Rutherford County (25,316) with the same representation; Decatur County (5,563) has the same representation as Carter (23,303) though the latter has four times the population; likewise, Loudon County (13,264), Houston (3,084), and Anderson County (33,990) have the same representation, i.e., 1.25 each. But it is said that in this illustration all of the underrepresented counties contain municipalities of over 10,000 population and they therefore should be included under the 'urban' classification, rationalizing this disparity as an attempt to effect a rural-urban political balance. But in so doing one is caught up in the backlash of his own bull whip, for many counties have municipalities with a population exceeding 10,000, yet the same invidious discrimination is present.

Likewise, counties with no municipality of over 10,000 suffer a similar discrimination.

Mr. Justice FRANKFURTER, whom Mr. Justice HARLAN joins, dissenting.

The Court today reverses a uniform course of decision established by a dozen cases, including one by which the very claim now sustained was unanimously rejected only five years ago. The impressive body of rulings thus cast aside reflected the equally uniform course of our political history regarding the relationship between population and legislative representation—a wholly different matter from denial of the franchise to individuals because of race, color, religion or sex. Such a massive repudiation of the experience of our whole past in asserting destructively novel judicial power demands a detailed analysis of the role of this Court in our constitutional scheme. Disregard of inherent limits in the effective exercise of the Court's 'judicial Power' not only presages the futility of judicial intervention in the essentially political conflict of forces by which the relation between population and representation has time out of mind been and now is determined. It may well impair the Court's position as the ultimate organ of 'the supreme Law of the Land' in that vast range of legal problems, often strongly entangled in popular feeling, on which this Court must pronounce. The Court's authority—possessed of neither the purse nor the sword—ultimately rests on sustained public confidence in its moral sanction. Such feeling must be nourished by the Court's complete detachment, in fact and in appearance, from political entanglements and by abstention from injecting itself into the clash of political forces in political settlements. ...

Dissenting opinion of Mr. Justice HARLAN, whom Mr. Justice FRANKFURTER joins

The dissenting opinion of Mr. Justice FRANKFURTER, in which I join, demonstrates the abrupt departure the majority makes from judicial history by putting the federal courts into this area of state concerns—an area which, in this instance, the Tennessee state courts themselves have refused to enter. ...

Notes and Questions

1. *Is this new law?* The dissents assert that this was a new decision in the law, which permits a case to proceed that otherwise would have been dismissed. Do you find the majority or dissent more persuasive? What good could come of a court reviewing redistricting? What bad? Is the Court taking jurisdiction in this case consistent with *Marbury*?
2. *Political questions and violations of constitutional rights.* In *Davis v. Bandemer,* 478 U.S. 109 (1986), the Court ruled that Indiana's state apportionment did not violate the Equal Protection Clause. Is this a natural result of the reasoning in *Baker*? Does it make sense to you that here, as elsewhere, the Court has ruled that under the Equal Protection Clause the principle is "one person, one vote"? Id. at 118.
3. *The nonjusticiability of direct democracy.* Article IV, Section 4 of the Constitution says, "The United States shall guarantee to every State in this Union a Republican Form of Government." "Republican" here means representative. The Framers believed that direct democracy (where voters make laws directly) is dangerous to the public good because the decision makers are not accountable to the public. A republican democracy—a representative democracy—is more likely to serve the larger public good. Therefore, states, like the federal government, should be representative in structure. Before *Baker* was decided, the Court had ruled in *Luther v. Borden*, 48 U.S. 1 (1849) that whether Rhode Island's government was a republican form of government was a political question that the courts should not hear. States today have elements of direct democracy as part of governance in the form of referenda and initiatives, in part because the Supreme Court found the Guarantee Clause nonjusticiable, which makes it unenforceable.
4. *Presidential authority and justiciability.* In *Goldwater v. Carter,* 444 U.S. 996 (1979), President Jimmy Carter ended a treaty with Taiwan. Senator Barry Goldwater and the Congress challenged Carter's authority to do so under the Constitution. The Court found that the case was not justiciable, and, therefore, Carter won. In dissent, Justice Brennan would have decided the case on the merits because it involved a legal question of the president's authority, saying "[o]ur cases firmly establish that the Constitution commits to the President alone the power to recognize, and withdraw recognition from, foreign regimes." Id. at 1007.
5. *Justiciability of State Department determinations.* A federal statute permitted those born anywhere in Israel to indicate the place of birth as "City, Israel" rather than just the city of birth for purposes of passports and other identifying documents. But the State Department had a policy that required the passports for those born in Jerusalem to indicate "Jerusalem" without reference to Israel. That might seem like a political question, but the Court held it could hear the merits. In *Zivotofsky v. Clinton*, 566 U.S. 189 (2012), parents argued that their son's place of birth should be recorded as "Israel" and not Jerusalem, based on the federal statute. The Court

held it was justiciable, but the parents did not prevail until 2020 when the State Department policy was reversed.

6. *Is there a reliable standard for political geryymandering cases?* In *Vieth v. Jubelirer*, 541 U.S. 267 (2004), no 5 Justices agreed on whether there can be a standard that makes gerrymandering disputes justiciable. Scalia wrote an opinion concluding gerrymandering was nonjusticiable, joined by Rehnquist, O'Connor, and Thomas. Kennedy provided the fifth vote to that plurality in a concurrence in the judgment, suggesting that the Court had not yet found a standard for political gerrymandering but might in the future. Breyer, Souter, Stevens, and Ginsburg dissented saying that there are available standards.
7. *Behind the scenes in* Baker v. Carr. The Justices' discussions during their Conference meeting on *Baker v. Carr* are available and were published in the book, Del Dickson, *The Supreme Court in Conference 1940–1985: the private discussions behind nearly 300 Supreme Court decisions 845–51* (2001). What do the following excerpts from the book tell you about the case and why the Justices voted as they did?

Conference of April 20, 1961

WARREN: I agree with the case as presented by the United States, and I reverse on that argument. But I think that we should say that the complaint states a cause of action. The district court has jurisdiction. I would reverse.

BLACK: I reverse. My dissent in *Colegrove v. Green* covers this I also still agree with my *Peters* dissent. There should be a trial on this complaint.

FRANKFURTER: I affirm. Unless we affirm, we will get into great difficulty and this Court will rue the results. I think that the solicitor general was irresponsible in stating that there is a permissible remedy. In *Colegrove*, Stone and Jackson supported my view. The costs will be very serious. The Tennessee constitution has nothing to do with the case-this must be a violation of the federal Constitution for the petitioner to get in federal court. Every machinery of every state puts everyone on a par with everyone else. The solicitor general said that he was not arguing for "equality" in voting but that history, the congregation of populations, and the like could be considered. All of these factors are not capable of being determined by the court. No one state is free of gerrymandering-how can courts determine what is fair in this area? The subject matter is not proper for judicial inquiry—Look at *Luther v. Borden*. Also look at our initiative and referenda cases. Also look at our decisions in *Massachusetts v. Mellon*.

DOUGLAS: I reverse.

CLARK The precedents are against us. If we upset the Tennessee system, it would have no legislature. Equality is not the basis of voting in the electoral college. Equality is not a basic principle in American political voting.

HARLAN: I agree wholly with Felix's views. I think that the solicitor general was reckless in his desire to inject the judiciary into this field. There is no federally protected right in an individual based on equality of voting. Moreover, this is not a justiciable issue. This Court is not competent to solve this type of problem. I affirm.

BRENNAN: Our decisions have not yet held that this is not a federally protected right. The purpose of the Fourteenth Amendment was to give equality. Much of its history pertained to voting rights. I would rely on the equal protection clause. I do not believe that the remedies are insoluble—I have worked it out with a judicial remedy. I reverse.

WHITTAKER: If we wrote on a clean slate, I would say that petitioners have standing to sue and that they are being denied equal protection of the laws—then no relief in the state courts. If there is a constitutional right involved, the chancellor should not withhold relief. Precedents, however, say that this is a political issue. I am reluctant to overrule those cases. So I affirm, but I would do so only on an equity ground.

STEWART: I am not at rest on the issue. I have trouble seeing that disproportionate voting is a violation of equal protection. A state can divide up its jurisdiction into unequal political units. I would uphold the Michigan system that is here in another case we are holding. Tennessee is different, because it has a law that requires equality, and the state's failure to apply it may raise an equal protection point. I have sufficient doubt that I pass.

Conference of April 28, 1961

STEWART: [DOUGLAS: This case was passed, for him.] I think that this is as important a case as our school segregation cases. Under our precedents, we can go either way. It will establish a big precedent if we go in and let the federal courts supervise these affairs. I would suggest putting the case down for rehearing. [DOUGLAS: Since Potter has the critical vote, everyone agreed to put case down for reargument in October.]

After Reargument. Conference of October 13, 1961

WARREN: There is a violation of equal protection shown here. I don't think that we have to decide the merits on the question of republican form of government. All we have to decide is that there is jurisdiction. We have jurisdiction—no case says we do not. We don't have to say that the state must give precise equality. Here, we have a classification that denies some classes the right to cast their ballots with the strength that others cast theirs.

We can't say that we must stay out of state election problems, since Congress has put us in it as the defense procedure for inquiring into the denial of the vote on racial grounds. Congress in the Civil Rights Acts has put watchers on the polls in state elections. We come in only where the line of arbitrariness has been crossed. All we need to do here is to say that this shows an arbitrary and capricious practice. The Court has jurisdiction. I would reverse solely on jurisdiction, and leave the rest of the case and the form of decree to the district court. I would not at this time say what decree should be entered, although I would suggest certain guidelines.

BLACK: I adhere to my views in *Colegrove v. Green.* Felix's memo in this case is a good brief for a weak cause. *Colegrove v. Green* is a weak read on which to hang any notion of an established rule. That opinion was only agreed to by Frankfurter, Reed, and Burton. It did not rest on *Luther v. Borden.* I agree with *Luther v. Borden*, with each party having claimed to represent the state. It wasn't a dispute over a law passed by state, but an argument about which group was the state. Congress has the power to resolve that issue. Felix cited an Oregon case which said that Congress must decide "all" questions of whether states have a republican form of government. But as Wilson said, it is different when you attack a law that is not an attack on the state's form of government and whether it denies a republican form of government. Here, no interlopers have tried to seize the government.

Here, it is simply a question of whether the law passed bears so unequally—capriciously—as to deny equal protection. Does this act bear so unequally and arbitrarily as to deny equal protection? I think that it does, and I reverse. In *Luther v. Borden*, Congress could give relief. Here, Congress has no power to give relief to these people, whatever their power may be to pass legislation under the Fourteenth Amendment.

FRANKFURTER: (DOUGLAS: He refers to his long memo that has been circulated.) To reverse this, we will have to reverse the *Kidd* case, where we dismissed the appeal. Asserting jurisdiction in this case is fraught with such consequences that to me are so dangerous to our whole system that I would stay out. Principles fundamental to society may sometimes be unenforceable by the Courts, as witness Part IV of the Indian Constitution. What are the standards to which a remedy is to be fashioned?

DOUGLAS: *Gomillion* is a precedent leading to reversal here. The equal protection clause is not designed just for Negroes—even he has to show an arbitrary discrimination. Negroes have no greater right under equal protection than whites. The difficulties of the Judiciary doing anything about it, as great as they are, can't deter us from doing our job.

CLARK: I would dismiss. The petitioners failed to show that they had exhausted other avenues to relief (1) in congress and (2) there was no campaign in Tennessee to include in its case this problem. Even if there was jurisdiction, I would not exercise it. Congress could act to end discrimination in the twenty-odd states where this discrimination exists. There are a dozen cases since 1932 when the Court has stayed out of this problem. Look at MacDougall and all of the cases that came to us after *Colgrove.* I think that we should adhere to *Colegrove.*

HARLAN: My earlier views have been reinforced by reargument. If Tennessee had enacted this scheme in its constitution or by statute, an attack would assert no claim of violation of the Constitution. If a state can distribute its organs of government as it wishes without subjecting itself to federal judicial supervision or interference, then I can't see why a state may not—free of judicial federal restraint—choose the means whereby these organs are to be created and the rules enforced. I would not deal with this on an equal protection basis—there is no federally protected right involved here. But even if you got over this and say that there is an equal protection claim, I still can't see under our standards any disparity between urban and rural voters that offends equal protection. It is the fact that it is a violation of the state constitution that brings this case about. There is no jurisdiction here, because no federal cause of action is stated. It makes no difference whether the votes are loaded one way or the other. The *Tuskegee* case, on the other hand, was a denial of the right to vote, and that can't be denied because of race under the Fifteenth Amendment. I would plead, for the protection of this Court, against getting into these political contests. The protection of this Court has been in refraining from getting involved in these problems.

[DOUGLAS: My God—what does he think the Segregation Cases were—or the *Tuskegee* case?]

BRENNAN: There is an equal protection problem presented here. By historic tradition, one house in the states is always elected by the people. Here, there is a capricious and arbitrary denial of equal protection. I would assert jurisdiction, but not direct a specific decree. I think that an assertion of power will cause the Tennessee legislature to act. Look at Senate Bill No.2579 of September 19, 1961, which would amend the Constitution to provide for equitable representation, plus a bill which provides a standard. This was introduced by Senator Joseph Clark of Pennsylvania. I do not think that *Kidd* should be taken too seriously. We passed over quite a few Sunday Law cases before last term, when we took the cases and decided them. I would reverse for a hearing on the merits of the complaint.

WHITTAKER: I affirmed last term but was very shaky on it. I have written two memos diametrically opposed to each other- one for asserting jurisdiction and one for affirmance. I now affirm, but not for lack of judicial power or jurisdiction. The district court dismissed this case on that ground, but it was wrong. That court also dismissed on the ground that the complaint failed to state a cause of action on which relief might be granted. We do not enforce state law, but equal protection of rights granted by state law. In *Kidd*, it was alleged that apportionment was not made in accord with the Tennessee constitution. It refused to pass on the de facto issue for Tennessee, because they would be without a government.

But the Tennessee constitution and statute have been read by the Tennessee Supreme Court. The Tennessee court held that the1901 apportionment act is not judicially cognizable or enforceable, and the effect of that decision was to amend the state constitution and statute to say that neither shall be justiciable in the courts. If that is so, then the claim here that the petitioners have been deprived of a right granted by state law fails, for no right granted them by state law has been denied. The federal court has jurisdiction to entertain this type of claim, but there is no right to enforce.

STEWART: The district court had jurisdiction. This is not a so-called political question. A "political" question is a problem the determination of which the Constitution has precluded from the courts and placed in another branch of government. There is standing on the part of these petitioners. This is not a "republican form of government" case that involves the other branches of government. Given jurisdiction and standing, I can't say whether the district court can or cannot afford appropriate relief. Some of the suggestions of the solicitor general seem to me to be impractical. I can't follow here Rutledge's abstention in *Colegrove*, as the election is a year away. On the merits, there is an assumption that equal protection requires the legislature to apportion votes so that there is no discrimination. I would reject that view. Our entire American history presumes the contrary, and on that history I follow Frankfurter's memo.

I couldn't say that equal protection requires representation approximately commensurate with voting strength. States could give towns only one vote, whatever their size. States could allocate voting rights by taxes paid, education, and so forth. The only equality demanded is that of the Fifteenth Amendment. Every presumption here is in favor of every state action, like with the cases last term involving the Sunday Laws. So the state does not have to justify every departure from a one-man one-vote basis, and the greatest burden of proof is on the plaintiff to show an arbitrary and capricious system.

Basically, this is the same as if Tennessee had by its constitution ordained the present system. What is done by inaction is the same as what is done by direct action. Conceivably, there can be a denial of equal protection in an apportionment case-so there is a cause of action stated here. There was one in the Sunday Laws cases. If this was discrimination against red-haired people or those over fifty years of age, then we would have a cause for action. It would then be wholly capricious. The giving of greater weight of votes to rural blocs is O.K. There may be difficulty here in justifying discrimination in contiguous counties. The fact that the state court says that the issue is not justiciable is not binding on the federal courts. On that score, I disagree with Whittaker—a state can't take away one's right to enforce a constitutional right. This is like the *Shelley* case, in that there is much being held for this case. I think that decision has unusual wisdom. On the merits, I agree more or less with Bill Brennan.

2. Or Doesn't!

Does the following case, *Rucho v. Common Cause*, answer the question whether redistricting cases can be justiciable? Why is *Rucho* another 5–4 decision even though the Justices on the Court have changed? Can you tell from the oral argument, on the case's website, https://www.oyez.org/cases/2018/18-422, how the Justices would vote? If you prefer, you can listen to the oral argument at https://www.c-span.org/video/?458085-1/supreme-court-dismisses-north-carolina-gerrymandering-case-5-4-ruling.

Rucho v. Common Cause

SUPREME COURT OF THE UNITED STATES, 2019

588 U.S. ___, 139 S.Ct. 2484

ROBERTS, C. J., delivered the opinion of the Court, in which THOMAS, ALITO, GORSUCH, and KAVANAUGH, JJ., joined. KAGAN, J., filed a dissenting opinion, in which GINSBURG, BREYER, and SOTOMAYOR, JJ., joined.

Chief Justice ROBERTS delivered the opinion of the Court.

Voters and other plaintiffs in North Carolina and Maryland challenged their States' congressional districting maps as unconstitutional partisan gerrymanders. The North Carolina plaintiffs complained that the State's districting plan discriminated against Democrats; the Maryland plaintiffs complained that their State's plan discriminated against Republicans. The plaintiffs alleged that the gerrymandering violated the First Amendment, the Equal Protection Clause of the Fourteenth Amendment, the Elections Clause, and Article I, § 2, of the Constitution. The District Courts in both cases ruled in favor of the plaintiffs, and the defendants appealed directly to this Court.

These cases require us to consider once again whether claims of excessive partisanship in districting are "justiciable"—that is, properly suited for resolution by the federal courts. This Court has not previously struck down a districting plan as an unconstitutional partisan gerrymander, and has struggled without success over the past several decades to discern judicially manageable standards for deciding such claims. The districting plans at issue here are highly partisan, by any measure. The question is whether the courts below appropriately exercised judicial power when they found them unconstitutional as well.

...

II B

Partisan gerrymandering is nothing new. Nor is frustration with it. The practice was known in the Colonies prior to Independence, and the Framers were familiar with it at the time of the drafting and ratification of the Constitution. George Washington and his Federalist allies accused Patrick Henry of trying to gerrymander Virginia's districts against their candidates—in particular James Madison, who ultimately prevailed over fellow future President James Monroe.

In 1812, Governor of Massachusetts and future Vice President Elbridge Gerry notoriously approved congressional districts that the legislature had drawn to aid the Democratic-Republican Party. The moniker "gerrymander" was born when an outraged Federalist newspaper observed that one of the misshapen districts resembled a salamander.

The Framers addressed the election of Representatives to Congress in the Elections Clause. Art. I, § 4, cl. 1. That provision assigns to state legislatures the power to prescribe the "Times, Places and Manner of holding Elections" for Members of Congress, while giving Congress the power to "make or alter" any such regulations. ...

Appellants suggest that, through the Elections Clause, the Framers set aside electoral issues such as the one before us as questions that only Congress can resolve. We do not agree. In two areas—one-person, one-vote and racial gerrymandering—our cases have held that there is a role for the courts with respect to at least some issues that could arise from a State's drawing of congressional districts.

But the history is not irrelevant. The Framers were aware of electoral districting problems and considered what to do about them. They settled on a characteristic approach, assigning the issue to the state legislatures, expressly checked and balanced by the Federal Congress. As Alexander Hamilton explained, "it will ... not be denied that a discretionary power over elections ought to exist somewhere. It will, I presume, be as readily conceded that there were only three ways in which this power could have been reasonably modified and disposed: that it must either have been lodged wholly in the national legislature, or wholly in the State legislatures, or primarily in the latter, and ultimately in the former." At no point was there a suggestion that the federal courts had a role to play. Nor was there any indication that the Framers had ever heard of courts doing such a thing.

II C

...

Partisan gerrymandering claims have proved far more difficult to adjudicate. The basic reason is that, while it is illegal for a jurisdiction to depart from the one-person, one-vote rule, or to engage in racial discrimination in districting, "a jurisdiction may engage in constitutional political gerrymandering." ...

III A

In considering whether partisan gerrymandering claims are justiciable, we are mindful of Justice Kennedy's counsel in *Vieth*; Any standard for resolving such claims must be grounded in a "limited and precise rationale" and be "clear, manageable, and politically neutral." ...

IV A

Appellees and the dissent propose a number of "tests" for evaluating partisan gerrymandering claims, but none meets the need for a limited and precise standard that is judicially discernible and manageable. And none provides a solid grounding for judges to take the extraordinary step of reallocating power and influence between political parties. ...

V

Excessive partisanship in districting leads to results that reasonably seem unjust. But the fact that such gerrymandering is "incompatible with democratic principles," does not mean that the solution lies with the federal judiciary. We conclude that partisan gerrymandering claims present political questions beyond the reach of the federal courts. Federal judges have no license to reallocate political power between the two major political parties, with no plausible grant of authority in the Constitution, and no legal standards to limit and direct their decisions. "[J]udicial action must be governed by *standard*, by *rule*," and must be "principled, rational, and based upon reasoned distinctions" found in the Constitution or laws. *Vieth*. Judicial review of partisan gerrymandering does not meet those basic requirements.

Today the dissent essentially embraces the argument that the Court unanimously rejected in *Gill*: "this Court *can* address the problem of partisan gerrymandering because it *must*." That is not the test of our authority under the Constitution; that document instead "confines the federal courts to a properly judicial role."

What the appellees and dissent seek is an unprecedented expansion of judicial power. We have never struck down a partisan gerrymander as unconstitutional—despite various requests over the past 45 years. The expansion of judicial authority would not be into just any area of controversy, but into one of the most intensely partisan aspects of American political life. That intervention would be unlimited in scope and duration—it would recur over and over again around the country with each new round of districting, for state as well as federal representatives. Consideration of the impact of today's ruling on democratic principles cannot ignore the effect of the unelected and politically unaccountable branch of the Federal Government assuming such an extraordinary and unprecedented role. …

No one can accuse this Court of having a crabbed view of the reach of its competence. But we have no commission to allocate political power and influence in the absence of a constitutional directive or legal standards to guide us in the exercise of such authority. "It is emphatically the province and duty of the judicial department to say what the law is." *Marbury*. In this rare circumstance, that means our duty is to say "this is not law." …

Justice KAGAN, with whom Justice GINSBURG, Justice BREYER, and Justice SOTOMAYOR join, dissenting.

For the first time ever, this Court refuses to remedy a constitutional violation because it thinks the task beyond judicial capabilities.

And not just any constitutional violation. The partisan gerrymanders in these cases deprived citizens of the most fundamental of their constitutional rights: the rights to participate equally in the political process, to join with others to advance political beliefs, and to choose their political representatives. In so doing, the partisan gerrymanders here debased and dishonored our democracy, turning upside-down the core American idea that all governmental power derives from the people. These gerrymanders enabled politicians to entrench themselves in office as against voters' preferences. They promoted partisanship above respect for the popular will. They encouraged a politics of polarization and dysfunction. If left unchecked, gerrymanders like the ones here may irreparably damage our system of government.

And checking them is *not* beyond the courts. The majority's abdication comes just when courts across the country, including those below, have coalesced around manageable judicial standards to resolve partisan gerrymandering claims. Those standards satisfy the majority's own benchmarks. They do not require—indeed, they do not permit—courts to rely on their own ideas of electoral fairness, whether proportional representation or any other. And they limit courts to correcting only egregious gerrymanders, so judges do not become omnipresent players in the political process. But yes, the standards used here do allow—as well they should—judicial intervention in the worst-of-the-worst cases of democratic subversion, causing blatant constitutional harms. In other words, they allow courts to undo partisan gerrymanders of the kind we face today from North Carolina and Maryland. In giving such gerrymanders a pass from judicial review, the majority goes tragically wrong. …

I C

Partisan gerrymandering of the kind before us not only subverts democracy (as if that weren't bad enough). It violates individuals' constitutional rights as well. That statement is not the lonesome cry of a dissenting Justice. This Court has recognized extreme partisan gerrymandering as such a violation for many years.

Partisan gerrymandering operates through vote dilution—the devaluation of one citizen's vote as compared to others. A mapmaker draws district lines to "pack" and "crack" voters likely to support the disfavored party. He packs supermajorities of those voters into a relatively few districts, in numbers far greater than needed for their preferred candidates to prevail. Then he cracks the rest across many more districts, spreading them so thin that their candidates will not be able to win. Whether the person is packed or cracked, his vote carries less weight—has less consequence—than it would under a neutrally drawn (non-partisan) map. In short, the mapmaker has made some votes count for less, because they are likely to go for the other party.

That practice implicates the Fourteenth Amendment's Equal Protection Clause. The Fourteenth Amendment, we long ago recognized, "guarantees the opportunity for equal participation by all voters in the election" of legislators. And that opportunity "can be denied by a debasement or dilution of the weight of a citizen's vote just as effectively as by wholly prohibiting the free exercise of the franchise." …

II

…

But in throwing up its hands, the majority misses something under its nose: What it says can't be done *has* been done. Over the past several years, federal courts across the country—including, but not exclusively, in the decisions below—have largely converged on a standard for adjudicating partisan gerrymandering claims (striking down both Democratic and Republican districting plans in the process). And that standard does what the majority says is impossible.

The standard does not use any judge-made conception of electoral fairness—either proportional representation or any other; instead, it takes as its baseline a State's *own* criteria of fairness, apart from partisan gain. And by requiring plaintiffs to make difficult showings relating to both purpose and effects, the standard invalidates the most extreme, but only the most extreme, partisan gerrymanders. ...

Notes and Questions

1. *The tests.* Why does the majority say there is no feasible test for gerrymandering disputes? What test does the dissent choose, and from where did they get it?
2. *Voting rights and justiciability.* What is the role of the judiciary with respect to the rights of voters? What should it be?
3. *An analysis of the case.* What do you think of Professor Chambers's analysis of the case in The Synopsis: *Rucho v. Common Cause*, 2019, Jul. 8, 2019, posted at https://www.youtube.com/watch?v=8GuOSHe4KhU&list=PLsFE_Nvl6h_Y75KGR5pkGqcFisGvBnO9S&index=26?

A Look Ahead

This chapter introduced you to the case and controversy requirement for federal courts, the standing doctrine, and the justiciability of political questions. Each doctrine fills in the gaps after the Court decides in *Marbury v. Madison* that it holds the power to interpret the Constitution and to be the last word on the meaning of the Constitution. While *Marbury* could have justified the Court deciding every constitutional dispute brought to it, the cases in this chapter show you that there are meaningful limits to the Court's exercise of its judicial power, which have been set by the Court's own interpretations.

In the next chapter, we introduce another branch of the federal government, Congress, whose power is delineated by the Court's interpretation of Article 1 of the Constitution.

Two

Article I: Congress

Introduction

Before the Constitution, the relationship between the states was a "confederation" or essentially a committee. The United States's first governing document was the Articles of Confederation. Under the Articles, law was generated by each individual state. When the Confederation broke down due to the inability of the Articles to bring the states together for defense or trade, the states convened a gathering in Philadelphia to repair the Articles. When it was clear they were beyond repair, the Framers of the Constitution embarked on establishing a national government. It was assumed that the states would continue to maintain power over most issues, e.g., family law and contract law, but they had to grant some lawmaking power to this new federal government to institute enforceable coordination among the states.

Article I, Section 1 of the Constitution gives all legislative powers to the Congress of the United States, which is composed of a Senate and a House of Representatives. Early Supreme Court cases had to determine just how much power the Congress had and why. The Court has said that the federal government is one of enumerated powers. What does that mean? Is there anything you see in Article I that explains why? Article I, Section 8, says:

> The Congress shall have power to lay and collect taxes, duties, imposts and excises, to pay the debts and provide for the common defense and general welfare of the United States; but all duties, imposts and excises shall be uniform throughout the United States;
>
> To borrow money on the credit of the United States;
>
> To regulate commerce with foreign nations, and among the several states, and with the Indian tribes;
>
> To establish a uniform rule of naturalization, and uniform laws on the subject of bankruptcies throughout the United States;
>
> To coin money, regulate the value thereof, and of foreign coin, and fix the standard of weights and measures;
>
> To provide for the punishment of counterfeiting the securities and current coin of the United States;
>
> To establish post offices and post roads;

To promote the progress of science and useful arts, by securing for limited times to authors and inventors the exclusive right to their respective writings and discoveries;

To constitute tribunals inferior to the Supreme Court;

To define and punish piracies and felonies committed on the high seas, and offenses against the law of nations;

To declare war, grant letters of marque and reprisal, and make rules concerning captures on land and water;

To raise and support armies, but no appropriation of money to that use shall be for a longer term than two years;

To provide and maintain a navy;

To make rules for the government and regulation of the land and naval forces;

To provide for calling forth the militia to execute the laws of the union, suppress insurrections and repel invasions;

To provide for organizing, arming, and disciplining, the militia, and for governing such part of them as may be employed in the service of the United States, reserving to the states respectively, the appointment of the officers, and the authority of training the militia according to the discipline prescribed by Congress;

To exercise exclusive legislation in all cases whatsoever, over such District (not exceeding ten miles square) as may, by cession of particular states, and the acceptance of Congress, become the seat of the government of the United States, and to exercise like authority over all places purchased by the consent of the legislature of the state in which the same shall be, for the erection of forts, magazines, arsenals, dockyards, and other needful buildings;—And

To make all laws which shall be necessary and proper for carrying into execution the foregoing powers, and all other powers vested by this Constitution in the government of the United States, or in any department or officer thereof.

Thus, the Framers enumerated the powers of Congress. To further make clear that these were not unbounded powers, the Tenth Amendment of the U.S. Constitution says the "powers not delegated to the United States by the Constitution, nor prohibited by it to the states, are reserved to the states respectively, or to the people."

Having *two* sets of governments is a distinctive feature of the United States. Early cases had to figure out the boundaries of the federal and state governments. There are three answers in terms of line-drawing: an issue belongs to the federal government; it belongs to the state governments; or it is shared between the state and federal governments.

Article VI contains a Supremacy Clause, which says: "This Constitution, and the laws of the United States which shall be made in pursuance thereof; and all treaties made, or which shall be made, under the authority of the United States, shall be the supreme law of the land; and the judges in every state shall be bound thereby, anything in the Constitution or laws of any State to the contrary notwithstanding." The Court has emphatically stated that federal laws are supreme. How would supremacy be affected if state governments could tax a federal bank? Whose interests would be affected? Whose would not?

Section A of this chapter looks at "how we started," meaning it looks at early Supreme Court cases that set out the role of Congress and the states. The Court does mention the Supremacy Clause. What do you think of the Court's reasoning in these cases? What does Justice Marshall mean when he writes "we must never forget that it is *a Constitution* we are expounding." What is the necessary and proper clause?

A. How We Started

1. The Early Court Explains the Relationship Between the Federal and State Governments

This case is recognized as one of the important early Supreme Court cases. It is especially important because it explains the relationship of the federal and state governments. Why is the federal government supreme? Does supremacy leave any power to the states? If so, which powers and how much? Does this video help you to understand what the case decided? See Quimbee's video, *McCulloch v. Maryland* Summary, Oct. 13, 2017, posted at https://www.youtube.com/watch?v=tPdhWW6Bz-Q&list=PLsFE_Nvl6h_Y75KGR5pkGqcFisGvBnO9S&index=36.

McCulloch v. Maryland

SUPREME COURT OF THE UNITED STATES, 1819

17 U.S. 316

MARSHALL, Chief Justice, delivered the [unanimous] decision of the Court.

In the case now to be determined, the defendant, a sovereign State, denies the obligation of a law enacted by the legislature of the Union, and the plaintiff, on his part, contests the validity of an act which has been passed by the legislature of that State. ...

The first question made in the cause is—has Congress power to incorporate a bank?

... The power now contested was exercised by the first Congress elected under the present Constitution.

The bill for incorporating the Bank of the United States did not steal upon an unsuspecting legislature and pass unobserved. Its principle was completely understood, and was opposed with equal zeal and ability. After being resisted first in the fair and open field of debate, and afterwards in the executive cabinet, with as much persevering talent as any measure has ever experienced, and being supported by arguments which convinced minds as pure and as intelligent as this country can boast, it became a law. The original act was permitted to expire, but a short experience of the embarrassments to which the refusal to revive it exposed the Government convinced those who were most prejudiced against the measure of its necessity, and induced the passage of the present law. It would require no ordinary share of intrepidity to assert that a measure adopted under these circumstances was a bold and plain usurpation to which the Constitution gave no countenance. These observations belong to the cause; but they are not made under the impression that, were the question entirely new, the law would be found irreconcilable with the Constitution.

In discussing this question, the counsel for the State of Maryland have deemed it of some importance, in the construction of the Constitution, to consider that instrument not as emanating from the people, but as the act of sovereign and independent States. The powers of the General Government, it has been said, are delegated by the States, who alone are truly sovereign, and must be exercised in subordination to the States, who alone possess supreme dominion.

It would be difficult to sustain this proposition. The convention which framed the Constitution was indeed elected by the State legislatures. But the instrument, when it came from their hands, was a mere proposal, without obligation or pretensions to it. It was reported to the then existing Congress of the United States with a request that it might "be submitted to a convention of delegates, chosen in each State by the people thereof, under the recommendation of its legislature, for their assent and ratification."

This mode of proceeding was adopted, and by the convention, by Congress, and by the State legislatures, the instrument was submitted to the people. They acted upon it in the only manner in which they can act safely, effectively and wisely, on such a subject—by assembling in convention. It is true, they assembled in their several States—and where else should they have assembled? No political dreamer was ever wild enough to think of breaking down the lines which separate the States, and of compounding the American people into one common mass. Of consequence, when they act, they act in their States. But the measures they adopt do not, on that account, cease to be the measures of the people themselves, or become the measures of the State governments.

From these conventions the Constitution derives its whole authority. The government proceeds directly from the people; is "ordained and established" in the name of the people, and is declared to be ordained, "in order to form a more perfect union, establish justice, insure domestic tranquillity, and secure the blessings of liberty to themselves and to their posterity." ...

This Government is acknowledged by all to be one of enumerated powers. The principle that it can exercise only the powers granted to it would seem too apparent to have required to be enforced by all those arguments which its enlightened friends, while it was depending before the people, found it necessary to urge; that principle is now universally admitted. But the question respecting the extent of the powers actually granted is perpetually arising, and will probably continue to arise so long as our system shall exist. In discussing these questions, the conflicting powers of the General and State Governments must be brought into view, and the supremacy of their respective laws, when they are in opposition, must be settled. ...

But this question is not left to mere reason; the people have, in express terms, decided it by saying,

> "this Constitution, and the laws of the United States, which shall be made in pursuance thereof," "shall be the supreme law of the land," and by requiring that the members of the State legislatures and the officers of the executive and judicial departments of the States shall take the oath of fidelity to it. The Government of the United States, then, though limited in its powers, is supreme, and its laws, when made in pursuance of the Constitution, form the supreme law of the land, "anything in the Constitution or laws of any State to the contrary notwithstanding."

Among the enumerated powers, we do not find that of establishing a bank or creating a corporation. But there is no phrase in the instrument which, like the Articles of Confederation, excludes incidental or implied powers and which requires that everything granted shall be expressly and minutely described. Even the 10th Amendment, which was framed for the purpose of quieting the excessive jealousies which had been excited, omits the word "expressly," and declares only that the powers "not delegated to the United States, nor prohibited to the States, are reserved to the States or to the people," thus leaving the question whether the particular power which may become the subject of contest has been delegated to the one Government, or prohibited to the other, to depend on a fair construction of the whole instrument. The men who drew and adopted this amendment had experienced the embarrassments resulting from the insertion of this word in the Articles of Confederation, and probably omitted it to avoid those embarrassments. A Constitution, to contain an accurate detail of all the subdivisions of which its great powers will admit, and of all the means by which they may be carried into execution, would partake of the prolixity of a legal code, and could scarcely be embraced by the human mind. It would probably never be understood by the public. Its nature, therefore, requires that only its great outlines should be marked, its important objects designated, and the minor ingredients which compose those objects be deduced from the nature of the objects themselves. That this idea was entertained by the framers of the American Constitution is not only to be inferred from the nature of the instrument, but from the language. Why else were some of the limitations found in the 9th section of the 1st article introduced? It is also in some degree warranted by their having omitted to use any restrictive term which might prevent its receiving a fair and just interpretation. In considering this question, then, we must never forget that it is *a Constitution* we are expounding.

Although, among the enumerated powers of Government, we do not find the word "bank" or "incorporation," we find the great powers, to lay and collect taxes; to borrow money; to regulate commerce; to declare and conduct a war; and to raise and support armies and navies. The sword and the purse, all the external relations, and no inconsiderable portion of the industry of the nation are intrusted to its Government. It can never be pretended that these vast powers draw after them others of inferior importance merely because they are inferior. ...

But the Constitution of the United States has not left the right of Congress to employ the necessary means for the execution of the powers conferred on the Government to general reasoning. To its enumeration of powers is added that of making "all laws which shall be necessary and proper for carrying into execution the foregoing powers, and all other powers vested by this Constitution in the Government of the United States or in any department thereof." ...

But the argument on which most reliance is placed is drawn from that peculiar language of this clause. Congress is not empowered by it to make all laws which may have relation to the powers conferred on the Government, but such only as may be "necessary and proper" for carrying them into execution. The word "necessary" is considered as controlling the whole sentence, and as limiting the right to pass laws for the execution of the granted powers to such as are indispensable, and without which the power would be nugatory. That it excludes the choice of means, and leaves to Congress in each case that only which is most direct and simple.

Is it true that this is the sense in which the word "necessary" is always used? Does it always import an absolute physical necessity so strong that one thing to which another may be termed necessary cannot exist without that other? We think it does not. If reference be had to its use in the common affairs of the world or in approved authors, we find that it frequently imports no more than that one thing is convenient, or useful, or essential to another. To employ the means necessary to an end is generally understood as employing any means calculated to produce the end, and not as being confined to those single means without which the end would be entirely unattainable. Such is the character of human language that no word conveys to the mind in all situations one single definite idea, and nothing is more common than to use words in a figurative sense. Almost all compositions contain words which, taken in a their rigorous sense, would convey a meaning different from that which is obviously intended. It is essential to just construction that many words which import something excessive should be understood in a more mitigated sense—in that sense which common usage justifies. The word "necessary" is of this description. It has not a fixed character peculiar to itself. It admits of all degrees of comparison, and is often connected with other words which increase or diminish the impression the mind receives of the urgency it imports. A thing may be necessary, very necessary, absolutely or indispensably necessary. To no mind would the same idea be conveyed by these several phrases. The comment on the word is well illustrated by the passage cited at the bar from the 10th section of the 1st article of the Constitution. It is, we think, impossible to compare the sentence which prohibits a State from laying "imposts, or duties on imports or exports, except what may be absolutely necessary for executing its inspection laws," with that which authorizes Congress "to make all laws which shall be necessary and proper for carrying into execution" the powers of the General Government without feeling a conviction that the convention understood itself to change materially the meaning of the word "necessary," by prefixing the word "absolutely." This word, then, like others, is used in various senses, and, in its construction, the subject, the context, the intention of the person using them are all to be taken into view.

Let this be done in the case under consideration. The subject is the execution of those great powers on which the welfare of a Nation essentially depends. It must have been the intention of those who gave these powers to insure, so far as human prudence could insure, their beneficial execution. This could not be done by confiding the choice of means to such narrow limits as not to leave it in the power of Congress to adopt any which might be appropriate, and which were conducive to the end. This provision is made in a Constitution intended to endure for ages to come, and consequently to be adapted to the various crises of human affairs. To have prescribed the means by which Government should, in all future time, execute its powers would have been to change entirely the character of the instrument and give it the properties of a legal code. It would have been an unwise attempt to provide by immutable rules for exigencies which, if foreseen at all, must have been seen dimly, and which can be best provided for as they occur. To have declared that the best means shall not be used, but those alone without which the power given would be nugatory, would have been to deprive the legislature of the capacity to avail itself of experience, to exercise its reason, and to accommodate its legislation to circumstances. ...

The result of the most careful and attentive consideration bestowed upon this clause is that, if it does not enlarge, it cannot be construed to restrain, the powers of Congress, or to impair the right of the legislature to exercise its best judgment in the selection of measures to carry into execution the Constitutional powers of the Government. If no other motive for its insertion can be suggested, a sufficient one is found in the desire to remove all doubts respecting the right to legislate on that vast mass of incidental powers which must be involved in the Constitution if that instrument be not a splendid bauble.

We admit, as all must admit, that the powers of the Government are limited, and that its limits are not to be transcended. But we think the sound construction of the Constitution must allow to the national legislature that discretion with respect to the means by which the powers it confers are to be carried into execution which will enable that body to perform the high duties assigned to it in the manner most beneficial to the people. Let the end be legitimate, let it be within the scope of the Constitution, and all means which are appropriate, which are plainly adapted to that end, which are not prohibited, but consist with the letter and spirit of the Constitution, are Constitutional. ...

After the most deliberate consideration, it is the unanimous and decided opinion of this Court that the act to incorporate the Bank of the United States is a law made in pursuance of the Constitution, and is a part of the supreme law of the land.

The branches, proceeding from the same stock and being conducive to the complete accomplishment of the object, are equally constitutional. It would have been unwise to locate them in the charter, and it would be unnecessarily inconvenient to employ the legislative power in making those subordinate arrangements. The great duties of the bank are prescribed; those duties require branches; and the bank itself may, we think, be safely trusted with the selection of places where those branches shall be fixed, reserving always to the Government the right to require that a branch shall be located where it may be deemed necessary.

It being the opinion of the Court that the act incorporating the bank is constitutional, and that the power of establishing a branch in the State of Maryland might be properly exercised by the bank itself, we proceed to inquire:

1. Whether the State of Maryland may, without violating the Constitution, tax that branch?

That the power of taxation is one of vital importance; that it is retained by the States; that it is not abridged by the grant of a similar power to the Government of the Union; that it is to be concurrently exercised by the two Governments—are truths which have never been denied. But such is the paramount character of the Constitution that its capacity to withdraw any subject from the action of even this power is admitted. The States are expressly forbidden to lay any duties on imports or exports except what may be absolutely necessary for executing their inspection laws. If the obligation of this prohibition must be conceded—if it may restrain a State from the exercise of its taxing power on imports and exports—the same paramount character would seem to restrain, as it certainly may restrain, a State from such other exercise of this power as is in its nature incompatible with, and repugnant to, the constitutional laws of the Union. A law absolutely repugnant to another as entirely repeals that other as if express terms of repeal were used.

On this ground, the counsel for the bank place its claim to be exempted from the power of a State to tax its operations. There is no express provision for the case, but the claim has been sustained on a principle which so entirely pervades the Constitution, is so intermixed with the materials which compose it, so interwoven with its web, so blended with its texture, as to be incapable of being separated from it without rending it into shreds.

This great principle is that the Constitution and the laws made in pursuance thereof are supreme; that they control the Constitution and laws of the respective States, and cannot be controlled by them. From this, which may be almost termed an axiom, other propositions are deduced as corollaries, on the truth or error of which, and on their application to this case, the cause has been supposed to depend. These are, 1st. That a power to create implies a power to preserve; 2d. That a power to destroy, if wielded by a different hand, is hostile to, and incompatible with these powers to create and to preserve; 3d. That, where this repugnancy exists, that authority which is supreme must control, not yield to that over which it is supreme. ...

That the power of taxing it by the States may be exercised so as to destroy it is too obvious to be denied. But taxation is said to be an absolute power which acknowledges no other limits than those expressly prescribed in the Constitution, and, like sovereign power of every other description, is intrusted to the discretion of those who use it. But the very terms of this argument admit that the sovereignty of the State, in the article of taxation itself, is subordinate to, and may be controlled by, the Constitution of the United States. How far it has been controlled by that instrument must be a question of construction. In making this construction, no principle, not declared, can be admissible which would defeat the legitimate operations of a supreme Government. It is of the very essence of supremacy to remove all obstacles to its action within its own sphere, and so to modify every power vested in subordinate governments as to exempt its own operations from their own influence. This effect need not be stated in terms. It is so involved in the declaration of supremacy, so necessarily implied in it, that the expression of it could not make it more certain. We must, therefore, keep it in view while construing the Constitution. ...

The people of a State, therefore, give to their Government a right of taxing themselves and their property, and as the exigencies of Government cannot be limited, they prescribe no limits to the exercise of this right, resting confidently on the interest of the legislator and on the influence of the constituent over their representative to guard them against its abuse. But the means employed by the Government of the Union have no such security, nor is the right of a State to tax them sustained by the same theory. Those means are not given by the people of a particular State, not given by the constituents of the legislature which claim the right to tax them, but by the people of all the States They are given by all, for the benefit of all—and, upon theory, should be subjected to that Government only which belongs to all. ...

We have a principle which leaves the power of taxing the people and property of a State unimpaired; which leaves to a State the command of all its resources, and which places beyond its reach all those powers which are conferred by the people of the United States on the Government of the Union, and all those means which are given for the purpose of carrying those powers into execution. ...

We find, then, on just theory, a total failure of this original right to tax the means employed by the Government of the Union, for the execution of its powers. The right never existed, and the question whether it has been surrendered cannot arise. ...

That the power to tax involves the power to destroy; that the power to destroy may defeat and render useless the power to create; that there is a plain repugnance in conferring on one Government a power to control the constitutional measures of another, which other, with respect to those very measures, is declared to be supreme over that which exerts the control, are propositions not to be denied. But all inconsistencies are to be reconciled by the magic of the word CONFIDENCE. Taxation, it is said, does not necessarily and unavoidably destroy. To carry it to the excess of destruction would be an abuse, to presume which would banish that confidence which is essential to all Government.

But is this a case of confidence? Would the people of any one State trust those of another with a power to control the most insignificant operations of their State Government? We know they would not. Why, then, should we suppose that the people of any one State should be willing to trust those of another with a power to control the operations of a Government to which they have confided their most important and most valuable interests? In the Legislature of the Union alone are all represented. The Legislature of the Union alone, therefore, can be trusted by the people with the power of controlling measures which concern all, in the confidence that it will not be abused. This, then, is not a case of confidence, and we must consider it is as it really is.

If we apply the principle for which the State of Maryland contends, to the Constitution generally, we shall find it capable of changing totally the character of that instrument. We shall find it capable of arresting all the measures of the Government, and of prostrating it at the foot of the States. The American people have declared their Constitution and the laws made in pursuance thereof to be supreme, but this principle would transfer the supremacy, in fact, to the States. ...

The people of all the States have created the General Government, and have conferred upon it the general power of taxation. The people of all the

States, and the States themselves, are represented in Congress, and, by their representatives, exercise this power. When they tax the chartered institutions of the States, they tax their constituents, and these taxes must be uniform. But when a State taxes the operations of the Government of the United States, it acts upon institutions created not by their own constituents, but by people over whom they claim no control. It acts upon the measures of a Government created by others as well as themselves, for the benefit of others in common with themselves. The difference is that which always exists, and always must exist, between the action of the whole on a part, and the action of a part on the whole—between the laws of a Government declared to be supreme, and those of a Government which, when in opposition to those laws, is not supreme. ...

The Court has bestowed on this subject its most deliberate consideration. The result is a conviction that the States have no power, by taxation or otherwise, to retard, impede, burden, or in any manner control the operations of the constitutional laws enacted by Congress to carry into execution the powers vested in the General Government. This is, we think, the unavoidable consequence of that supremacy which the Constitution has declared.

We are unanimously of opinion that the law passed by the Legislature of Maryland, imposing a tax on the Bank of the United States is unconstitutional and void. ...

Notes and Questions

1. *Representation.* Voting is a key part of a constitutional representative democracy. By voting, voters select their representatives to make the governing decisions. The Framers considered submitting representatives to a "right to instruct" their representatives but ultimately rejected the notion. The voters have two ways to connect with their representatives: (1) vote and (2) communicate. What were the implications for voters if Maryland had been allowed to tax a federal bank? Whose interests would be protected? Whose would not? *See generally* John Hart Ely, Democracy and Distrust: A Theory of Judicial Review (1981).

2. The Early Court Rules on the Commerce Power

As you saw above when you read the sections of Article I, that portion of the Constitution lists the Congress's enumerated power "To regulate commerce with foreign nations, and among the several states, and with the Indian tribes." The commerce power has been one of Congress's greatest sources of power and controversy at the Court. The following case, *Gibbons v. Ogden*, gives an early and broad analysis of how far Congress's commerce powers go in a case of shipping. What definition of commerce do you take away from this case? Does this video help you to understand the case? See the Bill of Right Institute's video, *Gibbons v. Ogden*: BRI's Homework Help Series, Feb. 7, 2017, posted at https://www.youtube.com/watch?v=XvyqfJ1nhNM&list=PLsFE_Nvl6h_Y75KGR5pkGqcFisGvBnO9S&index=42.

Gibbons v. Ogden
SUPREME COURT OF THE UNITED STATES, 1824
22 U.S. 1

DECREE. This cause came on to be heard on the transcript of the record of the Court for the Trial of Impeachments and Correction of Errors of the State of New-York, and was argued by counsel. On consideration whereof, this Court is of opinion, that the several licenses to the steam boats the Stoudinger and the Bellona, to carry on the coasting trade, which are set up by the appellant, Thomas Gibbons, in his answer to the bill of the respondent, Aaron Ogden, filed in the Court of Chancery for the State of New-York, which were granted under an act of Congress, passed in pursuance of the constitution of the United States, gave full authority to those vessels to navigate the waters of the United States, by steam or otherwise, for the purpose of carrying on the coasting trade, any law of the State of New-York to the contrary notwithstanding; and that so much of the several laws of the State of New-York, as prohibits vessels, licensed according to the laws of the United States, from navigating the waters of the State of New-York, by means of fire or steam, is repugnant to the said constitution, and void. This Court is, therefore, of opinion, that the decree of the Court of New-York for the Trial of Impeachments and the Correction of Errors, affirming the decree of the Chancellor of that State, which perpetually enjoins the said Thomas Gibbons, the appellant, from navigating the waters of the State of New-York with the steam boats the Stoudinger and the Bellona, by steam or fire, is erroneous, and ought to be reversed, and the same is hereby reversed and annulled: and this Court doth further DIRECT, ORDER, and DECREE, that the bill of the said Aaron Ogden be dismissed, and the same is hereby dismissed accordingly.

Mr. Chief Justice MARSHALL delivered the opinion of the Court, and, after stating the case, proceeded as follows:

The appellant contends that this decree is erroneous, because the laws which purport to give the exclusive privilege it sustains, are repugnant to the constitution and laws of the United States.

They are said to be repugnant——

1st. To that clause in the constitution which authorizes Congress to regulate commerce.

2d. To that which authorizes Congress to promote the progress of science and useful arts.

The State of New-York maintains the constitutionality of these laws; and their Legislature, their Council of Revision, and their Judges, have repeatedly concurred in this opinion. It is supported by great names—by names which have all the titles to consideration that virtue, intelligence, and office, can bestow. No tribunal can approach the decision of this question, without feeling a just and real respect for that opinion which is sustained by such authority; but it is the province of this Court, while it respects, not to bow to it implicitly; and the Judges must exercise, in the examination of the subject, that understanding which Providence has bestowed upon them, with that independence which the people of the United States expect from this department of the government.

As preliminary to the very able discussions of the constitution, which we have heard from the bar, and as having some influence on its construction, reference has been made to the political situation of these States, anterior to its formation. It has been said, that they were sovereign, were completely independent, and were connected with each other only by a league. This is true. But, when these allied sovereigns converted their league into a government, when they converted their Congress of Ambassadors, deputed to deliberate on their common concerns, and to recommend measures of general utility, into a Legislature, empowered to enact laws on the most interesting subjects, the whole character in which the States appear, underwent a change, the extent of which must be determined by a fair consideration of the instrument by which that change was effected.

This instrument contains an enumeration of powers expressly granted by the people to their government. It has been said, that these powers ought to be construed strictly. But why ought they to be so construed? Is there one sentence in the constitution which gives countenance to this rule? In the last of the enumerated powers, that which grants, expressly, the means for carrying all others into execution, Congress is authorized 'to make all laws which shall be necessary and proper' for the purpose. But this limitation on the means which may be used, is not extended to the powers which are conferred; nor is there one sentence in the constitution, which has been pointed out by the gentlemen of the bar, or which we have been able to discern, that prescribes this rule. ...

We know of no rule for construing the extent of such powers, other than is given by the language of the instrument which confers them, taken in connexion with the purposes for which they were conferred.

The words are, 'Congress shall have power to regulate commerce with foreign nations, and among the several States, and with the Indian tribes.'

The subject to be regulated is commerce; and our constitution being, as was aptly said at the bar, one of enumeration, and not of definition, to ascertain the extent of the power, it becomes necessary to settle the meaning of the word. The counsel for the appellee would limit it to traffic, to buying and selling, or the interchange of commodities, and do not admit that it comprehends navigation. This would restrict a general term, applicable to many objects, to one of its significations. Commerce, undoubtedly, is traffic, but it is something more: it is intercourse. It describes the commercial intercourse between nations, and parts of nations, in all its branches, and is regulated by prescribing rules for carrying on that intercourse. The mind can scarcely conceive a system for regulating commerce between nations, which shall exclude all laws concerning navigation, which shall be silent on the admission of the vessels of the one nation into the ports of the other, and be confined to prescribing rules for the conduct of individuals, in the actual employment of buying and selling, or of barter.

If commerce does not include navigation, the government of the Union has no direct power over that subject, and can make no law prescribing what shall constitute American vessels, or requiring that they shall be navigated by American seamen. Yet this power has been exercised from the commencement of the government, has been exercised with the consent of all, and has been understood by all to be a commercial regulation. All America understands, and has uniformly understood, the word 'commerce,' to comprehend navigation. It was so understood, and must have been so understood, when the constitution was framed. The power over commerce, including navigation, was one of the primary objects for which the people of America adopted their government, and must have been contemplated in forming it. The convention must have used the word in that sense, because all have understood it in that sense; and the attempt to restrict it comes too late.

If the opinion that 'commerce,' as the word is used in the constitution, comprehends navigation also, requires any additional confirmation, that additional confirmation is, we think, furnished by the words of the instrument itself.

It is a rule of construction, acknowledged by all, that the exceptions from a power mark its extent; for it would be absurd, as well as useless, to except from a granted power, that which was not granted—that which the words of the grant could not comprehend. If, then, there are in the constitution plain exceptions from the power over navigation, plain inhibitions to the exercise of that power in a particular way, it is a proof that those who made these exceptions, and prescribed these inhibitions, understood the power to which they applied as being granted. ...

The word used in the constitution, then, comprehends, and has been always understood to comprehend, navigation within its meaning; and a power to regulate navigation, is as expressly granted, as if that term had been added to the word 'commerce.'

To what commerce does this power extend? The constitution informs us, to commerce 'with foreign nations, and among the several States, and with the Indian tribes.'

It has, we believe, been universally admitted, that these words comprehend every species of commercial intercourse between the United States and foreign nations. No sort of trade can be carried on between this country and any other, to which this power does not extend. It has been truly said, that commerce, as the word is used in the constitution, is a unit, every part of which is indicated by the term.

If this be the admitted meaning of the word, in its application to foreign nations, it must carry the same meaning throughout the sentence, and remain a unit, unless there be some plain intelligible cause which alters it.

The subject to which the power is next applied, is to commerce 'among the several States.' The word 'among' means intermingled with. A thing which is among others, is intermingled with them. Commerce among the States, cannot stop at the external boundary line of each State, but may be introduced into the interior.

It is not intended to say that these words comprehend that commerce, which is completely internal, which is carried on between man and man in a State, or between different parts of the same State, and which does not extend to or affect other States. Such a power would be inconvenient, and is certainly unnecessary.

Comprehensive as the word 'among' is, it may very properly be restricted to that commerce which concerns more States than one. The phrase is not one which would probably have been selected to indicate the completely interior traffic of a State, because it is not an apt phrase for that purpose; and the enumeration of the particular classes of commerce, to which the power was to be extended, would not have been made, had the intention been to extend the power to every description. The enumeration presupposes something not enumerated; and that something, if we regard the language or the subject of the sentence, must be the exclusively internal commerce of a State. The genius and character of the whole government seem to be, that its action is to be applied to all the external concerns of the nation, and to those internal concerns which affect the States generally; but not to those which are completely within a particular State, which do not affect other States, and with which it is not necessary to interfere, for the purpose of executing some of the general powers of the government. The completely internal commerce of a State, then, may be considered as reserved for the State itself.

But, in regulating commerce with foreign nations, the power of Congress does not stop at the jurisdictional lines of the several States. It would be a very useless power, if it could not pass those lines. The commerce of the United States with foreign nations, is that of the whole United States. Every district has a right to participate in it. The deep streams which penetrate our country in every direction, pass through the interior of almost every State in the Union, and furnish the means of exercising this right. If Congress has the power to regulate it, that power must be exercised whenever the subject exists. If it exists within the States, if a foreign voyage may commence or terminate at a port within a State, then the power of Congress may be exercised within a State. ...

We are now arrived at the inquiry—What is this power?

It is the power to regulate; that is, to prescribe the rule by which commerce is to be governed. This power, like all others vested in Congress, is complete in itself, may be exercised to its utmost extent, and acknowledges no limitations, other than are prescribed in the constitution. These are expressed in plain terms, and do not affect the questions which arise in this case, or which have been discussed at the bar. If, as has always been understood, the sovereignty of Congress, though limited to specified objects, is plenary as to those objects, the power over commerce with foreign nations, and among the several States, is vested in Congress as absolutely as it would be in a single government, having in its constitution the same restrictions on the exercise of the power as are found in the constitution of the United States. The wisdom and the discretion of Congress, their identity with the people, and the influence which their constituents possess at elections, are, in this, as in many other instances, as that, for example, of declaring war, the sole restraints on which they have relied, to secure them from its abuse. They are the restraints on which the people must often rely solely, in all representative governments.

The power of Congress, then, comprehends navigation, within the limits of every State in the Union; so far as that navigation may be, in any manner, connected with 'commerce with foreign nations, or among the several States, or with the Indian tribes.' It may, of consequence, pass the jurisdictional line of New-York, and act upon the very waters to which the prohibition now under consideration applies.

But it has been urged with great earnestness, that, although the power of Congress to regulate commerce with foreign nations, and among the several States, be co-extensive with the subject itself, and have no other limits than are prescribed in the constitution, yet the States may severally exercise the same power, within their respective jurisdictions. In support of this argument, it is said, that they possessed it as an inseparable attribute of sovereignty, before the formation of the constitution, and still retain it, except so far as they have surrendered it by that instrument; that this principle results from the nature of the government, and is secured by the tenth amendment; that an affirmative grant of power is not exclusive, unless in its own nature it be such that the continued exercise of it by the former possessor is inconsistent with the grant, and that this is not of that description. ...

Both parties have appealed to the constitution, to legislative acts, and judicial decisions; and have drawn arguments from all these sources, to support and illustrate the propositions they respectively maintain.

The grant of the power to lay and collect taxes is, like the power to regulate commerce, made in general terms, and has never been understood to interfere with the exercise of the same power by the State; and hence has been drawn an argument which has been applied to the question under consideration. But the two grants are not, it is conceived, similar in their terms or their nature. Although many of the powers formerly exercised by the States, are transferred to the government of the Union, yet the State governments remain, and constitute a most important part of our system. The power of taxation is indispensable to their existence, and is a power which, in its own nature, is capable of residing in, and being exercised by, different authorities at the same time. We are accustomed to see it placed, for different purposes, in different hands. Taxation is the simple operation of taking small portions from a perpetually accumulating mass, susceptible of almost infinite division; and a power in one to take what is necessary for certain purposes, is not, in its nature, incompatible with a power in another to take what is necessary for other purposes. Congress is authorized to lay and collect taxes, &c. to pay the debts, and provide for the common defence and general welfare of the United States. This does not interfere with the power of the States to tax for the support of their own governments; nor is the exercise of that power by the States, an exercise of any portion of the power that is granted to the United States. In imposing taxes for State purposes, they are not doing what Congress is empowered to do. Congress is not empowered to tax for those purposes which are within the exclusive province of the States. When, then, each government exercises the power of taxation, neither is exercising the power of the other. But, when a State proceeds to regulate commerce with foreign nations, or among the several States, it is exercising the very power that is granted to Congress, and is doing the very thing which Congress is authorized to do. There is no analogy, then, between the power of taxation and the power of regulating commerce. ...

The acts of Congress, passed in 1796 and 1799, empowering and directing the officers of the general government to conform to, and assist in the execution of the quarantine and health laws of a State, proceed, it is said, upon the idea that these laws are constitutional. It is undoubtedly true, that they do proceed upon that idea; and the constitutionality of such laws has never, so far as we are informed, been denied. But they do not imply an acknowledgment that a State may rightfully regulate commerce with foreign nations, or among the States; for they do not imply that such laws are an exercise of that power, or enacted with a view to it. On the contrary, they are treated as quarantine and health laws, are so denominated in the acts of Congress, and are considered as flowing from the acknowledged power of a State, to provide for the health of its citizens. But, as it was apparent that some of the provisions made for this purpose, and in virtue of this power, might interfere with, and be affected by the laws of the United States, made for the regulation of commerce, Congress, in that spirit of harmony and concilitation, which ought always to characterize the conduct of governments standing in the relation which that of the Union and those of the States bear to each other, has directed its officers to aid in the execution of these laws; and has, in some measure, adapted its own legislation to this object, by making provisions in aid of those of the States. But, in making these provisions, the opinion is unequivocally manifested, that Congress may control the State laws, so far as it may be necessary to control them, for the regulation of commerce. ...

Since, however, in exercising the power of regulating their own purely internal affairs, whether of trading or police, the States may sometimes enact laws, the validity of which depends on their interfering with, and being contrary to, an act of Congress passed in pursuance of the constitution, the Court will enter upon the inquiry, whether the laws of New-York, as expounded by the highest tribunal of that State, have, in their application to this case, come into collision with an act of Congress, and deprived a citizen of a right to which that act entitles him. Should this collision exist, it will be immaterial whether those laws were passed in virtue of a concurrent power 'to regulate commerce with foreign nations and among the several States,' or, in virtue of a power to regulate their domestic trade and police. In one case and the other, the acts of New-York must yield to the law of Congress; and the decision sustaining the privilege they confer, against a right given by a law of the Union, must be erroneous.

This opinion has been frequently expressed in this Court, and is founded, as well on the nature of the government as on the words of the constitution. In argument, however, it has been contended, that if a law passed by a State, in the exercise of its acknowledged sovereignty, comes into conflict with a law passed by Congress in pursuance of the constitution, they affect the subject, and each other, like equal opposing powers.

But the framers of our constitution foresaw this state of things, and provided for it, by declaring the supremacy not only of itself, but of the laws made in pursuance of it. The nullity of any act, law. The appropriate inconsistent with the constitution, is produced by the declaration, that the constitution is the supreme law. The appropriate application of that part of the clause which confers the same supremacy on laws and treaties, is to such acts of the State Legislatures as do not transcend their powers, but, though enacted in the execution of acknowledged State powers, interfere with, or are contrary to the laws of Congress, made in pursuance of the constitution, or some treaty made under the authority of the United States. In every such case, the act of Congress, or the treaty, is supreme; and the law of the State, though enacted in the exercise of powers not controverted, must yield to it. ...

But all inquiry into this subject seems to the Court to be put completely at rest, by the act already mentioned, entitled, 'An act for the enrolling and licensing of steam boats.'

This act authorizes a steam boat employed, or intended to be employed, only in a river or bay of the United States, owned wholly or in part by an alien, resident within the United States, to be enrolled and licensed as if the same belonged to a citizen of the United States.

This act demonstrates the opinion of Congress, that steam boats may be enrolled and licensed, in common with vessels using sails. They are, of course, entitled to the same privileges, and can no more be restrained from navigating waters, and entering ports which are free to such vessels, than if they were wafted on their voyage by the winds, instead of being propelled by the agency of fire. The one element may be as legitimately used as the other, for every commercial purpose authorized by the laws of the Union; and the act of a State inhibiting the use of either to any vessel having a license under the act of Congress, comes, we think, in direct collision with that act.

As this decides the cause, it is unnecessary to enter in an examination of that part of the constitution which empowers Congress to promote the progress of science and the useful arts. ...

Mr. Justice JOHNSON.

... Commerce, in its simplest signification, means an exchange of goods; but in the advancement of society, labour, transportation, intelligence, care, and various mediums of exchange, become commodities, and enter into commerce; the subject, the vehicle, the agent, and their various operations, become the objects of commercial regulation. Ship building, the carrying trade, and propagation of seamen, are such vital agents of commercial prosperity, that the nation which could not legislate over these subjects, would not possess power to regulate commerce. That such was the understanding of the framers of the constitution, is conspicuous from provisions contained in that instrument. ...

Notes and Questions

1. *The breadth of the commerce power:* How much regulation could Congress undertake pursuant to the Commerce Clause under Justice Marshall's opinion for the majority? Is it unlimited? If not, what are the sources of limitation?
2. *The limits:* What state activities could not be regulated by Congress according to this case?

B. What Is Congress's Commerce Power and Its Power to Tax and Spend?

1. The Most Commerce Power Ever?

The following case, *Wickard v. Filburn*, is often recognized as the case in which the Supreme Court interpreted the Commerce Clause to conclude that Congress has expansive commerce power. *Wickard* was decided in 1942. It appeared in the midst of a development on the Court. The Great Depression began in 1929, and once elected in 1933, President Franklin Roosevelt instituted the New Deal, government programs that were supposed to end the effects of the depression and raise everyone's standard of living. The Court frequently blocked Roosevelt's programs.

Cases limiting Congress's power appeared even before the Depression. In *Hammer v. Dagenhart,* 247 U.S. 251 (1918), which is often referred to as "The Child Labor Case," the federal law barred the transportation in interstate commerce of items produced by employers who employed workers under age 14 or children between 14 and 16 who worked more than 8 hours a day, 6 days a week, or at night. The Court ruled that the case was not about transportation but instead regulated the working hours of children. According to the Court, the commerce power did not give Congress power over children's labor. That issue belonged to the states.

Two years after President Roosevelt took office, the Court found unconstitutional the Railroad Requirement Act of 1934, which was the first compulsory retirement and pension plan for non-governmental employees administered by the federal government. It was not sufficiently related to commerce as the Court had been defining it. *Railroad Retirement Board v. Alton Railroad Co.,* 295 U.S. 330 (1935). *Schechter Poultry Corp. v. United States,* 295 U.S. 495 (1935), invalidated the National Industrial Recovery Act of 1933, which regulated wages, hours, unfair trade practices, and collective bargaining for private sector workers. *Schechter* involved the Live Poultry Industry of New York and is often referred to as the "Sick Chicken" case. The Court found that the wages and hours were local and could not be subject to federal control. Another law that regulated maximum hours and minimum wages in coal mines was also deemed unconstitutional, *Carter v. Carter Coal Co.,* 298 U.S. 238 (1936).

These anti-New Deal opinions led Franklin Delano Roosevelt to propose the famous 1937 court-packing plan. Roosevelt commented on the aging Court and its capacity. He proposed that for each justice who had reached 70 years of age, who had been on the court at least ten years, and who had not retired from the Court, they would nominate an additional justice, up to 15 justices total.

The Senate Judiciary Committee eventually rejected Roosevelt's plan, but while the court-packing discussion was continuing, the Court changed its approach to the commerce power. In *West Coast Hotel v. Parrish*, 300 U.S. 379 (1937), a 5–4 Court upheld a minimum wage law for women. Scholars have debated whether the first Justice Roberts's "switch in time that saved the Nine" in this opinion really kept Roosevelt from expanding the Court.

The Supreme Court then upheld Congress's commerce power in *NLRB v. Jones & Laughlin Steel Corp.,* 301 U.S. 1 (1937), which ruled that the National Labor Relations Board's actions regulating unfair labor practices were constitutional.

In a 1941 case, *United States v. Darby*, 312 U.S. 100 (1941), the Court overruled *Hammer v. Dagenhart* and unanimously upheld Congress's Fair Labor Standards Act, which regulated child labor and working wages and hours. Relying on *Gibbons v. Ogden*, which you read above, the Court ruled that the FLSA had a significant impact on interstate commerce and so, was a constitutional use of Congress's commerce powers. Do you understand what the significant impact was?

What was the commerce in the following case? Why do people think this was a broad interpretation of congressional power?

Wickard v. Filburn

SUPREME COURT OF THE UNITED STATES, 1942

317 U.S. 111, 63 S.Ct. 82

Mr. Justice JACKSON delivered the opinion of the Court.

The appellee filed his complaint against the Secretary of Agriculture of the United States, three members of the County Agricultural Conservation Committee for Montgomery County, Ohio, and a member of the State Agricultural Conservation Committee for Ohio. He sought to enjoin enforcement against himself of the marketing penalty imposed by the amendment of May 26, 1941, to the Agricultural Adjustment Act of 1938, upon that part of his 1941 wheat crop which was available for marketing in excess of the marketing quota established for his farm. He also sought a declaratory judgment that the wheat marketing quota provisions of the Act as amended and applicable to him were unconstitutional because not sustainable under the Commerce Clause or consistent with the Due Process Clause of the Fifth Amendment. ...

The appellee for many years past has owned and operated a small farm in Montgomery County, Ohio, maintaining a herd of dairy cattle, selling milk, raising poultry, and selling poultry and eggs. It has been his practice to raise a small acreage of winter wheat, sown in the Fall and harvested in the following July; to sell a portion of the crop; to feed part to poultry and livestock on the farm, some of which is sold; to use some in making flour for home consumption; and to keep the rest for the following seeding. ...

II

It is urged that under the Commerce Clause of the Constitution, Article I, s 8, clause 3, Congress does not possess the power it has in this instance sought to exercise. The question would merit little consideration since our decision in *United States v. Darby*, sustaining the federal power to regulate production of goods for commerce except for the fact that this Act extends federal regulation to production not intended in any part for commerce but wholly for consumption on the farm. The Act includes a definition of 'market' and its derivatives so that as related to wheat in addition to its conventional meaning it also means to dispose of 'by feeding (in any form) to poultry or livestock which, or the products of which, are sold, bartered, or exchanged, or to be so disposed of.' Hence, marketing quotas not only embrace all that may be sold without penalty but also what may be consumed on the premises. Wheat produced on excess acreage is designated as 'available for marketing' as so defined and the penalty is imposed thereon. Penalties do not depend upon whether any part of the wheat either within or without the quota is sold or intended to be sold. The sum of this is that the Federal Government fixes a quota including all that the farmer may harvest for sale or for his own farm needs, and declares that wheat produced on excess acreage may neither be disposed of nor used except upon payment of the penalty or except it is stored as required by the Act or delivered to the Secretary of Agriculture.

Appellee says that this is a regulation of production and consumption of wheat. Such activities are, he urges, beyond the reach of Congressional power under the Commerce Clause, since they are local in character, and their effects upon interstate commerce are at most 'indirect.' In answer the Government argues that the statute regulates neither production nor consumption, but only marketing; and, in the alternative, that if the Act does go beyond the regulation of marketing it is sustainable as a 'necessary and proper' implementation of the power of Congress over interstate commerce.

The Government's concern lest the Act be held to be a regulation of production or consumption rather than of marketing is attributable to a few dicta and decisions of this Court which might be understood to lay it down that activities such as 'production,' 'manufacturing,' and 'mining' are strictly 'local' and, except in special circumstances which are not present here, cannot be regulated under the commerce power because their effects upon interstate commerce are, as matter of law, only 'indirect.' Even today, when this power has been held to have great latitude, there is no decision of this Court that such activities may be regulated where no part of the product is intended for interstate commerce or intermingled with the subjects thereof. We believe that a review of the course of decision under the Commerce Clause will make plain, however, that questions of the power of Congress are not to be decided by reference to any formula which would give controlling force to nomenclature such as 'production' and 'indirect' and foreclose consideration of the actual effects of the activity in question upon interstate commerce.

At the beginning Chief Justice Marshall described the Federal commerce power with a breadth never yet exceeded. *Gibbons v. Ogden.* He made emphatic the embracing and penetrating nature of this power by warning that effective restraints on its exercise must proceed from political rather than from judicial processes.

For nearly a century, however, decisions of this Court under the Commerce Clause dealt rarely with questions of what Congress might do in the exercise of its granted power under the Clause and almost entirely with the permissibility of state activity which it was claimed discriminated against or burdened interstate commerce. During this period there was perhaps little occasion for the affirmative exercise of the commerce power, and the influence of the Clause on American life and law was a negative one, resulting almost wholly from its operation as a restraint upon the powers of the states. In discussion and decision the point of reference instead of being what was 'necessary and proper' to the exercise by Congress of its granted power, was often some concept of sovereignty thought to be implicit in the status of statehood. Certain activities such as 'production,' 'manufacturing,' and 'mining' were occasionally said to be within the province of state governments and beyond the power of Congress under the Commerce Clause.

It was not until 1887 with the enactment of the Interstate Commerce Act that the interstate commerce power began to exert positive influence in American law and life. This first important federal resort to the commerce power was followed in 1890 by the Sherman Anti-Trust Act and, thereafter, mainly after 1903, by many others. These statutes ushered in new phases of adjudication, which required the Court to approach the interpretation of the Commerce Clause in the light of an actual exercise by Congress of its power thereunder.

When it first dealt with this new legislation, the Court adhered to its earlier pronouncements, and allowed but little scope to the power of Congress. United States v. E. C. Knight Co., 156 U.S. 1, 15 S.Ct. 249, 39 L.Ed. 325. These earlier pronouncements also played an important part in several of the five cases in which this Court later held that Acts of Congress under the Commerce Clause were in excess of its power.[1]

Even while important opinions in this line of restrictive authority were being written, however, other cases called forth broader interpretations of the Commerce Clause destined to supersede the earlier ones, and to bring about a return to the principles first enunciated by Chief Justice Marshall in *Gibbons v. Ogden*, supra.

Not long after the decision of *United States v. E. C. Knight Co.*, supra, Mr. Justice Holmes, in sustaining the exercise of national power over intrastate activity, stated for the Court that 'commerce among the states is not a technical legal conception, but a practical one, drawn from the course of business.' *Swift & Co. v. United States.* It was soon demonstrated that the effects of many kinds of intrastate activity upon interstate commerce were such as to make them a proper subject of federal regulation. In some cases sustaining the exercise of federal power over intrastate matters the term 'direct' was used for the purpose of stating, rather than of reaching, a result; in others it was treated as synonymous with 'substantial' or 'material;' and in others it was not used at all. Of late its use has been abandoned in cases dealing with questions of federal power under the Commerce Clause.

In the *Shreveport Rate Cases (Houston, E. & W.T.R. Co. v. United States)*, 234 U.S. 342, 34 S.Ct. 833, 58 L.Ed. 1341, the Court held that railroad rates of an admittedly intrastate character and fixed by authority of the state might, nevertheless, be revised by the Federal Government because of the economic effects which they had upon interstate commerce. The opinion of Mr. Justice Hughes found federal intervention constitutionally authorized because of 'matters having such a close and substantial relation to interstate traffic that

1. Employers Liability Cases (Howard v. Illinois Central R. Co.), 207 U.S. 463, 28 S.Ct. 141, 52 L.Ed. 297; Hammer v. Dagenhart, 247 U.S. 251, 38 S.Ct. 529, 62 L.Ed. 1101, 3 A.L.R. 649, Ann.Cas.1918E, 724; Railroad Retirement Board v. Alton R. Co., 295 U.S. 330, 55 S.Ct. 758, 79 L.Ed. 1468; Schechter Corp. v. United States, 295 U.S. 495, 55 S.Ct. 837, 79 L.Ed. 1570, 97 A.L.R. 947; Carter v. Carter Coal Co., 298 U.S. 238, 56 S.Ct. 855, 80 L.Ed. 1160; cf. United States v. Dewitt, 9 Wall. 41, 19 L.Ed. 593; Trade Mark Cases (United States v. Steffens), 100 U.S. 82, 25 L.Ed. 550; Hill v. Wallace, 259 U.S. 44, 42 S.Ct. 453, 66 L.Ed. 822; Heisler v. Thomas Colliery Co., 260 U.S. 245, 259, 260, 43 S.Ct. 83, 86, 67 L.Ed. 237; Oliver Iron Co. v. Lord, 262 U.S. 172, 178, 179, 43 S.Ct. 526, 529, 67 L.Ed. 929; Utah Power & Light Co. v. Pfost, 286 U.S. 165, 52 S.Ct. 548, 76 L.Ed. 1038.

the control is essential or appropriate to the security of that traffic, to the efficiency of the interstate service, and to the maintenance of the conditions under which interstate commerce may be conducted upon fair terms and without molestation or hindrance.'

The Court's recognition of the relevance of the economic effects in the application of the Commerce Clause exemplified by this statement has made the mechanical application of legal formulas no longer feasible. Once an economic measure of the reach of the power granted to Congress in the Commerce Clause is accepted, questions of federal power cannot be decided simply by finding the activity in question to be 'production' nor can consideration of its economic effects be foreclosed by calling them 'indirect.' The present Chief Justice has said in summary of the present state of the law: 'The commerce power is not confined in its exercise to the regulation of commerce among the states. It extends to those activities intrastate which so affect interstate commerce, or the exertion of the power of Congress over it, as to make regulation of them appropriate means to the attainment of a legitimate end, the effective execution of the granted power to regulate interstate commerce. * * * The power of Congress over interstate commerce is plenary and complete in itself, may be exercised to its utmost extent, and acknowledges no limitations other than are prescribed in the Constitution. * * * It follows that no form of state activity can constitutionally thwart the regulatory power granted by the commerce clause to Congress. Hence the reach of that power extends to those intrastate activities which in a substantial way interfere with or obstruct the exercise of the granted power.'

Whether the subject of the regulation in question was 'production,' 'consumption,' or 'marketing' is, therefore, not material for purposes of deciding the question of federal power before us. That an activity is of local character may help in a doubtful case to determine whether Congress intended to reach it. The same consideration might help in determining whether in the absence of Congressional action it would be permissible for the state to exert its power on the subject matter, even though in so doing it to some degree affected interstate commerce. But even if appellee's activity be local and though it may not be regarded as commerce, it may still, whatever its nature, be reached by Congress if it exerts a substantial economic effect on interstate commerce and this irrespective of whether such effect is what might at some earlier time have been defined as 'direct' or 'indirect.'

The parties have stipulated a summary of the economics of the wheat industry. Commerce among the states in wheat is large and important. Although wheat is raised in every state but one, production in most states is not equal to consumption. Sixteen states on average have had a surplus of wheat above their own requirements for feed, seed, and food. Thirty-two states and the District of Columbia, where production has been below consumption, have looked to these surplus-producing states for their supply as well as for wheat for export and carryover.

The wheat industry has been a problem industry for some years. Largely as a result of increased foreign production and import restrictions, annual exports of wheat and flour from the United States during the ten-year period ending in 1940 averaged less than 10 per cent of total production, while during the 1920's they averaged more than 25 per cent. The decline in the export trade has left a large surplus in production which in connection with an abnormally large supply of wheat and other grains in recent years caused congestion in a number of markets; tied up railroad cars; and caused elevators in some instances to turn away grains, and railroads to institute embargoes to prevent further congestion. ...

The effect of consumption of homegrown wheat on interstate commerce is due to the fact that it constitutes the most variable factor in the disappearance of the wheat crop. Consumption on the farm where grown appears to vary in an amount greater than 20 per cent of average production. The total amount of wheat consumed as food varies but relatively little, and use as seed is relatively constant.

The maintenance by government regulation of a price for wheat undoubtedly can be accomplished as effectively by sustaining or increasing the demand as by limiting the supply. The effect of the statute before us is to restrict the amount which may be produced for market and the extent as well to which one may forestall resort to the market by producing to meet his own needs. That appellee's own contribution to the demand for wheat may be trivial by itself is not enough to remove him from the scope of federal regulation where, as here, his contribution, taken together with that of many others similarly situated, is far from trivial. *National Labor Relations Board v. Fainblatt*; *United States v. Darby*.

It is well established by decisions of this Court that the power to regulate commerce includes the power to regulate the prices at which commodities in that commerce are dealt in and practices affecting such prices. One of the primary purposes of the Act in question was to increase the market price of wheat and to that end to limit the volume thereof that could affect the market. It can hardly be denied that a factor of such volume and variability as home-consumed wheat would have a substantial influence on price and market conditions. This may arise because being in marketable condition such wheat overhangs the market and if induced by rising prices tends to flow into the market and check price increases. But if we assume that it is never marketed, it supplies a need of the man who grew it which would otherwise be reflected by purchases in the open market. Home-grown wheat in this sense competes with wheat in commerce. The stimulation of commerce is a use of the regulatory function quite as definitely as prohibitions or restrictions thereon. This record leaves us in no doubt that Congress may properly have considered that wheat consumed on the farm where grown if wholly outside the scheme of regulation would have a substantial effect in defeating and obstructing its purpose to stimulate trade therein at increased prices.

It is said, however, that this Act, forcing some farmers into the market to buy what they could provide for themselves, is an unfair promotion of the markets and prices of specializing wheat growers. It is of the essence of regulation that it lays a restraining hand on the self interest of the regulated and that advantages from the regulation commonly fall to others. The conflicts of economic interest between the regulated and those who advantage by it are wisely left under our system to resolution by the Congress under its more flexible and responsible legislative process. Such conflicts rarely lend themselves to judicial determination. And with the wisdom, workability, or fairness, of the plan of regulation we have nothing to do. ...

That appellee is the worse off for the aggregate of this legislation does not appear; it only appears that if he could get all that the Government gives and do nothing that the Government asks, he would be better off than this law allows. To deny him this is not to deny him due process of law.

Notes and Questions

1. *How far does* Wickard *go?* The Court states that once they recognized that economic impact of a federal regulation is relevant to determining commerce power, it was too late for "mechanical application of legal formulas." Does this decision mean that the powers of Congress are not really limited or enumerated? Can Congress do anything once it identifies some economic impact of its actions?
2. *Video.* Does this video help you to understand the history and significance of the case? See Quimbee's video, *Wickard v. Filburn* Case Brief Summary/Law Case Explained, Apr. 2, 2019, posted at https://www.youtube.com/watch?v=UGZIAf_-Ckw&list=PLsFE_Nvl6h_Y75KGR5pkGqcFisGvBnO9S&index=48.
3. *The Justices discuss* Wickard. The Justices' discussions from the vote on *Wickard v. Filburn* are available and were published in Del Dickson, *The Supreme Court in Conference 1940–1985: the private discussions behind nearly 300 Supreme Court decisions 221–222* (2001). What do the following comments tell you about the case and why the Justices voted as they did?

Conference of May 7, 1942

STONE: The respondent planted grain when provisions of the act respecting quotas were different. Before he planted his wheat, he had notice of his quota allotment. At the same time, the secretary of agriculture made a speech failing to mention that there was an amendment of the law. Prior to this, there had been a penalty on marketing in interstate commerce. The farmer could ship it if he paid a penalty or fed it to his stock, etc. The amendment provided for an increase in the penalty to 49 cents, and he could turn the Wheat over to the secretary, or store it, or borrow on it. Respondent says that the law is bad: (a) as a regulation of production; and (b) it is being applied retroactive as to him in such an offensive way as to violate the Fifth Amendment. As to the latter, we can assume there was no act at all when the crop was planted. If the act forbade shipment, in interstate commerce, it would still be okay as a regulation of commerce under *Mulford*." The retroactivity issue drops out if it is an exercise of commerce power. If the government can regulate by regulating goods planted before the act came in, then it can do this, provided that this is a regulation of Congress's commerce power. The government says that this is a regulation of commerce, because to fix the amount that moves in commerce is the very purpose of regulation. This is a regulation of commerce, and it is no more retroactive than the regulation in the *Mulford* case. The act is applicable to goods which may be used only intrastate. Here, we only know that some of his crop was used on his farm. The government says that it is regulating commerce, since the purpose is to regulate a crop which moves in commerce. They have to take control of the whole crop—if he can feed this to his stock, then it affects commerce. I find it difficult to say as a matter of logic and economics that this is not a means of regulating commerce-perhaps even an indispensable means. This raises the question of where the permissible regulation of commerce ends. Congress can regulate intrastate commerce where it has fair relation to interstate commerce. We said that in the *milk* case. This case is closely parallel. Also the *Darby* case. I do not care for the result.

ROBERTS: I pass. I am in doubt on both features of this case.

BLACK: I agree with the Chief Justice.

REED: I take no part. I have money invested in a farm.

FRANKFURTER: I agree with the Chief Justice.

DOUGLAS: I agree.

MURPHY: I agree.

BYRNES: I agree.

JACKSON: I agree.

Conference of October 17, 1942

STONE: On the two main issues: (1) On the retroactive increase of the penalty for over-production, I am guided by the *Mulford* case. (2) On the constitutional scope of the commerce power, previous regulation of amounts for shipment without including farm consumption was ineffective. This is an appropriate regulation of something which affects Commerce.

ROBERTS: I am for reversal.

2. Are There Any Limits on the Spending Power?

The plain language of the enumerated powers includes a commerce power and a spending power. The Court has found that the spending power allows Congress to attach conditions to the granting of federal funds. The case below asks whether a state can be required to change its drinking age to 21 in order to obtain more funds to build highways. If Congress provides the funding, it is a Spending Clause action. The following case tells you what limits the Court has put on that power.

Read the oral argument in this case, which is available on the case's website, https://www.oyez.org/cases/1986/86-260. This spending case is unusual in that it contrasts the federal government's spending powers with the states' powers under the Twenty-First Amendment, the amendment that eliminated Prohibition and gave each state the power to regulate alcohol as it chose. Can you tell what the Justices think about spending in the oral argument? Who seems most supportive of the spending power? Is any Justice supportive of the states' powers under the Twenty-First Amendment? After reading the argument and before you read the opinion, predict how each Justice would vote on the power of Congress to persuade the states to change their drinking age. What is the total number of justices you get on each side? Is your opinion 7–2 as the Justices voted in the case itself?

South Dakota v. Dole
SUPREME COURT OF THE UNITED STATES, 1987
483 U.S. 203, 107 S.Ct. 2793

REHNQUIST, C.J., delivered the opinion of the Court, in which WHITE, MARSHALL, BLACKMUN, POWELL, STEVENS, and SCALIA, JJ., joined. BRENNAN, J., and O'CONNOR, J., filed dissenting opinions.

Petitioner South Dakota permits persons 19 years of age or older to purchase beer containing up to 3.2% alcohol. S.D.Codified Laws § 35-6-27 (1986). In 1984 Congress enacted 23 U.S.C. § 158 (1982 ed., Supp. III), which directs the Secretary of Transportation to withhold a percentage of federal highway funds otherwise allocable from States "in which the purchase or public possession ... of any alcoholic beverage by a person who is less than twenty-one years of age is lawful." The State sued in United States District Court seeking a declaratory judgment that § 158 violates the constitutional limitations on congressional exercise of the spending power and violates the Twenty-first Amendment to the United States Constitution. ...

Despite the extended treatment of the question by the parties, however, we need not decide in this case whether that Amendment would prohibit an attempt by Congress to legislate directly a national minimum drinking age. Here, Congress has acted indirectly under its spending power to encourage uniformity in the States' drinking ages. As we explain below, we find this legislative effort within constitutional bounds even if Congress may not regulate drinking ages directly.

The Constitution empowers Congress to "lay and collect Taxes, Duties, Imposts, and Excises, to pay the Debts and provide for the common Defence and general Welfare of the United States." Art. I, § 8, cl. 1. Incident to this power, Congress may attach conditions on the receipt of federal funds, and has repeatedly employed the power "to further broad policy objectives by conditioning receipt of federal moneys upon compliance by the recipient with federal statutory and administrative directives." The breadth of this power was made clear in *United States v. Butler,* 297 U.S. 1, 66, 56 S.Ct. 312, 319, 80 L.Ed. 477 (1936), where the Court, resolving a longstanding debate over the scope of the Spending Clause, determined that "the power of Congress to authorize expenditure of public moneys for public purposes is not limited by the direct grants of legislative power found in the Constitution." Thus, objectives not thought to be within Article I's "enumerated legislative fields," *id.,* at 65, 56 S.Ct., at 319, may nevertheless be attained through the use of the spending power and the conditional grant of federal funds.

The spending power is of course not unlimited, but is instead subject to several general restrictions articulated in our cases. The first of these limitations is derived from the language of the Constitution itself: the exercise of the spending power must be in pursuit of "the general welfare In considering whether a particular expenditure is intended to serve general public purposes, courts should defer substantially to the judgment of Congress. Second, we have required that if Congress desires to condition the States' receipt of federal funds, it "must do so unambiguously ..., enabl[ing] the States to exercise their choice knowingly, cognizant of the consequences of their participation." Third, our cases have suggested (without significant elaboration) that conditions on federal grants might be illegitimate if they are unrelated "to the federal interest in particular national projects or programs." Finally, we have noted that other constitutional provisions may provide an independent bar to the conditional grant of federal funds.

South Dakota does not seriously claim that § 158 is inconsistent with any of the first three restrictions mentioned above. ...

The remaining question about the validity of § 158—and the basic point of disagreement between the parties—is whether the Twenty-first Amendment constitutes an "independent constitutional bar" to the conditional grant of federal funds. Petitioner, relying on its view that the Twenty-first Amendment prohibits *direct* regulation of drinking ages by Congress, asserts that "Congress may not use the spending power to regulate that which it is prohibited from regulating directly under the Twenty-first Amendment." But our cases show that this "independent constitutional bar" limitation on the spending power is not of the kind petitioner suggests. *United States v. Butler, supra,* for example, established that the constitutional limitations on Congress when exercising its spending power are less exacting than those on its authority to regulate directly. ...

Our decisions have recognized that in some circumstances the financial inducement offered by Congress might be so coercive as to pass the point at which "pressure turns into compulsion." *Steward Machine Co. v. Davis, supra,* 301 U.S., at 590, 57 S.Ct., at 892. Here, however, Congress has directed only that a State desiring to establish a minimum drinking age lower than 21 lose a relatively small percentage of certain federal highway funds. Petitioner contends that the coercive nature of this program is evident from the degree of success it has achieved. We cannot conclude, however, that a conditional grant of federal money of this sort is unconstitutional simply by reason of its success in achieving the congressional objective.

When we consider, for a moment, that all South Dakota would lose if she adheres to her chosen course as to a suitable minimum drinking age is 5% of the funds otherwise obtainable under specified highway grant programs, the argument as to coercion is shown to be more rhetoric than fact. ... Even if Congress might lack the power to impose a national minimum drinking age directly, we conclude that encouragement to state action found in § 158 is a valid use of the spending power.

Justice BRENNAN, dissenting.

I agree with Justice O'CONNOR that regulation of the minimum age of purchasers of liquor falls squarely within the ambit of those powers reserved to the States by the Twenty-first Amendment. Since States possess this constitutional power, Congress cannot condition a federal grant in a manner that abridges this right. The Amendment, itself, strikes the proper balance between federal and state authority. I therefore dissent.

Justice O'CONNOR, dissenting.

... As discussed above, a condition that a State will raise its drinking age to 21 cannot fairly be said to be reasonably related to the expenditure of funds for highway construction. The only possible connection, highway safety, has nothing to do with how the funds Congress has appropriated are expended. Rather than a condition determining how federal highway money shall be expended, it is a regulation determining who shall be able to drink liquor. As such it is not justified by the spending power.

Of the other possible sources of congressional authority for regulating the sale of liquor only the commerce power comes to mind. But in my view, the regulation of the age of the purchasers of liquor, just as the regulation of the price at which liquor may be sold, falls squarely within the scope of those powers reserved to the States by the Twenty-first Amendment.

The immense size and power of the Government of the United States ought not obscure its fundamental character. It remains a Government of enumerated powers. *McCulloch v. Maryland,* 4 Wheat. 316, 405, 4 L.Ed. 579 (1819). Because 23 U.S.C. § 158 (1982 ed., Supp. III) cannot be justified as an exercise of any power delegated to the Congress, it is not authorized by the Constitution. The Court errs in holding it to be the law of the land, and I respectfully dissent.

Notes and Questions

1. *Who is more persuasive?* Why? What would be the practical impact on federal power if O'Connor's reasoning were followed?
2. *How far can the federal government go?* What is the limit on the ability of the federal government to persuade the states to act with federal funds? Has Chief Justice Rehnquist's majority opinion established a test for future instances of the federal government conditioning funding on forcing the states to act?
3. *Video.* What do you think of this video's analysis of the case? See Quimbee's video on *South Dakota v. Dole* Case Brief Summary/Law Case Explained, Jun. 9, 2017, posted at https://www.youtube.com/watch?v=Pj_qNXyC9Xw&list=PLsFE_Nvl6h_Y75KGR5pkGqcFisGvBnO9S&index=68.

3. The Court Restricts Commerce Power Again

As you learned in Part B1, during the Great Depression, the Court cut back on Congress's commerce power, repeatedly ruling against the President's labor legislation. With cases like *Wickard*, however, the Court let Congress do many other things under its commerce power. We will see in Chapter 10, for example, that Congress used its Commerce Clause power to pass the Civil Rights Act.

However, in 1995, the Court ruled that Congress's Gun-Free School Zones Act was not within Congress's commerce powers. Therefore, a student who brought a gun to school could not be prosecuted under that statute. The Court seemed more sympathetic to the states, under the Tenth Amendment, than to Congress, under Article I. Why do you think the Court ruled that way? Which is the most persuasive opinion in the following case? Which is the least?

Read the oral argument in this case before you read the case itself. It is available on this website, https://www.oyez.org/cases/1994/93-1260. This case was decided in 1995. Which advocate did the best job supporting the client's case? Why do you think that advocate was the best? Which Justices were most committed to protecting states' power? Do Rehnquist and O'Connor show more interest in state power than the other Justices? Are there any questions that the advocates cannot answer? Did any question by the Justices strike you as particularly hard?

Why are there so many different opinions in the decided case?

Lopez, of course, informed Congress that the Court would be following *Lopez*'s test in future Commerce Clause cases. What would you recommend Representatives and Senators do in passing legislation to accord with the *Lopez* Commerce Clause analysis?

United States v. Lopez

SUPREME COURT OF THE UNITED STATES, 1995

514 U.S. 549, 115 S.Ct. 1624

REHNQUIST, C.J., delivered the opinion of the Court, in which O'CONNOR, SCALIA, KENNEDY, and THOMAS, JJ., joined. KENNEDY, J., filed a concurring opinion, in which O'CONNOR, J., joined. THOMAS, J., filed a concurring opinion. STEVENS, J., and SOUTER, J., filed dissenting opinions. BREYER, J., filed a dissenting opinion, in which STEVENS, SOUTER, and GINSBURG, JJ., joined.

In the Gun-Free School Zones Act of 1990, Congress made it a federal offense "for any individual knowingly to possess a firearm at a place that the individual knows, or has reasonable cause to believe, is a school zone." The Act neither regulates a commercial activity nor contains a requirement that the possession be connected in any way to interstate commerce. We hold that the Act exceeds the authority of Congress "[t]o regulate Commerce ... among the several States. ..." ...

We start with first principles. The Constitution creates a Federal Government of enumerated powers. See Art. I, § 8. As James Madison wrote: "The powers delegated by the proposed Constitution to the federal government are few and defined. Those which are to remain in the State governments are numerous and indefinite." The Federalist No. 45. This constitutionally mandated division of authority "was adopted by the Framers to ensure protection of our fundamental liberties." "Just as the separation and independence of the coordinate branches of the Federal Government serve to prevent the accumulation of excessive power in any one branch, a healthy balance of power between the States and the Federal Government will reduce the risk of tyranny and abuse from either front." ...

Consistent with this structure, we have identified three broad categories of activity that Congress may regulate under its commerce power. First, Congress may regulate the use of the channels of interstate commerce. Second, Congress is empowered to regulate and protect the instrumentalities of interstate commerce, or persons or things in interstate commerce, even though the threat may come only from intrastate activities. Finally, Congress' commerce authority includes the power to regulate those activities having a substantial relation to interstate commerce.

Within this final category, admittedly, our case law has not been clear whether an activity must "affect" or "substantially affect" interstate commerce in order to be within Congress' power to regulate it under the Commerce Clause. We conclude, consistent with the great weight of our case law, that the proper test requires an analysis of whether the regulated activity "substantially affects" interstate commerce.

We now turn to consider the power of Congress, in the light of this framework, to enact the statute. The first two categories of authority may be quickly disposed of: § 922(q) is not a regulation of the use of the channels of interstate commerce, nor is it an attempt to prohibit the interstate transportation of a commodity through the channels of commerce; nor can § 922(q) be justified as a regulation by which Congress has sought to protect an instrumentality of interstate commerce or a thing in interstate commerce. Thus, if § 922(q) is to be sustained, it must be under the third category as a regulation of an activity that substantially affects interstate commerce. ...

[This] is a criminal statute that by its terms has nothing to do with "commerce" or any sort of economic enterprise, however broadly one might define those terms. Section 922(q) is not an essential part of a larger regulation of economic activity, in which the regulatory scheme could be undercut unless the intrastate activity were regulated. It cannot, therefore, be sustained under our cases upholding regulations of activities that arise out of or are connected with a commercial transaction, which viewed in the aggregate, substantially affects interstate commerce.

Second, § 922(q) contains no jurisdictional element which would ensure, through case-by-case inquiry, that the firearm possession in question affects interstate commerce. ...

Although as part of our independent evaluation of constitutionality under the Commerce Clause we of course consider legislative findings, and indeed even congressional committee findings, regarding effect on interstate commerce, the Government concedes that "[n]either the statute nor its legislative history contain[s] express congressional findings regarding the effects upon interstate commerce of gun possession in a school zone." We agree with the Government that Congress normally is not required to make formal findings as to the substantial burdens that an activity has on interstate commerce. But to the extent that congressional findings would enable us to evaluate the legislative judgment that the activity in question substantially affected interstate commerce, even though no such substantial effect was visible to the naked eye, they are lacking here. ...

Although Justice BREYER argues that acceptance of the Government's rationales would not authorize a general federal police power, he is unable to identify any activity that the States may regulate but Congress may not. Justice BREYER posits that there might be some limitations on Congress' commerce power, such as family law or certain aspects of education. These suggested limitations, when viewed in light of the dissent's expansive analysis, are devoid of substance.

Justice BREYER focuses, for the most part, on the threat that firearm possession in and near schools poses to the educational process and the potential economic consequences flowing from that threat. Specifically, the dissent reasons that (1) gun-related violence is a serious problem; (2) that problem, in turn, has an adverse effect on classroom learning; and (3) that adverse effect on classroom learning, in turn, represents a substantial threat to trade and commerce. This analysis would be equally applicable, if not more so, to subjects such as family law and direct regulation of education. ...

To uphold the Government's contentions here, we would have to pile inference upon inference in a manner that would bid fair to convert congressional authority under the Commerce Clause to a general police power of the sort retained by the States. Admittedly, some of our prior cases have taken long steps down that road, giving great deference to congressional action. The broad language in these opinions has suggested the possibility of additional expansion, but we decline here to proceed any further. To do so would require us to conclude that the Constitution's enumeration of powers does not presuppose something not enumeratedand that there never will be a distinction between what is truly national and what is truly local. This we are unwilling to do.

Justice KENNEDY, with whom Justice O'CONNOR joins, concurring.

... The case that seems to mark the Court's definitive commitment to the practical conception of the commerce power is *NLRB v. Jones & Laughlin Steel Corp.*, where the Court sustained labor laws that applied to manufacturing facilities, making no real attempt to distinguish *Carter, supra*, and *Schechter, supra*. The deference given to Congress has since been confirmed. *United States v. Darby*, overruled *Hammer v. Dagenhart, supra*. And in *Wickard v. Filburn*, the Court disapproved *E.C. Knight* and the entire line of direct-indirect and manufacture-production cases, explaining that "broader interpretations of the Commerce Clause [were] destined to supersede the earlier ones," and "[w]hatever terminology is used, the criterion is necessarily one of degree and must be so defined. This does not satisfy those who seek mathematical or rigid formulas. But such formulas are not provided by the great concepts of the Constitution." Later examples of the exercise of federal power where commercial transactions were the subject of regulation include *Heart of Atlanta Motel, Inc. v. United States*, 379 U.S. 241, 85 S.Ct. 348, 13 L.Ed.2d 258 (1964), *Katzenbach v. McClung*, 379 U.S. 294, 85 S.Ct. 377, 13 L.Ed.2d 290 (1964), and *Perez v. United States*, 402 U.S. 146, 91 S.Ct. 1357, 28 L.Ed.2d 686 (1971). These and like authorities are within the fair ambit of the Court's practical conception of commercial regulation and are not called in question by our decision today.

The history of our Commerce Clause decisions contains at least two lessons of relevance to this case. The first, as stated at the outset, is the imprecision of content-based boundaries used without more to define the limits of the Commerce Clause. The second, related to the first but of even greater consequence, is that the Court as an institution and the legal system as a whole have an immense stake in the stability of our Commerce Clause jurisprudence as it has evolved to this point. *Stare decisis* operates with great force in counseling us not to call in question the essential principles now in place respecting the congressional power to regulate transactions of a commercial nature. That fundamental restraint on our power forecloses us from reverting to an understanding of commerce that would serve only an 18th-century economy, dependent then upon production and trading practices that had changed but little over the preceding centuries; it also mandates against returning to the time when congressional authority to regulate undoubted commercial activities was limited by a judicial determination that those matters had an insufficient connection to an interstate system. Congress can regulate in the commercial sphere on the assumption that we have a single market and a unified purpose to build a stable national economy. ...

The statute now before us forecloses the States from experimenting and exercising their own judgment in an area to which States lay claim by right of history and expertise, and it does so by regulating an activity beyond the realm of commerce in the ordinary and usual sense of that term. The tendency of this statute to displace state regulation in areas of traditional state concern is evident from its territorial operation. There are over 100,000 elementary and secondary schools in the United States. Each of these now has an invisible federal zone extending 1,000 feet beyond the (often irregular) boundaries of the school property. In some communities no doubt it would be difficult to navigate without infringing on those zones. Yet throughout these areas, school officials would find their own programs for the prohibition of guns in danger of displacement by the federal authority unless the State chooses to enact a parallel rule. ...

For these reasons, I join in the opinion and judgment of the Court.

Justice THOMAS, concurring.

... Although I join the majority, I write separately to observe that our case law has drifted far from the original understanding of the Commerce Clause. In a future case, we ought to temper our Commerce Clause jurisprudence in a manner that both makes sense of our more recent case law and is more faithful to the original understanding of that Clause. ...

This extended discussion of the original understanding and our first century and a half of case law does not necessarily require a wholesale abandonment of our more recent opinions. It simply reveals that our substantial effects test is far removed from both the Constitution and from our early case law and that the Court's opinion should not be viewed as "radical" or another "wrong turn" that must be corrected in the future. The analysis also suggests that we ought to temper our Commerce Clause jurisprudence.

Unless the dissenting Justices are willing to repudiate our long-held understanding of the limited nature of federal power, I would think that they, too, must be willing to reconsider the substantial effects test in a future case. If we wish to be true to a Constitution that does not cede a police power to the Federal Government, our Commerce Clause's boundaries simply cannot be "defined" as being "'commensurate with the national needs'" or self-consciously intendedto let the

Federal Government "'defend itself against economic forces that Congress decrees inimical or destructive of the national economy.'" Such a formulation of federal power is no test at all: It is a blank check.

At an appropriate juncture, I think we must modify our Commerce Clause jurisprudence. Today, it is easy enough to say that the Clause certainly does not empower Congress to ban gun possession within 1,000 feet of a school.

Justice STEVENS, dissenting.

... Guns are both articles of commerce and articles that can be used to restrain commerce. Their possession is the consequence, either directly or indirectly, of commercial activity. In my judgment, Congress' power to regulate commerce in firearms includes the power to prohibit possession of guns at any location because of their potentially harmful use; it necessarily follows that Congress may also prohibit their possession in particular markets. The market for the possession of handguns by school-age children is, distressingly, substantial. Whether or not the national interest in eliminating that market would have justified federal legislation in 1789, it surely does today.

Justice SOUTER, dissenting.

... It was not ever thus, however, as even a brief overview of Commerce Clause history during the past century reminds us. The modern respect for the competence and primacy of Congress in matters affecting commerce developed only after one of this Court's most chastening experiences, when it perforce repudiated an earlier and untenably expansive conception of judicial review in derogation of congressional commerce power. A look at history's sequence will serve to show how today's decision tugs the Court off course, leading it to suggest opportunities for further developments that would be at odds with the rule of restraint to which the Court still wisely states adherence. ...

Because Justice BREYER's opinion demonstrates beyond any doubt that the Act in question passes the rationality review that the Court continues to espouse, today's decision may be seen as only a misstep, its reasoning and its suggestionsnot quite in gear with the prevailing standard, but hardly an epochal case. I would not argue otherwise, but I would raise a caveat. Not every epochal case has come in epochal trappings. *Jones & Laughlin* did not reject the direct-indirect standard in so many words; it just said the relation of the regulated subject matter to commerce was direct enough. But we know what happened.

I respectfully dissent.

Justice BREYER, with whom Justice STEVENS, Justice SOUTER, and Justice GINSBURG join, dissenting.

The issue in this case is whether the Commerce Clause authorizes Congress to enact a statute that makes it a crime to possess a gun in, or near, a school. In my view, the statute falls well within the scope of the commerce power as this Court has understood that power over the last half century.

In reaching this conclusion, I apply three basic principles of Commerce Clause interpretation. First, the power to "regulate Commerce ... among the several States," U.S. Const., Art. I, § 8, cl. 3, encompasses the power to regulate local activities insofar as they significantly affect interstate commerce. See, *e.g., Gibbons v. Ogden*; *Wickard v. Filburn.* As the majority points out, the Court, in describing how much of an effect the Clause requires, sometimes has used the word "substantial" and sometimes has not. And, as the majority also recognizes in quoting Justice Cardozo, the question of degree (how *much* effect) requires an estimate of the "size" of the effect that no verbal formulation can capture with precision. I use the word "significant" because the word "substantial" implies a somewhat narrower power than recent precedent suggests. But to speak of "substantial effect" rather than "significant effect" would make no difference in this case.

Second, in determining whether a local activity will likely have a significant effect upon interstate commerce, a court must consider, not the effect of an individual act (a single instance of gun possession), but rather the cumulative effect of all similar instances (*i.e.,* the effect of all guns possessed in or near schools). See, *e.g., Wickard. ...*

Third, the Constitution requires us to judge the connection between a regulated activity and interstate commerce, not directly, but at one remove. Courts must give Congress a degree of leeway in determining the existence of a significant factual connection between the regulated activity and interstate commerce—both because the Constitution delegates the commerce power directly to Congress and because the determination requires an empirical judgment of a kind that a legislature is more likely than a court to make with accuracy. The traditional words "rational basis" capture this leeway. Thus, the specific question before us, as the Court recognizes, is not whether the "regulated activity sufficiently affected interstate commerce," but, rather, whether Congress could have had "*a rational basis*" for so concluding. ...

Applying these principles to the case at hand, we must ask whether Congress could have had a *rational basis* for finding a significant (or substantial) connection between gun-related school violence and interstate commerce. Or, to put the question in the language of the *explicit* finding that Congress made when it amended this law in 1994: Could Congress rationally have found that "violent crime in school zones," through its effect on the "quality of education," significantly (or substantially) affects "interstate" or "foreign commerce"? As long as one views the commerce connection, not as a "technical legal conception," but as "a practical one," *Swift & Co. v. United States,* 196 U.S. 375, 398, 25 S.Ct. 276, 280, 49 L.Ed. 518 (1905) (Holmes, J.), the answer to this question must be yes. Numerous reports and studies—generated both inside and outside government—make clear that Congress could reasonably have found the empirical connection that its law, implicitly or explicitly, asserts. ...

In sum, a holding that the particular statute before us falls within the commerce power would not expand the scope of that Clause. Rather, it simply would apply preexisting law to changing economic circumstances. ...

It would recognize that, in today's economic world, gun-related violence near the classroom makes a significant difference to our economic, as well as our social, well-being. In accordance with well-accepted precedent, such a holding would permit Congress "to act in terms of economic ... realities," would interpret the commerce power as "an affirmative power commensurate with the national needs," and would acknowledge that the "commerce clause does not operate so as to render the nation powerless to defend itself against economic forces that Congress decrees inimical or destructive of the national economy." ...

In sum, to find this legislation within the scope of the Commerce Clause would permit "Congress ... to act in terms of economic ... realities." It would interpret the Clause as this Court has traditionally interpreted it, with the exception of one wrong turn subsequently corrected. See *Gibbons v. Ogden,* 9 Wheat., at 195 (holding that the commerce power extends "to all the external concerns of the nation, and to those internal concerns which affect the States generally"); *United States v. Darby,* 312 U.S., at 116–117, 61 S.Ct., at 458 ("The conclusion is inescapable that *Hammer v. Dagenhart* [the child labor case] was a departure from the principles which have prevailed in the interpretation of the Commerce Clause both before and since the decision. ... It should be and now is overruled"). Upholding this legislation would do no more than simply recognize that Congress had a "rational basis" for finding a significant connection between guns in or near schools and (through their effect on education) the interstate and foreign commerce they threaten. For these reasons, I would reverse the judgment of the Court of Appeals.

Respectfully, I dissent.

Notes and Questions

1. *Which Justice in this opinion expresses the most accurate understanding of Court history on the Commerce Clause?*
2. *The majority states that there are arenas that naturally belong to the states.* Which ones? Do you agree?
3. *Video.* What do you think of this video's analysis of the case? See Quimbee's video on *United States v. Lopez* Summary, Sep. 15, 2017, posted at https://www.youtube.com/watch?v=vQ1weu4-U0k&list=PLsFE_Nvl6h_braQ_NxoD1jg8oDdM_l8uI&index=1&t=30s.

4. Health Insurance Is a Valid Tax But Not a Valid Exercise of the Commerce Power

Health insurance has been an ongoing issue at the Court, subject to intense constitutional debate. Remember that in 1995, in *Lopez,* the Court apparently cut back on the commerce power. In 2010,

Congress passed the Affordable Care Act (ACA), which became more popularly known after the president who sponsored it, Obamacare. When it was enacted, Congress thought health insurance was surely an economic issue and definitely a matter of interstate commerce. By the time the case got to the Court, however, many anticommerce arguments had developed. The press was full of accounts of whether requiring people to either get health insurance or pay a penalty involved commerce or not. Do you have any first instincts from reading the earlier cases—*Gibbons, Wickard, Lopez*—whether health insurance is commerce?

The debate about commerce made this case very intense and difficult. Reporters even started misreading the conclusion when the case was released by the Court in 2012. Spend time going over the Court's oral argument on the case's website, https://www.oyez.org/cases/2011/11-393. The argument went on for several days and is long and complex. Can you tell *anything* about how the case will turn out from reading through the oral argument? How significant was *Lopez* for the Commerce Clause reasoning? *Wickard*?

National Federation of Independent Business v. Sebelius

SUPREME COURT OF THE UNITED STATES, 2012

567 U.S. 519, 132 S.Ct. 2566

ROBERTS, C.J., announced the judgment of the Court and delivered the opinion of the Court with respect to Parts I, II, and III–C, in which GINSBURG, BREYER, SOTOMAYOR, and KAGAN, JJ., joined; an opinion with respect to Part IV, in which BREYER and KAGAN, JJ., joined; and an opinion with respect to Parts III–A, III–B, and III–D. GINSBURG, J., filed an opinion concurring in part, concurring in the judgment in part, and dissenting in part, in which SOTOMAYOR, J., joined, and in which BREYER and KAGAN, JJ., joined as to Parts I, II, III, and IV. SCALIA, KENNEDY, THOMAS, and ALITO, JJ., filed a dissenting opinion. THOMAS, J., filed a dissenting opinion.

Today we resolve constitutional challenges to two provisions of the Patient Protection and Affordable Care Act of 2010: the individual mandate, which requires individuals to purchase a health insurance policy providing a minimum level of coverage; and the Medicaid expansion, which gives funds to the States on the condition that they provide specified health care to all citizens whose income falls below a certain threshold. We do not consider whether the Act embodies sound policies. That judgment is entrusted to the Nation's elected leaders. We ask only whether Congress has the power under the Constitution to enact the challenged provisions.

In our federal system, the National Government possesses only limited powers; the States and the people retain the remainder. Nearly two centuries ago, Chief Justice Marshall observed that "the question respecting the extent of the powers actually granted" to the Federal Government "is perpetually arising, and will probably continue to arise, as long as our system shall exist." *McCulloch v. Maryland,* 4 Wheat. 316, 405, 4 L.Ed. 579 (1819). In this case we must again determine whether the Constitution grants Congress powers it now asserts, but which many States and individuals believe it does not possess. Resolving this controversy requires us to examine both the limits of the Government's power, and our own limited role in policing those boundaries.

The Federal Government "is acknowledged by all to be one of enumerated powers." That is, rather than granting general authority to perform all the conceivable functions of government, the Constitution lists, or enumerates, the Federal Government's powers. Congress may, for example, "coin Money," "establish Post Offices," and "raise and support Armies." Art. I, § 8, cls. 5, 7, 12. The enumeration of powers is also a limitation of powers, because "[t]he enumeration presupposes something not enumerated." *Gibbons v. Ogden,* 9 Wheat. 1, 195, 6 L.Ed. 23 (1824). The Constitution's express conferral of some powers makes clear that it does not grant others. And the Federal Government "can exercise only the powers granted to it." *McCulloch, supra,* at 405.

Today, the restrictions on government power foremost in many Americans' minds are likely to be affirmative prohibitions, such as contained in the Bill of Rights. These affirmative prohibitions come into play, however, only where the Government possesses authority to act in the first place. If no enumerated power authorizes Congress to pass a certain law, that law may not be enacted, even if it would not violate any of the express prohibitions in the Bill of Rights or elsewhere in the Constitution. ...

The Framers thus ensured that powers which "in the ordinary course of affairs, concern the lives, liberties, and properties of the people" were held by governments more local and more accountable than a distant federal bureaucracy. The Federalist No. 45, at 293 (J. Madison). The independent power of the States also serves as a check on the power of the Federal Government: "By denying any one government complete jurisdiction over all the concerns of public life, federalism protects the liberty of the individual from arbitrary power."

This case concerns two powers that the Constitution does grant the Federal Government, but which must be read carefully to avoid creating a general federal authority akin to the police power. The Constitution authorizes Congress to "regulate Commerce with foreign Nations, and among the several States, and with the Indian Tribes." Art. I, § 8, cl. 3. Our precedents read that to mean that Congress may regulate "the channels of interstate commerce," "persons or things in interstate commerce," and "those activities that substantially affect interstate commerce." *Morrison, supra,* at 609, 120 S.Ct. 1740 (internal quotation marks omitted). The power over activities that substantially affect interstate commerce can be expansive. That power has been held to authorize federal regulation of such seemingly local matters as a farmer's decision to grow wheat for himself and his livestock, and a loan shark's extortionate collections from a neighborhood butcher shop. See *Wickard v. Filburn,* 317 U.S. 111, 63 S.Ct. 82, 87 L.Ed. 122 (1942); *Perez v. United States,* 402 U.S. 146, 91 S.Ct. 1357, 28 L.Ed.2d 686 (1971).

Congress may also "lay and collect Taxes, Duties, Imposts and Excises, to pay the Debts and provide for the common Defence and general Welfare of the United States." U.S. Const., Art. I, § 8, cl. 1. Put simply, Congress may tax and spend. This grant gives the Federal Government considerable influence even in areas where it cannot directly regulate. The Federal Government may enact a tax on an activity that it cannot authorize, forbid, or otherwise control. And in exercising its spending power, Congress may offer funds to the States, and may condition those offers on compliance with specified conditions. These offers may well induce the States to adopt policies that the Federal Government itself could not impose. See, *e.g., South Dakota v. Dole,* 483 U.S. 203, 205–206, 107 S.Ct. 2793, 97 L.Ed.2d 171 (1987) (conditioning federal highway funds on States raising their drinking age to 21).

The reach of the Federal Government's enumerated powers is broader still because the Constitution authorizes Congress to "make all Laws which shall be necessary and proper for carrying into Execution the foregoing Powers." Art. I, § 8, cl. 18. We have long read this provision to give Congress great latitude in exercising its powers: "Let the end be legitimate, let it be within the scope of the constitution, and all means which are appropriate, which are plainly adapted to that end, which are not prohibited, but consist with the letter and spirit of the constitution, are constitutional." *McCulloch,* 4 Wheat., at 421.

Our deference in matters of policy cannot, however, become abdication in matters of law. "The powers of the legislature are defined and limited; and that those limits may not be mistaken, or forgotten, the constitution is written." *Marbury v. Madison,* 1 Cranch 137, 176, 2 L.Ed. 60 (1803). Our respect for Congress's policy judgments thus can never extend so far as to disavow restraints on federal power that the Constitution carefully constructed. "The peculiar circumstances of the moment may render a measure more or less wise, but cannot render it more or less constitutional." Chief Justice John Marshall, A Friend of the Constitution No. V, Alexandria Gazette, July 5, 1819, in John Marshall's Defense of *McCulloch v. Maryland* 190–191 (G. Gunther ed. 1969). And there can be no question that it is the responsibility of this Court to enforce the limits on federal powerby striking down acts of Congress that transgress those limits. *Marbury v. Madison, supra,* at 175–176.

The questions before us must be considered against the background of these basic principles.

I

In 2010, Congress enacted the Patient Protection and Affordable Care Act, 124 Stat. 119. The Act aims to increase the number of Americans covered by health insurance and decrease the cost of health care. The Act's 10 titles stretch over 900 pages and contain hundreds of provisions. This case concerns constitutional challenges to two key provisions, commonly referred to as the individual mandate and the Medicaid expansion.

The individual mandate requires most Americans to maintain "minimum essential" health insurance coverage. The mandate does not apply to some individuals, such as prisoners and undocumented aliens. Many individuals will receive the required coverage through their employer, or from a government program such as Medicaid or Medicare. But for individuals who are not exempt and do not receive health insurance through a third party, the means of satisfying the requirement is to purchase insurance from a private company.

Beginning in 2014, those who do not comply with the mandate must make a "[s]hared responsibility payment" to the Federal Government. That payment, which the Act describes as a "penalty," is calculated as a percentage of household income, subject to a floor based on a specified dollar amount and a ceiling based on the average annual premium the individual would have to pay for qualifying private health insurance. In 2016, for example, the penalty will be 2.5 percent of an individual's household income, but no less than $695 and no more than the average yearly premium for insurance that covers 60 percent of the cost of 10 specified services (*e.g.*, prescription drugs and hospitalization). ...

The second provision of the Affordable Care Act directly challenged here is the Medicaid expansion. Enacted in 1965, Medicaid offers federal funding to States to assist pregnant women, children, needy families, the blind, the elderly, and the disabled in obtaining medical care. In order to receive that funding, States must comply with federal criteria governing matters such as who receives care and what services are provided at what cost. By 1982 every State had chosen to participate in Medicaid. Federal funds received through the Medicaid program have become a substantial part of state budgets, now constituting over 10 percent of most States' total revenue.

The Affordable Care Act expands the scope of the Medicaid program and increases the number of individuals the States must cover. For example, the Act requires state programs to provide Medicaid coverage to adults with incomes up to 133 percent of the federal poverty level, whereas many States now cover adults with children only if their income is considerably lower, and do not cover childless adults at all. The Act increases federal funding to cover the States' costs in expanding Medicaid coverage, although States will bear a portion of the costs on their own. If a State does not comply with the Act's new coverage requirements, it may lose not only the federal funding for those requirements, but all of its federal Medicaid funds. ...

III

The Government advances two theories for the proposition that Congress had constitutional authority to enact the individual mandate. First, the Government argues that Congress had the power to enact the mandate under the Commerce Clause. Under that theory, Congress may order individuals to buy health insurance because the failure to do so affects interstate commerce, and could undercut the Affordable Care Act's other reforms. Second, the Government argues that if the commerce power does not support the mandate, we should nonetheless uphold it as an exercise of Congress's power to tax. According to the Government, even if Congress lacks the power to direct individuals to buy insurance, the only effect of the individual mandate is to raise taxes on those who do not do so, and thus the law may be upheld as a tax. ...

A 1

The Government contends that the individual mandate is within Congress's power because the failure to purchase insurance "has a substantial and deleterious effect on interstate commerce" by creating the cost-shifting problem. The path of our Commerce Clause decisions has not always run smooth, see *United States v. Lopez,* 514 U.S. 549, 552–559, 115 S.Ct. 1624, 131 L.Ed.2d 626 (1995), but it is now well established that Congress has broad authority under the Clause. We have recognized, for example, that "[t]he power of Congress over interstate commerce is not confined to the regulation of commerce among the states," but extends to activities that "have a substantial effect on interstate commerce." *United States v. Darby,* 312 U.S. 100, 118–119, 61 S.Ct. 451, 85 L.Ed. 609 (1941). Congress's power, moreover, is not limited to regulation of an activity that by itself substantially affects interstate commerce, but also extends to activities that do so only when aggregated with similar activities of others. See *Wickard,* 317 U.S., at 127–128, 63 S.Ct. 82. ...

Our precedent also reflects this understanding. As expansive as our cases construing the scope of the commerce power have been, they all have one thing in common: They uniformly describe the power as reaching "activity." It is nearly impossible to avoid the word when quoting them. See, *e.g., Lopez, supra,* at 560, 115 S.Ct. 1624 ("Where economic activity substantially affects interstate commerce, legislation regulating that activity will be sustained"). ...

The individual mandate, however, does not regulate existing commercial activity. It instead compels individuals to *become* active in commerce by purchasing a product, on the ground that their failure to do so affects interstate commerce. Construing the Commerce Clause to permit Congress to regulate individuals precisely *because* they are doing nothing would open a new and potentially vast domain to congressional authority. Every day individuals do not do an infinite number of things. In some cases they decide not to do something; in others they simply fail to do it. Allowing Congress to justify federal regulation by pointing to the effect of inaction on commerce would bring countless decisions an individual could *potentially* make within the scope of federal regulation, and—under the Government's theory—empower Congress to make those decisions for him. ...

Wickard has long been regarded as "perhaps the most far reaching example of Commerce Clause authority over intrastate activity," *Lopez,* 514 U.S., at 560, 115 S.Ct. 1624, but the Government's theory in this case would go much further. Under *Wickard* it is within Congress's power to regulate the market for wheat by supporting its price. But price can be supported by increasing demand as well as by decreasing supply. The aggregated decisions of some consumers not to purchase wheat have a substantial effect on the price of wheat, just as decisions not to purchase health insurance have on the price of insurance. Congress can therefore command that those not buying wheat do so, just as it argues here that it may command that those not buying health insurance do so. The farmer in *Wickard* was at least actively engaged in the production of wheat, and the Government could regulate that activity because of its effect on commerce. The Government's theory here would effectively override that limitation, by establishing that individuals may be regulated under the Commerce Clause whenever enough of them are not doing something the Government would have them do. ...

To consider a different example in the health care market, many Americans do not eat a balanced diet. That group makes up a larger percentage of the total population than those without health insurance. The failure of that group to have a healthy diet increases health care costs, to a greater extent than the failure of the uninsured to purchase insurance. Those increased costs are borne in part by other Americans who must pay more, just as the uninsured shift costs to the insured. Congress addressed the insurance problem by ordering everyone to buy insurance. Under the Government's theory, Congress could address the diet problem by ordering everyone to buy vegetables.

People, for reasons of their own, often fail to do things that would be good for them or good for society. Those failures—joined with the similar failures of others—can readily have a substantial effect on interstate commerce. Under the Government's logic, that authorizes Congress to use its commerce power to compel citizens to act as the Government would have them act.

That is not the country the Framers of our Constitution envisioned. James Madison explained that the Commerce Clause was "an addition which few oppose and from which no apprehensions are entertained." The Federalist No. 45, at 293. ...

The Government sees things differently. It argues that because sickness and injury are unpredictable but unavoidable, "the uninsured as a class are active in the market for health care, which they regularly seek and obtain." The individual mandate "merely regulates how individuals finance and pay for that active participation—requiring that they do so through insurance, rather than through attempted self-insurance with the back-stop of shifting costs to others."

The Government repeats the phrase "active in the market for health care" throughout its brief, but that concept has no constitutional significance. An individual who bought a car two years ago and may buy another in the future is not "active in the car market" in any pertinent sense. ...

The individual mandate's regulation of the uninsured as a class is, in fact, particularly divorced from any link to existing commercial activity. The mandate primarily affects healthy, often young adults who are less likely to need significant health care and have other priorities for spending their money. ...

The Government argues that the individual mandate can be sustained as a sort of exception to this rule, because health insurance is a unique product. According to the Government, upholding the individual mandate would not justify mandatory purchases of items such as cars or broccoli because, as the Government puts it, "[h]ealth insurance is not purchased for its own sake like a car or broccoli; it is a means of financing health-care consumption and covering universal risks." But cars and broccoli are no more purchased for their "own sake" than health insurance. They are purchased to cover the need for transportation and food. ...

The Government next contends that Congress has the power under the Necessary and Proper Clause to enact the individual mandate because the mandate is an "integral part of a comprehensive scheme of economic regulation"—the guaranteed-issue and community-rating insurance reforms. Under this argument, it is not necessary to consider the effect that an individual's inactivity may have on interstate commerce; it is enough that Congress regulate commercial activity in a way that requires regulation of inactivity to be effective. ...

This is in no way an authority that is "narrow in scope," *Comstock, supra,* at 148, 130 S.Ct., at 1964, or "incidental" to the exercise of the commerce power, *McCulloch, supra,* at 418. Rather, such a conception of the Necessary and Proper Clause would work a substantial expansion of federal authority. ...

Just as the individual mandate cannot be sustained as a law regulating the substantial effects of the failure to purchase health insurance, neither can it be upheld as a "necessary and proper" component of the insurance reforms. The commerce power thus does not authorize the mandate. Accord, *post,* at 2644 – 2650 (joint opinion of SCALIA, KENNEDY, THOMAS, and ALITO, JJ., dissenting).

B

That is not the end of the matter. Because the Commerce Clause does not support the individual mandate, it is necessary to turn to the Government's second argument: that the mandate may be upheld as within Congress's enumerated power to "lay and collect Taxes." ...

Under the mandate, if an individual does not maintain health insurance, the only consequence is that he must make an additional payment to the IRS when he pays his taxes. That, according to the Government, means the mandate can be regarded as establishing a condition—not owning health insurance—that triggers a tax—the required payment to the IRS. Under that theory, the mandate is not a legal command to buy insurance. Rather, it makes going without insurance just another thing the Government taxes, like buying gasoline or earning income. And if the mandate is in effect just a tax hike on certain taxpayers who do not have health insurance, it may be within Congress's constitutional power to tax.

The question is not whether that is the most natural interpretation of the mandate, but only whether it is a "fairly possible" one. ...

C

... It is of course true that the Act describes the payment as a "penalty," not a "tax." But while that label is fatal to the application of the Anti–Injunction Act, it does not determine whether the payment may be viewed as an exercise of Congress's taxing power. It is up to Congress whether to apply the Anti–Injunction Act to any particular statute, so it makes sense to be guided by Congress's choice of label on that question. That choice does not, however, control whether an exaction is within Congress's constitutional power to tax.

The Affordable Care Act's requirement that certain individuals pay a financial penalty for not obtaining health insurance may reasonably be characterized as a tax. Because the Constitution permits such a tax, it is not our role to forbid it, or to pass upon its wisdom or fairness.

D

Justice GINSBURG questions the necessity of rejecting the Government's commerce power argument, given [it] can be upheld under the taxing power. But the statute reads more naturally as a command to buy insurance than as a tax, and I would uphold it as a command if the Constitution allowed it. It is only because the Commerce Clause does not authorize such a command that it is necessary to reach the taxing power question. And it is only because we have a duty to construe a statute to save it, if fairly possible, that [it] can be interpreted as a tax. Without deciding the Commerce Clause question, I would find no basis to adopt such a saving construction.

The Federal Government does not have the power to order people to buy health insurance. [It] would therefore be unconstitutional if read as a command. The Federal Government does have the power to impose a tax on those without health insurance. [It] is therefore constitutional, because it can reasonably be read as a tax.

IV

A

The States also contend that the Medicaid expansion exceeds Congress's authority under the Spending Clause. They claim that Congress is coercing the States to adopt the changes it wants by threatening to withhold all of a State's Medicaid grants, unless the State accepts the new expanded funding and complies with the conditions that come with it. This, they argue, violates the basic principle that the "Federal Government may not compel the States to enact or administer a federal regulatory program." *New York,* 505 U.S., at 188, 112 S.Ct. 2408.

There is no doubt that the Act dramatically increases state obligations under Medicaid. The current Medicaid program requires States to cover only certain discrete categories of needy individuals—pregnant women, children, needy families, the blind, the elderly, and the disabled. There is no mandatory coverage for most childless adults, and the States typically do not offer any such coverage. The States also enjoy considerable flexibility with respect to the coverage levels for parents of needy families. On average States cover only those unemployed parents who make less than 37 percent of the federal poverty level, and only those employed parents who make less than 63 percent of the poverty line.

The Medicaid provisions of the Affordable Care Act, in contrast, require States to expand their Medicaid programs by 2014 to cover *all* individuals under the age of 65 with incomes below 133 percent of the federal poverty line. The Act also establishes a new "[e]ssential health benefits" package, which States must provide to all new Medicaid recipients—a level sufficient to satisfy a recipient's obligations under the individual mandate. The Affordable Care Act provides that the Federal Government will pay 100 percent of the costs of covering these newly eligible individuals through 2016. In the following years, the federal payment level gradually decreases, to a minimum of 90 percent. In light of the expansion in coverage mandated by the Act, the Federal Government estimates that its Medicaid spending will increase by approximately $100 billion per year, nearly 40 percent above current levels. ...

Permitting the Federal Government to force the States to implement a federal program would threaten the political accountability key to our federal system. "[W]here the Federal Government directs the States to regulate, it may be state officials who will bear the brunt of public disapproval, while the federal officials who devised the regulatory program may remain insulated from the electoral ramifications of their decision." Spending Clause programs do not pose this danger when a State has a legitimate choice whether to accept the federal conditions in exchange for federal funds. In such a situation, state officials can fairly be held politically accountable for choosing to accept or refuse the federal offer. But when the State has no choice, the Federal Government can achieve its objectives without accountability, just as in *New York* and *Printz.* Indeed, this danger is heightened when Congress acts under the Spending Clause, because Congress can use that power to implement federal policy it could not impose directly under its enumerated powers. ...

B

Nothing in our opinion precludes Congress from offering funds under the Affordable Care Act to expand the availability of health care, and requiring that States accepting such funds comply with the conditions on their use. What Congress is not free to do is to penalize States that choose not to participate in that new program by taking away their existing Medicaid funding. [It] gives the Secretary of Health and Human Services the authority to do just that. It allows her to withhold *all* "further [Medicaid] payments ... to the State" if she determines that the State is out of compliance with any Medicaid requirement, including those contained in the expansion. In light of the Court's holding, the Secretary cannot apply [the law] to withdraw existing Medicaid funds for failure to comply with the requirements set out in the expansion. ...

This is not to say, as the joint dissent suggests, that we are "rewriting the Medicaid Expansion." Instead, we determine, first, that [the act] is unconstitutional when applied to withdraw existing Medicaid funds from States that decline to comply with the expansion. We then follow Congress's explicit textual instruction to leave unaffected "the remainder of the chapter, and the application of [the challenged] provision to other persons or circumstances." When we invalidate an application of a statute because that application is unconstitutional, we are not "rewriting" the statute; we are merely enforcing the Constitution. ...

The question here is whether Congress would have wanted the rest of the Act to stand, had it known that States would have a genuine choice whether to participate in the new Medicaid expansion. Unless it is "evident" that the answer is no, we must leave the rest of the Act intact. ...

Justice GINSBURG, with whom Justice SOTOMAYOR joins, and with whom Justice BREYER and Justice KAGAN join as to Parts I, II, III, and IV, concurring in part, concurring in the judgment in part, and dissenting in part.

I agree with THE CHIEF JUSTICE that the Anti-Injunction Act does not bar the Court's consideration of these cases, and that the minimum coverage provision is a proper exercise of Congress' taxing power. I therefore join Parts I, II, and III–C of THE CHIEF JUSTICE's opinion. Unlike THE CHIEF JUSTICE, however, I would hold, alternatively, that the Commerce Clause authorizes Congress to enact the minimum coverage provision. I would also hold that the Spending Clause permits the Medicaid expansion exactly as Congress enacted it.

I A

... The health-care market's size is not its only distinctive feature. Unlike the market for almost any other product or service, the market for medical care is one in which all individuals inevitably participate. Virtually every person residing in the United States, sooner or later, will visit a doctor or other health-care professional. Most people will do so repeatedly. ...

D

Aware that a national solution was required, Congress could have taken over the health-insurance market by establishing a tax-and-spend federal program like Social Security. Such a program, commonly referred to as a single-payer system (where the sole payer is the Federal Government), would have left little, if any, room for private enterprise or the States. Instead of going this route, Congress enacted the ACA, a solution that retains a robust role for private insurers and state governments. To make its chosen approach work, however, Congress had to use some new tools, including a requirement that most individuals obtain private health insurance coverage. As explained below, by employing these tools, Congress was able to achieve a practical, altogether reasonable, solution. ...

In sum, Congress passed the minimum coverage provision as a key component of the ACA to address an economic and social problem that has plagued the Nation for decades: the large number of U.S. residents who are unable or unwilling to obtain health insurance. Whatever one thinks of the policy decision Congress made, it was Congress' prerogative to make it. Reviewed with appropriate deference, the minimum coverage provision, allied to the guaranteed-issue and community-rating prescriptions, should survive measurement under the Commerce and Necessary and Proper Clauses. ...

II B

... Until today, this Court's pragmatic approach to judging whether Congress validly exercised its commerce power was guided by two familiar principles. First, Congress has the power to regulate economic activities "that substantially affect interstate commerce." This capacious power extends even to local activities that, viewed in the aggregate, have a substantial impact on interstate commerce. See also *Wickard,* 317 U.S., at 125, 63 S.Ct. 82 ("[E]ven if appellee's activity be local and though it may not be regarded as commerce, it may still, *whatever its nature,* be reached by Congress if it exerts a substantial economic effect on interstate commerce." (emphasis added)).

Second, we owe a large measure of respect to Congress when it frames and enacts economic and social legislation. ...

D 1a

... Maintaining that the uninsured are not active in the health-care market, THE CHIEF JUSTICE draws an analogy to the car market. An individual "is not 'active in the car market,'" THE CHIEF JUSTICE observes, simply because he or she may someday buy a car. The analogy is inapt. The inevitable yet unpredictable need for medical care and the guarantee that emergency care will be provided when required are conditions nonexistent in other markets. That is so of the market for cars, and of the market for broccoli as well. Although an individual *might* buy a car or a crown of broccoli one day, there is no certainty she will ever do so. And if she eventually wants a car or has a craving for broccoli, she will be obliged to pay at the counter before receiving the vehicle or nourishment. She will get no free ride or food, at the expense of another consumer forced to pay an inflated price. Upholding the minimum coverage provision on the ground that all are participants or will be participants in the health-care market would therefore carry no implication that Congress may justify under the Commerce Clause a mandate to buy other products and services.

Nor is it accurate to say that the minimum coverage provision "compel[s] individuals ... to purchase an unwanted product," or "suite of products." If unwanted today, medical service secured by insurance may be desperately needed tomorrow. Virtually everyone, I reiterate, consumes health care at some point in his or her life. Health insurance is a means of paying for this care, nothing more. In requiring individuals to obtain insurance, Congress is therefore not mandating the purchase of a discrete, unwanted product. Rather, Congress is merely defining the terms on which individuals pay for an interstate good they consume: Persons subject to the mandate must now pay for medical care in advance (instead of at the point of service) and through insurance (instead of out of pocket). Establishing payment terms for goods in or affecting interstate commerce is quintessential economic regulation well within Congress' domain. ...

In the fullness of time, moreover, today's young and healthy will become society's old and infirm. Viewed over a lifespan, the costs and benefits even out: The young who pay more than their fair share currently will pay less than their fair share when they become senior citizens. And even if, as undoubtedly will be the case, some individuals, over their lifespans, will pay more for health insurance than they receive in health services, they have little to complain about, for that is how insurance works. Every insured person receives protection against a catastrophic loss, even though only a subset of the covered class will ultimately need that protection.

b

In any event, THE CHIEF JUSTICE's limitation of the commerce power to the regulation of those actively engaged in commerce finds no home in the text of the Constitution or our decisions. Article I, § 8, of the Constitution grants Congress the power "[t]o regulate Commerce ... among the several States." Nothing in this language implies that Congress' commerce power is limited to regulating those actively engaged in commercial transactions. Indeed, as the D.C. Circuit observed, "[a]t the time the Constitution was [framed], to 'regulate' meant," among other things, "to require action." ...

This argument is difficult to fathom. Requiring individuals to obtain insurance unquestionably regulates the interstate health-insurance and health-care markets, both of them in existence well before the enactment of the ACA. See *Wickard,* 317 U.S., at 128, 63 S.Ct. 82 ("The stimulation of commerce is a use of the regulatory function quite as definitely as prohibitions or restrictions thereon."). Thus, the "something to be regulated" was surely there when Congress created the minimum coverage provision. ...

In concluding that the Commerce Clause does not permit Congress to regulate commercial "inactivity," and therefore does not allow Congress to adopt the practical solution it devised for the health-care problem, THE CHIEF JUSTICE views the Clause as a "technical legal conception," precisely what our case law tells us not to do. *Wickard,* 317 U.S., at 122, 63 S.Ct. 82 (internal quotation marks omitted). This Court's former endeavors to impose categorical limits on the commerce power have not fared well. In several pre-New Deal cases, the Court attempted to cabin Congress' Commerce Clause authority by distinguishing "commerce" from activity once conceived to be noncommercial, notably, "production," "mining," and "manufacturing."

These line-drawing exercises were untenable, and the Court long ago abandoned them. "[Q]uestions of the power of Congress [under the Commerce Clause]," we held in *Wickard,* "are not to be decided by reference to any formula which would give controlling force to nomenclature such as 'production' and 'indirect' and foreclose consideration of the actual effects of the activity in question upon interstate commerce. Failing to learn from this history, THE CHIEF JUSTICE plows ahead with his formalistic distinction between those who are "active in commerce," and those who are not.

It is not hard to show the difficulty courts (and Congress) would encounter in distinguishing statutes that regulate "activity" from those that regulate "inactivity." As Judge Easterbrook noted, "it is possible to restate most actions as corresponding inactions with the same effect." ...

III B

... Asserting that the Necessary and Proper Clause does not authorize the minimum coverage provision, THE CHIEF JUSTICE focuses on the word "proper." A mandate to purchase health insurance is not "proper" legislation, THE CHIEF JUSTICE urges, because the command "undermine[s] the structure of government established by the Constitution." If long on rhetoric, THE CHIEF JUSTICE's argument is short on substance. ...

V

Medicaid, as amended by the ACA, however, is not two spending programs; it is a single program with a constant aim—to enable poor persons to receive basic health care when they need it. Given past expansions, plus express statutory warning that Congress may change the requirements participating States must meet, there can be no tenable claim that the ACA fails for lack of notice. Moreover, States have no entitlement to receive any Medicaid funds; they enjoy only the opportunity to accept funds on Congress' terms. Future Congresses are not bound by their predecessors' dispositions; they have authority to spend federal revenue as they see fit. The Federal Government, therefore, is not, as THE CHIEF JUSTICE charges, threatening States with the loss of "existing" funds from one spending program in order to induce them to opt into another program. Congress is simply requiring States to do what States have long been required to do to receive Medicaid funding: comply with the conditions Congress prescribes for participation.

A majority of the Court, however, buys the argument that prospective withholding of funds formerly available exceeds Congress' spending power. Given that holding, I entirely agree with THE CHIEF JUSTICE as to the appropriate remedy. It is to bar the withholding found impermissible—not, as the joint dissenters would have it, to scrap the expansion altogether. The dissenters' view that the ACA must fall in its entirety is a radical departure from the Court's normal course. ... Congress' extension of Medicaid remains available to any State that affirms its willingness to participate. ...

Justice SCALIA, Justice KENNEDY, Justice THOMAS, and Justice ALITO, dissenting.

... Whatever may be the conceptual limits upon the Commerce Clause and upon the power to tax and spend, they cannot be such as will enable the Federal Government to regulate all private conduct and to compel the States to function as administrators of federal programs.

That clear principle carries the day here. The striking case of *Wickard v. Filburn,* 317 U.S. 111, 63 S.Ct. 82, 87 L.Ed. 122 (1942), which held that the economic activity of growing wheat, even for one's own consumption, affected commerce sufficiently that it could be regulated, always has been regarded as the *ne plus ultra* of expansive Commerce Clause jurisprudence. To go beyond that, and to say the *failure* to grow wheat (which is *not* an economic activity, or any activity at all) nonetheless affects commerce and therefore can be federally regulated, is to make mere breathing in and out the basis for federal prescription and to extend federal power to virtually all human activity. ...

The Act before us here exceeds federal power both in mandating the purchase of health insurance and in denying nonconsenting States all Medicaid funding. These parts of the Act are central to its design and operation, and all the Act's other provisions would not have been enacted without them. In our view it must follow that the entire statute is inoperative.

I

The Individual Mandate

... We do not doubt that the buying and selling of health insurance contracts is commerce generally subject to federal regulation. But when Congress provides that (nearly) all citizens must buy an insurance contract, it goes beyond "adjust[ing] by rule or method," Johnson, *supra,* or "direct[ing] according to rule," Ash, *supra;* it directs the creation of commerce. ...

A

... The Government was invited, at oral argument, to suggest what federal controls over private conduct (other than those explicitly prohibited by the Bill of Rights or other constitutional controls) could *not* be justified as necessary and proper for the carrying out of a general regulatory scheme. It was unable to name any. As we said at the outset, whereas the precise scope of the Commerce Clause and the Necessary and Proper Clause is uncertain, the proposition that the Federal Government cannot do everything is a fundamental precept. See *Lopez,* 514 U.S., at 564, 115 S.Ct. 1624 ("[I]f we were to accept the Government's arguments, we are hard pressed to posit any activity by an individual that Congress is without power to regulate"). [The ACA] is defeated by that proposition. ...

C

A few respectful responses to Justice GINSBURG's dissent on the issue of the Mandate are in order. That dissent duly recites the test of Commerce Clause power that our opinions have applied, but disregards the premise the test contains. It is true enough that Congress needs only a "'rational basis' for concluding that the *regulated activity* substantially affects interstate commerce." But it must be *activity* affecting commerce that is regulated, and not merely the failure to engage in commerce. And one is not now purchasing the health care covered by the insurance mandate simply because one is likely to be purchasing it in the future. Our test's premise of regulated activity is not invented out of whole cloth, but rests upon the Constitution's requirement that it be commerce which is regulated. If all inactivity affecting commerce is commerce, commerce is everything. Ultimately the dissent is driven to saying that there is really no difference between action and inaction, a proposition that has never recommended itself, neither to the law nor to common sense. To say, for example, that the inaction here consists of activity in "the self-insurance market," seems to us wordplay. By parity of reasoning the failure to buy a car can be called participation in the non-private-car-transportation market. Commerce becomes everything. ...

II

The Taxing Power

... Quite separately, the fact that Congress (in its own words) "imposed ... a penalty," for failure to buy insurance is alone sufficient to render that failure unlawful. It is one of the canons of interpretation that a statute that penalizes an act makes it unlawful: "[W]here the statute inflicts a penalty for doing an act, although the act itself is not expressly prohibited, yet to do the act is unlawful, because it cannot be supposed that the Legislature intended that a penalty should be inflicted for a lawful act." Or in the words of Chancellor Kent: "If a statute inflicts a penalty for doing an act, the penalty implies a prohibition, and the thing is unlawful, though there be no prohibitory words in the statute." 1 J. Kent, Commentaries on American Law 436 (1826).

We never have classified as a tax an exaction imposed for violation of the law, and so too, we never have classified as a tax an exaction described in the legislation itself as a penalty. To be sure, we have sometimes treated as a tax a statutory exaction (imposed for something other than a violation of law) which bore an agnostic label that does not entail the significant constitutional consequences of a penalty—such as "license" or "surcharge." But we have never—*never*—treated as a tax an exaction which faces up to the critical difference between a tax and a penalty, and explicitly denominates the exaction a "penalty." Eighteen times in [the act] tself and elsewhere throughout the Act, Congress called the exaction a "penalty."

That [the act] imposes not a simple tax but a mandate to which a penalty is attached is demonstrated by the fact that some are exempt from the tax who are not exempt from the mandate—a distinction that would make no sense if the mandate were not a mandate. ...

IV

The Medicaid Expansion

We now consider respondents' second challenge to the constitutionality of the ACA, namely, that the Act's dramatic expansion of the Medicaid program exceeds Congress' power to attach conditions to federal grants to the States.

The ACA does not legally compel the States to participate in the expanded Medicaid program, but the Act authorizes a severe sanction for any State that refuses to go along: termination of all the State's Medicaid funding. For the average State, the annual federal Medicaid subsidy is equal to more than one-fifth of the State's expenditures.[7] A State forced out of the program would not only lose this huge sum but would almost certainly find it necessary to increase its own health care expenditures substantially, requiring either a drastic reduction in funding for other programs or a large increase in state taxes. And these new taxes would come on top of the federal taxes already paid by the State's citizens to fund the Medicaid program in other States.

The States challenging the constitutionality of the ACA's Medicaid Expansion contend that, for these practical reasons, the Act really does not give them any choice at all. As proof of this, they point to the goal and the structure of the ACA. The goal of the Act is to provide near-universal medical coverage, and without 100% state participation in the Medicaid program, attainment of this goal would be thwarted. Even if States could elect to remain in the old Medicaid program, while declining to participate in the Expansion, there would be a gaping hole in coverage. And if a substantial number of States were entirely expelled from the program, the number of persons without coverage would be even higher.

In light of the ACA's goal of near-universal coverage, petitioners argue, if Congress had thought that anything less than 100% state participation was a realistic possibility, Congress would have provided a backup scheme. But no such scheme is to be found anywhere in the more than 900 pages of the Act. This shows, they maintain, that Congress was certain that the ACA's Medicaid offer was one that no State could refuse.

In response to this argument, the Government contends that any congressional assumption about uniform state participation was based on the simple fact that the offer of federal funds associated with the expanded coverage is such a generous gift that no State would want to turn it down. ...

C

... Recognizing this potential for abuse, our cases have long held that the power to attach conditions to grants to the States has limits. See, *e.g., Dole,* 483 U.S., at 207–208, 107 S.Ct. 2793; *id.*, at 207, 107 S.Ct. 2793 (spending power is "subject to several general restrictions articulated in our cases"). ...

Coercing States to accept conditions risks the destruction of the "unique role of the States in our system." ...

Once it is recognized that spending-power legislation cannot coerce state participation, two questions remain: (1) What is the meaning of coercion in this context? (2) Is the ACA's expanded Medicaid coverage coercive? We now turn to those questions.

D

... In sum, it is perfectly clear from the goal and structure of the ACA that the offer of the Medicaid Expansion was one that Congress understood no State could refuse. The Medicaid Expansion therefore exceeds Congress' spending power and cannot be implemented.

F

Seven Members of the Court agree that the Medicaid Expansion, as enacted by Congress, is unconstitutional. See Parts IV–A to IV–E, *supra*; Part IV–A (opinion of ROBERTS, C.J., joined by BREYER and KAGAN, JJ.). Because the Medicaid Expansion is unconstitutional, the question of remedy arises. The most natural remedy would be to invalidate the Medicaid Expansion. However, the Government proposes—in two cursory sentences at the very end of its brief—preserving the Expansion. Under its proposal, States would receive the additional Medicaid funds if they expand eligibility, but States would keep their pre-existing Medicaid funds if they do not expand eligibility. We cannot accept the Government's suggestion. ...

The Constitution, though it dates from the founding of the Republic, has powerful meaning and vital relevance to our own times. The constitutional protections that this case involves are protections of structure. Structural protections—notably, the restraints imposed by federalism and separation of powers—are less romantic and have less obvious a connection to personal freedom than the provisions of the Bill of Rights or the Civil War Amendments. Hence they tend to be undervalued or even forgotten by our citizens. It should be the responsibility of the Court to teach otherwise, to remind our people that the Framers considered structural protections of freedom the most important ones, for which reason they alone were embodied in the original Constitution and not left to later amendment. The fragmentation of power produced by the structure of our Government is central to liberty, and when we destroy it, we place liberty at peril. Today's decision should have vindicated, should have taught, this truth; instead, our judgment today has disregarded it.

For the reasons here stated, we would find the Act invalid in its entirety. We respectfully dissent.

Justice THOMAS, dissenting.

... I adhere to my view that "the very notion of a 'substantial effects' test under the Commerce Clause is inconsistent with the original understanding of Congress' powers and with this Court's early Commerce Clause cases." *United States v. Morrison,* 529 U.S. 598, 627, 120 S.Ct. 1740, 146 L.Ed.2d 658 (2000) (THOMAS, J., concurring); see also *Lopez, supra,* at 584–602, 115 S.Ct. 1624 (same); *Gonzales v. Raich,* 545 U.S. 1, 67–69, 125 S.Ct. 2195, 162 L.Ed.2d 1 (2005) (THOMAS, J., dissenting). As I have explained, the Court's continued use of that test "has encouraged the Federal Government to persist in its view that the Commerce Clause has virtually no limits." *Morrison, supra,* at 627, 120 S.Ct. 1740. The Government's unprecedented claim in this suit that it may regulate not only economic activity but also *inactivity* that substantially affects interstate commerce is a case in point.

Notes and Questions

1. *Chief Justice Roberts.* How do you explain Chief Justice Roberts upholding the ACA as a tax but not as a valid exercise of the Commerce Clause? Why is the ACA part of Congress's taxing powers? And is it part of Congress's tax powers even though Congress never called the bill a "tax" when it passed the legislation? Why do you think Roberts found the taxing power argument persuasive?
2. *The commerce power.* Which Justices believe Congress had the Commerce Clause power to pass the ACA? Which Justices believe that it did not? What history of the Commerce Clause do they write? How do they back that historical account of commerce?
3. *The Medicaid provisions.* Are you surprised that seven of the Justices ruled that the Medicaid provisions were unconstitutional? Why did those seven think that Congress had surpassed its powers in the Medicaid section of the bill? Why do you think Justices Ginsburg and Sotomayor dissented on this issue?
4. *Severability.* Note that the Court frequently talks about sections of the law that are severable. Severability means that the Court may declare one portion of an act unconstitutional but sever that from the rest of the act so that the remainder remains constitutional. The Court did that here, invalidating the Medicaid section but upholding the rest of the ACA nonetheless. Some of the Justices thought that once one section was unconstitutional, the whole thing should be ruled unconstitutional. Who is more persuasive on severability?
5. *Video.* Does this video help you to understand the case? See Quimbee's video on *National Federation of Independent Business v. Sebelius* Case Brief Summary/Law Case Explained, Aug. 18, 2015, posted at https://www.youtube.com/watch?v=tQoe3EnwMfk&list=PLsFE_Nvl6h_Y75KGR5p-kGqcFisGvBnO9S&index=72.

5. The Court Considers the ACA Again

During the Trump administration, 2017–2021, some members of Congress repeatedly talked about ending the ACA. They did not obtain the votes necessary. They did, however, reduce the mandate penalty for not paying for insurance to $0. In other words, the tax was 0. The district court ruled that it was no longer valid as a taxing power and, therefore, the whole ACA was invalid because the mandate could not be severed from the rest of the legislation. The Court of Appeals agreed but remanded for severability to be reviewed in more detail. You can read the oral argument in *California v. Texas* here, https://www.oyez.org/cases/2020/19-840 or listen to it here, https://www.youtube.com/watch?v=yw-ioWSE8DE or here, https://www.c-span.org/video/?471185-1/health-care-law-supreme-court-oral-argument. Can you gain any insight from the argument about who will win or lose the case?

California v. Texas

SUPREME COURT OF THE UNITED STATES, 2021

593 U.S. ___, 141 S.Ct. 2104

BREYER, J., delivered the opinion of the Court, in which ROBERTS, C.J., and THOMAS, SOTOMAYOR, KAGAN, KAVANAUGH, and BARRETT, JJ., joined. Thomas, J., filed a concurring opinion. ALITO, J., filed a dissenting opinion, in which GORSUCH. J., joined.

As originally enacted in 2010, the Patient Protection and Affordable Care Act required most Americans to obtain minimum essential health insurance coverage. The Act also imposed a monetary penalty, scaled according to income, upon individuals who failed to do so. In 2017, Congress effectively nullified the penalty by setting its amount at $0.

Texas and 17 other States brought this lawsuit against the United States and federal officials. They were later joined by two individuals (Neill Hurley and John Nantz). The plaintiffs claim that without the penalty the Act's minimum essential coverage requirement is unconstitutional. Specifically, they say neither the Commerce Clause nor the Tax Clause (nor any other enumerated power) grants Congress the power to enact it. See U.S. Const., Art. I, § 8. They also argue that the minimum essential coverage requirement is not severable from the rest of the Act. Hence, they believe the Act as a whole is invalid. We do not reach these questions of the Act's validity, however, for Texas and the other plaintiffs in this suit lack the standing necessary to raise them. ...

Neither the individual nor the state plaintiffs have shown that the injury they will suffer or have suffered is "fairly traceable" to the "allegedly unlawful conduct" of which they complain. ...

Their problem lies in the fact that the statutory provision, while it tells them to obtain that coverage, has no means of enforcement. With the penalty zeroed out, the IRS can no longer seek a penalty from those who fail to comply. Because of this, there is no possible Government action that is causally connected to the plaintiffs' injury—the costs of purchasing health insurance. Or to put the matter conversely, that injury is not "fairly traceable" to any "allegedly unlawful conduct" of which the plaintiffs complain. ...

To consider the matter from the point of view of another standing requirement, namely, redressability, makes clear that the statutory language alone is not sufficient. To determine whether an injury is redressable, a court will consider the relationship between "the judicial relief requested" and the "injury" suffered. The plaintiffs here sought injunctive relief and a declaratory judgment. The injunctive relief, however, concerned the Act's other provisions that they say are inseverable from the minimum essential coverage requirement. The relief they sought in respect to the only provision they attack as unconstitutional—the minimum essential coverage provision—is declaratory relief, namely, a judicial statement that the provision they attacked is unconstitutional.

... At a minimum, this means that the dispute must "be 'real and substantial' and 'admit of specific relief through a decree of a conclusive character, as distinguished from an opinion advising what the law would be upon a hypothetical state of facts.'" ... The matter is not simply technical. To find standing here to attack an unenforceable statutory provision would allow a federal court to issue what would amount to "an advisory opinion without the possibility of any judicial relief." ...

Next, we turn to the state plaintiffs. We conclude that Texas and the other state plaintiffs have similarly failed to show that they have alleged an "injury fairly traceable to the defendant's allegedly *unlawful* conduct." ...

But setting aside that pure issue of law, we need only examine the initial factual premise of their claim to uncover another fatal weakness: The state plaintiffs have failed to show that the challenged minimum essential coverage provision, without any prospect of penalty, will harm them by leading more individuals to enroll in these programs. ...

For these reasons, we conclude that the plaintiffs in this suit failed to show a concrete, particularized injury fairly traceable to the defendants' conduct in enforcing the specific statutory provision they attack as unconstitutional. They have failed to show that they have standing to attack as unconstitutional the Act's minimum essential coverage provision. Therefore, we reverse the Fifth Circuit's judgment in respect to standing, vacate the judgment, and remand the cases with instructions to dismiss.

Justice THOMAS, concurring.

... But, whatever the Act's dubious history in this Court, we must assess the current suit on its own terms. And, here, there is a fundamental problem with the arguments advanced by the plaintiffs in attacking the Act—they have not identified any unlawful action that has injured them. Today's result is thus not the consequence of the Court once again rescuing the Act, but rather of us adjudicating the particular claims the plaintiffs chose to bring. ...

The Constitution gives this Court only the power to resolve "Cases" or "Controversies." As everyone agrees, we have interpreted this language to require a plaintiff to present an injury that is traceable to a particular "unlawful" action. And in light of the specific theories and arguments advanced in this suit, I do not believe that the plaintiffs have carried this burden. As the majority explains in detail, the individual plaintiffs allege only harm caused by the bare existence of an unlawful statute that does not impose any obligations or consequences. That is not enough. The state plaintiffs' arguments fail for similar reasons. Although they claim harms flowing from enforcement of certain parts of the Act, they attack only the lawfulness of a *different* provision. None of these theories trace a clear connection between an injury and unlawful conduct. ...

The plaintiffs failed to demonstrate that the harm they suffered is traceable to unlawful conduct. Although this Court has erred twice before in cases involving the Affordable Care Act, it does not err today.

Justice ALITO, with whom Justice GORSUCH joins, dissenting.

Today's decision is the third installment in our epic Affordable Care Act trilogy, and it follows the same pattern as installments one and two. In all three episodes, with the Affordable Care Act facing a serious threat, the Court has pulled off an improbable rescue. ...

In this suit, as I will explain, Texas and the other state plaintiffs have standing, and now that the "tax" imposed by the individual mandate is set at $0, the mandate cannot be sustained under the taxing power. As a result, it is clearly unconstitutional, and to the extent that the provisions of the ACA that burden the States are inextricably linked to the individual mandate, they too are unenforceable. ...

It is certainly true that the repeal of the tax or penal *NFIB* dissent is not whether the ACA could operate in *some* way without the individual mandate but whether it could operate in anything like the manner Congress designed. The answer to that question is clear. When the tax or penalty was collected, costs were shifted from individuals previously denied coverage due to their medical conditions and placed on others who purchased insurance only because the failure to do so was taxed or penalized. The repeal of the tax or penalty has not made the costs of the guaranteed-issue and community-rating requirements disappear. Those costs have obviously been shifted to others—in all likelihood to individuals who now pay higher premiums or face higher deductibles or to the taxpayers. This shift fundamentally changed the operation of the scheme Congress adopted. ...

The repeal of the tax or penalty also provides no reason to doubt our previous conclusion about Congress's intent. While the 2017 Act repealed the tax or penalty, it did not alter the statutory finding noted above, and the 2017 Act cannot plausibly be viewed as the manifestation of a congressional intent to preserve the ACA in altered form. The 2017 Act would not have passed the House without the votes of the Members who had voted to scrap the ACA just a few months earlier,[10] and the repeal of the tax or penalty, which they obviously found particularly offensive, was their fallback option. They eliminated the tax or penalty and left the chips to fall as they might. Thus, under the reasoning of the *NFIB* dissent, the provisions burdening the States are inseverable from the individual mandate. ...

No one can fail to be impressed by the lengths to which this Court has been willing to go to defend the ACA against all threats. A penalty is a tax. The United States is a State. And 18 States who bear costly burdens under the ACA cannot even get a foot in the door to raise a constitutional challenge. So a tax that does not tax is allowed to stand and support one of the biggest Government programs in our Nation's history. Fans of judicial inventiveness will applaud once again.

Notes and Questions

1. *Standing.* Are you surprised that the case was dismissed for lack of standing? Who would have standing?
2. *Justice Thomas.* Why did Justice Thomas concur, not dissent?
3. *Justice Alito.* Why did Justice Alito dissent?
4. *Comparing interpretations of the $0 tax provision.* Who had the best analysis of the $0 tax provision?

A Look Ahead

In the next chapter, we study Article II of the Constitution, which is the source of the Executive's power. We have studied two out of three federal branches to this point: the federal courts, which interpret the Constitution, and Congress, which enacts the law. The Executive branch enforces the law and makes administrative law.

Three

Article II: The Executive

Introduction

The first three Articles distribute governing power to the three branches. Article II, Section 1 says that the "executive power shall be vested in a President of the United States of America." Article II, Section 3 says "he shall take care that the laws be faithfully executed." What does it mean that the President "executes" the laws? How is that different from the work of Congress in Article I? And how do their powers overlap? Can a president "execute" a law if Congress has not passed a law? What if Congress considered a law but did not pass it?

Article II, Section 2 says the "President shall be commander in chief of the Army and Navy of the United States." What kind of power does the President get from that clause? Does it mean the President has complete power over the decisions of the United States to enter into warfare? Or just to execute warfare, not to begin it?

A. The President's Powers

Does the President possess emergency powers? Does the Constitution outline what happens in emergency situations? The Framers, at one point, considered a committee of presidents but eventually landed on just one. What does that tell you, if anything, about the constitutional design?

The following case, usually called "The Steel Seizure Case," involves a decision by President Harry Truman to seize the steel mills after they threatened to go on strike. This case remains the most famous Court treatment of executive powers. What does the Court say executive power is? How does it interpret the executive power that is identified in Article II? Do you agree with the majority, the concurrences, or the dissent in the following case? Does this reasoning apply when the President acts as Commander in Chief?

Does this case brief summary help you understand the case more? See Quimbee's video, *Youngstown Sheet and Tube Co. v. Sawyer* Case Brief Summary/Law Case Explained, Aug. 4, 2015, posted at https://www.youtube.com/watch?v=TqePUkGtm4o.

Youngstown Sheet & Tube Co. v. Sawyer

SUPREME COURT OF THE UNITED STATES, 1952.

343 U.S. 579, 72 S.Ct. 863

MR. JUSTICE BLACK delivered the opinion of the Court. [He was joined by Justices FRANKFURTER, DOUGLAS, JACKSON and BURTON.]

We are asked to decide whether the President was acting within his constitutional power when he issued an order directing the Secretary of Commerce to take possession of and operate most of the Nation's steel mills. The mill owners argue that the President's order amounts to lawmaking, a legislative function which the Constitution has expressly confided to the Congress and not to the President. The Government's position is that the order was made on findings of the President that his action was necessary to avert a national catastrophe which would inevitably result from a stoppage of steel production, and that in meeting this grave emergency the President was acting within the aggregate of his constitutional powers as the Nation's Chief Executive and the Commander in Chief of the Armed Forces of the United States. ...

On April 4, 1952, the Union gave notice of a nation-wide strike called to begin at 12:01 a.m. April 9. The indispensability of steel as a component of substantially all weapons and other war materials led the President to believe that the proposed work stoppage would immediately jeopardize our national defense and that governmental seizure of the steel mills was necessary in order to assure the continued availability of steel. Reciting these considerations for his action, the President, a few hours before the strike was to begin, issued Executive Order 10340. The order directed the Secretary of Commerce to take possession of most of the steel mills and keep them running. The Secretary immediately issued his own possessory orders, calling upon the presidents of the various seized companies to serve as operating managers for the United States. They were directed to carry on their activities in accordance with regulations and directions of the Secretary. The next morning the President sent a message to Congress reporting his action. Twelve days later he sent a second message. Cong. Rec., April 21, 1952. Congress has taken no action. ...

Two crucial issues have developed: First. Should final determination of the constitutional validity of the President's order be made in this case which has proceeded no further than the preliminary injunction stage? Second. If so, is the seizure order within the constitutional power of the President?

I

We agree with the District Court and can see no reason why that question was not ripe for determination on the record presented. We shall therefore consider and determine that question now.

II

The President's power, if any, to issue the order must stem either from an act of Congress or from the Constitution itself. There is no statute that expressly authorizes the President to take possession of property as he did here. Nor is there any act of Congress to which our attention has been directed from which such a power can fairly be implied. Indeed, we do not understand the Government to rely on statutory authorization for this seizure. There are two statutes which do authorize the President to take both personal and real property under certain conditions.[2] However, the Government admits that these conditions were not met and that the President's order was not rooted in either of the statutes. The Government refers to the seizure provisions of one of these statutes (s 201(b) of the Defense Production Act) as "much too cumbersome, involved, and time-consuming for the crisis which was at hand."

Moreover, the use of the seizure technique to solve labor disputes in order to prevent work stoppages was not only unauthorized by any congressional enactment; prior to this controversy, Congress had refused to adopt that method of settling labor disputes. When the Taft-Hartley Act was under consideration in 1947, Congress rejected an amendment which would have authorized such governmental seizures in cases of emergency. Apparently it was thought that the technique of seizure, like that of compulsory arbitration, would interfere with the process of collective bargaining. Consequently, the plan Congress adopted in that Act did not provide for seizure under any circumstances. Instead, the plan sought to bring about settlements by use of the customary devices of mediation, conciliation, investigation by boards of inquiry, and public reports. In some instances temporary injunctions were authorized to provide cooling-off periods. All this failing, unions were left free to strike after a secret vote by employees as to whether they wished to accept their employers' final settlement offer.

It is clear that if the President had authority to issue the order he did, it must be found in some provisions of the Constitution. And it is not claimed that express constitutional language grants this power to the President. The contention is that presidential power should be implied from the aggregate of his powers under the Constitution. Particular reliance is placed on provisions in Article II which say that "the executive Power shall be vested in a President * * *"; that "he shall take Care that the Laws be faithfully executed"; and that he "shall be Commander in Chief of the Army and Navy of the United States."

The order cannot properly be sustained as an exercise of the President's military power as Commander in Chief of the Armed Forces. The Government attempts to do so by citing a number of cases upholding broad powers in military commanders engaged in day-to-day fighting in a theater of war. Such cases need not concern us here. Even though 'theater of war' be an expanding concept, we cannot with faithfulness to our constitutional system hold that the Commander in Chief of the Armed Forces has the ultimate power as such to take possession of private property in order to keep labor disputes from stopping production. This is a job for the Nation's lawmakers, not for its military authorities.

Nor can the seizure order be sustained because of the several constitutional provisions that grant executive power to the President. In the framework of our Constitution, the President's power to see that the laws are faithfully executed refutes the idea that he is to be a lawmaker. The Constitution limits his functions in the lawmaking process to the recommending of laws he thinks wise and the vetoing of laws he thinks bad. And the Constitution is neither silent nor equivocal about who shall make laws which the President is to execute. The first section of the first article says that "All legislative Powers herein granted shall be vested in a Congress of the United States * * *." After granting many powers to the Congress, Article I goes on to provide that Congress may "make all Laws which shall be necessary and proper for carrying into Execution the foregoing Powers and all other Powers vested by this Constitution in the Government of the United States, or in any Department or Officer thereof."

The President's order does not direct that a congressional policy be executed in a manner prescribed by Congress—it directs that a presidential policy be executed in a manner prescribed by the President. The preamble of the order itself, like that of many statutes, sets out reasons why the President believes certain policies should be adopted, proclaims these policies as rules of conduct to be followed, and again, like a statute, authorizes a government official to promulgate additional rules and regulations consistent with the policy proclaimed and needed to carry that policy into execution. The power of Congress to adopt such public policies as those proclaimed by the order is beyond question. It can authorize the taking of private property for public use. It can makes laws regulating the relationships between employers and employees, prescribing rules designed to settle labor disputes, and fixing wages and working conditions in certain fields of our economy. The Constitution did not subject this law-making power of Congress to presidential or military supervision or control.

It is said that other Presidents without congressional authority have taken possession of private business enterprises in order to settle labor disputes. But even if this be true, Congress has not thereby lost its exclusive constitutional authority to make laws necessary and proper to carry out the powers vested by the Constitution "in the Government of the United States, or in any Department or Officer thereof."

The Founders of this Nation entrusted the law making power to the Congress alone in both good and bad times. It would do no good to recall the historical events, the fears of power and the hopes for freedom that lay behind their choice. Such a review would but confirm our holding that this seizure order cannot stand.

The judgment of the District Court is affirmed.

Mr. Justice JACKSON, concurring in the judgment and opinion of the Court. [Jackson was Attorney General of the United States before he joined the Court.]

... A judge, like an executive adviser, may be surprised at the poverty of really useful and unambiguous authority applicable to concrete problems of executive power as they actually present themselves. Just what our forefathers did envision, or would have envisioned had they foreseen modern conditions, must be divined from materials almost as enigmatic as the dreams Joseph was called upon to interpret for Pharaoh.

A century and a half of partisan debate and scholarly speculation yields no net result but only supplies more or less apt quotations from respected sources on each side of any question. They largely cancel each other. And court decisions are indecisive because of the judicial practice of dealing with the largest questions in the most narrow way.

The actual art of governing under our Constitution does not and cannot conform to judicial definitions of the power of any of its branches based on isolated clauses or even single Articles torn from context. While the Constitution diffuses power the better to secure liberty, it also contemplates that practice will integrate the dispersed powers into a workable government. It enjoins upon its branches separateness but interdependence, autonomy but reciprocity. Presidential powers are not fixed but fluctuate, depending upon their disjunction or conjunction with those of Congress. We may well begin by a somewhat over-simplified grouping of practical situations in which a President may doubt, or others may challenge, his powers, and by distinguishing roughly the legal consequences of this factor of relativity.

1. When the President acts pursuant to an express or implied authorization of Congress, his authority is at its maximum, for it includes all that he possesses in his own right plus all that Congress can delegate. In these circumstances, and in these only, may he be said (for what it be worth), to personify the federal sovereignty. If his act is held unconstitutional under these circumstances, it usually means that the Federal Government as an undivided whole lacks power. A seizure executed by the President pursuant to an Act of Congress would be supported by the strongest of presumptions and the widest latitude of judicial interpretation, and the burden of persuasion would rest heavily upon any who might attack it.
2. When the President acts in absence of either a congressional grant or denial of authority, he can only rely upon his own independent powers, but there is a zone of twilight in which he and Congress may have concurrent authority, or in which its distribution is uncertain. Therefore, congressional inertia, indifference or quiescence may sometimes, at least as a practical matter, enable, if not invite, measures on independent presidential responsibility. In this area, any actual test of power is likely to depend on the imperatives of events and contemporary imponderables rather than on abstract theories of law.
3. When the President takes measures incompatible with the expressed or implied will of Congress, his power is at its lowest ebb, for then he can rely only upon his own constitutional powers minus any constitutional powers of Congress over the matter. Courts can sustain exclusive Presidential control in such a case only be disabling the Congress from acting upon the subject.[4] Presidential claim to a power at once so conclusive and preclusive must be scrutinized with caution, for what is at stake is the equilibrium established by our constitutional system.

Into which of these classifications does this executive seizure of the steel industry fit? It is eliminated from the first by admission, for it is conceded that no congressional authorization exists for this seizure. That takes away also the support of the many precedents and declarations which were made in relation, and must be confined, to this category. ...

Can it then be defended under flexible tests available to the second category? It seems clearly eliminated from that class because Congress has not left seizure of private property an open field but has covered it by three statutory policies inconsistent with this seizure. In cases where the purpose is to supply needs of the Government itself, two courses are provided: one, seizure of a plant which fails to comply with obligatory orders placed by the Government, another, condemnation of facilities, including temporary use under the power of eminent domain.[7] The third is applicable where it is the general economy of the country that is to be protected rather than exclusive governmental interests.[8] None of these were invoked. In choosing a different and inconsistent way of his own, the President cannot claim that it is necessitated or invited by failure of Congress to legislate upon the occasions, grounds and methods for seizure of industrial properties.

This leaves the current seizure to be justified only by the severe tests under the third grouping, where it can be supported only by any remainder of executive power after subtraction of such powers as Congress may have over the subject. In short, we can sustain the President only by holding that seizure of such strike-bound industries is within his domain and beyond control by Congress. Thus, this Court's first review of such seizures occurs under circumstances which leave

Presidential power most vulnerable to attack and in the least favorable of possible constitutional postures.

The Solicitor General seeks the power of seizure in three clauses of the Executive Article, the first reading, "The executive Power shall be vested in a President of the United States of America." Lest I be thought to exaggerate, I quote the interpretation which his brief puts upon it: "In our view, this clause constitutes a grant of all the executive powers of which the Government is capable." If that be true, it is difficult to see why the forefathers bothered to add several specific items, including some trifling ones.

The example of such unlimited executive power that must have most impressed the forefathers was the prerogative exercised by George III, and the description of its evils in the Declaration of Independence leads me to doubt that they were creating their new Executive in his image. Continental European examples were no more appealing. And if we seek instruction from our own times, we can match it only from the executive powers in those governments we disparagingly describe as totalitarian. I cannot accept the view that this clause is a grant in bulk of all conceivable executive power but regard it as an allocation to the presidential office of the generic powers thereafter stated.

The clause on which the Government next relies is that "The President shall be Commander in Chief of the Army and Navy of the United States * * *." These cryptic words have given rise to some of the most persistent controversies in our constitutional history. Of course, they imply something more than an empty title. But just what authority goes with the name has plagued Presidential advisers who would not waive or narrow it by nonassertion yet cannot say where it begins or ends. ...

There are indications that the Constitution did not contemplate that the title Commander-in-Chief of the Army and Navy will constitute him also Commander-in-Chief of the country, its industries and its inhabitants. He has no monopoly of 'war powers,' whatever they are. While Congress cannot deprive the President of the command of the army and navy, only Congress can provide him an army or navy to command. It is also empowered to make rules for the "Government and Regulation of land and naval forces," by which it may to some unknown extent impinge upon even command functions.

That military powers of the Commander-in-Chief were not to supersede representative government of internal affairs seems obvious from the Constitution and from elementary American history. ...

The third clause in which the Solicitor General finds seizure powers is that "he shall take Care that the Laws be faithfully executed * * *. That authority must be matched against words of the Fifth Amendment that "No person shall be * * * deprived of life, liberty, or property, without due process of law * * *." One gives a governmental authority that reaches so far as there is law, the other gives a private right that authority shall go no farther. These signify about all there is of the principle that ours is a government of laws, not of men, and that we submit ourselves to rulers only if under rules.

The Solicitor General lastly grounds support of the seizure upon nebulous, inherent powers never expressly granted but said to have accrued to the office from the customs and claims of preceding administrations. The plea is for a resulting power to deal with a crisis or an emergency according to the necessities of the case, the unarticulated assumption being that necessity knows no law.

Loose and irresponsible use of adjectives colors all non-legal and much legal discussion of presidential powers. Inherent' powers, 'implied' powers, 'incidental' powers, 'plenary' powers, 'war' powers and 'emergency' powers are used, often interchangeably and without fixed or ascertainable meanings. ...

Mr. BURTON's and Mr. CLARK's concurrences are omitted

Mr. Justice FRANKFURTER, concurring.

... The pole-star for constitutional adjudications is John Marshall's greatest judicial utterance that "it is a constitution we are expounding." McCulloch v. Maryland, 4 Wheat. 316, 407, 4 L.Ed. 579. That requires both a spacious view in applying an instrument of government "made for an underfined and expanding future," and as narrow a delimitation of the constitutional issues as the circumstances permit. Not the least characteristic of great statesmanship which the Framers manifested was the extent to which they did not attempt to bind the future. It is no less incumbent upon this Court to avoid putting fetters upon the future by needless pronouncements today.

Marshall's admonition that "it is a constitution we are expounding" is especially relevant when the Court is required to give legal sanctions to an underlying principle of the Constitution—that of separation of powers. "The great ordinances of the Constitution do not establish and divide fields of black and white."

The issue before us can be met, and therefore should be, without attempting to define the President's powers comprehensively. I shall not attempt to delineate what belongs to him by virtue of his office beyond the power even of Congress to contract; what authority belongs to him until Congress acts; what kind of problems may be dealt with either by the Congress or by the President or by both; what power must be exercised by the Congress and cannot be delegated to the President. It is as unprofitable to lump together in an undiscriminating hotch-potch past presidential actions claimed to be derived from occupancy of the office, as it is to conjure up hypothetical future cases. The judiciary may, as this case proves, have to intervene in determining where authority lies as between the democratic forces in our scheme of government. But in doing so we should be wary and humble. Such is the teaching of this Court's role in the history of the country. ...

To be sure, the content of the three authorities of government is not to be derived from an abstract analysis. The areas are partly interacting, not wholly disjointed. The Constitution is a framework for government. Therefore the way the framework has consistently operated fairly establishes that it has operated according to its true nature. Deeply embedded traditional ways of conducting government cannot supplant the Constitution or legislation, but they give meaning to the words of a text or supply them. It is an inadmissibly narrow conception of American constitutional law to confine it to the words of the Constitution and to disregard the gloss which life has written upon them. In short, a systematic, unbroken, executive practice, long pursued to the knowledge of the Congress and never before questioned, engaged in by Presidents who have also sworn to uphold the Constitution, making as it were such exercise of power part of the structure of our government, may be treated as a gloss on 'executive Power' vested in the President by s 1 of Art. II. ...

It is not a pleasant judicial duty to find that the President has exceeded his powers and still less so when his purposes were dictated by concern for the Nation's wellbeing, in the assured conviction that he acted to avert danger. But it would stultify one's faith in our people to entertain even a momentary fear that the patriotism and the wisdom of the President and the Congress, as well as the long view of the immediate parties in interest, will not find ready accommodation for differences on matters which, however close to their concern and however intrinsically important, are overshadowed by the awesome issues which confront the world. ...

In reaching the conclusion that conscience compels, I too derive consolation from the reflection that the President and the Congress between them will continue to safeguard the heritage which comes to them straight from George Washington.

Mr. Chief Justice VINSON, with whom Mr. Justice REED and Mr. Justice MINTON join, dissenting.

The President of the United States directed the Secretary of Commerce to take temporary possession of the Nation's steel mills during the existing emergency because "a work stoppage would immediately jeopardize and imperil our national defense and the defense of those joined with us in resisting aggression, and would add to the continuing danger of our soldiers, sailors and airmen engaged in combat in the field." The District Court ordered the mills returned to their private owners on the ground that the President's action was beyond his powers under the Constitution.

This Court affirms. Some members of the Court are of the view that the President is without power to act in time of crisis in the absence of express statutory authorization. Other members of the Court affirm on the basis of their reading of certain statutes. Because we cannot agree that affirmance is proper on any ground, and because of the transcending importance of the questions presented not only in this critical litigation but also to the powers the President and of future Presidents to act in time of crisis, we are compelled to register this dissent. ...

The President has the duty to execute the foregoing legislative programs. Their successful execution depends upon continued production of steel and stabilized prices for steel. Accordingly, when the collective bargaining agreements between the Nation's steel producers and their employees, represented by the United Steel Workers, were due to expire on December 31, 1951, and a strike shutting down the entire basic steel industry was threatened, the President acted to avert a complete shutdown of steel production. …

Accordingly, if the President has any power under the Constitution to meet a critical situation in the absence of express statutory authorization, there is no basis whatever for criticizing the exercise of such power in this case. …

In passing upon the grave constitutional question presented in this case, we must never forget, as Chief Justice Marshall admonished, that the Constitution is "intended to endure for ages to come, and consequently, to be adapted to the various crises of human affairs," and that "(i)ts means are adequate to its ends."[28] Cases do arise presenting questions which could not have been foreseen by the Framers. In such cases, the Constitution has been treated as a living document adaptable to new situations. But we are not called upon today to expand the Constitution to meet a new situation. For, in this case, we need only look to history and time-honored principles of constitutional law—principles that have been applied consistently by all branches of the Government throughout our history. It is those who assert the invalidity of the Executive Order who seek to amend the Constitution in this case. …

As the District Judge stated, this is no time for 'timorous' judicial action. But neither is this a time for timorous executive action. Faced with the duty of executing the defense programs which Congress had enacted and the disastrous effects that any stoppage in steel production would have on those programs, the President acted to preserve those programs by seizing the steel mills. There is no question that the possession was other than temporary in character and subject to congressional direction—either approving, disapproving or regulating the manner in which the mills were to be administered and returned to the owners. The President immediately informed Congress of his action and clearly stated his intention to abide by the legislative will. No basis for claims of arbitrary action, unlimited powers or dictatorial usurpation of congressional power appears from the facts of this case. On the contrary, judicial, legislative and executive precedents throughout our history demonstrate that in this case the President acted in full conformity with his duties under the Constitution. Accordingly, we would reverse the order of the District Court.

Notes and Questions

1. *Justice Black vs. Justice Jackson.* What is the difference between Black's and Jackson's approaches?
2. *The prevailing standard.* Jackson's approach became the guide in these cases. Is that appropriate when Jackson wrote his opinion solely for himself?
3. *Video.* Does this video explain the reasoning of the Court's opinion? See Quimbee's video, *Youngstown Sheet and Tube Co. v. Sawyer* Case Brief Summary/Law Case Explained, Aug. 4, 2015, posted at https://www.youtube.com/watch?v=TqePUkGtm4o&list=PLsFE_Nvl6h_braQ_Nxo-D1jg8oDdM_l8uI&index=8.

B. The President's War Powers

Youngstown ruled that the Commander in Chief's power did not give the President authority to seize the steel mills. A different situation arises, however, when the nation is at war. Article I, Section 8 of the Constitution gives the Congress the power to "declare war." But the President is the Commander in Chief of the military. Is the President constrained to wait for Congress to declare war before ordering troops to a battlefront?

1. When the War Is a War on Terror

The "war" in earlier cases is different from the war on terror, thus, raising numerous questions. Those questions were addressed in the following cases. Read the oral argument in *Hamdi* on the case's website, https://www.oyez.org/cases/2003/03-6696. What are the most important questions that the Justice(s) raise? Who does the best job answering them? Can you tell from their questions which Justices would interpret the Constitution to provide a broad executive power? Or those that would endorse a weaker power? As you read through this chapter, try to identify which Justice has the strongest account of executive power. What is the spectrum of executive power in these cases?

Hamdi v. Rumsfeld

SUPREME COURT OF THE UNITED STATES, 2004
542 U.S. 507, 124 S.Ct. 2633

O'CONNOR, J., announced the judgment of the Court and delivered an opinion, in which REHNQUIST, C. J., and KENNEDY and BREYER, JJ., joined. SOUTER, J., filed an opinion concurring in part, dissenting in part, and concurring in the judgment, in which GINSBURG, J., joined. SCALIA, J., filed a dissenting opinion, in which STEVENS, J., joined. THOMAS, J., filed a dissenting opinion.

At this difficult time in our Nation's history, we are called upon to consider the legality of the Government's detention of a United States citizen on United States soil as an "enemy combatant" and to address the process that is constitutionally owed to one who seeks to challenge his classification as such. The United States Court of Appeals for the Fourth Circuit held that petitioner Yaser Hamdi's detention was legally authorized and that he was entitled to no further opportunity to challenge his enemy-combatant label. We now vacate and remand. We hold that although Congress authorized the detention of combatants in the narrow circumstances alleged here, due process demands that a citizen held in the United States as an enemy combatant be given a meaningful opportunity to contest the factual basis for that detention before a neutral decisionmaker.

I

On September 11, 2001, the al Qaeda terrorist network used hijacked commercial airliners to attack prominent targets in the United States. Approximately 3,000 people were killed in those attacks. One week later, in response to these "acts of treacherous violence," Congress passed a resolution authorizing the President to "use all necessary and appropriate force against those nations, organizations, or persons he determines planned, authorized, committed, or aided the terrorist attacks" or "harbored such organizations or persons, in order to prevent any future acts of international terrorism against the United States by such nations, organizations or persons." Authorization for Use of Military Force (AUMF), 115 Stat. 224. Soon thereafter, the President ordered United States Armed Forces to Afghanistan, with a mission to subdue al Qaeda and quell the Taliban regime that was known to support it.

This case arises out of the detention of a man whom the Government alleges took up arms with the Taliban during this conflict. His name is Yaser Esam Hamdi. Born in Louisiana in 1980, Hamdi moved with his family to Saudi Arabia as a child. By 2001, the parties agree, he resided in Afghanistan. At some point that year, he was seized by members of the Northern Alliance, a coalition of military groups opposed to the Taliban government, andeventually was turned over to the United States military. The Government asserts that it initially detained and interrogated Hamdi in Afghanistan before transferring him to the United States Naval Base in Guantanamo Bay in January 2002. In April 2002, upon learning that Hamdi is an American citizen, authorities transferred him to a naval brig in Norfolk, Virginia, where he remained until a recent transfer to a brig in Charleston, South Carolina. The Government contends that Hamdi is an "enemy combatant," and that this status justifies holding him in the United States indefinitely—without formal charges or proceedings—unless and until it makes the determination that access to counsel or further process is warranted.

In June 2002, Hamdi's father, Esam Fouad Hamdi, filed the present petition for a writ of habeas corpus under 28 U.S.C. § 2241 in the Eastern District of Virginia, naming as petitioners his son and himself as next friend. The elder Hamdi alleges in the petition that he has had no contact with his son since the Government took custody of him in 2001, and that the Government has held his son "without access to legal counsel or notice of any charges pending against him." The petition contends that Hamdi's detention was not legally authorized. It argues that, "[a]s an American citizen, ... Hamdi enjoys the full protections of the Constitution," and that Hamdi's detention in the United States without charges, access to an impartial tribunal, or assistance of counsel "violated and continue[s] to violate the Fifth and Fourteenth Amendments to the United States Constitution." The habeas petition asks that the court, among other things, (1) appoint counsel for Hamdi; (2) order respondents to cease interrogating him; (3) declare that he is being held in violation of the Fifth and Fourteenth Amendments; (4) "[t]o the extent Respondents contest any material factual allegations in this Petition, schedule an evidentiary hearing, at which Petitioners may adduce proof in support of their allegations"; and (5) order that Hamdi be released from his "unlawful custody." Although his habeas petition provides no details with regard to the factual circumstances surrounding his son's capture and detention, Hamdi's father has asserted in documents found elsewhere in the record that his son went to Afghanistan to do "relief work," and that he had been in that country less than two months before September 11, 2001, and could not have received military training. The 20-year-old was traveling on his own for the first time, his father says, and "[b]ecause of his lack of experience, he was trapped in Afghanistan once the military campaign began."

The District Court found that Hamdi's father was a proper next friend, appointed the federal public defender as counsel for the petitioners, and ordered that counsel be given access to Hamdi. The United States Court of Appeals for the Fourth Circuit reversed that order, holding that the District Court had failed to extend appropriate deference to the Government's security and intelligence interests. It directed the District Court to consider "the most cautious procedures first," and to conduct a deferential inquiry into Hamdi's status.. It opined that "if Hamdi is indeed an 'enemy combatant' who was captured during hostilities in Afghanistan, the government's present detention of him is a lawful one."

On remand, the Government filed a response and a motion to dismiss the petition. It attached to its response a declaration from one Michael Mobbs (hereinafter Mobbs Declaration), who identified himself as Special Advisor to the Under Secretary of Defense for Policy. Mobbs indicated that in this position, he has been "substantially involved with matters related to the detention of enemy combatants in the current war against the al Qaeda terrorists and those who support and harbor them (including the Taliban)." He expressed his "familiar[ity]" with Department of Defense and United States military policies and procedures applicable to the detention, control, and transfer of al Qaeda and Taliban personnel, and declared that "[b]ased upon my review of relevant records and reports, I am also familiar with the facts and circumstances related to the capture of ... Hamdi and his detention by U.S. military forces."

Mobbs then set forth what remains the sole evidentiary support that the Government has provided to the courts for Hamdi's detention. The declaration states that Hamdi "traveled to Afghanistan" in July or August 2001, and that he thereafter "affiliated with a Taliban military unit and received weapons training." It asserts that Hamdi "remained with his Taliban unit following the attacks of September 11" and that, during the time when Northern Alliance forces were "engaged in battle with the Taliban," "Hamdi's Taliban unit surrendered" to those forces, after which he "surrender[ed] his Kalishnikov assault rifle" to them. The Mobbs Declaration also states that, because al Qaeda and the Taliban "were and are hostile forces engaged in armed conflict with the armed forces of the United States," "individuals associated with" those groups "were and continue to be enemy combatants." Mobbs states that Hamdi was labeled an enemy combatant "[b]ased upon his interviews and in light of his association with the Taliban." According to the declaration, a series of "U.S. military screening team[s]" determined that Hamdi met "the criteria for enemy combatants," and "[a] subsequent interview of Hamdi has confirmed the fact that he surrendered and gave his firearm to Northern Alliance forces, which supports his classification as an enemy combatant."

After the Government submitted this declaration, the Fourth Circuit directed the District Court to proceed in accordance with its earlier ruling and, specifically, to "'consider the sufficiency of the Mobbs declaration as an independent matter before proceeding further.'" The District Court found that the Mobbs Declaration fell "far short" of supporting Hamdi's detention. It criticized the generic and hearsay nature of the affidavit, calling it "little more than the government's 'say-so.'" It ordered the Government to turn over numerous materials for *in camera* review, including copies of all of Hamdi's statements and the notes taken from interviews with him that related to his reasons for going to Afghanistan and his activities therein; a list of all interrogators who had questioned Hamdi and their names and addresses; statements by members of the Northern Alliance regarding Hamdi's surrender and capture; a list of the dates and locations of his capture and subsequent detentions; and the names and titles of the United States Government officials who made the determinations that Hamdi was an enemy combatant and that he should be moved to a naval brig. The court indicated that all of these materials were necessary for "meaningful judicial review" of whether Hamdi's detention was legally authorized and whether Hamdi had received sufficient process to satisfy the Due Process Clause of the Constitution and relevant treaties or military regulations. *[The Fourth Circuit then ruled for the government.] ...*

II

The threshold question before us is whether the Executive has the authority to detain citizens who qualify as "enemy combatants." There is some debate as to the proper scope of this term, and the Government has never provided any court with the full criteria that it uses in classifying individuals as such. It has made clear, however, that, for purposes of this case, the "enemy combatant" that it is seeking to detain is an individual who, it alleges, was "'part of or supporting forces hostile to the United States or coalition partners'" in Afghanistan and who "'engaged in an armed conflict against the United States'" there. We therefore answer only the narrow question before us: whether the detention of citizens falling within that definition is authorized.

The Government maintains that no explicit congressional authorization is required, because the Executive possesses plenary authority to detain pursuant to Article II of the Constitution. We do not reach the question whether Article II provides such authority, however, because we agree with the Government's alternative position, that Congress has in fact authorized Hamdi's detention, through the AUMF.

Our analysis on that point, set forth below, substantially overlaps with our analysis of Hamdi's principal argument for the illegality of his detention. He posits that his detention is forbidden by 18 U.S.C. § 4001(a). Section 4001(a) states that "[n]o citizen shall be imprisoned or otherwise detained by the United States except pursuant to an Act of Congress." Congress passed § 4001(a) in 1971 as part of a bill to repeal the Emergency Detention Act of 1950, 50 U.S.C. § 811 *et seq.*, which provided procedures for executive detention, during times of emergency, of individuals deemed likely to engage in espionage or sabotage. Congress was particularly concerned about the possibility that the Act could be used to reprise the Japanese-American internment camps of World War II. The Government again presses two alternative positions. First, it argues that § 4001(a), in light of its legislative history and its location in Title 18, applies only to "the control of civilian prisons and related detentions," not to military detentions. Second, it maintains that § 4001(a) is satisfied, because Hamdi is being detained "pursuant to an Act of Congress"—the AUMF. Again, because we conclude that the Government's second assertion is correct, we do not address the first. In other words, for the reasons that follow, we conclude that the AUMF is explicit congressional authorization for the detention of individuals in the narrow category we describe (assuming, without deciding, that such authorization is required), and that the AUMF satisfied § 4001(a)'s requirement that a detention be "pursuant to an Act of Congress" (assuming, without deciding, that § 4001(a) applies to military detentions). ...

There is no bar to this Nation's holding one of its own citizens as an enemy combatant. ...

In light of these principles, it is of no moment that the AUMF does not use specific language of detention. Because detention to prevent a combatant's return to the battlefield is a fundamental incident of waging war, in permitting the use of "necessary and appropriate force," Congress has clearly and unmistakably authorized detention in the narrow circumstances considered here. ...

The United States may detain, for the duration of these hostilities, individuals legitimately determined to be Taliban combatants who "engaged in an armed conflict against the United States." If the record establishes that United States troops are still involved in active combat in Afghanistan, those detentions are part of the exercise of "necessary and appropriate force," and therefore are authorized by the AUMF. ...

III

Even in cases in which the detention of enemy combatants is legally authorized, there remains the question of what process is constitutionally due to a citizen who disputes his enemy-combatant status. ...

B

First, the Government urges the adoption of the Fourth Circuit's holding below—that because it is "undisputed" that Hamdi's seizure took place in a combat zone, the habeas determination can be made purely as a matter of law, with no further hearing or factfinding necessary. This argument is easily rejected. ...

C

The Government's second argument requires closer consideration. This is the argument that further factual exploration is unwarranted and inappropriate in light of the extraordinary constitutional interests at stake. ...

Under this review, a court would assume the accuracy of the Government's articulated basis for Hamdi's detention, as set forth in the Mobbs Declaration, and assess only whether that articulated basis was a legitimate one. ...

With due recognition of these competing concerns, we believe that neither the process proposed by the Government nor the process apparently envisioned by the District Court below strikes the proper constitutional balance when a United States citizen is detained in the United States as an enemy combatant. That is, "the risk of an erroneous deprivation" of a detainee's liberty interest is unacceptably high under the Government's proposed rule, while some of the "additional or substitute procedural safeguards" suggested by the District Court are unwarranted in light of their limited "probable value" and the burdens they may impose on the military in such cases. *Mathews,* 424 U.S., at 335, 96 S.Ct. 893.

We therefore hold that a citizen-detainee seeking to challenge his classification as an enemy combatant must receive notice of the factual basis for his classification, and a fair opportunity to rebut the Government's factual assertions before a neutral decisionmaker. "For more than a century the central meaning of procedural due process has been clear: 'Parties whose rights are to be affected are entitled to be heard; and in order that they may enjoy that right they must first be notified.' It is equally fundamental that the right to notice and an opportunity to be heard 'must be granted at a meaningful time and in a meaningful manner.'" These essential constitutional promises may not be eroded.

At the same time, the exigencies of the circumstances may demand that, aside from these core elements, enemy-combatant proceedings may be tailored to alleviate their uncommon potential to burden the Executive at a time of ongoing military conflict. Hearsay, for example, may need to be accepted as the most reliable available evidence from the Government in such a proceeding. Likewise, the Constitution would not be offended by a presumption in favor of the Government's evidence, so long as that presumption remained a rebuttable one and fair opportunity for rebuttal were provided. Thus, once the Government puts forth credible evidence that the habeas petitioner meets the enemy-combatant criteria, the onus could shift to the petitioner to rebut that evidence with more persuasive evidence that he falls outside the criteria. A burden-shifting scheme of this sort would meet the goal of ensuring that the errant tourist, embedded journalist, or local aid worker has a chance to prove military error while giving due regard to the Executive once it has put forth meaningful support for its conclusion that the detainee is in fact an enemy combatant. In the words of *Mathews,* process of this sort would sufficiently address the "risk of an erroneous deprivation" of a detainee's liberty interest while eliminating certain procedures that have questionable additional value in light of the burden on the Government.

We think it unlikely that this basic process will have the dire impact on the central functions of warmaking that the Government forecasts. The parties agree that initial captures on the battlefield need not receive the process we have discussed here; that process is due only when the determination is made to *continue* to hold those who have been seized. The Government has made clear in its briefing that documentation regarding battlefield detainees already is kept in the ordinary course of military affairs. Any factfinding imposition created by requiring a knowledgeable affiant to summarize these records to an independent tribunal is a minimal one. Likewise, arguments that military officers ought not have to wage war under the threat of litigation lose much of their steam when factual disputes at enemy-combatant hearings are limited to the alleged combatant's acts. This focus meddles little, if at all, in the strategy or conduct of war, inquiring only into the appropriateness of continuing to detain an individual claimed to have taken up arms against the United States. While we accord the greatest respect and consideration to the judgments of military authorities in matters relating to the actual prosecution of a war, and recognize that the scope of that discretion necessarily is wide, it does not infringe on the core role of the military for the courts to exercise their own time-honored and constitutionally mandated roles of reviewing and resolving claims like those presented here. Cf. *Korematsu v. United States,* 323 U.S. 214, 233–234, 65 S.Ct. 193, 89 L.Ed. 194 (1944) (Murphy, J., dissenting) ("[L]ike other claims conflicting with the asserted constitutional rights of the individual, the military claim must subject itself to the judicial process of having its reasonableness determined and its conflicts with other interests reconciled").

In sum, while the full protections that accompany challenges to detentions in other settings may prove unworkable and inappropriate in the enemy-combatant setting, the threats to military operations posed by a basic system of independent review are not so weighty as to trump a citizen's core rights to challenge meaningfully the Government's case and to be heard by an impartial adjudicator. ...

The judgment of the United States Court of Appeals for the Fourth Circuit is vacated, and the case is remanded for further proceedings.

It is so ordered.

Justice SOUTER, with whom Justice GINSBURG joins, concurring in part, dissenting in part, and concurring in the judgment.

... The plurality rejects any such limit on the exercise of habeas jurisdiction and so far I agree with its opinion. The plurality does, however, accept the Government's position that if Hamdi's designation as an enemy combatant is correct, his detention (at least as to some period) is authorized by an Act of Congress as required by § 4001(a), that is, by the Authorization for Use of Military Force. Here, I disagree and respectfully dissent. The Government has failed to demonstrate that the Force Resolution authorizes the detention complained of here even on the facts the Government claims. If the Government raises nothing further than the record now shows, the Non–Detention Act entitles Hamdi to be released. ...

II

... The fact that Congress intended to guard against a repetition of the World War II internments when it repealed the 1950 statute and gave us § 4001(a) provides a powerful reason to think that § 4001(a) was meant to require clear congressional authorization before any citizen can be placed in a cell. It is not merely that the legislative history shows that § 4001(a) was thought necessary in anticipation of times just like the present, in which the safety of the country is threatened. To appreciate what is most significant, one must only recall that the internments of the 1940s were accomplished by Executive action. Although an Act of Congress ratified and confirmed an Executive order authorizing the military to exclude individuals from defined areas and to accommodate those it might remove, the statute said nothing whatever about the detention of those who might be removed; internment camps were creatures of the Executive, and confinement in them rested on assertion of Executive authority. When, therefore, Congress repealed the 1950 Act and adopted § 4001(a) for the purpose of avoiding another *Korematsu,* it intended to preclude reliance on vague congressional authority (for example, providing "accommodations" for those subject to removal) as authority for detention or imprisonment at the discretion of the Executive (maintaining detention camps of American citizens, for example). In requiring that any Executive detention be "pursuant to an Act of Congress," then, Congress necessarily meant to require a congressional enactment that clearly authorized detention or imprisonment. ...

III

Under this principle of reading § 4001(a) robustly to require a clear statement of authorization to detain, none of the Government's arguments suffices to justify Hamdi's detention. ...

IV

Because I find Hamdi's detention forbidden by § 4001(a) and unauthorized by the Force Resolution, I would not reach any questions of what process he may be due in litigating disputed issues in a proceeding under the habeas statute or prior to the habeas enquiry itself. For me, it suffices that the Government has failed to justify holding him in the absence of a further Act of Congress, criminal charges, a showing that the detention conforms to the laws of war, or a demonstration that § 4001(a) is unconstitutional. I would therefore vacate the judgment of the Court of Appeals and remand for proceedings consistent with this view.

Since this disposition does not command a majority of the Court, however, the need to give practical effect to the conclusions of eight Members of the Court rejecting the Government's position calls for me to join with the plurality in ordering remand on terms closest to those I would impose. Although I think litigation of Hamdi's status as an enemy combatant is unnecessary, the terms of the plurality's remand will allow Hamdi to offer evidence that he is not an enemy combatant, and he should at the least have the benefit of that opportunity. ...

Justice SCALIA, with whom Justice STEVENS joins, dissenting.

... Where the Government accuses a citizen of waging war against it, our constitutional tradition has been to prosecute him in federal court for treason or some other crime. Where the exigencies of war prevent that, the Constitution's Suspension Clause, Art. I, § 9, cl. 2, allows Congress to relax the usual protections temporarily. Absent suspension, however, the Executive's assertion of military exigency has not been thought sufficient to permit detention without charge. No one contends that the congressional Authorization for Use of Military Force, on which the Government relies to justify its actions here, is an implementation of the Suspension Clause. Accordingly, I would reverse the judgment below. ...

II A

Justice O'CONNOR, writing for a plurality of this Court, asserts that captured enemy combatants (other than those suspected of war crimes) have traditionally been detained until the cessation of hostilities and then released. That is probably an accurate description of wartime practice with respect to enemy *aliens*. The tradition with respect to American citizens, however, has been quite different. Citizens aiding the enemy have been treated as traitors subject to the criminal process. ...

III

... Writings from the founding generation also suggest that, without exception, the only constitutional alternatives are to charge the crime or suspend the writ.

... A view of the Constitution that gives the Executive authority to use military force rather than the force of law against citizens on American soil flies in the face of the mistrust that engendered these provisions. ...

IV

... Absent suspension of the writ, a citizen held where the courts are open is entitled either to criminal trial or to a judicial decree requiring his release.

V

It follows from what I have said that Hamdi is entitled to a habeas decree requiring his release unless (1) criminal proceedings are promptly brought, or (2) Congress has suspended the writ of habeas corpus. ...

[The AUMF] is not remotely a congressional suspension of the writ, and no one claims that it is. Contrary to the plurality's view, I do not think this statute even authorizes detention of a citizen with the clarity necessary to satisfy the interpretive canon that statutes should be construed so as to avoid grave constitutional concerns, ... or with the clarity necessary to overcome the statutory prescription that "[n]o citizen shall be imprisoned or otherwise detained by the United States except pursuant to an Act of Congress." ...

It should not be thought, however, that the plurality's evisceration of the Suspension Clause augments, principally, the power of Congress. As usual, the major effect of its constitutional improvisation is to increase the power of the Court. Having found a congressional authorization for detention of citizens where none clearly exists; and having discarded the categorical procedural protection of the Suspension Clause; the plurality then proceeds, under the guise of the Due Process Clause, to prescribe what procedural protections *it* thinks appropriate. It "weigh[s] the private interest ... against the Government's asserted interest," and—just as though writing a new Constitution—comes up with an unheard-of system in which the citizen rather than the Government bears the burden of proof, testimony is by hearsay rather than live witnesses, and the presiding officer may well be a "neutral" military officer rather than judge and jury. It claims authority to engage in this sort of "judicious balancing" from *Mathews v. Eldridge*, 424 U.S. 319, 96 S.Ct. 893, 47 L.Ed.2d 18 (1976), a case involving ... *the withdrawal of disability benefits!* Whatever the merits of this technique when newly recognized property rights are at issue (and even there they are questionable), it has no place where the Constitution and the common law already supply an answer.

Having distorted the Suspension Clause, the plurality finishes up by transmogrifying the Great Writ—disposing of the present habeas petition by remanding for the District Court to "engag[e] in a factfinding process that is both prudent and incremental." "In the absence of [the Executive's prior provision of procedures that satisfy due process], ... a court that receives a petition for a writ of habeas corpus from an alleged enemy combatant must itself ensure that the minimum requirements of due process are achieved." This judicial remediation of executive default is unheard of. The role of habeas corpus is to determine the legality of executive detention, not to supply the omitted process necessary to make it legal. It is not the habeas court's function to make illegal detention legal by supplying a process that the Government could have provided, but chose not to. If Hamdi is being imprisoned in violation of the Constitution (because without due process of law), then his habeas petition should be granted; the Executive may then hand him over to the criminal authorities, whose detention for the purpose of prosecution will be lawful, or else must release him.

There is a certain harmony of approach in the plurality's making up for Congress's failure to invoke the Suspension Clause and its making up for the Executive's failure to apply what it says are needed procedures—an approach that reflects what might be called a Mr. Fix-it Mentality. The plurality seems to view it as its mission to Make Everything Come Out Right, rather than merely to decree the consequences, as far as individual rights are concerned, of the other two branches' actions and omissions. Has the Legislature failed to suspend the writ in the current dire emergency? Well, we will remedy that failure by prescribing the reasonable conditions that a suspension should have included. And has the Executive failed to live up to those reasonable conditions? Well, we will ourselves make that failure good, so that this dangerous fellow (if he is dangerous) need not be set free. The problem with this approach is not only that it steps out of the courts' modest and limited role in a democratic society; but that by repeatedly doing what it thinks the political branches ought to do it encourages their lassitude and saps the vitality of government by the people. ...

Justice THOMAS, dissenting.

The Executive Branch, acting pursuant to the powers vested in the President by the Constitution and with explicit congressional approval, has determined that Yaser Hamdi is an enemy combatant and should be detained. This detention falls squarely within the Federal Government's war powers, and we lack the expertise and capacity to second-guess that decision. As such, petitioners' habeas challenge should fail, and there is no reason to remand the case. The plurality reaches a contrary conclusion by failing adequately to consider basic principles of the constitutional structure as it relates to national security and foreign affairs and by using the balancing scheme of *Mathews v. Eldridge*, 424 U.S. 319, 96 S.Ct. 893, 47 L.Ed.2d 18 (1976). I do not think that the Federal Government's war powers can be balanced away by this Court. Arguably, Congress could provide for additional procedural protections, but until it does, we have no right to insist upon them. But even if I were to agree with the general approach the plurality takes, I could not accept the particulars. The plurality utterly fails to account for the Government's compelling interests and for our own institutional inability to weigh competing concerns correctly. I respectfully dissent.

I

... I acknowledge that the question whether Hamdi's executive detention is lawful is a question properly resolved by the Judicial Branch, though the question comes to the Court with the strongest presumptions in favor of the Government. The plurality agrees that Hamdi's detention is lawful if he is an enemy combatant. But the question whether Hamdi is actually an enemy combatant is "of a kind for which the Judiciary has neither aptitude, facilities nor responsibility and which has long been held to belong in the domain of political power not subject to judicial intrusion or inquiry." That is, although it is appropriate for the Court to determine the judicial question whether the President has the asserted authority, we lack the information and expertise to question whether Hamdi is actually an enemy combatant, a question the resolution of which is committed to other branches. ...

III

I agree with the plurality that the Federal Government has power to detain those that the Executive Branch determines to be enemy combatants. But I do not think that the plurality has adequately explained the breadth of the President's authority to detain enemy combatants, an authority that includes making virtually conclusive factual findings. In my view, the structural considerations discussed above, as recognized in our precedent, demonstrate that we lack the capacity and responsibility to second-guess this determination. ...

Accordingly, I conclude that the Government's detention of Hamdi as an enemy combatant does not violate the Constitution. By detaining Hamdi, the President, in the prosecution of a war and authorized by Congress, has acted well within his authority. Hamdi thereby received all the process to which he was due under the circumstances. I therefore believe that this is no occasion to balance the competing interests, as the plurality unconvincingly attempts to do. ...

Notes and Questions

1. *The AUMF.* What is the AUMF? How much power did it give to the President? Is there any time limit on the AUMF? Can it be invoked indefinitely because the war on terror does not have a definable end?
2. *Korematsu and Hamdi. Korematsu* is the Supreme Court case that upheld the imprisonment of Japanese Americans during World War II. The Japanese were removed from their homes and sent to different prison camps. You will read *Korematsu* in Chapter 7. Most people today are critical of *Korematsu.* Why? How did the *Korematsu* precedent affect this opinion?
3. *Video.* Does this video give an adequate summary of the law of *Hamdi*? See Quimbee's video, *Hamdi v. Rumsfeld* Case Brief Summary/Law Case Explained, Sep. 5, 2015, posted at https://www.youtube.com/watch?v=yP2KbkEHp-M&list=PLsFE_Nvl6h_Y75KGR5pkGqcFisGvBnO9S&index=95.

2. The Prisoners Have the Constitutional Privilege of Habeas Corpus

Four years post-*Hamdi,* the Court faced another aspect of the war on terror in a case about the prisoners held in Guantanamo Bay, Cuba. Once again, the Court faced the question of how much power the Executive had over prisoners of war. The result in the following case is a 5–4 decision. Why was the decision so close?

Read the oral argument on the case's webpage, https://www.oyez.org/cases/2007/06-1195. Assess the quality of the lawyers' arguments. Did they all do a good job? Was any one a better advocate than the others? Can you tell from the argument that the Justices would split 5–4?

Boumediene v. Bush

SUPREME COURT OF THE UNITED STATES, 2008

553 U.S. 723, 128 S.Ct. 2229

KENNEDY, J., delivered the opinion of the Court, in which STEVENS, SOUTER, GINSBURG, and BREYER, JJ., joined. SOUTER, J., filed a concurring opinion, in which GINSBURG and BREYER, JJ., joined. ROBERTS, C. J., filed a dissenting opinion, in which SCALIA, THOMAS, and ALITO, JJ., joined. SCALIA, J., filed a dissenting opinion, in which ROBERTS, C. J., and THOMAS and ALITO, JJ., joined.

Petitioners are aliens designated as enemy combatants and detained at the United States Naval Station at Guantanamo Bay, Cuba. There are others detained there, also aliens, who are not parties to this suit.

Petitioners present a question not resolved by our earlier cases relating to the detention of aliens at Guantanamo: whether they have the constitutional privilege of habeas corpus, a privilege not to be withdrawn except in conformance with the Suspension Clause, Art. I, § 9, cl. 2. We hold these petitioners do have the habeas corpus privilege. Congress has enacted a statute, the Detainee Treatment Act of 2005 (DTA), 119 Stat. 2739, that provides certain procedures for review of the detainees' status. We hold that those procedures are not an adequate and effective substitute for habeas corpus. Therefore § 7 of the Military Commissions Act of 2006(MCA), 28 U.S.C. § 2241(e), operates as an unconstitutional suspension of the writ. We do not address whether the President has authority to detain these petitioners nor do we hold that the writ must issue. These and other questions regarding the legality of the detention are to be resolved in the first instance by the District Court. ...

II

As a threshold matter, we must decide whether MCA § 7 denies the federal courts jurisdiction to hear habeas corpus actions pending at the time of its enactment. We hold the statute does deny that jurisdiction, so that, if the statute is valid, petitioners' cases must be dismissed. ...

III

In deciding the constitutional questions now presented we must determine whether petitioners are barred from seeking the writ or invoking the protections of the Suspension Clause either because of their status, *i.e.*, petitioners' designation by the Executive Branch as enemy combatants, or their physical location, *i.e.*, their presence at Guantanamo Bay. The Government contends that noncitizens designated as enemy combatants and detained in territory located outside our Nation's borders have no constitutional rights and no privilege of habeas corpus. Petitioners contend they do have cognizable constitutional rights and that Congress, in seeking to eliminate recourse to habeas corpus as a means to assert those rights, acted in violation of the Suspension Clause. ...

IV

Drawing from its position that at common law the writ ran only to territories over which the Crown was sovereign, the Government says the Suspension Clause affords petitioners no rights because the United States does not claim sovereignty over the place of detention. ...

We therefore do not question the Government's position that Cuba, not the United States, maintains sovereignty, in the legal and technical sense of the term, over Guantanamo Bay. But this does not end the analysis. Our cases do not hold it is improper for us to inquire into the objective degree of control the Nation asserts over foreign territory. As commentators have noted, "'[s]overeignty' is a term used in many senses and is much abused." When we have stated that sovereignty is a political question, we have referred not to sovereignty in the general, colloquial sense, meaning the exercise of dominion or power, but sovereignty in the narrow, legal sense of the term, meaning a claim of right. Indeed, it is not altogether uncommon for a territory to be under the *de jure* sovereignty of one nation, while under the plenary control, or practical sovereignty, of another. This condition can occur when the territory is seized during war, as Guantanamo was during the Spanish–American War. Accordingly, for purposes of our analysis, we accept the Government's position that Cuba, and not the United States, retains *de jure* sovereignty over Guantanamo Bay. As we did in *Rasul,* however, we take notice of the obvious and uncontested fact that the United States, by virtue of its complete jurisdiction and control over the base, maintains *de facto* sovereignty over this territory. ...

A

The Court has discussed the issue of the Constitution's extraterritorial application on many occasions. These decisions undermine the Government's argument that, at least as applied to noncitizens, the Constitution necessarily stops where *de jure* sovereignty ends. ...

Practical considerations weighed heavily as well in *Johnson v. Eisentrager,* 339 U.S. 763, 70 S.Ct. 936, 94 L.Ed. 1255 (1950), where the Court addressed whether habeas corpus jurisdiction extended to enemy aliens who had been convicted of violating the laws of war. The prisoners were detained at Landsberg Prison in Germany during the Allied Powers' post-war occupation. The Court stressed the difficulties of ordering the Government to produce the prisoners in a habeas corpus proceeding. It "would require allocation of shipping space, guarding personnel, billeting and rations" and would damage the prestige of military commanders at a sensitive time. In considering these factors the Court sought to balance the constraints of military occupation with constitutional necessities.

True, the Court in *Eisentrager* denied access to the writ, and it noted the prisoners "at no relevant time were within any territory over which the United States is sovereign, and [that] the scenes of their offense, their capture, their trial and their punishment were all beyond the territorial jurisdiction of any court of the United States." The Government seizes upon this language as proof positive that the *Eisentrager* Court adopted a formalistic, sovereignty-based test for determining the reach of the Suspension Clause. We reject this reading for three reasons.

First, we do not accept the idea that the above-quoted passage from *Eisentrager* is the only authoritative language in the opinion and that all the rest is dicta. The Court's further determinations, based on practical considerations, were integral to Part II of its opinion and came before the decision announced its holding.

Second, because the United States lacked both *de jure* sovereignty and plenary control over Landsberg Prison, it is far from clear that the *Eisentrager* Court used the term sovereignty only in the narrow technical sense and not to connote the degree of control the military asserted over the facility. The Justices who decided *Eisentrager* would have understood sovereignty as a multifaceted concept. ...

[Third] A constricted reading of *Eisentrager* overlooks what we see as a common thread uniting the Insular Cases, *Eisentrager,* and *Reid:* the idea that questions of extraterritoriality turn on objective factors and practical concerns, not formalism.

B

The Government's formal sovereignty-based test raises troubling separation-of-powers concerns as well. The political history of Guantanamo illustrates the deficiencies of this approach. The United States has maintained complete and uninterrupted control of the bay for over 100 years. At the close of the Spanish–American War, Spain ceded control over the entire island of Cuba to the United States and specifically "relinquishe[d] all claim[s] of sovereignty ... and title." From the date the treaty with Spain was signed until the Cuban Republic was established on May 20, 1902, the United States governed the territory "in trust" for the benefit of the Cuban people. And although it recognized, by entering into the 1903 Lease Agreement, that Cuba retained "ultimate sovereignty" over Guantanamo, the United States continued to maintain the same plenary control it had enjoyed since 1898. Yet the Government's view is that the Constitution had no effect there, at least as to noncitizens, because the United States disclaimed sovereignty in the formal sense of the term. The necessary implication of the argument is that by surrendering formal sovereignty over any unincorporated territory to a third party, while at the same time entering into a lease that grants total control over the territory back to the United States, it would be possible for the political branches to govern without legal constraint.

Our basic charter cannot be contracted away like this. The Constitution grants Congress and the President the power to acquire, dispose of, and govern territory, not the power to decide when and where its terms apply. Even when the United States acts outside its borders, its powers are not "absolute and unlimited" but are subject "to such restrictions as are expressed in the Constitution." Abstaining from questions involving formal sovereignty and territorial governance is one thing. To hold the political branches have the power to switch the Constitution on or off at will is quite another. The former position reflects this Court's recognition that certain matters requiring political judgments are best left to the political branches. The latter would permit a striking anomaly in our tripartite system of government, leading to a regime in which Congress and the President, not this Court, say "what the law is." *Marbury v. Madison.* ...

C

As we recognized in *Rasul,* the outlines of a framework for determining the reach of the Suspension Clause are suggested by the factors the Court relied upon in *Eisentrager.* In addition to the practical concerns discussed above, the *Eisentrager* Court found relevant that each petitioner:

> "(a) is an enemy alien; (b) has never been or resided in the United States; (c) was captured outside of our territory and there held in military custody as a prisoner of war; (d) was tried and convicted by a Military

Commission sitting outside the United States; (e) for offenses against laws of war committed outside the United States; (f) and is at all times imprisoned outside the United States."

Based on this language from *Eisentrager*, and the reasoning in our other extraterritoriality opinions, we conclude that at least three factors are relevant in determining the reach of the Suspension Clause: (1) the citizenship and status of the detainee and the adequacy of the process through which that status determination was made; (2) the nature of the sites where apprehension and then detention took place; and (3) the practical obstacles inherent in resolving the prisoner's entitlement to the writ. ...

We hold that Art. I, § 9, cl. 2, of the Constitution has full effect at Guantanamo Bay. If the privilege of habeas corpus is to be denied to the detainees now before us, Congress must act in accordance with the requirements of the Suspension Clause. This Court may not impose a *de facto* suspension by abstaining from these controversies. The MCA does not purport to be a formal suspension of the writ; and the Government, in its submissions to us, has not argued that it is. Petitioners, therefore, are entitled to the privilege of habeas corpus to challenge the legality of their detention.

V

In light of this holding the question becomes whether the statute stripping jurisdiction to issue the writ avoids the Suspension Clause mandate because Congress has provided adequate substitute procedures for habeas corpus. The Government submits there has been compliance with the Suspension Clause because the DTA review process in the Court of Appeals, see DTA § 1005(e), provides an adequate substitute. ...

Under the circumstances we believe the costs of further delay substantially outweigh any benefits of remanding to the Court of Appeals to consider the issue it did not address in these cases. ...

C

We now consider whether the DTA allows the Court of Appeals to conduct a proceeding meeting these standards. ...

The absence of a release remedy and specific language allowing AUMF challenges are not the only constitutional infirmities from which the statute potentially suffers, however. The more difficult question is whether the DTA permits the Court of Appeals to make requisite findings of fact. The DTA enables petitioners to request "review" of their CSRT determination in the Court of Appeals; but the "Scope of Review" provision confines the Court of Appeals' role to reviewing whether the CSRT followed the "standards and procedures" issued by the Department of Defense and assessing whether those "standards and procedures" are lawful, Among these standards is "the requirement that the conclusion of the Tribunal be supported by a preponderance of the evidence ... allowing a rebuttable presumption in favor of the Government's evidence."

Assuming the DTA can be construed to allow the Court of Appeals to review or correct the CSRT's factual determinations, as opposed to merely certifying that the tribunal applied the correct standard of proof, we see no way to construe the statute to allow what is also constitutionally required in this context: an opportunity for the detainee to present relevant exculpatory evidence that was not made part of the record in the earlier proceedings. ...

Although we do not hold that an adequate substitute must duplicate § 2241 in all respects, it suffices that the Government has not established that the detainees' access to the statutory review provisions at issue is an adequate substitute for the writ of habeas corpus. MCA § 7 thus effects an unconstitutional suspension of the writ. In view of our holding we need not discuss the reach of the writ with respect to claims of unlawful conditions of treatment or confinement.

VI A

... Our decision today holds only that petitioners before us are entitled to seek the writ; that the DTA review procedures are an inadequate substitute for habeas corpus; and that petitioners in these cases need not exhaust the review procedures in the Court of Appeals before proceeding with their habeas actions in the District Court. The only law we identify as unconstitutional is MCA § 7. Accordingly, both the DTA and the CSRT process remain intact. Our holding with regard to exhaustion should not be read to imply that a habeas court should intervene the moment an enemy combatant steps foot in a territory where the writ runs. The Executive is entitled to a reasonable period of time to determine a detainee's status before a court entertains that detainee's habeas corpus petition. The CSRT process is the mechanism Congress and the President set up to deal with these issues. Except in cases of undue delay, federal courts should refrain from entertaining an enemy combatant's habeas corpus petition at least until after the Department, acting via the CSRT, has had a chance to review his status. ...

***

It bears repeating that our opinion does not address the content of the law that governs petitioners' detention. That is a matter yet to be determined. We hold that petitioners may invoke the fundamental procedural protections of habeas corpus. The laws and Constitution are designed to survive, and remain in force, in extraordinary times. Liberty and security can be reconciled; and in our system they are reconciled within the framework of the law. The Framers decided that habeas corpus, a right of first importance, must be a part of that framework, a part of that law.

The determination by the Court of Appeals that the Suspension Clause and its protections are inapplicable to petitioners was in error. The judgment of the Court of Appeals is reversed. The cases are remanded to the Court of Appeals with instructions that it remand the cases to the District Court for proceedings consistent with this opinion.

Justice SOUTER, with whom Justice GINSBURG and Justice BREYER join, concurring.

I join the Court's opinion in its entirety and add this afterword only to emphasize two things one might overlook after reading the dissents.

Four years ago, this Court in *Rasul v. Bush,* held that statutory habeas jurisdiction extended to claims of foreign nationals imprisoned by the United States at Guantanamo Bay, "to determine the legality of the Executive's potentially indefinite detention" of them. Subsequent legislation eliminated the statutory habeas jurisdiction over these claims, so that now there must be constitutionally based jurisdiction or none at all. Justice SCALIA is thus correct that here, for the first time, this Court holds there is (he says "confers") constitutional habeas jurisdiction over aliens imprisoned by the military outside an area of *de jure* national sovereignty. But no one who reads the Court's opinion in *Rasul* could seriously doubt that the jurisdictional question must be answered the same way in purely constitutional cases, given the Court's reliance on the historical background of habeas generally in answering the statutory question. Indeed, the Court in *Rasul* directly answered the very historical question that Justice SCALIA says is dispositive; it wrote that "[a]pplication of the habeas statute to persons detained at [Guantanamo] is consistent with the historical reach of the writ of habeas corpus." Justice SCALIA dismisses the statement as dictum, but if dictum it was, it was dictum well considered, and it stated the view of five Members of this Court on the historical scope of the writ. Of course, it takes more than a quotation from *Rasul,* however much on point, to resolve the constitutional issue before us here, which the majority opinion has explored afresh in the detail it deserves. But whether one agrees or disagrees with today's decision, it is no bolt out of the blue.

A second fact insufficiently appreciated by the dissents is the length of the disputed imprisonments, some of the prisoners represented here today having been locked up for six years. Hence the hollow ring when the dissenters suggest that the Court is somehow precipitating the judiciary into reviewing claims that the military (subject to appeal to the Court of Appeals for the District of Columbia Circuit) could handle within some reasonable period of time. These suggestions of judicial haste are all the more out of place given the Court's realistic acknowledgment that in periods of exigency the tempo of any habeas review must reflect the immediate peril facing the country. ...

After six years of sustained executive detentions in Guantanamo, subject to habeas jurisdiction but without any actual habeas scrutiny, today's decision is no judicial victory, but an act of perseverance in trying to make habeas review, and the obligation of the courts to provide it, mean something of value both to prisoners and to the Nation.

Chief Justice ROBERTS, with whom Justice SCALIA, Justice THOMAS, and Justice ALITO join, dissenting.

Today the Court strikes down as inadequate the most generous set of procedural protections ever afforded aliens detained by this country as enemy combatants. The political branches crafted these procedures amidst an ongoing military conflict, after much careful investigation and thorough debate. The Court rejects them today out of hand, without bothering to say what due process rights the detainees possess, without explaining how the statute fails to vindicate those rights, and before a single petitioner has exhausted the procedures under the law. And to what effect? The majority merely replaces a review system designed by the people's representatives with a set of shapeless procedures to be defined by federal courts at some future date. One cannot help but think, after surveying the modest practical results of the majority's ambitious opinion, that this decision is not really about the detainees at all, but about control of federal policy regarding enemy combatants.

The majority is adamant that the Guantanamo detainees are entitled to the protections of habeas corpus—its opinion begins by deciding that question. I regard the issue as a difficult one, primarily because of the unique and unusual jurisdictional status of Guantanamo Bay. I nonetheless agree with Justice SCALIA's analysis of our precedents and the pertinent history of the writ, and accordingly join his dissent. The important point for me, however, is that the Court should have resolved these cases on other grounds. Habeas is most fundamentally a procedural right, a mechanism for contesting the legality of executive detention. The critical threshold question in these cases, prior to any inquiry about the writ's scope, is whether the system the political branches designed protects whatever rights the detainees may possess. If so, there is no need for any additional process, whether called "habeas" or something else.

Congress entrusted that threshold question in the first instance to the Court of Appeals for the District of Columbia Circuit, as the Constitution surely allows Congress to do. But before the D.C. Circuit has addressed the issue, the Court cashiers the statute, and without answering this critical threshold question itself. The Court does eventually get around to asking whether review under the DTA is, as the Court frames it, an "adequate substitute" for habeas, but even then its opinion fails to determine what rights the detainees possess and whether the DTA system satisfies them. The majority instead compares the undefined DTA process to an equally undefined habeas right—one that is to be given shape only in the future by district courts on a case-by-case basis. This whole approach is misguided.

It is also fruitless. How the detainees' claims will be decided now that the DTA is gone is anybody's guess. But the habeas process the Court mandates will most likely end up looking a lot like the DTA system it replaces, as the district court judges shaping it will have to reconcile review of the prisoners' detention with the undoubted need to protect the American people from the terrorist threat—precisely the challenge Congress undertook in drafting the DTA. All that today's opinion has done is shift responsibility for those sensitive foreign policy and national security decisions from the elected branches to the Federal Judiciary.

I believe the system the political branches constructed adequately protects any constitutional rights aliens captured abroad and detained as enemy combatants may enjoy. I therefore would dismiss these cases on that ground. With all respect for the contrary views of the majority, I must dissent. ...

***

So who has won? Not the detainees. The Court's analysis leaves them with only the prospect of further litigation to determine the content of their new habeas right, followed by further litigation to resolve their particular cases, followed by further litigation before the D.C. Circuit—where they could have started had they invoked the DTA procedure. Not Congress, whose attempt to "determine—through democratic means—how best" to balance the security of the American people with the detainees' liberty interests, has been unceremoniously brushed aside. Not the Great Writ, whose majesty is hardly enhanced by its extension to a jurisdictionally quirky outpost, with no tangible benefit to anyone. Not the rule of law, unless by that is meant the rule of lawyers, who will now arguably have a greater role than military and intelligence officials in shaping policy for alien enemy combatants. And certainly not the American people, who today lose a bit more control over the conduct of this Nation's foreign policy to unelected, politically unaccountable judges.

I respectfully dissent.

Justice SCALIA, with whom THE CHIEF JUSTICE, Justice THOMAS, and Justice ALITO join, dissenting.

Today, for the first time in our Nation's history, the Court confers a constitutional right to habeas corpus on alien enemies detained abroad by our military forces in the course of an ongoing war. THE CHIEF JUSTICE's dissent, which I join, shows that the procedures prescribed by Congress in the Detainee Treatment Act provide the essential protections that habeas corpus guarantees; there has thus been no suspension of the writ, and no basis exists for judicial intervention beyond what the Act allows. My problem with today's opinion is more fundamental still: The writ of habeas corpus does not, and never has, run in favor of aliens abroad; the Suspension Clause thus has no application, and the Court's intervention in this military matter is entirely *ultra vires.*

I shall devote most of what will be a lengthy opinion to the legal errors contained in the opinion of the Court. Contrary to my usual practice, however, I think it appropriate to begin with a description of the disastrous consequences of what the Court has done today. ...

The game of bait-and-switch that today's opinion plays upon the Nation's Commander in Chief will make the war harder on us. It will almost certainly cause more Americans to be killed. That consequence would be tolerable if necessary to preserve a time-honored legal principle vital to our constitutional Republic. But it is this Court's blatant *abandonment* of such a principle that produces the decision today. The President relied on our settled precedent in *Johnson v. Eisentrager,* when he established the prison at Guantanamo Bay for enemy aliens. Citing that case, the President's Office of Legal Counsel advised him "that the great weight of legal authority indicates that a federal district court could not properly exercise habeas jurisdiction over an alien detained at [Guantanamo Bay]." Had the law been otherwise, the military surely would not have transported prisoners there, but would have kept them in Afghanistan, transferred them to another of our foreign military bases, or turned them over to allies for detention. Those other facilities might well have been worse for the detainees themselves.

In the long term, then, the Court's decision today accomplishes little, except perhaps to reduce the well-being of enemy combatants that the Court ostensibly seeks to protect. In the short term, however, the decision is devastating. At least 30 of those prisoners hitherto released from Guantanamo Bay have returned to the battlefield. Some have been captured or killed. But others have succeeded in carrying on their atrocities against innocent civilians. In one case, a detainee released from Guantanamo Bay masterminded the kidnapping of two Chinese dam workers, one of whom was later shot to death when used as a human shield against Pakistani commandoes. ...

The Court today decrees that no good reason to accept the judgment of the other two branches is "apparent." "The Government," it declares, "presents no credible arguments that the military mission at Guantanamo would be compromised if habeas corpus courts had jurisdiction to hear the detainees' claims." What competence does the Court have to second-guess the judgment of Congress and the President on such a point? None whatever. But the Court blunders in nonetheless. Henceforth, as today's opinion makes unnervingly clear, how to handle enemy prisoners in this war will ultimately lie with the branch that knows least about the national security concerns that the subject entails. ...

The Court purports to derive from our precedents a "functional" test for the extraterritorial reach of the writ, which shows that the Military Commissions Act unconstitutionally restricts the scope of habeas. That is remarkable because the most pertinent of those precedents, *Johnson v. Eisentrager,* conclusively establishes the opposite. There we were confronted with the claims of 21 Germans held at Landsberg Prison, an American military facility located in the American Zone of occupation in postwar Germany. They had been captured in China, and an American military commission sitting there had convicted them of war crimes—collaborating with the Japanese after Germany's surrender. Like the petitioners here, the Germans claimed that their detentions violated the Constitution and international law, and sought a writ of habeas corpus. Writing for the Court, Justice Jackson held that American courts lacked habeas jurisdiction[,] ...

Lest there be any doubt about the primacy of territorial sovereignty in determining the jurisdiction of a habeas court over an alien, Justice Jackson distinguished two cases in which aliens had been permitted to seek habeas relief, on the ground that the prisoners in those cases were in custody within the sovereign territory of the United States.

Eisentrager thus held—*held* beyond any doubt—that the Constitution does not ensure habeas for aliens held by the United States in areas over which our Government is not sovereign.

The Court would have us believe that *Eisentrager* rested on "[p]ractical considerations," such as the "difficulties of ordering the Government to produce the prisoners in a habeas corpus proceeding." Formal sovereignty, says the Court, is merely one consideration "that bears upon which constitutional guarantees apply" in a given location. This is a sheer rewriting of the case. *Eisentrager* mentioned practical concerns, to be sure—but not for the purpose of determining *under what circumstances* American courts could issue writs of habeas corpus for aliens abroad. It cited them to support *its holding* that the Constitution does not empower courts to issue writs of habeas corpus to aliens abroad *in any circumstances*. As Justice Black accurately said in dissent, "the Court's opinion inescapably denies courts power to afford the least bit of protection for any alien who is subject to our occupation government abroad, even if he is neither enemy nor belligerent and even after peace is officially declared." ...

There is simply no support for the Court's assertion that constitutional rights extend to aliens held outside U.S. sovereign territory, and *Eisentrager* could not be clearer that the privilege of habeas corpus does not extend to aliens abroad. By blatantly distorting *Eisentrager*, the Court avoids the difficulty of explaining why it should be overruled. ...

What drives today's decision is neither the meaning of the Suspension Clause, nor the principles of our precedents, but rather an inflated notion of judicial supremacy. ...

***

Today the Court warps our Constitution in a way that goes beyond the narrow issue of the reach of the Suspension Clause, invoking judicially brainstormed separation-of-powers principles to establish a manipulable "functional" test for the extraterritorial reach of habeas corpus (and, no doubt, for the extraterritorial reach of other constitutional protections as well). It blatantly misdescribes important precedents, most conspicuously Justice Jackson's opinion for the Court in *Johnson v. Eisentrager*. It breaks a chain of precedent as old as the common law that prohibits judicial inquiry into detentions of aliens abroad absent statutory authorization. And, most tragically, it sets our military commanders the impossible task of proving to a civilian court, under whatever standards this Court devises in the future, that evidence supports the confinement of each and every enemy prisoner.

The Nation will live to regret what the Court has done today. I dissent.

Notes and Questions

1. *The best opinion?* Which of the above opinions was the "best" in your view? Do you judge the "best" according to the conclusion? The reasoning? Something else?
2. *Responsibility toward the prisoners.* Are you surprised that the majority held that there is a responsibility to prisoners held at Guantanamo Bay?
3. *The writ of habeas corpus.* What is the writ of habeas corpus? Why do prisoners have it? What can Congress do with the writ of habeas corpus?
4. *Video.* Does this video capture the main legal arguments of the Justices in *Boumediene*? See Quimbee's video on *Boumediene v. Bush* Case Brief Summary/Law Case Explained, Apr. 30, 2018, posted at https://www.youtube.com/watch?v=hEDhKN5YKT0&list=PLsFE_Nvl6h_Y75KGR5pkGqcFisGvBnO9S&index=97.

C. Immigration

Article I, Section 8 of the Constitution gives Congress the power to "establish a uniform rule of naturalization," which gives it the authority to determine when and how people become citizens of the United States. The President would execute those laws, according to Art. II. There is also another pathway to presidential action: the President can write "executive orders" to the executive branch agencies, etc. The following case asks if President Trump had the power to restrict entry into the United States from predominantly Muslim countries.

Once again, *Korematsu* was important to the Justices who disagreed about this case. Note that Chief Justice Roberts states *Korematsu* is overruled. Do you agree with Justice Sotomayor that this case is a duplication of the horrors of *Korematsu*? Who provides the best analysis of *Korematsu*?

The First Amendment says, "Congress shall make no law respecting an establishment of religion, or prohibiting the free exercise thereof." Did an immigration policy focused on Muslim nations violate the First Amendment? This is yet another 5–4 opinion. Why was the vote so close? Can you anticipate what the final vote will be by reading the oral argument on the case's website, https://www.oyez.org/cases/2017/17-965? What do you think was the hardest question asked by a Justice in this case? Does this ABA preview capture the important issues in the case? Can you tell from the video who will win the case and what the result of it will be? See Quimbee's video on *Trump v. Hawaii*—ABA Preview, Apr. 23, 2018, posted at https://www.youtube.com/watch?v=g6LvBmFA3KU&list=PLsFE_Nvl6h_Y75KGR5pkGqcFisGvBnO9S&index=101&t=8s.

Trump v. Hawaii

SUPREME COURT OF THE UNITED STATES, 2018

585 U.S. ____, 138 S.Ct. 2392

ROBERTS, C.J., delivered the opinion of the Court, in which KENNEDY, THOMAS, ALITO, and GORSUCH, JJ., joined. KENNEDY, J., and THOMAS, J., filed concurring opinions. BREYER, J., filed a dissenting opinion, in which KAGAN, J., joined. SOTOMAYOR, J., filed a dissenting opinion, in which GINSBURG, J., joined.

Under the Immigration and Nationality Act, foreign nationals seeking entry into the United States undergo a vetting process to ensure that they satisfy the numerous requirements for admission. The Act also vests the President with authority to restrict the entry of aliens whenever he finds that their entry "would be detrimental to the interests of the United States." Relying on that delegation, the President concluded that it was necessary to impose entry restrictions on nationals of countries that do not share adequate information for an informed entry determination, or that otherwise present national security risks. The plaintiffs in this litigation, respondents here, challenged the application of those entry restrictions to certain aliens abroad. We now decide whether the President had authority under the Act to issue the Proclamation, and whether the entry policy violates the Establishment Clause of the First Amendment.

I A

Shortly after taking office, President Trump signed Executive Order No. 13769, Protecting the Nation From Foreign Terrorist Entry Into the United States. (EO-1). EO-1 directed the Secretary of Homeland Security to conduct a review to examine the adequacy of information provided by foreign governments about their nationals seeking to enter the United States. Pending that review, the order suspended for 90 days the entry of foreign nationals from seven countries—Iran, Iraq, Libya, Somalia, Sudan, Syria, and Yemen—that had been previously identified by Congress or prior administrations as posing heightened terrorism risks. ...

On September 24, 2017, after completion of the worldwide review, the President issued the Proclamation before us—Proclamation No. 9645, Enhancing Vetting Capabilities and Processes for Detecting Attempted Entry Into the United States by Terrorists or Other Public–Safety Threats. The Proclamation (as its title indicates) sought to improve vetting procedures by identifying ongoing deficiencies in the information needed to assess whether nationals of particular countries present "public safety threats." To further that purpose, the Proclamation placed entry restrictions on the nationals of eight foreign states whose systems for managing and sharing information about their nationals the President deemed inadequate. ...

[T]he Acting Secretary of Homeland Security concluded that eight countries—Chad, Iran, Iraq, Libya, North Korea, Syria, Venezuela, and Yemen—remained deficient in terms of their risk profile and willingness to provide requested information. The Acting Secretary recommended that the President impose entry restrictions on certain nationals from all of those countries except Iraq. She also concluded that although Somalia generally satisfied the information-sharing component of the baseline standards, its "identity-management deficiencies" and "significant terrorist presence" presented special circumstances justifying additional limitations. She therefore recommended entry limitations for certain nationals of that country. As for Iraq, the Acting Secretary found that entry limitations on its nationals were not warranted given the close cooperative relationship between the U.S. and Iraqi Governments and Iraq's commitment to combating ISIS.

After consulting with multiple Cabinet members and other officials, the President adopted the Acting Secretary's recommendations and issued the Proclamation. Invoking his authority under 8 U.S.C. §§ 1182(f) and 1185(a), the President determined that certain entry restrictions were necessary to "prevent the entry of those foreign nationals about whom the United States Government lacks sufficient information"; "elicit improved identity-management and information-sharing protocols and practices from foreign governments"; and otherwise "advance [the] foreign policy, national security, and counterterrorism objectives" of the United States. The President explained that these restrictions would be the "most likely to encourage cooperation" while "protect[ing] the United States until such time as improvements occur." ...

The Proclamation exempts lawful permanent residents and foreign nationals who have been granted asylum. It also provides for case-by-case waivers when a foreign national demonstrates undue hardship, and that his entry is in the national interest and would not pose a threat to public safety. The Proclamation further directs DHS to assess on a continuing basis whether entry restrictions should be modified or continued, and to report to the President every 180 days. Upon completion of the first such review period, the President, on the recommendation of the Secretary of Homeland Security, determined that Chad had sufficiently improved its practices, and he accordingly lifted restrictions on its nationals. ...

III

... By its plain language, § 1182(f) grants the President broad discretion to suspend the entry of aliens into the United States. The President lawfully exercised that discretion based on his findings—following a worldwide, multi-agency review—that entry of the covered aliens would be detrimental to the national interest. And plaintiffs' attempts to identify a conflict with other provisions in the INA, and their appeal to the statute's purposes and legislative history, fail to overcome the clear statutory language.

A

... The Proclamation falls well within this comprehensive delegation. The sole prerequisite set forth in § 1182(f) is that the President "find[ ]" that the entry of the covered aliens "would be detrimental to the interests of the United States." The President has undoubtedly fulfilled that requirement here. He first ordered DHS and other agencies to conduct a comprehensive evaluation of every single country's compliance with the information and risk assessment baseline. The President then issued a Proclamation setting forth extensive findings describing how deficiencies in the practices of select foreign governments—several of which are state sponsors of terrorism—deprive the Government of "sufficient information to assess the risks [those countries' nationals] pose to the United States." Based on that review, the President found that it was in the national interest to restrict entry of aliens who could not be vetted with adequate information—both to protect national security and public safety, and to induce improvement by their home countries. The Proclamation therefore "craft[ed] ... country-specific restrictions that would be most likely to encourage cooperation given each country's distinct circumstances," while securing the Nation "until such time as improvements occur." ...

Like its predecessors, the Proclamation makes clear that its "conditional restrictions" will remain in force only so long as necessary to "address" the identified "inadequacies and risks" within the covered nations. To that end, the Proclamation establishes an ongoing process to engage covered nations and assess every 180 days whether the entry restrictions should be modified or terminated. Indeed, after the initial review period, the President determined that Chad had made sufficient improvements to its identity-management protocols, and he accordingly lifted the entry suspension on its nationals.

Finally, the Proclamation properly identifies a "class of aliens"—nationals of select countries—whose entry is suspended. Plaintiffs argue that "class" must refer to a well-defined group of individuals who share a common "characteristic" apart from nationality. But the text of § 1182(f), of course, does not say that, and the word "class" comfortably encompasses a group of people linked by nationality. Plaintiffs also contend that the class cannot be "overbroad." But that simply amounts to an unspoken tailoring requirement found nowhere in Congress's grant of authority to suspend entry of not only "any class of aliens" but "all aliens."

In short, the language of § 1182(f) is clear, and the Proclamation does not exceed any textual limit on the President's authority. ...

C

Plaintiffs' final statutory argument is that the President's entry suspension violates § 1152(a)(1)(A), which provides that "no person shall ... be discriminated against in the issuance of an immigrant visa because of the person's race, sex, nationality, place of birth, or place of residence." They contend that we should interpret the provision as prohibiting nationality-based discrimination throughout the *entire* immigration process, despite the reference in § 1152(a)(1)(A) to the act of visa issuance alone. Specifically, plaintiffs argue that § 1152(a)(1)(A) applies to the predicate question of a visa applicant's eligibility for admission and the subsequent question whether the holder of a visa may in fact enter the country. Any other conclusion, they say, would allow the President to circumvent the protections against discrimination enshrined in § 1152(a)(1)(A). ... [W]e reject plaintiffs' interpretation because it ignores the basic distinction between admissibility determinations and visa issuance that runs throughout the INA. ...

The Proclamation is squarely within the scope of Presidential authority under the INA. Indeed, neither dissent even attempts any serious argument to the contrary, despite the fact that plaintiffs' primary contention below and in their briefing before this Court was that the Proclamation violated the statute.

IV A

We now turn to plaintiffs' claim that the Proclamation was issued for the unconstitutional purpose of excluding Muslims. ...

B

... At the heart of plaintiffs' case is a series of statements by the President and his advisers casting doubt on the official objective of the Proclamation. For example, while a candidate on the campaign trail, the President published a "Statement on Preventing Muslim Immigration" that called for a "total and complete shutdown of Muslims entering the United States until our country's representatives can figure out what is going on." That statement remained on his campaign website until May 2017. Then-candidate Trump also stated that "Islam hates us" and asserted that the United States was "having problems with Muslims coming into the country." Shortly after being elected, when asked whether violence in Europe had affected his plans to "ban Muslim immigration," the President replied, "You know my plans. All along, I've been proven to be right." ...

D

... The Proclamation is expressly premised on legitimate purposes: preventing entry of nationals who cannot be adequately vetted and inducing other nations to improve their practices. The text says nothing about religion. Plaintiffs and the dissent nonetheless emphasize that five of the seven nations currently included in the Proclamation have Muslim-majority populations. Yet that fact alone does not support an inference of religious hostility, given that the policy covers just 8% of the world's Muslim population and is limited to countries that were previously designated by Congress or prior administrations as posing national security risks.

The Proclamation, moreover, reflects the results of a worldwide review process undertaken by multiple Cabinet officials and their agencies. Plaintiffs seek to discredit the findings of the review, pointing to deviations from the review's baseline criteria resulting in the inclusion of Somalia and omission of Iraq. But as the Proclamation explains, in each case the determinations were justified by the distinct conditions in each country. ...

Finally, the dissent invokes *Korematsu*. Whatever rhetorical advantage the dissent may see in doing so, *Korematsu* has nothing to do with this case. The forcible relocation of U.S. citizens to concentration camps, solely and explicitly on the basis of race, is objectively unlawful and outside the scope of Presidential authority. But it is wholly inapt to liken that morally repugnant order to a facially neutral policy denying certain foreign nationals the privilege of admission. The entry suspension is an act that is well within executive authority and could have been taken by any other President—the only question is evaluating the actions of this particular President in promulgating an otherwise valid Proclamation.

The dissent's reference to *Korematsu*, however, affords this Court the opportunity to make express what is already obvious: *Korematsu* was gravely wrong the day it was decided, has been overruled in the court of history, and—to be clear—"has no place in law under the Constitution."

Under these circumstances, the Government has set forth a sufficient national security justification to survive rational basis review. We express no view on the soundness of the policy. We simply hold today that plaintiffs have not demonstrated a likelihood of success on the merits of their constitutional claim. ...

Justice KENNEDY, concurring.

I join the Court's opinion in full. ...

The First Amendment prohibits the establishment of religion and promises the free exercise of religion. From these safeguards, and from the guarantee of freedom of speech, it follows there is freedom of belief and expression. It is an urgent necessity that officials adhere to these constitutional guarantees and mandates in all their actions, even in the sphere of foreign affairs. An anxious world must know that our Government remains committed always to the liberties the Constitution seeks to preserve and protect, so that freedom extends outward, and lasts.

THOMAS, J., concurring.

... Merits aside, I write separately to address the remedy that the plaintiffs sought and obtained in this case. The District Court imposed an injunction that barred the Government from enforcing the President's Proclamation against anyone, not just the plaintiffs. Injunctions that prohibit the Executive Branch from applying a law or policy against anyone—often called "universal" or "nationwide" injunctions—have become increasingly common. ...

I am skeptical that district courts have the authority to enter universal injunctions. These injunctions did not emerge until a century and a half after the founding. And they appear to be inconsistent with longstanding limits on equitable relief and the power of Article III courts. If their popularity continues, this Court must address their legality. ...

In sum, universal injunctions are legally and historically dubious. If federal courts continue to issue them, this Court is dutybound to adjudicate their authority to do so.

Justice BREYER, with whom Justice KAGAN joins, dissenting.

... Unfortunately there is evidence that supports the second possibility, *i.e.*, that the Government is not applying the Proclamation as written.

Declarations, anecdotal evidence, facts, and numbers taken from *amicus* briefs are not judicial fact-findings. The Government has not had an opportunity to respond, and a court has not had an opportunity to decide. But, given the importance of the decision in this case, the need for assurance that the Proclamation does not rest upon a "Muslim ban," and the assistance in deciding the issue that answers to the "exemption and waiver" questions may provide, I would send this case back to the District Court for further proceedings. And, I would leave the injunction in effect while the matter is litigated. Regardless, the Court's decision today leaves the District Court free to explore these issues on remand.

If this Court must decide the question without this further litigation, I would, on balance, find the evidence of antireligious bias, including statements on a website taken down only after the President issued the two executive orders preceding the Proclamation, along with the other statements also set forth in Justice SOTOMAYOR's opinion, a sufficient basis to set the Proclamation aside. And for these reasons, I respectfully dissent.

Justice SOTOMAYOR, with whom Justice GINSBURG joins, dissenting.

The United States of America is a Nation built upon the promise of religious liberty. Our Founders honored that core promise by embedding the principle of religious neutrality in the First Amendment. The Court's decision today fails to safeguard that fundamental principle. It leaves undisturbed a policy first advertised openly and unequivocally as a "total and complete shutdown of Muslims entering the United States" because the policy now masquerades behind a facade of national-security concerns. But this repackaging does little to cleanse Presidential Proclamation No. 9645 of the appearance of discrimination that the President's words have created. Based on the evidence in the record, a reasonable observer would conclude that the Proclamation was motivated by anti-Muslim animus. That alone suffices to show that plaintiffs are likely to succeed on the merits of their Establishment Clause claim. The majority holds otherwise by ignoring the facts, misconstruing our legal precedent, and turning a blind eye to the pain and suffering the Proclamation inflicts upon countless families and individuals, many of whom are United States citizens. Because that troubling result runs contrary to the Constitution and our precedent, I dissent. ...

I B 1

… Although the majority briefly recounts a few of the statements and background events that form the basis of plaintiffs' constitutional challenge, that highly abridged account does not tell even half of the story. The full record paints a far more harrowing picture, from which a reasonable observer would readily conclude that the Proclamation was motivated by hostility and animus toward the Muslim faith. …

B 2

… Taking all the relevant evidence together, a reasonable observer would conclude that the Proclamation was driven primarily by anti-Muslim animus, rather than by the Government's asserted national-security justifications. Even before being sworn into office, then-candidate Trump stated that "Islam hates us," warned that "[w]e're having problems with the Muslims, and we're having problems with Muslims coming into the country," promised to enact a "total and complete shutdown of Muslims entering the United States," and instructed one of his advisers to find a "lega[l]" way to enact a Muslim ban. The President continued to make similar statements well after his inauguration, as detailed above.

Moreover, despite several opportunities to do so, President Trump has never disavowed any of his prior statements about Islam. Ultimately, what began as a policy explicitly "calling for a total and complete shutdown of Muslims entering the United States" has since morphed into a "Proclamation" putatively based on national-security concerns. … But this new window dressing cannot conceal an unassailable fact: the words of the President and his advisers create the strong perception that the Proclamation is contaminated by impermissible discriminatory animus against Islam and its followers. …

IV

… Today's holding is all the more troubling given the stark parallels between the reasoning of this case and that of *Korematsu*. In *Korematsu*, the Court gave "a pass [to] an odious, gravely injurious racial classification" authorized by an executive order. As here, the Government invoked an ill-defined national-security threat to justify an exclusionary policy of sweeping proportion. As here, the exclusion order was rooted in dangerous stereotypes about, *inter alia*, a particular group's supposed inability to assimilate and desire to harm the United States. See *Korematsu*, (Murphy, J., dissenting). As here, the Government was unwilling to reveal its own intelligence agencies' views of the alleged security concerns to the very citizens it purported to protect. And as here, there was strong evidence that impermissible hostility and animus motivated the Government's policy.

Although a majority of the Court in *Korematsu* was willing to uphold the Government's actions based on a barren invocation of national security, dissenting Justices warned of that decision's harm to our constitutional fabric. Justice Murphy recognized that there is a need for great deference to the Executive Branch in the context of national security, but cautioned that "it is essential that there be definite limits to [the government's] discretion," as "[i]ndividuals must not be left impoverished of their constitutional rights on a plea of military necessity that has neither substance nor support." (Murphy, J., dissenting). Justice Jackson lamented that the Court's decision upholding the Government's policy would prove to be "a far more subtle blow to liberty than the promulgation of the order itself," for although the executive order was not likely to be long lasting, the Court's willingness to tolerate it would endure.

In the intervening years since *Korematsu*, our Nation has done much to leave its sordid legacy behind. Today, the Court takes the important step of finally overruling *Korematsu*, denouncing it as "gravely wrong the day it was decided." (*citing Korematsu*, (Jackson, J., dissenting)). This formal repudiation of a shameful precedent is laudable and long overdue. But it does not make the majority's decision here acceptable or right. By blindly accepting the Government's misguided invitation to sanction a discriminatory policy motivated by animosity toward a disfavored group, all in the name of a superficial claim of national security, the Court redeploys the same dangerous logic underlying *Korematsu* and merely replaces one "gravely wrong" decision with another.

Our Constitution demands, and our country deserves, a Judiciary willing to hold the coordinate branches to account when they defy our most sacred legal commitments. Because the Court's decision today has failed in that respect, with profound regret, I dissent.

Notes and Questions

1. *Comparing the opinions.* Assess each one of these opinions. Which is the most persuasive? Why did you pick the opinion that you chose?
2. *The majority opinion.* Does this opinion set a good precedent for immigration or a bad one? How did you reach your conclusion?
3. *Justice Kennedy.* What was the point of Justice Kennedy's concurrence?

A Look Ahead

Think of the federal government as a watch. We have studied the powers of each of the three federal branches. Consider them as cogs in the watch. Next, we turn to the separation of powers doctrine that determines how the cogs operate together. The Court in the following chapter is making the branches into an operational machine.

Four

Articles I, II, and III: Separation of Powers

Introduction

When the Framers gathered to amend the Articles of Confederation and ultimately drafted an entirely new Constitution, they came to Philadelphia with a shared assessment of human nature: you can't trust anyone with power. And the more power they have, the less they can be trusted. To state it slightly differently, unchecked power leads to tyranny. Thus, the Constitution divides power horizontally between three branches (and vertically between the states and the newly configured federal government). The "separation of powers" is, therefore, a legal doctrine built on the assumption that powers granted also need to be checked and challenged. The reasoning extends to the branches, which were expected to aggrandize themselves at the expense of the other branches. Of course, the branches cannot work in hermetically sealed universes. They must interact and coordinate. Think of the system as a watch, as the framing generation did, with independent cogs that are interlinked together to achieve the goal of the public good.

For the system to operate successfully, it is, therefore, important to empower and constrain at the same time. That is true of the horizontal separation of power; think of the constitutional cases you have already read about in Articles I, II, and III delineating the federal legislative, executive, and judicial powers. It is also true of the vertical separation of power between the federal government and the states as you will read later in the course; it is a unique combination with two sets of governments in play. As this book continues, you will learn a lot more about which jobs are assigned to the federal and state governments and how the Constitution keeps each of them doing their jobs.

Following *Marbury v. Madison*, the Court held the power to draw the boundaries between the many exercises of power. The Court has said repeatedly that it must protect the proper separation of powers between the branches. One way to think about this is to say the legislature must do legislative jobs; the executive must do executive jobs, and the judiciary must do judicial jobs. Think of what you've learned from the first three chapters about the job each of the branches is assigned. Does that give you enough insight to figure out when the separation of powers is violated?

There are numerous tools the Constitution provides to guide how those with power will be constrained. One of the tools to preserve separation is the power of impeachment, which allows one branch of government to impeach and indict a member of another branch. As you read the impeachment cases, ask yourself how the Court's interpretation of the separation of powers adds power to one branch at the expense of another. As the Court lays down the boundary lines between branches, there are winners and losers. The question is whether the line-drawing creates the possibility of tyranny through unchecked power.

A. The Impeachment Power

1. Presidential Privilege

The Constitution contains the following sections about impeachment, which is discussed in the *Nixon* case. What do these provisions tell you about how impeachment should operate?

Article II, Section 4 of the Constitution says, "The President, Vice President and all civil officers of the United States, shall be removed from office on impeachment for, and conviction of, treason, bribery, or other high crimes and misdemeanors."

Article I, Section 2 gives the House of Representatives "the sole power of impeachment."

Article I, Section 3 states, "The Senate shall have the sole power to try all impeachments. When sitting for that purpose, they shall be on oath or affirmation. When the President of the United States is tried, the Chief Justice shall preside: And no person shall be convicted without the concurrence of two thirds of the members present. Judgment in cases of impeachment shall not extend further than to removal from office, and disqualification to hold and enjoy any office of honor, trust or profit under the United States: but the party convicted shall nevertheless be liable and subject to indictment, trial, judgment and punishment, according to law."

When should a President be impeached? What is the difference between being impeached by the House and being tried in an impeachment by the Senate? Are there rules or policies that must govern House and Senate procedures?

PBS authored a DVD called *Watergate Plus 30* that goes over details of the case against Richard Nixon. There is also background to the Watergate events at The Watergate Scandal: Timeline and Background, Jan. 10, 2012, posted at https://www.youtube.com/watch?v=IHnmriyXYeg&list=PLsFE_Nvl6h_braQ_NxoD1jg8oDdM_l8uI&index=33. What does this tell you about the executive branch's role in the scandal?

Listen to the oral argument in *United States v. Nixon.* Can you predict from listening to it who is going to win? Can you predict the vote of all the Justices? The argument is available on the case's website, https://www.oyez.org/cases/1973/73-1766. The full case is also included there.

United States v. Nixon

SUPREME COURT OF THE UNITED STATES, 1974

418 U.S. 683, 94 S.Ct. 3090

BURGER, Chief Justice, delivered the [unanimous] decision of the Court. With DOUGLAS, BRENNAN, STEWART, WHITE, MARSHALL, BLACKMUN AND POWELL.

This litigation presents for review the denial of a motion, filed in the District Court on behalf of the President of the United States, in the case of United States v. Mitchell et al. (D.C.Crim. No. 74—110), to quash a third-party subpoena duces tecum issued by the United States District Court for the District of Columbia, pursuant to Fed.Rule Crim.Proc. 17(c). The subpoena directed the President to produce certain tape recordings and documents relating to his conversations with aides and advisers. The court rejected the President's claims of absolute executive privilege, of lack of jurisdiction, and of failure to satisfy the requirements of Rule 17(c). The President appealed to the Court of Appeals. We granted both the United States' petition for certiorari before judgment (No. 73—1766), and also the President's cross-petition for certiorari before judgment (No. 73—1834), because of the public importance of the issues presented and the need for their prompt resolution. ...

II

Justiciability

In the District Court, the President's counsel argued that the court lacked jurisdiction to issue the subpoena because the matter was an intra-branch dispute between a subordinate and superior officer of the Executive Branch and hence not subject to judicial resolution. That argument has been renewed in this Court with emphasis on the contention that the dispute does not present a 'case' or 'controversy' which can be adjudicated in the federal courts. The President's counsel argues that the federal courts should not intrude into areas committed to the other branches of Government. He views the present dispute as essentially a 'jurisdictional' dispute within the Executive Branch which he analogizes to a dispute between two congressional committees. Since the Executive Branch has exclusive authority and absolute discretion to decide whether to prosecute a case, it is contended that a President's decision is final in determining what evidence is to be used in a given criminal case. Although his counsel concedes that the President has delegated certain specific powers to the Special Prosecutor, he has not 'waived nor delegated to the Special Prosecutor the President's duty to claim privilege as to all materials ... which fall within the President's inherent authority to refuse to disclose to any executive officer.' The Special Prosecutor's demand for the items therefore presents, in the view of the President's counsel, a political question under *Baker v. Carr*. ...

Here, as in *Accardi*, it is theoretically possible for the Attorney General to amend or revoke the regulation defining the Special Prosecutor's authority. But he has not done so. So long as this regulation remains in force the Executive Branch is bound by it, and indeed the United States as the sovereign composed of the three branches is bound to respect and to enforce it. Moreover, the delegation of authority to the Special Prosecutor in this case is not an ordinary delegation by the Attorney General to a subordinate officer: with the authorization of the President, the Acting Attorney General provided in the regulation that the Special Prosecutor was not to be removed without the 'consensus' of eight designated leaders of Congress.

The demands of and the resistance to the subpoena present an obvious controversy in the ordinary sense, but that alone is not sufficient to meet constitutional standards. In the constitutional sense, controversy means more than disagreement and conflict; rather it means the kind of controversy courts traditionally resolve. Here at issue is the production or nonproduction of specified evidence deemed by the Special Prosecutor to be relevant and admissible in a pending criminal case. It is sought by one official of the Executive Branch within the scope of his express authority; it is resisted by the Chief Executive on the ground of his duty to preserve the confidentiality of the communications of the President. Whatever the correct answer on the merits, these issues are 'of a type which are traditionally justiciable.' The independent Special Prosecutor with his asserted need for the subpoenaed material in the underlying criminal prosecution is opposed by the President with his steadfast assertion of privilege against disclosure of the material. This setting assures there is 'that concrete adverseness which sharpens the presentation of issues upon which the court so largely depends for illumination of difficult constitutional questions.' *Baker v. Carr*. Moreover, since the matter is one arising in the regular course of a federal criminal prosecution, it is within the traditional scope of Art. III power.

In light of the uniqueness of the setting in which the conflict arises, the fact that both parties are officers of the Executive Branch cannot be viewed as a barrier to justiciability. It would be inconsistent with the applicable law and regulation, and the unique facts of this case to conclude other than that the Special Prosecutor has standing to bring this action and that a justiciable controversy is presented for decision. ...

IV

The Claim of Privilege

A

Having determined that the requirements of Rule 17(c) were satisfied, we turn to the claim that the subpoena should be quashed because it demands 'confidential conversations between a President and his close advisors that it would be inconsistent with the public interest to produce.' The first contention is a broad claim that the separation of powers doctrine precludes judicial review of a President's claim of privilege. The second contention is that if he does not prevail on the claim of absolute privilege, the court should hold as a matter of constitutional law that the privilege prevails over the subpoena duces tecum.

In the performance of assigned constitutional duties each branch of the Government must initially interpret the Constitution, and the interpretation of its powers by any branch is due great respect from the others. The President's counsel, as we have noted, reads the Constitution as providing an absolute privilege of confidentiality for all Presidential communications. Many decisions of this Court, however, have unequivocally reaffirmed the holding of Marbury v. Madison, 1 Cranch, 137, 2 L.Ed. 60 (1803), that '(i)t is emphatically the province and duty of the judicial department to say what the law is.'

No holding of the Court has defined the scope of judicial power specifically relating to the enforcement of a subpoena for confidential Presidential communications for use in a criminal prosecution, but other exercises of power by the Executive Branch and the Legislative Branch have been found invalid as in conflict with the Constitution. *Powell v. McCormack; Youngstown, Sheet & Tube Co. v. Sawyer.* In a series of cases, the Court interpreted the explicit immunity conferred by express provisions of the Constitution on Members of the House and Senate by the Speech or Debate Clause. Since this Court has consistently exercised the power to construe and delineate claims arising under express powers, it must follow that the Court has authority to interpret claims with respect to powers alleged to derive from enumerated powers.

Our system of government 'requires that federal courts on occasion interpret the Constitution in a manner at variance with the construction given the document by another branch.' And in *Baker v. Carr*, the Court stated:

> '(D)eciding whether a matter has in any measure been committed by the Constitution to another branch of government, or whether the action of that branch exceeds whatever authority has been committed, is itself a delicate exercise in constitutional interpretation, and is a responsibility of this Court as ultimate interpreter of the Constitution.'

Notwithstanding the deference each branch must accord the others, the 'judicial Power of the United States' vested in the federal courts by Art. III, s 1, of the Constitution can no more be shared with the Executive Branch than the Chief Executive, for example, can share with the Judiciary the veto power, or the Congress share with the Judiciary the power to override a Presidential veto. Any other conclusion would be contrary to the basic concept of separation of powers and the checks and balances that flow from the scheme of a tripartite government. The Federalist, No. 47, p. 313 (S. Mittell ed. 1938). We therefore reaffirm that it is the province and duty of this Court 'to say what the law is' with respect to the claim of privilege presented in this case. *Marbury v. Madison.*

B

In support of his claim of absolute privilege, the President's counsel urges two grounds, one of which is common to all governments and one of which is peculiar to our system of separation of powers. ...

The second ground asserted by the President's counsel in support of the claim of absolute privilege rests on the doctrine of separation of powers. Here it is argued that the independence of the Executive Branch within its own sphere, insulates a President from a judicial subpoena in an ongoing criminal prosecution, and thereby protects confidential Presidential communications.

However, neither the doctrine of separation of powers, nor the need for confidentiality of high-level communications, without more, can sustain an absolute, unqualified Presidential privilege of immunity from judicial process under all circumstances. The President's need for complete candor and objectivity from advisers calls for great deference from the courts. However, when the privilege depends solely on the broad, undifferentiated claim of public interest in the confidentiality of such conversations, a confrontation with other values arises. Absent a claim of need to protect military, diplomatic, or sensitive national security secrets, we find it difficult to accept the argument that even the very important interest in confidentiality of Presidential communications is significantly diminished by production of such material for in camera inspection with all the protection that a district court will be obliged to provide.

The impediment that an absolute, unqualified privilege would place in the way of the primary constitutional duty of the Judicial Branch to do justice in criminal prosecutions would plainly conflict with the function of the courts under Art. III. In designing the structure of our Government and dividing and allocating the sovereign power among three co-equal branches, the Framers of the Constitution sought to provide a comprehensive system, but the separate powers were not intended to operate with absolute independence. 'While the Constitution diffuses power the better to secure liberty, it also contemplates that practice will integrate the dispersed powers into a workable government. It enjoins upon its branches separateness but interdependence, autonomy but reciprocity.' *Youngstown Sheet & Tube Co. v. Sawyer.*

To read the Art. II powers of the President as providing an absolute privilege as against a subpoena essential to enforcement of criminal statutes on no more than a generalized claim of the public interest in confidentiality of nonmilitary and nondiplomatic discussions would upset the constitutional balance of 'a workable government' and gravely impair the role of the courts under Art. III.

C

Since we conclude that the legitimate needs of the judicial process may outweigh Presidential privilege, it is necessary to resolve those competing interests in a manner that preserves the essential functions of each branch. The right and indeed the duty to resolve that question does not free the Judiciary from according high respect to the representations made on behalf of the President. ...

The privilege is fundamental to the operation of Government and inextricably rooted in the separation of powers under the Constitution. In *Nixon v. Sirica*, the Court of Appeals held that such Presidential communications are 'presumptively privileged,' and this position is accepted by both parties in the present litigation. We agree with Mr. Chief Justice Marshall's observation, therefore, that '(i)n no case of this kind would a court be required to proceed against the president as against an ordinary individual.'

But this presumptive privilege must be considered in light of our historic commitment to the rule of law. This is nowhere more profoundly manifest than in our view that 'the twofold aim (of criminal justice) is that guilt shall not escape or innocence suffer. e have elected to employ an adversary system of criminal justice in which the parties contest all issues before a court of law. The need to develop all relevant facts in the adversary system is both fundamental and comprehensive. The ends of criminal justice would be defeated if judgments were to be founded on a partial or speculative presentation of the facts. The very integrity of the judicial system and public confidence in the system depend on full disclosure of all the facts, within the framework of the rules of evidence. To ensure that justice is done, it is imperative to the function of courts that compulsory process be available for the production of evidence needed either by the prosecution or by the defense. ...

In this case the President challenges a subpoena served on him as a third party requiring the production of materials for use in a criminal prosecution; he does so on the claim that he has a privilege against disclosure of confidential communications. He does not place his claim of privilege on the ground they are military or diplomatic secrets. ...

No case of the Court, however, has extended this high degree of deference to a President's generalized interest in confidentiality. Nowhere in the Constitution, as we have noted earlier, is there any explicit reference to a privilege of confidentiality, yet to the extent this interest relates to the effective discharge of a President's powers, it is constitutionally based. ...

In this case we must weigh the importance of the general privilege of confidentiality of Presidential communications in performance of the President's responsibilities against the inroads of such a privilege on the fair administration of criminal justice. The interest in preserving confidentiality is weighty indeed and entitled to great respect. However, we cannot conclude that advisers will be moved to temper the candor of their remarks by the infrequent occasions of disclosure because of the possibility that such conversations will be called for in the context of a criminal prosecution.

On the other hand, the allowance of the privilege to withhold evidence that is demonstrably relevant in a criminal trial would cut deeply into the guarantee of due process of law and gravely impair the basic function of the courts. A President's acknowledged need for confidentiality in the communications of his office is general in nature, whereas the constitutional need for production of relevant evidence in a criminal proceeding is specific and central to the fair adjudication of a particular criminal case in the administration of justice. Without access to specific facts a criminal prosecution may be totally frustrated. The President's broad interest in confidentiality of communications will not be vitiated by disclosure of a limited number of conversations preliminarily shown to have some bearing on the pending criminal cases.

We conclude that when the ground for asserting privilege as to subpoenaed materials sought for use in a criminal trial is based only on the generalized interest in confidentiality, it cannot prevail over the fundamental demands of due process of law in the fair administration of criminal justice. The generalized assertion of privilege must yield to the demonstrated, specific need for evidence in a pending criminal trial.

D

... On the basis of our examination of the record we are unable to conclude that the District Court erred in ordering the inspection. Accordingly we affirm the order of the District Court that subpoenaed materials be transmitted to that court. ...

Notes and Questions

1. *Judges and impeachment.* Like the President, federal judges can be impeached by the House and tried by the Senate. There was a different Nixon, Judge Walter L. Nixon, Jr., on the United States District Court for the District of Mississippi, who was impeached following conviction and sentencing by a court on fraud. The House impeached and the Senate convicted and removed him. He sued to invalidate the Senate conviction so he could retain his salary and benefits. He challenged Senate Impeachment Rule XI, which allows a committee of Senators to hear evidence against a judge and report the evidence to the full Senate. The Supreme Court unanimously held that the claim was nonjusticiable, i.e., could not be heard by the courts. In making this ruling, the Court cited the political question cases, *Baker v. Carr* and *Powell v. McCormick*, and the Court ruled there was no judicially manageable standard to apply to Judge Nixon's challenge. *See Nixon v. United States*, 506 U.S. 224 (1993).

   The Court also observed that impeachment is the "*only* check on the Judicial Branch by the legislature," and, therefore, should not be undermined by the courts' involvement. *Id.* Does this mean that court review of judicial impeachment is different from court review of presidential impeachment?

   Justice Souter concurred, but noted, "If the Senate were to act in a manner seriously threatening the integrity of its results, convicting, say, upon a coin-toss, or upon a summary determination that an officer of the United States was simply 'a bad guy,' judicial interference might well be appropriate." Id. Do you agree?

   You can watch a video description of Judge Nixon's case *at Nixon v. United States* Summary, Oct. 3, 2017, posted at https://www.youtube.com/watch?v=b6T_DQz5nKE&list=PLsFE_Nvl6h_Y75KGR5pkGqcFisGvBnO9S&index=34.

2. *Rule XI.* Do you agree with the Court that Nixon's Rule XI challenge should not be heard by the courts?
3. *The Justices conversing.* The Justices' discussions from the vote on *United States v. Nixon* are available, and were published in Del Dickson, *The Supreme Court in Conference 1940–1985: the private discussions behind nearly 300 Supreme Court decisions 182–86* (2001). What do the following comments tell you about the legal issues in the case and why the Justices voted as they did?

The first conference centered on whether the Court should allow the special prosecutor to skip the court of appeals, while the second conference focused on the merits of the case.

First Conference

BURGER: I see three different categories of executive privilege: (1) congressional committees; (2) grand jury; and (3) criminal prosecution. In the first category, I think that the executive branch has a very broad privilege. In the second category, the privilege remains broad but is narrower. Number three is the tough one-it is the Burr situation.

DOUGLAS: *Nixon v. Sirica* seems to cover this, and that may be a good reason to let it stay in the court of appeals. I see no merits in the question raised. It would be shocking to withhold exculpatory materials that would free a man. I would prefer not to bypass, but will acquiesce if the Court grants cert.

STEWART: I agree that the court of appeals has canvassed the executive privilege issue. On the issue of "requiring immediate settlement in this Court," I don't see that this qualifies. The criminal trial can be put off without real damage. Other issues that the court of appeals hasn't yet confronted: exculpatory evidence, and whether this is an intra-branch fight. Is identification of material here as good as last fall's? If we deny, I hope that we would have a per curiam opinion saying, "We'll stand by." I'm with Bill Douglas.

WHITE: I am reluctant to bypass. The government's application does not really demonstrate an immediate need for review. It is just a transparent effort to have an impact on the impeachment proceedings. I don't think we should let ourselves be used that way. In addition to Potter's points as to other issues, there is the question of appealability and whether we can take mandamus out of the court of appeals. And I don't want, before the court of appeals, to examine the secret material. I would prefer to deny.

MARSHALL: I don't see that the impeachment proceeding is a relevant consideration here. I also don't see why we should go to the court of appeals when the president didn't appeal *Nixon v. Sirica.*

BLACKMUN: There has been no past expedited case except when the executive was on one side and a private party on the other side. A six-month delay in a criminal case is noirreparable injury. If the court of appeals has crossed the bridge already, their decision of this must be prompt. The politics of the thing are that impeachment is the real issue. It may be an unpopular decision, and I would deny.

POWELL: I agree with Douglas, Marshall, Stewart and White. On the merits, I am inclined to say that the president can't claim privilege to keep material from the defense. I would expedite any appeal from court of appeals, but not under Rule 20.

[BRENNAN: From 6–2, votes changed: Powell and Stewart, on the ground that every other institution has delayed, and we have a duty to our institution and to the public not to be one of them—so the case will be set for July 8.]

Second Conference

BURGER: No claim of internal security, state secrets, or military secrets. It is essentially a confidentiality claim. Jurisdiction: this was an appealable order, and I do not reach mandamus or the All Writs Act question. Justiciability: on whether this is an intra-branch dispute, the president has diluted his own discretion to control this case. What about Rule 17(c) on the admissibility of the president's and Colon's statements? He is an unindicted co-conspirator, so I doubt it is necessary. Can we dismiss as improvidently granted the cross-petition? On executive privilege, I think that this is different from a presidential privilege. When communication is required for a criminal trial, there is still a presidential privilege. It is a qualified privilege, limited to official duties. Who decides when it is becomes crucial. Conduct outside of Article 2 is not covered.

DOUGLAS: On the unindicted co-conspirator issue, I say that constitutionally a president can be named as an unindicted co-conspirator, and under the Constitution we can't go back of grand jury's action. I would DIG the cross-petition: (1) because it is not relevant to the issue of discovery; and (2) because insofar as it is relevant to Watergate, it is a political question.

WHITE: I would prefer mandamus, but will go along.

BLACKMUN: I prefer mandamus but will go along.

2. When Can the President Be Sued by a Citizen?

In contrast to President Nixon, who faced impeachment and then resigned because of the charges and the Watergate scandal, President Bill Clinton faced a lawsuit by Paula Corbin Jones for alleged sexual misconduct before he was President when he was governor of Arkansas. Clinton and his lawyers argued that he should not be subject to such a lawsuit because of his duties as president. Which rule would you prefer for a lawsuit based on pre-presidential conduct? That it be dismissed? That it be held while the President is in office, and be conducted as a normal trial would be? That it be held while the President is in office but with great attention paid to changing the trial's date and requirements in deference to the President's schedule? That it be delayed until the President's term is over? Why did you choose your answer?

This case, *Clinton v. Jones*, focused on the Governor of Arkansas's misconduct. As you read the oral argument, which is on the case's website, https://www.oyez.org/cases/1996/95-1853, ask yourself what attitude the Justices and lawyers have toward the idea of a president facing a trial about non-presidential conduct. The oral arguments are also available on youtube, at https://www.youtube.com/watch?v=y75541q8zHQ&list=PLsFE_Nvl6h_braQ_NxoD1jg8oDdM_l8uI&index=14.

During this case and its focus on the President, investigators learned about President Clinton's affair with Monica Lewinsky. This eventually led to his being impeached by the House. The Senate, however, did not convict Clinton. Does that result make you more or less willing to agree with the result in *Clinton v. Jones*? The decision was unanimous. Could you predict that from the oral argument?

Clinton v. Jones

SUPREME COURT OF THE UNITED STATES, 1997

520 U.S. 681, 117 S.Ct. 1636

STEVENS, J., delivered the opinion of the Court, in which REHNQUIST, C.J., and O'CONNOR, SCALIA, KENNEDY, SOUTER, THOMAS, and GINSBURG, JJ., joined. BREYER, J., filed an opinion concurring in the judgment.

This case raises a constitutional and a prudential question concerning the Office of the President of the United States. Respondent, a private citizen, seeks to recover damages from the current occupant of that office based on actions allegedly taken before his term began. The President submits that in all but the most exceptional cases the Constitution requires federal courts to defer such litigation until his term ends and that, in any event, respect for the office warrants such a stay. Despite the force of the arguments supporting the President's submissions, we conclude that they must be rejected.

I

Petitioner, William Jefferson Clinton, was elected to the Presidency in 1992, and re-elected in 1996. His term of office expires on January 20, 2001. In 1991 he was the Governor of the State of Arkansas. Respondent, Paula Corbin Jones, is a resident of California. In 1991 she lived in Arkansas, and was an employee of the Arkansas Industrial Development Commission.

On May 6, 1994, she commenced this action in the United States District Court for the Eastern District of Arkansas by filing a complaint naming petitioner and Danny Ferguson, a former Arkansas State Police officer, as defendants. The complaint alleges two federal claims, and two state-law claims over which the federal court has jurisdiction because of the diverse citizenship of the parties. As the case comes to us, we are required to assume the truth of the detailed—but as yet untested—factual allegations in the complaint.

Those allegations principally describe events that are said to have occurred on the afternoon of May 8, 1991, during an official conference held at the Excelsior Hotel in Little Rock, Arkansas. The Governor delivered a speech at the conference; respondent—working as a state employee—staffed the registration desk. She alleges that Ferguson persuaded her to leave her desk and to visit the Governor in a business suite at the hotel, where he made "abhorrent"[2] sexual advances that she vehemently rejected. She further claims that her superiors at work subsequently dealt with her in a hostile and rude manner, and changed her duties to punish her for rejecting those advances. Finally, she alleges that after petitioner was elected President, Ferguson defamed her by making a statement to a reporter that implied she had accepted petitioner's alleged overtures, and that various persons authorized to speak for the President publicly branded her a liar by denying that the incident had occurred.

Respondent seeks actual damages of $75,000 and punitive damages of $100,000. Her complaint contains four counts. The first charges that petitioner, acting under color of state law, deprived her of rights protected by the Constitution, in violation of Rev. Stat. § 1979, 42 U.S.C. § 1983. The second charges that petitioner and Ferguson engaged in a conspiracy to violate her federal rights, also actionable under federal law. The third is a state common law claim for intentional infliction of emotional distress, grounded primarily on the incident at the hotel. The fourth count, also based on state law, is for defamation, embracing both the comments allegedly made to the press by Ferguson and the statements of petitioner's agents. Inasmuch as the legal sufficiency of the claims has not yet been challenged, we assume, without deciding, that each of the four counts states a cause of action as a matter of law. With the exception of the last charge, which arguably may involve conduct within the outer perimeter of the President's official responsibilities, it is perfectly clear that the alleged misconduct of petitioner was unrelated to any of his official duties as President of the United States and, indeed, occurred before he was elected to that office. ...

III

The President, represented by private counsel, filed a petition for certiorari. The Acting Solicitor General, representing the United States, supported the petition, arguing that the decision of the Court of Appeals was "fundamentally mistaken" and created "serious risks for the institution of the Presidency." In her brief in opposition to certiorari, respondent argued that this "one-of-a-kind case is singularly inappropriate" for the exercise of our certiorari jurisdiction because it did not create any conflict among the Courts of Appeals, it "does not pose any conceivable threat to the functioning of the Executive Branch," and there is no precedent supporting the President's position. ...

[O]ur decision rejecting the immunity claim and allowing the case to proceed does not require us to confront the question whether a court may compel the attendance of the President at any specific time or place. We assume that the testimony of the President, both for discovery and for use at trial, may be taken at the White House at a time that will accommodate his busy schedule, and that, if a trial is held, there would be no necessity for the President to attend in person, though he could elect to do so.

IV

Petitioner's principal submission—that "in all but the most exceptional cases," the Constitution affords the President temporary immunity from civil damages litigation arising out of events that occurred before he took office—cannot be sustained on the basis of precedent. ...

The principal rationale for affording certain public servants immunity from suits for money damages arising out of their official acts is inapplicable to unofficial conduct. In cases involving prosecutors, legislators, and judges we have repeatedly explained that the immunity serves the public interest in enabling such officials to perform their designated functions effectively without fear that a particular decision may give rise to personal liability. ...

This reasoning provides no support for an immunity for *unofficial* conduct. As we explained in *Fitzgerald,* "the sphere of protected action must be related closely to the immunity's justifying purposes." Because of the President's broad responsibilities, we recognized in that case an immunity from damages claims arising out of official acts extending to the "outer perimeter of his authority." But we have never suggested that the President, or any other official, has an immunity that extends beyond the scope of any action taken in an official capacity. ...

Petitioner's effort to construct an immunity from suit for unofficial acts grounded purely in the identity of his office is unsupported by precedent.

V

... In the end, as applied to the particular question before us, we reach the same conclusion about these historical materials that Justice Jackson described when confronted with an issue concerning the dimensions of the President's power. "Just what our forefathers did envision, or would have envisioned had they foreseen modern conditions, must be divined from materials almost as enigmatic as the dreams Joseph was called upon to interpret for Pharoah. A century and a half of partisan debate and scholarly speculation yields no net result but only supplies more or less apt quotations from respected sources on each side. ... They largely cancel each other." *Youngstown Sheet & Tube Co. v. Sawyer.*

VI

Petitioner's strongest argument supporting his immunity claim is based on the text and structure of the Constitution. He does not contend that the occupant of the Office of the President is "above the law," in the sense that his conduct is entirely immune from judicial scrutiny. The President argues merely for a postponement of the judicial proceedings that will determine whether he violated any law. His argument is grounded in the character of the office that was created by Article II of the Constitution, and relies on separation-of-powers principles that have structured our constitutional arrangement since the founding.

As a starting premise, petitioner contends that he occupies a unique office with powers and responsibilities so vast and important that the public interest demands that he devote his undivided time and attention to his public duties. He submits that—given the nature of the office—the doctrine of separation of powers places limits on the authority of the Federal Judiciary to interfere with the Executive Branch that would be transgressed by allowing this action to proceed.

We have no dispute with the initial premise of the argument. ...

It does not follow, however, that separation-of-powers principles would be violated by allowing this action to proceed. The doctrine of separation of powers is concerned with the allocation of official power among the three coequal branches of our Government. The Framers "built into the tripartite Federal Government ... a self-executing safeguard against the encroachment or aggrandizement of one branch at the expense of the other." ...

Petitioner's predictive judgment finds little support in either history or the relatively narrow compass of the issues raised in this particular case. As we have already noted, in the more than 200-year history of the Republic, only three sitting Presidents have been subjected to suits for their private actions. If the past is any indicator, it seems unlikely that a deluge of such litigation will ever engulf the Presidency. As for the case at hand, if properly managed by the District Court, it appears to us highly unlikely to occupy any substantial amount of petitioner's time.

Of greater significance, petitioner errs by presuming that interactions between the Judicial Branch and the Executive, even quite burdensome interactions, necessarily rise to the level of constitutionally forbidden impairment of the Executive's ability to perform its constitutionally mandated functions. "[O]ur ... system imposes upon the Branches a degree of overlapping responsibility, a duty of interdependence as well as independence the absence of which 'would preclude the establishment of a Nation capable of governing itself effectively.'" As Madison explained, separation of powers does not mean that the branches "ought to have no *partial agency* in, or no *controul* over the acts of each other." The fact that a federal court's exercise of its traditional Article III jurisdiction may significantly burden the time and attention of the Chief Executive is not sufficient to establish a violation of the Constitution. Two long-settled propositions, first announced by Chief Justice Marshall, support that conclusion.

First, we have long held that when the President takes official action, the Court has the authority to determine whether he has acted within the law. Perhaps the most dramatic example of such a case is our holding that President Truman exceeded his constitutional authority when he issued an order directing the Secretary of Commerce to take possession of and operate most of the Nation's steel mills in order to avert a national catastrophe. *Youngstown Sheet & Tube Co. v. Sawyer*. Despite the serious impact of that decision on the ability of the Executive Branch to accomplish its assigned mission, and the substantial time that the President must necessarily have devoted to the matter as a result of judicial involvement, we exercised our Article III jurisdiction to decide whether his official conduct conformed to the law. Our holding was an application of the principle established in *Marbury v. Madison,* that "[i]t is emphatically the province and duty of the judicial department to say what the law is."

Second, it is also settled that the President is subject to judicial process in appropriate circumstances. Although Thomas Jefferson apparently thought otherwise, Chief Justice Marshall, when presiding in the treason trial of Aaron Burr, ruled that a subpoena *duces tecum* could be directed to the President. We unequivocally and emphatically endorsed Marshall's position when we held that President Nixon was obligated to comply with a subpoena commanding him to produce certain tape recordings of his conversations with his aides. *United States v. Nixon*. As we explained, "neither the doctrine of separation of powers, nor the need for confidentiality of high-level communications, without more, can sustain an absolute, unqualified Presidential privilege of immunity from judicial process under all circumstances."

Sitting Presidents have responded to court orders to provide testimony and other information with sufficient frequency that such interactions between the Judicial and Executive Branches can scarcely be thought a novelty. President Monroe responded to written interrogatories, President Nixon—as noted above—produced tapes in response to a subpoena *duces tecum,* see *United States v. Nixon,* President Ford complied with an order to give a deposition in a criminal trial, and President Clinton has twice given videotaped testimony in criminal proceedings, Moreover, sitting Presidents have also voluntarily complied with judicial requests for testimony. President Grant gave a lengthy deposition in a criminal case under such circumstances, and President Carter similarly gave videotaped testimony for use at a criminal trial.

In sum, "[i]t is settled law that the separation-of-powers doctrine does not bar every exercise of jurisdiction over the President of the United States." If the Judiciary may severely burden the Executive Branch by reviewing the legality of the President's official conduct, and if it may direct appropriate process to the President himself, it must follow that the federal courts have power to determine the legality of his unofficial conduct. The burden on the President's time and energy that is a mere byproduct of such review surely cannot be considered as onerous as the direct burden imposed by judicial review and the occasional invalidation of his official actions. We therefore hold that the doctrine of separation of powers does not require federal courts to stay all private actions against the President until he leaves office.

The reasons for rejecting such a categorical rule apply as well to a rule that would require a stay "in all but the most exceptional cases." Indeed, if the Framers of the Constitution had thought it necessary to protect the President from the burdens of private litigation, we think it far more likely that they would have adopted a categorical rule than a rule that required the President to litigate the question whether a specific case belonged in the "exceptional case" subcategory. In all events, the question whether a specific case should receive exceptional treatment is more appropriately the subject of the exercise of judicial discretion than an interpretation of the Constitution. Accordingly, we turn to the question whether the District Court's decision to stay the trial until after petitioner leaves office was an abuse of discretion.

VII

... [W]e are persuaded that it was an abuse of discretion for the District Court to defer the trial until after the President leaves office. Such a lengthy and categorical stay takes no account whatever of the respondent's interest in bringing the case to trial. The complaint was filed within the statutory limitations period—albeit near the end of that period—and delaying trial would increase the danger of prejudice resulting from the loss of evidence, including the inability of witnesses to recall specific facts, or the possible death of a party. ...

Justice BREYER, concurring in the judgment.

... To obtain a postponement the President must "bea[r] the burden of establishing its need."

In my view, however, once the President sets forth and explains a conflict between judicial proceeding and public duties, the matter changes. At that point, the Constitution permits a judge to schedule a trial in an ordinary civil damages action (where postponement normally is possible without overwhelming damage to a plaintiff) only within the constraints of a constitutional principle—a principle that forbids a federal judge in such a case to interfere with the President's discharge of his public duties. I have no doubt that the Constitution contains such a principle applicable to civil suits, based upon Article II's vesting of the entire "executive Power" in a single individual, implemented through the Constitution's structural separation of powers, and revealed both by history and case precedent.

I recognize that this case does not require us now to apply the principle specifically, thereby delineating its contours; nor need we now decide whether lower courts are to apply it directly or categorically through the use of presumptions or rules of administration. Yet I fear that to disregard it now may appear to deny it. I also fear that the majority's description of the relevant precedents de-emphasizes the extent to which they support a principle of the President's independent authority to control his own time and energy. Further, if the majority is wrong in predicting the future infrequency of private civil litigation against sitting Presidents, acknowledgment and future delineation of the constitutional principle will prove a practically necessary institutional safeguard. For these reasons, I think it important to explain how the Constitution's text, history, and precedent support this principle of judicial noninterference with Presidential functions in ordinary civil damages actions. ...

III

... I concede the possibility that district courts, supervised by the Courts of Appeals and perhaps this Court, might prove able to manage private civil damages actions against sitting Presidents without significantly interfering with the discharge of Presidential duties—at least if they manage those actions with the constitutional problem in mind. Nonetheless, predicting the future is difficult, and I am skeptical. Should the majority's optimism turn out to be misplaced, then, in my view, courts will have to develop administrative rules applicable to such cases (including postponement rules of the sort at issue in this case) in order to implement the basic constitutional directive. A Constitution that separates powers in order to prevent one branch of Government from significantly threatening the workings of another could not grant a single judge more than a very limited power to second-guess a President's reasonable determination (announced in open court) of his scheduling needs, nor could it permit the issuance of a trial scheduling order that would significantly interfere with the President's discharge of his duties—in a private civil damages action the trial of which might be postponed without the plaintiff suffering enormous harm. As Madison pointed out in The Federalist No. 51: "The great security against a gradual concentration of the several powers in the same department consists in giving to those who administer each department the necessary constitutional means and personal motives to resist encroachments of the others. *The provision for defense must in this, as in all other cases, be made commensurate to the danger of attack.*" I agree with the majority's determination that a constitutional defense must await a more specific showing of need; I do not agree with what I believe to be an understatement of the "danger." And I believe that ordinary case-management principles are unlikely to prove sufficient to deal with private civil lawsuits for damages unless supplemented with a constitutionally based requirement that district courts schedule proceedings so as to avoid significant interference with the President's ongoing discharge of his official responsibilities.

IV

This case is a private action for civil damages in which, as the District Court here found, it is possible to preserve evidence and in which later payment of interest can compensate for delay. The District Court in this case determined that the Constitution required the postponement of trial during the sitting President's term. It may well be that the trial of this case cannot take place without significantly interfering with the President's ability to carry out his official duties. Yet, I agree with the majority that there is no automatic temporary immunity and that the President should have to provide the District Court with a reasoned explanation of why the immunity is needed; and I also agree that, in the absence of that explanation, the court's postponement of the trial date was premature. For those reasons, I concur in the result.

Notes and Questions

1. *The rule of law.* The "rule of law" means that the law applies to all, including elected representatives. Does this opinion vindicate the rule of law?
2. *The history of Presidential impeachment.* Lawyers for Paula Jones found out that President Bill Clinton had an affair with Monica Lewinsky, an aide to the President. President Clinton was impeached by the House of Representatives for two counts. One charged him with lying under oath to a grand jury, and the second charged obstruction of justice. He was not convicted by the Senate, so he remained President. He was the second President in history to be impeached;

Andrew Johnson was the first. President Nixon resigned before being impeached by the House although the House Judiciary Committee had voted on articles of impeachment.

3. *Is it useful?* What is the point of impeachment?
4. *Video.* Does Quimbee's video, *Clinton v. Jones* Case Brief Summary/Law Case Explained, Oct. 2, 2020, posted at https://www.youtube.com/watch?v=y75541q8zHQ&list=PLsFE_Nvl6h_braQ_NxoD1jg8oDdM_l8uI&index=14, explain the case's meaning and its implications?
5. *President Trump.* Why were there impeachment proceedings against President Donald Trump?

B. Separation of the Branches

1. The Court Draws the Line Between Congress and the Executive Branch

The Court has repeatedly said that the separation of power between the branches is one of the foundational elements of the Constitution.

Article I, Section 1 states, "All legislative powers herein granted shall be vested in a Congress of the United States, which shall consist of a Senate and House of Representatives." Article I, Section 7 states, "Every bill which shall have passed the House of Representatives and the Senate, shall, before it become a law, be presented to the President of the United States; if he approve he shall sign it, but if not he shall return it, with his objections to that House in which it shall have originated, who shall enter the objections at large on their journal, and proceed to reconsider it." "Every order, resolution, or vote to which the concurrence of the Senate and House of Representatives may be necessary (except on a question of adjournment) shall be presented to the President of the United States; and before the same shall take effect, shall be approved by him, or being disapproved by him, shall be repassed by two thirds of the Senate and House of Representatives, according to the rules and limitations prescribed in the case of a bill."

The following case considers whether every action of the Congress must be bicameral. Listen to the oral argument, available on the case's website, https://www.oyez.org/cases/1981/80-1832. Does the oral argument make clear what Congress was trying to accomplish with its legislation and why? What views about immigrants are expressed during the argument? Can you think of a simple way to describe what this case was about?

Immigration and Naturalization Service v. Chadha

SUPREME COURT OF THE UNITED STATES, 1983

462 U.S. 919, 103 S.Ct. 2764

Chief Justice BURGER delivered the opinion of the Court, with BRENNAN, MARSHALL, BLACKMUN, POWELL, STEVENS AND O'CONNOR. Justice POWELL concurred in the judgment and filed opinion. JUSTICE WHITE dissented. Justice REHNQUIST dissented and filed an opinion in which Justice WHITE joined.

...

I

Chadha is an East Indian who was born in Kenya and holds a British passport. He was lawfully admitted to the United States in 1966 on a nonimmigrant student visa. His visa expired on June 30, 1972. On October 11, 1973, the District Director of the Immigration and Naturalization Service ordered Chadha to show cause why he should not be deported for having "remained in the United States for a longer time than permitted." Pursuant to § 242(b) of the Immigration and Nationality Act (Act), a deportation hearing was held before an immigration judge on January 11, 1974. Chadha conceded that he was deportable for overstaying his visa and the hearing was adjourned to enable him to file an application for suspension of deportation. ...

After Chadha submitted his application for suspension of deportation, the deportation hearing was resumed on February 7, 1974. On the basis of evidence adduced at the hearing, affidavits submitted with the application, and the results of a character investigation conducted by the INS, the immigration judge, on June 25, 1974, ordered that Chadha's deportation be suspended. The immigration judge found that Chadha met the requirements of § 244(a)(1): he had resided continuously in the United States for over seven years, was of good moral character, and would suffer "extreme hardship" if deported.

Pursuant to § 244(c)(1) of the Act, the immigration judge suspended Chadha's deportation and a report of the suspension was transmitted to Congress. Section 244(c)(1) provides:

> "Upon application by any alien who is found by the Attorney General to meet the requirements of subsection (a) of this section the Attorney General may in his discretion suspend deportation of such alien. If the deportation of any alien is suspended under the provisions of this subsection, a complete and detailed statement of the facts and pertinent provisions of law in the case shall be reported to the Congress with the reasons for such suspension. Such reports shall be submitted on the first day of each calendar month in which Congress is in session."

Once the Attorney General's recommendation for suspension of Chadha's deportation was conveyed to Congress, Congress had the power to veto the Attorney General's determination that Chadha should not be deported. Section 244(c)(2) provides:

> "(2) In the case of an alien specified in paragraph (1) of subsection (a) of this subsection—if during the session of the Congress at which a case is reported, or prior to the close of the session of the Congress next following the session at which a case is reported, either the Senate or the House of Representatives passes a resolution stating in substance that it does not favor the suspension of such deportation, the Attorney General shall thereupon deport such alien or authorize the alien's voluntary departure at his own expense under the order of deportation in the manner provided by law. If, within the time above specified, neither the Senate nor the House of Representatives shall pass such a resolution, the Attorney General shall cancel deportation proceedings."

... Absent Congressional action, Chadha's deportation proceedings would have been cancelled after this date and his status adjusted to that of a permanent resident alien. ...

The resolution was passed without debate or recorded vote. Since the House action was pursuant to § 244(c)(2), the resolution was not treated as an Article I legislative act; it was not submitted to the Senate or presented to the President for his action. ...

III A

... By the same token, the fact that a given law or procedure is efficient, convenient, and useful in facilitating functions of government, standing alone, will not save it if it is contrary to the Constitution. Convenience and efficiency are not the primary objectives—or the hallmarks—of democratic government and our inquiry is sharpened rather than blunted by the fact that Congressional veto provisions are appearing with increasing frequency in statutes which delegate authority to executive and independent agencies. ...

Explicit and unambiguous provisions of the Constitution prescribe and define the respective functions of the Congress and of the Executive in the legislative process. Since the precise terms of those familiar provisions are critical to the resolution of this case, we set them out verbatim. ...

B

The Presentment Clauses

The records of the Constitutional Convention reveal that the requirement that all legislation be presented to the President before becoming law was uniformly accepted by the Framers. Presentment to the President and the Presidential veto were considered so imperative that the draftsmen took special pains to assure that these requirements could not be circumvented. During the final debate on Art. I, § 7, cl. 2, James Madison expressed concern that it might easily be evaded by the simple expedient of calling a proposed law a "resolution" or "vote" rather than a "bill." As a consequence, Art. I, § 7, cl. 3, was added.

The decision to provide the President with a limited and qualified power to nullify proposed legislation by veto was based on the profound conviction of the Framers that the powers conferred on Congress were the powers to be most carefully circumscribed. It is beyond doubt that lawmaking was a power to be shared by both Houses and the President. ...

The President's role in the lawmaking process also reflects the Framers' careful efforts to check whatever propensity a particular Congress might have to enact oppressive, improvident, or ill-considered measures. ...

C

Bicameralism

The bicameral requirement of Art. I, §§ 1, 7 was of scarcely less concern to the Framers than was the Presidential veto and indeed the two concepts are interdependent. By providing that no law could take effect without the concurrence of the prescribed majority of the Members of both Houses, the Framers reemphasized their belief, already remarked upon in connection with the Presentment Clauses, that legislation should not be enacted unless it has been carefully and fully considered by the Nation's elected officials. ...

We see therefore that the Framers were acutely conscious that the bicameral requirement and the Presentment Clauses would serve essential constitutional functions. The President's participation in the legislative process was to protect the Executive Branch from Congress and to protect the whole people from improvident laws. The division of the Congress into two distinctive bodies assures that the legislative power would be exercised only after opportunity for full study and debate in separate settings. The President's unilateral veto power, in turn, was limited by the power of two thirds of both Houses of Congress to overrule a veto thereby precluding final arbitrary action of one person. It emerges clearly that the prescription for legislative action in Art. I, §§ 1, 7 represents the Framers' decision that the legislative power of the Federal government be exercised in accord with a single, finely wrought and exhaustively considered, procedure.

IV

... Examination of the action taken here by one House pursuant to § 244(c)(2) reveals that it was essentially legislative in purpose and effect. In purporting to exercise power defined in Art. I, § 8, cl. 4 to "establish an uniform Rule of Naturalization," the House took action that had the purpose and effect of altering the legal rights, duties and relations of persons, including the Attorney General, Executive Branch officials and Chadha, all outside the legislative branch. Section 244(c)(2) purports to authorize one House of Congress to require the Attorney General to deport an individual alien whose deportation otherwise would be cancelled under § 244. The one-House veto operated in this case to overrule the Attorney General and mandate Chadha's deportation; absent the House action, Chadha would remain in the United States. Congress has *acted* and its action has altered Chadha's status.

The legislative character of the one-House veto in this case is confirmed by the character of the Congressional action it supplants. Neither the House of Representatives nor the Senate contends that, absent the veto provision in § 244(c)(2), either of them, or both of them acting together, could effectively require the Attorney General to deport an alien once the Attorney General, in the exercise of legislatively delegated authority,[16] had determined the alien should remain in the United States. Without the challenged provision in § 244(c)(2), this could have been achieved, if at all, only by legislation requiring deportation. Similarly, a veto by one House of Congress under § 244(c)(2) cannot be justified as an attempt at amending the standards set out in § 244(a)(1), or as a repeal of § 244 as applied to Chadha. Amendment and repeal of statutes, no less than enactment, must conform with Art. I.

The nature of the decision implemented by the one-House veto in this case further manifests its legislative character. After long experience with the clumsy, time consuming private bill procedure, Congress made a deliberate choice to delegate to the Executive Branch, and specifically to the Attorney General, the authority to allow deportable aliens to remain in this country in certain specified circumstances. It is not disputed that this choice to delegate authority is precisely the kind of decision that can be implemented only in accordance with the procedures set out in Art. I. Disagreement with the Attorney General's decision on Chadha's deportation—that is, Congress' decision to deport Chadha—no less than Congress' original choice to delegate to the Attorney General the authority to make that decision, involves determinations of policy that Congress can implement in only one way; bicameral passage followed by presentment to the President. Congress must abide by its delegation of authority until that delegation is legislatively altered or revoked.

Finally, we see that when the Framers intended to authorize either House of Congress to act alone and outside of its prescribed bicameral legislative role, they narrowly and precisely defined the procedure for such action. There are but four provisions in the Constitution, explicit and unambiguous, by which one House may act alone with the unreviewable force of law, not subject to the President's veto:

(a) The House of Representatives alone was given the power to initiate impeachments. Art. I, § 2, cl. 6;
(b) The Senate alone was given the power to conduct trials following impeachment on charges initiated by the House and to convict following trial. Art. I, § 3, cl. 5;
(c) The Senate alone was given final unreviewable power to approve or to disapprove presidential appointments. Art. II, § 2, cl. 2;
(d) The Senate alone was given unreviewable power to ratify treaties negotiated by the President. Art. II, § 2, cl. 2. ...

Justice POWELL, concurring in the judgment.

The Court's decision, based on the Presentment Clauses, Art. I, § 7, cls. 2 and 3, apparently will invalidate every use of the legislative veto. The breadth of this holding gives one pause. Congress has included the veto in literally hundreds of statutes, dating back to the 1930s. Congress clearly views this procedure as essential to controlling the delegation of power to administrative agencies. One reasonably may disagree with Congress' assessment of the veto's utility, but the respect due its judgment as a coordinate branch of Government cautions that our holding should be no more extensive than necessary to decide this case. In my view, the case may be decided on a narrower ground. When Congress finds that a particular person does not satisfy the statutory criteria for permanent residence in this country it has assumed a judicial function in violation of the principle of separation of powers. Accordingly, I concur only in the judgment. ...

On its face, the House's action appears clearly adjudicatory. The House did not enact a general rule; rather it made its own determination that six specific persons did not comply with certain statutory criteria. It thus undertook the type of decision that traditionally has been left to other branches. Even if the House did not make a *de novo* determination, but simply reviewed the Immigration and Naturalization Service's findings, it still assumed a function ordinarily entrusted to the federal courts. Where, as here, Congress has exercised a power "that cannot possibly be regarded as merely in aid of the legislative function of Congress," the decisions of this Court have held that Congress impermissibly assumed a function that the Constitution entrusted to another branch.

The impropriety of the House's assumption of this function is confirmed by the fact that its action raises the very danger the Framers sought to avoid—the exercise of unchecked power. In deciding whether Chadha deserves to be deported, Congress is not subject to any internal constraints that prevent it from arbitrarily depriving him of the right to remain in this country. Unlike the judiciary or an administrative agency, Congress is not bound by established substantive rules. Nor is it subject to the procedural safeguards, such as the right to counsel and a hearing before an impartial tribunal, that are present when a court or an agency adjudicates individual rights. The only effective constraint on Congress' power is political, but Congress is most accountable politically when it prescribes rules of general applicability. When it decides rights of specific persons, those rights are subject to "the tyranny of a shifting majority." ...

Justice WHITE, dissenting.

Today the Court not only invalidates § 244(c)(2) of the Immigration and Nationality Act, but also sounds the death knell for nearly 200 other statutory provisions in which Congress has reserved a "legislative veto." For this reason, the Court's decision is of surpassing importance. And it is for this reason that the Court would have been well-advised to decide the case, if possible, on the narrower grounds of separation of powers, leaving for full consideration the constitutionality of other congressional review statutes operating on such varied matters as war powers and agency rulemaking, some of which concern the independent regulatory agencies.

The prominence of the legislative veto mechanism in our contemporary political system and its importance to Congress can hardly be overstated. It has become a central means by which Congress secures the accountability of executive and independent agencies. Without the legislative veto, Congress is faced with a Hobson's choice: either to refrain from delegating the necessary authority, leaving itself with a hopeless task of writing laws with the requisite specificity to cover endless special circumstances across the entire policy landscape, or in the alternative, to abdicate its law-making function to the executive branch and independent agencies. To choose the former leaves major national problems unresolved; to opt for the latter risks unaccountable policymaking by those not elected to fill that role. Accordingly, over the past five decades, the legislative veto has been placed in nearly 200 statutes. The device is known in every field of governmental concern: reorganization, budgets, foreign affairs, war powers, and regulation of trade, safety, energy, the environment and the economy. ...

The power to exercise a legislative veto is not the power to write new law without bicameral approval or presidential consideration. The veto must be authorized by statute and may only negative what an Executive department or independent agency has proposed. On its face, the legislative veto no more allows one House of Congress to make law than does the presidential veto confer such power upon the President. Accordingly, the Court properly recognizes that it "must establish that the challenged action under § 244(c)(2) is of the kind to which the procedural requirements of Art. I, § 7 apply" and admits that "not every action taken by either House is subject to the bicameralism and presentation requirements of Art. I." ...

The Court heeded this counsel in approving the modern administrative state. The Court's holding today that all legislative-type action must be enacted through the lawmaking process ignores that legislative authority is routinely delegated to the Executive branch, to the independent regulatory agencies, and to private individuals and groups. ...

I regret that I am in disagreement with my colleagues on the fundamental questions that this case presents. But even more I regret the destructive scope of the Court's holding. It reflects a profoundly different conception of the Constitution than that held by the Courts which sanctioned the modern administrative state. Today's decision strikes down in one fell swoop provisions in more laws enacted by Congress than the Court has cumulatively invalidated in its history. I fear it will now be more difficult "to insure that the fundamental policy decisions in our society will be made not by an appointed official but by the body immediately responsible to the people[,]" I must dissent.

Justice REHNQUIST, with whom Justice WHITE joins, dissenting.

... Because I believe that Congress did not intend the one-House veto provision of § 244(c)(2) to be severable, I dissent. ...

The Court finds that the legislative history of § 244 shows that Congress intended § 244(c)(2) to be severable because Congress wanted to relieve itself of the burden of private bills. But the history elucidated by the Court shows that Congress was unwilling to give the Executive Branch permission to suspend deportation on its own. Over the years, Congress consistently rejected requests from the Executive for complete discretion in this area. Congress always insisted on retaining ultimate control, whether by concurrent resolution, as in the 1948 Act, or by one-House veto, as in the present Act. Congress has never indicated that it would be willing to permit suspensions of deportation unless it could retain some sort of veto.

It is doubtless true that Congress has the power to provide for suspensions of deportation without a one-House veto. But the Court has failed to identify any evidence that Congress intended to exercise that power. On the contrary, Congress' continued insistence on retaining control of the suspension process indicates that it has never been disposed to give the Executive Branch a free hand. By severing § 244(c)(2) the Court has "confounded" Congress' "intention" to permit suspensions of deportation "with their power to carry that intention into effect."

Because I do not believe that § 244(c)(2) is severable, I would reverse the judgment of the Court of Appeals.

Notes and Questions

1. *Pre-Justice Scalia.* Before he was a judge or Justice, Antonin Scalia filed an amicus brief for the American Bar Association with the Supreme Court urging affirmance. Why do you think he took that position? Is it consistent with his later cases as a Justice of the Supreme Court?
2. *How do the opinions differ?* How do the views of the majority, concurrence in the judgment (joining the majority result but not its reasoning), compare regarding (1) the role of the different branches of government and (2) the possibility of separation?
3. *Video.* Does Quimbee's video, *Immigration and Naturalization Service v. Chadha* Case Brief Summary/Law Case Explained, Mar. 6, 2017, posted at https://www.youtube.com/watch?v=qYtb3BbNbTA&list=PLsFE_Nvl6h_Y75KGR5pkGqcFisGvBnO9S&index=85, explain the case's importance?
4. *Who prosecutes?* We learned in the impeachment section that government workers may commit misconduct that makes them worthy of impeachment. This is related to the general problem that anyone can violate the law and be prosecuted. Who should do the prosecuting? The Watergate scandal led to passage of Ethics in Government Acts, which were supposed to ensure that government officials acted ethically.

2. Is an Independent Counsel Constitutional?

One section of the act created an independent counsel, who could be selected to investigate an alleged criminal and figure out if they had violated the law. Independent Counsel (also known as Special Prosecutor) Ken Starr investigated President Clinton, and the information received from the investigation was part of the evidence at Clinton's impeachment.

The next case is from 1988 and occurred before President Clinton was elected in 1992. As you read the case, determine whose misconduct is being investigated and who the independent counsel was. Can you tell from reading the opinion how the counsel was chosen? What process was used? What role did each of the Article I, II, or III branches play in the case? Can you sketch out the conduct of all the branches in this process?

The oral argument is available at https://www.oyez.org/cases/1987/87-1279. Can you tell from this oral argument that there would be only one dissenting Justice in this case? Who did the best job in this argument of stating the facts clearly? Of stating the constitutional argument clearly?

If you were a member of Congress, would you vote in favor of a statute authorizing an independent counsel? What are the pros and cons?

Morrison v. Olson

SUPREME COURT OF THE UNITED STATES, 1988

487 U.S. 654, 108 S.Ct. 2597

REHNQUIST, C.J., delivered the opinion of the Court, in which BRENNAN, WHITE, MARSHALL, BLACKMUN, STEVENS, and O'CONNOR, JJ., joined. SCALIA, J., filed a dissenting opinion. KENNEDY, J., took no part in the consideration or decision of the case.

This case presents us with a challenge to the independent counsel provisions of the Ethics in Government Act of 1978. We hold today that these provisions of the Act do not violate the Appointments Clause of the Constitution, Art. II, § 2, cl. 2, or the limitations of Article III, nor do they impermissibly interfere with the President's authority under Article II in violation of the constitutional principle of separation of powers.

I

Briefly stated, Title VI of the Ethics in Government Act allows for the appointment of an "independent counsel" to investigate and, if appropriate, prosecute certain high-ranking Government officials for violations of federal criminal laws. The Act requires the Attorney General, upon receipt of information that he determines is "sufficient to constitute grounds to investigate whether any person [covered by the Act] may have violated any Federal criminal law," to conduct a preliminary investigation of the matter. When the Attorney General has completed this investigation, or 90 days has elapsed, he is required to report to a special court (the Special Division) created by the Act "for the purpose of appointing independent counsels." If the Attorney General determines that "there are no reasonable grounds to believe that further investigation is warranted," then he must notify the Special Division of this result. In such a case, "the division of the court shall have no power to appoint an independent counsel." If, however, the Attorney General has determined that there are "reasonable grounds to believe that further investigation or prosecution is warranted," then he "shall apply to the division of the court for the appointment of an independent counsel." The Attorney General's application to the court "shall contain sufficient information to assist the [court] in selecting an independent counsel and in defining that independent counsel's prosecutorial jurisdiction." Upon receiving this application, the Special Division "shall appoint an appropriate independent counsel and shall define that independent counsel's prosecutorial jurisdiction."

With respect to all matters within the independent counsel's jurisdiction, the Act grants the counsel "full power and independent authority to exercise all investigative and prosecutorial functions and powers of the Department of Justice, the Attorney General, and any other officer or employee of the Department of Justice." The functions of the independent counsel include conducting grand jury proceedings and other investigations, participating in civil and criminal court proceedings and litigation, and appealing any decision in any case in which the counsel participates in an official capacity. Under § 594(a)(9), the counsel's powers include "initiating and conducting prosecutions in any court of competent jurisdiction, framing and signing indictments, filing informations, and handling all aspects of any case, in the name of the United States." The counsel may appoint employees, may request and obtain assistance from the Department of Justice, and may accept referral of matters from the Attorney General if the matter falls within the counsel's jurisdiction as defined by the Special Division. The Act also states that an independent counsel "shall, except where not possible, comply with the written or other established policies of the Department of Justice respecting enforcement of the criminal laws." In addition, whenever a matter has been referred to an independent counsel under the Act, the Attorney General and the Justice Department are required to suspend all investigations and proceedings regarding the matter. An independent counsel has "full authority to dismiss matters within [his or her] prosecutorial jurisdiction without conducting an investigation or at any subsequent time before prosecution, if to do so would be consistent" with Department of Justice policy.

Two statutory provisions govern the length of an independent counsel's tenure in office. The first defines the procedure for removing an independent counsel. Section 596(a)(1) provides:

> "An independent counsel appointed under this chapter may be removed from office, other than by impeachment and conviction, only by the personal action of the Attorney General and only for good cause, physical disability, mental incapacity, or any other condition that substantially impairs the performance of such independent counsel's duties."

If an independent counsel is removed pursuant to this section, the Attorney General is required to submit a report to both the Special Division and the Judiciary Committees of the Senate and the House "specifying the facts found and the ultimate grounds for such removal." Under the current version of the Act, an independent counsel can obtain judicial review of the Attorney General's action by filing a civil action in the United States District Court for the District of Columbia. Members of the Special Division "may not hear or determine any such civil action or any appeal of a decision in any such civil action." The reviewing court is authorized to grant reinstatement or "other appropriate relief."

The other provision governing the tenure of the independent counsel defines the procedures for "terminating" the counsel's office. Under § 596(b)(1), the office of an independent counsel terminates when he or she notifies the Attorney General that he or she has completed or substantially completed any investigations or prosecutions undertaken pursuant to the Act. In addition, the Special Division, acting either on its own or on the suggestion of the Attorney General, may terminate the office of an independent counsel at any time if it finds that "the investigation of all matters within the prosecutorial jurisdiction of such independent counsel ... have been completed or so substantially completed that it would be appropriate for the Department of Justice to complete such investigations and prosecutions."

Finally, the Act provides for congressional oversight of the activities of independent counsel. An independent counsel may from time to time send Congress statements or reports on his or her activities. The "appropriate committees of the Congress" are given oversight jurisdiction in regard to the official conduct of an independent counsel, and the counsel is required by the Act to cooperate with Congress in the exercise of this jurisdiction. The counsel is required to inform the House of Representatives of "substantial and credible information which [the counsel] receives ... that may constitute grounds for an impeachment." In addition, the Act gives certain congressional committee members the power to "request in writing that the Attorney General apply for the appointment of an independent counsel." The Attorney General is required to respond to this request within a specified time but is not required to accede to the request.

The proceedings in this case provide an example of how the Act works in practice. In 1982, two Subcommittees of the House of Representatives issued subpoenas directing the Environmental Protection Agency (EPA) to produce certain documents relating to the efforts of the EPA and the Land and Natural Resources Division of the Justice Department to enforce the "Superfund Law." At that time, appellee Olson was the Assistant Attorney General for the Office of Legal Counsel (OLC), appellee Schmults was Deputy Attorney General, and appellee Dinkins was the Assistant Attorney General for the Land and Natural Resources Division. Acting on the advice of the Justice Department, the President ordered the Administrator of EPA to invoke executive privilege to withhold certain of the documents on the ground that they contained "enforcement sensitive information." The Administrator obeyed this order and withheld the documents. In response, the House voted to hold the Administrator in contempt, after which the Administrator and the United States together filed a lawsuit against the House. The conflict abated in March 1983, when the administration agreed to give the House Subcommittees limited access to the documents.

The following year, the House Judiciary Committee began an investigation into the Justice Department's role in the controversy over the EPA documents. During this investigation, appellee Olson testified before a House Subcommittee on March 10, 1983. Both before and after that testimony, the Department complied with several Committee requests to produce certain documents. Other documents were at first withheld, although these documents were eventually disclosed by the Department after the Committee learned of their existence. In 1985, the majority members of the Judiciary Committee published a lengthy report on the Committee's investigation. Report on Investigation of the Role of the Department of Justice in the Withholding of Environmental Protection Agency Documents from Congress in 1982–83, H.R.Rep. No. 99–435 (1985). The report not only criticized various officials in the Department of Justice for their role in the EPA executive privilege dispute, but it also suggested that appellee Olson had given false and misleading testimony to the Subcommittee on March 10, 1983, and that appellees Schmults and Dinkins had wrongfully withheld certain documents from the Committee, thus obstructing the Committee's investigation. The Chairman of the Judiciary Committee forwarded a copy of the report to the Attorney General with a request, pursuant to 28 U.S.C. § 592(c), that he seek the appointment of an independent counsel to investigate the allegations against Olson, Schmults, and Dinkins.

The Attorney General directed the Public Integrity Section of the Criminal Division to conduct a preliminary investigation. The Section's report concluded that the appointment of an independent counsel was warranted to investigate the Committee's allegations with respect to all three appellees. After consulting with other Department officials, however, the Attorney

General chose to apply to the Special Division for the appointment of an independent counsel solely with respect to appellee Olson. The Attorney General accordingly requested appointment of an independent counsel to investigate whether Olson's March 10, 1983, testimony

> "regarding the completeness of [OLC's] response to the Judiciary Committee's request for OLC documents, and regarding his knowledge of EPA's willingness to turn over certain disputed documents to Congress, violated 18 U.S.C. § 1505, § 1001, or any other provision of federal criminal law."

The Attorney General also requested that the independent counsel have authority to investigate "any other matter related to that allegation."

On April 23, 1986, the Special Division appointed James C. McKay as independent counsel to investigate

> "whether the testimony of ... Olson and his revision of such testimony on March 10, 1983, violated either 18 U.S.C. § 1505 or § 1001, or any other provision of federal law."

The court also ordered that the independent counsel

> "shall have jurisdiction to investigate any other allegation of evidence of violation of any Federal criminal law by Theodore Olson developed during investigations, by the Independent Counsel, referred to above, and connected with or arising out of that investigation, and Independent Counsel shall have jurisdiction to prosecute for any such violation."

McKay later resigned as independent counsel, and on May 29, 1986, the Division appointed appellant Morrison as his replacement, with the same jurisdiction.

In January, 1987, appellant asked the Attorney General pursuant to § 594(e) to refer to her as "related matters" the Committee's allegations against appellees Schmults and Dinkins. The Attorney General refused to refer the matters, concluding that his decision not to request the appointment of an independent counsel in regard to those matters was final under § 592(b)(1). Appellant then asked the Special Division to order that the matters be referred to her under § 594(e). On April 2, 1987, the Division ruled that the Attorney General's decision not to seek appointment of an independent counsel with respect to Schmults and Dinkins was final and unreviewable under § 592(b)(1), and that therefore the court had no authority to make the requested referral. *In re Olson,* 260 U.S.App.D.C. 168, 818 F.2d 34. The court ruled, however, that its original grant of jurisdiction to appellant was broad enough to permit inquiry into whether Olson may have conspired with others, including Schmults and Dinkins, to obstruct the Committee's investigation.

Following this ruling, in May and June, 1987, appellant caused a grand jury to issue and serve subpoenas *ad testificandum* and *duces tecum* on appellees. All three appellees moved to quash the subpoenas, claiming, among other things, that the independent counsel provisions of the Act were unconstitutional, and that appellant accordingly had no authority to proceed. On July 20, 1987, the District Court upheld the constitutionality of the Act and denied the motions to quash. *In re Sealed Case,* 665 F. Supp. 56 (DC). The court subsequently ordered that appellees be held in contempt pursuant to 28 U.S.C. § 1826(a) for continuing to refuse to comply with the subpoenas. The court stayed the effect of its contempt orders pending expedited appeal.

A divided Court of Appeals reversed. *In re Sealed Case,* 267 U.S.App.D.C. 178, 838 F.2d 476 (1988). The majority ruled first that an independent counsel is not an "inferior Officer" of the United States for purposes of the Appointments Clause. Accordingly, the court found the Act invalid because it does not provide for the independent counsel to be nominated by the President and confirmed by the Senate, as the Clause requires for "principal" officers. The court then went on to consider several alternative grounds for its conclusion that the statute was unconstitutional. In the majority's view, the Act also violates the Appointments Clause insofar as it empowers a court of law to appoint an "inferior" officer who performs core executive functions; the Act's delegation of various powers to the Special Division violates the limitations of Article III; the Act's restrictions on the Attorney General's power to remove an independent counsel violate the separation of powers; and finally, the Act interferes with the Executive Branch's prerogative to "take care that the Laws be faithfully executed," Art. II, § 3. The dissenting judge was of the view that the Act was constitutional. 267 U.S.App.D.C. at 238, 838 F.2d at 536. Appellant then sought review by this Court, and we noted probable jurisdiction. 484 U.S. 1058 (1988). We now reverse. ...

III

The Appointments Clause of Article II reads as follows:

> "[The President] shall nominate, and by and with the Advice and Consent of the Senate, shall appoint Ambassadors, other public Ministers and Consuls, Judges of the Supreme Court, and all other Officers of the United States, whose Appointments are not herein otherwise provided for, and which shall be established by Law: but the Congress may by Law vest the Appointment of such inferior Officers, as they think proper, in the President alone, in the Courts of Law, or in the Heads of Departments." U.S. Const., Art. II, § 2, cl. 2.

The parties do not dispute that "[t]he Constitution for purposes of appointment ... divides all its officers into two classes." "[P]rincipal officers are selected by the President with the advice and consent of the Senate. Inferior officers Congress may allow to be appointed by the President alone, by the heads of departments, or by the Judiciary." The initial question is, accordingly, whether appellant is an "inferior" or a "principal" officer. If she is the latter, as the Court of Appeals concluded, then the Act is in violation of the Appointments Clause.

The line between "inferior" and "principal" officers is one that is far from clear, and the Framers provided little guidance into where it should be drawn. We need not attempt here to decide exactly where the line falls between the two types of officers, because in our view appellant clearly falls on the "inferior officer" side of that line. ... First, appellant is subject to removal by a higher Executive Branch official. ... Second, appellant is empowered by the Act to perform only certain, limited duties. ... Third, appellant's office is limited in jurisdiction.

This does not, however, end our inquiry under the Appointments Clause. Appellees argue that even if appellant is an "inferior" officer, the Clause does not empower Congress to place the power to appoint such an officer outside the Executive Branch. They contend that the Clause does not contemplate congressional authorization of "interbranch appointments," in which an officer of one branch is appointed by officers of another branch. The relevant language of the Appointments Clause is worth repeating. It reads: "... but the Congress may by Law vest the Appointment of such inferior Officers, as they think proper, in the President alone, in the courts of Law, or in the Heads of Departments." On its face, the language of this "excepting clause" admits of no limitation on interbranch appointments. Indeed, the inclusion of "as they think proper" seems clearly to give Congress significant discretion to determine whether it is "proper" to vest the appointment of, for example, executive officials in the "courts of Law." ...

In the light of the Act's provision making the judges of the Special Division ineligible to participate in any matters relating to an independent counsel they have appointed, we do not think that appointment of the independent counsel by the court runs afoul of the constitutional limitation on "incongruous" interbranch appointments.

IV

Appellees next contend that the powers vested in the Special Division by the Act conflict with Article III of the Constitution. ...

Most importantly, the Act vests in the Special Division the power to choose who will serve as independent counsel and the power to define his or her jurisdiction. Clearly, once it is accepted that the Appointments Clause gives Congress the power to vest the appointment of officials such as the independent counsel in the "courts of Law," there can be no Article III objection to the Special Division's exercise of that power, as the power itself derives from the Appointments Clause, a source of authority for judicial actionthat is independent of Article III.[16] Appellees contend, however, that the Division's Appointments Clause powers do not encompass the power to define the independent counsel's jurisdiction. ...

Leaving aside for the moment the Division's power to terminate an independent counsel, we do not think that Article III absolutely prevents Congress from vesting these other miscellaneous powers in the Special Division pursuant to the Act. As we observed above, one purpose of the broad prohibition upon the courts' exercise of "executive or administrative duties of a nonjudicial nature," is to maintain the separation between the Judiciary and the other branches of the Federal Government by ensuring that judges do not encroach upon executive or legislative authority or undertake tasks that are more properly accomplished by those branches. In this case, the miscellaneous powers described above do not impermissibly trespass upon the authority of the Executive Branch. ...

We emphasize, nevertheless, that the Special Division has *no* authority to take any action or undertake any duties that are not specifically authorized by the Act. The gradual expansion of the authority of the Special Division might in another context be a bureaucratic success story, but it would be one that would have serious constitutional ramifications. The record in other cases involving independent counsel indicate that the Special Division has at times given advisory opinions or issued orders that are not directly authorized by the Act. Two examples of this were cited by the Court of Appeals, which noted that the Special Division issued "orders" that ostensibly exempted the independent counsel from conflict-of-interest laws. In another case, the Division reportedly ordered that a counsel postpone an investigation into certain allegations until the completion of related state criminal proceedings. The propriety of the Special Division's actions in these instances is not before us as such, but we nonetheless think it appropriate to point out not only that there is no authorization for such actions in the Act itself, but that the Division's exercise of unauthorized powers risks the transgression of the constitutional limitations of Article III that we have just discussed.

V

We now turn to consider whether the Act is invalid under the constitutional principle of separation of powers. Two related issues must be addressed: The first is whether the provision of the Act restricting the Attorney General's power to remove the independent counsel to only those instances in which he can show "good cause," taken by itself, impermissibly interferes with the President's exercise of his constitutionally appointed functions. The second is whether, taken as a whole, the Act violates the separation of powers by reducing the President's ability to control the prosecutorial powers wielded by the independent counsel. ...

A

... Considering for the moment the "good cause" removal provision in isolation from the other parts of the Act at issue in this case, we cannot say that the imposition of a "good cause" standard for removal by itself unduly trammels on executive authority. There is no real dispute that the functions performed by the independent counsel are "executive" in the sense that they are law enforcement functions that typically have been undertaken by officials within the Executive Branch. As we noted above, however, the independent counsel is an inferior officer under the Appointments Clause, with limited jurisdiction and tenure and lacking policymaking or significant administrative authority. Although the counsel exercises no small amount of discretion and judgment in deciding how to carry out his or her duties under the Act, we simply do not see how the President's need to control the exercise of that discretion is so central to the functioning of the Executive Branch as to require as a matter of constitutional law that the counsel be terminable at will by the President.

Nor do we think that the "good cause" removal provision at issue here impermissibly burdens the President's power to control or supervise the independent counsel, as an executive official, in the execution of his or her duties under the Act. This is not a case in which the power to remove an executive official has been completely stripped from the President, thus providing no means for the President to ensure the "faithful execution" of the laws. Rather, because the independent counsel may be terminated for "good cause," the Executive, through the Attorney General, retains ample authority to assure that the counsel is competently performing his or her statutory responsibilities in a manner that comports with the provisions of the Act. Although we need not decide in this case exactly what is encompassed within the term "good cause" under the Act, the legislative history of the removal provision also makes clear that the Attorney General may remove an independent counsel for "misconduct." Here, as with the provision of the Act conferring the appointment authority of the independent counsel on the special court, the congressional determination to limit the removal power of the Attorney General was essential, in the view of Congress, to establish the necessary independence of the office. We do not think that this limitation as it presently stands sufficiently deprives the President of control over the independent counsel to interfere impermissibly with his constitutional obligation to ensure the faithful execution of the laws.

B

The final question to be addressed is whether the Act, taken as a whole, violates the principle of separation of powers by unduly interfering with the role of the Executive Branch. Time and again we have reaffirmed the importance in our constitutional scheme of the separation of governmental powers into the three coordinate branches. ...

We observe first that this case does not involve an attempt by Congress to increase its own powers at the expense of the Executive Branch. ... Similarly, we do not think that the Act works any *judicial* usurpation of properly executive functions. ... Finally, we do not think that the Act "impermissibly undermine[s]" the powers of the Executive Branch, or "disrupts the proper balance between the coordinate branches [by] prevent [ing] the Executive Branch from accomplishing its constitutionally assigned functions." ...

VI

In sum, we conclude today that it does not violate the Appointments Clause for Congress to vest the appointment of independent counsel in the Special Division; that the powers exercised by the Special Division under the Act do not violate Article III; and that the Act does not violate the separation-of-powers principle by impermissibly interfering with the functions of the Executive Branch. The decision of the Court of Appeals is therefore *Reversed.*

Justice SCALIA, dissenting.

... That is what this suit is about. Power. The allocation of power among Congress, the President, and the courts in such fashion as to preserve the equilibrium the Constitution sought to establish—so that "a gradual concentration of the several powers in the same department," Federalist No. 51, p. 321 (J. Madison), can effectively be resisted. Frequently an issue of this sort will come before the Court clad, so to speak, in sheep's clothing: the potential of the asserted principle to effect important change in the equilibrium of power is not immediately evident, and must be discerned by a careful and perceptive analysis. But this wolf comes as a wolf. ...

II

If to describe this case is not to decide it, the concept of a government of separate and coordinate powers no longer has meaning. The Court devotes most of its attention to such relatively technical details as the Appointments Clause and the removal power, addressing briefly and only at the end of its opinion the separation of powers. As my prologue suggests, I think that has it backwards. Our opinions are full of the recognition that it is the principle of separation of powers, and the inseparable corollary that each department's "defense must ... be made commensurate to the danger of attack," Federalist No. 51, p. 322 (J. Madison), which gives comprehensible content to the Appointments Clause, and determines the appropriate scope of the removal power. Thus, while I will subsequently discuss why our appointments and removal jurisprudence does not support today's holding, I begin with a consideration of the fountainhead of that jurisprudence, the separation and equilibration of powers. ...

To repeat, Article II, § 1, cl. 1, of the Constitution provides:

> "The executive Power shall be vested in a President of the United States." ...

It is not for us to determine, and we have never presumed to determine, how much of the purely executive powers of government must be within the full control of the President. The Constitution prescribes that they *all* are. ...

The Court has, nonetheless, replaced the clear constitutional prescription that the executive power belongs to the President with a "balancing test." What are the standards to determine how the balance is to be struck, that is, how much removal of Presidential power is too much? Many countries of the world get along with an executive that is much weaker than ours—in fact, entirely dependent upon the continued support of the legislature. Once we depart from the text of the Constitution, just where short of that do we stop? The most amazing feature of the Court's opinion is that it does not even purport to give an answer. It simply *announces,* with no analysis, that the ability to control the decision whether to investigate and prosecute the President's closest advisers, and indeed the President himself, is not "so central to the functioning of the Executive Branch" as to be constitutionally required to be within the President's control. Apparently that is so because we say it is so. Having abandoned as the basis for our decision-making the text of Article II that "the executive Power" must be vested in the President, the Court does not even attempt to craft a *substitute* criterion—a "justiciable standard," however remote from the Constitution—that today governs, and in the future will govern, the decision of such questions. Evidently, the governing standard is to be what might be called the unfettered wisdom of a majority of this Court, revealed to an obedient people on a case-by-case basis. This is not only not the government of laws that the Constitution established; it is not a government of laws at all. ...

In sum, this statute does deprive the President of substantial control over the prosecutory functions performed by the independent counsel, and it does substantially affect the balance of powers. That the Court could possibly conclude otherwise demonstrates both the wisdom of our former constitutional system, in which the degree of reduced control and political impairment were irrelevant, since *all* purely executive power had to be in the President; and the folly of the new system of standardless judicial allocation of powers we adopt today.

III

... The independent counsel is not even subordinate to the President. The Court essentially admits as much, noting that "appellant may not be 'subordinate' to the Attorney General (and the President) insofar as she possesses a degree of independent discretion to exercise the powers delegated to her under the Act." In fact, there is no doubt about it. As noted earlier, the Act specifically grants her the "*full* power and *independent* authority to exercise *all* investigative and prosecutorial functions of the Department of Justice," and makes her removable only for "good cause," a limitation specifically intended to ensure that she be *independent* of, not *subordinate* to, the President and the Attorney General.

Because appellant is not subordinate to another officer, she is not an "inferior" officer and her appointment other than by the President with the advice and consent of the Senate is unconstitutional.

Notes and Questions

1. *The sole dissent.* Why do you think Justice Scalia was the sole dissenter in this case? How does his argument compare to the majority's? Do you agree that this "wolf comes as a wolf"?
2. *Which is best?* Which opinion do you find most persuasive on the constitutionality of an independent counsel?
3. *Video.* Do you agree with this video that Justice Scalia's *Morrison* opinion was a "great dissent" and is recognized as correct today? Or was Scalia wrong then and wrong today? See The Federalist Society, The Great Dissent: Justice Scalia's Opinion in *Morrison v. Olson*, Oct. 7, 2018, posted at https://www.youtube.com/watch?v=gk8IKBWrTqw&list=PLsFE_Nvl6h_Y75KGR5p-kGqcFisGvBnO9S&index=89.

3. Recess Appointments

In *Morrison*, you read about the Appointments Clause. Usually, the Senate gives its advice and consent to someone the president has nominated. The next case, *NLRB v. Noel Canning*, determines the president's power to make an appointment while the Senate is in recess. Recess appointments permit the president to move forward on nominations to keep the government running when the Senate is in recess and can't act on a nominee.

President John F. Kennedy appointed Thurgood Marshall, later a Supreme Court Justice, to the Second Circuit Court of Appeals in October 1961, during a recess. The Senate approved Marshall in September 1962. President Dwight Eisenhower nominated Chief Justice Earl Warren (1953) and Associate Justices William Brennan (1956) and Potter Stewart (1958) to the Supreme Court during a Senate recess. The Senate later confirmed all three. President George Washington appointed John Rutledge as Chief Justice during a 1795 recess; the Senate later rejected him. See AP, A look at presidential recess appointments, *Chicago Tribune*, Aug. 1, 2015, https://www.chicagotribune.com/

sns-ap-recess-appointments-glance-story.html. Other presidents have made recess appointments to the courts and other government jobs that were later approved—or not—by the Senate.

The following opinion explains how recess appointments work and when they are constitutional. Why do you think all of the Justices agreed that President Barack Obama could not make his recess appointments? How does Justice Breyer's opinion differ from Justice Scalia's? Can you trace out the details of their arguments? Can you predict the opinions they would write, and which Justices would join them, from the oral argument, https://www.oyez.org/cases/2013/12-1281?

NLRB v. Noel Canning

SUPREME COURT OF THE UNITED STATES, 2014

573 U.S. 513, 134 S.Ct. 2550

BREYER, J., delivered the opinion of the Court, in which KENNEDY, GINSBURG, SOTOMAYOR, and KAGAN, JJ., joined. SCALIA, J., filed an opinion concurring in the judgment, in which ROBERTS, C.J., and THOMAS and ALITO, JJ., joined.

Ordinarily the President must obtain "the Advice and Consent of the Senate" before appointing an "Office[r] of the United States." U.S. Const., Art. II, § 2, cl. 2. But the Recess Appointments Clause creates an exception. It gives the President alone the power "to fill up all Vacancies that may happen during the Recess of the Senate, by granting Commissions which shall expire at the End of their next Session." Art. II, § 2, cl. 3. We here consider three questions about the application of this Clause.

The first concerns the scope of the words "recess of the Senate." Does that phrase refer only to an inter-session recess (*i.e.,* a break between formal sessions of Congress), or does it also include an intra-session recess, such as a summer recess in the midst of a session? We conclude that the Clause applies to both kinds of recess.

The second question concerns the scope of the words "vacancies that may happen." Does that phrase refer only to vacancies that first come into existence during a recess, or does it also include vacancies that arise prior to a recess but continue to exist during the recess? We conclude that the Clause applies to both kinds of vacancy.

The third question concerns calculation of the length of a "recess." The President made the appointments here at issue on January 4, 2012. At that time the Senate was in recess pursuant to a December 17, 2011, resolution providing for a series of brief recesses punctuated by "*pro forma* session[s]," with "no business ... transacted," every Tuesday and Friday through January 20, 2012. In calculating the length of a recess are we to ignore the *pro forma* sessions, thereby treating the series of brief recesses as a single, month-long recess? We conclude that we cannot ignore these *pro forma* sessions.

Our answer to the third question means that, when the appointments before us took place, the Senate was in the midst of a 3-day recess. Three days is too short a time to bring a recess within the scope of the Clause. Thus we conclude that the President lacked the power to make the recess appointments here at issue.

I

The case before us arises out of a labor dispute. The National Labor Relations Board (NLRB) found that a Pepsi-Cola distributor, Noel Canning, had unlawfully refused to reduce to writing and execute a collective-bargaining agreement with a labor union. The Board ordered the distributor to execute the agreement and to make employees whole for any losses.

The Pepsi-Cola distributor subsequently asked the Court of Appeals for the District of Columbia Circuit to set the Board's order aside. It claimed that three of the five Board members had been invalidly appointed, leaving the Board without the three lawfully appointed members necessary for it to act.

The three members in question were Sharon Block, Richard Griffin, and Terence Flynn. In 2011 the President had nominated each of them to the Board. As of January 2012, Flynn's nomination had been pending in the Senate awaiting confirmation for approximately a year. The nominations of each of the other two had been pending for a few weeks. On January 4, 2012, the President, invoking the Recess Appointments Clause, appointed all three to the Board.

The distributor argued that the Recess Appointments Clause did not authorize those appointments. It pointed out that on December 17, 2011, the Senate, by unanimous consent, had adopted a resolution providing that it would take a series of brief recesses beginning the following day. Pursuant to that resolution, the Senate held pro forma sessions every Tuesday and Friday until it returned for ordinary business on January 23, 2012. The President's January 4 appointments were made between the January 3 and January 6 pro forma sessions. In the distributor's view, each pro forma session terminated the immediately preceding recess. Accordingly, the appointments were made during a 3-day adjournment, which is not long enough to trigger the Recess Appointments Clause. …

…

III

The first question concerns the scope of the phrase "*the recess* of the Senate." Art. II, § 2, cl. 3 (emphasis added). The Constitution provides for congressional elections every two years. And the 2-year life of each elected Congress typically consists of two formal 1-year sessions, each separated from the next by an "inter-session recess." The Senate or the House of Representatives announces an inter-session recess by approving a resolution stating that it will "adjourn *sine die*," *i.e.*, without specifying a date to return (in which case Congress will reconvene when the next formal session is scheduled to begin).

The Senate and the House also take breaks in the midst of a session. The Senate or the House announces any such "intra-session recess" by adopting a resolution stating that it will "adjourn" to a fixed date, a few days or weeks or even months later. All agree that the phrase "the recess of the Senate" covers inter-session recesses. The question is whether it includes intra-session recesses as well.

In our view, the phrase "the recess" includes an intra-session recess of substantial length. Its words taken literally can refer to both types of recess. …

The upshot is that restricting the Clause to inter-session recesses would frustrate its purpose. It would make the President's recess-appointment power dependent on a formalistic distinction of Senate procedure. Moreover, the President has consistently and frequently interpreted the word "recess" to apply to intra-session recesses, and has acted on that interpretation. The Senate as a body has done nothing to deny the validity of this practice for at least three-quarters of a century. And three-quarters of a century of settled practice is long enough to entitle a practice to "great weight in a proper interpretation" of the constitutional provision. …

The greater interpretive problem is determining how long a recess must be in order to fall within the Clause. Is a break of a week, or a day, or an hour too short to count as a "recess"? The Clause itself does not say. And Justice SCALIA claims that this silence itself shows that the Framers intended the Clause to apply only to an inter-session recess. …

We agree with the Solicitor General that a 3-day recess would be too short. (Under Senate practice, "Sunday is generally not considered a day," and so is not counted for purposes of the Adjournments Clause. The Adjournments Clause reflects the fact that a 3-day break is not a significant interruption of legislative business. As the Solicitor General says, it is constitutionally *de minimis*. Brief for Petitioner 18. A Senate recess that is so short that it does not require the consent of the House is not long enough to trigger the President's recess-appointment power.

That is not to say that the President may make recess appointments during any recess that is "more than three days." Art. I, § 5, cl. 4. The Recess Appointments Clause seeks to permit the Executive Branch to function smoothly when Congress is unavailable. And though Congress has taken short breaks for almost 200 years, and there have been many thousands of recess appointments in that time, we have not found a single example of a recess appointment made during an intra-session recess that was shorter than 10 days. Nor has the Solicitor General. Indeed, the Office of Legal Counsel once informally advised against making a recess appointment during a 6-day intra-session recess. The lack of examples suggests that the recess-appointment power is not needed in that context. (The length of a recess is "ordinarily calculated by counting the calendar days running from the day after the recess begins and including the day the recess ends." …

In sum, we conclude that the phrase "the recess" applies to both intra-session and inter-session recesses. If a Senate recess is so short that it does not require the consent of the House, it is too short to trigger the Recess Appointments Clause. See Art. I, § 5, cl. 4. And a recess lasting less than 10 days is presumptively too short as well.

IV

The second question concerns the scope of the phrase "vacancies *that may happen* during the recess of the Senate." Art. II, § 2, cl. 3 (emphasis added). All agree that the phrase applies to vacancies that initially occur during a recess. But does it also apply to vacancies that initially occur before a recess and continue to exist during the recess? In our view the phrase applies to both kinds of vacancy. ...

While we concede that both interpretations carry with them some risk of undesirable consequences, we believe the narrower interpretation risks undermining constitutionally conferred powers more seriously and more often. It would prevent the President from making any recess appointment that arose before a recess, no matter who the official, no matter how dire the need, no matter how uncontroversial the appointment, and no matter how late in the session the office fell vacant. Overall, like Attorney General Wirt, we believe the broader interpretation more consistent with the Constitution's "reason and spirit." ...

In light of some linguistic ambiguity, the basic purpose of the Clause, and the historical practice we have described, we conclude that the phrase "all vacancies" includes vacancies that come into existence while the Senate is in session.

V

The third question concerns the calculation of the length of the Senate's "recess." ...

The President made the recess appointments before us on January 4, 2012, in between the January 3 and the January 6 *pro forma* sessions. We must determine the significance of these sessions—that is, whether, for purposes of the Clause, we should treat them as periods when the Senate was in session or as periods when it was in recess. If the former, the period between January 3 and January 6 was a 3-day recess, which is too short to trigger the President's recess-appointment power. If the latter, however, then the 3-day period was part of a much longer recess during which the President did have the power to make recess appointments.

The Solicitor General argues that we must treat the *pro forma* sessions as periods of recess. He says that these "sessions" were sessions in name only because the Senate was in recess as a *functional* matter. The Senate, he contends, remained in a single, unbroken recess from January 3, when the second session of the 112th Congress began by operation of the Twentieth Amendment, until January 23, when the Senate reconvened to do regular business.

In our view, however, the *pro forma* sessions count as sessions, not as periods of recess. We hold that, for purposes of the Recess Appointments Clause, the Senate is in session when it says it is, provided that, under its own rules, it retains the capacity to transact Senate business. The Senate met that standard here.

The standard we apply is consistent with the Constitution's broad delegation of authority to the Senate to determine how and when to conduct its business. The Constitution explicitly empowers the Senate to "determine the Rules of its Proceedings." Art. I, § 5, cl. 2. And we have held that "all matters of method are open to the determination" of the Senate, as long as there is "a reasonable relation between the mode or method of proceeding established by the rule and the result which is sought to be attained" and the rule does not "ignore constitutional restraints or violate fundamental rights." ...

For these reasons, we conclude that we must give great weight to the Senate's own determination of when it is and when it is not in session. But our deference to the Senate cannot be absolute. When the Senate is without the *capacity* to act, under its own rules, it is not in session even if it so declares. In that circumstance, the Senate is not simply unlikely or unwilling to act upon nominations of the President. It is *unable* to do so. The purpose of the Clause is to ensure the continued functioning of the Federal Government while the Senate is unavailable. This purpose would count for little were we to treat the Senate as though it were in session even when it lacks the ability to provide its "advice and consent." Art. II, § 2, cl. 2. Accordingly, we conclude that when the Senate declares that it is in session and possesses the capacity, under its own rules, to conduct business, it is in session for purposes of the Clause.

Applying this standard, we find that the *pro forma* sessions were sessions for purposes of the Clause. First, the Senate said it was in session. The Journal of the Senate and the Congressional Record indicate that the Senate convened for a series of twice-weekly "sessions" from December 20 through January 20. And these reports of the Senate "must be assumed to speak the truth."

Second, the Senate's rules make clear that during its *pro forma* sessions, despite its resolution that it would conduct no business, the Senate retained the power to conduct business. During any *pro forma* session, the Senate could have conducted business simply by passing a unanimous consent agreement. The Senate in fact conducts much of its business through unanimous consent. Senate rules presume that a quorum is present unless a present Senator questions it. And when the Senate has a quorum, an agreement is unanimously passed if, upon its proposal, no present Senator objects. It is consequently unsurprising that the Senate *has* enacted legislation during *pro forma* sessions even when it has said that no business will be transacted. Indeed, the Senate passed a bill by unanimous consent during the second *pro forma* session after its December 17 adjournment. And that bill quickly became law.

By way of contrast, we do not see how the Senate could conduct business during a recess. It could terminate the recess and then, when in session, pass a bill. But in that case, of course, the Senate would no longer be in recess. It would be in session. And that is the crucial point. Senate rules make clear that, once in session, the Senate can act even if it has earlier said that it would not. ...

VI

The Recess Appointments Clause responds to a structural difference between the Executive and Legislative Branches: The Executive Branch is perpetually in operation, while the Legislature only acts in intervals separated by recesses. The purpose of the Clause is to allow the Executive to continue operating while the Senate is unavailable. We believe that the Clause's text, standing alone, is ambiguous. It does not resolve whether the President may make appointments during intra-session recesses, or whether he may fill pre-recess vacancies. But the broader reading better serves the Clause's structural function. Moreover, that broader reading is reinforced by centuries of history, which we are hesitant to disturb. We thus hold that the Constitution empowers the President to fill any existing vacancy during any recess—intra-session or inter-session—of sufficient length.

Justice SCALIA would render illegitimate thousands of recess appointments reaching all the way back to the founding era. More than that: Calling the Clause an "anachronism," he would basically read it out of the Constitution. He performs this act of judicial excision in the name of liberty. We fail to see how excising the Recess Appointments Clause preserves freedom. In fact, Alexander Hamilton observed in the very first Federalist Paper that "the vigour of government is essential to the security of liberty." The Federalist No. 1, at 5. And the Framers included the Recess Appointments Clause to preserve the "vigour of government" at times when an important organ of Government, the United States Senate, is in recess. Justice SCALIA's interpretation of the Clause would defeat the power of the Clause to achieve that objective.

The foregoing discussion should refute Justice SCALIA's claim that we have "embrace[d]" an "adverse-possession theory of executive power." Instead, as in all cases, we interpret the Constitution in light of its text, purposes, and "our whole experience" as a Nation. And we look to the actual practice of Government to inform our interpretation.

Given our answer to the last question before us, we conclude that the Recess Appointments Clause does not give the President the constitutional authority to make the appointments here at issue. Because the Court of Appeals reached the same ultimate conclusion (though for reasons we reject), its judgment is affirmed.

It is so ordered.

Justice SCALIA, with whom THE CHIEF JUSTICE, Justice THOMAS, and Justice ALITO join, concurring in the judgment.

... Today's Court agrees that the appointments were invalid, but for the far narrower reason that they were made during a 3-day break in the Senate's session. On its way to that result, the majority sweeps away the key textual limitations on the recess-appointment power. It holds, first, that the President can make appointments without the Senate's participation even during short breaks in the middle of the Senate's session, and second, that those appointments can fill offices that became vacant long before the break in which they were filled. The majority justifies those atextual results on an adverse-possession theory of executive authority: Presidents have long claimed the powers in question, and the Senate has not disputed those claims with sufficient vigor, so the Court should not "upset the compromises and working arrangements that the elected branches of Government themselves have reached."

The Court's decision transforms the recess-appointment power from a tool carefully designed to fill a narrow and specific need into a weapon to be wielded by future Presidents against future Senates. To reach that result, the majority casts aside the plain, original meaning of the constitutional text in deference to late-arising historical practices that are ambiguous at best. The majority's insistence on deferring to the Executive's untenably broad interpretation of the power is in clear conflict with our precedent and forebodes a diminution of this Court's role in controversies involving the separation of powers and the structure of government. I concur in the judgment only. ...

II. Intra-Session Breaks

The first question presented is whether "the Recess of the Senate," during which the President's recess-appointment power is active, is (a) the period between two of the Senate's formal sessions, or (b) any break in the Senate's proceedings. I would hold that "the Recess" is the gap between sessions and that the appointments at issue here are invalid because they undisputedly were made *during* the Senate's session. The Court's contrary conclusion—that "the Recess" includes "breaks in the midst of a session,"—is inconsistent with the Constitution's text and structure, and it requires judicial fabrication of vague, unadministrable limits on the recess-appointment power (thus defined) that overstep the judicial role. And although the majority relies heavily on "historical practice," no practice worthy of our deference supports the majority's conclusion on this issue. ...

What does all this amount to? In short: Intra-session recess appointments were virtually unheard of for the first 130 years of the Republic, were deemed unconstitutional by the first Attorney General to address them, were not openly defended by the Executive until 1921, were not made in significant numbers until after World War II, and have been repeatedly criticized as unconstitutional by Senators of both parties. It is astonishing for the majority to assert that this history lends "strong support," to its interpretation of the Recess Appointments Clause. And the majority's contention that recent executive practice in this area merits deference because the Senate has not done more to oppose it is utterly divorced from our precedent.

Moreover, the majority's insistence that the Senate gainsay an executive practice "as a body" in order to prevent the Executive from acquiring power by adverse possession, will systematically favor the expansion of executive power at the expense of Congress. In any controversy between the political branches over a separation-of-powers question, staking out a position and defending it over time is far easier for the Executive Branch than for the Legislative Branch. All Presidents have a high interest in expanding the powers of their office, since the more power the President can wield, the more effectively he can implement his political agenda; whereas individual Senators may have little interest in opposing Presidential encroachment on legislative prerogatives, especially when the encroacher is a President who is the leader of their own party. (The majority would not be able to point to a lack of "formal action" by the Senate "as a body" challenging intra-session recess appointments, had the appointing President's party in the Senate not blocked such action on multiple occasions.) And when the President wants to assert a power and establish a precedent, he faces neither the collective-action problems nor the procedural inertia inherent in the legislative process. The majority's methodology thus all but guarantees the continuing aggrandizement of the Executive Branch.

...

III B. Historical Practice

For the reasons just given, it is clear that the Constitution authorizes the President to fill unilaterally only those vacancies that arise during a recess, not every vacancy that happens to exist during a recess. Again, however, the majority says "[h]istorical practice" requires the broader interpretation. And again the majority is mistaken. Even if the Constitution were wrongly thought to be ambiguous on this point, a fair recounting of the relevant history does not support the majority's interpretation. ...

IV. Conclusion

What the majority needs to sustain its judgment is an ambiguous text and a clear historical practice. What it has is a clear text and an at-best-ambiguous historical practice. Even if the Executive could accumulate power through adverse possession by engaging in a *consistent* and *unchallenged* practice over a long period of time, the oft-disputed practices at issue here would not meet that standard. Nor have those practices created any justifiable expectations that could be disappointed by enforcing the Constitution's original meaning. There is thus no ground for the majority's deference to the unconstitutional recess-appointment practices of the Executive Branch.

The majority replaces the Constitution's text with a new set of judge-made rules to govern recess appointments. Henceforth, the Senate can avoid triggering the President's now-vast recess-appointment power by the odd contrivance of never adjourning for more than three days without holding a *pro forma* session at which it is understood that no business will be conducted. How this new regime will work in practice remains to be seen. Perhaps it will reduce the prevalence of recess appointments. But perhaps not: Members of the President's party in Congress may be able to prevent the Senate from holding *pro forma* sessions with the necessary frequency, and if the House and Senate disagree, the President may be able to adjourn both "to such Time as he shall think proper." U.S. Const., Art. II, § 3. In any event, the limitation upon the President's appointment power is there not for the benefit of the Senate, but for the protection of the people; it should not be dependent on Senate action for its existence.

The real tragedy of today's decision is not simply the abolition of the Constitution's limits on the recess-appointment power and the substitution of a novel framework invented by this Court. It is the damage done to our separation-of-powers jurisprudence more generally. It is not every day that we encounter a proper case or controversy requiring interpretation of the Constitution's structural provisions. Most of the time, the interpretation of those provisions is left to the political branches—which, in deciding how much respect to afford the constitutional text, often take their cues from this Court. We should therefore take every opportunity to affirm the primacy of the Constitution's enduring principles over the politics of the moment. Our failure to do so today will resonate well beyond the particular dispute at hand. Sad, but true: The Court's embrace of the adverse-possession theory of executive power (a characterization the majority resists but does not refute) will be cited in diverse contexts, including those presently unimagined, and will have the effect of aggrandizing the Presidency beyond its constitutional bounds and undermining respect for the separation of powers.

I concur in the judgment only.

Notes and Questions

1. *This was the Court's first opinion on recess appointments.* Do you agree that "the majority set some limits but still kept that authority mostly intact"? Lyle Denniston, *Opinion analysis: Pragmatism triumphs over formalism*, SCOTUSblog (Jun. 26, 2014, 12:56 PM), https://www.scotusblog.com/2014/06/opinion-analysis-pragmatism-triumphs-over-formalism/.
2. *Are you persuaded by the dissenters' intent "to strip presidents of nearly all power to make such appointments. ..."* *Id.* Do you agree that "the scope of that defeat for Obama in particular and presidents in general seemed quite small." *Id.*
3. *What do you think of Denniston's further analysis of the opinion:*

> Whatever those who wrote the original Constitution might actually have intended by what they wrote in that clause, the Court majority said the real clues to its meaning are found in some two centuries of "compromises and working arrangements" between the branches of government at opposite ends of Pennsylvania Avenue in Washington.
>
> The split within the Court was as vivid an example as can be given of constitutional pragmatism winning out over constitutional formalism, and a very clear illustration of how the Constitution gets some of its most basic meaning from experience rather than from logic or hard-and-fast legal rules.
>
> It thus was absolutely no surprise that the majority opinion would have been written by Justice Stephen G. Breyer, who has established himself as the most pragmatic of the Justices, and that the separate opinion (a concurrence but reading much like a dissent) would have been written by Justice Antonin Scalia, long recognized as the devotee of a Constitution of rules rooted in Founding era understandings. *Id.*

Does this distinction between the Justices' reasoning make sense to you?

4. The President's Power to Remove

The following case, *Seila Law*, is a very hard separation-of-powers case. It describes the Consumer Financial Protection Bureau, an agency that had *one* Director. The case concluded that the provision violated the Constitution. The case was decided 5–4. The dissenters agreed with majority author Chief Justice Roberts that the Director provision could be severed from the rest of the law but left the rest of the law intact.

You will notice the case says that usually there are no limitations on the President's ability to fire an agency head but that there are two exceptions. One exception is the case you read about above, *Morrison*, which upheld the independent counsel provision of the Ethics in Government Act. The second exemption is an older case from 1935, *Humphrey's Executor* v. *United States*. Humphrey was appointed head of the Federal Trade Commission (FTC) by the President and confirmed by the Senate. President Franklin Roosevelt later asked Humphrey to resign, but he did not. Therefore, Roosevelt fired Humphrey. The Court unanimously upheld the FTC Act, which limited the President's power to fire Humphrey to "inefficiency, neglect of duty, or malfeasance in office." At the time *Seila* was argued, some people wondered if *Morrison* and *Humphrey* might be overruled.

Does *Humphrey* mean that the President can be limited in his abilities to remove the Director of the CFPB? This Court says "no" because the CFPB Director was the sole director and not one of a group of directors. Justices Thomas and Gorsuch asked for *Humphrey* to be overruled. Justice Kagan's dissent followed *Humphrey*.

Read the oral argument, available at https://www.oyez.org/cases/2019/19-7. Do the Justices' questions in this case predict how they all will vote? Did either side's attorney do a better job than the *other*?

Seila Law LLC v. Consumer Financial Protection Bureau

SUPREME COURT OF THE UNITED STATES, 2020

591 U.S. ___, 140 S.Ct. 2183

ROBERTS, C. J., delivered the opinion of the Court with respect to Parts I, II, and III, in which THOMAS, ALITO, GORSUCH, and KAVANAUGH, JJ., joined, and an opinion with respect to Part IV, in which ALITO and KAVANAUGH, JJ., joined. THOMAS, J., filed an opinion concurring in part and dissenting in part, in which GORSUCH, J., joined. KAGAN, J., filed an opinion concurring in the judgment with respect to severability and dissenting in part, in which GINSBURG, BREYER, and SOTOMAYOR, JJ., joined.

In the wake of the 2008 financial crisis, Congress established the Consumer Financial Protection Bureau (CFPB), an independent regulatory agency tasked with ensuring that consumer debt products are safe and transparent. In organizing the CFPB, Congress deviated from the structure of nearly every other independent administrative agency in our history. Instead of placing the agency under the leadership of a board with multiple members, Congress provided that the CFPB would be led by a single Director, who serves for a longer term than the President and cannot be removed by the President except for inefficiency, neglect, or malfeasance. The CFPB Director has no boss, peers, or voters to report to. Yet the Director wields vast rulemaking, enforcement, and adjudicatory authority over a significant portion of the U.S. economy. The question before us is whether this arrangement violates the Constitution's separation of powers. ...

The President's power to remove—and thus supervise—those who wield executive power on his behalf follows from the text of Article II, was settled by the First Congress, and was confirmed in the landmark decision *Myers v. United States*, 272 U.S. 52, 47 S.Ct. 21, 71 L.Ed. 160 (1926). Our precedents have recognized only two exceptions to the President's unrestricted removal power. In *Humphrey's Executor* v. *United States*, 295 U.S. 602, 55 S.Ct. 869, 79 L.Ed. 1611 (1935), we held that Congress could create expert agencies led by a *group* of principal officers removable by the President only for good cause. And in *United States v. Perkins*, 116 U.S. 483, 6 S.Ct. 449, 29 L.Ed. 700 (1886), and *Morrison v. Olson*, 487 U.S. 654, 108 S.Ct. 2597, 101 L.Ed.2d 569 (1988), we held that Congress could provide tenure protections to certain *inferior* officers with narrowly defined duties.

We are now asked to extend these precedents to a new configuration: an independent agency that wields significant executive power and is run by a single individual who cannot be removed by the President unless certain statutory criteria are met. We decline to take that step. While we need not and do not revisit our prior decisions allowing certain limitations on the President's removal power, there are compelling reasons not to extend those precedents to the novel context of an independent agency led by a single Director. Such an agency lacks a foundation in historical practice and clashes with constitutional structure by concentrating power in a unilateral actor insulated from Presidential control.

We therefore hold that the structure of the CFPB violates the separation of powers. We go on to hold that the CFPB Director's removal protection is severable from the other statutory provisions bearing on the CFPB's authority. The agency may therefore continue to operate, but its Director, in light of our decision, must be removable by the President at will.

I A

... Congress's design for the CFPB differed from the proposals of Professor Warren and the Obama administration in one critical respect. Rather than create a traditional independent agency headed by a multimember board or commission, Congress elected to place the CFPB under the leadership of a single Director. The CFPB Director is appointed by the President with the advice and consent of the Senate. The Director serves for a term of five years, during which the President may remove the Director from office only for "inefficiency, neglect of duty, or malfeasance in office."

Unlike most other agencies, the CFPB does not rely on the annual appropriation sprocess for funding. Instead, the CFPB receives funding directly from the Federal Reserve, which is itself funded outside the appropriations process through bank assessments. Each year, the CFPB requests an amount that the Director deems "reasonably necessary to carry out" the agency's duties, and the Federal Reserve grants that request so long as it does not exceed 12% of the total operating expenses of the Federal Reserve (inflation adjusted). In recent years, the CFPB's annual budget has exceeded half a billion dollars.

B

Seila Law LLC is a California-based law firm that provides debt-related legal services to clients. In 2017, the CFPB issued a civil investigative demand to Seila Law to determine whether the firm had "engag[ed] in unlawful acts or practices in the advertising, marketing, or sale of debt relief services." The demand (essentially a subpoena) directed Seila Law to produce information and documents related to its business practices.

Seila Law asked the CFPB to set aside the demand, objecting that the agency's leadership by a single Director removable only for cause violated the separation of powers. The CFPB declined to address that claim and directed Seila Law to comply with the demand. ...

III

We hold that the CFPB's leadership by a single individual removable only for inefficiency, neglect, or malfeasance violates the separation of powers.

A

... These two exceptions—one for multimember expert agencies that do not wield substantial executive power, and one for inferior officers with limited duties and no policymaking or administrative authority—"represent what up to now have been the outermost constitutional limits of permissible congressional restrictions on the President's removal power."

B

Neither *Humphrey's Executor* nor *Morrison* resolves whether the CFPB Director's insulation from removal is constitutional. Start with *Humphrey's Executor.* Unlike the New Deal-era FTC upheld there, the CFPB is led by a single Director who cannot be described as a "body of experts" and cannot be considered "non-partisan" in the same sense as a group of officials drawn from both sides of the aisle. ...

The logic of *Morrison* also does not apply. Everyone agrees the CFPB Director is not an inferior officer, and her duties are far from limited. Unlike the independent counsel, who lacked policymaking or administrative authority, the Director has the sole responsibility to administer 19 separate consumer-protection statutes that cover everything from credit cards and car payments to mortgages and student loans. It is true that the independent counsel in *Morrison* was empowered to initiate criminal investigations and prosecutions, and in that respect wielded core executive power. But that power, while significant, was trained inward to high-ranking Governmental actors identified by others, and was confined to a specified matter in which the Department of Justice had a potential conflict of interest. By contrast, the CFPB Director has the authority to bring the coercive power of the state to bear on millions of private citizens and businesses, imposing even billion-dollar penalties through administrative adjudications and civil actions.

In light of these differences, the constitutionality of the CFPB Director's insulation from removal cannot be settled by *Humphrey's Executor* or *Morrison* alone.

C2

...

In addition to being a historical anomaly, the CFPB's single-Director configuration is incompatible with our constitutional structure. Aside from the sole exception of the Presidency, that structure scrupulously avoids concentrating power in the hands of any single individual. ...

The CFPB Director's insulation from removal by an accountable President is enough to render the agency's structure unconstitutional. But several other features of the CFPB combine to make the Director's removal protection even more problematic. In addition to lacking the most direct method of presidential control—removal at will—the agency's unique structure also forecloses certain indirect methods of Presidential control.

Because the CFPB is headed by a single Director with a five-year term, some Presidents may not have any opportunity to shape its leadership and thereby influence its activities. A President elected in 2020 would likely not appoint a CFPB Director until 2023, and a President elected in 2028 may *never* appoint one. That means an unlucky President might get elected on a consumer-protection platform and enter office only to find herself saddled with a holdover Director from a competing political party who is dead set *against* that agenda. To make matters worse, the agency's single-Director structure means the President will not have the opportunity to appoint any other leaders—such as a chair or fellow members of a Commission or Board—who can serve as a check on the Director's authority and help bring the agency in line with the President's preferred policies.

The CFPB's receipt of funds outside the appropriations process further aggravates the agency's threat to Presidential control. ...

IV

Having concluded that the CFPB's leadership by a single independent Director violates the separation of powers, we now turn to the appropriate remedy. We directed the parties to brief and argue whether the Director's removal protection was severable from the other provisions of the Dodd-Frank Act that establish the CFPB. If so, then the CFPB may continue to exist and operate notwithstanding Congress's unconstitutional attempt to insulate the agency's Director from removal by the President. There is a live controversy between the parties on that question, and resolving it is a necessary step in determining petitioner's entitlement to its requested relief. ...

If the removal restriction is not severable, then we must grant the relief requested, promptly rejecting the demand outright. If, on the other hand, the removal restriction is severable, we must instead remand for the Government to press its ratification arguments in further proceedings. Unlike the lingering ratification issue, severability presents a pure question of law that has been fully briefed and argued by the parties. ...

Because we find the Director's removal protection severable from the other provisions of Dodd-Frank that establish the CFPB, we remand for the Court of Appeals to consider whether the civil investigative demand was validly ratified.

* * *

A decade ago, we declined to extend Congress's authority to limit the President's removal power to a new situation, never before confronted by the Court. We do the same today. In our constitutional system, the executive power belongs to the President, and that power generally includes the ability to supervise and remove the agents who wield executive power in his stead. While we have previously upheld limits on the President's removal authority in certain contexts, we decline to do so when it comes to principal officers who, acting alone, wield significant executive power. The Constitution requires that such officials remain dependent on the President, who in turn is accountable to the people.

The judgment of the United States Court of Appeals for the Ninth Circuit is vacated, and the case is remanded for further proceedings consistent with this opinion.

It is so ordered.

Justice THOMAS, with whom Justice GORSUCH joins, concurring in part and dissenting in part.

The Court's decision today takes a restrained approach on the merits by limiting *Humphrey's Executor* v. *United States*, 295 U.S. 602, 55 S.Ct. 869, 79 L.Ed. 1611 (1935), rather than overruling it. At the same time, the Court takes an aggressive approach on severability by severing a provision when it is not necessary to do so. I would do the opposite.

Because the Court takes a step in the right direction by limiting *Humphrey's Executor* to "multimember expert agencies that *do not wield substantial executive power*," (emphasis added), I join Parts I, II, and III of its opinion. I respectfully dissent from the Court's severability analysis, however, because I do not believe that we should address severability in this case.

I

The decision in *Humphrey's Executor* poses a direct threat to our constitutional structure and, as a result, the liberty of the American people. The Court concludes that it is not strictly necessary for us to overrule that decision. But with today's decision, the Court has repudiated almost every aspect of *Humphrey's Executor*. In a future case, I would repudiate what is left of this erroneous precedent.

* * *

... Continued reliance on *Humphrey's Executor* to justify the existence of independent agencies creates a serious, ongoing threat to our Government's design. Leaving these unconstitutional agencies in place does not enhance this Court's legitimacy; it subverts political accountability and threatens individual liberty. We have a "responsibility to 'examin[e] without fear, and revis[e] without reluctance,' any 'hasty and crude decisions' rather than leaving 'the character of [the] law impaired, and the beauty and harmony of the [American constitutional] system destroyed by the perpetuity of error.'" We simply cannot compromise when it comes to our Government's structure. Today, the Court does enough to resolve this case, but in the future, we should reconsider *Humphrey's Executor in toto*. And I hope that we will have the will to do so.

II

While I think that the Court correctly resolves the merits of the constitutional question, I do not agree with its decision to sever the removal restriction. To resolve this case, I would simply deny the Consumer Financial Protection Bureau (CFPB) petition to enforce the civil investigative demand. ...

* * *

Given my concerns about our modern severability doctrine and the fact that severability makes no difference to the dispute before us, I would resolve this case by simply denying the CFPB's petition to enforce the civil investigative demand.

Justice KAGAN, with whom Justice GINSBURG, Justice BREYER, and Justice SOTOMAYOR join, concurring in the judgment with respect to severability and dissenting in part.

Throughout the Nation's history, this Court has left most decisions about how to structure the Executive Branch to Congress and the President, acting through legislation they both agree to. In particular, the Court has commonly allowed those two branches to create zones of administrative independence by limiting the President's power to remove agency heads. The Federal Reserve Board. The Federal Trade Commission (FTC). The National Labor Relations Board. Statute after statute establishing such entities instructs the President that he may not discharge their directors except for cause—most often phrased as inefficiency, neglect of duty, or malfeasance in office. Those statutes, whose language the Court has repeatedly approved, provide the model for the removal restriction before us today. If precedent were any guide, that provision would have survived its encounter with this Court—and so would the intended independence of the Consumer Financial Protection Bureau (CFPB). ...

I

The text of the Constitution, the history of the country, the precedents of this Court, and the need for sound and adaptable governance—all stand against the majority's opinion. They point not to the majority's "general rule" of "unrestricted removal power" with two grudgingly applied "exceptions." Rather, they bestow discretion on the legislature to structure administrative institutions as the times demand, so long as the President retains the ability to carry out his constitutional duties. And most relevant here, they give Congress wide leeway to limit the President's removal power in the interest of enhancing independence from politics in regulatory bodies like the CFPB.

A

What does the Constitution say about the separation of powers—and particularly about the President's removal authority? (Spoiler alert: about the latter, nothing at all.) ...

Finally, recall the Constitution's telltale silence: Nowhere does the text say anything about the President's power to remove subordinate officials at will. The majority professes unconcern. After all, it says, "neither is there a 'separation of powers clause' or a 'federalism clause.'" But those concepts are carved into the Constitution's text—the former in its first three articles separating powers, the latter in its enumeration of federal powers and its reservation of all else to the States. And anyway, at-will removal is hardly such a "foundational doctrine[ ]," *ibid.*: You won't find it on a civics class syllabus. That's because removal is a *tool*—one means among many, even if sometimes an important one, for a President to control executive officials. To find that authority hidden in the Constitution as a "general rule" is to discover what is nowhere there. ...

C

... So caselaw joins text and history in establishing the general permissibility of for-cause provisions giving some independence to agencies. Contrary to the majority's view, those laws do not represent a suspicious departure from illimitable presidential control over administration. For almost a century, this Court has made clear that Congress has broad discretion to enact for-cause protections in pursuit of good governance.

D

... Our Constitution, as shown earlier, entrusts such decisions to more accountable and knowledgeable actors. The document—with great good sense—sets out almost no rules about the administrative sphere. As Chief Justice Marshall wrote when he upheld the first independent financial agency: "To have prescribed the means by which government should, in all future time, execute its powers, would have been to change, entirely, the character of the instrument." *McCulloch*, 4 Wheat. at 415. That would have been, he continued, "an unwise attempt to provide, by immutable rules, for exigencies which, if foreseen at all, must have been seen dimly." And if the Constitution, for those reasons, does not lay out immutable rules, then neither should judges. This Court has usually respected that injunction. It has declined to second-guess the work of the political branches in creating independent agencies like the CFPB. In reversing course today—in spurning a "pragmatic, flexible approach to American governance" in favor of a dogmatic, inflexible one,—the majority makes a serious error.

II

... The analysis is as simple as simple can be. The CFPB Director exercises the same powers, and receives the same removal protections, as the heads of other, constitutionally permissible independent agencies. How could it be that this opinion is a dissent? ...

And in doing so, the majority again reveals its lack of interest in how agencies work. First, the premise of the majority's argument—that the CFPB head is a mini-dictator, not subject to meaningful presidential control—is wrong. As this Court has seen in the past, independent agencies are not fully independent. A for-cause removal provision, as noted earlier, leaves "ample" control over agency heads in the hands of the President. *Morrison*, 487 U.S., at 692, 108 S.Ct. 2597. He can discharge them for failing to perform their duties competently or in accordance with law, and so ensure that the laws are "faithfully executed." U.S. Const., Art. II, § 3. And he can use the many other tools attached to the Office of the Presidency—including in the CFPB's case, rulemaking review—to exert influence over discretionary policy calls. Second, the majority has nothing but intuition to back up its essentially functionalist claim that the CFPB would be less capable of exercising power if it had more than one Director (even supposing that were a suitable issue for a court to address). Maybe the CFPB would be. Or maybe not. Although a multimember format tends to frustrate the President's control over an agency, it may not lessen the agency's own ability to act with decision and dispatch. (Consider, for a recent example, the Federal Reserve Board.) That effect presumably would depend on the agency's internal organization, voting rules, and similar matters. At the least: If the Court is going to invalidate statutes based on empirical assertions like this one, it should offer some empirical support. It should not pretend that its assessment that the CFPB wields more power more dangerously than the SEC comes from someplace in the Constitution. But today the majority fails to accord even that minimal respect to Congress.

III

Recall again how this dispute got started. In the midst of the Great Recession, Congress and the President came together to create an agency with an important mission. It would protect consumers from the reckless financial practices that had caused the then-ongoing economic collapse. Not only Congress but also the President thought that the new agency, to fulfill its mandate, needed a measure of independence. So the two political branches, acting together, gave the CFPB Director the same job protection that innumerable other agency heads possess. All in all, those branches must have thought, they had done a good day's work. Relying on their experience and knowledge of administration, they had built an agency in the way best suited to carry out its functions. They had protected the public from financial chicanery and crisis. They had governed.

And now consider how the dispute ends—with five unelected judges rejecting the result of that democratic process. The outcome today will not shut down the CFPB: A different majority of this Court, including all those who join this opinion, believes that *if* the agency's removal provision is unconstitutional, it should be severed. But the majority on constitutionality jettisons a measure Congress and the President viewed as integral to the way the agency should operate. The majority does so even though the Constitution grants to Congress, acting with the President's approval, the authority to create and shape administrative bodies. And even though those branches, as compared to courts, have far greater understanding of political control mechanisms and agency design.

Nothing in the Constitution requires that outcome; to the contrary. "While the Constitution diffuses power the better to secure liberty, it also contemplates that practice will integrate the dispersed powers into a workable government." *Youngstown Sheet & Tube Co. v. Sawyer*, (Jackson, J., concurring). The Framers took pains to craft a document that would allow the structures of governance to change, as times and needs change. The Constitution says only a few words about administration. As Chief Justice Marshall wrote: Rather than prescribing "immutable rules," it enables Congress to choose "the means by which government should, in all future time, execute its powers." *McCulloch*, 4 Wheat. at 415. It authorizes Congress to meet new exigencies with new devices. So Article II does not generally prohibit independent agencies. Nor do any supposed structural principles. Nor do any odors wafting from the document. Save for when those agencies impede the President's performance of his own constitutional duties, the matter is left up to Congress.

Our history has stayed true to the Framers' vision. Congress has accepted their invitation to experiment with administrative forms—nowhere more so than in the field of financial regulation. And this Court has mostly allowed it to do so. The result is a broad array of independent agencies, no two exactly alike but all with a measure of insulation from the President's removal power. The Federal Reserve Board; the FTC; the SEC; maybe some you've never heard of. As to each, Congress thought that formal job protection for policymaking would produce regulatory outcomes in greater accord with the long-term public interest. Congress may have been right; or it may have been wrong; or maybe it was some of both. No matter—the branches accountable to the people have decided how the people should be governed.

The CFPB should have joined the ranks. Maybe it will still do so, even under today's opinion: The majority tells Congress that it may "pursu[e] alternative responses" to the identified constitutional defect—"for example, converting the CFPB into a multimember agency." But there was no need to send Congress back to the drawing board. The Constitution does not distinguish between single-director and multimember independent agencies. It instructs Congress, not this Court, to decide on agency design. Because this Court ignores that sensible—indeed, that obvious—division of tasks, I respectfully dissent.

Notes and Questions

1. *What happened here?* Read the title of a SCOTUSblog essay on *Seila Law*: Opinion analysis: Court strikes down restrictions on removal of CFPB director but leaves bureau in place. Amy Howe, SCOTUSblog (Jun. 29, 2020, 4:41 PM), https://www.scotusblog.com/2020/06/opinion-analysis-court-strikes-down-restrictions-on-removal-of-cfpb-director-but-leaves-bureau-in-place/. How does that title capture what happened in the case?
2. "Today, in ***Seila Law v. Consumer Financial Protection Bureau***, a divided Supreme Court ruled that these restrictions on the removal of the CFPB director are unconstitutional. But the justices stopped there, rejecting a request by a California law firm to hold that, if the leadership structure is unconstitutional, the court should strike down the rest of the act creating the CFPB as well." *Id.* Should the Justices have gone farther and invalidated the whole act?
3. *Congress's power?* Do you agree that this case "may place Congress on solid constitutional footing to establish what's known as 'for-cause removal protections' for inspectors general, whose independence from political influence is critical to their ability to root out waste, fraud, and abuse in the federal government"? How is an inspector general different from the CFPB director? Why would different rules apply to the two of them? Do you agree we "need watchdogs, not lapdogs," and for-cause removal provides independence? See Rebecca Jones, *Seila Law v. CFPB*: What's Unconstitutional for One May Not Be Unconstitutional for All, POGO, Jul. 1, 2020, at https://www.pogo.org/analysis/2020/07/seila-law-v-cfpb-whats-unconstitutional-for-one-may-not-be-unconstitutional-for-all/#:~:text=Essentially%2C%20Seila%20Law%20argued%20that,removal%20protections%20violated%20the%20Constitution.
4. *Another analysis.* How do you analyze Professor Steven Schwinn's analysis of *Seila*, which is available at Seila Law: Court Strikes Independence of CFPB Director, Jun. 29, 2020, posted at https://www.youtube.com/watch?v=GNSKvHt7B0s?

A Look Ahead

In Chapter 5, we study the power that the Constitution gives to the states through the Tenth Amendment. The next chapter takes us to the powers and limits of the states. Once again, think of the Constitution as a watch. Now we are adding the states' cog(s).

Five

Amendment X: The States

Introduction

In Chapter 4, we focused on the federal system constructed by Articles I, II, and III of the Constitution. We examined the assigned powers for each branch and where the Supreme Court has drawn the boundary lines between branches. The Constitution also separates power between the federal government and the states. The Tenth Amendment states: "The powers not delegated to the United States by the Constitution, nor prohibited by it to the states, are reserved to the states respectively, or to the people."

When we study Congress, we learn repeatedly that the federal government is one of *enumerated* powers, which means that the Constitution must give Congress the power if it is to act. In other words, Congress only has commerce power because Article I has a Commerce Clause.

In Part A, we examine what powers the states possess under the Tenth Amendment. Parts B and C raise the vertical separation of powers questions. The states have their own powers, which means the Court must draw boundary lines between Congress and the states just as it does for the branches. Part B examines when and how the Tenth Amendment limits Congress's powers.

Part C includes cases where the Court reads the Commerce Clause as not only a power of Congress, e.g., the Affordable Care Act cases, but also a limitation on state power. The Court has recognized something called the "Dormant Commerce Clause" or the "negative implication of the Commerce Clause." This means that the states cannot interfere with Congress's interstate commerce powers. Generally speaking, the Court says Congress has power over interstate commerce while states have power over intrastate. Can you help the Court figure out what is interstate and what is intrastate? And just how much power the states have?

A. The Tenth Amendment

The following case is part of a controversy about the Tenth Amendment powers of the states. In 1976, the Court decided the *National League of Cities* case, which "ruled that the Commerce Clause does not empower Congress to enforce the minimum-wage and overtime provisions of the Fair Labor Standards Act (FLSA) against the States 'in areas of traditional governmental functions.'" *National*

League was a 5–4 decision. Justice Blackmun was the fifth vote in the majority, joining Justices Burger, Stewart, Powell, and Rehnquist.

A first oral argument took place in the following case, *Garcia*, on March 19, 1984. After that argument, Justice Blackmun was assigned to write the majority opinion for the Court. Blackmun, however, changed his mind and decided he could not vote to uphold *National League.* So, a second oral argument was heard on October 1, 1984. You can listen to (but not read) those two oral arguments at the case's website, https://www.oyez.org/cases/1983/82-1913. In *Garcia*, Blackmun joined the four dissenters in *National League*, Brennan, White, Marshall and Stevens, to overrule *National League.*

What can you tell from the two different oral arguments in the same case? Does the second argument emphasize the same matters as the first? Does Justice Blackmun ask the same questions in both cases? Why do you think Justice Blackmun changed his mind?

Garcia v. San Antonio Metropolitan Transit Authority [SAMTA]

SUPREME COURT OF THE UNITED STATES, 1985
469 U.S. 528, 105 S.Ct. 1005

Justice BLACKMUN delivered the opinion of the Court [with BRENNAN, WHITE, MARSHALL, and STEVENS]. Justice POWELL filed dissenting opinion in which Chief Justice BURGER and Justice REHNQUIST and Justice O'CONNOR joined. Justice REHNQUIST filed dissenting opinion. Justice O'CONNOR filed dissenting opinion in which Justice POWELL and Justice REHNQUIST joined.

We revisit in these cases an issue raised in *National League of Cities v. Usery,* 426 U.S. 833, 96 S.Ct. 2465, 49 L.Ed.2d 245 (1976). In that litigation, this Court, by a sharply divided vote, ruled that the Commerce Clause does not empower Congress to enforce the minimum-wage and overtime provisions of the Fair Labor Standards Act (FLSA) against the States "in areas of traditional governmental functions." Although *National League of Cities* supplied some examples of "traditional governmental functions," it did not offer a general explanation of how a "traditional" function is to be distinguished from a "nontraditional" one. Since then, federal and state courts have struggled with the task, thus imposed, of identifying a traditional function for purposes of state immunity under the Commerce Clause.

In the present cases, a Federal District Court concluded that municipal ownership and operation of a mass-transit system is a traditional governmental function and thus, under *National League of Cities,* is exempt from the obligations imposed by the FLSA. Faced with the identical question, three Federal Courts of Appeals and one state appellate court have reached the opposite conclusion.

Our examination of this "function" standard applied in these and other cases over the last eight years now persuades us that the attempt to draw the boundaries of state regulatory immunity in terms of "traditional governmental function" is not only unworkable but is also inconsistent with established principles of federalism and, indeed, with those very federalism principles on which *National League of Cities* purported to rest. That case, accordingly, is overruled.

I

... The present controversy concerns the extent to which SAMTA may be subjected to the minimum-wage and overtime requirements of the FLSA. When the FLSA was enacted in 1938, its wage and overtime provisions did not apply to local mass-transit employees or, indeed, to employees of state and local governments. In 1961, Congress extended minimum-wage coverage to employees of any private mass-transit carrier whose annual gross revenue was not less than $1 million. Five years later, Congress extended FLSA coverage to state and local-government employees for the first time by withdrawing the minimum-wage and overtime exemptions from public hospitals, schools, and mass-transit carriers whose rates and services were subject to state regulation. At the same time, Congress eliminated the overtime exemption for all mass-transit employees other than drivers, operators, and conductors. The application of the FLSA to public schools and hospitals was ruled to be within Congress' power under the Commerce Clause. ...

II

... The prerequisites for governmental immunity under *National League of Cities* were summarized by this Court in *Hodel, supra.* Under that summary, four conditions must be satisfied before a state activity may be deemed immune from a particular federal regulation under the Commerce Clause. First, it is said that the federal statute at issue must regulate "the 'States as States.'" Second, the statute must "address matters that are indisputably 'attribute[s] of state sovereignty.'" Third, state compliance with the federal obligation must "directly impair [the States'] ability 'to structure integral operations in areas of traditional governmental functions.'" Finally, the relation of state and federal interests must not be such that "the nature of the federal interest ... justifies state submission." ...

We believe, however, that there is a more fundamental problem at work here, a problem that explains why the Court was never able to provide a basis for the governmental/proprietary distinction in the intergovernmental tax-immunity cases and why an attempt to draw similar distinctions with respect to federal regulatory authority under *National League of Cities* is unlikely to succeed regardless of how the distinctions are phrased. The problem is that neither the governmental/proprietary distinction nor any other that purports to separate out important governmental functions can be faithful to the role of federalism in a democratic society. The essence of our federal system is that within the realm of authority left open to them under the Constitution, the States must be equally free to engage in any activity that their citizens choose for the common weal, no matter how unorthodox or unnecessary anyone else—including the judiciary—deems state involvement to be. Any rule of state immunity that looks to the "traditional," "integral," or "necessary" nature of governmental functions inevitably invites an unelected federal judiciary to make decisions about which state policies it favors and which ones it dislikes. "The science of government ... is the science of experiment," and the States cannot serve as laboratories for social and economic experiment, if they must pay an added price when they meet the changing needs of their citizenry by taking up functions that an earlier day and a different society left in private hands. ...

We therefore now reject, as unsound in principle and unworkable in practice, a rule of state immunity from federal regulation that turns on a judicial appraisal of whether a particular governmental function is "integral" or "traditional." Any such rule leads to inconsistent results at the same time that it disserves principles of democratic self-governance, and it breeds inconsistency precisely because it is divorced from those principles. If there are to be limits on the Federal Government's power to interfere with state functions—as undoubtedly there are—we must look elsewhere to find them. We accordingly return to the underlying issue that confronted this Court in *National League of Cities*—the manner in which the Constitution insulates States from the reach of Congress' power under the Commerce Clause.

III

... We doubt that courts ultimately can identify principled constitutional limitations on the scope of Congress' Commerce Clause powers over the States merely by relying on *a priori* definitions of state sovereignty. In part, this is because of the elusiveness of objective criteria for "fundamental" elements of state sovereignty, a problem we have witnessed in the search for "traditional governmental functions." There is, however, a more fundamental reason: the sovereignty of the States is limited by the Constitution itself. A variety of sovereign powers, for example, are withdrawn from the States by Article I, § 10. Section 8 of the same Article works an equally sharp contraction of state sovereignty by authorizing Congress to exercise a wide range of legislative powers and (in conjunction with the Supremacy Clause of Article VI) to displace contrary state legislation. By providing for final review of questions of federal law in this Court, Article III curtails the sovereign power of the States' judiciaries to make authoritative determinations of law. See *Martin v. Hunter's Lessee,* 1 Wheat. 304, 4 L.Ed. 97 (1816). Finally, the developed application, through the Fourteenth Amendment, of the greater part of the Bill of Rights to the States limits the sovereign authority that States otherwise would possess to legislate with respect to their citizens and to conduct their own affairs. ...

IV

This analysis makes clear that Congress' action in affording SAMTA employees the protections of the wage and hour provisions of the FLSA contravened no affirmative limit on Congress' power under the Commerce Clause. The judgment of the District Court therefore must be reversed.

Of course, we continue to recognize that the States occupy a special and specific position in our constitutional system and that the scope of Congress' authority under the Commerce Clause must reflect that position. But the principal and basic limit on the federal commerce power is that inherent in all congressional action—the built-in restraints that our system provides through state participation in federal governmental action. The political process ensures that laws that unduly burden the States will not be promulgated. In the factual setting of these cases the internal safeguards of the political process have performed as intended.

Justice POWELL, with whom THE CHIEF JUSTICE, Justice REHNQUIST, and Justice O'CONNOR join, dissenting.

... Because I believe this decision substantially alters the federal system embodied in the Constitution, I dissent.

... The Court apparently thinks that the State's success at obtaining federal funds for various projects and exemptions from the obligations of some federal statutes is indicative of the "effectiveness of the federal political process in preserving the States' interests. ..." But such political success is not relevant to the question whether the political *processes* are the proper means of enforcing constitutional limitations. The fact that Congress generally does not transgress constitutional limits on its power to reach state activities does not make judicial review any less necessary to rectify the cases in which it does do so. The States' role in our system of government is a matter of constitutional law, not of legislative grace. "The powers not delegated to the United States by the Constitution, nor prohibited by it to the States, are reserved to the States, respectively, or to the people." U.S. Const., Amdt. 10.

More troubling than the logical infirmities in the Court's reasoning is the result of its holding, *i.e.,* that federal political officials, invoking the Commerce Clause, are the sole judges of the limits of their own power. This result is inconsistent with the fundamental principles of our constitutional system. See, *e.g.,* The Federalist No. 78 (Hamilton). At least since *Marbury v. Madison,* 1 Cranch 137, 177, 2 L.Ed. 60 (1803), it has been the settled province of the federal judiciary "to say what the law is" with respect to the constitutionality of Acts of Congress. In rejecting the role of the judiciary in protecting the States from federal overreaching, the Court's opinion offers no explanation for ignoring the teaching of the most famous case in our history. ...

The opinion for the Court in *National League of Cities* was faithful to history in its understanding of federalism. The Court observed that "our federal system of government imposes definite limits upon the authority of Congress to regulate the activities of States as States by means of the commerce power." The Tenth Amendment was invoked to prevent Congress from exercising its "'power in a fashion that impairs the States' integrity or their ability to function effectively in a federal system.'"

This Court has recognized repeatedly that state sovereignty is a fundamental component of our system of government. More than a century ago, the Court stated that the Constitution recognized "the necessary existence of the States, and, within their proper spheres, the independent authority of the States." It concluded, as Madison did, that this authority extended to "nearly the whole charge of interior regulation ...; to [the States] and to the people all powers not expressly delegated to the national government are reserved." Recently, the Court recognized that the state action exemption from the antitrust laws was based on state sovereignty. Similarly, although finding the Railway Labor Act applicable to a state-owned railroad, the unanimous Court was careful to say that the States possess constitutionally preserved sovereign powers. ...

III D

In contrast, the Court today propounds a view of federalism that pays only lipservice to the role of the States. ...

IV

The question presented in these cases is whether the extension of the FLSA to the wages and hours of employees of a city-owned transit system unconstitutionally impinges on fundamental state sovereignty. The Court's sweeping holding does far more than simply answer this question in the negative. In overruling *National League of Cities,* today's opinion apparently authorizes federal control, under the auspices of the Commerce Clause, over the terms and conditions of employment of all state and local employees. Thus, for purposes of federal regulation, the Court rejects the distinction between public and private employers that had been drawn carefully in *National League of Cities*. The Court's action reflects a serious misunderstanding, if not an outright rejection, of the history of our country and the intention of the Framers of the Constitution. ...

V

Although the Court's opinion purports to recognize that the States retain some sovereign power, it does not identify even a single aspect of state authority that would remain when the Commerce Clause is invoked to justify federal regulation. ...

Justice REHNQUIST, dissenting.

I join both Justice POWELL's and Justice O'CONNOR's thoughtful dissents. Justice POWELL's reference to the "balancing test" approved in *National League of Cities* is not identical with the language in that case, which recognized that Congress could not act under its commerce power to infringe on certain fundamental aspects of state sovereignty that are essential to "the States' separate and independent existence." Nor is either test, or Justice O'CONNOR's suggested approach, precisely congruent with Justice BLACKMUN's views in 1976, when he spoke of a balancing approach which did not outlaw federal power in areas "where the federal interest is demonstrably greater." But under any one of these approaches the judgment in these cases should be affirmed, and I do not think it incumbent on those of us in dissent to spell out further the fine points of a principle that will, I am confident, in time again command the support of a majority of this Court.

Justice O'CONNOR, with whom Justice POWELL and Justice REHNQUIST join, dissenting.

The Court today surveys the battle scene of federalism and sounds a retreat. Like Justice POWELL, I would prefer to hold the field and, at the very least, render a little aid to the wounded. I join Justice POWELL's opinion. I also write separately to note my fundamental disagreement with the majority's views of federalism and the duty of this Court. ...

In my view, federalism cannot be reduced to the weak "essence" distilled by the majority today. There is more to federalism than the nature of the constraints that can be imposed on the States in "the realm of authority left open to them by the Constitution." The central issue of federalism, of course, is whether any realm *is* left open to the States by the Constitution—whether any area remains in which a State may act free of federal interference. "The issue ... is whether the federal system has any *legal* substance, any core of constitutional right that courts will enforce." The true "essence" of federalism is that the States *as States* have legitimate interests which the National Government is bound to respect even though its laws are supreme. If federalism so conceived and so carefully cultivated by the Framers of our Constitution is to remain meaningful, this Court cannot abdicate its constitutional responsibility to oversee the Federal Government's compliance with its duty to respect the legitimate interests of the States. ...

Notes and Questions

1. *The holding.* What did *National League of Cities* hold? What test came out of it? Why did five Justices vote to overrule it? What test did the majority employ here? What are the strengths and weaknesses of that test?
2. *The dissent.* Why did four Justices dissent in this case? What did they like about *National League*? What do they dislike about Justice Blackmun's new test? What do they say is wrong with it? What test do they prefer? Why do they suggest the future Court will spend time working out an adequate test?
3. Marbury. Why is there a reference to *Marbury* and to other fundamental principles of the Constitution in this case? You have read *Marbury*, the Court's lead case on the power of judicial review. Why is it relevant in this case?
4. *What is the Tenth Amendment?* Do these Justices have different interpretations of what the Tenth Amendment means? What would be the best interpretation of the amendment for today's United States?

5. *The Justices conversing.* The following parts of the Justices' discussions of *Garcia* are available and were published in Del Dickson, *The Supreme Court in Conference 1940–1985: the private discussions behind nearly 300 Supreme Court decisions 229–33* (2001). What do the following comments tell you about the case and why the Justices voted as they did?

BURGER: National League of Cities is at a crossroads in this case. Private mass transit has faded out and large cities have gone public. Federal funds subsidize 75 percent of the cost and only 25 percent of operating costs come from revenue. Still, transit systems are essentially local. This is like water in that respect and is here to stay. The federal government can attach conditions. I don't think that Long Island controls this case.

BRENNAN: The question presented in this case is whether the operation of a publicly owned and operated mass transit system is a "traditional state function" for purposes of the 10th Amendment. In my view, it is not. In *United Transportation Union v. Long Island Railroad*, we held that the determination whether a federal regulation affects a traditional state function, rests on whether that regulation "affects basic state prerogatives in such a way as would be likely to hamper the state government's ability to fulfill its role in the Union and endanger its separate and independent existence." Although we also stated in Long Island Railroad that the traditional state function inquiry does not impose a "static historical view of state functions," there can be no question that history plays a vital role in this inquiry. In Long Island Railroad itself, we relied heavily on history. For example, we stated that "It is certainly true that some passenger railroads have come under state control in recent years ... but that does not alter the historical reality that operation of the railroads is not among the functions traditionally performed by state and local governments." Indeed, if the states have not traditionally performed a particular function, they have, of course, survived as independent entities without performing that function at all. It is, therefore, difficult to see how federal regulation of that function can threaten the states' independent existence.

In this case, there is no question that the states have not traditionally operated mass transit systems. Until recently, these systems were largely privately operated. Thus, the history of private operation of mass transit strongly suggests that operation of mass transit systems is not a traditional state function.

The recent large scale entry of the states into the mass transit field does not alter this conclusion. This development occurred when massive amounts of federal funds were made available to the states to operate mass transit systems. Additionally, the various conditions on grants under the Urban Mass Transit Act have undoubtedly played a vital role in determining the nature of the mass transit services that the states provide. Thus, the states' large scale involvement in mass transit has been a joint venture with the federal government, rather than a matter of purely local concern. Because the federal government has been so involved in mass transit during the period in which the states acquired mass transit facilities, it is difficult to conceive of mass transit as the kind of state function that must be free of federal regulation to preserve the independent existence of the states. To my knowledge, none of the other functions which we have previously identified as traditional state functions is characterized by an absence of historical state involvement and the presence of federal funding in the states' development of that function. Finally, it is worth noting that over 80 percent of the publicly owned mass transit systems became public after 1966, when the Fair Labor Standards Act was amended to apply to publicly owned mass transit. As in Long Island Railroad, these states acquired their mass transit operations knowing that the operations would be subject to federal regulation.

For these reasons, I believe that the operation of a mass transit system is not a traditional state function. As a result, the Tenth Amendment is not violated when the Fair Labor Standards Act is applied to state-operated mass transit systems. I reverse.

WHITE: I agree with Brennan.

MARSHALL: I agree with Brennan.

BLACKMUN: This is a tough case for me after my concurrence in National League. Municipal mass transit reeks of localism, like police, fire, and so forth. I agree that a good opinion can be written either way. I come down on the side that this is local, and I will vote to affirm.

POWELL: One can write a principled decision either way, and I agree with Harry. We are talking here of driving people to and from their work—a service that is essential to provide.

REHNQUIST: I agree with Harry and Lewis.

STEVENS: How much should be entrusted to the democratic process is a guide for me. It is anomalous to think that municipalities, with their political powers, should be protected against Congress. It is too much for me.

O'CONNOR: The third National League test is my focus. I don't think that history freezes traditional public service—the test is whether Congress goes too far.

After Reargument

BURGER: Mass transit should not be subject to federal control.

BRENNAN: I was fully ready to join in Harry's opinion last term, and I continue to stand ready to do so. It is a splendid piece of scholarship, and it properly emphasizes that the federalism restraints on Congress commerce clause power lie primarily in the political process-not the judicial process.

I would only add that, if there is sentiment for expressly overruling *National League of Cities*, I would join in such a disposition without hesitation. Such an outcome may, in fact, be required by Harry's analysis. Of course, there would continue to be restraints on Congress's commerce power. As we emphasized in *Maryland v. Wirtz* and *United States v. California*, the courts must ensure that challenged legislation is a valid regulation of interstate commerce. Beyond that, I believe that further judicial inquiry is not required by the Constitution—indeed, it is prohibited. Reverse.

WHITE: I would reconsider National League and reverse.

MARSHALL: I am still with Harry and would overrule National League.

BLACKMUN: It was a disappointing argument from all concerned. The traditional government function test doesn't approach.

POWELL: I would treat the traditional function test as whether it is essentially a matter of local or national concern. I don't think that the federal interest here is that great.

REHNQUIST: I am still to affirm.

STEVENS: There is no doubt what Congress meant here. Any balancing here is for Congress to do, as Brennan says. Indeed, this is a classic case where it is wrong for the judiciary to intervene.

O'CONNOR: This is a watershed case. The Framers encouraged a system of state and federal sovereignty, and pay of state employees is for the states to determine.

B. Does the Tenth Amendment Limit Congress's Powers?

1. The Limits on Congress's Power to Order the States to Act

Think about the questions that the Justices are considering in the following case. Does the Tenth Amendment set limits on Congress's powers? The majority here says yes, that under the Tenth Amendment the federal government cannot "commandeer" the state governments. Justice O'Connor concludes that the "take title" provisions in the following waste policy statute were unconstitutional although other parts of the legislation were constitutional under Congress's powers. The dissenting justices thought that the take title provisions were constitutional. Can you tell why? How do the Justices disagree about this aspect of the Tenth Amendment?

Read through the oral argument in this case, which is available on the case's website, at https://www.oyez.org/cases/1991/91-543. Who is most persuasive that the Congress does not have power to pass the take title provision? Who is most persuasive that it does have that power? Can you tell from the questions how the Justices will vote?

New York v. United States
SUPREME COURT OF THE UNITED STATES, 1992
505 U.S. 144, 112 S.Ct. 2408

O'CONNOR, J., delivered the opinion of the Court, in which REHNQUIST, C.J., and SCALIA, KENNEDY, SOUTER, and THOMAS, JJ., joined, and in Parts III–A and III–B of which WHITE, BLACKMUN, and STEVENS, JJ., joined. WHITE, J., filed an opinion concurring in part and dissenting in part, in which BLACKMUN and STEVENS, JJ., joined. STEVENS, J., filed an opinion concurring in part and dissenting in part.

These cases implicate one of our Nation's newest problems of public policy and perhaps our oldest question of constitutional law. The public policy issue involves the disposal of radioactive waste: In these cases, we address the constitutionality of three provisions of the Low–Level Radioactive Waste Policy Amendments Act of 1985. The constitutional question is as old as the Constitution: It consists of discerning the proper division of authority between the Federal Government and the States. We conclude that while Congress has substantial power under the Constitution to encourage the States to provide for the disposal of the radioactive waste generated within their borders, the Constitution does not confer upon Congress the ability simply to compel the States to do so. We therefore find that only two of the Act's three provisions at issue are consistent with the Constitution's allocation of power to the Federal Government.

I

... [S]ince 1979 only three disposal sites—those in Nevada, Washington, and South Carolina—have been in operation. Waste generated in the rest of the country must be shipped to one of these three sites for disposal. ...

Faced with the possibility that the Nation would be left with no disposal sites for low level radioactive waste, Congress responded by enacting the Low–Level Radioactive Waste Policy Act. Relying largely on a report submitted by the National Governors' Association, Congress declared a federal policy of holding each State "responsible for providing for the availability of capacity either within or outside the State for the disposal of low-level radioactive waste generated within its borders," and found that such waste could be disposed of "most safely and efficiently ... on a regional basis." The 1980 Act authorized States to enter into regional compacts that, once ratified by Congress, would have the authority beginning in 1986 to restrict the use of their disposal facilities to waste generated within member States. The 1980 Act included no penalties for States that failed to participate in this plan.

By 1985, only three approved regional compacts had operational disposal facilities; not surprisingly, these were the compacts formed around South Carolina, Nevada, and Washington, the three sited States. The following year, the 1980 Act would have given these three compacts the ability to exclude waste from nonmembers, and the remaining 31 States would have had no assured outlet for their low level radioactive waste. With this prospect looming, Congress once again took up the issue of waste disposal. The result was the legislation challenged here, the Low–Level Radioactive Waste Policy Amendments Act of 1985.

The 1985 Act was again based largely on a proposal submitted by the National Governors' Association. In broad outline, the Act embodies a compromise among the sited and unsited States. The sited States agreed to extend for seven years the period in which they would accept low level radioactive waste from other States. In exchange, the unsited States agreed to end their reliance on the sited States by 1992. ...

The Act provides three types of incentives to encourage the States to comply with their statutory obligation to provide for the disposal of waste generated within their borders.

1. *Monetary incentives.* One quarter of the surcharges collected by the sited States must be transferred to an escrow account held by the Secretary of Energy. The Secretary then makes payments from this account to each State that has complied with a series of deadlines. ...
2. *Access incentives.* The second type of incentive involves the denial of access to disposal sites. States that fail to meet the July 1986 deadline may be charged twice the ordinary surcharge for the remainder of 1986 and may be denied access to disposal facilities thereafter. ...
3. *The take title provision.* The third type of incentive is the most severe. The Act provides:

> "If a State (or, where applicable, a compact region) in which low-level radioactive waste is generated is unable to provide for the disposal of all such waste generated within such State or compact region by January 1, 1996, each State in which such waste is generated, upon the request of the generator or owner of the waste, shall take title to the waste, be obligated to take possession of the waste, and shall be liable for all damages directly or indirectly incurred by such generator or owner as a consequence of the failure of the State to take possession of the waste as soon after January 1, 1996, as the generator or owner notifies the State that the waste is available for shipment."

These three incentives are the focus of petitioners' constitutional challenge.

... [A]s the cases stand before us, petitioners claim only that the Act is inconsistent with the Tenth Amendment and the Guarantee Clause [the Guarantee Clause claim lost].

IIA

... [T]he Tenth Amendment "states but a truism that all is retained which has not been surrendered." ...

Congress exercises its conferred powers subject to the limitations contained in the Constitution. Thus, for example, under the Commerce Clause Congress may regulate publishers engaged in interstate commerce, but Congress is constrained in the exercise of that power by the First Amendment. The Tenth Amendment likewise restrains the power of Congress, but this limit is not derived from the text of the Tenth Amendment itself, which, as we have discussed, is essentially a tautology. Instead, the Tenth Amendment confirms that the power of the Federal Government is subject to limits that may, in a given instance, reserve power to the States. The Tenth Amendment thus directs us to determine, as in this case, whether an incident of state sovereignty is protected by a limitation on an Article I power. ...

The actual scope of the Federal Government's authority with respect to the States has changed over the years, therefore, but the constitutional structure underlying and limiting that authority has not. In the end, just as a cup may be half empty or half full, it makes no difference whether one views the question at issue in these cases as one of ascertaining the limits of the power delegated to the Federal Government under the affirmative provisions of the Constitution or one of discerning the core of sovereignty retained by the States under the Tenth Amendment. Either way, we must determine whether any of the three challenged provisions of the Low-Level Radioactive Waste Policy Amendments Act of 1985 oversteps the boundary between federal and state authority.

IIB

... Petitioners contend only that the Tenth Amendment limits the power of Congress to regulate in the way it has chosen. Rather than addressing the problem of waste disposal by directly regulating the generators and disposers of waste, petitioners argue, Congress has impermissibly directed the States to regulate in this field.

This litigation instead concerns the circumstances under which Congress may use the States as implements of regulation; that is, whether Congress may direct or otherwise motivate the States to regulate in a particular field or a particular way. Our cases have established a few principles that guide our resolution of the issue.

IIB1

As an initial matter, Congress may not simply "commandee[r] the legislative processes of the States by directly compelling them to enact and enforce a federal regulatory program." ...

While Congress has substantial powers to govern the Nation directly, including in areas of intimate concern to the States, the Constitution has never been understood to confer upon Congress the ability to require the States to govern according to Congress' instructions. ...

In the end, the Convention opted for a Constitution in which Congress would exercise its legislative authority directly over individuals rather than over States. ...

In providing for a stronger central government, therefore, the Framers explicitly chose a Constitution that confers upon Congress the power to regulate individuals, not States. As we have seen, the Court has consistently respected this choice. We have always understood that even where Congress has the authority under the Constitution to pass laws requiring or prohibiting certain acts, it lacks the power directly to compel the States to require or prohibit those acts. The allocation of power contained in the Commerce Clause, for example, authorizes Congress to regulate interstate commerce directly; it does not authorize Congress to regulate state governments' regulation of interstate commerce.

IIB2

This is not to say that Congress lacks the ability to encourage a State to regulate in a particular way, or that Congress may not hold out incentives to the States as a method of influencing a State's policy choices. ...

First, under Congress' spending power, "Congress may attach conditions on the receipt of federal funds." ...

Second, where Congress has the authority to regulate private activity under the Commerce Clause, we have recognized Congress' power to offer States the choice of regulating that activity according to federal standards or having state law pre-empted by federal regulation. ...

By either of these methods, as by any other permissible method of encouraging a State to conform to federal policy choices, the residents of the State retain the ultimate decision as to whether or not the State will comply. If a State's citizens view federal policy as sufficiently contrary to local interests, they may elect to decline a federal grant. If state residents would prefer their government to devote its attention and resources to problems other than those deemed important by Congress, they may choose to have the Federal Government rather than the State bear the expense of a federally mandated regulatory program, and they may continue to supplement that program to the extent state law is not pre-empted. Where Congress encourages state regulation rather than compelling it, state governments remain responsive to the local electorate's preferences; state officials remain accountable to the people.

By contrast, where the Federal Government compels States to regulate, the accountability of both state and federal officials is diminished. If the citizens of New York, for example, do not consider that making provision for the disposal of radioactive waste is in their best interest, they may elect state officials who share their view. That view can always be pre-empted under the Supremacy Clause if it is contrary to the national view, but in such a case it is the Federal Government that makes the decision in full view of the public, and it will be federal officials that suffer the consequences if the decision turns out to be detrimental or unpopular. But where the Federal Government directs the States to regulate, it may be state officials who will bear the brunt of public disapproval, while the federal officials who devised the regulatory program may remain insulated from the electoral ramifications of their decision. Accountability is thus diminished when, due to federal coercion, elected state officials cannot regulate in accordance with the views of the local electorate in matters not pre-empted by federal regulation. ...

IIIA

... The Act's first set of incentives, in which Congress has conditioned grants to the States upon the States' attainment of a series of milestones, is thus well within the authority of Congress under the Commerce and Spending Clauses. Because the first set of incentives is supported by affirmative constitutional grants of power to Congress, it is not inconsistent with the Tenth Amendment.

IIIB

... The Act's second set of incentives thus represents a conditional exercise of Congress' commerce power, along the lines of those we have held to be within Congress' authority. As a result, the second set of incentives does not intrude on the sovereignty reserved to the States by the Tenth Amendment.

IIIC

The take title provision is of a different character. This third so-called "incentive" offers States, as an alternative to regulating pursuant to Congress' direction, the option of taking title to and possession of the low level radioactive waste generated within their borders and becoming liable for all damages waste generators suffer as a result of the States' failure to do so promptly. In this provision, Congress has crossed the line distinguishing encouragement from coercion. ...

Because an instruction to state governments to take title to waste, standing alone, would be beyond the authority of Congress, and because a direct order to regulate, standing alone, would also be beyond the authority of Congress, it follows that Congress lacks the power to offer the States a choice between the two. Unlike the first two sets of incentives, the take title incentive does not represent the conditional exercise of any congressional power enumerated in the Constitution. In this provision, Congress has not held out the threat of exercising its spending power or its commerce power; it has instead held out the threat, should the States not regulate according to one federal instruction, of simply forcing the States to submit to another federal instruction. A choice between two unconstitutionally coercive regulatory techniques is no choice at all. Either way, "the Act commandeers the legislative processes of the States by directly compelling them to enact and enforce a federal regulatory program," an outcome that has never been understood to lie within the authority conferred upon Congress by the Constitution. ...

The take title provision appears to be unique. No other federal statute has been cited which offers a state government no option other than that of implementing legislation enacted by Congress. Whether one views the take title provision as lying outside Congress' enumerated powers, or as infringing upon the core of state sovereignty reserved by the Tenth Amendment, the provision is inconsistent with the federal structure of our Government established by the Constitution. ...

VII

... Whatever the outer limits of that sovereignty may be, one thing is clear: The Federal Government may not compel the States to enact or administer a federal regulatory program. The Constitution permits both the Federal Government and the States to enact legislation regarding the disposal of low level radioactive waste. The Constitution enables the Federal Government to pre-empt state regulation contrary to federal interests, and it permits the Federal Government to hold out incentives to the States as a means of encouraging them to adopt suggested regulatory schemes. It does not, however, authorize Congress simply to direct the States to provide for the disposal of the radioactive waste generated within their borders. While there may be many constitutional methods of achieving regional self-sufficiency in radioactive waste disposal, the method Congress has chosen is not one of them. The judgment of the Court of Appeals is accordingly

Affirmed in part and reversed in part.

Justice WHITE, with whom Justice BLACKMUN and Justice STEVENS join, concurring in part and dissenting in part.

... I can only join Parts III–A and III–B, and I respectfully dissent from the rest of its opinion and the judgment reversing in part the judgment of the Court of Appeals.

I

... There is no need to resummarize the essentials of the 1985 legislation, which the Court does. It does, however, seem critical to emphasize what is accurately described in one *amicus* brief as the assumption by Congress of "the role of arbiter of disputes among the several States." Unlike legislation that directs action from the Federal Government to the States, the 1980 and 1985 Acts reflected hard-fought agreements among States as refereed by Congress. The distinction is key, and the Court's failure properly to characterize this legislation ultimately affects its analysis of the take title provision's constitutionality. ...

III

... Ultimately, I suppose, the entire structure of our federal constitutional government can be traced to an interest in establishing checks and balances to prevent the exercise of tyranny against individuals. But these fears seem extremely far distant to me in a situation such as this. We face a crisis of national proportions in the disposal of low-level radioactive waste, and Congress has acceded to the wishes of the States by permitting local decisionmaking rather than imposing a solution from Washington. New York itself participated and supported passage of this legislation at both the gubernatorial and federal representative levels, and then enacted state laws specifically to comply with the deadlines and timetables agreed upon by the States in the 1985 Act. For me, the Court's civics lecture has a decidedly hollow ring at a time when action, rather than rhetoric, is needed to solve a national problem. ...

IV

Though I disagree with the Court's conclusion that the take title provision is unconstitutional, I do not read its opinion to preclude Congress from adopting a similar measure through its powers under the Spending or Commerce Clauses. The Court makes clear that its objection is to the alleged "commandeer[ing]" quality of the take title provision. As its discussion of the surcharge and rebate incentives reveals, the spending power offers a means of enacting a take title provision under the Court's standards. Congress could, in other words, condition the payment of funds on the State's willingness to take title if it has not already provided a waste disposal facility. Under the scheme upheld in these cases, for example, moneys collected in the surcharge provision might be withheld or disbursed depending on a State's willingness to take title to or otherwise accept responsibility for the low-level radioactive waste generated in state after the statutory deadline for establishing its own waste disposal facility has passed.

Similarly, should a State fail to establish a waste disposal facility by the appointed deadline, Congress has the power pursuant to the Commerce Clause to regulate directly the producers of the waste. Thus, as I read it, Congress could amend the statute to say that if a State fails to meet the January 1, 1996, deadline for achieving a means of waste disposal, and has not taken title to the waste, no low-level radioactive waste may be shipped out of the State of New York. As the legislative history of the 1980 and 1985 Acts indicates, faced with the choice of federal pre-emptive regulation and self-regulation pursuant to interstate agreement with congressional consent and ratification, the States decisively chose the latter. This background suggests that the threat of federal pre-emption may suffice to induce States to accept responsibility for failing to meet critical time deadlines for solving their low-level radioactive waste disposal problems, especially if that federal intervention also would strip state and local authorities of any input in locating sites for low-level radioactive waste disposal facilities. And should Congress amend the statute to meet the Court's objection and a State refuse to act, the National Legislature will have ensured at least a federal solution to the waste management problem.

Finally, our precedents leave open the possibility that Congress may create federal rights of action in the generators of low-level radioactive waste against persons acting under color of state law for their failure to meet certain functions designated in federal-state programs. ...

V

The ultimate irony of the decision today is that in its formalistically rigid obeisance to "federalism," the Court gives Congress fewer incentives to defer to the wishes of state officials in achieving local solutions to local problems. This legislation was a classic example of Congress acting as arbiter among the States in their attempts to accept responsibility for managing a problem of grave import. The States urged the National Legislature not to impose from Washington a solution to the country's low-level radioactive waste management problems. Instead, they sought a reasonable level of local and regional autonomy consistent with Art. I, § 10, cl. 3, of the Constitution. By invalidating the measure designed to ensure compliance for recalcitrant States, such as New York, the Court upsets the delicate compromise achieved among the States and forces Congress to erect several additional formalistic hurdles to clear before achieving exactly the same objective. Because the Court's justifications for undertaking this step are unpersuasive to me, I respectfully dissent.

Justice STEVENS, concurring in part and dissenting in part.

... The notion that Congress does not have the power to issue "a simple command to state governments to implement legislation enacted by Congress," is incorrect and unsound. There is no such limitation in the Constitution. The Tenth Amendment[1] surely does not impose any limit on Congress' exercise of the powers delegated to it by Article I. Nor does the structure of the constitutional order or the values of federalism mandate such a formal rule. To the contrary, the Federal Government directs state governments in many realms. The Government regulates state-operated railroads, state school systems, state prisons, state elections, and a host of other state functions. Similarly, there can be no doubt that, in time of war, Congress could either draft soldiers itself or command the States to supply their quotas of troops. I see no reason why Congress may not also command the States to enforce federal water and air quality standards or federal standards for the disposition of low-level radioactive wastes. ...

Notes and Questions

1. *Justice O'Connor.* Why does Justice O'Connor conclude Congress does not have the authority to require the states to do one of the items of this legislation? Does she strike a proper balance between federal and state sovereignty? What are the three parts of the legislation, and how does the Court treat each one?
2. *The other Justices.* Why do Justices White, Blackmun, and Stevens join only Parts IIIA and IIIB of the opinion? Where do they differ from Justice O'Connor on federal and state sovereignty? Why do they both concur and dissent?
3. *Justice Stevens and where to draw the line.* What does Justice Stevens conclude about the relationship between federal and state sovereignty?
4. *The scope of Congress's power.* What implications does this decision have for current waste and other regulations by Congress of the states?
5. *Video.* Does Quimbee's video, *New York v. United States* Case Brief Summary/Law Case Explained, Nov. 27, 2015, posted at https://www.youtube.com/watch?v=G3QU9R2BkFY&list=PLsFE_Nvl6h_braQ_NxoD1jg8oDdM_l8uI&index=5&t=31s, explain the details of the case to you?

2. Can Congress Commandeer the States?

The last case, *New York,* and the next case, *Printz,* have similar issues. What are the similar issues in both cases? Why do the Justices disagree about them? Does knowing about *New York* help you understand *Printz?* Why or why not? Does *New York* help you understand the oral argument in *Printz,* https://www.oyez.org/cases/1996/95-1478? Do you understand the core constitutional issues that are at stake in both cases?

Oyez gives you the following pictures of how the Justices voted in these two cases. Are these votes predictable from the oral arguments?

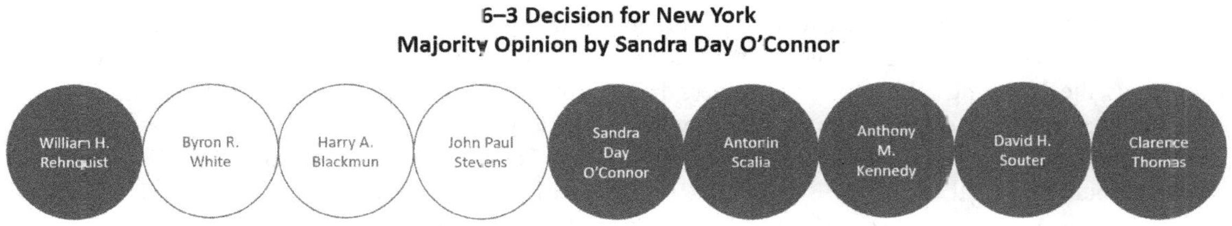

FIGURE 5.1

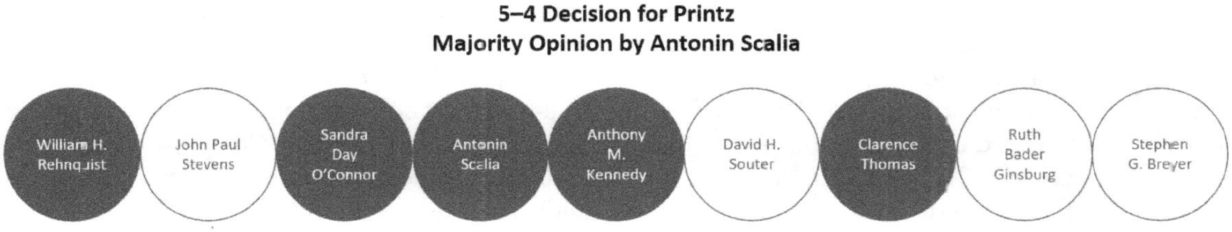

FIGURE 5.2

Printz v. United States
SUPREME COURT OF THE UNITED STATES, 1997
521 U.S. 898, 117 S.Ct. 2365

SCALIA, J., delivered the opinion of the Court, in which REHNQUIST, C. J., and O'CONNOR, KENNEDY, and THOMAS, JJ., joined. O'CONNOR, J., and THOMAS, J., filed concurring opinions. STEVENS, J., filed a dissenting opinion, in which SOUTER, GINSBURG, and BREYER, JJ., joined. SOUTER, J., filed a dissenting opinion. BREYER, J., filed a dissenting opinion, in which STEVENS, J., joined

The question presented in these cases is whether certain interim provisions of the Brady Handgun Violence Prevention Act, commanding state and local law enforcement officers to conduct background checks on prospective handgun purchasers and to perform certain related tasks, violate the Constitution.

I

... In 1993, Congress amended the GCA [Gun Control Act] by enacting the Brady Act.

... Under the interim provisions, a firearms dealer who proposes to transfer a handgun must first: (1) receive from the transferee a statement (the Brady Form), containing the name, address, and date of birth of the proposed transferee along with a sworn statement that the transferee is not among any of the classes of prohibited purchasers; (2) verify the identity of the transferee by examining an identification document; and (3) provide the "chief law enforcement officer" (CLEO) of the transferee's residence with notice of the contents (and a copy) of the Brady Form. With some exceptions, the dealer must then wait five business days before consummating the sale, unless the CLEO earlier notifies the dealer that he has no reason to believe the transfer would be illegal.

The Brady Act creates two significant alternatives to the foregoing scheme. A dealer may sell a handgun immediately if the purchaser possesses a state handgun permit issued after a background check, or if state law provides for an instant background check. In States that have not rendered one of these alternatives applicable to all gun purchasers, CLEOs are required to perform certain duties. When a CLEO receives the required notice of a proposed transfer from the firearms dealer, the CLEO must "make a reasonable effort to ascertain within 5 business days whether receipt or possession would be in violation of the law, including research in whatever State and local recordkeeping systems are available and in a national system designated by the Attorney General." The Act does not require the CLEO to take any particular action if he determines that a pending transaction would be unlawful; he may notify the firearms dealer to that effect, but is not required to do so. If, however, the CLEO notifies a gun dealer that a prospective purchaser is ineligible to receive a handgun, he must, upon request, provide the would-be purchaser with a written statement of the reasons for that determination. Moreover, if the CLEO does not discover any basis for objecting to the sale, he must destroy any records in his possession relating to the transfer, including his copy of the Brady Form. Under a separate provision of the GCA, any person who "knowingly violates [the section of the GCA amended by the Brady Act] shall be fined under this title, imprisoned for not more than 1 year, or both."

II

... Petitioners here object to being pressed into federal service, and contend that congressional action compelling state officers to execute federal laws is unconstitutional. ...

These early laws establish, at most, that the Constitution was originally understood to permit imposition of an obligation on state *judges* to enforce federal prescriptions, insofar as those prescriptions related to matters appropriate for the judicial power. ...

For these reasons, we do not think the early statutes imposing obligations on state courts imply a power of Congress to impress the state executive into its service. Indeed, it can be argued that the numerousness of these statutes, contrasted with the utter lack of statutes imposing obligations on the States' executive (notwithstanding the attractiveness of that course to Congress), suggests an assumed *absence* of such power. ...

To complete the historical record, we must note that there is not only an absence of executive-commandeering statutes in the early Congresses, but there is an absence of them in our later history as well, at least until very recent years. ...

III A

... This separation of the two spheres is one of the Constitution's structural protections of liberty. "Just as the separation and independence of the coordinate branches of the Federal Government serve to prevent the accumulation of excessive power in any one branch, a healthy balance of power between the States and the Federal Government will reduce the risk of tyranny and abuse from either front." ...

V

What we have said makes it clear enough that the central obligation imposed upon CLEOs by the interim provisions of the Brady Act—the obligation to "make a reasonable effort to ascertain within 5 business days whether receipt or possession [of a handgun] would be in violation of the law, including research in whatever State and local recordkeeping systems are available and in a national system designated by the Attorney General,"—is unconstitutional. Extinguished with it, of course, is the duty implicit in the background-check requirement that the CLEO accept notice of the contents of, and a copy of, the completed Brady 934 Form, which the firearms dealer is required to provide to him. ...

* * *

We held in *New York* that Congress cannot compel the States to enact or enforce a federal regulatory program. Today we hold that Congress cannot circumvent that prohibition by conscripting the State's officers directly. The Federal Government may neither issue directives requiring the States to address particular problems, nor command the States' officers, or those of their political subdivisions, to administer or enforce a federal regulatory program. It matters not whether policymaking is involved, and no case-by-case weighing of the burdens or benefits is necessary; such commands are fundamentally incompatible with our constitutional system of dual sovereignty. Accordingly, the judgment of the Court of Appeals for the Ninth Circuit is reversed.

It is so ordered.

Justice O'CONNOR, concurring.

Our precedent and our Nation's historical practices support the Court's holding today. ... [T]he Court appropriately refrains from deciding whether other purely ministerial reporting requirements imposed by Congress on state and local authorities pursuant to its Commerce Clause powers are similarly invalid. See, *e.g.*, 42 U.S.C. § 5779(a) (requiring state and local law enforcement agencies to report cases of missing children to the Department of Justice). The provisions invalidated here, however, which directly compel state officials to administer a federal regulatory program, utterly fail to adhere to the design and structure of our constitutional scheme.

Justice THOMAS, concurring.

... In my "revisionist" view, the Federal Government's authority under the Commerce Clause, which merely allocates to Congress the power "to regulate Commerce ... among the several States," does not extend to the regulation of wholly *intra* state, point-of-sale transactions. Absent the underlying authority to regulate the intrastate transfer of firearms, Congress surely lacks the corollary power to impress state law enforcement officers into administering and enforcing such regulations. Although this Court has long interpreted the Constitution as ceding Congress extensive authority to regulate commerce (interstate or otherwise), I continue to believe that we must "temper our Commerce Clause jurisprudence" and return to an interpretation better rooted in the Clause's original understanding. ...

Justice STEVENS, with whom Justice SOUTER, Justice GINSBURG, and Justice BREYER join, dissenting.

When Congress exercises the powers delegated to it by the Constitution, it may impose affirmative obligations on executive and judicial officers of state and local governments as well as ordinary citizens. This conclusion is firmly supported by the text of the Constitution, the early history of the Nation, decisions of this Court, and a correct understanding of the basic structure of the Federal Government. ...

Indeed, the historical materials strongly suggest that the founders intended to enhance the capacity of the Federal Government by empowering it—as a part of the new authority to make demands directly on individual citizens—to act through local officials. Hamilton made clear that the new Constitution, "by extending the authority of the federal head to the individual citizens of the several States, will enable the government to employ the ordinary magistracy of each in the execution of its laws." The Federalist No. 27, at 180. Hamilton's meaning was unambiguous; the Federal Government was to have the power to demand that local officials implement national policy programs. As he went on to explain: "It is easy to perceive that this will tend to destroy, in the common apprehension, all distinction between the sources from which [the State and Federal Governments] might proceed; and will give the federal government the same advantage for securing a due obedience to its authority which is enjoyed by the government of each State." ...

* * *

The provision of the Brady Act that crosses the Court's newly defined constitutional threshold is more comparable to a statute requiring local police officers to report the identity of missing children to the Crime Control Center of the Department of Justice than to an offensive federal command to a sovereign State. If Congress believes that such a statute will benefit the people of the Nation, and serve the interests of cooperative federalism better than an enlarged federal bureaucracy, we should respect both its policy judgment and its appraisal of its constitutional power.

Accordingly, I respectfully dissent.

Justice SOUTER, dissenting.

... In deciding these cases, which I have found closer than I had anticipated, it is The Federalist that finally determines my position. I believe that the most straightforward reading of No. 27 is authority for the Government's position here, and that this reading is both supported by No. 44 and consistent with Nos. 36 and 45. ...

In the light of all these passages, I cannot persuade myself that the statements from No. 27 speak of anything less than the authority of the National Government, when exercising an otherwise legitimate power (the commerce power, say), to require state "auxiliaries" to take appropriate action. ...

Justice BREYER, with whom Justice STEVENS joins, dissenting.

I would add to the reasons Justice STEVENS sets forth the fact that the United States is not the only nation that seeks to reconcile the practical need for a central authority with the democratic virtues of more local control. At least some other countries, facing the same basic problem, have found that local control is better maintained through application of a principle that is the direct opposite of the principle the majority derives from the silence of our Constitution. The federal systems of Switzerland, Germany, and the European Union, for example, all provide that constituent states, not federal bureaucracies, will themselves implement many of the laws, rules, regulations, or decrees enacted by the central "federal" body. ...

Notes and Questions

1. *Justice O'Connor and federalism.* Notice what Justice O'Connor says in her concurrence: "the Court appropriately refrains from deciding whether other purely ministerial reporting requirements imposed by Congress on state and local authorities pursuant to its Commerce Clause powers are similarly invalid. See, *e.g.,* 42 U.S.C. § 5779(a) (requiring state and local law enforcement agencies to report cases of missing children to the Department of Justice)." What would the Court say about an obligation for state and local agencies to report cases of missing children? Constitutional or unconstitutional? If having such a requirement would be unconstitutional, does it show that the dissent has a better analysis of the Constitution's powers than the majority does?
2. *The other Justices. Printz* has opinions from Justices Scalia, O'Connor, Thomas, Stevens, Souter, and Breyer. What does each Justice argue? Why are there so many opinions? What does each Justice think about state sovereignty?
3. *State sovereignty.* What does this case say about state sovereignty?
4. *Video.* Do you agree with or find helpful Quimbee's video summary of *Printz,* Dec. 4, 2017, available at https://www.youtube.com/watch?v=SBPAkZVj-UU? What about their video summary of *New York,* Nov.27, 2015, at https://www.youtube.com/watch?v=G3QU9R2BkFY? Do these videos summarize the points you learned in reading these two cases?

5. The Indian Child Welfare Act establishes a preference that Native American children be placed with Native American families whenever they are adopted. Individuals and states challenged the law, arguing that it commandeered the states by requiring them to place children in homes in violation of the Tenth Amendment. The oral argument in *Haaland v. Brackeen* is available at https://www.oyez.org/cases/2022/21-376. Do you think this law is commandeering the states, or is it a federal law that should be obeyed by the states? What power gives Congress the right to pass the Indian Child Welfare Act?

C. Can the States Intrude on Congress's Commerce Powers?

1. What Happens When One State Regulated Another's City?

You can tell from the name of the following case, *Philadelphia v. New Jersey*, that there was a dispute between two states. They were fighting over a New Jersey law that banned solid waste from Philadelphia from being imported into New Jersey. Can you tell why this is a significant constitutional question? If New Jersey can do this, what does it tell you about state powers? If New Jersey cannot do this, what does it tell you about state powers? What does interstate commerce have to do with it?

Why are there two dissenting Justices? If you read the oral argument, at https://www.oyez.org/cases/1977/77-404, who does a better job, the lawyer supporting Philadelphia or the lawyer supporting New Jersey? Which is the hardest question that a Justice asks?

City of Philadelphia v. New Jersey

SUPREME COURT OF THE UNITED STATES, 1978
437 U.S. 617, 98 S.Ct. 2531

Mr. Justice STEWART delivered the opinion of the Court [joined by BRENNAN, STEWART, WHITE, MARSHALL, BLACKMUN, POWELL, and STEVENS]. Mr. Justice REHNQUIST filed a dissenting opinion in which Mr. Chief Justice BURGER joined.

A New Jersey law prohibits the importation of most "solid or liquid waste which originated or was collected outside the territorial limits of the State. ..." In this case we are required to decide whether this statutory prohibition violates the Commerce Clause of the United States Constitution. ...

IIIA

... The opinions of the Court through the years have reflected an alertness to the evils of "economic isolation" and protectionism, while at the same time recognizing that incidental burdens on interstate commerce may be unavoidable when a State legislates to safeguard the health and safety of its people. Thus, where simple economic protectionism is effected by state legislation, a virtually *per se* rule of invalidity has been erected. The clearest example of such legislation is a law that overtly blocks the flow of interstate commerce at a State's borders. But where other legislative objectives are credibly advanced and there is no patent discrimination against interstate trade, the Court has adopted a much more flexible approach, the general contours of which were outlined in *Pike v. Bruce Church, Inc.* ...

The crucial inquiry, therefore, must be directed to determining whether ch. 363 is basically a protectionist measure, or whether it can fairly be viewed as a law directed to legitimate local concerns, with effects upon interstate commerce that are only incidental. ...

III B

... This dispute about ultimate legislative purpose need not be resolved, because its resolution would not be relevant to the constitutional issue to be decided in this case. Contrary to the evident assumption of the state court and the parties, the evil of protectionism can reside in legislative means as well as legislative ends. Thus, it does not matter whether the ultimate aim of ch. 363 is to reduce the waste disposal costs of New Jersey residents or to save remaining open lands from pollution, for we assume New Jersey has every right to protect its residents' pocketbooks as well as their environment. And it may be assumed as well that New Jersey may pursue those ends by sl'wing the flow of *all* waste into the State's remaining landfills, even though interstate commerce may incidentally be affected. But whatever New Jersey's ultimate purpose, it may not be accomplished by discriminating against articles of commerce coming from outside the State unless there is some reason, apart from their origin, to treat them differently. Both on its face and in its plain effect, ch. 363 violates this principle of nondiscrimination.

The Court has consistently found parochial legislation of this kind to be constitutionally i'valid, whether the ultimate aim of the legislation was to assure a steady supply of milk by erecting barriers to allegedly ruinous outside competition, or to create jobs by keeping industry within the State, or to preserve the State's financial resources from depletion by fencing out indigent immigrants. In each of these cases, a presumably legitimate goal was sought to be achieved by the illegitimate means of isolating the State from the national economy. ...

The New Jersey law at issue in this case falls squarely within the area that the Commerce Clause puts off limits to state regulation. On its face, it imposes on out-of-state commercial interests the full burden of conserving the State's remaining landfill space. It is true that in our previous cases the scarce natural resource was itself the article of commerce, whereas here the scarce resource and the article of commerce are distinct. But that difference is without consequence. In both instances, the State has overtly moved to slow or freeze the flow of commerce for protectionist reasons. It does not matter that the State has shut the article of commerce inside the State in one case and outside the State in the other. What is crucial is the attempt by one State to isolate itself from a problem common to many by erecting a barrier against the movement of interstate trade. ...

It is true that certain quarantine laws have not been considered forbidden protectionist measures, even though they were directed against out-of-state commerce. But those quarantine laws banned the importation of articles such as diseased livestock that required destruction as soon as possible because their very movement risked contagion and other evils. Those laws thus did not discriminate against interstate commerce as such, but simply prevented traffic in noxious articles, whatever their origin.

The New Jersey statute is not such a quarantine law. There has been no claim here that the very movement of waste into or through New Jersey endangers health, or that waste must be disposed of as soon and as close to its point of generation as possible. The harms caused by waste are said to arise after its disposal in landfill sites, and at that point, as New Jersey concedes, there is no basis to distinguish out-of-state waste from domestic waste. If one is inherently harmful, so is the other. Yet New Jersey has banned the former while leaving its landfill sites open to the latter. The New Jersey law blocks the importation of waste in an obvious effort to saddle those outside the State with the entire burden of slowing the flow of refuse into New Jersey's remaining landfill sites. That legislative effort is clearly impermissible under the Commerce Clause of the Constitution.

Today, cities in Pennsylvania and New York find it expedient or necessary to send their waste into New Jersey for disposal, and New Jersey claims the right to close its borders to such traffic. Tomorrow, cities in New Jersey may find it expedient or necessary to send their waste into Pennsylvania or New York for disposal, and those States might then claim the right to close their borders. The Commerce Clause will protect New Jersey in the future, just as it protects her neighbors now, from efforts by one State to isolate itself in the stream of interstate commerce from a problem shared by all. The judgment is *Reversed.*

Mr. Justice REHNQUIST, with whom THE CHIEF JUSTICE joins, dissenting.

... In my opinion, these [quarantine] cases are dispositive of the present one. Under them, New Jersey may require germ-infected rags or diseased meat to be disposed of as best as possible within the State, but at the same time prohibit the *importation* of such items for disposal at the facilities that are set up within New Jersey for disposal of such material generated *within* the State. The physical fact of life that New Jersey must somehow dispose of its own noxious items does not mean that it must serve as a depository for those of every other State. Similarly, New Jersey should be free under our past precedents to prohibit the importation of solid waste because of the health and safety problems that such waste poses to its citizens. The fact that New Jersey continues to, and indeed must continue to, dispose of its own solid waste does not mean that New Jersey may not prohibit the importation of even more solid waste into the State. I simply see no way to distinguish solid waste, on the record of this case, from germ-infected rags, diseased meat, and other noxious items.

The Court's effort to distinguish these prior cases is unconvincing. It first asserts that the quarantine laws which have previously been upheld "banned the importation of articles such as diseased livestock that required destruction as soon as possible because their very movement risked contagion and other evils." According to the Court, the New Jersey law is distinguishable from these other laws, and invalid, because the concern of New Jersey is not with the *movement* of solid waste but with the present inability to safely *dispose* of it once it reaches its destination. But I think it far from clear that the State's law has as limited a focus as the Court imputes to it: Solid waste which is a health hazard when it reaches its destination may in all likelihood be an equally great health hazard in transit. ...

Notes and Questions

1. *Quarantines.* Why do the Justices talk about quarantines? When may the states use a quarantine? Does this case explain how quarantines for deadly diseases can be regulated by the states?
2. *The Dissent.* What is the dissent's reasoning to uphold the New Jersey ban?
3. *The Articles of Confederation.* Remember that the Articles of Confederation failed, in part, because the states were not cooperating. The Constitution was designed to create cooperation toward a national good. How much independence can or should the Constitution give each state?
4. *Video.* Does Quimbee's video, *City of Philadelphia v. New Jersey* Case Brief Summary, Feb. 5, 2018, posted at https://www.youtube.com/watch?v=7TROkQLsD4c&list=PLsFE_Nvl6h_Y75KGR5pkGqcFisGvBnO9S&index=114, explain the case to you?

2. State Burdens on Interstate Commerce and the Dormant Commerce Clause

Can you identify what the issues are of state power between Wisconsin and Illinois in the following case? Why do two Justices dissent? The oral argument for this case is unavailable online. What questions do you think the Justices asked of the lawyers?

Dean Milk Co. v. City of Madison

SUPREME COURT OF THE UNITED STATES, 1951

340 U.S. 349, 71 S.Ct. 295

Mr. Justice CLARK delivered the opinion of the Court, with VINSON, REED, FRANKFURTER, JACKSON, BURTON. Mr. Justice BLACK, Mr. Justice DOUGLAS and Mr. Justice MINTON dissented.

This appeal challenges the constitutional validity of two sections of an ordinance of the City of Madison, Wisconsin, regulating the sale of milk and milk products within the municipality's jurisdiction. One section in issue makes it unlawful to sell any milk as pasteurized unless it has been processed and bottled at an approved pasteurization plant within a radius of five miles from the central square of Madison. Another section, which prohibits the sale of milk, or the importation, receipt or storage of milk for sale, in Madison unless from a source of supply possessing a permit issued after inspection by Madison officials, is attacked insofar as it expressly relieves municipal authorities from any duty to inspect farms located beyond twenty-five miles from the center of the city.

Appellant is an Illinois corporation engaged in distributing milk and milk products in Illinois and Wisconsin. It contended below, as it does here, that both the five-mile limit on pasteurization plants and the twenty-five-mile limit on sources of milk violate the Commerce Clause and the Fourteenth Amendment to the Federal Constitution. ...

The area defined by the ordinance with respect to milk sources encompasses practically all of Dane County and includes some 500 farms which supply milk for Madison. Within the five-mile area for pasteurization are plants of five processors, only three of which are engaged in the general wholesale and retail trade in Madison. Inspection of these farms and plants is scheduled once every thirty days and is performed by two municipal inspectors, one of whom is full-time. The courts below found that the ordinance in question promotes convenient, economical and efficient plant inspection.

Appellant purchases and gathers milk from approximately 950 farms in northern Illinois and southern Wisconsin, none being within twenty-five miles of Madison. Its pasteurization plants are located at Chemung and Huntley, Illinois, about 65 and 85 miles respectively from Madison. Appellant was denied a license to sell its products within Madison solely because its pasteurization plants were more than five miles away.

It is conceded that the milk which appellant seeks to sell in Madison is supplied from farms and processed in plants licensed and inspected by public health authorities of Chicago, and is labeled 'Grade A' under the Chicago ordinance which adopts the rating standards recommended by the United States Public Health Service. ...

[W]e agree with appellant that the ordinance imposes an undue burden on interstate commerce. ...

But this regulation, like the provision invalidated in Baldwin v. G.A.F. Seelig, Inc., supra, in practical effect excludes from distribution in Madison wholesome milk produced and pasteurized in Illinois. 'The importer * * * may keep his milk or drink it, but sell it he may not.' In thus erecting an economic barrier protecting a major local industry against competition from without the State, Madison plainly discriminates against interstate commerce. This it cannot do, even in the exercise of its unquestioned power to protect the health and safety of its people, if reasonable nondiscriminatory alternatives, adequate to conserve legitimate local interests, are available. ...

To permit Madison to adopt a regulation not essential for the protection of local health interests and placing a discriminatory burden on interstate commerce would invite a multiplication of preferential trade areas destructive of the very purpose of the Commerce Clause. Under the circumstances here presented, the regulation must yield to the principle that 'one state in its dealings with another may not place itself in a position of economic isolation.'

For these reasons we conclude that the judgment below sustaining the five-mile provision as to pasteurization must be reversed.

The Supreme Court of Wisconsin thought it unnecessary to pass upon the validity of the twenty-five-mile limitation, apparently in part for the reason that this issue was made academic by its decision upholding the five-mile section. In view of our conclusion as to the latter provision, a determination of appellant's contention as to the other section is now necessary. As to this issue, therefore, we vacate the judgment below and remand for further proceedings not inconsistent with the principles announced in this opinion. It is so ordered.

Mr. Justice BLACK, with whom Mr. Justice DOUGLAS and Mr. Justice MINTON concur, dissenting.

Today's holding invalidates s 7.21 of the Madison, Wisconsin, ordinance on the following reasoning: (1) the section excludes wholesome milk coming from Illinois; (2) this imposes a discriminatory burden on interstate commerce; (3) such a burden cannot be imposed where, as here, there are reasonable, nondiscriminatory and adequate alternatives available. I disagree with the Court's premises, reasoning, and judgment.

... But both state courts below found that s 7.21 represents a good-faith attempt to safeguard public health by making adequate sanitation inspection possible. While we are not bound by these findings, I do not understand the Court to overturn them. Therefore, the fact that s 7.21, like all health regulations, imposes some burden on trade, does not mean that it 'discriminates' against interstate commerce. ...

From what this record shows, and from what it fails to show, I do not think that either of the alternatives suggested by the Court would assure the people of Madison as pure a supply of milk as they receive under their own ordinance. On this record I would uphold the Madison law. At the very least, however, I would not invalidate it without giving the parties a chance to present evidence and get findings on the ultimate issues the Court thinks crucial—namely, the relative merits of the Madison ordinance and the alternatives suggested by the Court today.

Notes and Questions

1. *Another milk case.* In *Baldwin v. G.A.F. Seeling, Inc.*, 294 U.S. 511 (1935), the Court ruled that the New York Milk Control Act was unconstitutional in requiring businesses who bought their milk out of state to pay the out-of-state producers what the New York regulations required be paid to its in-state producers. Why is that case consistent with the outcome of *Dean Milk*?
2. *The votes.* Why does Justice Clark conclude the law is unconstitutional? Why does Justice Black dissent? Why does this legislation involve the Dormant Commerce Clause?
3. *Video.* Does Quimbee's video, *Dean Milk Co. v. City of Madison*, Wisconsin Case Brief Summary, Jan. 14, 2021, posted at https://www.youtube.com/watch?v=kteLWFQ17xc&list=PLsFE_Nvl6h_Y75KGR5pkGqcFisGvBnO9S&index=118, explain the holding of the case?

3. The Standard of the Dormant Commerce Clause

The next case is from 1970. It is always remembered for providing an early test for figuring out when a state regulation interferes with interstate commerce. Can you tell what the test is from the decision below? Are you surprised the decision was unanimous (with eight justices on the Court)? Can you tell from the oral argument, https://www.oyez.org/cases/1969/301, that all the justices were going to agree?

Pike v. Bruce Church, Inc.

SUPREME COURT OF THE UNITED STATES, 1970

397 U.S. 137, 90 S.Ct. 844

Justice STEWART delivered the opinion of the Court, joined by Justices BURGER, BLACK, DOUGLAS, HARLAN, BRENNAN, WHITE, and MARSHALL.

The appellee is a company engaged in extensive commercial farming operations in Arizona and California. The appellant is the official charged with enforcing the Arizona Fruit and Vegetable Standardization Act. A provision of the Act requires that, with certain exceptions, all cantaloupes grown in Arizona and offered for sale must 'be packed in regular compact arrangement in closed standard containers approved by the supervisor * * *.' Invoking his authority under that provision, the appellant issued an order prohibiting the appellee company from transporting uncrated cantaloupes from its Parker, Arizona, ranch to nearby Blythe, California, for packing and processing. The company then brought this action in a federal court to enjoin the order as unconstitutional. ...

The facts are not in dispute, having been stipulated by the parties. The appellee company has for many years been engaged in the business of growing, harvesting, processing, and packing fruits and vegetables at numerous locations in Arizona and California for interstate shipment to markets throughout the Nation. One of the company's newest operations is at Parker, Arizona, where, pursuant to a 1964 lease with the Secretary of the Interior, the Colorado River Indian Agency, and the Colorado River Indian Tribes, it undertook to develop approximately 6,400 acres of uncultivated, arid land for agricultural use. The company has spent more than $3,000,000 in clearing, leveling, irrigating, and otherwise developing this land.

The company began growing cantaloupes on part of the land in 1966, and has harvested a large cantaloupe crop there in each subsequent year. The cantaloupes are considered to be of higher quality that those grown in other areas of the State. Because they are highly perishable, cantaloupes must upon maturity be immediately harvested, processed, packed, and shipped in order to prevent spoliage. The processing and packing operations can be performed only in packing sheds. Because the company had no such facilities at Parker, it transported its 1966 Parker cantaloupe harvest in bulk loads to Blythe, California, 31 miles away, where it operated centralized and efficient packing shed facilities. There the melons were sorted, inspected, packed, and shipped. In 1967 the company again sent its Parker cantaloupe crop to Blythe for sorting, packing, and shipping. In 1968, however, the appellant entered the order here in issue, prohibiting the company from shipping its cantaloupes out of the State unless they were packed in containers in a manner and of a kind approved by the appellant. ...

But in any event, the decisions do not support the argument that the order in the present case does not offect [sic] interstate commerce. ...

Although the criteria for determining the validity of state statutes affecting interstate commerce have been variously stated, the general rule that emerges can be phrased as follows: Where the statute regulates even-handedly to effectuate a legitimate local public interest, and its effects on interstate commerce are only incidental, it will be upheld unless the burden imposed on such commerce is clearly excessive in relation to the putative local benefits. If a legitimate local purpose is found, then the question becomes one of degree. And the extent of the burden that will be tolerated will of course depend on the nature of the local interest involved, and on whether it could be promoted as well with a lesser impact on interstate activities. Occasionally the Court has candidly undertaken a balancing approach in resolving these issues, but more frequently it has spoken in terms of 'direct' and 'indirect' effects and burdens. ...

We are not, then, dealing here with 'state legislation in the field of safety where the propriety of local regulation has long been recognized,'[6] or with an Act designed to protect consumers in Arizona from contaminated or unfit goods. Its purpose and design are simply to protect and enhance the reputation of growers within the State. These are surely legitimate state interest. We have upheld a State's power to require that produce packaged in the State be packaged in a particular kind of receptacle. And we have recognized the legitimate interest of a State in maximizing the financial return to an industry within it. Therefore, as applied to Arizona growers who package their produce in Arizona, we may assume the constitutional validity of the Act. We may further assume that Arizona has full constitutional power to forbid the misleading use of its name on produce that was grown or packed elsewhere. And, to the extent the Act forbids the shipment of contaminated or unfit produce, it clearly rests on sure footing. For, as the Court has said, such produce is 'not the legitimate subject of trade or commerce, nor within the protection of the commerce clause of the Constitution.'

But application of the Act through the appellant's order to the appellee company has a far different impact, and quite a different purpose. The cantaloupes grown by the company at Parker are of exceptionally high quality. The company does not pack them in Arizona and cannot do so without making a capital expenditure of approximately $200,000. It transports them in bulk to nearby Blythe, California, where they are sorted, inspected, packed, and shipped in containers that do not identify them as Arizona cantaloupes, but bear the name of their California packer.[7] The appellant's order would forbid the company to pack its cantaloupes outside Arizona, not for the purpose of keeping the reputation of its growers unsullied, but to enhance their reputation through the reflected good will of the company's superior produce. The appellant, in other words, is not complaining because the company is putting the good name of Arizona on an inferior or deceptively packaged product, but because it is not putting that name on a product that is superior and well packaged. As the appellant's brief puts the matter, 'It is within Arizona's legitimate interest to require that interstate cantaloupe purchasers be informed that this high quality Parker fruit was grown in Arizona.'

Although it is not easy to see why the other growers of Arizona are entitled to benefit at the company's expense from the fact that it produces superior crops, we may assume that the asserted state interest is a legitimate one. But the State's tenuous interest in having the company's cantaloupes identified as originating in Arizona cannot constitutionally justify the requirement that the company build and operate an unneeded $200,000 packing plant in the State. The nature of that burden is, constitutionally, more significant than its extent. For the Court has viewed with particular suspicion state statutes requiring business operations to be performed in the home State that could more efficiently be performed elsewhere. Even where the State is pursuing a clearly legitimate local interest, this particular burden on commerce has been declared to be virtually per se illegal.

The appellant argues that the above cases are different because they involved statutes whose express or concealed purpose was to preserve or secure employment for the home State, while here the statute is a regulatory one and there is no hint of such a purpose. But in *Toomer v. Witsell*, supra, the Court indicated that such a burden upon interstate commerce is unconstitutional even in the absence of such a purpose. In Toomer the Court held invalid a South Carolina statute requiring that owners of shrimp boats licensed by the State to fish in the maritime belt off South Carolina must unload and pack their catch in that State before 'shipping or transporting it to another State.' What we said there applies to this case as well. ...

While the order issued under the Arizona statute does not impose such rigidity on an entire industry, it does impose just such a straitjacket on the appellee company with respect to the allocation of its interstate resources. Such an incidental consequence of a regulatory scheme could perhaps be tolerated if a more compelling state interest were involved. But here the State's interest is minimal at best—certainly less substantial than a State's interest in securing employment for its people. If the Commerce Clause forbids a State to require work to be done within its jurisdiction to promote local employment, then surely it cannot permit a State to require a person to go into a local packing business solely for the sake of enhancing the reputation of other producers within its borders.

Notes and Questions

1. *The Pike test. Pike* is remembered for its test that even if a law does not discriminate on its face against interstate commerce, it can still violate the Dormant Commerce Clause. What test does the Court use to show a Dormant Commerce Clause violation in such circumstances?
2. *Unanimous!* Why was this decision unanimous?
3. *Minimal?* Why is the state's interest in this case minimal?
4. *Fruits and vegetables!* Does this case about fruits and vegetables make sense to you?
5. *The lesson.* Is there a lesson in this case for today, more than 50 years later?
6. *Pike's importance.* Why should this case be in the book?
7. *Does this explanation help to understand the Dormant Commerce Clause's tests?* Constitutional Law: Dormant Commerce Clause: Residual Balance Test, Oct. 22, 2018, posted at https://www.youtube.com/watch?v=bfv4CdRw5dw&list=PLsFE_Nvl6h_Y75KGR5pkGqcFisGvB-nO9S&index=120?
8. California's Proposition 12 requires pork meat sold in California to be born of an adult female pig housed within 24 square feet and with room for that sow to turn around without touching her surroundings. Petitioners argue that most pigs do not live in such circumstances. They note that while the law provides criminal and civil penalties in California only, 99% of sows live outside of California. They argue that the law's influence on out-of-state sows has a tremendous out-of-state effect, and thus violates the dormant commerce clause. Petitioners also allege that the *Pike* test is failed because California's defense of its laws is invalid. They say California has no valid interest in preventing animal cruelty outside of California's borders and has proved no human health interest in the legislation. The oral argument in this case, *National Pork Producers Council v. Ross*, is available at https://www.oyez.org/cases/2022/21-468. Can you tell from the argument what the Justices think about the dormant commerce clause and how it will work here? Do you think they will rule that Proposition 12 violates the dormant commerce clause?

4. Market Participants vs. Market Regulators

The following case looks at an Alaska requirement that timber taken from Alaska be processed within the state prior to export. The Court relies on a distinction between market participants and market regulators to analyze the case. What do those terms mean? Why would the Court distinguish between them here, with the majority saying that market regulators do not get an exemption from the Commerce Clause? Do you agree with the majority? With Justice Brennan's concurrence that the distinction is weak? With Justices Rehnquist's and O'Connor's conclusion that the distinction is "artificial and unconvincing"?

Read through the oral argument, available at https://www.oyez.org/cases/1983/82-1608. If market participant and regulator are hard to understand in this written opinion, do they make sense in the oral argument? What, if anything, did you learn from the oral argument? Some people believe the Justices Rehnquist and O'Connor were more sympathetic to states' rights (which is an awkward phrase for state power) than other Justices. Can you tell that in the oral argument? Can you see that below? Why would they have that perspective?

South-Central Timber Development, Inc. v. Wunnicke

SUPREME COURT OF THE UNITED STATES, 1984

467 U.S. 82, 104 S.Ct. 2237

Justice WHITE announced the judgment of the Court and delivered the opinion of the Court with respect to Parts I and II, and an opinion with respect to Parts III and IV, in which Justice BRENNAN, Justice BLACKMUN, and Justice STEVENS joined.

We granted certiorari in this case to review a decision of the Court of Appeals for the Ninth Circuit that held that Alaska's requirement that timber taken from state lands be processed within the State prior to export was "implicitly authorized" by Congress and therefore does not violate the Commerce Clause. We hold that it was not authorized and reverse the judgment of the Court of Appeals.

I

In September 1980, the Alaska Department of Natural Resources published a notice that it would sell approximately 49 million board-feet of timber in the area of Icy Cape, Alaska, on October 23, 1980. The notice of sale, the prospectus, and the proposed contract for the sale all provided, pursuant to 11 Alaska Admin.Code § 76.130 (1974), that "[p]rimary manufacture within the State of Alaska will be required as a special provision of the contract." Under the primary-manufacture requirement, the successful bidder must partially process the timber prior to shipping it outside of the State. The requirement is imposed by contract and does not limit the export of unprocessed timber not owned by the State. The stated purpose of the requirement is to "protect existing industries, provide for the establishment of new industries, derive revenue from all timber resources, and manage the State's forests on a sustained yield basis." ...

Petitioner, South-Central Timber Development, Inc., is an Alaska corporation engaged in the business of purchasing standing timber, logging the timber, and shipping the logs into foreign commerce, almost exclusively to Japan. It does not operate a mill in Alaska and customarily sells unprocessed logs. When it learned that the primary-manufacture requirement was to be imposed on the Icy Cape sale, it brought an action in Federal District Court seeking an injunction, arguing that the requirement violated *the negative implications of the Commerce Clause* (emphasis added). ...

II

Although the Commerce Clause is by its text an affirmative grant of power to Congress to regulate interstate and foreign commerce, the Clause has long been recognized as a self-executing limitation on the power of the States to enact laws imposing substantial burdens on such commerce. ...

The fact that the state policy in this case appears to be consistent with federal policy—or even that state policy furthers the goals we might believe that Congress had in mind—is an insufficient indicium of congressional intent. Congress acted only with respect to federal lands; we cannot infer from that fact that it intended to authorize a similar policy with respect to state lands. Accordingly, we reverse the contrary judgment of the Court of Appeals.

III

We now turn to the issues left unresolved by the Court of Appeals. The first of these issues is whether Alaska's restrictions on export of unprocessed timber from state-owned lands are exempt from Commerce Clause scrutiny under the "market-participant doctrine."

Our cases make clear that if a State is acting as a market participant, rather than as a market regulator, the dormant Commerce Clause places no limitation on its activities. The precise contours of the market-participant doctrine have yet to be established, however, the doctrine having been applied in only three cases of this Court to date.

The first of the cases, *Hughes v. Alexandria Scrap Corp.*, involved a Maryland program designed to reduce the number of junked automobiles in the State. A "bounty" was established on Maryland-licensed junk cars, and the State imposed more stringent documentation requirements on out- of-state scrap processors than on in-state ones. The Court rejected a Commerce Clause attack on the program, although it noted that under traditional Commerce Clause analysis the program might well be invalid because it had the effect of reducing the flow of goods in interstate commerce. The Court concluded that Maryland's action was not "the kind of action with which the Commerce Clause is concerned," because "[n]othing in the purposes animating the Commerce Clause prohibits a State, in the absence of congressional action, from participating in the market and exercising the right to favor its own citizens over others."

In *Reeves, Inc. v. Stake*, the Court upheld a South Dakota policy of restricting the sale of cement from a state-owned plant to state residents, declaring that "[t]he basic distinction drawn in Alexandria Scrap between States as market participants and States as market regulators makes good sense and sound law." The Court relied upon "'the long recognized right of trader or manufacturer, engaged in an entirely private business, freely to exercise his own independent discretion as to parties with whom he will deal.'" In essence, the Court recognized the principle that the Commerce Clause places no limitations on a State's refusal to deal with particular parties when it is participating in the interstate market in goods.

The most recent of this Court's cases developing the market-participant doctrine is *White v. Massachusetts Council of Construction Employers, Inc.*, in which the Court sustained against a Commerce Clause challenge an executive order of the Mayor of Boston that required all construction projects funded in whole or in part by city funds or city-administered funds to be performed by a work force of at least 50% city residents. The Court rejected the argument that the city was not entitled to the protection of the doctrine because the order had the effect of regulating employment contracts between public contractors and their employees. Recognizing that "there are some limits on a state or local government's ability to impose restrictions that reach beyond the immediate parties with which the government transacts business," the Court found it unnecessary to define those limits because "[e]veryone affected by the order [was], in a substantial if informal sense, 'working for the city.'" The fact that the employees were "working for the city" was "crucial" to the market-participant analysis in White. ...

The limit of the market-participant doctrine must be that it allows a State to impose burdens on commerce within the market in which it is a participant, but allows it to go no further. The State may not impose conditions, whether by statute, regulation, or contract, that have a substantial regulatory effect outside of that particular market. Unless the "market" is relatively narrowly defined, the doctrine has the potential of swallowing up the rule that States may not impose substantial burdens on interstate commerce even if they act with the permissible state purpose of fostering local industry.

At the heart of the dispute in this case is disagreement over the definition of the market. Alaska contends that it is participating in the processed timber market, although it acknowledges that it participates in no way in the actual processing. South-Central argues, on the other hand, that although the State may be a participant in the timber market, it is using its leverage in that market to exert a regulatory effect in the processing market, in which it is not a participant. We agree with the latter position.

... We reject the contention that a State's action as a market regulator may be upheld against Commerce Clause challenge on the ground that the State could achieve the same end as a market participant. We therefore find it unimportant for present purposes that the State could support its processing industry by selling only to Alaska processors, by vertical integration, or by direct subsidy.

Second, downstream restrictions have a greater regulatory effect than do limitations on the immediate transaction. Instead of merely choosing its own trading partners, the State is attempting to govern the private, separate economic relationships of its trading partners; that is, it restricts the post-purchase activity of the purchaser, rather than merely the purchasing activity. In contrast to the situation in White, this restriction on private economic activity takes place after the completion of the parties' direct commercial obligations, rather than during the course of an ongoing commercial relationship in which the city retained a continuing proprietary interest in the subject of the contract. In sum, the State may not avail itself of the market-participant doctrine to immunize its downstream regulation of the timber-processing market in which it is not a participant.

IV

... Because of the protectionist nature of Alaska's local-processing requirement and the burden on commerce resulting therefrom, we conclude that it falls within the rule of virtual per se invalidity of laws that "bloc[k] the flow of interstate commerce at a State's borders." City of Philadelphia v. New Jersey. ...

Justice BRENNAN, concurring.

... In my view, Justice WHITE's treatment of the market-participant doctrine and the response of Justice REHNQUIST point up the inherent weakness of the doctrine.

Justice POWELL, with whom THE CHIEF JUSTICE joins, concurring in part and concurring in the judgment.

I join Parts I and II of Justice WHITE's opinion. I would remand the case to the Court of Appeals to allow that court to consider whether Alaska was acting as a "market participant" and whether Alaska's primary-manufacture requirement substantially burdened interstate commerce under the holding of Pike v. Bruce Church.

Justice REHNQUIST, with whom Justice O'CONNOR joins, dissenting.

In my view, the line of distinction drawn in the plurality opinion between the State as market participant and the State as market regulator is both artificial and unconvincing. ...

Perhaps the State's actions do raise antitrust problems. But what the plurality overlooks is that the antitrust laws apply to a State only when it is acting as a market participant. When the State acts as a market regulator, it is immune from antitrust scrutiny. Of course, the line of distinction in cases under the Commerce Clause need not necessarily parallel the line drawn in antitrust law. But the plurality can hardly justify placing Alaska in the market-regulator category, in this Commerce Clause case, by relying on antitrust cases that are relevant only if the State is a market participant.

The contractual term at issue here no more transforms Alaska's sale of timber into "regulation" of the processing industry than the resident-hiring preference imposed by the city of Boston in White v. Massachusetts. Alaska is merely paying the buyer of the timber indirectly, by means of a reduced price, to hire Alaska residents to process the timber. ... It seems to me unduly formalistic to conclude that the one path chosen by the State as best suited to promote its concerns is the path forbidden it by the Commerce Clause.

Notes and Questions

1. *Market participant or regulator?* What is the constitutional difference between Alaska being a participant in the market and Alaska being a regulator of the market? Why does Justice White conclude that Alaska is acting as a regulator in this case and, therefore, limited by the Dormant Commerce Clause?

2. *Justice Brennan?* Why does Justice Brennan concur that "Justice WHITE's treatment of the market-participant doctrine and the response of Justice REHNQUIST point up the inherent weakness of the doctrine." Do you agree? Is there any way for you to make the doctrine stronger?
3. *Justice Powell and remand.* Why would Justice Powell remand the case?
4. *The dissent.* Do you agree with Rehnquist's dissent that "the line of distinction drawn in the plurality opinion between the state as market participant and the state as market regulator is both artificial and unconvincing"? Why does he cite antitrust law?
5. *The three cited cases.* Justice White discusses three cases that had discussed the market participant exception. In *Hughes*, 426 U.S. 794 (1976), the Court allowed Maryland to put more regulations on out-of-state junk cars than in-state cars. The Court concluded the Dormant Commerce Clause did not prevent the state "from participating in the market and exercising the right to favor its own citizens over others." The Court reaffirmed *Hughes* in *Reeves*, 447 U.S. 429 (1980), ruling that South Dakota could participate in the market and favor its own citizens over citizens of other states. In *White*, 460 U.S. 204 (1983), the mayor of Boston's executive order required that construction projects funded by the city be performed by a workplace made up of at least half the residents of the city. Boston was also a market participant and, therefore, not subject to the Dormant Commerce Clause. What are those cases about? Why are they relevant here?
6. *Federal and state sovereigns.* What does it mean to have two sovereigns—federal and state? Do you understand their role now? What questions do you have about each sovereign?
7. *The market participant exception. How* would you assess Professor Opderbeck's analysis of the market participant exception, in Constitutional Law: Unit 6: Market Participant Exception, Oct. 19, 2018, at https://www.youtube.com/watch?v=I_k2RrCwfZw&list=PLsFE_Nvl6h_Y75KGR5pkGqcFisGvBnO9S&index=124?
8. *Clarkstown, New York, undermines competition and violates the Dormant Commerce Clause.* Clarkstown, New York, had a law that promoted a privately owned local waste transfer station so that all waste would go there and finance the local revenue transfer facility. All waste had to be processed at the local processing facility before leaving the state. The Court ruled that the ordinance violated the Dormant Commerce Clause because it undermined competition with in-state and out-of-state competitors. *C & A Carbone, Inc. v. Town of Clarkstown*, 511 U.S. 383 (1994).

   In 2007, the Court ruled that a different flow control ordinance, which required haulers to bring their waste to a state-created public benefit corporation, was constitutional. The Court ruled that the public corporation was not a private business and that state and local governments have different responsibilities than private businesses. The government was allowed to protect the health, safety, and welfare of its citizens. *United Haulers Association, Inc. v. Herkimer Solid Waste Management Authority*, 550 U.S. 330 (2007). Do you agree with the Court that the private or public nature of the facility affects the commerce analysis?

9. *Is there a Dormant Commerce Clause?* Justices Scalia and Thomas argued that the Constitution does not contain a "negative Commerce Clause." It contains a Commerce Clause. "The Clause says nothing about prohibiting state laws that burden commerce. Much less does it

say anything about authorizing judges to set aside state laws *they believe* burden commerce." They conclude it is a "judicial fraud" to allow Congress to approve impermissible burdens on interstate commerce. Therefore, they dissented from an opinion concluding that Maryland's personal income tax violated the Commerce Clause because it favored intrastate over interstate economic activity. *Comptroller of the Treasury of Maryland v. Wynne*, 575 I/S/ 542 (2015). Do you agree with Scalia and Thomas, or do you think the Dormant Commerce Clause plays an important constitutional role?

10. *A Summary.* A summary of the Dormant Commerce Clause says that if a law discriminates against out-of-state laws, it can violate the Dormant Commerce Clause unless its action is necessary to achieve an important governmental purpose. There is no violation if Congress approves of the legislation, using its commerce powers, or if the market participant exception applies. If the law does not discriminate against out-of-state commerce, it can still violate the Dormant Commerce Clause if its burdens exceed its benefits. What does this case law contribute to your understanding of federal and state sovereignty?

The Privileges and Immunities Clause of Article IV of the Constitution also involves discrimination against out-of-staters. We study Article IV in Chapter 8.

A Look Ahead

Having studied the structure of the Constitution, we now turn to the rights recognized by the Constitution. In Chapter 6, we study the place of slavery in the Constitution and history of the United States.

Credits

Fig. 5.1: Adapted from: Oyez, "How the Justices Voted in New York," https://www.oyez.org/cases/1991/91-543. Copyright © 2022 by Oyez, Inc.

Fig. 5.2: Adapted from: Oyez, "How the Justices Voted in Printz," https://www.oyez.org/cases/1996/95-1478. Copyright © 2022 by Oyez, Inc.

Six

The Constitution Protected Slavery Until the Civil War Amendments Ended It

Introduction

Are you surprised that the U.S. Constitution protected slavery? You should know that the Framers were not in agreement on whether slavery should be abolished or grandfathered in. They compromised, embedding a conflict that would later erupt in war. Here are three relevant constitutional texts that protected slavery and allowed it to continue:

> Article 1, Section 2, Clause 3. Representatives and direct Taxes shall be apportioned among the several States which may be included within this Union, according to their respective Numbers, which shall be determined by adding to the whole Number of free Persons, including those bound to Service for a Term of Years, and excluding Indians not taxed, three fifths of all other Persons.

> Article 1, Section 9, Clause 1. The Migration or Importation of such Persons as any of the States now existing shall think proper to admit, shall not be prohibited by the Congress prior to the Year one thousand eight hundred and eight, but a Tax or duty may be imposed on such Importation, not exceeding ten dollars for each Person.

> Article 4, Section 2, Clause 3. No Person held to Service or Labour in one State, under the Laws thereof, escaping into another, shall, in Consequence of any Law or Regulation therein, be discharged from such Service or Labour, but shall be delivered up on Claim of the Party to whom such Service or Labour may be due.

After the Civil War was fought, three amendments—the Thirteenth, Fourteenth, and Fifteenth Amendments—were added to the Constitution. The Thirteenth Amendment ended slavery. The Fourteenth Amendment protected the privileges or immunities of citizens, as well as due process and equal protection. The Fifteenth Amendment defended voting rights. These three amendments were directly concerned with overcoming the preslavery constitutional texts that you just read.

In this chapter, after you read the Court's decision accepting slavery, the *Dred Scott* case, you will read about how the Thirteenth, Fourteenth, and Fifteenth Amendments opposed slavery and protected civil rights. Ask yourself if the Court interpreting those amendments has protected all the rights that the amendments were expected to defend. Are there more rights that you think the three constitutional amendments could protect? Has slavery finally ended?

The last section of the chapter asks if the Civil War amendments mean that the Bill of Rights now applies not only to the federal government but to the state governments. Are the states required to protect their citizens according to the rights amendments to the U.S. Constitution?

A. The Constitutional Texts

The following case, *Dred Scott*, is often viewed as one of the Supreme Court's worst cases ever. Do you agree? Why was this case so important? Why is the Court's refusal of jurisdiction such a negative thing?

The case involved a slave, Dred Scott, who belonged to Dr. Emerson. They lived in the State of Missouri. Then, Emerson took Scott to the State of Illinois for about two years. Then, Dr. Emerson took Scott to Upper Louisiana, which was north of the State of Missouri. Dred married a fellow slave, Harriet, and they had two children. All of them wound up in the State of Missouri. Emerson died. Scott brought a lawsuit for their freedom against Emerson's estate, arguing that there was diversity jurisdiction because they were citizens of different states and that his residence in a free state had made him free.

The case involved the Missouri Compromise, where Missouri was admitted as a slave state and Maine as a free state, while legislation passed prohibiting slavery in Louisiana Purchase lands north of the 36´30″ parallel except for Missouri.

Do you understand why constitutional amendments were necessary in response to *Dred Scott*?

Dred Scott v. Sandford

SUPREME COURT OF THE UNITED STATES, 1857

60 U.S. 393, 19 How. 393

Mr. Chief Justice TANEY delivered the opinion of the court.

... There are two leading questions presented by the record:

1. Had the Circuit Court of the United States jurisdiction to hear and determine the case between these parties? And
2. If it had jurisdiction, is the judgment it has given erroneous or not? ...

If the question raised by it is legally before us, and the court should be of opinion that the facts stated in it disqualify the plaintiff from becoming a citizen, in the sense in which that word is used in the Constitution of the United States, then the judgment of the Circuit Court is erroneous, and must be reversed. ...

The question is simply this: Can a negro, whose ancestors were imported into this country, and sold as slaves, become a member of the political community formed and brought into existence by the Constitution of the United States, and as such become entitled to all the rights, and privileges, and immunities, guarantied by that instrument to the citizen? One of which rights is the privilege of suing in a court of the United States in the cases specified in the Constitution.

It will be observed, that the plea applies to that class of persons only whose ancestors were negroes of the African race, and imported into this country, and sold and held as slaves. The only matter in issue before the court, therefore, is, whether the descendants of such slaves, when they shall be emancipated, or who are born of parents who had become free before their birth, are citizens of a State, in the sense in which the word citizen is used in the Constitution of the United States. And this being the only matter in dispute on the pleadings, the court must be understood as speaking in this opinion of that class only, that is, of those persons who are the descendants of Africans who were imported into this country, and sold as slaves.

The situation of this population was altogether unlike that of the Indian race. The latter, it is true, formed no part of the colonial communities, and never amalgamated with them in social connections or in government. But although they were uncivilized, they were yet a free and independent people, associated together in nations or tribes, and governed by their own laws. Many of these political communities were situated in territories to which the white race claimed the ultimate right of dominion. But that claim was acknowledged to be subject to the right of the Indians to occupy it as long as they thought proper, and neither the English nor colonial Governments claimed or exercised any dominion over the tribe or nation by whom it was occupied, nor claimed the right to the possession of the territory, until the tribe or nation consented to cede it. These Indian Governments were regarded and treated as foreign Governments, as much so as if an ocean had separated the red man from the white; and their freedom has constantly been acknowledged, from the time of the first emigration to the English colonies to the present day, by the different Governments which succeeded each other. Treaties have been negotiated with them, and their alliance sought for in war; and the people who compose these Indian political communities have always been treated as foreigners not living under our Government. It is true that the course of events has brought the Indian tribes within the limits of the United States under subjection to the white race; and it has been found necessary, for their sake as well as our own, to regard them as in a state of pupilage, and to legislate to a certain extent over them and the territory they occupy. But they may, without doubt, like the subjects of any other foreign Government, be naturalized by the authority of Congress, and become citizens of a State, and of the United States; and if an individual should leave his nation or tribe, and take up his abode among the white population, he would be entitled to all the rights and privileges which would belong to an emigrant from any other foreign people.

We proceed to examine the case as presented by the pleadings.

The words 'people of the United States' and 'citizens' are synonymous terms, and mean the same thing. They both describe the political body who, according to our republican institutions, form the sovereignty, and who hold the power and conduct the Government through their representatives. They are what we familiarly call the 'sovereign people,' and every citizen is one of this people, and a constituent member of this sovereignty. The question before us is, whether the class of persons described in the plea in abatement compose a portion of this people, and are constituent members of this sovereignty? We think they are not, and that they are not included, and were not intended to be included, under the word 'citizens' in the Constitution, and can therefore claim none of the rights and privileges which that instrument provides for and secures to citizens of the United States. On the contrary, they were at that time considered as a subordinate and inferior class of beings, who had been subjugated by the dominant race, and, whether emancipated or not, yet remained subject to their authority, and had no rights or privileges but such as those who held the power and the Government might choose to grant them.

It is not the province of the court to decide upon the justice or injustice, the policy or impolicy, of these laws. The decision of that question belonged to the political or law-making power; to those who formed the sovereignty and framed the Constitution. The duty of the court is, to interpret the instrument they have framed, with the best lights we can obtain on the subject, and to administer it as we find it, according to its true intent and meaning when it was adopted. ...

Each State may still confer them upon an alien, or any one it thinks proper, or upon any class or description of persons; yet he would not be a citizen in the sense in which that word is used in the Constitution of the United States, nor entitled to sue as such in one of its courts, nor to the privileges and immunities of a citizen in the other States. The rights which he would acquire would be restricted to the State which gave them. The Constitution has conferred on Congress the right to establish an uniform rule of naturalization, and this right is evidently exclusive, and has always been held by this court to be so. Consequently, no State, since the adoption of the Constitution, can by naturalizing an alien invest him with the rights and privileges secured to a citizen of a State under the Federal Government, although, so far as the State alone was concerned, he would undoubtedly be entitled to the rights of a citizen, and clothed with all the rights and immunities which the Constitution and laws of the State attached to that character.

It is very clear, therefore, that no State can, by any act or law of its own, passed since the adoption of the Constitution, introduce a new member into the political community created by the Constitution of the United States. It cannot make him a member of this community by making him a member of its own. And for the same reason it cannot introduce any person, or description of persons, who were not intended to be embraced in this new political family, which the Constitution brought into existence, but were intended to be excluded from it. ...

In the opinion of the court, the legislation and histories of the times, and the language used in the Declaration of Independence, show, that neither the class of persons who had been imported as slaves, nor their descendants, whether they had become free or not, were then acknowledged as a part of the people, nor intended to be included in the general words used in that memorable instrument. ...

They had for more than a century before been regarded as beings of an inferior order, and altogether unfit to associate with the white race, either in social or political relations; and so far inferior, that they had no rights which the white man was bound to respect; and that the negro might justly and lawfully be reduced to slavery for his benefit. He was bought and sold, and treated as an ordinary article of merchandise and traffic, whenever a profit could be made by it. This opinion was at that time fixed and universal in the civilized portion of the white race. It was regarded as an axiom in morals as well as in politics, which no one thought of disputing, or supposed to be open to dispute; and men in every grade and position in society daily and habitually acted upon it in their private pursuits, as well as in matters of public concern, without doubting for a moment the correctness of this opinion. ...

[The Declaration of Independence] proceeds to say: 'We hold these truths to be self-evident: that all men are created equal; that they are endowed by their Creator with certain unalienable rights; that among them is life, liberty, and the pursuit of happiness; that to secure these rights, Governments are instituted, deriving their just powers from the consent of the governed.'

The general words above quoted would seem to embrace the whole human family, and if they were used in a similar instrument at this day would be so understood. But it is too clear for dispute, that the enslaved African race were not intended to be included, and formed no part of the people who framed and adopted this declaration; for if the language, as understood in that day, would embrace them, the conduct of the distinguished men who framed the Declaration of Independence would have been utterly and flagrantly inconsistent with the principles they asserted; and instead of the sympathy of mankind, to which they so confidently appealed, they would have deserved and received universal rebuke and reprobation.

... The unhappy black race were separated from the white by indelible marks, and laws long before established, and were never thought of or spoken of except as property, and when the claims of the owner or the profit of the trader were supposed to need protection. ...

But there are two clauses in the Constitution which point directly and specifically to the negro race as a separate class of persons, and show clearly that they were not regarded as a portion of the people or citizens of the Government then formed.

One of these clauses reserves to each of the thirteen States the right to import slaves until the year 1808, if it thinks proper. And the importation which it thus sanctions was unquestionably of persons of the race of which we are speaking, as the traffic in slaves in the United States had always been confined to them. And by the other provision the States pledge themselves to each other to maintain the right of property of the master, by delivering up to him any slave who may have escaped from his service, and be found within their respective territories. By the first above-mentioned clause, therefore, the right to purchase and hold this property is directly sanctioned and authorized for twenty years by the people who framed the Constitution. And by the second, they pledge themselves to maintain and uphold the right of the master in the manner specified, as long as the Government they then formed should endure. And these two provisions show, conclusively, that neither the description of persons therein referred to, nor their descendants, were embraced in any of the other provisions of the Constitution; for certainly these two clauses were not intended to confer on them or their posterity the blessings of liberty, or any of the personal rights so carefully provided for the citizen. ...

We proceed, therefore, to inquire whether the facts relied on by the plaintiff entitled him to his freedom.

The case, as he himself states it, on the record brought here by his writ of error, is this:

The plaintiff was a negro slave, belonging to Dr. Emerson, who was a surgeon in the army of the United States. In the year 1834, he took the plaintiff from the State of Missouri to the military post at Rock Island, in the State of Illinois, and held him there as a slave until the month of April or May, 1836. At the time last mentioned, said Dr. Emerson removed the plaintiff from said military post at Rock Island to the military post at Fort Snelling, situate on the west bank of the Mississippi river, in the Territory known as Upper Louisiana, acquired by the United States of France, and situate north of the latitude of thirty-six degrees thirty minutes north, and north of the State of Missouri. Said Dr. Emerson held the plaintiff in slavery at said Fort Snelling, from said last-mentioned date until the year 1838. ...

In considering this part of the controversy [on the merits], two questions arise: 1. Was he, together with his family, free in Missouri by reason of the stay in the territory of the United States hereinbefore mentioned? And 2. If they were not, is Scott himself free by reason of his removal to Rock Island, in the State of Illinois, as stated in the above admissions? ...

The act of Congress, upon which the plaintiff relies, declares that slavery and involuntary servitude, except as a punishment for crime, shall be forever prohibited in all that part of the territory ceded by France, under the name of Louisiana, which lies north of thirty-six degrees thirty minutes north latitude, and not included within the limits of Missouri. And the difficulty which meets us at the threshold of this part of the inquiry is, whether Congress was authorized to pass this law under any of the powers granted to it by the Constitution; for if the authority is not given by that instrument, it is the duty of this court to declare it void and inoperative, and incapable of conferring freedom upon any one who is held as a slave under the have of any one of the States. ...

But the power of Congress over the person or property of a citizen can never be a mere discretionary power under our Constitution and form of Government. The powers of the Government and the rights and privileges of the citizen are regulated and plainly defined by the Constitution itself. And when the Territory becomes a part of the United States, the Federal Government enters into possession in the character impressed upon it by those who created it. It enters upon it with its powers over the citizen strictly defined, and limited by the Constitution, from which it derives its own existence, and by virtue of which alone it continues to exist and act as a Government and sovereignty. It has no power of any kind beyond it; and it cannot, when it enters a Territory of the United States, put off its character, and assume discretionary or despotic powers which the Constitution has denied to it. It cannot create for itself a new character separated from the citizens of the United States, and the duties it owes them under the provisions of the Constitution. The Territory being a part of the United States, the Government and the citizen both enter it under the authority of the Constitution, with their respective rights defined and marked out; and the Federal Government can exercise no power over his person or property, beyond what that instrument confers, nor lawfully deny any right which it has reserved. ...

It seems, however, to be supposed, that there is a difference between property in a slave and other property, and that different rules may be applied to it in expounding the Constitution of the United States. And the laws and usages of nations, and the writings of eminent jurists upon the relation of master and slave and their mutual rights and duties, and the powers which Governments may exercise over it, have been dwelt upon in the argument.

But in considering the question before us, it must be borne in mind that there is no law of nations standing between the people of the United States and their Government, and interfering with their relation to each other. The powers of the Government, and the rights of the citizen under it, are positive and practical regulations plainly written down. The people of the United States have delegated to it certain enumerated powers, and forbidden it to exercise others. It has no power over the person or property of a citizen but what the citizens of the United States have granted. And no laws or usages of other nations, or reasoning of statesmen or jurists upon the relations of master and slave, can enlarge the powers of the Government, or take from the citizens the rights they have reserved. And if the Constitution recognizes the right of property of the master in a slave, and makes no distinction between that description of property and other property owned by a citizen, no tribunal, acting under the authority of the United States, whether it be legislative, executive, or judicial, has a right to draw such a distinction, or deny to it the benefit of the provisions and guarantees which have been provided for the protection of private property against the encroachments of the Government.

Now, as we have already said in an earlier part of this opinion, upon a different point, the right of property in a slave is distinctly and expressly affirmed in the Constitution. The right to traffic in it, like an ordinary article of merchandise and property, was guarantied to the citizens of the United States, in every State that might desire it, for twenty years. And the Government in express terms is pledged to protect it in all future time, if the slave escapes from his owner. This is done in plain words—too plain to be misunderstood. And no word can be found in the Constitution which gives Congress a greater power over slave property, or which entitles property of that kind to less protection that property of any other description. The only power conferred is the power coupled with the duty of guarding and protecting the owner in his rights.Upon these considerations, it is the opinion of the court that the act of Congress which prohibited a citizen from holding and owning property of this kind in the territory of the United States north of the line therein mentioned, is not warranted by the Constitution, and is therefore void; and that neither Dred Scott himself, nor any of his family, were made free by being carried into this territory; even if they had been carried there by the owner, with the intention of becoming a permanent resident. ...

But there is another point in the case which depends on State power and State law. And it is contended, on the part of the plaintiff, that he is made free by being taken to Rock Island, in the State of Illinois, independently of his residence in the territory of the United States; and being so made free, he was not again reduced to a state of slavery by being brought back to Missouri.

Our notice of this part of the case will be very brief; for the principle on which it depends was decided in this court, upon much consideration, in the case of Strader et al. *v.* Graham, reported in 10th Howard, 82. In that case, the slaves had been taken from Kentucky to Ohio, with the consent of the owner, and afterwards brought back to Kentucky. And this court held that their *status* or condition, as free or slave, depended upon the laws of Kentucky, when they were brought back into that State, and not of Ohio; and that this court had no jurisdiction to revise the judgment of a State court upon its own laws. This was the point directly before the court, and the decision that this court had not jurisdiction turned upon it, as will be seen by the report of the case.

So in this case. As Scott was a slave when taken into the State of Illinois by his owner, and was there held as such, and brought back in that character, his *status*, as free or slave, depended on the laws of Missouri, and not of Illinois. ...

Upon the whole, therefore, it is the judgment of this court, that it appears by the record before us that the plaintiff in error is not a citizen of Missouri, in the sense in which that word is used in the Constitution; and that the Circuit Court of the United States, for that reason, had no jurisdiction in the case, and could give no judgment in it. Its judgment for the defendant must, consequently, be reversed, and a mandate issued, directing the suit to be dismissed for want of jurisdiction.

Mr. Justice CURTIS dissenting.

... To determine whether any free persons, descended from Africans held in slavery, were citizens of the United States under the Confederation, and consequently at the time of the adoption of the Constitution of the United States, it is only necessary to know whether any such persons were citizens of either of the States under the Confederation, at the time of the adoption of the Constitution.

Of this there can be no doubt. At the time of the ratification of the Articles of Confederation, all free native-born inhabitants of the States of New Hampshire, Massachusetts, New York, New Jersey, and North Carolina, though descended from African slaves, were not only citizens of those States, but such of them as had the other necessary qualifications possessed the franchise of electors, on equal terms with other citizens. ...

Did the Constitution of the United States deprive them or their descendants of citizenship?

That Constitution was ordained and established by the people of the United States, through the action, in each State, or those persons who were qualified by its laws to act thereon, in behalf of themselves and all other citizens of that State. In some of the States, as we have seen, colored persons were among those qualified by law to act on this subject. These colored persons were not only included in the body of 'the people of the United States,' by whom the Constitution was ordained and established, but in at least five of the States they had the power to act, and doubtless did act, by their suffrages, upon the question of its adoption. It would be strange, if we were to find in that instrument anything which deprived of their citizenship any part of the people of the United States who were among those by whom it was established.

I can find nothing in the Constitution which, *proprio vigore*, deprives of their citizenship any class of persons who were citizens of the United States at the time of its adoption, or who should be native-born citizens of any State after its adoption; nor any power enabling Congress to disfranchise persons born on the soil of any State, and entitled to citizenship of such State by its Constitution and laws. And my opinion is, that, under the Constitution of the United States, every free person born on the soil of a State, who is a citizen of that State by force of its Constitution or laws, is also a citizen of the United States. …

To convert this temporary stipulation of the treaty, in behalf of French subjects who then inhabited a small portion of Louisiana, into a permanent restriction upon the power of Congress to regulate territory then uninhabited, and to assert that it not only restrains Congress from affecting the rights of property of the then inhabitants, but enabled them and all other citizens of the United States to go into any part of the ceded territory with their slaves, and hold them there, is a construction of this treaty so opposed to its natural meaning, and so far beyond its subject-matter and the evident design of the parties, that I cannot assent to it. In my opinion, this treaty has no bearing on the present question. …

For these reasons, I am of opinion that so much of the several acts of Congress as prohibited slavery and involuntary servitude within that part of the Territory of Wisconsin lying north of thirty-six degrees thirty minutes north latitude, and west of the river Mississippi, were constitutional and valid laws.

Notes and Questions

1. *The decision and the historico-political context.* Justice Stephen Breyer delivered an address for the Supreme Court Historical Society in 2009, which provides illuminating history and analysis that aid in putting *Dred Scott* in the proper historical context. Read it at Guardian of the Constitution, The Counter Example of *Dred Scott*, June 1, 2000, at https://www.supremecourt.gov/publicinfo/speeches/sp_06-01-09.html. What other Supreme Court cases have generated a backlash? What happened?
2. *Defining "citizen."* What does it mean to be a citizen of the United States? A citizen of a state? What do those mean at the time of this opinion?
3. *The Framers and slavery.* The Framers differed on whether to eliminate slavery or grandfather it in. Why did the Constitution allow for slavery in the first place?
4. *Video.* Does this video, Bill of Rights Institute, *Dred v. Scott*: Homework Help, Mar. 21, 2017, adequately capture the meaning of the case, https://www.youtube.com/watch?v=OazGts1xC9w? Does this video, Khan Academy, The Dred Scott case and citizenship, Sept. 1, 2020, give you the background on the case, https://www.youtube.com/watch?v=U3vK0RuwZMc?

B. The Civil War Amendments: XIII, XIV, XV

Dred Scott was decided four years before the Civil War began in 1861; the war lasted four years, ending on April 9, 1865. Eight months later, the Thirteenth Amendment abolishing slavery was ratified. Over three years later, the Fourteenth Amendment was ratified, which protects privileges or immunities, due process, and equal protection. Approximately a year and a half later, the Fifteenth Amendment was ratified, which protects the right to vote. Of course, those amendments changed the law as explained in *Dred Scott*. How did they change it? Why do these amendments remain important today? What would the Constitution mean without them?

1. The Thirteenth Amendment

This is Amendment XIII:

> Section 1.
>
> Neither slavery nor involuntary servitude, except as a punishment for crime whereof the party shall have been duly convicted, shall exist within thited States, or any place subject to their jurisdiction.
>
> Section 2.
>
> Congress shall have power to enforce this article by appropriate legislation.

If we said this was the United States's most important constitutional amendment, would you agree with us? Why or why not? If not, what amendment or section of the Constitution would you choose?

a. Peonage, or Debt Servitude, Violates the Thirteenth Amendment

The following case, *Bailey*, was decided in 1911. What does it say about the Thirteenth Amendment? Is that an important point for the Court to make? Does *Bailey* remain relevant today?

Bailey v. Alabama

SUPREME COURT OF THE UNITED STATES, 1911

219 U.S. 219, 31 S.Ct. 145

Mr. Justice HUGHES delivered the opinion of the court:

This is a writ of error to review a judgment of the supreme court of the state of Alabama, affirming a judgment of conviction in the Montgomery city court. The statute upon which the conviction was based is assailed as in violation ... of the 13th Amendment, and of the act of Congress providing for the enforcement of that Amendment, in that the effect of the statute is to enforce involuntary servitude by compelling personal service in liquidation of a debt. ...

Bailey, the plaintiff in error, was committed for detention on the charge of obtaining $15 under a contract in writing with intent to injure or defraud his employer. ...

Having failed to obtain his release on habeas corpus, Bailey was indicted on the following charge:

'The grand jury of said county charge that before the finding of this indictment Alonzo Bailey, with intent to injure or defraud his employer, the Riverside Company, a corporation, entered into a written contract to perform labor or services for the Riverside Company, a corporation, and obtained thereby the sum of $15 from the said the Riverside Company, and afterwards with like intent, and without just cause, failed or refused to perform such labor or services, or to refund such money, against the peace and dignity of the state of Alabama.' ...

In the present case it is urged that the statute as amended, through the operation of the presumption for which it provides, violates the 13th Amendment of the Constitution of the United States and the act of Congress passed for its enforcement.

The 13th Amendment provides:

> 'Section 1. Neither slavery nor involuntary servitude, except as a punishment for crime whereof the party shall have been duly convicted, shall exist within the United States, or any place subject to their jurisdiction.
>
> 'Section 2. Congress shall have power to enforce this article by appropriate legislation.'

Pursuant to the authority thus conferred, Congress passed the act of March 2, 1867, chap. 187, 14 Stat. at L. 546, the provisions of which are now found in §§ 1990 and 5526 of the Revised Statutes (U.S. Comp. Stat. 1901, pp. 1266, 3715), as follows:

> 'Sec. 1990. The holding of any person to service or labor under the system known as peonage is abolished and forever prohibited in the territory of New Mexico, or in any other territory or state of the United States; and all acts, laws, resolutions, orders, regulations, or usages of the territory of New Mexico, or of any other territory or state, which have heretofore established, maintained, or enforced, or by virtue of which any attempt shall hereafter be made to establish, maintain, or enforce, directly or indirectly, the voluntary or involuntary service or labor of any persons as peons, in liquidation of any debt or obligation, or otherwise, are declared null and void.'
>
> 'Sec. 5526. Every person who holds, arrests, returns, or causes to be held, arrested, or returned, or in any manner aids in the arrest or return, of any person to a condition of peonage, shall be punished by a fine of not less than one thousand nor more than five thousand dollars, or by imprisonment not less than one year nor more than five years, or by both.'

The language of the 13th Amendment was not new. It reproduced the historice words of the ordinance of 1787 for the government of the Northwest territory, and gave them unrestricted application within the United States and all places subject to their jurisdiction. While the immediate concern was with African slavery, the Amendment was not limited to that. It was a charter of universal civil freedom for all persons, of whatever race, color, or estate, under the flag.

The words involuntary servitude have a 'larger meaning than slavery.'

'It was very well understood that, in the form of apprenticeship for long terms, as it had been practised in the West India Islands, on the abolition of slavery by the English government, or by reducing the slaves to the condition of serfs attached to the plantation, the purpose of the article might have been evaded, if only the word 'slavery' had been used.' Slaughter-House Cases, 16 Wall. p. 69, 21 L. ed. 406. The plain intention was to abolish slavery of whatever name and form and all its badges and incidents; to render impossible any state of bondage; to make labor free, by prohibiting that control by which the personal service of one man is disposed of or coerced for another's benefit, which is the essence of involuntary servitude.

While the Amendment was self-executing, so far as its terms were applicable to any existing condition, Congress was authorized to secure its complete enforcement by appropriate legislation. As was said in the Civil Rights Cases: 'By its own unaided force and effect it abolished slavery, and established universal freedom. Still, legislation may be necessary and proper to meet all the various cases and circumstances to be affected by it, and to prescribe proper modes of redress for its violation in letter or spirit. And such legislation may be primary and direct in its character; for the Amendment is not a mere prohibition of state laws establishing or upholding slavery, but an absolute declaration that slavery or involuntary servitude shall not exist in any part of the United States.'

The act of March 2, 1867 (Rev. Stat. §§ 1990 and 5526, supra), a was a valid exercise of this express authority. It declared that all laws of any state, by virtue of which any attempt should be made 'to establish, maintain, or enforce, directly or indirectly, the voluntary or involuntary service or labor of any person as peons, in liquidation of any debt or obligation, or otherwise,' should be null and void.

Peonage is a term descriptive of a condition which has existed in Spanish America, and especially in Mexico. The essence of the thing is compulsory service in payment of a debt. A peon is one who is compelled to work for his creditor until his debt is paid. And in this explicit and comprehensive enactment, Congress was not concerned with mere names or manner of description, or with a particular place or section of the country. It was concerned with a fact, wherever it might exist; with a condition, however named and wherever it might be established, maintained, or enforced. ...

The act of Congress, nullifying all state laws by which it should be attempted to enforce the 'service or labor of any persons as peons, in liquidation of any debt or obligation, or otherwise,' necessarily embraces all legislation which seeks to compel the service or labor by making it a crime to refuse or fail to perform it. Such laws would furnish the readiest means of compulsion.

The 13th Amendment prohibits involuntary servitude except as punishment for crime. But the exception, allowing full latitude for the enforcement of penal laws, does not destroy the prohibition. It does not permit slavery or involuntary servitude to be established or maintained through the operation of the criminal law by making it a crime to refuse to submit to the one or to render the service which would constitute the other. The state may impose involuntary servitude as a punishment for crime, but it may not compel one man to labor for another in payment of a debt, by punishing him as a criminal if he does not perform the service or pay the debt. ...

Mr. Justice HOLMES, dissenting:

... The 13th Amendment does not outlaw contracts for labor. That would be at least as great a misfortune for the laborer as for the man that employed him. For it certainly would affect the terms of the bargain unfavorably for the laboring man if it were understood that the employer could do nothing in case the laborer saw fit to break his word. But any legal liability for breach of a contract is a disagreeable consequence which tends to make the contractor do as he said he would. Liability to an action for damages has that tendency as well a fine. If the mere imposition of such consequences as tend to make a man keep to his promise is the creation of peonage when the contract happens to be for labor, I do not see why the allowance of a civil action is not, as well as an indictment ending in fine. Peonage is service to a private master at which a man is kept by bodily compulsion against his will. But the creation of the ordinary legal motives for right conduct does not produce it. Breach of a legal contract without excuse is wrong conduct, even if the contract is for labor; and if a state adds to civil liability a criminal liability to fine, it simply intensifies the legal motive for doing right; it does not make the laborer a slave. ...

In my opinion, the statute embodies little if anything more than what I should have told the jury was the law without it. The right of the state to regulate laws of evidence is admitted, and the statute does not go much beyond the common law. ...

To sum up, I think that obtaining money by fraud may be made a crime as well as murder or theft; that a false representation, expressed or implied, at the time of making a contract of labor, that one intends to perform it, and thereby obtaining an advance, may be declared a case of fraudulently obtaining money as well as any other; that if made a crime it may be punished like any other crime; and that an unjustified departure from the promised service without repayment may be declared a sufficient case to go to the jury for their judgment; all without in any way infringing the 13th Amendment or the statutes of the United States.

Mr. Justice LURTON concurs in this dissent.

Notes and Questions

1. *The breadth of the Thirteenth Amendment.* Justice Hughes reads the Thirteenth Amendment broadly. Why should the Thirteenth Amendment allow Congress to apply something to private persons and not just to the states?
2. *Justice Holmes.* Justice Oliver Wendell Holmes is a historically important Justice, frequently acknowledged for his powerful dissents. What do you think of this dissent in *Bailey*? Is he more accurate about the state of the law and the Thirteenth Amendment than the majority is?
3. *The Thirteenth Amendment today.* Are there any laws today that raise Thirteenth Amendment questions that should be decided by the federal courts all the way up to the Supreme Court?
4. *Success?* Some might think the Thirteenth Amendment has been the most successful of the amendments because we no longer have slavery. Do you agree?
5. *Video.* What do you think of this video summary of *Bailey*, Lipton Legal Group, January 3—*Bailey v. Alabama,* Jan. 2, 2020, at https://www.youtube.com/watch?v=0ZZvoxvCE58?

b. The Thirteenth Amendment and Racial Housing Laws

The following case is about the Thirteenth Amendment's relationship to a racial housing law. The oral argument is available on the case's website, https://www.oyez.org/cases/1967/645. Can you tell from the oral argument what the Thirteenth Amendment is supposed to protect? Who does the best job explaining what the amendment was about? Can you tell from the argument that the result is a 7–2 decision? Are there any questions that you think are especially good?

Jones v. Alfred H. Mayer Co.

SUPREME COURT OF THE UNITED STATES, 1968

392 U.S. 409, 88 S.Ct. 2186

Mr. Justice STEWART delivered the opinion of the Court. STEWART was joined by WARREN, BLACK, DOUGLAS, BRENNAN, FORTAS, and MARSHALL. Justices HARLAN and WHITE dissented.

In this case we are called upon to determine the scope and constitutionality of an Act of Congress, 42 U.S.C. § 1982, which provides that:

> "All citizens of the United States shall have the same right, in every State and Territory, as is enjoyed by white citizens thereof to inherit, purchase, lease, sell, hold, and convey real and personal property." ...

We hold that § 1982 bars all racial discrimination, private as well as public, in the sale or rental of property, and that the statute, thus construed, is a valid exercise of the power of Congress to enforce the Thirteenth Amendment.

...

III

We begin with the language of the statute itself. In plain and unambiguous terms, § 1982 grants to all citizens, without regard to race or color, "the same right" to purchase and lease property "as is enjoyed by white citizens." ...

On its face, therefore, § 1982 appears to prohibit all discrimination against Negroes in the sale or rental of property—discrimination by private owners as well as discrimination by public authorities. Indeed, even the respondents seem to concede that, if s 1982 "means what it says"—to use the words of the respondents' brief—then it must encompass every racially motivated refusal to sell or rent and cannot be confined to officially sanctioned segregation in housing. Stressing what they consider to be the revolutionary implications of so literal a reading of s 1982, the respondents argue that Congress cannot possibly have intended any such result. Our examination of the relevant history, however, persuades us that Congress meant exactly what it said.

...

V

The remaining question is whether Congress has power under the Constitution to do what s 1982 purports to do: to prohibit all racial discrimination, private and public, in the sale and rental of property. Our starting point is the Thirteenth Amendment, for it was pursuant to that constitutional provision that Congress originally enacted what is now s 1982. The Amendment consists of two parts. Section 1 states:

> "Neither slavery nor involuntary servitude, except as a punishment for crime whereby the party shall have been duly convicted, shall exist within the United States, or any place subject to their jurisdiction."

Section 2 provides:

> "Congress shall have power to enforce this article by appropriate legislation."

As its text reveals, the Thirteenth Amendment "is not a mere prohibition of state laws establishing or upholding slavery, but an absolute declaration that slavery or involuntary servitude shall not exist in any part of the United States." Civil Rights Cases. It has never been doubted, therefore, "that the power vested in Congress to enforce the article by appropriate legislation," ibid., includes the power to enact laws "direct and primary, operating upon the acts of individuals, whether sanctioned by state legislation or not."

Thus, the fact that s 1982 operates upon the unofficial acts of private individuals, whether or not sanctioned by state law, presents no constitutional problem. If Congress has power under the Thirteenth Amendment to eradicate conditions that prevent Negroes from buying and renting property because of their race or color, then no federal statute calculated to achieve that objective can be thought to exceed the constitutional power of Congress simply because it reaches beyond state action to regulate the conduct of private individuals. The constitutional question in this case, therefore, comes to this: Does the authority of Congress to enforce the Thirteenth Amendment "by appropriate legislation" include the power to eliminate all racial barriers to the acquisition of real and personal property? We think the answer to that question is plainly yes. ...

Those who opposed passage of the Civil Rights Act of 1866 argued in effect that the Thirteenth Amendment merely authorized Congress to dissolve the legal bond by which the Negro slave was held to his master. Yet many had earlier opposed the Thirteenth Amendment on the very ground that it would give Congress virtually unlimited power to enact laws for the protection of Negroes in every State. ...

Negro citizens, North and South, who saw in the Thirteenth Amendment a promise of freedom—freedom to "go and come at pleasure" and to "buy and sell when they please"—would be left with "a mere paper guarantee" if Congress were powerless to assure that a dollar in the hands of a Negro will purchase the same thing as a dollar in the hands of a white man. At the very least, the freedom that Congress is empowered to secure under the Thirteenth Amendment includes the freedom to buy whatever a white man can buy, the right to live wherever a white man can live. If Congress cannot say that being a free man means at least this much, then the Thirteenth Amendment made a promise the Nation cannot keep. ...

Mr. Justice HARLAN, whom Mr. Justice WHITE joins, dissenting.

The decision in this case appears to me to be most ill-considered and ill-advised. ...

For reasons which follow, I believe that the Court's construction of s 1982 as applying to purely private action is almost surely wrong, and at the least is open to serious doubt. The issues of the constitutionality of s 1982, as construed by the Court, and of liability under the Fourteenth Amendment alone, also present formidable difficulties. Moreover, the political processes of our own era have, since the date of oral argument in this case, given birth to a civil rights statute embodying "fair housing" provisions which would at the end of this year make available to others, though apparently not to the petitioners themselves, the type of relief which the petitioners now seek. It seems to me that this latter factor so diminishes the public importance of this case that by far the wisest course would be for this Court to refrain from decision and to dismiss the writ as improvidently granted.

IC

... The remarks just quoted constitute the plainest possible statement that the civil rights bill was intended to apply only to state-sanctioned conduct and not to purely activate action. The Court has attempted to negate the force of these statements by citing other declarations by Senator Trumbull and others that the bill would operate everywhere in the country. However, the obvious and natural way to reconcile these two sets of statements is to read the ones about the bill's nationwide application as declarations that the enactment of a racially discriminatory law in any State would bring the bill into effect there. It seems to me that very great weight must be given these statements of Senator Trumbull, for they were clearly made to reassure Northern and Border State Senators about the extent of the bill's operation in their States. ...

ID

The foregoing analysis of the language, structure, and legislative history of the 1866 Civil Rights Act shows, I believe, that the Court's thesis that the Act was meant to extend to purely private action is open to the most serious doubt, if indeed it does not render that thesis wholly untenable. Another, albeit less tangible, consideration points in the same direction. Many of the legislators who took part in the congressional debates inevitably must have shared the individualistic ethic of their time, which emphasized personal freedom and embodied a distaste for governmental interference which was soon to culminate in the era of laissez-faire. It seems to me that most of these men would have regarded it as a great intrusion on individual liberty for the Government to take from a man the power to refuse for personal reasons to enter into a purely private transaction involving the disposition of property, albeit those personal reasons might reflect racial bias. It should be remembered that racial prejudice was not uncommon in 1866, even outside the South. Although Massachusetts had recently enacted the Nation's first law prohibiting racial discrimination in public accommodations, Negroes could not ride within Philadelphia streetcars or attend public schools with white children in New York City. Only five States accorded equal voting rights to Negroes, and it appears that Negroes were allowed to serve on juries only in Massachusetts. Residential segregation was the prevailing pattern almost everywhere in the North. There were no state "fair housing" laws in 1866, and it appears that none had ever been proposed. In this historical context, I cannot conceive that a bill thought to prohibit purely private discrimination not only in the sale or rental of housing but in all property transactions would not have received a great deal of criticism explicitly directed to this feature. The fact that the 1866 Act received *no* criticism of this kind is for me strong additional evidence that it was not regarded as extending so far.

In sum, the most which can be said with assurance about the intended impact of the 1866 Civil Rights Act upon purely private discrimination is that the Act probably was envisioned by most members of Congress as prohibiting official, community-sanctioned discrimination in the South, engaged in pursuant to local "customs" which in the recent time of slavery probably were embodied in laws or regulations. Acts done under the color of such "customs" were, of course, said by the Court in the Civil Rights Cases to constitute "state action" prohibited by the Fourteenth Amendment. Adoption of a "state action" construction of the Civil Rights Act would therefore have the additional merit of bringing its interpretation into line with that of the Fourteenth Amendment, which this Court has consistently held to reach only "state action." This seems especially desirable in light of the wide agreement that a major purpose of the Fourteenth Amendment, at least in the minds of its congressional proponents, was to assure that the rights conferred by the then recently enacted Civil Rights Act could not be taken away by a subsequent Congress. ...

For these reasons, I would dismiss the writ of certiorari as improvidently granted.

Notes and Questions

1. *Justice Stewart.* How does Justice Stewart interpret the Thirteenth Amendment in this case? Why should the Thirteenth Amendment be read to cover private actions and not just state actions? Reread the language of the Thirteenth Amendment. Does he take the meaning of the amendment too far, just right, or not far enough?
2. *Justice Harlan.* Justice Harlan is often remembered as a careful reader of the Constitution. Do you think his dissent is more faithful to the Constitution than the majority's opinion? Do you agree with him that the decision is "most ill-considered and ill-advised"? Why or why not?
3. *State action.* Why does the Court talk about "state action"? What is state action? Can you think of reasons why state action is treated differently from private action in the law?
4. *The scope of the Thirteenth Amendment.* Do you agree with the majority's statement: "At the very least, the freedom that Congress is empowered to secure under the Thirteenth Amendment includes the freedom to buy whatever a white man can buy, the right to live wherever a white man can live. If Congress cannot say that being a free man means at least this much, then the Thirteenth Amendment made a promise the Nation cannot keep." Would the dissenters agree with that statement? Why or why not? If they disagree, what would they say?
5. *The power of Congress.* How much power does Congress have to enforce the Thirteenth Amendment?
6. *The Thirteenth Amendment today.* Do you think the Thirteenth Amendment could be used more frequently today? How would you use it?

7. *Video.* What do you think of this video presentation of the opinion, Quimbee, *Jones v. Alfred H. Mayer Co.* Case Brief Summary, Dec. 21, 2020, at https://www.youtube.com/watch?v=pJq04PQIzqs?

2. The Fourteenth Amendment

The Fourteenth Amendment contains the following sections:

> Section 1.
>
> All persons born or naturalized in the United States, and subject to the jurisdiction thereof, are citizens of the United States and of the state wherein they reside. No state shall make or enforce any law which shall abridge the privileges or immunities of citizens of the United States; nor shall any state deprive any person of life, liberty, or property, without due process of law; nor deny to any person within its jurisdiction the equal protection of the laws.
>
> Section 5.
>
> The Congress shall have power to enforce, by appropriate legislation, the provisions of this article.

The Court has argued about just how much power Congress has under Section 5. Should it be a broad power or a narrow power? When should it be used? You can see from Section 1 that the Fourteenth Amendment protects equal protection, which has been interpreted to include the equal protection of the races, women, and LGBTQs. And, as we will focus on in Section C, the Fourteenth Amendment has held state governments, not only the federal government, responsible to be committed to the first eight constitutional amendments, part of the Bill of Rights.

Pre-*Boerne*, the Supreme Court had decided a free exercise of religion case, *Employment Division v. Smith,* 494 U.S. 872 (1990), which held that all persons, including religious persons, must obey neutral laws of general applicability. Congress disagreed with that decision and passed the Religious Freedom Restoration Act of 1993, which imposed the highest scrutiny on all laws that substantially burden religion. That meant the government had to prove the law served a compelling interest in the least restrictive means (for the believer). *Smith* is a decision that had surveyed all of the Supreme Court's free exercise jurisprudence and announced the Court's definitive free exercise standard. Under pressure of organized religion, Congress enacted RFRA to "fix" the Court's doctrine by imposing the standard organized religion preferred.

a. How Much Power Does Section 5 Give Congress?

Read the oral argument in *Boerne*, which is available at https://www.oyez.org/cases/1996/95-2074. Professor Hamilton was the lawyer for the petitioner City of Boerne. Can you tell why she won the case? Is there any point where she was especially effective at getting the Court to see things from the petitioner's perspective? What was the best argument that opposing counsel made? Does Professor Hamilton say it is a religious liberty or a federalism case at the start?

City of Boerne v. Flores

SUPREME COURT OF THE UNITED STATES, 1997
521 U.S. 507, 117 S.Ct. 2157

KENNEDY, J., delivered the opinion of the Court, in which REHNQUIST, C.J., and STEVENS, THOMAS, and GINSBURG, JJ., joined, and in which SCALIA, J., joined as to all but Part III–A–1. STEVENS, J., filed a concurring opinion. SCALIA, J., filed an opinion concurring in part, in which STEVENS, J., joined. O'CONNOR, J., filed a dissenting opinion, in which BREYER, J., joined except as to the first paragraph of Part I. SOUTER, J., and BREYER, J., filed dissenting opinions.

A decision by local zoning authorities to deny a church a building permit was challenged under the Religious Freedom Restoration Act of 1993 (RFRA or Act). The case calls into question the authority of Congress to enact RFRA. We conclude the statute exceeds Congress' power.

...

II

Congress enacted RFRA in direct response to the Court's decision in *Employment Div., Dept. of Human Resources of Oregon v. Smith*. ...

Many criticized the Court's reasoning, and this disagreement resulted in the passage of RFRA. Congress announced:

> "(1) [T]he framers of the Constitution, recognizing free exercise of religion as an unalienable right, secured its protection in the First Amendment to the Constitution;
>
> "(2) laws 'neutral' toward religion may burden religious exercise as surely as laws intended to interfere with religious exercise;
>
> "(3) governments should not substantially burden religious exercise without compelling justification;
>
> "(4) in *Employment Division v. Smith*, the Supreme Court virtually eliminated the requirement that the government justify burdens on religious exercise imposed by laws neutral toward religion; and
>
> "(5) the compelling interest test as set forth in prior Federal court rulings is a workable test for striking sensible balances between religious liberty and competing prior governmental interests."

The Act's stated purposes are:

> "(1) to restore the compelling interest test as set forth in *Sherbert v. Verner* and *Wisconsin v. Yoder*, and to guarantee its application in all cases where free exercise of religion is substantially burdened; and
>
> "(2) to provide a claim or defense to persons whose religious exercise is substantially burdened by government." ..

IIIA

... Congress relied on its Fourteenth Amendment enforcement power in enacting the most far-reaching and substantial of RFRA's provisions, those which impose its requirements on the States. ...

The parties disagree over whether RFRA is a proper exercise of Congress' § 5 power "to enforce" by "appropriate legislation" the constitutional guarantee that no State shall deprive any person of "life, liberty, or property, without due process of law" nor deny any person "equal protection of the laws." ...

Legislation which deters or remedies constitutional violations can fall within the sweep of Congress' enforcement power even if in the process it prohibits conduct which is not itself unconstitutional and intrudes into "legislative spheres of autonomy previously reserved to the States." ... It is also true, however, that "[a]s broad as the congressional enforcement power is, it is not unlimited."

In assessing the breadth of § 5's enforcement power, we begin with its text. Congress has been given the power "to enforce" the "provisions of this article." ... Congress' power under § 5, however, extends only to "enforc[ing]" the provisions of the Fourteenth Amendment. The Court has described this power as "remedial." The design of the Amendment and the text of § 5 are inconsistent with the suggestion that Congress has the power to decree the substance of the Fourteenth Amendment's restrictions on the States. Legislation which alters the meaning of the Free Exercise Clause cannot be said to be enforcing the Clause. Congress does not enforce a constitutional right by changing what the right is. It has been given the power "to enforce," not the power to determine what constitutes a constitutional violation. Were it not so, what Congress would be enforcing would no longer be, in any meaningful sense, the "provisions of [the Fourteenth Amendment]."

While the line between measures that remedy or prevent unconstitutional actions and measures that make a substantive change in the governing law is not easy to discern, and Congress must have wide latitude in determining where it lies, the distinction exists and must be observed. There must be a congruence and proportionality between the injury to be prevented or remedied and the means adopted to that end. Lacking such a connection, legislation may become substantive in operation and effect. History and our case law support drawing the distinction, one apparent from the text of the Amendment.

1

The Fourteenth Amendment's history confirms the remedial, rather than substantive, nature of the Enforcement Clause. ...

2

The remedial and preventive nature of Congress' enforcement power, and the limitation inherent in the power, were confirmed in our earliest cases on the Fourteenth Amendment. ...

Recent cases have continued to revolve around the question whether § 5 legislation can be considered remedial. ...

3

Any suggestion that Congress has a substantive, non-remedial power under the Fourteenth Amendment is not supported by our case law. ...

If Congress could define its own powers by altering the Fourteenth Amendment's meaning, no longer would the Constitution be "superior paramount law, unchangeable by ordinary means." It would be "on a level with ordinary legislative acts, and, like other acts, ... alterable when the legislature shall please to alter it." *Marbury v. Madison.* Under this approach, it is difficult to conceive of a principle that would limit congressional power. Shifting legislative majorities could change the Constitution and effectively circumvent the difficult and detailed amendment process contained in Article V. ...

B

...

Regardless of the state of the legislative record, RFRA cannot be considered remedial, preventive legislation, if those terms are to have any meaning. RFRA is so out of proportion to a supposed remedial or preventive object that it cannot be understood as responsive to, or designed to prevent, unconstitutional behavior. It appears, instead, to attempt a substantive change in constitutional protections. Preventive measures prohibiting certain types of laws may be appropriate when there is reason to believe that many of the laws affected by the congressional enactment have a significant likelihood of being unconstitutional. Remedial legislation under § 5 "should be adapted to the mischief and wrong which the [Fourteenth] [A]mendment was intended to provide against." *Civil Rights Cases.*

RFRA is not so confined. Sweeping coverage ensures its intrusion at every level of government, displacing laws and prohibiting official actions of almost every description and regardless of subject matter. RFRA's restrictions apply to every agency and official of the Federal, State, and local Governments. RFRA applies to all federal and state law, statutory or otherwise, whether adopted before or after its enactment. RFRA has no termination date or termination mechanism. Any law is subject to challenge at any time by any individual who alleges a substantial burden on his or her free exercise of religion.

The reach and scope of RFRA distinguish it from other measures passed under Congress' enforcement power, even in the area of voting rights. ...

The stringent test RFRA demands of state laws reflects a lack of proportionality or congruence between the means adopted and the legitimate end to be achieved. If an objector can show a substantial burden on his free exercise, the State must demonstrate a compelling governmental interest and show that the law is the least restrictive means of furthering its interest. Claims that a law substantially burdens someone's exercise of religion will often be difficult to contest. Requiring a State to demonstrate a compelling interest and show that it has adopted the least restrictive means of achieving that interest is the most demanding test known to constitutional law. If "'compelling interest' really means what it says ..., many laws will not meet the test. ... [The test] would open the prospect of constitutionally required religious exemptions from civic obligations of almost every conceivable kind." Laws valid under *Smith* would fall under RFRA without regard to whether they had the object of stifling or punishing free exercise. We make these observations not to reargue the position of the majority in *Smith* but to illustrate the substantive alteration of its holding attempted by RFRA. Even assuming RFRA would be interpreted in effect to mandate some lesser test, say, one equivalent to intermediate scrutiny, the statute nevertheless would require searching judicial scrutiny of state law with the attendant likelihood of invalidation. This is a considerable congressional intrusion into the States' traditional prerogatives and general authority to regulate for the health and welfare of their citizens.

The substantial costs RFRA exacts, both in practical terms of imposing a heavy litigation burden on the States and in terms of curtailing their traditional general regulatory power, far exceed any pattern or practice of unconstitutional conduct under the Free Exercise Clause as interpreted in *Smith*. Simply put, RFRA is not designed to identify and counteract state laws likely to be unconstitutional because of their treatment of religion. ...

Broad as the power of Congress is under the Enforcement Clause of the Fourteenth Amendment, RFRA contradicts vital principles necessary to maintain separation of powers and the federal balance. The judgment of the Court of Appeals sustaining the Act's constitutionality is reversed.

Justice STEVENS, concurring.

In my opinion, the Religious Freedom Restoration Act of 1993 (RFRA) is a "law respecting an establishment of religion" that violates the First Amendment to the Constitution. ...

Justice SCALIA, with whom Justice STEVENS joins, concurring in part.

I write to respond briefly to the claim of Justice O'CONNOR's dissent (hereinafter "the dissent") that historical materials support a result contrary to the one reached in *Employment Div., Dept. of Human Resources of Oregon v. Smith*, 494 U.S. 872, 110 S.Ct. 1595, 108 L.Ed.2d 876 (1990). We held in *Smith* that the Constitution's Free Exercise Clause "does not relieve an individual of the obligation to comply with a 'valid and neutral law of general applicability on the ground that the law proscribes (or prescribes) conduct that his religion prescribes. The material that the dissent claims is at odds with *Smith* either has little to say about the issue or is in fact more consistent with *Smith* than with the dissent's interpretation of the Free Exercise Clause. The dissent's extravagant claim that the historical record shows *Smith* to have been wrong should be compared with the assessment of the most prominent scholarly critic of *Smith*, who, after an extensive review of the historical record, was willing to venture no more than that "constitutionally compelled exemptions [from generally applicable laws regulating conduct] were *within the contemplation* of the framers and ratifiers as a *possible interpretation* of the free exercise clause."

Justice O'CONNOR, with whom Justice BREYER joins except as to the first paragraph of Part I, dissenting.

... I remain of the view that *Smith* was wrongly decided, and I would use this case to reexamine the Court's holding there. Therefore, I would direct the parties to brief the question whether *Smith* represents the correct understanding of the Free Exercise Clause and set the case for reargument. If the Court were to correct the misinterpretation of the Free Exercise Clause set forth in *Smith*, it would simultaneously put our First Amendment jurisprudence back on course and allay the legitimate concerns of a majority in Congress who believed that *Smith* improperly restricted religious liberty. We would then be in a position to review RFRA in light of a proper interpretation of the Free Exercise Clause.

Justice SOUTER, dissenting.

To decide whether the Fourteenth Amendment gives Congress sufficient power to enact the Religious Freedom Restoration Act of 1993, the Court measures the legislation against the free-exercise standard of *Employment Div., Dept. of Human Resources of Oregon v. Smith*, 494 U.S. 872, 110 S.Ct. 1595, 108 L.Ed.2d 876 (1990). For the reasons stated in my opinion in *Church of Lukumi Babalu Aye, Inc. v. Hialeah*, 508 U.S. 520, 564–577, 113 S.Ct. 2217, 2242–2250, 124 L.Ed.2d 472 (1993) (opinion concurring in part and concurring in judgment), I have serious doubts about the precedential value of the *Smith* rule and its entitlement to adherence. ...

Justice BREYER, dissenting.

I agree with Justice O'CONNOR that the Court should direct the parties to brief the question whether *Employment Div., Dept. of Human Resources of Oregon v. Smith*, 494 U.S. 872, 110 S.Ct. 1595, 108 L.Ed.2d 876 (1990), was correctly decided, and set this case for reargument. I do not, however, find it necessary to consider the question whether, assuming *Smith* is correct, § 5 of the Fourteenth Amendment would authorize Congress to enact the legislation before us.

Notes and Questions

1. *Which governments?* What governments are limited by the 14th Amendment, according to its language?
2. *Can there be more than one constitutional violation?* The court lays out three constitutional bases for overturning RFRA: *Marbury v. Madison*; dual sovereignty of the state and federal governments; and Article V. In short, the Court points to separation of powers, federalism, and the constitutional amendment process to explain RFRA's defects. Can a law be unconstitutional for three different reasons?
3. *Which governments, take 2.* The 1993 RFRA attempted to dramatically increase religious liberty against all governments, local, state, and federal, as well as legislative, executive, and judicial. After *Boerne*, Congress reenacted RFRA to apply to federal law in 2000. What is the difference between a federal RFRA that governs the federal government and a federal RFRA that governs state and local governments? Does Justice Kennedy's opinion see a difference between them? Does *Boerne* say a federal RFRA governing state laws is unconstitutional? If so, why? Does *Boerne* say a federal RFRA covering the federal government is constitutional? Why or why not?

   The Court holds that the enforcement mechanism of the 14th Amendment—Sec. 5—is remedial. In other words, it does not confer on Congress the power to unilaterally establish the substance of constitutional rights against the states. Congress does not have the power to enact substance for the Amendment. What test does Justice Kennedy provide for Section 5 of the 14th Amendment? "Proportionality" is drawn from the law of remedies; for example, a jail sentence should be proportional to the crime.

4. *The Establishment Clause.* Do you know what the Establishment Clause is? Where is it in the First Amendment? Why does Justice Stevens think RFRA violates the Establishment Clause?
5. *Justice O'Connor.* Why does Justice O'Connor think *Smith* was wrongly decided? She embraced a different free exercise test than the *Smith* majority; in *Smith*, she endorsed the same text but agreed with the majority's result. Do you agree or disagree with her?

b. The Power of Congress to Protect Women's Rights Using Its Section 5 Power

The Equal Protection Clause of the Fourteenth Amendment protects women's rights, too. In protection of women's rights, Congress passed the Violence Against Women Act, which allowed women to file lawsuits against those who had committed violence against them. In the case below, Christy Brzonkala alleged she was raped by students Antonio Morrison and James Crawford. She sued under VAWA for her damages. The Court ruled that Congress did not have commerce power, under Article I, Section 8, to pass this legislation. Can you remember why the Court would not view this as commerce?

In the following part of the opinion, the Court also ruled that Congress did not have § 5 power either. Why not? Because the legislation governed private individuals and not the states. Is that good reasoning? What do the Justices and lawyers say about § 5 in the oral argument of the case, which is available at https://www.oyez.org/cases/1999/99-5. If Congress cannot pass state RFRA or VAWA under § 5, when can it use it? Could § 5 be used to enact the federal RFRA?

United States v. Morrison

SUPREME COURT OF THE UNITED STATES, 2000

529 U.S. 598, 120 S.Ct. 1740

REHNQUIST, C.J., delivered the opinion of the Court, in which O'CONNOR, SCALIA, KENNEDY, and THOMAS, JJ., joined. THOMAS, J., filed a concurring opinion. SOUTER, J., filed a dissenting opinion, in which STEVENS, GINSBURG, and BREYER, JJ., joined. BREYER, J., filed a dissenting opinion, in which STEVENS, J., joined, and in which SOUTER and GINSBURG, JJ., joined as to Part I–A.

...

I

...

Section 13981 was part of the Violence Against Women Act of 1994, § 40302, 108 Stat. 1941–1942. It states that "[a]ll persons within the United States shall have the right to be free from crimes of violence motivated by gender." To enforce that right, subsection (c) declares:

> "A person (including a person who acts under color of any statute, ordinance, regulation, custom, or usage of any State) who commits a crime of violence motivated by gender and thus deprives another of the right declared in subsection (b) of this section shall be liable to the party injured, in an action for the recovery of compensatory and punitive damages, injunctive and declaratory relief, and such other relief as a court may deem appropriate." ...

Every law enacted by Congress must be based on one or more of its powers enumerated in the Constitution. "The powers of the legislature are defined and limited; and that those limits may not be mistaken, or forgotten, the constitution is written." *Marbury v. Madison,* 1 Cranch 137, 176, 2 L.Ed. 60 (1803) (Marshall, C. J.). Congress explicitly identified the sources of federal authority on which it relied in enacting § 13981. It said that a "Federal civil rights cause of action" is established "[p]ursuant to the affirmative power of Congress ... under section 5 of the Fourteenth Amendment to the Constitution, as well as under section 8 of Article I of the Constitution." ...

III

Because we conclude that the Commerce Clause does not provide Congress with authority to enact § 13981, we address petitioners' alternative argument that the section's civil remedy should be upheld as an exercise of Congress' remedial power under § 5 of the Fourteenth Amendment. As noted above, Congress expressly invoked the Fourteenth Amendment as a source of authority to enact § 13981. ...

Petitioners' § 5 argument is founded on an assertion that there is pervasive bias in various state justice systems against victims of gender-motivated violence. This assertion is supported by a voluminous congressional record. ...

However, the language and purpose of the Fourteenth Amendment place certain limitations on the manner in which Congress may attack discriminatory conduct. These limitations are necessary to prevent the Fourteenth Amendment from obliterating the Framers' carefully crafted balance of power between the States and the National Government. ...

Shortly after the Fourteenth Amendment was adopted, we decided two cases interpreting the Amendment's provisions, *United States v. Harris,* 106 U.S. 629, 1 S.Ct. 601, 27 L.Ed. 290 (1883), and the *Civil Rights Cases,* 109 U.S. 3, 3 S.Ct. 18, 27 L.Ed. 835 (1883). In *Harris,* the Court considered a challenge to § 2 of the Civil Rights Act of 1871. That section sought to punish "private persons" for "conspiring to deprive any one of the equal protection of the laws enacted by the State." We concluded that this law exceeded Congress' § 5 power because the law was "directed exclusively against the action of private persons, without reference to the laws of the State, or their administration by her officers." ...

We reached a similar conclusion in the *Civil Rights Cases.* In those consolidated cases, we held that the public accommodation provisions of the Civil Rights Act of 1875, which applied to purely private conduct, were beyond the scope of the § 5 enforcement power. ...

Section 13981 is not aimed at proscribing discrimination by officials which the Fourteenth Amendment might not itself proscribe; it is directed not at any State or state actor, but at individuals who have committed criminal acts motivated by gender bias. ...

For these reasons, we conclude that Congress' power under § 5 does not extend to the enactment of § 13981.

IV

Petitioner Brzonkala's complaint alleges that she was the victim of a brutal assault. But Congress' effort in § 13981 to provide a federal civil remedy can be sustained neither under the Commerce Clause nor under § 5 of the Fourteenth Amendment. If the allegations here are true, no civilized system of justice could fail to provide her a remedy for the conduct of respondent Morrison. But under our federal system that remedy must be provided by the Commonwealth of Virginia, and not by the United States.

Justice BREYER, with whom Justice STEVENS joins, dissenting.

...

II

Given my conclusion on the Commerce Clause question, I need not consider Congress' authority under § 5 of the Fourteenth Amendment. Nonetheless, I doubt the Court's reasoning rejecting that source of authority. The Court points out that in *United States v. Harris,* and the *Civil Rights Cases,* the Court held that § 5 does not authorize Congress to use the Fourteenth Amendment as a source of power to remedy the conduct of *private persons.* That is certainly so. The Federal Government's argument, however, is that Congress used § 5 to remedy the actions of *state actors,* namely, those States which, through discriminatory design or the discriminatory conduct of their officials, failed to provide adequate (or any) state remedies for women injured by gender-motivated violence—a failure that the States, and Congress, documented in depth.

Neither *Harris* nor the *Civil Rights Cases* considered this kind of claim. The Court in *Harris* specifically said that it treated the federal laws in question as "directed *exclusively* against the action of private persons, without reference to the laws of the State or their administration by her officers."; see also *Civil Rights Cases,* (observing that the statute did "not profess to be corrective of any constitutional wrong committed by the States" and that it established "rules for the conduct of individuals in society towards each other, ... without referring in any manner to any supposed action of the State or its authorities"). ...

But why can Congress not provide a remedy against private actors? Those private actors, of course, did not themselves violate the Constitution. But this Court has held that Congress at least sometimes can enact remedial "[l]egislation ... [that] prohibits conduct which is not itself unconstitutional." The statutory remedy does not in any sense purport to "determine what constitutes a constitutional violation." It intrudes little upon either States or private parties. It may lead state actors to improve their own remedial systems, primarily through example. It restricts private actors only by imposing liability for private conduct that is, in the main, already forbidden by state law. Why is the remedy "disproportionate"? And given the relation between remedy and violation—the creation of a federal remedy to substitute for constitutionally inadequate state remedies—where is the lack of "congruence"?

But Congress had before it the task force reports of at least 21 States documenting constitutional violations. And it made its own findings about pervasive gender-based stereotypes hampering many state legal systems, sometimes unconstitutionally so. The record nowhere reveals a congressional finding that the problem "does not exist" elsewhere. Why can Congress not take the evidence before it as evidence of a national problem? This Court has not previously held that Congress must document the existence of a problem in every State prior to proposing a national solution. ...

Notes and Questions

1. *Video.* Does this video help you to understand the case? See Quimbee, *United States v. Morrison* Case Brief Summary, Nov. 16, 2017, at https://www.youtube.com/watch?v=CtBR1PfKU-vM&list=PLsFE_Nvl6h_Y75KGR5pkGqcFisGvBnO9S&index=55. What questions do you still have?
2. *The role of state opinion.* What role does the states' opinion that the country needs a VAWA have on this case?
3. *Private persons.* Why is the role of private persons so important to this case?
4. *Compare the majority and the dissent.* What argument does each side make? Which side makes the better argument? Why?
5. *Different or similar powers?* What is the difference between the Fourteenth Amendment and the Commerce Clause?
6. *VAWA amended.* What did VAWA look like after the Court announced these opinions? What sections would still be constitutional? Congress is reconsidering VAWA in 2022. https://www.congress.gov/bill/117th-congress/senate-bill/3623/text?r=1&s=1. The bill includes protection for Native American women. Where does Congress get the power to do that? It authorizes grants to states that apply for funding under the Act. What power is Congress exercising there? What case you have already read is relevant to such a provision? It also provides grants to schools and universities to combat violent sexual abuse and assault on campus. If the sex abuse and assault violates local and state laws, can Congress regulate it in this way?

3. The Fifteenth Amendment

Amendment XV protects the right to vote. Its text follows:

> Section 1.
>
> The right of citizens of the United States to vote shall not be denied or abridged by the United States or by any state on account of race, color, or previous condition of servitude.
>
> Section 2.
>
> The Congress shall have power to enforce this article by appropriate legislation.

The Voting Rights Act was passed to enforce the Fifteenth Amendment. Sections 2, 4, and 5 of the Voting Rights Act became important in the cases that follow. Section 2 of the Act bans any "standard, practice, or procedure" that "results in a denial or abridgement of the right of any citizen ... to vote on account of race or color." Section 4 of the Act provides the "coverage formula," defining the "covered jurisdictions" as states or political subdivisions that maintained tests or devices as prerequisites to voting and had low voter registration or turnout in the 1960s and early 1970s. In the areas covered under § 4, § 5 of the Act provides that no change in voting procedures can take effect until approved by specified federal authorities in Washington, D.C. This procedure is called "preclearance."

a. The Court Deploys Its Assessment of Race-Based Discrimination to Invalidate Section 4 of the Voting Rights Act

Given what the Court said about § 5 in *Boerne* and *Morrison*, how much power do you think § 2 of the Fifteenth Amendment will have? *Shelby County* involves the Voting Rights Act, legislation that was first passed in 1965 to protect voters against the racial discrimination that voters frequently confronted. The Voting Rights Act was supposed to enforce the Fifteenth Amendment. In *Shelby County*, the Court ruled that § 4 of the act, which requires certain states and counties to get preclearance for voting changes from the federal government before they went into effect, was illegal because it was no longer needed.

How much racial discrimination do you think there is in voting? Why do you hold that opinion? What do you learn about the Voting Rights Act in the oral argument in *Shelby County*, available at https://www.oyez.org/cases/2012/12-96. Do the lawyers and Justices talk about racism? Do they talk about the history of the Act? This is another 5–4 opinion. Do the Justices' questions in this case predict the way they vote in the following opinion? What is the most important issue they are arguing about? Be prepared to explain which of the Justice's opinions you think is best in the following case.

Shelby County v. Holder
SUPREME COURT OF THE UNITED STATES, 2013
570 U.S. 529, 133 S.Ct. 2612

ROBERTS, C.J., delivered the opinion of the Court, in which SCALIA, KENNEDY, THOMAS, and ALITO, JJ., joined. THOMAS, J., filed a concurring opinion. GINSBURG, J., filed a dissenting opinion, in which BREYER, SOTOMAYOR, and KAGAN, JJ., joined.

The Voting Rights Act of 1965 employed extraordinary measures to address an extraordinary problem. Section 5 of the Act required States to obtain federal permission before enacting any law related to voting—a drastic departure from basic principles of federalism. And § 4 of the Act applied that requirement only to some States—an equally dramatic departure from the principle that all States enjoy equal sovereignty. This was strong medicine, but Congress determined it was needed to address entrenched racial discrimination in voting, "an insidious and pervasive evil which had been perpetuated in certain parts of our country through unremitting and ingenious defiance of the Constitution." As we explained in upholding the law, "exceptional conditions can justify legislative measures not otherwise appropriate." Reflecting the unprecedented nature of these measures, they were scheduled to expire after five years.

Nearly 50 years later, they are still in effect; indeed, they have been made more stringent, and are now scheduled to last until 2031. There is no denying, however, that the conditions that originally justified these measures no longer characterize voting in the covered jurisdictions. By 2009, "the racial gap in voter registration and turnout [was] lower in the States originally covered by § 5 than it [was] nationwide." Since that time, Census Bureau data indicate that African-American voter turnout has come to exceed white voter turnout in five of the six States originally covered by § 5, with a gap in the sixth State of less than one half of one percent.

At the same time, voting discrimination still exists; no one doubts that. The question is whether the Act's extraordinary measures, including its disparate treatment of the States, continue to satisfy constitutional requirements. As we put it a short time ago, "the Act imposes current burdens and must be justified by current needs."

IA

The Fifteenth Amendment was ratified in 1870, in the wake of the Civil War. It provides that "[t]he right of citizens of the United States to vote shall not be denied or abridged by the United States or by any State on account of race, color, or previous condition of servitude," and it gives Congress the "power to enforce this article by appropriate legislation."

"The first century of congressional enforcement of the Amendment, however, can only be regarded as a failure." In the 1890s, Alabama, Georgia, Louisiana, Mississippi, North Carolina, South Carolina, and Virginia began to enact literacy tests for voter registration and to employ other methods designed to prevent African-Americans from voting. Congress passed statutes outlawing some of these practices and facilitating litigation against them, but litigation remained slow and expensive, and the States came up with new ways to discriminate as soon as existing ones were struck down. Voter registration of African-Americans barely improved.

Inspired to action by the civil rights movement, Congress responded in 1965 with the Voting Rights Act. Section 2 was enacted to forbid, in all 50 States, any "standard, practice, or procedure ... imposed or applied ... to deny or abridge the right of any citizen of the United States to vote on account of race or color." The current version forbids any "standard, practice, or procedure" that "results in a denial or abridgement of the right of any citizen of the United States to vote on account of race or color." Both the Federal Government and individuals have sued to enforce § 2, and injunctive relief is available in appropriate cases to block voting laws from going into effect. Section 2 is permanent, applies nationwide, and is not at issue in this case.

Other sections targeted only some parts of the country. At the time of the Act's passage, these "covered" jurisdictions were those States or political subdivisions that had maintained a test or device as a prerequisite to voting as of November 1, 1964, and had less than 50 percent voter registration or turnout in the 1964 Presidential election. § 4(b). Such tests or devices included literacy and knowledge tests, good moral character requirements, the need for vouchers from registered voters, and the like. § 4(c). A covered jurisdiction could "bail out" of coverage if it had not used a test or device in the preceding five years "for the purpose or with the effect of denying or abridging the right to vote on account of race or color." § 4(a). In 1965, the covered States included Alabama, Georgia, Louisiana, Mississippi, South Carolina, and Virginia. The additional covered subdivisions included 39 counties in North Carolina and one in Arizona.

In those jurisdictions, § 4 of the Act banned all such tests or devices. Section 5 provided that no change in voting procedures could take effect until it was approved by federal authorities in Washington, D.C.—either the Attorney General or a court of three judges. A jurisdiction could obtain such "preclearance" only by proving that the change had neither "the purpose [nor] the effect of denying or abridging the right to vote on account of race or color."

Sections 4 and 5 were intended to be temporary; they were set to expire after five years. [However, the act was passed and reauthorized in 1970, 1975, 1982, and 2006 (for 25 years for the 2006 bill).] ...

B

Shelby County is located in Alabama, a covered jurisdiction. It has not sought bailout, as the Attorney General has recently objected to voting changes proposed from within the county Instead, in 2010, the county sued the Attorney General in Federal District Court in Washington, D.C., seeking a declaratory judgment that sections 4(b) and 5 of the Voting Rights Act are facially unconstitutional, as well as a permanent injunction against their enforcement. ...

IIA

...

The Constitution and laws of the United States are "the supreme Law of the Land." U.S. Const., Art. VI, cl. 2. State legislation may not contravene federal law. The Federal Government does not, however, have a general right to review and veto state enactments before they go into effect. A proposal to grant such authority to "negative" state laws was considered at the Constitutional Convention, but rejected in favor of allowing state laws to take effect, subject to later challenge under the Supremacy Clause.

Outside the strictures of the Supremacy Clause, States retain broad autonomy in structuring their governments and pursuing legislative objectives. Indeed, the Constitution provides that all powers not specifically granted to the Federal Government are reserved to the States or citizens. Amdt. 10. This "allocation of powers in our federal system preserves the integrity, dignity, and residual sovereignty of the States." But the federal balance "is not just an end in itself: Rather, federalism secures to citizens the liberties that derive from the diffusion of sovereign power."

More specifically, "'the Framers of the Constitution intended the States to keep for themselves, as provided in the Tenth Amendment, the power to regulate elections.'" ...

Not only do States retain sovereignty under the Constitution, there is also a "fundamental principle of *equal* sovereignty" among the States. ...

The Voting Rights Act sharply departs from these basic principles. It suspends "*all* changes to state election law—however innocuous—until they have been precleared by federal authorities in Washington, D.C." States must beseech the Federal Government for permission to implement laws that they would otherwise have the right to enact and execute on their own, subject of course to any injunction in a § 2 action. The Attorney General has 60 days to object to a preclearance request, longer if he requests more information. If a State seeks preclearance from a three-judge court, the process can take years.

And despite the tradition of equal sovereignty, the Act applies to only nine States (and several additional counties). ...

C

Nearly 50 years later, things have changed dramatically. Shelby County contends that the preclearance requirement, even without regard to its disparate coverage, is now unconstitutional. Its arguments have a good deal of force. In the covered jurisdictions, "[v]oter turnout and registration rates now approach parity. Blatantly discriminatory evasions of federal decrees are rare. And minority candidates hold office at unprecedented levels." The tests and devices that blocked access to the ballot have been forbidden nationwide for over 40 years.

Those conclusions are not ours alone. Congress said the same when it reauthorized the Act in 2006, writing that "[s]ignificant progress has been made in eliminating first generation barriers experienced by minority voters, including increased numbers of registered minority voters, minority voter turnout, and minority representation in Congress, State legislatures, and local elected offices." The House Report elaborated that "the number of African-Americans who are registered and who turn out to cast ballots has increased significantly over the last 40 years, particularly since 1982," and noted that "[i]n some circumstances, minorities register to vote and cast ballots at levels that surpass those of white voters." That Report also explained that there have been "significant increases in the number of African-Americans serving in elected offices"; more specifically, there has been approximately a 1,000 percent increase since 1965 in the number of African-American elected officials in the six States originally covered by the Voting Rights Act.

The following chart, compiled from the Senate and House Reports, compares voter registration numbers from 1965 to those from 2004 in the six originally covered States. These are the numbers that were before Congress when it reauthorized the Act in 2006:

	1965			2004		
	White	Black	Gap	White	Black	Gap
Alabama	69.2	19.3	49.9	73.8	72.9	0.9
Georgia	62.[6]	27.4	35.2	63.5	64.2	−0.7
Louisiana	80.5	31.6	48.9	75.1	71.1	4.0
Mississippi	69.9	6.7	63.2	72.3	76.1	−3.8
South Carolina	75.7	37.3	38.4	74.4	71.1	3.3
Virginia	61.1	38.3	22.8	68.2	57.4	10.8

... The provisions of § 5 apply only to those jurisdictions singled out by § 4. We now consider whether that coverage formula is constitutional in light of current conditions.

III

...

Coverage today is based on decades-old data and eradicated practices. The formula captures States by reference to literacy tests and low voter registration and turnout in the 1960s and early 1970s. But such tests have been banned nationwide for over 40 years. And voter registration and turnout numbers in the covered States have risen dramatically in the years since. ...

In 1965, the States could be divided into two groups: those with a recent history of voting tests and low voter registration and turnout, and those without those characteristics. Congress based its coverage formula on that distinction. Today the Nation is no longer divided along those lines, yet the Voting Rights Act continues to treat it as if it were. ...

But history did not end in 1965. By the time the Act was reauthorized in 2006, there had been 40 more years of it. In assessing the "current need [ ]" for a preclearance system that treats States differently from one another today, that history cannot be ignored. During that time, largely because of the Voting Rights Act, voting tests were abolished, disparities in voter registration and turnout due to race were erased, and African-Americans attained political office in record numbers. And yet the coverage formula that Congress reauthorized in 2006 ignores these developments, keeping the focus on decades-old data relevant to decades-old problems, rather than current data reflecting current needs.

The Fifteenth Amendment commands that the right to vote shall not be denied or abridged on account of race or color, and it gives Congress the power to enforce that command. The Amendment is not designed to punish for the past; its purpose is to ensure a better future. To serve that purpose, Congress—if it is to divide the States—must identify those jurisdictions to be singled out on a basis that makes sense in light of current conditions. It cannot rely simply on the past....

There is no valid reason to insulate the coverage formula from review merely because it was previously enacted 40 years ago. If Congress had started from scratch in 2006, it plainly could not have enacted the present coverage formula. It would have been irrational for Congress to distinguish between States in such a fundamental way based on 40-year-old data, when today's statistics tell an entirely different story. And it would have been irrational to base coverage on the use of voting tests 40 years ago, when such tests have been illegal since that time. But that is exactly what Congress has done....

Our decision in no way affects the permanent, nationwide ban on racial discrimination in voting found in § 2. We issue no holding on § 5 itself, only on the coverage formula. Congress may draft another formula based on current conditions. Such a formula is an initial prerequisite to a determination that exceptional conditions still exist justifying such an "extraordinary departure from the traditional course of relations between the States and the Federal Government." Our country has changed, and while any racial discrimination in voting is too much, Congress must ensure that the legislation it passes to remedy that problem speaks to current conditions.

Justice THOMAS, concurring.

I join the Court's opinion in full but write separately to explain that I would find § 5 of the Voting Rights Act unconstitutional as well. The Court's opinion sets forth the reasons....

Justice GINSBURG, with whom Justice BREYER, Justice SOTOMAYOR, and Justice KAGAN join, dissenting.

In the Court's view, the very success of § 5 of the Voting Rights Act demands its dormancy. Congress was of another mind. Recognizing that large progress has been made, Congress determined, based on a voluminous record, that the scourge of discrimination was not yet extirpated. The question this case presents is who decides whether, as currently operative, § 5 remains justifiable, this Court, or a Congress charged with the obligation to enforce the post-Civil War Amendments "by appropriate legislation." With overwhelming support in both Houses, Congress concluded that, for two prime reasons, § 5 should continue in force, unabated. First, continuance would facilitate completion of the impressive gains thus far made; and second, continuance would guard against backsliding. Those assessments were well within Congress' province to make and should elicit this Court's unstinting approbation.

I

"[V]oting discrimination still exists; no one doubts that." But the Court today terminates the remedy that proved to be best suited to block that discrimination. The Voting Rights Act of 1965 (VRA) has worked to combat voting discrimination where other remedies had been tried and failed. Particularly effective is the VRA's requirement of federal preclearance for all changes to voting laws in the regions of the country with the most aggravated records of rank discrimination against minority voting rights....

Congress learned from experience that laws targeting particular electoral practices or enabling case-by-case litigation were inadequate to the task. In the Civil Rights Acts of 1957, 1960, and 1964, Congress authorized and then expanded the power of "the Attorney General to seek injunctions against public and private interference with the right to vote on racial grounds." ...

Answering that need, the Voting Rights Act became one of the most consequential, efficacious, and amply justified exercises of federal legislative power in our Nation's history. Requiring federal preclearance of changes in voting laws in the covered jurisdictions—those States and localities where opposition to the Constitution's commands were most virulent—the VRA provided a fit solution for minority voters as well as for States. Under the preclearance regime established by § 5 of the VRA, covered jurisdictions must submit proposed changes in voting laws or procedures to the Department of Justice (DOJ), which has 60 days to respond to the changes. A change will be approved unless DOJ finds it has "the purpose [or] ... the effect of denying or abridging the right to vote on account of race or color." In the alternative, the covered jurisdiction may seek approval by a three-judge District Court in the District of Columbia.

After a century's failure to fulfill the promise of the Fourteenth and Fifteenth Amendments, passage of the VRA finally led to signal improvement on this front. "The Justice Department estimated that in the five years after [the VRA's] passage, almost as many blacks registered [to vote] in Alabama, Mississippi, Georgia, Louisiana, North Carolina, and South Carolina as in the entire century before 1965." And in assessing the overall effects of the VRA in 2006, Congress found that "[s]ignificant progress has been made in eliminating first generation barriers experienced by minority voters, including increased numbers of registered minority voters, minority voter turnout, and minority representation in Congress, State legislatures, and local elected offices. This progress is the direct result of the Voting Rights Act of 1965." On that matter of cause and effects there can be no genuine doubt.

Although the VRA wrought dramatic changes in the realization of minority voting rights, the Act, to date, surely has not eliminated all vestiges of discrimination against the exercise of the franchise by minority citizens. Jurisdictions covered by the preclearance requirement continued to submit, in large numbers, proposed changes to voting laws that the Attorney General declined to approve, auguring that barriers to minority voting would quickly resurface were the preclearance remedy eliminated. ...

Second-generation barriers come in various forms. One of the blockages is racial gerrymandering, the redrawing of legislative districts in an "effort to segregate the races for purposes of voting." Another is adoption of a system of at-large voting in lieu of district-by-district voting in a city with a sizable black minority. By switching to at-large voting, the overall majority could control the election of each city council member, effectively eliminating the potency of the minority's votes. A similar effect could be achieved if the city engaged in discriminatory annexation by incorporating majority-white areas into city limits, thereby decreasing the effect of VRA-occasioned increases in black voting. Whatever the device employed, this Court has long recognized that vote dilution, when adopted with a discriminatory purpose, cuts down the right to vote as certainly as denial of access to the ballot. ...

The question before the Court is whether Congress had the authority under the Constitution to act as it did.

II

In answering this question, the Court does not write on a clean slate. It is well established that Congress' judgment regarding exercise of its power to enforce the Fourteenth and Fifteenth Amendments warrants substantial deference. The VRA addresses the combination of race discrimination and the right to vote, which is "preservative of all rights." When confronting the most constitutionally invidious form of discrimination, and the most fundamental right in our democratic system, Congress' power to act is at its height. ...

Until today, in considering the constitutionality of the VRA, the Court has accorded Congress the full measure of respect its judgments in this domain should garner. ...

...

III

The 2006 reauthorization of the Voting Rights Act fully satisfies the standard stated in *McCulloch,* 4 Wheat., at 421: Congress may choose any means "appropriate" and "plainly adapted to" a legitimate constitutional end. As we shall see, it is implausible to suggest otherwise. ...

The Court criticizes Congress for failing to recognize that "history did not end in 1965." But the Court ignores that "what's past is prologue." W. Shakespeare, The Tempest, act 2, sc. 1. And "[t]hose who cannot remember the past are condemned to repeat it." 1 G. Santayana, The Life of Reason 284 (1905). Congress was especially mindful of the need to reinforce the gains already made and to prevent backsliding. ...

Although covered jurisdictions account for less than 25 percent of the country's population, the Katz study revealed that they accounted for 56 percent of successful § 2 litigation since 1982. ...

This experience exposes the inaccuracy of the Court's portrayal of the Act as static, unchanged since 1965. Congress designed the VRA to be a dynamic statute, capable of adjusting to changing conditions. True, many covered jurisdictions have not been able to bail out due to recent acts of noncompliance with the VRA, but that truth reinforces the congressional judgment that these jurisdictions were rightfully subject to preclearance, and ought to remain under that regime.

IV

...

Throwing out preclearance when it has worked and is continuing to work to stop discriminatory changes is like throwing away your umbrella in a rainstorm because you are not getting wet. ...

The sad irony of today's decision lies in its utter failure to grasp why the VRA has proven effective. The Court appears to believe that the VRA's success in eliminating the specific devices extant in 1965 means that preclearance is no longer needed. With that belief, and the argument derived from it, history repeats itself. The same assumption—that the problem could be solved when particular methods of voting discrimination are identified and eliminated—was indulged and proved wrong repeatedly prior to the VRA's enactment. Unlike prior statutes, which singled out particular tests or devices, the VRA is grounded in Congress' recognition of the "variety and persistence" of measures designed to impair minority voting rights. In truth, the evolution of voting discrimination into more subtle second-generation barriers is powerful evidence that a remedy as effective as preclearance remains vital to protect minority voting rights and prevent backsliding.

Beyond question, the VRA is no ordinary legislation. It is extraordinary because Congress embarked on a mission long delayed and of extraordinary importance: to realize the purpose and promise of the Fifteenth Amendment. For a half century, a concerted effort has been made to end racial discrimination in voting. Thanks to the Voting Rights Act, progress once the subject of a dream has been achieved and continues to be made.

The record supporting the 2006 reauthorization of the VRA is also extraordinary. It was described by the Chairman of the House Judiciary Committee as "one of the most extensive considerations of any piece of legislation that the United States Congress has dealt with in the 27 & half; years" he had served in the House. After exhaustive evidence-gathering and deliberative process, Congress reauthorized the VRA, including the coverage provision, with overwhelming bipartisan support. It was the judgment of Congress that "40 years has not been a sufficient amount of time to eliminate the vestiges of discrimination following nearly 100 years of disregard for the dictates of the 15th amendment and to ensure that the right of all citizens to vote is protected as guaranteed by the Constitution." That determination of the body empowered to enforce the Civil War Amendments "by appropriate legislation" merits this Court's utmost respect. In my judgment, the Court errs egregiously by overriding Congress' decision.

Notes and Questions

1. *The need for a Voting Rights Act.* Why did Congress think a Voting Rights Act was necessary? Do you think it is still necessary or not?
2. *Are you persuaded?* Which Justice wrote the opinion most persuasive to you? Why was it persuasive?
3. *Justice Thomas.* Why does Justice Thomas think § 5 is unconstitutional?
4. *Video.* Does this video help you understand the case? Supreme Court Briefs, Suppressing the Vote, Oct. 2, 2020, at https://www.youtube.com/watch?v=UAu2APOafvw&list=PLsFE_Nvl6h_Y75KGR5pkGqcFisGvBnO9S&index=70.
5. *The VRA and 2021 and 2022 voting laws.* How could an individual win a VRA case today? Consider the voting bills that were passed following the 2020 election, which are summarized in the Brennan Center's Voting Roundup at https://www.brennancenter.org/our-work/research-reports/voting-laws-roundup-october-2021. Do any of them violate the VRA? How could you prove they do? How could you prove they do not? What similarities and differences are there between the 2021 laws and the 2022 laws, also detailed by the Brennan Center at https://www.brennancenter.org/our-work/research-reports/voting-laws-roundup-february-2022?
6. *How to enforce.* What is the best way to enforce the Fifteenth Amendment?

After the *Shelby* decision regarding Sections 4 and 5 of the Voting Rights Act, many people argued that Section 2 of the VRA was still valid; section 2 of the Voting Rights Act prohibits racial discrimination in voting. A 1982 amendment to the section provided that a plaintiff could win if the local electoral process or the standard, practice, or procedure being challenged denied an equal opportunity to participate in the political process of a racial or language minority. The next case discusses how the Supreme Court dealt with Sec. 2 following *Shelby*.

b. Section 2 of the Voting Rights Act Is Read Narrowly

In 2021, in the following case, the Supreme Court ruled 6–3 that Arizona had not violated Section 2 when it required out-of-precinct ballots to be discarded and limited the ability of third parties to help people mail their ballots. *Brnovich v. Democratic Nat'l Comm.*, 141 S. Ct. 2321 (2021). Justice Alito wrote the majority opinion. Justice Kagan wrote the dissent. Justices Gorsuch and Thomas concurred.

Read the oral argument of the case, available at https://www.oyez.org/cases/2020/19-1257. Consider the Justices' questions. Can you link their questions to their vote in the final opinion? As you consider the oral argument, would you be able to predict who would win?

Brnovich v. Democratic National Committee

SUPREME COURT OF THE UNITED STATES, 2021

594 U.S. ___, 141 S.Ct. 2321

ALITO, J., delivered the opinion of the Court, in which ROBERTS, C. J., and THOMAS, GORSUCH, KAVANAUGH, and BARRETT, JJ., joined. GORSUCH, J., filed a concurring opinion, in which THOMAS, J., joined. KAGAN, J., filed a dissenting opinion, in which BREYER and SOTOMAYOR, JJ., joined.

In these cases, we are called upon for the first time to apply § 2 of the Voting Rights Act of 1965 to regulations that govern how ballots are collected and counted. Arizona law generally makes it very easy to vote. All voters may vote by mail or in person for nearly a month before election day, but Arizona imposes two restrictions that are claimed to be unlawful. First, in some counties, voters who choose to cast a ballot in person on election day must vote in their own precincts or else their ballots will not be counted. Second, mail-in ballots cannot be collected by anyone other than an election official, a mail carrier, or a voter's family member, household member, or caregiver. ...

IA

Congress enacted the landmark Voting Rights Act of 1965, 79 Stat. 437, as amended, 52 U.S.C. § 10301 *et seq.*, in an effort to achieve at long last what the Fifteenth Amendment had sought to bring about 95 years earlier: an end to the denial of the right to vote based on race. Ratified in 1870, the Fifteenth Amendment provides in § 1 that "[t]he right of citizens of the United States to vote shall not be denied or abridged by the United States or by any State on account of race, color, or previous condition of servitude." Section 2 of the Amendment then grants Congress the "power to enforce [the Amendment] by appropriate legislation."

Despite the ratification of the Fifteenth Amendment, the right of African-Americans to vote was heavily suppressed for nearly a century. States employed a variety of notorious methods, including poll taxes, literacy tests, property qualifications, "'white primar[ies],'" and "'grandfather clause[s].'" Challenges to some blatant efforts reached this Court and were held to violate the Fifteenth Amendment.

Invoking the power conferred by § 2 of the Fifteenth Amendment, Congress enacted the Voting Rights Act (VRA) to address this entrenched problem. The Act and its amendments in the 1970s specifically forbade some of the practices that had been used to suppress black voting. ...

As originally enacted, § 2 closely tracked the language of the Amendment it was adopted to enforce. Section 2 stated simply that "[n]o voting qualification or prerequisite to voting, or standard, practice, or procedure shall be imposed or applied by any State or political subdivision to deny or abridge the right of any citizen of the United States to vote on account of race or color."

Unlike other provisions of the VRA, § 2 attracted relatively little attention during the congressional debates and was "little-used" for more than a decade after its passage. ...

Shortly after *Bolden* was handed down, Congress amended § 2 of the VRA. The oft-cited Report of the Senate Judiciary Committee accompanying the 1982 Amendment stated that the amendment's purpose was to repudiate *Bolden* and establish a new vote-dilution test based on what the Court had said in *White*. The bill that was initially passed by the House of Representatives included what is now § 2(a). In place of the phrase "to deny or abridge the right ... to vote on account of race or color," the amendment substituted "in a manner which *results in* a denial or abridgement of the right ... to vote on account of race or color." ...

What is now § 2(b) was added, and that provision sets out what must be shown to prove a § 2 violation. It requires consideration of "the totality of circumstances" in each case and demands proof that "the political processes leading to nomination or election in the State or political subdivision are not *equally open* to participation" by members of a protected class "*in that its members have less opportunity* than other members of the electorate to participate in the political process and to elect representatives of their choice." Reflecting the Senate Judiciary Committee's stated focus on the issue of vote dilution, this language was taken almost verbatim from *White*. ...

B

... In 2016, the Democratic National Committee and certain affiliates brought this suit and named as defendants (among others) the Arizona attorney general and secretary of state in their official capacities. Among other things, the plaintiffs claimed that both the State's refusal to count ballots cast in the wrong precinct and its ballot-collection restriction "adversely and disparately affect Arizona's American Indian, Hispanic, and African American citizens," in violation of § 2 of the VRA. In addition, they alleged that the ballot-collection restriction was "enacted with discriminatory intent" and thus violated both § 2 of the VRA and the Fifteenth Amendment. ...

II

... But as this is our first foray into the area, we think it sufficient for present purposes to identify certain guideposts that lead us to our decision in these cases.

B

... Putting these terms together, it appears that the core of § 2(b) is the requirement that voting be "equally open." The statute's reference to equal "opportunity" may stretch that concept to some degree to include consideration of a person's ability to *use* the means that are equally open. But equal openness remains the touchstone.

C

One other important feature of § 2(b) stands out. The provision requires consideration of "the totality of circumstances." Thus, any circumstance that has a logical bearing on whether voting is "equally open" and affords equal "opportunity" may be considered. We will not attempt to compile an exhaustive list, but several important circumstances should be mentioned.

1

First, the size of the burden imposed by a challenged voting rule is highly relevant. ...

For similar reasons, the degree to which a voting rule departs from what was standard practice when § 2 was amended in 1982 is a relevant consideration. ...

The size of any disparities in a rule's impact on members of different racial or ethnic groups is also an important factor to consider. Small disparities are less likely than large ones to indicate that a system is not equally open. ...

Next, courts must consider the opportunities provided by a State's entire system of voting when assessing the burden imposed by a challenged provision. ...

Finally, the strength of the state interests served by a challenged voting rule is also an important factor that must be taken into account. ...

One strong and entirely legitimate state interest is the prevention of fraud. ...

2

While the factors set out above are important, others considered by some lower courts are less helpful in a case like the ones at hand. First, it is important to keep in mind that the *Gingles* or "Senate" factors grew out of and were designed for use in vote-dilution cases. But in cases involving neutral time, place, and manner rules, the only relevance of these and the remaining factors is to show that minority group members suffered discrimination in the past (factor one) and that effects of that discrimination persist (factor five). We do not suggest that these factors should be disregarded. After all, § 2(b) requires consideration of "the totality of circumstances." But their relevance is much less direct.

We also do not find the disparate-impact model employed in Title VII and Fair Housing Act cases useful here. ...

D

... The dissent, by contrast, would rewrite the text of § 2 and make it turn almost entirely on just one circumstance—disparate impact.

That is a radical project, and the dissent strains mightily to obscure its objective. ...

IV

A

In light of the principles set out above, neither Arizona's out-of-precinct rule nor its ballot-collection law violates § 2 of the VRA. Arizona's out-of-precinct rule enforces the requirement that voters who choose to vote in person on election day must do so in their assigned precincts. Having to identify one's own polling place and then travel there to vote does not exceed the "usual burdens of voting." *Crawford*, 553 U.S. at 198, 128 S.Ct. 1610 (opinion of STEVENS, J.) (noting the same about making a trip to the department of motor vehicles). On the contrary, these tasks are quintessential examples of the usual burdens of voting. ...

Next, the racial disparity in burdens allegedly caused by the out-of-precinct policy is small in absolute terms. The District Court accepted the plaintiffs' evidence that, of the Arizona counties that reported out-of-precinct ballots in the 2016 general election, a little over 1% of Hispanic voters, 1% of African-American voters, and 1% of Native American voters who voted on election day cast an out-of-precinct ballot. For non-minority voters, the rate was around 0.5%. A policy that appears to work for 98% or more of voters to whom it applies—minority and non-minority alike—is unlikely to render a system unequally open. ...

In light of the modest burdens allegedly imposed by Arizona's out-of-precinct policy, the small size of its disparate impact, and the State's justifications, we conclude the rule does not violate § 2 of the VRA.

B

HB 2023 likewise passes muster under the results test of § 2. ...

The plaintiffs were unable to provide statistical evidence showing that HB 2023 had a disparate impact on minority voters. Instead, they called witnesses who testified that third-party ballot collection tends to be used most heavily in disadvantaged communities and that minorities in Arizona—especially Native Americans—are disproportionately disadvantaged. But from that evidence the District Court could conclude only that prior to HB 2023's enactment, "minorities generically were more likely than non-minorities to return their early ballots with the assistance of third parties." How much more, the court could not say from the record. Neither can we. And without more concrete evidence, we cannot conclude that HB 2023 results in less opportunity to participate in the political process. ...

V

We also granted certiorari to review whether the Court of Appeals erred in concluding that HB 2023 was enacted with a discriminatory purpose. The District Court found that it was not. ...

We are more than satisfied that the District Court's interpretation of the evidence is permissible. The spark for the debate over mail-in voting may well have been provided by one Senator's enflamed partisanship, but partisan motives are not the same as racial motives. ...

* * *

Arizona's out-of-precinct policy and HB 2023 do not violate § 2 of the VRA, and HB 2023 was not enacted with a racially discriminatory purpose. The judgment of the Court of Appeals is reversed, and the cases are remanded for further proceedings consistent with this opinion.

Justice GORSUCH, with whom Justice THOMAS joins, concurring.

I join the Court's opinion in full, but flag one thing it does not decide. Our cases have assumed—without deciding—that the Voting Rights Act of 1965 furnishes an implied cause of action under § 2. Lower courts have treated this as an open question. Because no party argues that the plaintiffs lack a cause of action here, and because the existence (or not) of a cause of action does not go to a court's subject-matter jurisdiction this Court need not and does not address that issue today.

Justice KAGAN, with whom Justice BREYER and Justice SOTOMAYOR join, dissenting.

... Today, the Court undermines Section 2 and the right it provides. The majority fears that the statute Congress wrote is too "radical"—that it will invalidate too many state voting laws. So the majority writes its own set of rules, limiting Section 2 from multiple directions. Wherever it can, the majority gives a cramped reading to broad language. And then it uses that reading to uphold two election laws from Arizona that discriminate against minority voters. I could say—and will in the following pages—that this is not how the Court is supposed to interpret and apply statutes. But that ordinary critique woefully undersells the problem. What is tragic here is that the Court has (yet again) rewritten—in order to weaken—a statute that stands as a monument to America's greatness, and protects against its basest impulses. What is tragic is that the Court has damaged a statute designed to bring about "the end of discrimination in voting." I respectfully dissent. ...

Momentous as the Fifteenth Amendment was, celebration of its achievements soon proved premature. The Amendment's guarantees "quickly became dead letters in much of the country." African Americans daring to go to the polls often "met with coordinated intimidation and violence." And almost immediately, legislators discovered that bloodless actions could also suffice to limit the electorate to white citizens. Many States, especially in the South, suppressed the black vote through a dizzying array of methods: literacy tests, poll taxes, registration requirements, and property qualifications. Most of those laws, though facially neutral, gave enough discretion to election officials to prevent significant effects on poor or uneducated whites. The idea, as one Virginia representative put it, was "to disfranchise every negro that [he] could disfranchise," and "as few white people as possible." Decade after decade after decade, election rules blocked African Americans—and in some States, Hispanics and Native Americans too—from making use of the ballot. By 1965, only 27% of black Georgians, 19% of black Alabamians, and 7%—yes, 7%—of black Mississippians were registered to vote. ...

"After a century's failure to fulfill the promise" of the Fifteenth Amendment, "passage of the VRA finally led to signal improvement." *Shelby County*, 570 U.S. at 562, 133 S.Ct. 2612 (GINSBURG, J., dissenting). ...

Yet efforts to suppress the minority vote continue. No one would know this from reading the majority opinion. It hails the "good news" that legislative efforts had mostly shifted by the 1980s from vote denial to vote dilution. And then it moves on to other matters, as though the Voting Rights Act no longer has a problem to address—as though once literacy tests and poll taxes disappeared, so too did efforts to curb minority voting. But as this Court recognized about a decade ago, "racial discrimination and racially polarized voting are not ancient history." Indeed, the problem of voting discrimination has become worse since that time—in part because of what this Court did in *Shelby County*. Weaken the Voting Rights Act, and predictable consequences follow: yet a further generation of voter suppression laws. ...

Once Section 5's strictures came off, States and localities put in place new restrictive voting laws, with foreseeably adverse effects on minority voters. ...

So the Court decides this Voting Rights Act case at a perilous moment for the Nation's commitment to equal citizenship. It decides this case in an era of voting-rights retrenchment—when too many States and localities are restricting access to voting in ways that will predictably deprive members of minority groups of equal access to the ballot box. If "any racial discrimination in voting is too much," as the *Shelby County* Court recited, then the Act still has much to do. Or more precisely, the fraction of the Act remaining—the Act as diminished by the Court's hand. Congress never meant for Section 2 to bear all of the weight of the Act's commitments. That provision looks to courts, not to the Executive Branch, to restrain discriminatory voting practices. And litigation is an after-the-fact remedy, incapable of providing relief until an election—usually, more than one election—has come and gone. So Section 2 was supposed to be a back-up, for all its sweep and power. But after *Shelby County*, the vitality of Section 2—a "permanent, nationwide ban on racial discrimination in voting"—matters more than ever. For after *Shelby County*, Section 2 is what voters have left. ...

So the text of Section 2, as applied in our precedents, tells us the following, every part of which speaks to the ambition of Congress's action. Section 2 applies to any voting rule, of any kind. The provision prohibits not just the denial but also the abridgment of a citizen's voting rights on account of race. The inquiry is focused on effects: It asks not about why state officials enacted a rule, but about whether that rule results in racial discrimination. The discrimination that is of concern is inequality of voting opportunity. That kind of discrimination can arise from facially neutral (not just targeted) rules. There is a Section 2 problem when an election rule, operating against the backdrop of historical, social, and economic conditions, makes it harder for minority citizens than for others to cast ballots. And strong state interests may save an otherwise discriminatory rule, but only if that rule is needed to achieve them—that is, only if a less discriminatory rule will not attain the State's goal. ...

The majority's opinion mostly inhabits a law-free zone. ...

In sum, the majority skates over the strong words Congress drafted to accomplish its equally strong purpose: ensuring that minority citizens can access the electoral system as easily as whites. ...

The majority instead founds its decision on a list of mostly made-up factors, at odds with Section 2 itself. ...

Congress enacted Section 2 to prevent those maneuvers from working. It knew that States and localities had over time enacted measure after measure imposing discriminatory voting burdens. And it knew that governments were proficient in justifying those measures on non-racial grounds. So Congress called a halt. It enacted a statute that would strike down all unnecessary laws, including facially neutral ones, that result in members of a racial group having unequal access to the political process. ...

The Voting Rights Act was meant to replace state and local election rules that needlessly make voting harder for members of one race than for others. The text of the Act perfectly reflects that objective. The "democratic" principle it upholds is not one of States' rights as against federal courts. The democratic principle it upholds is the right of every American, of every race, to have equal access to the ballot box. The majority today undermines that principle as it refuses to apply the terms of the statute. By declaring some racially discriminatory burdens inconsequential, and by refusing to subject asserted state interests to serious means-end scrutiny, the majority enables voting discrimination.

Just look at Arizona. Two of that State's policies disproportionately affect minority citizens' opportunity to vote. The first—the out-of-precinct policy—results in Hispanic and African American voters' ballots being thrown out at a statistically higher rate than those of whites. And whatever the majority might say about the ordinariness of such a rule, Arizona applies it in extra-ordinary fashion: Arizona is *the* national outlier in dealing with out-of-precinct votes, with the next-worst offender nowhere in sight. The second rule—the ballot-collection ban—makes voting meaningfully more difficult for Native American citizens than for others. And nothing about how that ban is applied is "usual" either—this time because of how many of the State's Native American citizens need to travel long distances to use the mail. Both policies violate Section 2, on a straightforward application of its text. Considering the "totality of circumstances," both "result in" members of some races having "less opportunity than other members of the electorate to participate in the political process and to elect a representative of their choice." § 10301(b). The majority reaches the opposite conclusion because it closes its eyes to the facts on the ground. ...

This Court has no right to remake Section 2. Maybe some think that vote suppression is a relic of history—and so the need for a potent Section 2 has come and gone. Cf. *Shelby County*, 570 U.S. at 547, 133 S.Ct. 2612 ("[T]hings have changed dramatically"). But Congress gets to make that call. Because it has not done so, this Court's duty is to apply the law as it is written. The law that confronted one of this country's most enduring wrongs; pledged to give every American, of every race, an equal chance to participate in our democracy; and now stands as the crucial tool to achieve that goal. That law, of all laws, deserves the sweep and power Congress gave it. That law, of all laws, should not be diminished by this Court.

Notes and Questions

1. *The tests.* What do you think of Justice Alito's analysis of Section 2? How does it differ from Justice Kagan's? If you were to summarize each of their tests, how would you plead a Section 2 case today? What facts would you need to win a Section 2 case?

2. *Persuaded?* Which Justice wrote the opinion most persuasive to you? Why was it persuasive?
3. *Reactions.* What do you think of the Arizona Attorney General's reaction to the Court's opinion, Breaking News, AZ Attorney General Mark Brnovich reacts to Supreme Court decision, Jul. 1, 2021, at https://www.youtube.com/watch?v=8eqIYvSnMbQ? What can the voters complain about now that the decision is written, see Voting rights activists to protest voter suppression at Arizona AG Mark Brnovich's office, Jul. 8, 2021, at https://www.youtube.com/watch?v=yrV1KVQGkHk?
4. *Challenge to Georgia law.* The Justice Department filed a Section 2 lawsuit against Georgia on June 25, 2021. The description of the lawsuit says it challenges Georgia laws "including a provision banning government entities from distributing unsolicited absentee ballot applications; the imposition of costly and onerous fines on civil organizations, churches and advocacy groups that distribute follow-up absentee ballot applications; the shortening of the deadline to request absentee ballots of 11 days before Election Day; the requirement that voters who do not have identification issued by the Georgia Department of Driver Services photocopy another form of identification in order to request an absentee ballot without allowing for use of the last four digits of a social security number for such applications; significant limitations on counties' use of absentee ballot drop boxes; the prohibition on efforts by churches and civic groups to provide food or water to persons waiting in long lines to vote; and the prohibition on counting out-of-precinct provisional ballots before 5 p.m. on Election Day." Justice Department Files Lawsuit Against the State of Georgia to Stop Racially Discriminatory Provisions of New Voting Law, Justice News, June 25, 2021, at https://www.justice.gov/opa/pr/justice-department-files-lawsuit-against-state-georgia-stop-racially-discriminatory. The district court rejected the state's motions to dismiss the lawsuit, and so it will proceed. *United States v. Georgia*, No. 1:21-CV-02575-JPB, 2021 WL 5833000, at *2 (N.D. Ga. Dec. 9, 2021). How can the DOJ win this lawsuit? How can Georgia win this lawsuit?
5. *Current Texas law.* What is the current voting law in Texas? See Eric Bradner, The new Texas voting law includes these 7 major changes, CNN.com, Sept. 8, 2021, at https://www.cnn.com/2021/09/07/politics/what-texas-voting-bill-does/index.html. Does it violate the Voting Rights Act in any way? Why do you think the NAACP would have sued Texas, challenging limitations on early voting hours and the elimination of drive-through voting centers, among other sections of the law?
6. *After the 2020 census, Alabama redistricted its seven districts for the House of Representatives and included one majority Black district.* The NAACP and other organizations sued, alleging the redistricting had packed too many Blacks into one district and spread the rest of the Blacks around the other districts. Plaintiffs asked for two majority Black districts. A three-member district court issued an injunction, ruling that Alabama had violated Section 2 of the Voting Rights Act, stating that "Black voters have less opportunity than other Alabamians to elect candidates of their choice to Congress." *Singleton v. Merrill*, 2022 WL 265001 (N.D.Ala.), 2. The court concluded that the maps had to have two majority Black districts or something close to that situation in order to be legal, issuing an injunction. The Supreme Court then stayed the injunction.

The Supreme Court later considered those facts in *Merrill v. Milligan,* and heard oral argument in that case on October 4, 2022. The Court granted cert. on the question "Whether the state of Alabama's 2021 redistricting plan for its seven seats in the United States House of Representatives violated Section 2 of the Voting Rights Act." See *Merrill v. Milligan*, https://www.scotusblog.com/case-files/cases/merrill-v-milligan-2/. You can listen to the oral argument at https://www.c-span.org/video/?523311-1/merrill-v-milligan-oral-argument. How do you think the Court will vote in this case? How will its earlier cases on the Voting Rights Act affect its outcome here?

7. Can you find another existing or proposed state law that you think violates Section 2? Could federal legislation solve this problem? What would the legislation say?
8. The Supreme Court has also granted cert. in *Moore v. Harper*, which asks the question "Whether a state's judicial branch may nullify the regulations governing the 'Manner of holding Elections for Senators and Representatives ... prescribed ... by the Legislature thereof,' and replace them with regulations of the state courts' own devising, based on vague state constitutional provisions purportedly vesting the state judiciary with power to prescribe whatever rules it deems appropriate to ensure a 'fair' or 'free' election." See *Moore v. Harper*, https://www.scotusblog.com/case-files/cases/moore-v-harper-2/. This is the "independent state legislature theory," which would change who decides what elections are constitutional. The oral argument is available at https://www.oyez.org/cases/2022/21-1271. How do you think the Court will vote in this case?

C. The Federal Constitution's Bill of Rights Applied to the States

The Bill of Rights is the first ten amendments to the U.S. Constitution. As the name suggests, the amendments are supposed to protect rights. The Framers produced the Constitution's Articles with the hope that they had at least designed a usable federal government. It was ratified June 21, 1788. Some states, however, were concerned that the Articles would be read to give the new federal government power to infringe individual rights and to interfere with the states' determination of state constitutional rights (articulated in each state's constitution). James Madison drafted the Bill of Rights, which was ratified December 15, 1791.

Think of the opening words of the First Amendment: "Congress shall make no law." The plain language states that the First Amendment limits Congress. What does it say about the states? Nothing, right? Then there is the Fourteenth Amendment, which states: "No State shall make or enforce any law ..." What does it say about the federal government? Nothing again.

Yet, the Court has an established jurisprudence applying the Bill of Rights to the states through the Fourteenth Amendment. In other words, the Fourteenth Amendment is read to include at least some rights enumerated in the Bill of Rights. That means the rights enforceable against the federal government under the Bill of Rights become enforceable against the states by being read into the Fourteenth Amendment. This doctrine is called "incorporation." Think of it this way: the 14th Amendment's rights provide portals to read in the rights from the Bill of Rights that the Court determines should be incorporated.

Justice Hugo Black long argued that the Privileges or Immunities Clause of the 14th Amendment "incorporated" the whole Bill of Rights, meaning that the rights may be invoked against both the federal government and the states. The Court did not take that total incorporation approach, however, and has reviewed each section of the Bill of Rights, text by text. This is called "selective" rather than "total" incorporation. The first incorporation case was in 1925, but we have the most recent 2020 case below, *Ramos v. Louisiana*, about the Sixth Amendment's jury provisions.

The next case involves the Second Amendment, which states, "A well regulated militia, being necessary to the security of a free state, the right of the people to keep and bear arms, shall not be infringed." What do you think the text of the amendment means? Does it protect the right of the militia to bear arms? Or does it protect an individual right to bear arms? In *District of Columbia v. Heller*, 554 U.S. 570 (2008), the Court ruled 5–4 that the amendment protected an individual right. But *Heller* was a District of Columbia (federal) case, so the Court had to wait until it got an Illinois case to decide whether the Second Amendment applies to the states.

The following Justices voted 5–4 in *Heller* to find a constitutional right to bear arms, as the picture shows, https://www.oyez.org/cases/2007/07-290. Why do you think the vote was so close?

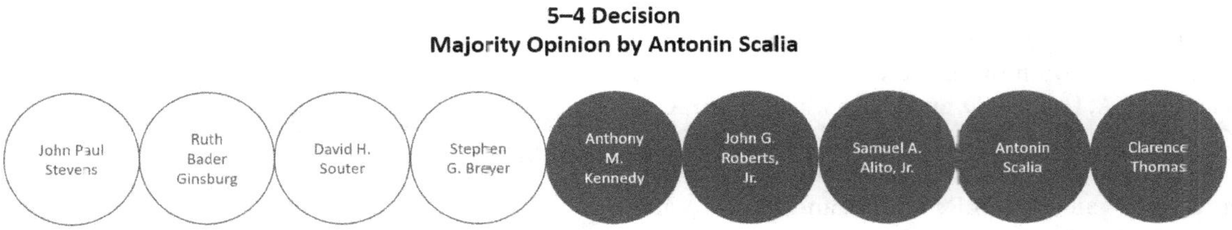

FIGURE 6.1 District of Columbia v Heller, 554 U.S. 570 (2008)

Why are there conflicting opinions about the Second Amendment, including in the *Heller* opinion? What do you think the amendment should protect? Is there anything about it that should apply to the states?

Note the key dispute about incorporation in the Illinois gun case and in later cases. To incorporate a right into the Fourteenth Amendment, there must be a gateway in the language. Justice Black would have funneled all of the rights through the Privileges and Immunities Clause. While his total incorporation theory was not embraced by the whole Court, some Justices have invoked the P & I Clause, like Justice Thomas. Others embrace the Due Process Clause. What difference does it make to say incorporation is a matter of due process or a privilege or immunity? How much difference would it make in your understanding of the amendment if one theory is adopted instead of another?

1. Adding the Second Amendment to the Rights that Are Incorporated Against the States

McDonald is a 5–4 opinion. Is that because of the Justices' interpretation of incorporation or the Second Amendment? The dissenters in *Heller* were Stevens, Souter, Ginsburg, and Breyer. The dissenters in *McDonald* were Stevens, Ginsburg, Breyer, and Sotomayor. Yet, the five in the majority remained the same five justices as shown in the illustration, https://www.oyez.org/cases/2009/08-1521.

5–4 Decision for Otis McDonald, et al.
Majority Opinion by Samuel A. Alito, Jr.

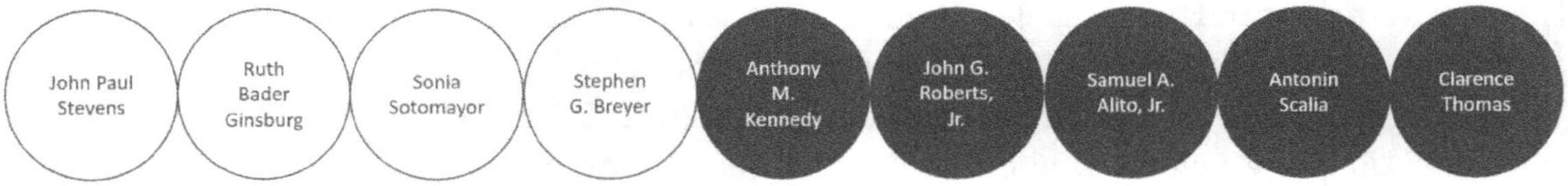

FIGURE 6.2 McDonald v. City of Chicago, Illinois, 561 U.S. 742 (2020)

Read the *McDonald* oral argument at https://www.oyez.org/cases/2009/08-1521. What did the Justices emphasize in their questions? Can you tell what their perspective on the Second Amendment is? On what the Fourteenth Amendment means? Can you tell yet that Scalia and Stevens have different perspectives on the role of history in the courts' opinions?

McDonald v. City of Chicago, Illinois

SUPREME COURT OF THE UNITED STATES, 2010

561 U.S. 742, 130 S.Ct. 2020

ALITO, J., announced the judgment of the Court and delivered the opinion of the Court with respect to Parts I, II–A, II–B, II–D, and III, in which ROBERTS, C. J., and SCALIA, KENNEDY, and THOMAS, JJ., joined, and an opinion with respect to Parts II–C, IV, and V, in which ROBERTS, C. J., and SCALIA and KENNEDY, JJ., join. SCALIA, J., filed a concurring opinion. THOMAS, J., filed an opinion concurring in part and concurring in the judgment. STEVENS, J., filed a dissenting opinion. BREYER, J., filed a dissenting opinion, in which GINSBURG and SOTOMAYOR, JJ., joined.

Two years ago, in *District of Columbia v. Heller,* 554 U.S. 570, 128 S.Ct. 2783, 171 L.Ed.2d 637 (2008), we held that the Second Amendment protects the right to keep and bear arms for the purpose of self-defense, and we struck down a District of Columbia law that banned the possession of handguns in the home. The city of Chicago (City) and the village of Oak Park, a Chicago suburb, have laws that are similar to the District of Columbia's, but Chicago and Oak Park argue that their laws are constitutional because the Second Amendment has no application to the States. We have previously held that most of the provisions of the Bill of Rights apply with full force to both the Federal Government and the States. Applying the standard that is well established in our case law, we hold that the Second Amendment right is fully applicable to the States. ...

IIA

Petitioners argue that the Chicago and Oak Park laws violate the right to keep and bear arms for two reasons. Petitioners' primary submission is that this right is among the "privileges or immunities of citizens of the United States" and that the narrow interpretation of the Privileges or Immunities Clause adopted in the *Slaughter–House Cases, supra,* should now be rejected. As a secondary argument, petitioners contend that the Fourteenth Amendment's Due Process Clause "incorporates" the Second Amendment right. ...

IIC

... We see no need to reconsider that interpretation here. For many decades, the question of the rights protected by the Fourteenth Amendment against state infringement has been analyzed under the Due Process Clause of that Amendment and not under the Privileges or Immunities Clause. We therefore decline to disturb the *Slaughter–House* holding. ...

IID1

In the late 19th century, the Court began to consider whether the Due Process Clause prohibits the States from infringing rights set out in the Bill of Rights. See *Hurtado v. California,* 110 U.S. 516, 4 S.Ct. 111, 28 L.Ed. 232 (1884) (due process does not require grand jury indictment); *Chicago, B. & Q.R. Co. v. Chicago,* 166 U.S. 226, 17 S.Ct. 581, 41 L.Ed. 979 (1897) (due process prohibits States from taking of private property for public use without just compensation). Five features of the approach taken during the ensuing era should be noted.

First, the Court viewed the due process question as entirely separate from the question whether a right was a privilege or immunity of national citizenship. See *Twining v. New Jersey,* 211 U.S. 78, 99, 29 S.Ct. 14, 53 L.Ed. 97 (1908).

Second, the Court explained that the only rights protected against state infringement by the Due Process Clause were those rights "of such a nature that they are included in the conception of due process of law." *Ibid.* See also, *e.g., Adamson v. California,* 332 U.S. 46, 67 S.Ct. 1672, 91 L.Ed. 1903 (1947); *Betts v. Brady,* 316 U.S. 455, 62 S.Ct. 1252, 86 L.Ed. 1595 (1942); *Palko v. Connecticut,* 302 U.S. 319, 58 S.Ct. 149, 82 L.Ed. 288 (1937); *Grosjean v. American Press Co.,* 297 U.S. 233, 56 S.Ct. 444, 80 L.Ed. 660 (1936); *Powell v. Alabama,* 287 U.S. 45, 53 S.Ct. 55, 77 L.Ed. 158 (1932). While it was "possible that some of the personal rights safeguarded by the first eight Amendments against National action [might] also be safeguarded against state action," the Court stated, this was "not because those rights are enumerated in the first eight Amendments." *Twining,* 211 U.S., at 99, 29 S.Ct. 14.

The Court used different formulations in describing the boundaries of due process. For example, in *Twining,* the Court referred to "immutable principles of justice which inhere in the very idea of free government which no member of the Union may disregard." *Id.,* at 102, 29 S.Ct. 14 (internal quotation marks omitted). In *Snyder v. Massachusetts,* 291 U.S. 97, 105, 54 S.Ct. 330, 78 L.Ed. 674 (1934), the Court spoke of rights that are "so rooted in the traditions and conscience of our people as to be ranked as fundamental." And in *Palko,* the Court famously said that due process protects those rights that are "the very essence of a scheme of ordered liberty" and essential to "a fair and enlightened system of justice." 302 U.S., at 325, 58 S.Ct. 149.

Third, in some cases decided during this era the Court "can be seen as having asked, when inquiring into whether some particular procedural safeguard was required of a State, if a civilized system could be imagined that would not accord the particular protection." *Duncan v. Louisiana,* 391 U.S. 145, 149, n. 14, 88 S.Ct. 1444, 20 L.Ed.2d 491 (1968). Thus, in holding that due process prohibits a State from taking private property without just compensation, the Court described the right as "a principle of natural equity, recognized by all temperate and civilized governments, from a deep and universal sense of its justice." *Chicago, B. & Q.R. Co., supra,* at 238, 17 S.Ct. 581. Similarly, the Court found that due process did not provide a right against compelled incrimination in part because this right "has no place in the jurisprudence of civilized and free countries outside the domain of the common law." *Twining, supra,* at 113, 29 S.Ct. 14.

Fourth, the Court during this era was not hesitant to hold that a right set out in the Bill of Rights failed to meet the test for inclusion within the protection of the Due Process Clause. The Court found that some such rights qualified. See, *e.g., Gitlow v. New York,* 268 U.S. 652, 666, 45 S.Ct. 625, 69 L.Ed. 1138 (1925) (freedom of speech and press); *Near v. Minnesota ex rel. Olson,* 283 U.S. 697, 51 S.Ct. 625, 75 L.Ed. 1357 (1931) (same); *Powell, supra* (assistance of counsel in capital cases); *De Jonge, supra* (freedom of assembly); *Cantwell v. Connecticut,* 310 U.S. 296, 60 S.Ct. 900, 84 L.Ed. 1213 (1940) (free exercise of religion). But others did not. See, *e.g., Hurtado, supra* (grand jury indictment requirement); *Twining, supra* (privilege against self-incrimination).

Finally, even when a right set out in the Bill of Rights was held to fall within the conception of due process, the protection or remedies afforded against state infringement sometimes differed from the protection or remedies provided against abridgment by the Federal Government. To give one example, in *Betts* the Court held that, although the Sixth Amendment required the appointment of counsel in all federal criminal cases in which the defendant was unable to retain an attorney, the Due Process Clause required appointment of counsel in state criminal proceedings only where "want of counsel in [the] particular case ... result[ed] in a conviction lacking in ... fundamental fairness." 316 U.S., at 473, 62 S.Ct. 1252. Similarly, in *Wolf v. Colorado,* 338 U.S. 25, 69 S.Ct. 1359, 93 L.Ed. 1782 (1949), the Court held that the "core of the Fourth Amendment" was implicit in the concept of ordered liberty and thus "enforceable against the States through the Due Process Clause" but that the exclusionary rule, which applied in federal cases, did not apply to the States. *Id.,* at 27–28, 33, 69 S.Ct. 1359.

IID2

An alternative theory regarding the relationship between the Bill of Rights and § 1 of the Fourteenth

Amendment was championed by Justice Black. This theory held that § 1 of the Fourteenth Amendment totally incorporated all of the provisions of the Bill of Rights. See, *e.g., Adamson, supra,* at 71–72, 67 S.Ct. 1672 (Black, J., dissenting); *Duncan, supra,* at 166, 88 S.Ct. 1444 (Black, J., concurring). As Justice Black noted, the chief congressional proponents of the Fourteenth Amendment espoused the view that the Amendment made the Bill of Rights applicable to the States and, in so doing, overruled this Court's decision in *Barron.Adamson, supra,* at 72, 67 S.Ct. 1672 (dissenting opinion). Nonetheless, the Court never has embraced Justice Black's "total incorporation" theory.

IID3

While Justice Black's theory was never adopted, the Court eventually moved in that direction by initiating what has been called a process of "selective incorporation," *i. e.*, the Court began to hold that the Due Process Clause fully incorporates particular rights contained in the first eight Amendments. See, *e.g., Gideon v. Wainwright,* 372 U.S. 335, 341, 83 S.Ct. 792, 9 L.Ed.2d 799 (1963); *Malloy v. Hogan,* 378 U.S. 1, 5–6, 84 S.Ct. 1489, 12 L.Ed.2d 653 (1964); *Pointer v. Texas,* 380 U.S. 400, 403–404, 85 S.Ct. 1065, 13 L.Ed.2d 923 (1965); *Washington v. Texas,* 388 U.S. 14, 18, 87 S.Ct. 1920, 18 L.Ed.2d 1019 (1967); *Duncan,* 391 U.S., at 147–148, 88 S.Ct. 1444; *Benton v. Maryland,* 395 U.S. 784, 794, 89 S.Ct. 2056, 23 L.Ed.2d 707 (1969).

The decisions during this time abandoned three of the previously noted characteristics of the earlier period. The Court made it clear that the governing standard is not whether *any* "civilized system [can] be imagined that would not accord the particular protection." *Duncan,* 391 U.S., at 149, n. 14, 88 S.Ct. 1444. Instead, the Court inquired whether a particular Bill of Rights guarantee is fundamental to *our* scheme of ordered liberty and system of justice. *Id.*, at 149, and n. 14, 88 S.Ct. 1444; see also *id.,* at 148, 88 S.Ct. 1444 (referring to those "fundamental principles of liberty and justice which lie at the base of all *our* civil and political institutions").

The Court also shed any reluctance to hold that rights guaranteed by the Bill of Rights met the requirements for protection under the Due Process Clause. The Court eventually incorporated almost all of the provisions of the Bill of Rights. Only a handful of the Bill of Rights protections remain unincorporated.[13]

Finally, the Court abandoned "the notion that the Fourteenth Amendment applies to the States only a watered-down, subjective version of the individual guarantees of the Bill of Rights," stating that it would be "incongruous" to apply different standards "depending on whether the claim was asserted in a state or federal court." *Malloy,* 378 U.S., at 10–11, 84 S.Ct. 1489 (internal quotation marks omitted). Instead, the Court decisively held that incorporated Bill of Rights protections "are all to be enforced against the States under the Fourteenth Amendment according to the same standards that protect those personal rights against federal encroachment." *Id.*, at 10, 84 S.Ct. 1489; see also *Mapp v. Ohio,* 367 U.S. 643, 655–656, 81 S.Ct. 1684, 6 L.Ed.2d 1081 (1961); *Ker v. California,* 374 U.S. 23, 33–34, 83 S.Ct. 1623, 10 L.Ed.2d 726 (1963); *Aguilar v. Texas,* 378 U.S. 108, 110, 84 S.Ct. 1509, 12 L.Ed.2d 723 (1964); *Pointer, supra,* at 406, 85 S.Ct. 1065; *Duncan, supra,* at 149, 157–158, 88 S.Ct. 1444; *Benton, supra,* at 794–795, 89 S.Ct. 2056; *Wallace v. Jaffree,* 472 U.S. 38, 48–49, 105 S.Ct. 2479, 86 L.Ed.2d 29 (1985).

Employing this approach, the Court overruled earlier decisions in which it had held that particular Bill of Rights guarantees or remedies did not apply to the States. See, *e.g., Mapp, supra* (overruling in part *Wolf,* 338 U.S. 25, 69 S.Ct. 1359, 93 L.Ed. 1782); *Gideon,* 372

13. In addition to the right to keep and bear arms (and the Sixth Amendment right to a unanimous jury verdict), the only rights not fully incorporated are (1) the Third Amendment's protection against quartering of soldiers; (2) the Fifth Amendment's grand jury indictment requirement; (3) the Seventh Amendment right to a jury trial in civil cases; and (4) the Eighth Amendment's prohibition on excessive fines.

We never have decided whether the Third Amendment or the Eighth Amendment's prohibition of excessive fines applies to the States through the Due Process Clause. See *Browning–Ferris Industries of Vt., Inc. v. Kelco Disposal, Inc.,* 492 U.S. 257, 276, n. 22, 109 S.Ct. 2909, 106 L.Ed.2d 219 (1989) (declining to decide whether the excessive-fines protection applies to the States); see also *Engblom v. Carey,* 677 F.2d 957, 961 (C.A.2 1982) (holding as a matter of first impression that the "Third Amendment is incorporated into the Fourteenth Amendment for application to the states").

Our governing decisions regarding the Grand Jury Clause of the Fifth Amendment and the Seventh Amendment's civil jury requirement long predate the era of selective incorporation.

U.S. 335, 83 S.Ct. 792, 9 L.Ed.2d 799 (overruling *Betts,* 316 U.S. 455, 62 S.Ct. 1252, 86 L.Ed. 1595); *Malloy, supra* (overruling *Adamson,* 332 U.S. 46, 67 S.Ct. 1672, 91 L.Ed. 1903, and *Twining,* 211 U.S. 78, 29 S.Ct. 14, 53 L.Ed. 97); *Benton,* 395 U.S., at 794, 89 S.Ct. 2056 (overruling *Palko,* 302 U.S. 319, 58 S.Ct. 149, 82 L.Ed. 288).

III

With this framework in mind, we now turn directly to the question whether the Second Amendment right to keep and bear arms is incorporated in the concept of due process. In answering that question, as just explained, we must decide whether the right to keep and bear arms is fundamental to *our* scheme of ordered liberty, *Duncan,* 391 U.S., at 149, 88 S.Ct. 1444, or as we have said in a related context, whether this right is "deeply rooted in this Nation's history and tradition," *Washington v. Glucksberg,* 521 U.S. 702, 721, 117 S.Ct. 2302, 138 L.Ed.2d 772 (1997) (internal quotation marks omitted).

IIIA

Our decision in *Heller* points unmistakably to the answer. Self-defense is a basic right, recognized by many legal systems from ancient times to the present day, and in *Heller,* we held that individual self-defense is "the *central component*" of the Second Amendment right. ...

Heller makes it clear that this right is "deeply rooted in this Nation's history and tradition." ...

IIIB1

... In sum, it is clear that the Framers and ratifiers of the Fourteenth Amendment counted the right to keep and bear arms among those fundamental rights necessary to our system of ordered liberty. ...

IV

Municipal respondents' remaining arguments are at war with our central holding in *Heller*: that the Second Amendment protects a personal right to keep and bear arms for lawful purposes, most notably for self-defense within the home. Municipal respondents, in effect, ask us to treat the right recognized in *Heller* as a second-class right, subject to an entirely different body of rules than the other Bill of Rights guarantees that we have held to be incorporated into the Due Process Clause.

Municipal respondents' main argument is nothing less than a plea to disregard 50 years of incorporation precedent and return (presumably for this case only) to a bygone era. ... Therefore, the municipal respondents continue, because such countries as England, Canada, Australia, Japan, Denmark, Finland, Luxembourg, and New Zealand either ban or severely limit handgun ownership, it must follow that no right to possess such weapons is protected by the Fourteenth Amendment. ...

V

A

We turn, finally, to the two dissenting opinions. Justice STEVENS' eloquent opinion covers ground already addressed, and therefore little need be added in response. Justice STEVENS would "'ground the prohibitions against state action squarely on due process, without intermediate reliance on any of the first eight Amendments.'" *Post,* at 3092 (quoting *Malloy,* 378 U.S., at 24, 84 S.Ct. 1489 (Harlan, J., dissenting)). The question presented in this case, in his view, "is whether the particular right asserted by petitioners applies to the States because of the Fourteenth Amendment itself, standing on its own bottom." *Post,* at 3103. He would hold that "[t]he rights protected against state infringement by the Fourteenth Amendment's Due Process Clause need not be identical in shape or scope to the rights protected against Federal Government infringement by the various provisions of the Bill of Rights." ...

In *Heller,* we held that the Second Amendment protects the right to possess a handgun in the home for the purpose of self-defense. Unless considerations of *stare decisis* counsel otherwise, a provision of the Bill of Rights that protects a right that is fundamental from an American perspective applies equally to the Federal Government and the States. See *Duncan,* 391 U.S., at 149, and n. 14, 88 S.Ct. 1444. We therefore hold that the Due Process Clause of the Fourteenth Amendment incorporates the Second Amendment right recognized in *Heller.* The judgment of the Court of Appeals is reversed, and the case is remanded for further proceedings.

Justice SCALIA, concurring.

... I write separately only to respond to some aspects of Justice STEVENS' dissent. Not that aspect which disagrees with the majority's application of our precedents to this case, which is fully covered by the Court's opinion. But much of what Justice STEVENS writes is a broad condemnation of the theory of interpretation which underlies the Court's opinion, a theory that makes the traditions of our people paramount. He proposes a different theory, which he claims is more "cautiou[s]" and respectful of proper limits on the judicial role. It is that claim I wish to address.

II

If Justice STEVENS' account of the constraints of his approach did not demonstrate that they do not exist, his application of that approach to the case before us leaves no doubt. He offers several reasons for concluding that the Second Amendment right to keep and bear arms is not fundamental enough to be applied against the States. None is persuasive, but more pertinent to my purpose, each is either intrinsically indeterminate, would preclude incorporation of rights we have already held incorporated, or both. His approach therefore does nothing to stop a judge from arriving at any conclusion he sets out to reach. ...

III

Justice STEVENS' response to this concurrence, makes the usual rejoinder of "living Constitution" advocates to the criticism that it empowers judges to eliminate or expand what the people have prescribed: The traditional, historically focused method, he says, reposes discretion in judges as well.[8] Historical analysis can be difficult; it sometimes requires resolving threshold questions, and making nuanced judgments about which evidence to consult and how to interpret it.

I will stipulate to that. But the question to be decided is not whether the historically focused method is a *perfect means* of restraining aristocratic judicial Constitution-writing; but whether it is the *best means available* in an imperfect world. Or indeed, even more narrowly than that: whether it is demonstrably much better than what Justice STEVENS proposes. I think it beyond all serious dispute that it is much less subjective, and intrudes much less upon the democratic process. It is less subjective because it depends upon a body of evidence susceptible of reasoned analysis rather than a variety of vague ethico-political First Principles whose combined conclusion can be found to point in any direction the judges favor. ...

Justice STEVENS abhors a system in which "majorities or powerful interest groups always get their way," but replaces it with a system in which unelected and life-tenured judges always get their way. ...

Justice THOMAS, concurring in part and concurring in the judgment.

I agree with the Court that the Fourteenth Amendment makes the right to keep and bear arms set forth in the Second Amendment "fully applicable to the States." I write separately because I believe there is a more straightforward path to this conclusion, one that is more faithful to the Fourteenth Amendment's text and history. I therefore do not join Parts II–C, IV, and V of the principal opinion.

Applying what is now a well-settled test, the Court concludes that the right to keep and bear arms applies to the States through the Fourteenth Amendment's Due Process Clause because it is "fundamental" to the American "scheme of ordered liberty," *ante*, at 3036 (citing *Duncan v. Louisiana*, 391 U.S. 145, 149, 88 S.Ct. 1444, 20 L.Ed.2d 491 (1968)), and "'deeply rooted in this Nation's history and tradition,'" *ante*, at 3036 (quoting *Washington v. Glucksberg*, 521 U.S. 702, 721, 117 S.Ct. 2302, 138 L.Ed.2d 772 (1997)). I agree with that description of the right. But I cannot agree that it is enforceable against the States through a Clause that speaks only to "process." Instead, the right to keep and bear arms is a privilege of American citizenship that applies to the States through the Fourteenth Amendment's Privileges or Immunities Clause. ...

The text examined so far demonstrates three points about the meaning of the Privileges or Immunities Clause in § 1. First, "privileges" and "immunities" were synonyms for "rights." Second, both the States and the Federal Government had long recognized the inalienable rights of their citizens. Third, Article IV, § 2, of the Constitution protected traveling citizens against state discrimination with respect to the fundamental rights of state citizenship. ...

This history confirms what the text of the Privileges or Immunities Clause most naturally suggests: Consistent with its command that "[n]o State shall ... abridge" the rights of United States citizens, the Clause establishes a minimum baseline of federal rights, and the constitutional right to keep and bear arms plainly was among them. ...

In my view, the record makes plain that the Framers of the Privileges or Immunities Clause and the ratifying-era public understood—just as the Framers of the Second Amendment did—that the right to keep and bear arms was essential to the preservation of liberty. The record makes equally plain that they deemed this right necessary to include in the minimum baseline of federal rights that the Privileges or Immunities Clause established in the wake of the war over slavery. There is nothing about *Cruikshank* 's contrary holding that warrants its retention.

I agree with the Court that the Second Amendment is fully applicable to the States. I do so because the right to keep and bear arms is guaranteed by the Fourteenth Amendment as a privilege of American citizenship.

Justice STEVENS, dissenting.

In *District of Columbia v. Heller,* 554 U.S. 570, 573, 128 S.Ct. 2783, 2788, 171 L.Ed.2d 637 (2008), the Court answered the question whether a federal enclave's "prohibition on the possession of usable handguns in the home violates the Second Amendment to the Constitution." The question we should be answering in this case is whether the Constitution "guarantees individuals a fundamental right," enforceable against the States, "to possess a functional, personal firearm, including a handgun, within the home." Complaint ¶ 34, App. 23. That is a different—and more difficult—inquiry than asking if the Fourteenth Amendment "incorporates" the Second Amendment. The so-called incorporation question was squarely and, in my view, correctly resolved in the late 19th century.[14] ...

In his own classic opinion in *Griswold,* 381 U.S., at 500, 85 S.Ct. 1678 (opinion concurring in judgment), Justice Harlan memorably distilled these precedents' lesson: "While the relevant inquiry may be aided by resort to one or more of the provisions of the Bill of Rights, it is not dependent on them or any of their radiations. The Due Process Clause of the Fourteenth Amendment stands ... on its own bottom." Inclusion in the Bill of Rights is neither necessary nor sufficient for an interest to be judicially enforceable under the Fourteenth Amendment. This Court's "'selective incorporation'" doctrine is not simply "related" to substantive due process; it is a subset thereof. ...

The basic inquiry was described by Justice Cardozo more than 70 years ago. When confronted with a substantive due process claim, we must ask whether the allegedly unlawful practice violates values "implicit in the concept of ordered liberty." *Palko v. Connecticut,* 302 U.S. 319, 325, 58 S.Ct. 149, 82 L.Ed. 288 (1937).[14] If the practice in question lacks any "oppressive and arbitrary" character, if judicial enforcement of the asserted right would not materially contribute to "a fair and enlightened system of justice," then the claim is unsuitable for substantive due process protection. *Id.,* at 327, 325, 58 S.Ct. 149. Implicit in Justice Cardozo's test is a recognition that the postulates of liberty have a universal character. Liberty claims that are inseparable from the customs that prevail in a certain region, the idiosyncratic expectations of a certain group, or the personal preferences of their champions, may be valid claims in some sense; but they are not of constitutional stature. Whether conceptualized as a "rational continuum" of legal precepts, *Poe,* 367 U.S., at 543, 81 S.Ct. 1752 (Harlan, J., dissenting), or a seamless web of moral commitments, the rights embraced by the liberty clause transcend the local and the particular. ...

The Court's flight from *Palko* leaves its analysis, careful and scholarly though it is, much too narrow to provide a satisfying answer to this case. The Court hinges its entire decision on one mode of intellectual history, culling selected pronouncements and enactments from the 18th and 19th centuries to ascertain what Americans thought about firearms. Relying on *Duncan* and *Glucksberg,* the principal opinion suggests that only interests that have proved "fundamental from an American perspective," *ante,* at 3046, 3050 (plurality opinion), or "'deeply rooted in this Nation's history and tradition,'" *ante,* at 3036 (majority opinion). (quoting *Glucksberg,* 521 U.S., at 721, 117 S.Ct. 2258), to the Court's satisfaction, may qualify for incorporation into the Fourteenth Amendment. To the extent the principal opinion could be read to imply that the historical pedigree of a right is the exclusive or dispositive determinant of its status under the Due Process Clause, the opinion is seriously mistaken. ...

At this point a difficult question arises. In considering such a majestic term as "liberty" and applying it to present circumstances, how are we to do justice to its urgent call and its open texture—and to the grant of interpretive discretion the latter

---

14. See *United States v. Cruikshank,* 92 U.S. 542, 553, 23 L.Ed. 588 (1876); *Presser v. Illinois,* 116 U.S. 252, 265, 6 S.Ct. 580, 29 L.Ed. 615 (1886); *Miller v. Texas,* 153 U.S. 535, 538, 14 S.Ct. 874, 38 L.Ed. 812 (1894). This is not to say that I agree with all other aspects of these decisions.

embodies—without injecting excessive subjectivity or unduly restricting the States' "broad latitude in experimenting with possible solutions to problems of vital local concern," *Whalen v. Roe,* 429 U.S. 589, 597, 97 S.Ct. 869, 51 L.Ed.2d 64 (1977)? One part of the answer, already discussed, is that we must ground the analysis in historical experience and reasoned judgment, and never on "merely personal and private notions." *Rochin v. California,* 342 U.S. 165, 170, 72 S.Ct. 205, 96 L.Ed. 183 (1952). Our precedents place a number of additional constraints on the decisional process. Although "guideposts for responsible decisionmaking in this unchartered area are scarce and open-ended," *Collins v. Harker Heights,* 503 U.S. 115, 125, 112 S.Ct. 1061, 117 L.Ed.2d 261 (1992), significant guideposts do exist

The most basic is that we have eschewed attempts to provide any all-purpose, top-down, totalizing theory of "liberty." That project is bound to end in failure or worse. The Framers did not express a clear understanding of the term to guide us, and the now-repudiated *Lochner* line of cases attests to the dangers of judicial overconfidence in using substantive due process to advance a broad theory of the right or the good. See, *e.g., Lochner v. New York,* 198 U.S. 45, 25 S.Ct. 539, 49 L.Ed. 937 (1905). In its most durable precedents, the Court "has not attempted to define with exactness the liberty ... guaranteed" by the Fourteenth Amendment. *Meyer,* 262 U.S., at 399, 43 S.Ct. 625; see also, *e.g., Bolling,* 347 U.S., at 499, 74 S.Ct. 693. By its very nature, the meaning of liberty cannot be "reduced to any formula; its content cannot be determined by reference to any code." *Poe,* 367 U.S., at 542, 81 S.Ct. 1752 (Harlan, J., dissenting).

Yet while "the 'liberty' specially protected by the Fourteenth Amendment" is "perhaps not capable of being fully clarified," *Glucksberg,* 521 U.S., at 722, 117 S.Ct. 2258, it is capable of being refined and delimited. ...

The question in this case, then, is not whether the Second Amendment right to keep and bear arms (whatever that right's precise contours) applies to the States because the Amendment has been incorporated into the Fourteenth Amendment. It has not been. The question, rather, is whether the particular right asserted by petitioners applies to the States because of the Fourteenth Amendment itself, standing on its own bottom. And to answer that question, we need to determine, first, the nature of the right that has been asserted and, second, whether that right is an aspect of Fourteenth Amendment "liberty." Even accepting the Court's holding in *Heller,* it remains entirely possible that the right to keep and bear arms identified in that opinion is not judicially enforceable against the States, or that only part of the right is so enforceable. It is likewise possible for the Court to find in this case that some part of the *Heller* right applies to the States, and then to find in later cases that other parts of the right also apply, or apply on different terms. ...

While I agree with the Court that our substantive due process cases offer a principled basis for holding that petitioners have a constitutional right to possess a usable firearm in the home, I am ultimately persuaded that a better reading of our case law supports the city of Chicago. I would not foreclose the possibility that a particular plaintiff—say, an elderly widow who lives in a dangerous neighborhood and does not have the strength to operate a long gun—may have a cognizable liberty interest in possessing a handgun. But I cannot accept petitioners' broader submission. ... firearms have a fundamentally ambivalent relationship to liberty. Just as they can help homeowners defend their families and property from intruders, they can help thugs and insurrectionists murder innocent victims. The threat that firearms will be misused is far from hypothetical, for gun crime has devastated many of our communities. ...

The liberty interest asserted by petitioners is also dissimilar from those we have recognized in its capacity to undermine the security of others. ...

I accept that the evolution in Americans' understanding of the Second Amendment may help shed light on the question whether a right to keep and bear arms is included within Fourteenth Amendment "liberty." But the reasons that motivated the Framers to protect the ability of militiamen to keep muskets available for military use when our Nation was in its infancy, or that motivated the Reconstruction Congress to extend full citizenship to the freedmen in the wake of the Civil War, have only a limited bearing on the question that confronts the homeowner in a crime-infested metropolis today. The many episodes of brutal violence against African-Americans that blight our Nation's history do not suggest that every American must be allowed to own whatever type of firearm he or she desires—just that no group of Americans should be systematically and discriminatorily disarmed and left to the mercy of racial terrorists. And the fact that some Americans may have thought or hoped that the Fourteenth Amendment would nationalize the Second Amendment hardly suffices to justify the conclusion that it did. ...

Which leads me to the final set of points I wish to make: Justice SCALIA's method invites not only bad history, but also bad constitutional law. As I have already explained, in evaluating a claimed liberty interest (or any constitutional claim for that matter), it makes perfect sense to give history significant weight: Justice SCALIA's position is closer to my own than he apparently feels comfortable acknowledging. But it makes little sense to give history dispositive weight in every case. And it makes *especially* little sense to answer questions like whether the right to bear arms is "fundamental" by focusing only on the past, given that both the practical significance and the public understandings of such a right often change as society changes. What if the evidence had shown that, whereas at one time firearm possession contributed substantially to personal liberty and safety, nowadays it contributes nothing, or even tends to undermine them? Would it still have been reasonable to constitutionalize the right? ...

The fact that the right to keep and bear arms appears in the Constitution should not obscure the novelty of the Court's decision to enforce that right against the States. By its terms, the Second Amendment does not apply to the States; read properly, it does not even apply to individuals outside of the militia context. The Second Amendment was adopted to protect the *States* from federal encroachment. And the Fourteenth Amendment has never been understood by the Court to have "incorporated" the entire Bill of Rights. There was nothing foreordained about today's outcome.

Although the Court's decision in this case might be seen as a mere adjunct to its decision in *Heller,* the consequences could prove far more destructive—quite literally—to our Nation's communities and to our constitutional structure. Thankfully, the Second Amendment right identified in *Heller* and its newly minted Fourteenth Amendment analogue are limited, at least for now, to the home. But neither the "assurances" provided by the plurality, nor the many historical sources cited in its opinion should obscure the reality that today's ruling marks a dramatic change in our law—or that the Justices who have joined it have brought to bear an awesome amount of discretion in resolving the legal question presented by this case.

I would proceed more cautiously. For the reasons set out at length above, I cannot accept either the methodology the Court employs or the conclusions it draws. Although impressively argued, the majority's decision to overturn more than a century of Supreme Court precedent and to unsettle a much longer tradition of state practice is not, in my judgment, built "upon respect for the teachings of history, solid recognition of the basic values that underlie our society, and wise appreciation of the great roles that the doctrines of federalism and separation of powers have played in establishing and preserving American freedoms." *Griswold,* 381 U.S., at 501, 85 S.Ct. 1678 (Harlan, J., concurring in judgment). ...

Justice BREYER, with whom Justice GINSBURG and Justice SOTOMAYOR join, dissenting.

... I can find nothing in the Second Amendment's text, history, or underlying rationale that could warrant characterizing it as "fundamental" insofar as it seeks to protect the keeping and bearing of arms for private self-defense purposes. Nor can I find any justification for interpreting the Constitution as transferring ultimate regulatory authority over the private uses of firearms from democratically elected legislatures to courts or from the States to the Federal Government. I therefore conclude that the Fourteenth Amendment does not "incorporate" the Second Amendment's right "to keep and bear Arms." And I consequently dissent. ...

In sum, the Framers did not write the Second Amendment in order to protect a private right of armed self-defense. There has been, and is, no consensus that the right is, or was, "fundamental." No broader constitutional interest or principle supports legal treatment of that right as fundamental. To the contrary, broader constitutional concerns of an institutional nature argue strongly against that treatment.

Moreover, nothing in 18th-, 19th-, 20th-, or 21st-century history shows a consensus that the right to private armed self-defense, as described in *Heller,* is "deeply rooted in this Nation's history [or] tradition" or is otherwise "fundamental." Indeed, incorporating the right recognized in *Heller* may change the law in many of the 50 States. Read in the majority's favor, the historical evidence is at most ambiguous. And, in the absence of any other support for its conclusion, ambiguous history cannot show that the Fourteenth Amendment incorporates a private right of self-defense against the States.

With respect, I dissent.

Notes and Questions

1. *Incorporation doctrine.* The case includes many citations to the incorporation cases. How would you characterize the history of incorporation? What are the different tests the Court has employed? Can you tell which one it employs today? Which test makes the most sense to you? Make a list of all the tests, and decide which is the best.
2. *What difference does the incorporation portal make?* Does the strength of the right change, depending on whether it is incorporated through the Due Process or Privileges or Immunities Clauses?
3. *Footnote 13.* Reread footnote 13: "In addition to the right to keep and bear arms (and the Sixth Amendment right to a unanimous jury verdict), the only rights not fully incorporated are (1) the Third Amendment's protection against quartering of soldiers; (2) the Fifth Amendment's grand jury indictment requirement; (3) the Seventh Amendment right to a jury trial in civil cases; and (4) the Eighth Amendment's prohibition on excessive fines." Note that the Court refers to sections of individual Bill of Rights that have not been incorporated. They include the Sixth Amendment right to a unanimous jury verdict and the Eighth Amendment's prohibition on excessive fines. Those rights are incorporated in the cases below. Can you predict whether there will be incorporation or not? What about the other rights listed in the footnote?
4. *Video.* What does this video, Bill of Rights Institute, *McDonald v. Chicago*, Oct. 6, 2019, at https://www.youtube.com/watch?v=6s_61iRNSO0&list=PLsFE_Nvl6h_Y75KGR5pkGqcFisGvBnO9S&index=131, teach you about the opinion?
5. *Incremental incorporation of the Eighth Amendment.* According to the Eighth Amendment, "Excessive bail shall not be required, nor excessive fines imposed, nor cruel and unusual punishments inflicted." In *Robinson v. California*, 370 U.S. 660 (1972), the Court incorporated the Cruel and Unusual Punishments Clause. In *Schilb v. Kuebel*, 404 U.S. 357 (1971), the Court incorporated the Excessive Bail Clause. Do you think the Excessive Fines Clause should also be incorporated? Why or why not?

2. The Eighth Amendment and Partial Incorporation

Can you tell from the oral argument in the following case, available at https://www.oyez.org/cases/2018/17-1091, that the Court's decision to incorporate the Excessive Fines Clause will be unanimous? Did the Court talk about which test to apply to decide if this section of the Eighth Amendment was incorporated? What do you think of this version of the oral argument, SCOTUS-Toons, *Timbs v. Indiana*, Nov. 30, 2018, at https://www.youtube.com/watch?v=fys0hvRXyz8&list=PLsFE_Nvl6h_Y75KGR5pkGqcFisGvBnO9S&index=136?

Timbs v. Indiana

SUPREME COURT OF THE UNITED STATES, 2019

586 U.S. ___, 139 S.Ct. 682

GINSBURG, J., delivered the opinion of the Court, in which ROBERTS, C.J., and BREYER, ALITO, SOTOMAYOR, KAGAN, GORSUCH, and KAVANAUGH, JJ., joined. GORSUCH, J., filed a concurring opinion. THOMAS, J., filed an opinion concurring in the judgment.

Tyson Timbs pleaded guilty in Indiana state court to dealing in a controlled substance and conspiracy to commit theft. The trial court sentenced him to one year of home detention and five years of probation, which included a court-supervised addiction-treatment program. The sentence also required Timbs to pay fees and costs totaling $1,203. At the time of Timbs's arrest, the police seized his vehicle, a Land Rover SUV Timbs had purchased for about $ 42,000. Timbs paid for the vehicle with money he received from an insurance policy when his father died.

The State engaged a private law firm to bring a civil suit for forfeiture of Timbs's Land Rover, charging that the vehicle had been used to transport heroin. After Timbs's guilty plea in the criminal case, the trial court held a hearing on the forfeiture demand. Although finding that Timbs's vehicle had been used to facilitate violation of a criminal statute, the court denied the requested forfeiture, observing that Timbs had recently purchased the vehicle for $42,000, more than four times the maximum $10,000 monetary fine assessable against him for his drug conviction. Forfeiture of the Land Rover, the court determined, would be grossly disproportionate to the gravity of Timbs's offense, hence unconstitutional under the Eighth Amendment's Excessive Fines Clause. The Court of Appeals of Indiana affirmed that determination, but the Indiana Supreme Court reversed. The Indiana Supreme Court did not decide whether the forfeiture would be excessive. Instead, it held that the Excessive Fines Clause constrains only federal action and is inapplicable to state impositions. We granted certiorari.

The question presented: Is the Eighth Amendment's Excessive Fines Clause an "incorporated" protection applicable to the States under the Fourteenth Amendment's Due Process Clause? Like the Eighth Amendment's proscriptions of "cruel and unusual punishment" and "[e]xcessive bail," the protection against excessive fines guards against abuses of government's punitive or criminal-law-enforcement authority. This safeguard, we hold, is "fundamental to our scheme of ordered liberty," with "dee[p] root[s] in [our] history and tradition." *McDonald v. Chicago*, 561 U.S. 742, 767, 130 S.Ct. 3020, 177 L.Ed.2d 894 (2010). The Excessive Fines Clause is therefore incorporated by the Due Process Clause of the Fourteenth Amendment. ...

IB

... Today, acknowledgment of the right's fundamental nature remains widespread. As Indiana itself reports, all 50 States have a constitutional provision prohibiting the imposition of excessive fines either directly or by requiring proportionality. Indeed, Indiana explains that its own Supreme Court has held that the Indiana Constitution should be interpreted to impose the same restrictions as the Eighth Amendment.

For good reason, the protection against excessive fines has been a constant shield throughout Anglo-American history: Exorbitant tolls undermine other constitutional liberties. Excessive fines can be used, for example, to retaliate against or chill the speech of political enemies, as the Stuarts' critics learned several centuries ago. Even absent a political motive, fines may be employed "in a measure out of accord with the penal goals of retribution and deterrence," for "fines are a source of revenue," while other forms of punishment "cost a State money." *Harmelin* v. *Michigan*, 501 U.S. 957, 979, n. 9, 111 S.Ct. 2680, 115 L.Ed.2d 836 (1991) (opinion of Scalia, J.) ("it makes sense to scrutinize governmental action more closely when the State stands to benefit"). This concern is scarcely hypothetical. See Brief for American Civil Liberties Union et al. as *Amici Curiae* 7 ("Perhaps because they are politically easier to impose than generally applicable taxes, state and local governments nationwide increasingly depend heavily on fines and fees as a source of general revenue.").

In short, the historical and logical case for concluding that the Fourteenth Amendment incorporates the Excessive Fines Clause is overwhelming. Protection against excessive punitive economic sanctions secured by the Clause is, to repeat, both "fundamental to our scheme of ordered liberty" and "deeply rooted in this Nation's history and tradition." *McDonald*, 561 U.S., at 767, 130 S.Ct. 3020 (internal quotation marks omitted; emphasis deleted).

II

The State of Indiana does not meaningfully challenge the case for incorporating the Excessive Fines Clause as a general matter. Instead, the State argues that the Clause does not apply to its use of civil *in rem* forfeitures because, the State says, the Clause's specific application to such forfeitures is neither fundamental nor deeply rooted. ... We thus decline the State's invitation to reconsider our unanimous judgment in *Austin* that civil *in rem* forfeitures are fines for purposes of the Eighth Amendment when they are at least partially punitive. ...

Similarly here, regardless of whether application of the Excessive Fines Clause to civil *in rem* forfeitures is itself fundamental or deeply rooted, our conclusion that the Clause is incorporated remains unchanged.

For the reasons stated, the judgment of the Indiana Supreme Court is vacated, and the case is remanded for further proceedings not inconsistent with this opinion.

Justice GORSUCH, concurring.

... As an original matter, I acknowledge, the appropriate vehicle for incorporation may well be the Fourteenth Amendment's Privileges or Immunities Clause, rather than, as this Court has long assumed, the Due Process Clause. ...

Justice THOMAS, concurring in the judgment.

I agree with the Court that the Fourteenth Amendment makes the Eighth Amendment's prohibition on excessive fines fully applicable to the States. But I cannot agree with the route the Court takes to reach this conclusion. Instead of reading the Fourteenth Amendment's Due Process Clause to encompass a substantive right that has nothing to do with "process," I would hold that the right to be free from excessive fines is one of the "privileges or immunities of citizens of the United States" protected by the Fourteenth Amendment. ...

The right against excessive fines traces its lineage back in English law nearly a millennium, and from the founding of our country, it has been consistently recognized as a core right worthy of constitutional protection. As a constitutionally enumerated right understood to be a privilege of American citizenship, the Eighth Amendment's prohibition on excessive fines applies in full to the States.

Notes and Questions

1. *Justice Ginsburg.* What did Justice Ginsburg say about incorporation in the majority opinion?
2. *Justice Thomas.* Why did Justice Thomas concur?
3. *Justice Gorsuch.* Why did Justice Gorsuch concur?
4. *Due process vs. P & I?* Does it matter if the Court uses due process or privileges or immunities? Why?
5. *Is there a case for total incorporation?* Does this case confirm that the Court should have used total incorporation as Justice Black suggested long ago? Could it avoid this case-by-case development and dispute over what should be incorporated?

3. The Sixth Amendment's Right to Trial by Jury and the Unanimity Requirement

According to the Sixth Amendment, "In all criminal prosecutions, the accused shall enjoy the right to a speedy and public trial, by an **impartial jury** of the state and district wherein the crime shall have been committed, which district shall have been previously ascertained by law, and to be informed of the nature and cause of the accusation; to be confronted with the witnesses against him; to have compulsory process for obtaining witnesses in his favor, and to have the assistance of counsel for his defense." In a 1971 case, *Apodaca v. Oregon*, the Court decided *not* to incorporate a requirement that the jury verdict be *unanimous*. The following Justices ruled 5–4 against incorporation, as the picture illustrates, Justice White wrote a plurality opinion (https://www.oyez.org/cases/1971/69-5046). Justice Powell provided the fifth vote. You will see as you read the following case that Powell had his own perspective on the Sixth Amendment and unanimity, saying that the rule applied to the federal but not the state governments, and the Justices are still debating the point.

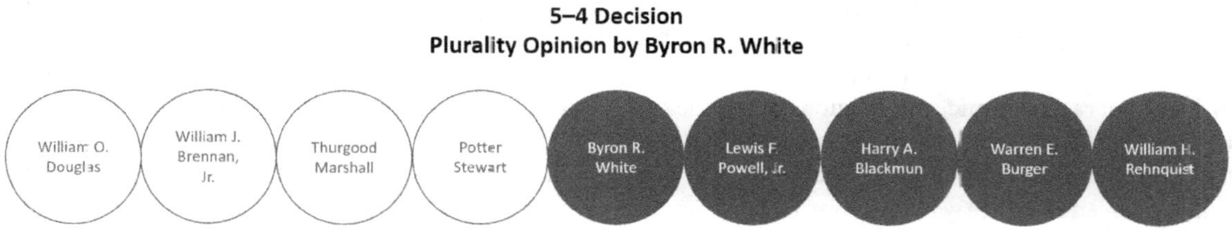

FIGURE 6.3 Apodaca v. Oregon, 406 U.S. 404 (1972)

Can you tell the importance of the *Apodaca* precedent in the oral argument in *Ramos*, available at https://www.oyez.org/cases/2019/18-5924? What role did racial discrimination play in the case? In the oral argument? What do you think of this video of *Ramos*? SCOTUS-Toons, *Ramos v. Louisiana*, Oct. 12, 2019, at https://www.youtube.com/watch?v=WqW3J4erGVc&list=PLsFE_Nvl6h_Y75KGR5pkGqcFisGvBnO9S&index=135.

Ramos v. Louisiana

SUPREME COURT OF THE UNITED STATES, 2020

590 U.S. ___, 140 S.Ct. 1390

GORSUCH, J., announced the judgment of the Court, and delivered the opinion of the Court with respect to Parts I, II–A, III, and IV–B–1, in which GINSBURG, BREYER, SOTOMAYOR, and KAVANAUGH, JJ., joined, an opinion with respect to Parts II–B, IV–B–2, and V, in which GINSBURG, BREYER, and SOTOMAYOR, JJ., joined, and an opinion with respect to Part IV–A, in which GINSBURG and BREYER, JJ., joined. SOTOMAYOR, J., filed an opinion concurring as to all but Part IV–A. KAVANAUGH, J., filed an opinion concurring in part. THOMAS, J., filed an opinion concurring in the judgment. ALITO, J., filed a dissenting opinion, in which ROBERTS, C. J., joined, and in which KAGAN, J., joined as to all but Part III–D.

... Accused of a serious crime, Evangelisto Ramos insisted on his innocence and invoked his right to a jury trial. Eventually, 10 jurors found the evidence against him persuasive. But a pair of jurors believed that the State of Louisiana had failed to prove Mr. Ramos's guilt beyond reasonable doubt; they voted to acquit.

In 48 States and federal court, a single juror's vote to acquit is enough to prevent a conviction. But not in Louisiana. Along with Oregon, Louisiana has long punished people based on 10-to-2 verdicts like the one here. So instead of the mistrial he would have received almost anywhere else, Mr. Ramos was sentenced to life in prison without the possibility of parole.

Why do Louisiana and Oregon allow nonunanimous convictions? Though it's hard to say why these laws persist, their origins are clear. Louisiana first endorsed nonunanimous verdicts for serious crimes at a constitutional convention in 1898. According to one committee chairman, the avowed purpose of that convention was to "establish the supremacy of the white race," and the resulting document included many of the trappings of the Jim Crow era: a poll tax, a combined literacy and property ownership test, and a grandfather clause that in practice exempted white residents from the most onerous of these requirements.

Nor was it only the prospect of African-Americans voting that concerned the delegates. Just a week before the convention, the U.S. Senate passed a resolution calling for an investigation into whether Louisiana was systemically excluding African-Americans from juries. Seeking to avoid unwanted national attention, and aware that this Court would strike down any policy of overt discrimination against African-American jurors as a violation of the Fourteenth Amendment, the delegates sought to undermine African-American participation on juries in another way. With a careful eye on racial demographics, the convention delegates sculpted a "facially race-neutral" rule permitting 10-to-2 verdicts in order "to ensure that African-American juror service would be meaningless."

Adopted in the 1930s, Oregon's rule permitting nonunanimous verdicts can be similarly traced to the rise of the Ku Klux Klan and efforts to dilute "the influence of racial, ethnic, and religious minorities on Oregon juries." In fact, no one before us contests any of this; courts in both Louisiana and Oregon have frankly acknowledged that race was a motivating factor in the adoption of their States' respective nonunanimity rules.

We took this case to decide whether the Sixth Amendment right to a jury trial—as incorporated against the States by way of the Fourteenth Amendment—requires a unanimous verdict to convict a defendant of a serious offense. Louisiana insists that this Court has never definitively passed on the question and urges us to find its practice consistent with the Sixth Amendment. By contrast, the dissent doesn't try to defend Louisiana's law on Sixth or Fourteenth Amendment grounds; tacitly, it seems to admit that the Constitution forbids States from using nonunanimous juries. Yet, unprompted by Louisiana, the dissent suggests our precedent requires us to rule for the State anyway. What explains all this? To answer the puzzle, it's necessary to say a bit more about the merits of the question presented, the relevant precedent, and, at last, the consequences that follow from saying what we know to be true.

I

... If the term "trial by an impartial jury" carried any meaning at all, it surely included a requirement as long and widely accepted as unanimity. ...

There can be no question either that the Sixth Amendment's unanimity requirement applies to state and federal criminal trials equally. This Court has long explained that the Sixth Amendment right to a jury trial is "fundamental to the American scheme of justice" and incorporated against the States under the Fourteenth Amendment. This Court has long explained, too, that incorporated provisions of the Bill of Rights bear the same content when asserted against States as they do when asserted against the federal government.[24] So if the Sixth Amendment's right to a jury trial requires a unanimous verdict to support a conviction in federal court, it requires no less in state court.

II A

How, despite these seemingly straightforward principles, have Louisiana's and Oregon's laws managed to hang on for so long? It turns out that the Sixth Amendment's otherwise simple story took a strange turn in 1972. That year, the Court confronted these States' unconventional schemes for the first time—in *Apodaca* v. *Oregon*[25] and a companion case, *Johnson* v. *Louisiana*.[26] Ultimately, the Court could do no more than issue a badly fractured set of opinions. Four dissenting Justices would not have hesitated to strike down the States' laws, recognizing that the Sixth Amendment requires unanimity and that this guarantee is fully applicable against the States under the Fourteenth Amendment. But a four-Justice plurality took a very different view of the Sixth Amendment. These Justices declared that the real question before them was whether unanimity serves an important "function" in "contemporary society." Then, having reframed the question, the plurality wasted few words before concluding that unanimity's costs outweigh its benefits in the modern era, so the Sixth Amendment should not stand in the way of Louisiana or Oregon.

The ninth Member of the Court adopted a position that was neither here nor there. On the one hand, Justice Powell agreed that, as a matter of "history and precedent, ... the Sixth Amendment requires a unanimous jury verdict to convict." But, on the other hand, he argued that the Fourteenth Amendment does not render this guarantee against the federal government fully applicable against the States. In this way, Justice Powell doubled down on his belief in "dual-track" incorporation—the idea that a single right can mean two different things depending on whether it is being invoked against the federal or a state government. ...

B

In the years following *Apodaca*, both Louisiana and Oregon chose to continue allowing nonunanimous verdicts. ... So what could we possibly describe as the "holding" of *Apodaca*?

Really, no one has found a way to make sense of it. In later cases, this Court has labeled *Apodaca* an "exception," "unusual," and in any event "not an endorsement" of Justice Powell's view of incorporation. At the same time, we have continued to recognize the historical need for unanimity. We've been studiously ambiguous, even inconsistent, about what *Apodaca* might mean. To its credit, Louisiana acknowledges the problem. The State expressly tells us it is not "asking the Court to accord Justice Powell's solo opinion in *Apodaca* precedential force." Instead, in an effort to win today's case, Louisiana embraces the idea that everything is up for grabs. It contends that this Court has never definitively ruled on the propriety of nonunanimous juries under the Sixth Amendment—and that we should use this case to hold for the first time that nonunanimous juries are permissible in state and federal courts alike.

III

... Our real objection here isn't that the *Apodaca* plurality's cost-benefit analysis was too skimpy. The deeper problem is that the plurality subjected the ancient guarantee of a unanimous jury verdict to its own functionalist assessment in the first place. And Louisiana asks us to repeat the error today, just replacing *Apodaca*'s functionalist assessment with our own updated version. All this overlooks the fact that, at the time of the Sixth Amendment's adoption, the right to trial by jury *included* a right to a unanimous verdict. When the American people chose to enshrine that right in the Constitution, they weren't suggesting fruitful topics for future cost-benefit analyses. They were seeking to ensure that their children's children would enjoy the same hard-won liberty they enjoyed. As judges, it is not our role to reassess whether the right to a unanimous jury is "important enough" to retain. With humility, we must accept that this right may serve purposes evading our current notice. We are entrusted to preserve and protect that liberty, not balance it away aided by no more than social statistics.

IVA

If Louisiana's path to an affirmance is a difficult one, the dissent's is trickier still. The dissent doesn't dispute that the Sixth Amendment protects the right to a unanimous jury verdict, or that the Fourteenth Amendment extends this right to state-court trials. But, it insists, we must affirm Mr. Ramos's conviction anyway. Why? Because the doctrine of *stare decisis* supposedly commands it. ...

The dissent's backup argument fares no better. In the end, even the dissent is forced to concede that Justice Powell's *reasoning* in *Apodaca* lacks controlling force. So far, so good. But then the dissent suggests *Apodaca* somehow still manages to supply a controlling precedent as to its *result*. Look closely, though. The dissent's account of *Apodaca*'s *result* looks suspiciously like the *reasoning* of Justice Powell's opinion: "In *Apodaca,* this means that when (1) a defendant is convicted in state court, (2) at least 10 of the 12 jurors vote to convict, and (3) the defendant argues that the conviction violates the Constitution because the vote was not unanimous, the challenge fails." Where does the convenient "state court" qualification come from? Neither the *Apodaca* plurality nor the dissent included any limitation like that—their opinions turned on the meaning of the Sixth Amendment. What the dissent characterizes as *Apodaca*'s result turns out to be nothing more than Justice Powell's reasoning about dual-track incorporation dressed up to look like a logical proof. ...

B1

There's another obstacle the dissent must overcome. Even if we accepted the premise that *Apodaca* established a precedent, no one on the Court today is prepared to say it was rightly decided, and *stare decisis* isn't supposed to be the art of methodically ignoring what everyone knows to be true. ...

... but prior convictions in only two States are potentially affected by our judgment. Those States credibly claim that the number of nonunanimous felony convictions still on direct appeal are somewhere in the hundreds, and retrying or plea bargaining these cases will surely impose a cost. But new rules of criminal procedures usually do, often affecting significant numbers of pending cases across the whole country. For example, after *Booker* v. *United States* held that the Federal Sentencing Guidelines must be advisory rather than mandatory, this Court vacated and remanded nearly 800 decisions to the courts of appeals. Similar consequences likely followed when *Crawford* v. *Washington* overturned prior interpretations of the Confrontation Clause or *Arizona* v. *Gant* changed the law for searches incident to arrests. Our decision here promises to cause less, and certainly nothing before us supports the dissent's surmise that it will cause wildly more, disruption than these other decisions.

2

... Whether the right to jury unanimity applies to cases on collateral review is a question for a future case where the parties will have a chance to brief the issue and we will benefit from their adversarial presentation. That litigation is sure to come, and will rightly take into account the States' interest in the finality of their criminal convictions. In this way, *Teague* frees us to say what we know to be true about the rights of the accused under our Constitution today, while leaving questions about the reliance interest States possess in their final judgments for later proceedings crafted to account for them. ...

Taken at its word, the dissent would have us discard a Sixth Amendment right in perpetuity rather than ask two States to retry a slice of their prior criminal cases. Whether that slice turns out to be large or small, it cannot outweigh the interest we all share in the preservation of our constitutionally promised liberties. Indeed, the dissent can cite no case in which the one-time need to retry defendants has *ever* been sufficient to inter a constitutional right forever. ...

V

On what ground would anyone have us leave Mr. Ramos in prison for the rest of his life? Not a single Member of this Court is prepared to say Louisiana secured his conviction constitutionally under the Sixth Amendment. No one before us suggests that the error was harmless. Louisiana does not claim precedent commands an affirmance. In the end, the best anyone can seem to muster against Mr. Ramos is that, if we dared to admit in his case what we all know to be true about the Sixth Amendment, we might have to say the same in some others. But where is the justice in that? Every judge must learn to live with the fact he or she will make some mistakes; it comes with the territory. But it is something else entirely to perpetuate something we all know to be wrong only because we fear the consequences of being right. The judgment of the Court of Appeals is

Reversed.

Justice SOTOMAYOR, concurring as to all but Part IV–A.

I agree with most of the Court's rationale, and so I join all but Part IV–A of its opinion. I write separately, however, to underscore three points. First, overruling precedent here is not only warranted, but compelled. Second, the interests at stake point far more clearly to that outcome than those in other recent cases. And finally, the racially biased origins of the Louisiana and Oregon laws uniquely matter here. ...

III

... Today, Louisiana's and Oregon's laws are fully—and rightly—relegated to the dustbin of history. And so, too, is *Apodaca*. While overruling precedent must be rare, this Court should not shy away from correcting its errors where the right to avoid imprisonment pursuant to unconstitutional procedures hangs in the balance.

Justice KAVANAUGH, concurring in part.

In *Apodaca* v. *Oregon*, this Court held that state juries need not be unanimous in order to convict a criminal defendant. 406 U.S. 404, 92 S.Ct. 1628, 32 L.Ed.2d 184 (1972). Two States, Louisiana and Oregon, have continued to use non-unanimous juries in criminal cases. Today, the Court overrules *Apodaca* and holds that state juries must be unanimous in order to convict a criminal defendant.

I agree with the Court that the time has come to overrule *Apodaca*. I therefore join the introduction and Parts I, II–A, III, and IV–B–1 of the Court's persuasive and important opinion. I write separately to explain my view of how *stare decisis* applies to this case.

I

... The *stare decisis* factors identified by the Court in its past cases include:

- the quality of the precedent's reasoning;
- the precedent's consistency and coherence with previous or subsequent decisions;
- changed law since the prior decision;
- changed facts since the prior decision;
- the workability of the precedent;
- the reliance interests of those who have relied on the precedent; and
- the age of the precedent. ...

As I read the Court's cases on precedent, those varied and somewhat elastic *stare decisis* factors fold into three broad considerations that, in my view, can help guide the inquiry and help determine what constitutes a "special justification" or "strong grounds" to overrule a prior constitutional decision.

First, is the prior decision not just wrong, but grievously or egregiously wrong? ... *Second*, has the prior decision caused significant negative jurisprudential or real-world consequences? ... *Third*, would overruling the prior decision unduly upset reliance interests? ...

Taken together, those three considerations set a high (but not insurmountable) bar for overruling a precedent, and they therefore limit the number of overrulings and maintain stability in the law. Those three considerations also constrain judicial discretion in deciding when to overrule an erroneous precedent. To be sure, applying those considerations is not a purely mechanical exercise, and I do not claim otherwise. I suggest only that those three considerations may better structure how to consider the many traditional *stare decisis* factors. ...

II

Applying the three broad *stare decisis* considerations to this case, I agree with the Court's decision to overrule *Apodaca*.

First, *Apodaca* is egregiously wrong. ... *Second*, *Apodaca* causes significant negative consequences. ... To state the point in simple terms: Why stick by an erroneous precedent that is egregiously wrong as a matter of constitutional law, that allows convictions of some who would not be convicted under the proper constitutional rule, and that tolerates and reinforces a practice that is thoroughly racist in its origins and has continuing racially discriminatory effects? *Third*, overruling *Apodaca* would not unduly upset reliance interests. ...

So assuming that the Court faithfully applies *Teague*, today's decision will not apply retroactively on federal habeas corpus review and will not disturb convictions that are final. ...

For those reasons, the reliance interests at stake in this case are not especially substantial, and they do not mandate adherence to *Apodaca*. ...

Justice THOMAS, concurring in the judgment.

I agree with the Court that petitioner Evangelisto Ramos' felony conviction by a nonunanimous jury was unconstitutional. I write separately because I would resolve this case based on the Court's longstanding view that the Sixth Amendment includes a protection against nonunanimous felony guilty verdicts, without undertaking a fresh analysis of the meaning of "trial ... by an impartial jury." I also would make clear that this right applies against the States through the Privileges or Immunities Clause of the Fourteenth Amendment, not the Due Process Clause. ...

I would accept petitioner's invitation to decide this case under the Privileges or Immunities Clause. The Court conspicuously avoids saying which clause it analyzes. But one assumes from its silence that the Court is either following our due process incorporation precedents or believes that "nothing in this case turns on" which clause applies, *Timbs*, *supra*, at ____, 139 S.Ct., at 691 (GORSUCH, J., concurring).

I have already rejected our due process incorporation cases as demonstrably erroneous, and I fundamentally disagree with applying that theory of incorporation simply because it reaches the same result in the case before us. Close enough is for horseshoes and hand grenades, not constitutional interpretation. The textual difference between protecting "citizens" (in the Privileges or Immunities Clause) and "person[s]" (in the Due Process Clause) will surely be relevant in another case. And our judicial duty—not to mention the candor we owe to our fellow citizens—requires us to put an end to this Court's due process prestidigitation, which no one is willing to defend on the merits.

I would simply hold that, because all of the opinions in *Apodaca* addressed the Due Process Clause, its Fourteenth Amendment ruling does not bind us because the proper question here is the scope of the Privileges or Immunities Clause. I cannot understand why the Court, having decided to abandon *Apodaca*, refuses to correctly root its holding in the Privileges or Immunities Clause. ...

Justice ALITO, with whom THE CHIEF JUSTICE joins, and with whom Justice KAGAN joins as to all but Part III–D, dissenting.

... I would not overrule *Apodaca*. Whatever one may think about the correctness of the decision, it has elicited enormous and entirely reasonable reliance. And before this Court decided to intervene, the decision appeared to have little practical importance going forward. Louisiana has now abolished non-unanimous verdicts, and Oregon seemed on the verge of doing the same until the Court intervened. ...

I

... If Louisiana and Oregon originally adopted their laws allowing non-unanimous verdicts for these reasons, that is deplorable, but what does that have to do with the broad constitutional question before us? The answer is: nothing. ...

Some years ago the British Parliament enacted a law allowing non-unanimous verdicts. Was Parliament under the sway of the Klan? The Constitution of Puerto Rico permits non-unanimous verdicts. Were the framers of that Constitution racists? Non-unanimous verdicts were once advocated by the American Law

Institute and the American Bar Association. Was their aim to promote white supremacy? And how about the prominent scholars who have taken the same position? Racists all? Of course not. So all the talk about the Klan, etc., is entirely out of place. We should set an example of rational and civil discourse instead of contributing to the worst current trends. ...

III

... Even now, our cases do not hold that *every* provision of the Bill of Rights applies in the same way to the Federal Government and the States. A notable exception is the Grand Jury Clause of the Fifth Amendment, a provision that, like the Sixth Amendment jury-trial right, reflects the importance that the founding generation attached to juries as safeguards against oppression. In *Hurtado v. California*, 110 U.S. 516, 538, 4 S.Ct. 292, 28 L.Ed. 232 (1884), the Court held that the Grand Jury Clause does not bind the States and that they may substitute preliminary hearings at which the decision to allow a prosecution to go forward is made by a judge rather than a defendant's peers. That decision was based on reasoning that is not easy to distinguish from Justice Powell's in *Apodaca*. *Hurtado* remains good law and is critically important to the 28 States that allow a defendant to be prosecuted for a felony without a grand jury indictment. If we took the same approach to the *Hurtado* question that the majority takes in this case, the holding in that case could be called into question. ...

While the majority worries that *Apodaca* is inconsistent with our cases on incorporation, the majority ignores something far more important: the way in which *Apodaca* is intertwined with the body of our Sixth Amendment case law. As I have explained, the *Apodaca* plurality's reasoning was based on the same fundamental mode of analysis as that in *Williams*, 399 U.S. 78, 90 S.Ct. 1893, 26 L.Ed.2d 446, which had held just two years earlier that the Sixth Amendment did not constitutionalize the common law's requirement that a jury have 12 members. Although only one State, Oregon, now permits non-unanimous verdicts, many more allow six-person juries. Repudiating the reasoning of *Apodaca* will almost certainly prompt calls to overrule *Williams*.

C

... What convinces me that *Apodaca* should be retained are the enormous reliance interests of Louisiana and Oregon. For 48 years, Louisiana and Oregon, trusting that *Apodaca* is good law, have conducted thousands and thousands of trials under rules allowing non-unanimous verdicts. Now, those States face a potential tsunami of litigation on the jury-unanimity issue. ...

The majority cannot have it both ways. As long as retroactive application on collateral review remains a real possibility, the crushing burden that this would entail cannot be ignored. And while it is true that this Court has been chary in recognizing new watershed rules, it is by no means clear that *Teague* will preclude the application of today's decision on collateral review. ...

D

... By striking down a precedent upon which there has been massive and entirely reasonable reliance, the majority sets an important precedent about *stare decisis*. I assume that those in the majority will apply the same standard in future cases.

Under the approach to *stare decisis* that we have taken in recent years, *Apodaca* should not be overruled. I would therefore affirm the judgment below, and I respectfully dissent.

Notes and Questions

1. *The debate about stare decisis.* Why do you think the Justices are arguing so much about stare decisis? For this case? For future cases? You will see this issue rise again in the abortion cases.
2. *Video.* What did *Apodaca* hold? Are there good reasons for it to be overruled? When should the Court overrule a case? Does this video explain the role of *Apodaca* in this case well? The Federalist Society, *Ramos v. Louisiana*, Oct. 6, 2019, at https://www.youtube.com/watch?v=VIH26MeGz_M&list=PLsFE_Nvl6h_Y75KGR5pkGqcFisGvBnO9S&index=133.

3. *The role of racism?* How was the issue of racism related to the Court's precedent on this issue?
4. *Justice Gorsuch.* Summarize Justice Gorsuch's argument for the Court. Why did he decide to incorporate?
5. *Justice Sotomayor.* Why did Justice Sotomayor concur?
6. *Justice Kavanaugh.* Why did Justice Kavanaugh concur?
7. *Justice Alito.* Why did Justice Alito dissent?
8. *Video.* Does this video explain the case to you, *Ramos v. Louisiana*, Oct. 6, 2019, at https://www.youtube.com/watch?v=VIH26MeGz_M&list=PLsFE_Nvl6h_Y75KGR5pkGqcFisGvBnO9S&index=134?
9. *The retroactivity of constitutional rulings.* In 2021, the Justices wrote a follow-up opinion to *Ramos*. In *Edwards v. Vannoy*, 593 U.S. ___, 141 S.Ct. 1547 (2021), the Court ruled 6–3 that inmates whose convictions occurred before *Ramos* was decided could not challenge their convictions on federal collateral review. Edwards was convicted of armed robbery, rape, and kidnapping by an 11–1 vote in Louisiana. Justice Kavanaugh wrote for the majority that *Ramos* was a new rule that did not apply retroactively. Kavanaugh was joined by Roberts, Thomas, Alito, Gorsuch, and Barrett. In dissent, Justice Kagan, joined by Breyer and Sotomayor, said *Ramos* was a watershed rule that should have been applied retroactively. She accused the majority of undermining the Court's precedents that watershed cases are applied retroactively.

   "The decision means that hundreds of people who were found guilty by non-unanimous juries in those two states [Louisiana and Oregon] before *Ramos* will not get to seek to have their convictions overturned." Amy Howe, *Justices divided on retroactive application of jury-unanimity rule*, SCOTUSblog (May. 17, 2021, 2:01 PM), https://www.scotusblog.com/2021/05/justices-divided-on-retroactive-application-of-jury-unanimity-rule/. What do you think of that conclusion?

10. *Your sample opinion.* Write a sample opinion about whether the Third Amendment is incorporated. Who would bring the case? What arguments would they make? What arguments would there be against it? Who would win in the Supreme Court? By what vote?

A Look Ahead

This chapter introduced us to the Civil War amendments, namely the Thirteenth, Fourteenth, and Fifteenth Amendments. The Fourteenth Amendment has received lengthy analysis by the Court in cases about liberty and equality. In Chapter 7, we study the details of the Court's Fourteenth Amendment jurisprudence, including racial equality, national origin discrimination, gender equality, and sexual orientation discrimination. Then, in Chapter 8, we ask how much and whether the Fourteenth Amendment grants protection to privileges or immunities; to economic rights, e.g., the freedom for employers and employees to contract; to abortion rights; and whether it protects a "right to die."

Credits

IMG 6.1: Supreme Court of the United States, "Voter Registration Numbers from 1965 to 2004, from 'Shelby County v. Holder'," https://supreme.justia.com/cases/federal/us/570/529/#tab-opinion-1970752, 2013.

Fig. 6.1: Adapted from: Oyez, "How the Justices Voted in Heller," https://www.oyez.org/cases/2007/07-290. Copyright © 2022 by Oyez, Inc.

Fig. 6.2: Adapted from: Oyez, "How the Justices Voted in McDonald," https://www.oyez.org/cases/2009/08-1521. Copyright © 2022 by Oyez, Inc.

Fig. 6.3: Adapted from: Oyez, "How the Justices Voted in Apodaca," https://www.oyez.org/cases/1971/69-5046. Copyright © 2022 by Oyez, Inc.

Seven

The Fourteenth Amendment Prohibits Racial, Gender, and Sexual Orientation Discrimination

Introduction

In Chapter 6, you learned about the role of slavery in the history of the Constitution and the Thirteenth, Fourteenth, and Fifteenth Amendments, which are the Reconstruction amendments following the end of the Civil War. The Fourteenth Amendment has garnered more of the Court's attention in opinions than either the Thirteenth or the Fifteenth. Remember that the Fourteenth Amendment was supposed to take care of the citizenship issue after the Court in *Dred Scott* ruled that African Americans could not be citizens, but it also establishes other rights against the states.

Refer to the text of Section 1 of the Fourteenth Amendment: "All persons born or naturalized in the United States, and subject to the jurisdiction thereof, are **citizens** of the United States and of the state wherein they reside. No state shall make or enforce any law which shall abridge the **privileges or immunities** of citizens of the United States; nor shall any state deprive any person of life, liberty, or property, without **due process of law**; nor deny to any person within its jurisdiction the **equal protection** of the laws."

Consider the terms that are written in bold print. The citizens language addresses the issue of *Dred Scott*. Then, there are three other categories: privileges or immunities, due process, and equal protection. As you read this chapter, ask yourself what those terms mean in the eyes of the Court. In an early case, the Court gave little meaning to privileges or immunities, so it has not received much analysis from the Court.

What is due process? Is due process a procedural protection, or does it have substantive content? Can you identify rights that are protected by the Due Process Clause? Do you think it is the due process part of the Constitution that protects those rights? Does it protect a right not to be censored by the government? To abortion? A right to die?

And what is equal protection in the eyes of the law? The Justices disagree about the best way to analyze equal protection. As you read these cases, consider what you think the best approach to equal protection is.

We start this chapter with racial equality, which should be protected by the Civil War amendments. How much equality does race receive in the laws of the United States? Why do the Justices sometimes disagree about its meaning? In the rest of the chapter, we also look at national origin discrimination, gender equality, and sexual orientation discrimination

A. Levels of Scrutiny

To understand the rights cases at the Supreme Court, it is necessary to learn the formulae that the Justices use to decide whether a law violates a right under the Bill of Rights or the Fourteenth Amendment. First, there is only one absolute right in the entire Constitution. That is the right to believe whatever you choose in the First Amendment. As the Court in *West Virginia Board of Education v. Barnette* (1943) declared: "no official, high or petty, can prescribe what shall be orthodox in matters of politics, nationalism, religion, or other matters of opinion. ..." This is a blanket prohibition and will be discussed at greater length in the cases in the following chapters. Compared to this one absolute right, all other rights can be weighed against the interests of the government in making the law. The Court has established "levels of scrutiny" that establish how closely the courts will review certain rights.

The following chart provides an overview of levels of scrutiny, which you should keep in mind as you read through the rest of the book. It is not applied with mathematical precision in every case, but it is a useful guide through the rights cases.

TABLE 7.1 **Levels of Scrutiny**

Level of Review	**Rational Basis**	**Intermediate Scrutiny**	**Strict Scrutiny**
Level of government interest required	The interest is not irrational	It is important	It is compelling
Level of tailoring required between the state's interest and the individual's right	None	Substantially related	Narrow tailoring*

→ Least rigorous judicial review of law — Most rigorous judicial review of law

**There is also a more demanding tailoring requirement that requires the law to be the "least restrictive means" of regulating the right possible, which appears in the Fourteenth Amendment's race equality cases. It also appears in the federal statutes for religious liberty, RFRA, and RLUIPA, which you will learn about in Chapter 10.*

The levels of scrutiny guide how hard the Justices will examine a law in order to test its constitutionality. Ultimately, they determine how deferential the Court will be to the legislators (or executive branch officials) who make a law. Under rationality review, the Court is giving lawmakers broad sway to use their judgment in solving a social problem through legislation. Strict scrutiny grants lawmakers little leeway to potentially violate the right. Keep this in mind as you read each case and then review the entire set of cases in this chapter.

B. Racial Equality

1. Separate but Equal

Does equal protection mean "separate but equal"? In other words, if the nation has Black schools and White schools, is equal protection safeguarded? The following case upheld separate spaces in transportation for different races. Why did it do so? Are you persuaded by the majority or the dissent in the following opinion?

Plessy v. Ferguson
SUPREME COURT OF THE UNITED STATES, 1896
163 U.S. 537, 16 S.Ct. 1138
[overruled by *Brown v. Board of Education*]

Mr. Justice BROWN delivered the opinion of the court.

This case turns upon the constitutionality of an act of the general assembly of the state of Louisiana, passed in 1890, providing for separate railway carriages for the white and colored races.

The first section of the statute enacts 'that all railway companies carrying passengers in their coaches in this state, shall provide equal but separate accommodations for the white, and colored races, by providing two or more passenger coaches for each passenger train, or by dividing the passenger coaches by a partition so as to secure separate accommodations: provided, that this section shall not be construed to apply to street railroads. No person or persons shall be permitted to occupy seats in coaches, other than the ones assigned to them, on account of the race they belong to.' ...

The information filed in the criminal district court charged, in substance, that Plessy, being a passenger between two stations within the state of Louisiana, was assigned by officers of the company to the coach used for the race to which he belonged, but he insisted upon going into a coach used by the race to which he did not belong. Neither in the information nor plea was his particular race or color averred.

The petition for the writ of prohibition averred that petitioner was seven-eights Caucasian and one-eighth African blood; that the mixture of colored blood was not discernible in him; and that he was entitled to every right, privilege, and immunity secured to citizens of the United States of the white race; and that, upon such theory, he took possession of a vacant seat in a coach where passengers of the white race were accommodated, and was ordered by the conductor to vacate said coach, and take a seat in another, assigned to persons of the colored race, and, having refused to comply with such demand, he was forcibly ejected, with the aid of a police officer, and imprisoned in the parish jail to answer a charge of having violated the above act. ...

That it does not conflict with the thirteenth amendment, which abolished slavery and involuntary servitude, except as a punishment for crime, is too clear for argument. ... A statute which implies merely a legal distinction between the white and colored races—a distinction which is founded in the color of the two races, and which must always exist so long as white men are distinguished from the other race by color—has no tendency to destroy the legal equality of the two races, or re-establish a state of involuntary servitude. ...

So far, then, as a conflict with the fourteenth amendment is concerned, the case reduces itself to the question whether the statute of Louisiana is a reasonable regulation, and with respect to this there must necessarily be a large discretion on the part of the legislature. In determining the question of reasonableness, it is at liberty to act with reference to the established usages, customs, and traditions of the people, and with a view to the promotion of their comfort, and the preservation of the public peace and good order. Gauged by this standard, we cannot say that a law which authorizes or even requires the separation of the two races in public conveyances is unreasonable, or more obnoxious to the fourteenth amendment than the acts of congress requiring separate schools for colored children in the District of Columbia, the constitutionality of which does not seem to have been questioned, or the corresponding acts of state legislatures.

We consider the underlying fallacy of the plaintiff's argument to consist in the assumption that the enforced separation of the two races stamps the colored race with a badge of inferiority. If this be so, it is not by reason of anything found in the act, but solely because the colored race chooses to put that construction upon it. The argument necessarily assumes that if, as has been more than once the case, and is not unlikely to be so again, the colored race should become the dominant power in the state legislature, and should enact a law in precisely similar terms, it would thereby relegate the white race to an inferior position. We imagine that the white race, at least, would not acquiesce in this assumption. The argument also assumes that social prejudices may be overcome by legislation, and that equal rights cannot be secured to the negro except by an enforced commingling of the two races. We cannot accept this proposition. If the two races are to meet upon terms of social equality, it must be the result of natural affinities, a mutual appreciation of each other's merits, and a voluntary consent of individuals. As was said by the court of appeals of New York in People v. Gallagher, 93 N.Y. 438, 448: 'This end can neither be accomplished nor promoted by laws which conflict with the general sentiment of the community upon whom they are designed to operate. When the government, therefore, has secured to each of its citizens equal rights before the law, and equal opportunities for improvement and progress, it has accomplished the end for which it was organized, and performed all of the functions respecting social advantages with which it is endowed.' Legislation is powerless to eradicate racial instincts, or to abolish distinctions based upon physical differences, and the attempt to do so can only result in accentuating the difficulties of the present situation. If the civil and political rights of both races be equal, one cannot be inferior to the other civilly or politically. If one race be inferior to the other socially, the constitution of the United States cannot put them upon the same plane.

It is true that the question of the proportion of colored blood necessary to constitute a colored person, as distinguished from a white person, is one upon which there is a difference of opinion in the different states; some holding that any visible admixture of black blood stamps the person as belonging to the colored race (State v. Chavers, 5 Jones [N. C.] 1); others, that it depends upon the preponderance of blood (Gray v. State, 4 Ohio, 354; Monroe v. Collins, 17 Ohio St. 665); and still others, that the predominance of white blood must only be in the proportion of three-fourths (People v. Dean, 14 Mich. 406; Jones v. Com., 80 Va. 544). But these are questions to be determined under the laws of each state, and are not properly put in issue in this case. Under the allegations of his petition, it may undoubtedly become a question of importance whether, under the laws of Louisiana, the petitioner belongs to the white or colored race.

The judgment of the court below is therefore affirmed.

Mr. Justice HARLAN dissenting.

By the Louisiana statute the validity of which is here involved, all railway companies (other than street-railroad companies) carry passengers in that state are required to have separate but equal accommodations for white and colored persons. ...

These notable additions to the fundamental law [i.e., the Civil War amendments] were welcomed by the friends of liberty throughout the world. They removed the race line from our governmental systems. They had, as this court has said, a common purpose, namely, to secure 'to a race recently emancipated, a race that through many generations have been held in slavery, all the civil rights that the superior race enjoy.' They declared, in legal effect, this court has further said, 'that the law in the states shall be the same for the black as for the white; that all persons, whether colored or white, shall stand equal before the laws of the states; and in regard to the colored race, for whose protection the amendment was primarily designed, that no discrimination shall be made against them by law because of their color.' We also said: 'The words of the amendment, it is true, are prohibitory, but they contain a necessary implication of a positive immunity or right, most valuable to the colored race,—the right to exemption from unfriendly legislation against them distinctively as colored; exemption from legal discriminations, implying inferiority in civil society, lessening the security of their enjoyment of the rights which others enjoy; and discriminations which are steps towards reducing them to the condition of a subject race.' It was, consequently, adjudged that a state law that excluded citizens of the colored race from juries, because of their race, however well qualified in other respects to discharge the duties of jurymen, was repugnant to the fourteenth amendment. ...

The white race deems itself to be the dominant race in this country. And so it is, in prestige, in achievements, in education, in wealth, and in power. So, I doubt not, it will continue to be for all time, if it remains true to its great heritage, and holds fast to the principles of constitutional liberty. But in view of the constitution, in the eye of the law, there is in this country no superior, dominant, ruling class of citizens. There is no caste here. Our constitution is color-blind, and neither knows nor tolerates classes among citizens. In respect of civil rights, all citizens are equal before the law. The humblest is the peer of the most powerful. The law regards man as man, and takes no account of his surroundings or of his color when his civil rights as guaranteed by the supreme law of the land are involved. It is therefore to be regretted that this high tribunal, the final expositor of the fundamental law of the land, has reached the conclusion that it is competent for a state to regulate the enjoyment by citizens of their civil rights solely upon the basis of race.

In my opinion, the judgment this day rendered will, in time, prove to be quite as pernicious as the decision made by this tribunal in the Dred Scott Case.

It was adjudged in that case that the descendants of Africans who were imported into this country, and sold as slaves, were not included nor intended to be included under the word 'citizens' in the constitution, and could not claim any of the rights and privileges which that instrument provided for and secured to citizens of the United States; that, at time of the adoption of the constitution, they were 'considered as a subordinate and inferior class of beings, who had been subjugated by the dominant race, and, whether emancipated or not, yet remained subject to their authority, and had no rights or privileges but such as those who held the power and the government might choose to grant them.' The recent amendments of the constitution, it was supposed, had eradicated these principles from our institutions. But it seems that we have yet, in some of the states, a dominant race,—a superior class of citizens,—which assumes to regulate the enjoyment of civil rights, common to all citizens, upon the basis of race. The present decision, it may well be apprehended, will not only stimulate aggressions, more or less brutal and irritating, upon the admitted rights of colored citizens, but will encourage the belief that it is possible, by means of state enactments, to defeat the beneficent purposes which the people of the United States had in view when they adopted the recent amendments of the constitution, by one of which the blacks of this country were made citizens of the United States and of the states in which they respectively reside, and whose privileges and immunities, as citizens, the states are forbidden to abridge. Sixty millions of whites are in no danger from the presence here of eight millions of blacks. The destinies of the two races, in this country, are indissolubly linked together, and the interests of both require that the common government of all shall not permit the seeds of race hate to be planted under the sanction of law. What can more certainly arouse race hate, what more certainly create and perpetuate a feeling of distrust between these races, than state enactments which, in fact, proceed on the ground that colored citizens are so inferior and degraded that they cannot be allowed to sit in public coaches occupied by white citizens? That, as all will admit, is the real meaning of such legislation as was enacted in Louisiana. ...

There is a race so different from our own that we do not permit those belonging to it to become citizens of the United States. Persons belonging to it are, with few exceptions, absolutely excluded from our country. I allude to the Chinese race. But, by the statute in question, a Chinaman can ride in the same passenger coach with white citizens of the United States, while citizens of the black race in Louisiana, many of whom, perhaps, risked their lives for the preservation of the Union, who are entitled, by law, to participate in the political control of the state and nation, who are not excluded, by law or by reason of their race, from public stations of any kind, and who have all the legal rights that belong to white citizens, are yet declared to be criminals, liable to imprisonment, if they ride in a public coach occupied by citizens of the white race. It is scarcely just to say that a colored citizen should not object to occupying a public coach assigned to his own race. He does not object, nor, perhaps, would he object to separate coaches for his race if his rights under the law were recognized. But he does object, and he ought never to cease objecting, that citizens of the white and black races can be adjudged criminals because they sit, or claim the right to sit, in the same public coach on a public highway.

The arbitrary separation of citizens, on the basis of race, while they are on a public highway, is a badge of servitude wholly inconsistent with the civil freedom and the equality before the law established by the constitution. It cannot be justified upon any legal grounds. ...

Notes and Questions

1. *The Louisiana law.* How do you assess the Louisiana law? Would you recommend having such a law in your state today? Why or why not? This case was overruled by *Brown v. Board of Education.* Is there anything worth salvaging in *Plessy*?
2. *What does equal mean?* The Fourteenth Amendment safeguards "equal protection." What do you think of the Court's argument that separate but equal is consistent with the amendment?

It is suggested that equal protection can be achieved by the separation of the races as long as they are treated equally. What do you think about that?

3. *States or DC?* Congress had approved separate-race schools in the District of Columbia? What constitutional significance does that have?
4. *Harlan.* Why did Justice Harlan dissent? Whose view of racial relations is more accurate, Justice Brown's or Justice Harlan's? How is the view of race different today than it was in the Court in 1896?
5. *Here yesterday, gone today.* Are you surprised this case was overruled in 1954? Are there any circumstances in which you would reinstate it? What, if anything, is good about its holding?
6. *Chinese Americans.* What does Justice Harlan say about Chinese Americans?

2. Japanese Americans in World War II

The following case raises these questions: Are Japanese Americans protected by the Fourteenth Amendment? By other sections of the Constitution? How would you assess the Japanese internment as described in the following case, *Korematsu*? Keep these issues in mind as you read the case.

Korematsu v. United States
SUPREME COURT OF THE UNITED STATES, 1944
323 U.S. 214, 65 S.Ct. 193

Mr. Justice BLACK delivered the opinion of the Court.

The petitioner, an American citizen of Japanese descent, was convicted in a federal district court for remaining in San Leandro, California, a 'Military Area', contrary to Civilian Exclusion Order No. 34 of the Commanding General of the Western Command, U.S. Army, which directed that after May 9, 1942, all persons of Japanese ancestry should be excluded from that area. No question was raised as to petitioner's loyalty to the United States. ...

Exclusion Order No. 34, which the petitioner knowingly and admittedly violated was one of a number of military orders and proclamations, all of which were substantially based upon Executive Order No. 9066, 7 Fed.Reg. 1407. That order, issued after we were at war with Japan, declared that "the successful prosecution of the war requires every possible protection against espionage and against sabotage to national-defense material, national-defense premises, and national-defense utilities. * * *"

One of the series of orders and proclamations, a curfew order, which like the exclusion order here was promulgated pursuant to Executive Order 9066, subjected all persons of Japanese ancestry in prescribed West Coast military areas to remain in their residences from 8 p.m. to 6 a.m. As is the case with the exclusion order here, that prior curfew order was designed as a "protection against espionage and against sabotage." In Hirabayashi v. United States, 320 U.S. 81, 63 S.Ct. 1375, 87 L.Ed. 1774, we sustained a conviction obtained for violation of the curfew order. The Hirabayashi conviction and this one thus rest on the same 1942 Congressional Act and the same basic executive and military orders, all of which orders were aimed at the twin dangers of espionage and sabotage. ...

In the light of the principles we announced in the Hirabayashi case, we are unable to conclude that it was beyond the war power of Congress and the Executive to exclude those of Japanese ancestry from the West Coast war area at the time they did. True, exclusion from the area in which one's home is located is a far greater deprivation than constant confinement to the home from 8 p.m. to 6 a.m. Nothing short of apprehension by the proper military authorities of the gravest imminent danger to the public safety can constitutionally justify either. But exclusion from a threatened area, no less than curfew, has a definite and close relationship to the prevention of espionage and sabotage. The military authorities, charged with the primary responsibility of defending our shores, concluded that curfew provided inadequate protection and ordered exclusion. They did so, as pointed out in our Hirabayashi opinion, in accordance with Congressional authority to the military to say who should, and who should not, remain in the threatened areas. …

Here, as in the Hirabayashi case, we cannot reject as unfounded the judgment of the military authorities and of Congress that there were disloyal members of that population, whose number and strength could not be precisely and quickly ascertained. We cannot say that the war-making branches of the Government did not have ground for believing that in a critical hour such persons could not readily be isolated and separately dealt with, and constituted a menace to the national defense and safety, which demanded that prompt and adequate measures be taken to guard against it."

Like curfew, exclusion of those of Japanese origin was deemed necessary because of the presence of an unascertained number of disloyal members of the group, most of whom we have no doubt were loyal to this country. It was because we could not reject the finding of the military authorities that it was impossible to bring about an immediate segregation of the disloyal from the loyal that we sustained the validity of the curfew order as applying to the whole group. In the instant case, temporary exclusion of the entire group was rested by the military on the same ground. The judgment that exclusion of the whole group was for the same reason a military imperative answers the contention that the exclusion was in the nature of group punishment based on antagonism to those of Japanese origin. That there were members of the group who retained loyalties to Japan has been confirmed by investigations made subsequent to the exclusion. Approximately five thousand American citizens of Japanese ancestry refused to swear unqualified allegiance to the United States and to renounce allegiance to the Japanese Emperor, and several thousand evacuees requested repatriation to Japan.

We uphold the exclusion order as of the time it was made and when the petitioner violated it. In doing so, we are not unmindful of the hardships imposed by it upon a large group of American citizens. But hardships are part of war, and war is an aggregation of hardships. All citizens alike, both in and out of uniform, feel the impact of war in greater or lesser measure. Citizenship has its responsibilities as well as its privileges, and in time of war the burden is always heavier. Compulsory exclusion of large groups of citizens from their homes, except under circumstances of direst emergency and peril, is inconsistent with our basic governmental institutions. But when under conditions of modern warfare our shores are threatened by hostile forces, the power to protect must be commensurate with the threatened danger. …

It is said that we are dealing here with the case of imprisonment of a citizen in a concentration camp solely because of his ancestry, without evidence or inquiry concerning his loyalty and good disposition towards the United States. Our task would be simple, our duty clear, were this a case involving the imprisonment of a loyal citizen in a concentration camp because of racial prejudice. Regardless of the true nature of the assembly and relocation centers—and we deem it unjustifiable to call them concentration camps with all the ugly connotations that term implies—we are dealing specifically with nothing but an exclusion order. To cast this case into outlines of racial prejudice, without reference to the real military dangers which were presented, merely confuses the issue. Korematsu was not excluded from the Military Area because of hostility to him or his race. He was excluded because we are at war with the Japanese Empire, because the properly constituted military authorities feared an invasion of our West Coast and felt constrained to take proper security measures, because they decided that the military urgency of the situation demanded that all citizens of Japanese ancestry be segregated from the West Coast temporarily, and finally, because Congress, reposing its confidence in this time of war in our military leaders—as inevitably it must—determined that they should have the power to do just this. There was evidence of disloyalty on the part of some, the military authorities considered that the need for action was great, and time was short. We cannot—by availing ourselves of the calm perspective of hindsight—now say that at that time these actions were unjustified.

Mr. Justice FRANKFURTER, concurring.

To find that the Constitution does not forbid the military measures now complained of does not carry with it approval of that which Congress and the Executive did. That is their business, not ours.

Mr. Justice ROBERTS.

I dissent, because I think the indisputable facts exhibit a clear violation of Constitutional rights.

In the dilemma that he dare not remain in his home, or voluntarily leave the area, without incurring criminal penalties, and that the only way he could avoid punishment was to go to an Assembly Center and submit himself to military imprisonment, the petitioner did nothing.

But the facts above recited, show that the exclusion was but a part of an over-all plan for forceable detention. This case cannot, therefore, be decided on any such narrow ground as the possible validity of a Temporary Exclusion Order under which the residents of an area are given an opportunity to leave and go elsewhere in their native land outside the boundaries of a military area. To make the case turn on any such assumption is to shut our eyes to reality.

We cannot shut our eyes to the fact that had the petitioner attempted to violate Proclamation No. 4 and leave the military area in which he lived he would have been arrested and tried and convicted for violation of Proclamation No. 4. The two conflicting orders, one which commanded him to stay and the other which commanded him to go, were nothing but a cleverly devised trap to accomplish the real purpose of the military authority, which was to lock him up in a concentration camp. The only course by which the petitioner could avoid arrest and prosecution was to go to that camp according to instructions to be given him when he reported at a Civil Control Center. We know that is the fact. Why should we set up a figmentary and artificial situation instead of addressing ourselves to the actualities of the case?

Mr. Justice MURPHY, dissenting.

This exclusion of "all persons of Japanese ancestry, both alien and non-alien," from the Pacific Coast area on a plea of military necessity in the absence of martial law ought not to be approved. Such exclusion goes over "the very brink of constitutional power" and falls into the ugly abyss of racism.

No adequate reason is given for the failure to treat these Japanese Americans on an individual basis by holding investigations and hearings to separate the loyal from the disloyal, as was done in the case of persons of German and Italian ancestry. It is asserted merely that the loyalties of this group "were unknown and time was of the essence." Yet nearly four months elapsed after Pearl Harbor before the first exclusion order was issued; nearly eight months went by until the last order was issued; and the last of these 'subversive' persons was not actually removed until almost eleven months had elapsed. Leisure and deliberation seem to have been more of the essence than speed. And the fact that conditions were not such as to warrant a declaration of martial law adds strength to the belief that the factors of time and military necessity were not as urgent as they have been represented to be.

I dissent, therefore, from this legalization of racism. Racial discrimination in any form and in any degree has no justifiable part whatever in our democratic way of life. It is unattractive in any setting but it is utterly revolting among a free people who have embraced the principles set forth in the Constitution of the United States. All residents of this nation are kin in some way by blood or culture to a foreign land. Yet they are primarily and necessarily a part of the new and distinct civilization of the United States. They must accordingly be treated at all times as the heirs of the American experiment and as entitled to all the rights and freedoms guaranteed by the Constitution.

Mr. Justice JACKSON, dissenting.

Korematsu was born on our soil, of parents born in Japan. The Constitution makes him a citizen of the United States by nativity and a citizen of California by residence. No claim is made that he is not loyal to this country. There is no suggestion that apart from the matter involved here he is not law-abiding and well disposed. Korematsu, however, has been convicted of an act not commonly a crime. It consists merely of being present in the state whereof he is a citizen, near the place where he was born, and where all his life he has lived. ...

A citizen's presence in the locality, however, was made a crime only if his parents were of Japanese birth. Had Korematsu been one of four-the others being, say, a German alien enemy, an Italian alien enemy, and a citizen of American-born ancestors, convicted of treason but out on parole—only Korematsu's presence would have violated the order. The difference between their innocence and his crime would result, not from anything he did, said, or thought, different than they, but only in that he was born of different racial stock. ...

My duties as a justice as I see them do not require me to make a military judgment as to whether General DeWitt's evacuation and detention program was a reasonable military necessity. I do not suggest that the courts should have attempted to interfere with the

Army in carrying out its task. But I do not think they may be asked to execute a military expedient that has no place in law under the Constitution. I would reverse the judgment and discharge the prisoner.

Notes and Questions

1. *Were the Japanese slaves?* Is this case better or worse than *Dred Scott?* Are there any parallels between the treatment of slaves before the Civil War and the treatment of Japanese Americans in World War II?
2. *Racism or national security?* Is this case about racism, as the dissent suggests, or about protecting the United States from harm as the majority argues?
3. *What the government did.* Korematsu's later appeal of his conviction, and a statement by the 2011 Acting Solicitor General of the United States, disclosed that the U.S. government had withheld information from the Court, specifically a report that said very few Japanese were a risk to the government and that the dangerous few were already in custody. There was no evidence that the Japanese community was a team of spies. How does that affect your evaluation of the case?
4. *Is* Korematsu *still good law?* The Justices referred to *Korematsu* in a 2018 decision upholding President Trump's decision to bar immigrants from primarily Muslim countries. According to Chief Justice Roberts, the author of the opinion, "Finally, the dissent invokes *Korematsu v. United States,* 323 U.S. 214, 65 S.Ct. 193, 89 L.Ed. 194 (1944). Whatever rhetorical advantage the dissent may see in doing so, *Korematsu* has nothing to do with this case. The forcible relocation of U.S. citizens to concentration camps, solely and explicitly on the basis of race, is objectively unlawful and outside the scope of Presidential authority. But it is wholly inapt to liken that morally repugnant order to a facially neutral policy denying certain foreign nationals the privilege of admission. The entry suspension is an act that is well within executive authority and could have been taken by any other President—the only question is evaluating the actions of this particular President in promulgating an otherwise valid Proclamation. The dissent's reference to *Korematsu,* however, affords this Court the opportunity to make express what is already obvious: *Korematsu* was gravely wrong the day it was decided, has been overruled in the court of history, and—to be clear—'**has no place in law under the Constitution.**' 323 U.S., at 248, 65 S.Ct. 193 (Jackson, J., dissenting)." *Trump v. Hawaii,* 138 S. Ct. 2392, 2423, 201 L. Ed. 2d 775 (2018).

   In contrast, Justice Sotomayor's dissent said, "Today's holding is all the more troubling given the stark parallels between the reasoning of this case and that of *Korematsu v. United States,* 323 U.S. 214, 65 S.Ct. 193, 89 L.Ed. 194 (1944)." What are the parallels? *Trump* at 2447. What do you think of the two Justices' reading of *Korematsu*? Do you agree *Korematsu* was "gravely wrong the day it was decided"? Or was it just a natural part of the law of nations?

5. *What do you learn about the* Korematsu *case from this video explaining its history?* See TED-Ed, Ugly History, Oct. 2, 2019, at https://www.youtube.com/watch?v=q-qlS_J4Mho.
6. *The Integration cases.* You have already read *Plessy v. Ferguson* and learned that the Court ruled separate could be equal in transportation laws. The case also referred to segregated DC schools as evidence that separation was consistent with equality at the time of the passage of the Fourteenth Amendment.

3. *Plessy* Is Replaced with *Brown v. Board of Education*

That conclusion was challenged for years by lawyers in the courts, leading to the famous *Brown v. Board of Education* decision. There were two oral arguments in *Brown*, one in December 1952, and the second in December 1953. Both arguments are available at https://apps.lib.umich.edu/brown-versus-board-education/oralarguments.htm, the first one and the tenth one listed. Justice Thurgood Marshall's oral argument in a related case, and the state's response, are listed second and third. The two Courts had a different Chief Justice: Vinson in 1952 and Warren in 1953. Compare one oral argument to the other. Are they different or the same? How is Chief Justice Warren different from Chief Justice Vinton?

While *Brown* was going through the courts, *Bolling v. Sharpe*, 347 U.S. 497 (1954), was also decided. *Bolling* was from the District of Columbia schools. The District of Columbia is not a state and so is not subject to the Fourteenth Amendment. The Court ruled that DC schools were regulated by the Fifth Amendment, which does not have an Equal Protection Clause. Yet, the Court read an equal protection analysis into the Fifth Amendment. Why did they do that?

You will be reading *Brown I* and *Brown II*. *Brown I* explained why segregation was illegal, and *Brown II* focused on the appropriate remedy to segregation. What do you think of the two cases below?

Brown v. Board of Education of Topeka [Brown I]

SUPREME COURT OF THE UNITED STATES, 1954

347 U.S. 483, 74 S.Ct. 686

Mr. Chief Justice WARREN delivered the opinion of the Court. [The unanimous decision was joined by Justices BLACK, REED, FRANKFURTER, DOUGLAS, JACKSON, BURTON, CLARK and MINTON.]

... In each of the cases, minors of the Negro race, through their legal representatives, seek the aid of the courts in obtaining admission to the public schools of their community on a nonsegregated basis. In each instance, they have been denied admission to schools attended by white children under laws requiring or permitting segregation according to race. This segregation was alleged to deprive the plaintiffs of the equal protection of the laws under the Fourteenth Amendment. In each of the cases other than the Delaware case, a three-judge federal district court denied relief to the plaintiffs on the so-called 'separate but equal' doctrine announced by this Court in Plessy v. Ferguson. Under that doctrine, equality of treatment is accorded when the races are provided substantially equal facilities, even though these facilities be separate. ...

In the first cases in this Court construing the Fourteenth Amendment, decided shortly after its adoption, the Court interpreted it as proscribing all state-imposed discriminations against the Negro race. The doctrine of "separate but equal" did not make its appearance in this court until 1896 in the case of Plessy v. Ferguson, supra, involving not education but transportation. American courts have since labored with the doctrine for over half a century. In this Court, there have been six cases involving the 'separate but equal' doctrine in the field of public education. In Cumming v. Board of Education of Richmond County, 175 U.S. 528, 20 S.Ct. 197, 44 L.Ed. 262, and Gong Lum v. Rice, 275 U.S. 78, 48 S.Ct. 91, 72 L.Ed. 172, the validity of the doctrine itself was not challenged. In more recent cases, all on the graduate school level, inequality was found in that specific benefits enjoyed by white students were denied to Negro students of the same educational qualifications. State of Missouri ex rel. Gaines v. Canada, 305 U.S. 337, 59 S.Ct. 232, 83 L.Ed. 208; Sipuel v. Board of Regents of University of Oklahoma, 332 U.S. 631, 68 S.Ct. 299, 92 L.Ed. 247; Sweatt v. Painter, 339 U.S. 629, 70 s.Ct. 848, 94 L.Ed. 1114; McLaurin v. Oklahoma State Regents, 339 U.S. 637, 70 S.Ct. 851, 94 L.Ed. 1149. In none of these cases was it necessary to re-examine the doctrine to grant relief to the Negro plaintiff. And in Sweatt v. Painter, supra, the Court expressly reserved decision on the question whether Plessy v. Ferguson should be held inapplicable to public education.

In the instant cases, that question is directly presented. Here, unlike Sweatt v. Painter, there are findings below that the Negro and white schools involved have been equalized, or are being equalized, with respect to buildings, curricula, qualifications and salaries of teachers, and other 'tangible' factors. Our decision, therefore, cannot turn on merely a comparison of these tangible factors in the Negro and white schools involved in each of the cases. We must look instead to the effect of segregation itself on public education. ...

We come then to the question presented: Does segregation of children in public schools solely on the basis of race, even though the physical facilities and other 'tangible' factors may be equal, deprive the children of the minority group of equal educational opportunities? We believe that it does. ...

We conclude that in the field of public education the doctrine of 'separate but equal' has no place. Separate educational facilities are inherently unequal. Therefore, we hold that the plaintiffs and others similarly situated for whom the actions have been brought are, by reason of the segregation complained of, deprived of the equal protection of the laws guaranteed by the Fourteenth Amendment. This disposition makes unnecessary any discussion whether such segregation also violates the Due Process Clause of the Fourteenth Amendment. ...

In order that we may have the full assistance of the parties in formulating decrees, the cases will be restored to the docket, and the parties are requested to present further argument. ...

Notes and Questions

1. *The Vote.* Why was this decision unanimous?
2. *When to overrule?* What is the Court's reasoning to overrule *Plessy v. Ferguson*?
3. *The pre-*Brown *cases.* Paragraph two of the opinion cites some of the pre-*Brown* race cases. In *Gaines,* Missouri did not have a Black law school and refused admission to a Black student who applied to the segregated University of Missouri law school. The Court ruled this violated equal protection. *State of Missouri ex rel. Gaines v. Canada*, 305 U.S. 33 (1938). In the Oklahoma case, the Court ruled a Black student was denied equal protection when she was not admitted to the state's only law school, which was at the University of Oklahoma. *Sipuel v. Board of Regents of University of Oklahoma*, 332 U.S. 631 (1948). In *Sweatt v. Painter*, 339 U.S. 629 (1950), the Court ruled that Texas had to admit Sweatt to the University of Texas law school and not to its new separate law school for Blacks. On the same day, the Court ruled that Oklahoma could not deny admission of a Black student to the University of Oklahoma's education department. *McLaurin v. Oklahoma State Regents*, 339 U.S. 637 (1968). How do you think these cases prepared the way for *Brown*? Why did the Plaintiffs win those cases?

   In *Gong Lum v. Rice*, the Court ruled that a student of Chinese descent was colored, and therefore could not attend white schools according to *Plessy v. Ferguson*. Since the student was of "the Mongolian or yellow race," she could not be considered white. Is this case another lesson about separate but equal?

4. *The dolls tests.* In the 1940s, Doctors Kenneth and Mamie Clark used different-colored dolls to test children's perceptions of race. Because a majority of students preferred the White dolls, the Clarks concluded that "'prejudice, discrimination, and segregation' created a feeling of inferiority among African-American children and damaged their self-esteem." See NAACP LDF, A Revealing Experiment: *Brown v. Board* and "The Dolls Test," at https://www.naacpldf.org/ldf-celebrates-60th-anniversary-brown-v-board-education/significance-doll-test/#. The Court cited the dolls studies in their opinion. What does the dolls test tell you about the effects of segregation?

5. *Your version.* If you were writing a *Brown v. Board* opinion today, how would you explain the right that is identified?
6. *Video.* What does this video, *Harvard University, Brown v. Board of Education* Explained, May 17, 2021, at https://www.youtube.com/watch?v=FwxprgouAYU, tell you about the case?

4. *Brown II*

Brown v. Board of Education of Topeka [Brown II]
SUPREME COURT OF THE UNITED STATES, 1955
349 U.S. 294, 75 S.Ct. 753

Mr. Chief Justice WARREN delivered the opinion of the Court. [The unanimous decision was joined by Justices BLACK, REED, FRANKFURTER, DOUGLAS, BURTON, CLARK, MINTON and HARLAN.]

These cases were decided on May 17, 1954. The opinions of that date, declaring the fundamental principle that racial discrimination in public education is unconstitutional, are incorporated herein by reference. All provisions of federal, state, or local law requiring or permitting such discrimination must yield to this principle. There remains for consideration the manner in which relief is to be accorded. …

Full implementation of these constitutional principles may require solution of varied local school problems. School authorities have the primary responsibility for elucidating, assessing, and solving these problems; courts will have to consider whether the action of school authorities constitutes good faith implementation of the governing constitutional principles. Because of their proximity to local conditions and the possible need for further hearings, the courts which originally heard these cases can best perform this judicial appraisal. Accordingly, we believe it appropriate to remand the cases to those courts.

In fashioning and effectuating the decrees, the courts will be guided by equitable principles. Traditionally, equity has been characterized by a practical flexibility in shaping its remedies and by a facility for adjusting and reconciling public and private needs. These cases call for the exercise of these traditional attributes of equity power. At stake is the personal interest of the plaintiffs in admission to public schools as soon as practicable on a nondiscriminatory basis. To effectuate this interest may call for elimination of a variety of obstacles in making the transition to school systems operated in accordance with the constitutional principles set forth in our May 17, 1954, decision. Courts of equity may properly take into account the public interest in the elimination of such obstacles in a systematic and effective manner. But it should go without saying that the vitality of these constitutional principles cannot be allowed to yield simply because of disagreement with them.

While giving weight to these public and private considerations, the courts will require that the defendants make a prompt and reasonable start toward full compliance with our May 17, 1954, ruling. Once such a start has been made, the courts may find that additional time is necessary to carry out the ruling in an effective manner. The burden rests upon the defendants to establish that such time is necessary in the public interest and is consistent with good faith compliance at the earliest practicable date. To that end, the courts may consider problems related to administration, arising from the physical condition of the school plant, the school transportation system, personnel, revision of school districts and attendance areas into compact units to achieve a system of determining admission to the public schools on a nonracial basis, and revision of local laws and regulations which may be necessary in solving the foregoing problems. They will also consider the adequacy of any plans the defendants may propose to meet these problems and to effectuate a transition to a racially nondiscriminatory school system. During this period of transition, the courts will retain jurisdiction of these cases.

The judgments below, except that in the Delaware case, are accordingly reversed and the cases are remanded to the District Courts to take such proceedings and enter such orders and decrees consistent with this opinion as are necessary and proper to admit to public schools on a racially nondiscriminatory basis with all deliberate speed the parties to these cases. …

Notes and Questions

1. *How fast?* What does "with all deliberate speed" mean? What was causing the delay in implementation of the *Brown* holding in school districts?
2. *Opposition to the* Brown *opinions.* Can you tell from this opinion how judges are to assess what is happening in the schools? In *Cooper v. Aaron*, 358 U.S. 1 (1958), Arkansas asked the Court to stop integration in the Little Rock schools. The Court refused the state's request, citing *Marbury v. Madison* and stating "the federal judiciary is supreme in the exposition of the law of the Constitution." The Court insisted that the states could not nullify *Brown*. Nonetheless, the states kept trying. In *Goss v. Board of Education*, 373 U.S. 683 (1963), the Court ruled that students were not allowed to transfer from a school where they were a racial minority to one where they were a racial majority. In *Griffin v. County School Bd.*, 377 U.S. 218 (1964), the Court ruled it was illegal to close the schools instead of integrating them. In *Green v. County School Board*, 291 U.S. 430 (1968), the Court ruled that a "freedom of choice" plan was unconstitutional because it undermined the integration of the schools.

   We will see in later sections that the Court has repeatedly argued over what *Brown* protects. What do you read it as protecting?

3. *What did* Brown *protect?* Does Brown identify a right to education or quality education? Or a right to the same education regardless of race? In *Island Trees School District v. Pico*, 457 U.S. 853 (1982), the Court nodded toward a potential right to education in a First Amendment case addressing whether books could be removed from libraries due to their content. How does that square with the right identified in *Brown I*?
4. Brown *eventually applied beyond the school context, e.g., segregated public pools.* In *Gilmore v. City of Montgomery, Ala.*, 417 U.S. 556 (1974) the Court ruled that the government could not give exclusive control of its athletic facilities, like swimming pools, to all-White private schools because it created segregated conclaves that deprived Blacks of equal access to recreational facilities. Are there any public facilities that should not be integrated?
5. *Seeing patterns in the cases.* Remember the Commerce Clause of Article I, Section 8, and all the time we spent studying it? Remember how the Court started with *Gibson*, then cut back on the Commerce Clause's coverage, then expanded it, and then cut back again. That is often how the Court works!

5. The Civil Rights Act and Racial Equality

Yet, in the following case from 1964, the Court ruled that Congress correctly relied on the commerce power to pass the Civil Rights Act of 1964. What does civil rights have to do with commerce? You see in the concurrence a suggestion that Section 5 of the 14th Amendment would have been a better source of congressional power for this legislation. Why did the Justices think that? What is the difference between the Commerce Clause power and Section 5 power? How should each of them be used? Do you think today's Supreme Court would still say the Civil Rights Act was correctly based on Congress's commerce power?

When should the Civil Rights Act be used today? How can someone win a civil rights suit?

Consider the oral argument in this case, available at https://www.oyez.org/cases/1964/515. What do you learn about commerce and Congress's powers in this argument? Which lawyer or Justice does the best job of explaining what is at stake in this case?

Heart of Atlanta Motel, Inc. v. United States

SUPREME COURT OF THE UNITED STATES, 1964

379 U.S. 241, 85 S.Ct. 348

Mr. Justice CLARK delivered the opinion of the Court.

This is a declaratory judgment action, 28 U.S.C. s 2201 and s 2202 (1958 ed.) attacking the constitutionality of Title II of the Civil Rights Act of 1964, 78 Stat. 241, 241. ... Prior to passage of the Act the motel had followed a practice of refusing to rent rooms to Negroes, and it alleged that it intended to continue to do so. In an effort to perpetuate that policy this suit was filed.

The appellant contends that Congress in passing this Act exceeded its power to regulate commerce under Art. I, s 8, cl. 3, of the Constitution of the United States. ...

This Title is divided into seven sections beginning with s 201(a) which provides that:

> 'All persons shall be entitled to the full and equal enjoyment of the goods, services, facilities, privileges, advantages, and accommodations of any place of public accommodation, as defined in this section, without discrimination or segregation on the ground of race, color, religion, or national origin.' ...

It is admitted that the operation of the motel brings it within the provisions of s 201(a) of the Act and that appellant refused to provide lodging for transient Negroes because of their race or color and that it intends to continue that policy unless restrained.

The sole question posed is, therefore, the constitutionality of the Civil Rights Act of 1964 as applied to these facts. The legislative history of the Act indicates that Congress based the Act on s 5 and the Equal Protection Clause of the Fourteenth Amendment as well as its power to regulate interstate commerce under Art. I, s 8, cl. 3, of the Constitution. ...

While the Act as adopted carried no congressional findings the record of its passage through each house is replete with evidence of the burdens that discrimination by race or color places upon interstate commerce. This testimony included the fact that our people have become increasingly mobile with millions of people of all races traveling from State to State; that Negroes in particular have been the subject of discrimination in transient accommodations, having to travel great distances ot secure the same; that often they have been unable to obtain accommodations and have had to call upon friends to put them up overnight; and that these conditions had become so acute as to require the listing of available lodging for Negroes in a special guidebook which was itself 'dramatic testimony to the difficulties' Negroes encounter in travel. These exclusionary practices were found to be nationwide, the Under Secretary of Commerce testifying that there is 'no question that this discrimination in the North still exists to a large degree' and in the West and Midwest as well. This testimony indicated a qualitative as well as quantitative effect on interstate travel by Negroes. The former was the obvious impairment of the Negro traveler's pleasure and convenience that resulted when he continually was uncertain of finding lodging. As for the latter, there was evidence that this uncertainty stemming from racial discrimination had the effect of discouraging travel on the part of a substantial portion of the Negro community. This was the conclusion not only of the Under Secretary of Commerce but also of the Administrator of the Federal Aviation Agency who wrote the Chairman of the Senate Commerce Committee that it was his 'belief that air commerce is adversely affected by the denial to a substantial segment of the traveling public of adequate and desegregated public accommodations.' We shall not burden this opinion with further details since the voluminous testimony presents overwhelming evidence that discrimination by hotels and motels impedes interstate travel. ...

In short, the determinative test of the exercise of power by the Congress under the Commerce Clause is simply whether the activity sought to be regulated is 'commerce which concerns more States than one' and has a real and substantial relation to the national interest. ...

Thus the power of Congress to promote interstate commerce also includes the power to regulate the local incidents thereof, including local activities in both the States of origin and destination, which might have a substantial and harmful effect upon that commerce. One need only examine the evidence which we have discussed above to see that Congress may—as it has—prohibit racial discrimination by motels serving travelers, however 'local' their operations may appear.

Nor does the Act deprive appellant of liberty or property under the Fifth Amendment. The commerce power invoked here by the Congress is a specific and plenary one authorized by the Constitution itself. The only questions are: (1) whether Congress had a rational basis for finding that racial discrimination by motels affected commerce, and (2) if it had such a basis, whether the means it selected to eliminate that evil are reasonable and appropriate. If they are, appellant has no 'right' to select its guests as it sees fit, free from governmental regulation. ...

We, therefore, conclude that the action of the Congress in the adoption of the Act as applied here to a motel which concededly serves interstate travelers is within the power granted it by the Commerce Clause of the Constitution, as interpreted by this Court for 140 years. It may be argued that Congress could have pursued other methods to eliminate the obstructions it found in interstate commerce caused by racial discrimination. But this is a matter of policy that rests entirely with the Congress not with the courts. How obstructions in commerce may be removed—what means are to be employed—is within the sound and exclusive discretion of the Congress. It is subject only to one caveat—that the means chosen by it must be reasonably adapted to the end permitted by the Constitution. We cannot say that its choice here was not so adapted. The Constitution requires no more.

Mr. Justice BLACK, concurring.

In the first of these two cases the Heart of Atlanta Motel, a large motel in downtown Atlanta, Georgia, appeals from an order of a three-judge United States District Court for the Northern District of Georgia enjoining it from continuing to violate Title II of the Civil Rights Act of 1964 by refusing to accept Negroes as lodgers solely because of their race. In the second case the Acting Attorney General of the United States and a United States Attorney appeal from a judgment of a three-judge United States District Court for the Northern District of Alabama holding that Title II cannot constitutionally be applied to Ollie's Barbecue, a restaurant in Birmingham, Alabama, which serves few if any interstate travelers but which buys a substantial quantity of food which has moved in interstate commerce. It is undisputed that both establishments had and intended to continue a policy against serving Negroes. Both claimed that Congress had exceeded its constitutional powers in attempting to compel them to use their privately owned businesses to serve customers whom they did not want to serve. ...

It requires no novel or strained interpretation of the Commerce Clause to sustain Title II as applied in either of these cases. ...

The Heart of Atlanta Motel is a large 216-room establishment strategically located in relation to Atlanta and interstate travelers. It advertises extensively by signs along interstate highways and in various advertising media. As a result of these circumstances approximately 75% of the motel guests are transient interstate travelers. It is thus an important facility for use by interstate travelers who travel on highways, since travelers in their own cars must find lodging places to make their journeys comfortably and safely.

The restaurant is located in a residential and industrial section of Birmingham, 11 blocks from the nearest interstate highway. Almost all, if not all, its patrons are local people rather than transients. It has seats for about 200 customers and annual gross sales of about $350,000. Most of its sales are of barbecued meat sandwiches and pies. Consequently, the main commodity it purchases is meat, of which during the 12 months before the District Court hearing it bought $69,683 worth (representing 46% of its total expenditures for supplies), which had been shipped into Alabama from outside the State. Plainly, 46% of the goods it sells is a 'substantial' portion and amount. Congress concluded that restaurants which purchase a substantial quantity of goods from other States might well burden and disrupt the flow of interstate commerce if allowed to practice racial discrimination, because of the stifling and distorting effect that such discrimination on a wide scale might well have on the sale of goods shipped across state lines. Certainly this belief would not be irrational even had there not been a large body of evidence before the Congress to show the probability of this adverse effect.

The foregoing facts are more than enough, in my judgment, to show that Congress acting within its discretion and judgment has power under the Commerce Clause and the Necessary and Proper Clause to bar racial discrimination in the Heart of Atlanta Motel and Ollie's Barbecue. ...

Mr. Justice DOUGLAS, concurring.

Though I join the Court's opinions, I am somewhat reluctant here, as I was in Edwards v. People of State of California, 314 U.S. 160, 177, 62 S.Ct. 164, 168, 86 L.Ed. 119 to rest solely on the Commerce Clause. My reluctance is not due to any conviction that Congress lacks power to regulate commerce in the interests of human rights. It is rather my belief that the right of people to be free of state action that discriminates against them because of race, like the 'right of persons to move freely from State to State' (Edwards v. People of State of California, supra, at 177, 62 S.Ct. at 169), 'occupies a more protected position in our constitutional system than does the movement of cattle, fruit, steel and coal across state lines.' Ibid. Moreover, when we come to the problem of abatement in Hamm v. City of Rock Hill, 379 U.S. 306, 85 S.Ct. 384, decided this day, the result reached by the Court is for me much more obvious as a protective measure under the Fourteenth Amendment than under the Commerce Clause. For the former deals with the constitutional status of the individual not with the impact on commerce of local activities or vice versa.

Hence I would prefer to rest on the assertion of legislative power contained in s 5 of the Fourteenth Amendment which states: 'The Congress shall have power to enforce, by appropriate legislation, the provisions of this article'—a power which the Court concedes was exercised at least in part in this Act. ...

Notes and Questions

1. *Which constitutional text?* By now you have read a lot about the Commerce Clause and the Fourteenth Amendment. What is the difference between those two parts of the Constitution? What is Congress's power under each of those constitutional sections? Which is a bigger source of power for Congress, commerce or the Fourteenth Amendment's § 5? How important is the Court's description of Congress's power under these sources? What do you learn about *Heart of Atlanta* in this video about it, Quimbee, *Heart of Atlanta Motel, Inc. v. United States* Case Brief Summary, Jan. 22, 2018, at https://www.youtube.com/watch?v=EsktEwEOII8&list=PLsFE_Nvl6h_Y75KGR5pkGqcFisGvBnO9S&index=50&t=7s?
2. *Edwards.* Justice Douglas referred to *Edwards v. California*, in which the Court ruled that Edwards could not be convicted of bringing an indigent person into California. Justice Douglas concurred, arguing that he would "express no view" on the Commerce power but did want to emphasize that the "right of persons to move freely from state to state" was fundamental and should be acknowledged by the Court. Why does he think there, and here, that there is more protection under the Fourteenth Amendment than under the Commerce Clause? Why did he assert § 5 of the Fourteenth Amendment as preferable to the Commerce Clause? Do you agree with Douglas?

6. Interracial Marriage

We've discussed the role of race and racial discrimination in transportation, warfare, schooling, and the Civil Rights Act. The following case extends the line of racial discrimination cases to interracial marriage.

In 1967, the Court assessed the constitutionality of a state statute that banned interracial marriage and ruled that the state statute violated the Fourteenth Amendment. Do you think this case is a precedent that would also rule same-sex marriage bans unconstitutional? Would same-sex marriage be protected by the Fourteenth Amendment? Why or why not? As you read, take note of the specific details of the Virginia statute that made the law unconstitutional.

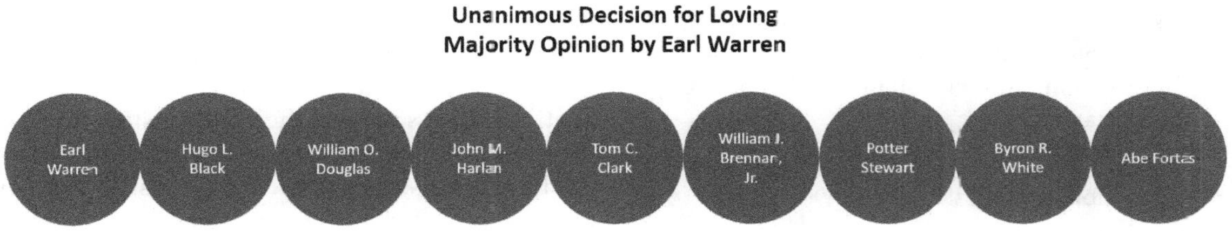

FIGURE 7.1 Loving et ux. V. Virginia, 388 US 1 (1967)

Can you tell from the oral argument, available at https://www.oyez.org/cases/1966/395, that the decision would be unanimous? Does the oral argument tell you anything about the difference between two parts of the Fourteenth Amendment, the Equal Protection Clause and the Due Process Clause, or which one provides a better fit for the right to marry? How are these two parts of the Fourteenth Amendment different from one another, and how are they similar?

Loving v. Virginia
SUPREME COURT OF THE UNITED STATES, 1967
388 U.S. 1, 87 S.Ct. 1817

Mr. Chief Justice WARREN delivered the opinion of the Court [with Justices BLACK, DOUGLAS, HARLAN, CLARK, BRENNAN, STEWART, WHITE, and FORTAS].

This case presents a constitutional question never addressed by this Court: whether a statutory scheme adopted by the State of Virginia to prevent marriages between persons solely on the basis of racial classifications violates the Equal Protection and Due Process Clauses of the Fourteenth Amendment. For reasons which seem to us to reflect the central meaning of those constitutional commands, we conclude that these statutes cannot stand consistently with the Fourteenth Amendment.

In June 1958, two residents of Virginia, Mildred Jeter, a Negro woman, and Richard Loving, a white man, were married in the District of Columbia pursuant to its laws. Shortly after their marriage, the Lovings returned to Virginia and established their marital abode in Caroline County. At the October Term, 1958, of the Circuit Court of Caroline County, a grand jury issued an indictment charging the Lovings with violating Virginia's ban on interracial marriages. On January 6, 1959, the Lovings pleaded guilty to the charge and were sentenced to one year in jail; however, the trial judge suspended the sentence for a period of 25 years on the condition that the Lovings leave the State and not return to Virginia together for 25 years. He stated in an opinion that:

> 'Almighty God created the races white, black, yellow, malay and red, and he placed them on separate continents. And but for the interference with his arrangement there would be no cause for such marriages. The fact that he separated the races shows that he did not intend for the races to mix.'

After their convictions, the Lovings took up residence in the District of Columbia. …

The two statutes under which appellants were convicted and sentenced are part of a comprehensive statutory scheme aimed at prohibiting and punishing interracial marriages. The Lovings were convicted of violating s 20—58 of the Virginia Code:

> 'Leaving State to evade law.—If any white person and colored person shall go out of this State, for the purpose of being married,

> and with the intention of returning, and be married out of it, and afterwards return to and reside in it, cohabiting as man and wife, they shall be punished as provided in s 20—59, and the marriage shall be governed by the same law as if it had been solemnized in this State. The fact of their cohabitation here as man and wife shall be evidence of their marriage.'

Section 20—59, which defines the penalty for miscegenation, provides:

> 'Punishment for marriage.—If any white person intermarry with a colored person, or any colored person intermarry with a white person, he shall be guilty of a felony and shall be punished by confinement in the penitentiary for not less than one nor more than five years.' ...

There can be no question but that Virginia's miscegenation statutes rest solely upon distinctions drawn according to race. The statutes proscribe generally accepted conduct if engaged in by members of different races. Over the years, this Court has consistently repudiated '(d)istinctions between citizens solely because of their ancestry' as being 'odious to a free people whose institutions are founded upon the doctrine of equality.' At the very least, the Equal Protection Clause demands that racial classifications, especially suspect in criminal statutes, be subjected to the 'most rigid scrutiny,' Korematsu v. United States, 323 U.S. 214, 216, 65 S.Ct. 193, 194, 89 L.Ed. 194 (1944), and, if they are ever to be upheld, they must be shown to be necessary to the accomplishment of some permissible state objective, independent of the racial discrimination which it was the object of the Fourteenth Amendment to eliminate. Indeed, two members of this Court have already stated that they 'cannot conceive of a valid legislative purpose * * * which makes the color of a person's skin the test of whether his conduct is a criminal offense.'

There is patently no legitimate overriding purpose independent of invidious racial discrimination which justifies this classification. The fact that Virginia prohibits only interracial marriages involving white persons demonstrates that the racial classifications must stand on their own justification, as measures designed to maintain White Supremacy. We have consistently denied the constitutionality of measures which restrict the rights of citizens on account of race. There can be no doubt that restricting the freedom to marry solely because of racial classifications violates the central meaning of the Equal Protection Clause.

These statutes also deprive the Lovings of liberty without due process of law in violation of the Due Process Clause of the Fourteenth Amendment. The freedom to marry has long been recognized as one of the vital personal rights essential to the orderly pursuit of happiness by free men.

Marriage is one of the 'basic civil rights of man,' fundamental to our very existence and survival. To deny this fundamental freedom on so unsupportable a basis as the racial classifications embodied in these statutes, classifications so directly subversive of the principle of equality at the heart of the Fourteenth Amendment, is surely to deprive all the State's citizens of liberty without due process of law. The Fourteenth Amendment requires that the freedom of choice to marry not be restricted by invidious racial discriminations. Under our Constitution, the freedom to marry or not marry, a person of another race resides with the individual and cannot be infringed by the State.

These convictions must be reversed. It is so ordered.

Notes and Questions

1. *Who is supreme?* Why does the decision talk about White supremacy? Was White supremacy involved in this marriage statute? Why? Exactly which marriages did the statute prohibit?
2. *What did God say about it?* Why did the trial judge talk about Almighty God and God's creation? What role does God play in the Constitution and in constitutional law?
3. *EP or DP?* What does the Equal Protection Clause say about the marriage law? What does the Due Process Clause say about it? Are there any similarities between the two arguments? Any differences?

4. *Video.* What do you learn about *Loving* from History, How *Loving v. Virginia* Led to Legalized Interracial Marriage, Feb. 27, 2018, at https://www.youtube.com/watch?v=q-qlS_J4Mho?
5. *Level of scrutiny. Loving* and other racial discrimination cases are remembered for applying the strictest scrutiny against the government as the Court did in *Korematsu.* What effect does that level of scrutiny have on the outcome of the cases? In *Hobby Lobby v. Burwell,* 573 U.S. 682 (2014), Justice Alito wrote that when the government faces a religious claimant under the Religious Freedom Restoration Act, the government must have a compelling state interest *and* use the least restrictive means of furthering that interest. Is that the same test that was used in *Korematsu* and *Loving?*

7. Affirmative Action

One question that has received continued attention from the courts is affirmative action. Affirmative action programs are set up to help disadvantaged groups that have suffered discrimination in the past. But lawyers and judges disagree about the constitutionality of affirmative action. If the Constitution is color-blind, does that mean that people of all races must be treated exactly alike? Or does equal protection require that those who are racially discriminated against should be made equal by according them affirmative action? Should people of color get affirmative action? Should women get affirmative action? Should LGBTQs get affirmative action? In other words, what is the baseline for equality?

Many legal challenges to affirmative action arose because of the Court's treatment of race in a variety of cases. Should all racial classifications get the strictest scrutiny? Or should there be different levels of scrutiny, strict for discriminatory ones but less strict for benign ones like affirmative action? How do you think *Brown* would answer that question?

In *Richmond v. J.A. Croson Co.,* 468 U.S. 469 (1980), the Court ruled 6–3, in an opinion by Justice O'Connor, that there should be a strict scrutiny standard for all racial classifications. Justice Thurgood Marshall was one of the dissenters. A year later, however, in *Metro Broadcasting, Inc. v. Federal Communications Commission,* 497 U.S. 547 (1990), Marshall was in the majority and O'Connor in the dissent, ruling that the *federal* FCC's minority policies were constitutional.

Metro Broadcasting was then overruled by *Adarand Constructors, Inc. v. Peña,* 515 U.S. 200 (1995), in a 5–4 opinion by Justice O'Connor. O'Connor was joined by Justice Clarence Thomas, who was Marshall's replacement on the Court. The Court held that all racial classifications, whether imposed by federal, state, or local authorities, must be judged by a strict scrutiny test. In other words, they must meet a compelling interest and be narrowly tailored to that interest, including laws intended to remedy racial discrimination.

In contrast, as he states in a dissent below, Justice Stevens "long adhered to the view that a decision to exclude a member of a minority because of his race is fundamentally different from a decision to include a member of a minority for that reason. See, e.g., *Adarand Constructors, Inc. v. Peña,* 515 U.S. 200, 243, 248, n. 6, 115 S.Ct. 2097, 132 L.Ed.2d 158 (1995) (STEVENS, J., dissenting); *Wygant v. Jackson Bd. of Ed.,* 476 U.S. 267, 316, 106 S.Ct. 1842, 90 L.Ed.2d 260 (1986) (same)."

In 2003, the Court released two opinions about affirmative action on the same day. One case, *Grutter,* involved the University of Michigan's law school, and a second, *Gratz,* involved its undergraduate program. The Court upheld the law school program but invalidated the undergraduate program. As you read these two opinions, ask yourself exactly how the programs worked. What was the difference between the law school program and the undergraduate program? Can you make sense of the Justices' two votes in the following two cases? What did the Justices disagree about? What do the Justices say about the *Bakke* case, an earlier affirmative action case that was 25 years old when these cases were decided? How does *Bakke* affect the outcome in *Grutter* and *Gratz*? What do you learn about *Bakke* in the Court's two decisions?

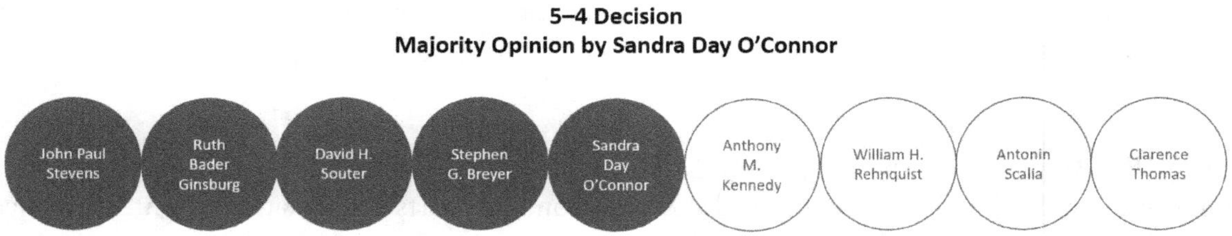

FIGURE 7.2 Grutter v. Bollinger, 539 US 306 (2003)

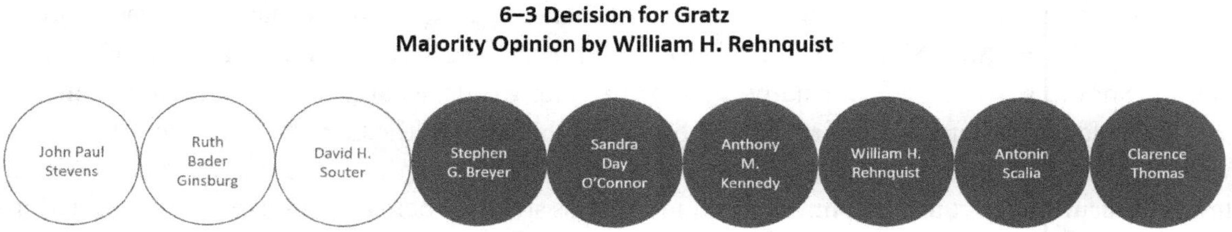

FIGURE 7.3 Gratz v. Bollinger, 539 US 244 (2003)

As you read the oral arguments in the two cases, ask yourself which lawyer does the best job defending their case. Can you tell what the Justices think about affirmative action from their questions? Is the tone or style of one oral argument different from the other? *Grutter* is available at https://www.oyez.org/cases/2002/02-241 and *Gratz* at https://www.oyez.org/cases/2002/02-516. What are the petitioners' injuries in these cases? Do their lawyers explain the injuries?

Grutter v. Bollinger

SUPREME COURT OF THE UNITED STATES, 2003

539 U.S. 306, 123 S.Ct. 2325

O'CONNOR, J., delivered the opinion of the Court, in which STEVENS, SOUTER, GINSBURG, and BREYER, JJ., joined, and in which SCALIA and THOMAS, JJ., joined in part insofar as it is consistent with the views expressed in Part VII of the opinion of THOMAS, J. GINSBURG, J., filed a concurring opinion, in which BREYER, J., joined. SCALIA, J., filed an opinion concurring in part and dissenting in part, in which THOMAS, J., joined. THOMAS, J., filed an opinion concurring in part and dissenting in part, in which SCALIA, J., joined as to Parts I–VII. REHNQUIST, C.J., filed a dissenting opinion, in which SCALIA, KENNEDY, and THOMAS, JJ., joined. KENNEDY, J., filed a dissenting opinion.

This case requires us to decide whether the use of race as a factor in student admissions by the University of Michigan Law School (Law School) is unlawful.

IA

The Law School ranks among the Nation's top law schools. It receives more than 3,500 applications each year for a class of around 350 students. Seeking to "admit a group of students who individually and collectively are among the most capable," the Law School looks for individuals with "substantial promise for success in law school" and "a strong likelihood of succeeding in the practice of law and contributing in diverse ways to the well-being of others." More broadly, the Law School seeks "a mix of students with varying backgrounds and experiences who will respect and learn from each other." In 1992, the dean of the Law School charged a faculty committee with crafting a written admissions policy to implement these goals. In particular, the Law School sought to ensure that its efforts to achieve student body diversity complied with this Court's most recent ruling on the use of race in university admissions. See *Regents of Univ. of Cal. v. Bakke,* 438 U.S. 265, 98 S.Ct. 2733, 57 L.Ed.2d 750 (1978). Upon the unanimous adoption of the committee's report by the Law School faculty, it became the Law School's official admissions policy. ...

The policy stresses that "no applicant should be admitted unless we expect that applicant to do well enough to graduate with no serious academic problems."

The policy makes clear, however, that even the highest possible score does not guarantee admission to the Law School. Nor does a low score automatically disqualify an applicant. Rather, the policy requires admissions officials to look beyond grades and test scores to other criteria that are important to the Law School's educational objectives. So-called "'soft' variables" such as "the enthusiasm of recommenders, the quality of the undergraduate institution, the quality of the applicant's essay, and the areas and difficulty of undergraduate course selection" are all brought to bear in assessing an "applicant's likely contributions to the intellectual and social life of the institution."

The policy aspires to "achieve that diversity which has the potential to enrich everyone's education and thus make a law school class stronger than the sum of its parts." The policy does not restrict the types of diversity contributions eligible for "substantial weight" in the admissions process, but instead recognizes "many possible bases for diversity admissions." The policy does, however, reaffirm the Law School's longstanding commitment to "one particular type of diversity," that is, "racial and ethnic diversity with special reference to the inclusion of students from groups which have been historically discriminated against, like African-Americans, Hispanics and Native Americans, who without this commitment might not be represented in our student body in meaningful numbers." By enrolling a "'critical mass' of [underrepresented] minority students," the Law School seeks to "ensur[e] their ability to make unique contributions to the character of the Law School." ...

IIA

We last addressed the use of race in public higher education over 25 years ago. In the landmark *Bakke* case, we reviewed a racial set-aside program that reserved 16 out of 100 seats in a medical school class for members of certain minority groups. The decision produced six separate opinions, none of which commanded a majority of the Court. Four Justices would have upheld the program against all attack on the ground that the government can use race to "remedy disadvantages cast on minorities by past racial prejudice." *Id.,* at 325, 98 S.Ct. 2733 (joint opinion of Brennan, White, Marshall, and Blackmun, JJ., concurring in judgment in part and dissenting in part). Four other Justices avoided the constitutional question altogether and struck down the program on statutory grounds. *Id.,* at 408, 98 S.Ct. 2733 (opinion of STEVENS, J., joined by Burger, C. J., and Stewart and REHNQUIST, JJ., concurring in judgment in part and dissenting in part). Justice Powell provided a fifth vote not only for invalidating the set-aside program, but also for reversing the state court's injunction against any use of race whatsoever. The only holding for the Court in *Bakke* was that a "State has a substantial interest that legitimately may be served by a properly devised admissions program involving the competitive consideration of race and ethnic origin." Thus, we reversed that part of the lower court's judgment that enjoined the university "from any consideration of the race of any applicant."

Since this Court's splintered decision in *Bakke,* Justice Powell's opinion announcing the judgment of the Court has served as the touchstone for constitutional analysis of race-conscious admissions policies. Public and private universities across the Nation have modeled their own admissions programs on Justice Powell's views on permissible race-conscious policies. We therefore discuss Justice Powell's opinion in some detail. ...

Justice Powell approved the university's use of race to further only one interest: "the attainment of a diverse student body." With the important proviso that "constitutional limitations protecting individual rights may not be disregarded," Justice Powell grounded his analysis in the academic freedom that "long has been viewed as a special concern of the First Amendment." Justice Powell emphasized that nothing less than the "'nation's future depends upon leaders trained through wide exposure' to the ideas and mores of students as diverse as this Nation of many peoples." In seeking the "right to select those students who will contribute the most to the 'robust exchange of ideas,'" a university seeks "to achieve a goal that is of paramount importance in the fulfillment of its mission. Both "tradition and experience lend support to the view that the contribution of diversity is substantial."

Justice Powell was, however, careful to emphasize that in his view race "is only one element in a range of factors a university properly may consider in attaining the goal of a heterogeneous student body." For Justice Powell, "[i]t is not an interest in simple ethnic diversity, in which a specified percentage of the student body is in effect guaranteed to be members of selected ethnic groups," that can justify the use of race. Rather, "[t]he diversity that furthers a compelling state interest encompasses a far broader array of qualifications and characteristics of which racial or ethnic origin is but a single though important element."

... today we endorse Justice Powell's view that student body diversity is a compelling state interest that can justify the use of race in university admissions. ...

IIIB

... To be narrowly tailored, a race-conscious admissions program cannot use a quota system—it cannot "insulat[e] each category of applicants with certain desired qualifications from competition with all other applicants." Instead, a university may consider race or ethnicity only as a "'plus' in a particular applicant's file," without "insulat[ing] the individual from comparison with all other candidates for the available seats." In other words, an admissions program must be "flexible enough to consider all pertinent elements of diversity in light of the particular qualifications of each applicant, and to place them on the same footing for consideration, although not necessarily according them the same weight."

We find that the Law School's admissions program bears the hallmarks of a narrowly tailored plan. As Justice Powell made clear in *Bakke,* truly individualized consideration demands that race be used in a flexible, nonmechanical way. It follows from this mandate that universities cannot establish quotas for members of certain racial groups or put members of those groups on separate admissions tracks. Nor can universities insulate applicants who belong to certain racial or ethnic groups from the competition for admission. Universities can, however, consider race or ethnicity more flexibly as a "plus" factor in the context of individualized consideration of each and every applicant.

We are satisfied that the Law School's admissions program, like the Harvard plan described by Justice Powell, does not operate as a quota. Properly understood, a "quota" is a program in which a certain fixed number or proportion of opportunities are "reserved exclusively for certain minority groups." ...

The Law School's goal of attaining a critical mass of underrepresented minority students does not transform its program into a quota. ...

We also find that, like the Harvard plan Justice Powell referenced in *Bakke,* the Law School's race-conscious admissions program adequately ensures that all factors that may contribute to student body diversity are meaningfully considered alongside race in admissions decisions. With respect to the use of race itself, all underrepresented minority students admitted by the Law School have been deemed qualified. By virtue of our Nation's struggle with racial inequality, such students are both likely to have experiences of particular importance to the Law School's mission, and less likely to be admitted in meaningful numbers on criteria that ignore those experiences. ...

Petitioner and the United States argue that the Law School's plan is not narrowly tailored because race-neutral means exist to obtain the educational benefits of student body diversity that the Law School seeks. We disagree. Narrow tailoring does not require exhaustion of every conceivable race-neutral alternative. Nor does it require a university to choose between maintaining a reputation for excellence or fulfilling a commitment to provide educational opportunities to members of all racial groups. Narrow tailoring does, however, require serious, good faith consideration of workable race-neutral alternatives that will achieve the diversity the university seeks. ...

The Law School's current admissions program considers race as one factor among many, in an effort to assemble a student body that is diverse in ways broader than race. Because a lottery would make that kind of nuanced judgment impossible, it would effectively sacrifice all other educational values, not to mention every other kind of diversity. So too with the suggestion that the Law School simply lower admissions standards for all students, a drastic remedy that would require the Law School to become a much different institution and sacrifice a vital component of its educational mission. The United States advocates "percentage plans," recently adopted by public undergraduate institutions in Texas, Florida, and California, to guarantee admission to all students above a certain class-rank threshold in every high school in the State. The United States does not, however, explain how such plans could work for graduate and professional schools. Moreover, even assuming such plans are race-neutral, they may preclude the university from conducting the individualized assessments necessary to assemble a student body that is not just racially diverse, but diverse along all the qualities valued by the university. We are satisfied that the Law School adequately considered race-neutral alternatives currently capable of producing a critical mass without forcing the Law School to abandon the academic selectivity that is the cornerstone of its educational mission. ...

We take the Law School at its word that it would "like nothing better than to find a race-neutral admissions formula" and will terminate its race-conscious admissions program as soon as practicable. It has been 25 years since Justice Powell first approved the use of race to further an interest in student body diversity in the context of public higher education. Since that time, the number of minority applicants with high grades and test scores has indeed increased. We expect that 25 years from now, the use of racial preferences will no longer be necessary to further the interest approved today.

IV

In summary, the Equal Protection Clause does not prohibit the Law School's narrowly tailored use of race in admissions decisions to further a compelling interest in obtaining the educational benefits that flow from a diverse student body. Consequently, petitioner's statutory claims based on Title VI and 42 U.S.C. § 1981 also fail.

Justice GINSBURG, with whom Justice BREYER joins, concurring.

... However strong the public's desire for improved education systems may be, it remains the current reality that many minority students encounter markedly inadequate and unequal educational opportunities. Despite these inequalities, some minority students are able to meet the high threshold requirements set for admission to the country's finest undergraduate and graduate educational institutions. As lower school education in minority communities improves, an increase in the number of such students may be anticipated. From today's vantage point, one may hope, but not firmly forecast, that over the next generation's span, progress toward nondiscrimination and genuinely equal opportunity will make it safe to sunset affirmative action.

Justice SCALIA, with whom Justice THOMAS joins, concurring in part and dissenting in part.

... Unlike a clear constitutional holding that racial preferences in state educational institutions are impermissible, or even a clear anticonstitutional holding that racial preferences in state educational institutions are OK, today's *Grutter-Gratz* split double header seems perversely designed to prolong the controversy and the litigation. Some future lawsuits will presumably focus on whether the discriminatory scheme in question contains enough evaluation of the applicant "as an individual," and sufficiently avoids "separate admissions tracks," to fall under *Grutter* rather than *Gratz*. Some will focus on whether a university has gone beyond the bounds of a "'good faith effort'" and has so zealously pursued its "critical mass" as to make it an unconstitutional *de facto* quota system, rather than merely "'a permissible goal.'" Other lawsuits may focus on whether, in the particular setting at issue, any educational benefits flow from racial diversity. Still other suits may challenge the bona fides of the institution's expressed commitment to the educational benefits of diversity that immunize the discriminatory scheme in *Grutter*. And still other suits may claim that the institution's racial preferences have gone below or above the mystical *Grutter*-approved "critical mass." Finally, litigation can be expected on behalf of minority groups intentionally short changed in the institution's composition of its generic minority "critical mass." I do not look forward to any of these cases. The Constitution proscribes government discrimination on the basis of race, and state-provided education is no exception.

Justice THOMAS, with whom Justice SCALIA joins as to Parts I–VII, concurring in part and dissenting in part.

... Like [Frederick] Douglass, I believe blacks can achieve in every avenue of American life without the meddling of university administrators. Because I wish to see all students succeed whatever their color, I share, in some respect, the sympathies of those who sponsor the type of discrimination advanced by the University of Michigan Law School (Law School). The Constitution does not, however, tolerate institutional devotion to the status quo in admissions policies when such devotion ripens into racial discrimination. Nor does the Constitution countenance the unprecedented deference the Court gives to the Law School, an approach inconsistent with the very concept of "strict scrutiny." ...

I respectfully dissent from the remainder of the Court's opinion and the judgment, however, because I believe that the Law School's current use of race violates the Equal Protection Clause and that the Constitution means the same thing today as it will in 300 months. ...

With the adoption of different admissions methods, such as accepting all students who meet minimum qualifications, the Law School could achieve its vision of the racially aesthetic student body without the use of racial discrimination. The Law School concedes this, but the Court holds, implicitly and under the guise of narrow tailoring, that the Law School has a compelling state interest in doing what it wants to do. I cannot agree. First, under strict scrutiny, the Law School's assessment of the benefits of racial discrimination and devotion to the admissions status quo are not entitled to any sort of deference, grounded in the First Amendment or anywhere else. Second, even if its "academic selectivity" must be maintained at all costs along with racial discrimination, the Court ignores the fact that other top law schools have succeeded in meeting their aesthetic demands without racial discrimination. ...

The absence of any articulated legal principle supporting the majority's principal holding suggests another rationale. I believe what lies beneath the Court's decision today are the benighted notions that one can tell when racial discrimination benefits (rather than hurts) minority groups, see *Adarand,* 515 U.S., at 239, 115 S.Ct. 2097 (SCALIA, J., concurring in part and concurring in judgment), and that racial discrimination is necessary to remedy general societal ills. This Court's precedents supposedly settled both issues, but clearly the majority still cannot commit to the principle that racial classifications are *per se* harmful and that almost no amount of benefit in the eye of the beholder can justify such classifications. ...

For the immediate future, however, the majority has placed its *imprimatur* on a practice that can only weaken the principle of equality embodied in the Declaration of Independence and the Equal Protection Clause. "Our Constitution is color-blind, and neither knows nor tolerates classes among citizens." *Plessy v. Ferguson,* 163 U.S. 537, 559, 16 S.Ct. 1138, 41 L.Ed. 256 (1896) (Harlan, J., dissenting). It has been nearly 140 years since Frederick Douglass asked the intellectual ancestors of the Law School to "[d]o nothing with us!" and the Nation adopted the Fourteenth Amendment. Now we must wait another 25 years to see this principle of equality vindicated. I therefore respectfully dissent from the remainder of the Court's opinion and the judgment.

Chief Justice REHNQUIST, with whom Justice SCALIA, Justice KENNEDY, and Justice THOMAS join, dissenting.

... Although the Court recites the language of our strict scrutiny analysis, its application of that review is unprecedented in its deference. ...

In practice, the Law School's program bears little or no relation to its asserted goal of achieving "critical mass." Respondents explain that the Law School seeks to accumulate a "critical mass" of *each* underrepresented minority group. See, *e.g., id.,* at 49, n. 79 ("The Law School's ... current policy ... provide[s] a special commitment to enrolling a 'critical mass' of 'Hispanics'"). But the record demonstrates that the Law School's admissions practices with respect to these groups differ dramatically and cannot be defended under any consistent use of the term "critical mass." ...

The Court, in an unprecedented display of deference under our strict scrutiny analysis, upholds the Law School's program despite its obvious flaws. We have said that when it comes to the use of race, the connection between the ends and the means used to attain them must be precise. But here the flaw is deeper than that; it is not merely a question of "fit" between ends and means. Here the means actually used are forbidden by the Equal Protection Clause of the Constitution.

Justice KENNEDY, dissenting.

... The Court, in a review that is nothing short of perfunctory, accepts the University of Michigan Law

School's (Law School) assurances that its admissions process meets with constitutional requirements. The majority fails to confront the reality of how the Law School's admissions policy is implemented. The dissenting opinion by THE CHIEF JUSTICE, which I join in full, demonstrates beyond question why the concept of critical mass is a delusion used by the Law School to mask its attempt to make race an automatic factor in most instances and to achieve numerical goals indistinguishable from quotas. An effort to achieve racial balance among the minorities the school seeks to attract is, by the Court's own admission, "patently unconstitutional." It remains to point out how critical mass becomes inconsistent with individual consideration in some more specific aspects of the admissions process. ...

The Law School has the burden of proving, in conformance with the standard of strict scrutiny, that it did not utilize race in an unconstitutional way. *Adarand Constructors,* 515 U.S., at 224, 115 S.Ct. 2097. At the very least, the constancy of admitted minority students and the close correlation between the racial breakdown of admitted minorities and the composition of the applicant pool, discussed by THE CHIEF JUSTICE, require the Law School either to produce a convincing explanation or to show it has taken adequate steps to ensure individual assessment. The Law School does neither. ...

It is difficult to assess the Court's pronouncement that race-conscious admissions programs will be unnecessary 25 years from now. *Ante,* at 2345–2347. If it is intended to mitigate the damage the Court does to the concept of strict scrutiny, neither petitioner nor other rejected law school applicants will find solace in knowing the basic protection put in place by Justice Powell will be suspended for a full quarter of a century. Deference is antithetical to strict scrutiny, not consistent with it. ...

If universities are given the latitude to administer programs that are tantamount to quotas, they will have few incentives to make the existing minority admissions schemes transparent and protective of individual review. The unhappy consequence will be to perpetuate the hostilities that proper consideration of race is designed to avoid. The perpetuation, of course, would be the worst of all outcomes. Other programs do exist which will be more effective in bringing about the harmony and mutual respect among all citizens that our constitutional tradition has always sought. They, and not the program under review here, should be the model, even if the Court defaults by not demanding it.

It is regrettable the Court's important holding allowing racial minorities to have their special circumstances considered in order to improve their educational opportunities is accompanied by a suspension of the strict scrutiny which was the predicate of allowing race to be considered in the first place. If the Court abdicates its constitutional duty to give strict scrutiny to the use of race in university admissions, it negates my authority to approve the use of race in pursuit of student diversity. The Constitution cannot confer the right to classify on the basis of race even in this special context absent searching judicial review. For these reasons, though I reiterate my approval of giving appropriate consideration to race in this one context, I must dissent in the present case.

Following is the undergraduate case. As you read it, consider how that program is different from the law school's admissions program.

Gratz v. Bollinger

SUPREME COURT OF THE UNITED STATES, 2003

539 U.S. 244, 123 S.Ct. 2411

REHNQUIST, C.J. delivered the opinion of the Court, in which O'CONNOR, SCALIA, KENNEDY, and THOMAS, JJ., joined. O'CONNOR, J., filed a concurring opinion, in which BREYER, J., joined in part. THOMAS, J., filed a concurring opinion. BREYER, J., filed an opinion concurring in the judgment. STEVENS, J., filed a dissenting opinion, in which SOUTER, J., joined. SOUTER, J., filed a dissenting opinion, in which GINSBURG, J., joined as to Part II. GINSBURG, J., filed a dissenting opinion, in which SOUTER, J., joined, and in which BREYER, J., joined as to Part I.

We granted certiorari in this case to decide whether "the University of Michigan's use of racial preferences in undergraduate admissions violate[s] the Equal Protection Clause of the Fourteenth Amendment, Title VI of the Civil Rights Act of 1964 (42 U.S.C. § 2000d), or 42 U.S.C. § 1981." Because we find that the manner in which the University considers the race of applicants in its undergraduate admissions guidelines violates these constitutional and statutory provisions, we reverse that portion of the District Court's decision upholding the guidelines. ...

IB

... OUA [the Office of Undergraduate Admissions] considers a number of factors in making admissions decisions, including high school grades, standardized test scores, high school quality, curriculum strength, geography, alumni relationships, and leadership. OUA also considers race. During all periods relevant to this litigation, the University has considered African-Americans, Hispanics, and Native Americans to be "underrepresented minorities," and it is undisputed that the University admits "virtually every qualified ... applicant" from these groups.

During 1995 and 1996, OUA counselors evaluated applications according to grade point average combined with what were referred to as the "SCUGA" factors. These factors included the quality of an applicant's high school (S), the strength of an applicant's high school curriculum (C), an applicant's unusual circumstances (U), an applicant's geographical residence (G), and an applicant's alumni relationships (A). After these scores were combined to produce an applicant's "GPA 2" score, the reviewing admissions counselors referenced a set of "Guidelines" tables, which listed GPA 2 ranges on the vertical axis, and American College Test/Scholastic Aptitude Test (ACT/SAT) scores on the horizontal axis. Each table was divided into cells that included one or more courses of action to be taken, including admit, reject, delay for additional information, or postpone for reconsideration.

In both years, applicants with the same GPA 2 score and ACT/SAT score were subject to different admissions outcomes based upon their racial or ethnic status. For example, as a Caucasian in-state applicant, Gratz's GPA 2 score and ACT score placed her within a cell calling for a postponed decision on her application. An in-state or out-of-state minority applicant with Gratz's scores would have fallen within a cell calling for admission.

In 1997, the University modified its admissions procedure. Specifically, the formula for calculating an applicant's GPA 2 score was restructured to include additional point values under the "U" category in the SCUGA factors. Under this new system, applicants could receive points for underrepresented minority status, socioeconomic disadvantage, or attendance at a high school with a predominantly underrepresented minority population, or underrepresentation in the unit to which the student was applying (for example, men who sought to pursue a career in nursing). Under the 1997 procedures, Hamacher's GPA 2 score and ACT score placed him in a cell on the in-state applicant table calling for postponement of a final admissions decision. An underrepresented minority applicant placed in the same cell would generally have been admitted.

Beginning with the 1998 academic year, the OUA dispensed with the Guidelines tables and the SCUGA point system in favor of a "selection index," on which an applicant could score a maximum of 150 points. This index was divided linearly into ranges generally calling for admissions dispositions as follows: 100–150 (admit); 95–99 (admit or postpone); 90–94 (postpone or admit); 75–89 (delay or postpone); 74 and below (delay or reject).

Each application received points based on high school grade point average, standardized test scores, academic quality of an applicant's high school, strength or weakness of high school curriculum, in-state residency, alumni relationship, personal essay, and personal achievement or leadership. Of particular significance here, under a "miscellaneous" category, an applicant was entitled to 20 points based upon his or her membership in an underrepresented racial or ethnic minority group. The University explained that the "'development of the selection index for admissions in 1998 changed only the mechanics, not the substance, of how race and ethnicity [were] considered in admissions.'" ...

IIB

Petitioners argue, first and foremost, that the University's use of race in undergraduate admissions violates the Fourteenth Amendment. Specifically, they contend that this Court has only sanctioned the use of racial classifications to remedy identified discrimination, a justification on which respondents have never relied. Petitioners further argue that "diversity as a basis for employing racial preferences is simply too open-ended, ill-defined, and indefinite to constitute a compelling interest capable of supporting narrowly-tailored means." But for the reasons set forth today in *Grutter v. Bollinger,* the Court has rejected these arguments of petitioners. …

The current LSA [Literature, Science, and the Arts] policy does not provide such individualized consideration. The LSA's policy automatically distributes 20 points to every single applicant from an "underrepresented minority" group, as defined by the University. The only consideration that accompanies this distribution of points is a factual review of an application to determine whether an individual is a member of one of these minority groups. Moreover, unlike Justice Powell's example, where the race of a "particular black applicant" could be considered without being decisive, see *Bakke,* 438 U.S., at 317, 98 S.Ct. 2733, the LSA's automatic distribution of 20 points has the effect of making "the factor of race … decisive" for virtually every minimally qualified underrepresented minority applicant. …

Even if student C's "extraordinary artistic talent" rivaled that of Monet or Picasso, the applicant would receive, at most, five points under the LSA's system. At the same time, every single underrepresented minority applicant, including students A and B, would automatically receive 20 points for submitting an application. …

Respondents contend that "[t]he volume of applications and the presentation of applicant information make it impractical for [LSA] to use the … admissions system" upheld by the Court today in *Grutter*. But the fact that the implementation of a program capable of providing individualized consideration might present administrative challenges does not render constitutional an otherwise problematic system. Nothing in Justice Powell's opinion in *Bakke* signaled that a university may employ whatever means it desires to achieve the stated goal of diversity without regard to the limits imposed by our strict scrutiny analysis.

We conclude, therefore, that because the University's use of race in its current freshman admissions policy is not narrowly tailored to achieve respondents' asserted compelling interest in diversity, the admissions policy violates the Equal Protection Clause of the Fourteenth Amendment. We further find that the admissions policy also violates Title VI and 42 U.S.C. § 1981. …

Justice O'CONNOR, concurring.

… But the selection index, by setting up automatic, predetermined point allocations for the soft variables, ensures that the diversity contributions of applicants cannot be individually assessed. This policy stands in sharp contrast to the law school's admissions plan, which enables admissions officers to make nuanced judgments with respect to the contributions each applicant is likely to make to the diversity of the incoming class. …

For these reasons, the record before us does not support the conclusion that the University's admissions program for its College of Literature, Science, and the Arts—to the extent that it considers race—provides the necessary individualized consideration. …

Justice THOMAS, concurring.

… I would hold that a State's use of racial discrimination in higher education admissions is categorically prohibited by the Equal Protection Clause. …

Justice BREYER's concurrence is omitted.

Justice STEVENS, with whom Justice SOUTER joins, dissenting.

Petitioners seek forward-looking relief enjoining the University of Michigan from continuing to use its current race-conscious freshman admissions policy. Yet unlike the plaintiff in *Grutter v. Bollinger,* the petitioners in this case had already enrolled at other schools before they filed their class-action complaint in this case. Neither petitioner was in the process of reapplying to Michigan through the freshman admissions process at the time this suit was filed, and neither has done so since. There is a total absence of evidence that either petitioner would receive any benefit from the prospective relief sought by their lawyer. While some unidentified members of the class may very well have standing to seek prospective relief, it is clear that neither petitioner does. Our precedents therefore require dismissal of the action. …

Both Hamacher and Gratz, of course, have standing to seek damages as compensation for the alleged wrongful denial of their respective applications under Michigan's old freshman admissions system. However, like the plaintiff in *Los Angeles v. Lyons,* 461 U.S. 95, 103 S.Ct. 1660, 75 L.Ed.2d 675 (1983), who had standing to recover damages caused by "chokeholds" administered by the police in the past but had no standing to seek injunctive relief preventing future chokeholds, petitioners' past injuries do not give them standing to obtain injunctive relief to protect third parties from similar harms. ...

Justice SOUTER, with whom Justice GINSBURG joins as to Part II, dissenting.

I agree with Justice STEVENS that Patrick Hamacher has no standing to seek declaratory or injunctive relief against a freshman admissions policy that will never cause him any harm. I write separately to note that even the Court's new gloss on the law of standing should not permit it to reach the issue it decides today. And because a majority of the Court has chosen to address the merits, I also add a word to say that even if the merits were reachable, I would dissent from the Court's judgment. ...

II

... Although the freshman admissions system here is subject to argument on the merits, I think it is closer to what *Grutter* approves than to what *Bakke* condemns, and should not be held unconstitutional on the current record. ...

In contrast to the college's forthrightness in saying just what plus factor it gives for membership in an underrepresented minority, it is worth considering the character of one alternative thrown up as preferable, because supposedly not based on race. Drawing on admissions systems used at public universities in California, Florida, and Texas, the United States contends that Michigan could get student diversity in satisfaction of its compelling interest by guaranteeing admission to a fixed percentage of the top students from each high school in Michigan.

While there is nothing unconstitutional about such a practice, it nonetheless suffers from a serious disadvantage. It is the disadvantage of deliberate obfuscation. The "percentage plans" are just as race conscious as the point scheme (and fairly so), but they get their racially diverse results without saying directly what they are doing or why they are doing it. In contrast, Michigan states its purpose directly and, if this were a doubtful case for me, I would be tempted to give Michigan an extra point of its own for its frankness. Equal protection cannot become an exercise in which the winners are the ones who hide the ball. ...

Justice GINSBURG, with whom Justice SOUTER joins, dissenting.

... Examining in this light the admissions policy employed by the University of Michigan's College of Literature, Science, and the Arts (College), and for the reasons well stated by Justice SOUTER, I see no constitutional infirmity. Like other top-ranking institutions, the College has many more applicants for admission than it can accommodate in an entering class. Every applicant admitted under the current plan, petitioners do not here dispute, is qualified to attend the College. The racial and ethnic groups to which the College accords special consideration (African-Americans, Hispanics, and Native-Americans) historically have been relegated to inferior status by law and social practice; their members continue to experience class-based discrimination to this day. There is no suggestion that the College adopted its current policy in order to limit or decrease enrollment by any particular racial or ethnic group, and no seats are reserved on the basis of race. Nor has there been any demonstration that the College's program unduly constricts admissions opportunities for students who do not receive special consideration based on race.

The stain of generations of racial oppression is still visible in our society, and the determination to hasten its removal remains vital. One can reasonably anticipate, therefore, that colleges and universities will seek to maintain their minority enrollment—and the networks and opportunities thereby opened to minority graduates—whether or not they can do so in full candor through adoption of affirmative action plans of the kind here at issue. Without recourse to such plans, institutions of higher education may resort to camouflage. For example, schools may encourage applicants to write of their cultural traditions in the essays they submit, or to indicate whether English is their second language. Seeking to improve their chances for admission, applicants may highlight the minority group associations to which they belong, or the Hispanic surnames of their mothers or grandparents. In turn, teachers' recommendations may emphasize who a student is as much as what he or she has accomplished. If honesty is the best policy, surely Michigan's accurately described, fully disclosed College affirmative action program is preferable to achieving similar numbers through winks, nods, and disguises.

Notes and Questions

1. *What is the level of scrutiny?* What is strict scrutiny? Consider each Justice on the Court. Does each Justice apply strict scrutiny in the same way? Why did each Justice vote the way they did?
2. *Texas developed percentage plans in which the top ten percent of any Texas high school receives automatic admission to any public university in the state.* Is this a race-neutral approach to admissions that guarantees diversity? Describe other race-neutral plans that could replace affirmative action.
3. *Another case.* In *Fisher v. University of Texas*, 570 U.S. 297 (2013), the university continued the top-ten admissions plan. For the remainder of admitted students, the school considered race as a factor. The Court ruled 7–1 that the lower courts had not applied the appropriate strictest level of scrutiny, namely whether the programs were "precisely tailored to serve a compelling governmental interest." The sole dissenter, Justice Ginsburg, would have upheld the program.

   On remand, the Fifth Circuit ruled that the university's use of race was justified by strict scrutiny. The case was reviewed again in the Supreme Court. In a 4–3 opinion, Justice Kennedy upheld the university's use of race in college admissions, concluding their programs met the compelling interest of diversity and were narrowly tailored to that interest. *Fisher v. University of Texas*, 579 U.S. 365 (2016).

4. *The history of racism.* One of the arguments that the Justices opposed to affirmative action have made is that racial discrimination is significantly less than it used to be. What do you think of that explanation?
5. *Videos.* What do you learn about the cases from these two videos, Gratz (2003), https://www.youtube.com/watch?v=fXlDE5wv-xM&list=PLsFE_Nvl6h_braQ_NxoD1jg8oDdM_l8uI&index=24&t=1s, and Grutter (2003), https://www.youtube.com/watch?v=UUB3TI87kd8&list=PLsFE_Nvl6h_braQ_NxoD1jg8oDdM_l8uI&index=25 in the Introduction to Constitutional Law series?
6. Will *Grutter* be overruled? Students for Fair Admissions asked for its overruling in their cases on behalf of students of Asian background at Harvard College and the University of North Carolina. Harvard is a Title VI case and *North Carolina* is an equal protection case. Do you know why the two cases are different in that respect? At the oral argument, Justice Thomas asked what diversity is. Can you give an answer to that question? You can listen to the oral argument at https://www.oyez.org/cases/2022/20-1199 and https://www.oyez.org/cases/2022/21-707. Can you tell how the Justices will vote on this topic? Which Justice asked the best questions? Which Justice asked the worst questions? Did the argument convince you *Grutter* should be overruled?

8. Should the Constitution Be Color-Blind?

The Court has repeatedly discussed what racial discrimination is and what *Brown* means. *Plessy* originally said "separate but equal" expressed the meaning of the Equal Protection Clause. But *Brown* overruled that. What does *Brown* mean now? Should the Constitution be color-blind so that race can never be a guiding factor by the government in any situation? Or is it necessary to incorporate race into some government programs and not others? Which ones? Should the government be allowed to distinguish good uses of race from bad, or should the government always be color-blind? This was at stake in the following *Parents Involved* case, which is a very long opinion with great details about two school systems. We provide a shorter version of it here so you can focus on the key arguments. Which Justice makes the best points about race?

Consider the facts of the following case as argued in the oral argument, https://www.oyez.org/cases/2006/05-908. You can also watch the argument on c-span, https://www.c-span.org/video/?195615-1/parents-involved-community-schools-v-seattle-school-district. Which lawyer does the best job defending their position? Can you tell from their questions where the Justices agree and disagree? Would a member of the 1975 Court agree with this majority opinion?

Parents Involved in Community Schools v. Seattle School District No. 1

SUPREME COURT OF THE UNITED STATES, 2007

551 U.S. 701, 127 S.Ct. 2738

Chief Justice ROBERTS announced the judgment of the Court, and delivered the opinion of the Court with respect to Parts I, II, III–A, and III–C, and an opinion with respect to Parts III–B and IV, in which Justice SCALIA, Justice THOMAS, and Justice ALITO join.

The school districts in these cases voluntarily adopted student assignment plans that rely upon race to determine which public schools certain children may attend. The Seattle school district classifies children as white or nonwhite; the Jefferson County school district as black or "other." In Seattle, this racial classification is used to allocate slots in oversubscribed high schools. In Jefferson County, it is used to make certain elementary school assignments and to rule on transfer requests. In each case, the school district relies upon an individual student's race in assigning that student to a particular school, so that the racial balance at the school falls within a predetermined range based on the racial composition of the school district as a whole. Parents of students denied assignment to particular schools under these plans solely because of their race brought suit, contending that allocating children to different public schools on the basis of race violated the Fourteenth Amendment guarantee of equal protection. The Courts of Appeals below upheld the plans. We granted certiorari, and now reverse.

I

Both cases present the same underlying legal question—whether a public school that had not operated legally segregated schools or has been found to be unitary may choose to classify students by race and rely upon that classification in making school assignments. Although we examine the plans under the same legal framework, the specifics of the two plans, and the circumstances surrounding their adoption, are in some respects quite different.

A

Seattle School District No. 1 operates 10 regular public high schools. In 1998, it adopted the plan at issue in this case for assigning students to these schools. The plan allows incoming ninth graders to choose from among any of the district's high schools, ranking however many schools they wish in order of preference.

Some schools are more popular than others. If too many students list the same school as their first choice, the district employs a series of "tiebreakers" to determine who will fill the open slots at the oversubscribed school. The first tiebreaker selects for admission students who have a sibling currently enrolled in the chosen school. The next tiebreaker depends upon the racial composition of the particular school and the race of the individual student. In the district's public schools approximately 41 percent of enrolled students are white; the remaining 59 percent, comprising all other racial groups, are classified by Seattle for assignment purposes as nonwhite. If an oversubscribed school is not within 10 percentage points of the district's overall white/nonwhite racial balance, it is what the district calls "integration positive," and the district employs a tiebreaker that selects for assignment students whose race "will serve to bring the school into balance." If it is still necessary to select students for the school after using the racial tiebreaker, the next tiebreaker is the geographic proximity of the school to the student's residence.

Seattle has never operated segregated schools—legally separate schools for students of different races—nor has it ever been subject to court-ordered desegregation. ...

Petitioner Parents Involved in Community Schools (Parents Involved) is a nonprofit corporation comprising the parents of children who have been or may be denied assignment to their chosen high school in the district because of their race. ...

B

Jefferson County Public Schools operates the public school system in metropolitan Louisville, Kentucky. In 1973 a federal court found that Jefferson County had maintained a segregated school system. ... Jefferson County operated under this decree until 2000, when the District Court dissolved the decree after finding that the district had achieved unitary status by eliminating "[t]o the greatest extent practicable" the vestiges of its prior policy of segregation. ... The plan requires all nonmagnet schools to maintain a minimum black enrollment of 15 percent, and a maximum black enrollment of 50 percent. ... If a school has reached the "extremes of the racial guidelines," a student whose race would contribute to the school's racial imbalance will not be assigned there. ...

III

A

It is well established that when the government distributes burdens or benefits on the basis of individual racial classifications, that action is reviewed under strict scrutiny. *Johnson v. California,* 543 U.S. 499, 505–506, 125 S.Ct. 1141, 160 L.Ed.2d 949 (2005); *Grutter v. Bollinger,* 539 U.S. 306, 326, 123 S.Ct. 2325, 156 L.Ed.2d 304 (2003); *Adarand, supra,* at 224, 115 S.Ct. 2097. As the Court recently reaffirmed, "'racial classifications are simply too pernicious to permit any but the most exact connection between justification and classification.'" *Gratz v. Bollinger,* 539 U.S. 244, 270, 123 S.Ct. 2411, 156 L.Ed.2d 257 (2003). In order to satisfy this searching standard of review, the school districts must demonstrate that the use of individual racial classifications in the assignment plans here under review is "narrowly tailored" to achieve a "compelling" government interest. *Adarand, supra,* at 227, 115 S.Ct. 2097.

Without attempting in these cases to set forth all the interests a school district might assert, it suffices to note that our prior cases, in evaluating the use of racial classifications in the school context, have recognized two interests that qualify as compelling. The first is the compelling interest of remedying the effects of past intentional discrimination. ...

The second government interest we have recognized as compelling for purposes of strict scrutiny is the interest in diversity in higher education upheld in *Grutter.* ...

In the present cases, by contrast, race is not considered as part of a broader effort to achieve "exposure to widely diverse people, cultures, ideas, and viewpoints,"; race, for some students, is determinative standing alone. ... Even when it comes to race, the plans here employ only a limited notion of diversity, viewing race exclusively in white/nonwhite terms in Seattle and black/"other" terms in Jefferson County.

B

... it is clear that the racial classifications employed by the districts are not narrowly tailored to the goal of achieving the educational and social benefits asserted to flow from racial diversity. In design and operation, the plans are directed only to racial balance, pure and simple, an objective this Court has repeatedly condemned as illegitimate. ...

The plans here are not tailored to achieving a degree of diversity necessary to realize the asserted educational benefits; instead the plans are tailored, in the words of Seattle's Manager of Enrollment Planning, Technical Support, and Demographics, to "the goal established by the school board of attaining a level of diversity within the schools that approximates the district's overall demographics." ...

This working backward to achieve a particular type of racial balance, rather than working forward from some demonstration of the level of diversity that provides the purported benefits, is a fatal flaw under our existing precedent. ...

C

... While we do not suggest that *greater* use of race would be preferable, the minimal impact of the districts' racial classifications on school enrollment casts doubt on the necessity of using racial classifications. ...

The districts have also failed to show that they considered methods other than explicit racial classifications to achieve their stated goals. ...

* * *

If the need for the racial classifications embraced by the school districts is unclear, even on the districts' own terms, the costs are undeniable. "[D]istinctions between citizens solely because of their ancestry are by their very nature odious to a free people whose institutions are founded upon the doctrine of equality." *Adarand,* 515 U.S., at 214, 115 S.Ct. 2097 (internal quotation marks omitted). Government action dividing us by race is inherently suspect because such classifications promote "notions of racial inferiority and lead to a politics of racial hostility," *Croson,* 488 U.S., at 493, 109 S.Ct. 706 (plurality opinion), "reinforce the belief, held by too many for too much of our history, that individuals should be judged by the color of their skin," *Shaw v. Reno,* 509 U.S. 630, 657, 113 S.Ct. 2816, 125 L.Ed.2d 511 (1993), and "endorse race-based reasoning and the conception of a Nation divided into racial blocs, thus contributing to an escalation of racial hostility and conflict." *Metro Broadcasting,* 497 U.S., at 603, 110 S.Ct. 2997 (O'Connor, J., dissenting). As the Court explained in *Rice v. Cayetano,* 528 U.S. 495, 517, 120 S.Ct. 1044, 145 L.Ed.2d 1007 (2000), "[o]ne of the principal reasons race is treated as a forbidden classification is that it demeans the dignity and worth of a person to be judged by ancestry instead of by his or her own merit and essential qualities."

All this is true enough in the contexts in which these statements were made—government contracting, voting districts, allocation of broadcast licenses, and electing state officers—but when it comes to using race to assign children to schools, history will be heard. In *Brown v. Board of Education,* 347 U.S. 483, 74 S.Ct. 686, 98 L.Ed. 873 (1954) (*Brown I*), we held that segregation deprived black children of equal educational opportunities regardless of whether school facilities and other tangible factors were equal, because government classification and separation on grounds of race themselves denoted inferiority. It was not the inequality of the facilities but the fact of legally separating children on the basis of race on which the Court relied to find a constitutional violation in 1954. The next Term, we accordingly stated that "full compliance" with *Brown I* required school districts "to achieve a system of determining admission to the public schools *on a nonracial basis.*" *Brown II,* 349 U.S., at 300–301, 75 S.Ct. 753 (emphasis added).

The parties and their *amici* debate which side is more faithful to the heritage of *Brown,* but the position of the plaintiffs in *Brown* was spelled out in their brief and could not have been clearer: "[T]he Fourteenth Amendment prevents states from according differential treatment to American children on the basis of their color or race." What do the racial classifications at issue here do, if not accord differential treatment on the basis of race? As counsel who appeared before this Court for the plaintiffs in *Brown* put it: "We have one fundamental contention which we will seek to develop in the course of this argument, and that contention is that no State has any authority under the equal-protection clause of the Fourteenth Amendment to use race as a factor in affording educational opportunities among its citizens." There is no ambiguity in that statement. And it was that position that prevailed in this Court, which emphasized in its remedial opinion that what was "[a]t stake is the personal interest of the plaintiffs in admission to public schools as soon as practicable *on a nondiscriminatory basis,*" and what was required was "determining admission to the public schools *on a nonracial basis.*" What do the racial classifications do in these cases, if not determine admission to a public school on a racial basis?

Before *Brown,* schoolchildren were told where they could and could not go to school based on the color of their skin. The school districts in these cases have not carried the heavy burden of demonstrating that we should allow this once again—even for very different reasons. For schools that never segregated on the basis of race, such as Seattle, or that have removed the vestiges of past segregation, such as Jefferson County, the way "to achieve a system of determining admission to the public schools on a nonracial basis," *Brown II, supra,* at 300–301, 75 S.Ct. 753, is to stop assigning students on a racial basis. The way to stop discrimination on the basis of race is to stop discriminating on the basis of race.

Justice THOMAS, concurring.

... Contrary to the dissent's arguments, resegregation is not occurring in Seattle or Louisville; these school boards have no present interest in remedying past segregation; and these race-based student-assignment programs do not serve any compelling state interest. Accordingly, the plans are unconstitutional. Disfavoring a colorblind interpretation of the Constitution, the dissent would give school boards a free hand to make decisions on the basis of race—an approach reminiscent of that advocated by the segregationists in *Brown v. Board of Education,* 347 U.S. 483, 74 S.Ct. 686, 98 L.Ed. 873 (1954). This approach is just as wrong today as it was a half century ago. The Constitution and our cases require us to be much more demanding before permitting local school boards to make decisions based on race. ...

III

Most of the dissent's criticisms of today's result can be traced to its rejection of the colorblind Constitution. The dissent attempts to marginalize the notion of a colorblind Constitution by consigning it to me and Members of today's plurality. But I am quite comfortable in the company I keep. My view of the Constitution is Justice Harlan's view in *Plessy:* "Our Constitution is color-blind, and neither knows nor tolerates classes among citizens." And my view was the rallying cry for the lawyers who litigated *Brown.* See In Memoriam: Honorable Thurgood Marshall, Proceedings of the Bar and Officers of the Supreme Court of the United States, p. X (1993) (remarks of Judge Motley) ("Marshall had a 'Bible' to which he turned during his most depressed moments. The 'Bible' would be known in the legal community as the first Mr. Justice Harlan's dissent in *Plessy v. Ferguson,* 163 U.S. 537, 552, 16 S.Ct. 1138, 41 L.Ed. 256 (1896). I do not know of any opinion which buoyed Marshall more in his pre-*Brown* days ..."). ...

Indeed, if our history has taught us anything, it has taught us to beware of elites bearing racial theories. See, *e.g., Dred Scott v. Sandford,* 19 How. 393, 406, 407, 15 L.Ed. 691 (1857) ("[T]hey [members of the "negro African race"] had no rights which the white man was bound to respect"). Can we really be sure that the racial theories that motivated *Dred Scott* and *Plessy* are a relic of the past or that future theories will be nothing but beneficent and progressive? That is a gamble I am unwilling to take, and it is one the Constitution does not allow.

* * *

The plans before us base school assignment decisions on students' race. Because "[o]ur Constitution is color-blind, and neither knows nor tolerates classes among citizens," such race-based decisionmaking is unconstitutional. *Plessy, supra,* at 559, 16 S.Ct. 1138 (Harlan, J., dissenting). I concur in THE CHIEF JUSTICE's opinion so holding.

Justice KENNEDY, concurring in part and concurring in the judgment.

... I agree with THE CHIEF JUSTICE that we have jurisdiction to decide the cases before us and join Parts I and II of the Court's opinion. I also join Parts III–A and III–C for reasons provided below. My views do not allow me to join the balance of the opinion by THE CHIEF JUSTICE, which seems to me to be inconsistent in both its approach and its implications with the history, meaning, and reach of the Equal Protection Clause. Justice BREYER's dissenting opinion, on the other hand, rests on what in my respectful submission is a misuse and mistaken interpretation of our precedents. This leads it to advance propositions that, in my view, are both erroneous and in fundamental conflict with basic equal protection principles. As a consequence, this separate opinion is necessary to set forth my conclusions in the two cases before the Court. ...

II

Our Nation from the inception has sought to preserve and expand the promise of liberty and equality on which it was founded. Today we enjoy a society that is remarkable in its openness and opportunity. Yet our tradition is to go beyond present achievements, however significant, and to recognize and confront the flaws and injustices that remain. This is especially true when we seek assurance that opportunity is not denied on account of race. The enduring hope is that race should not matter; the reality is that too often it does.

This is by way of preface to my respectful submission that parts of the opinion by THE CHIEF JUSTICE imply an all-too-unyielding insistence that race cannot be a factor in instances when, in my view, it may be taken into account. The plurality opinion is too dismissive of the legitimate interest government has in ensuring all people have equal opportunity regardless of their race. The plurality's postulate that "[t]he way to stop discrimination on the basis of race is to stop discriminating on the basis of race," is not sufficient to decide these cases. Fifty years of experience since *Brown v. Board of Education,* 347 U.S. 483, 74 S.Ct. 686, 98 L.Ed. 873 (1954), should teach us that the problem before us defies so easy a solution. School districts can seek to reach *Brown*'s objective of equal educational opportunity. The plurality opinion is at least open to the interpretation that the Constitution requires school districts to ignore the problem of *de facto* resegregation in schooling. I cannot endorse that conclusion. To the extent the plurality opinion suggests the Constitution mandates that state and local school authorities must accept the status quo of racial isolation in schools, it is, in my view, profoundly mistaken.

The statement by Justice Harlan that "[o]ur Constitution is color-blind" was most certainly justified in the context of his dissent in *Plessy v. Ferguson,* 163 U.S. 537, 559, 16 S.Ct. 1138, 41 L.Ed. 256 (1896). The Court's decision in that case was a grievous error it took far too long to overrule. *Plessy,* of course, concerned official classification by race applicable to all persons who sought to use railway carriages. And, as an aspiration, Justice Harlan's axiom must command our assent. In the real world, it is regrettable to say, it cannot be a universal constitutional principle. ...

School boards may pursue the goal of bringing together students of diverse backgrounds and races through other means, including strategic site selection of new schools; drawing attendance zones with general recognition of the demographics of neighborhoods; allocating resources for special programs; recruiting students and faculty in a targeted fashion; and tracking enrollments, performance, and other statistics by race. These mechanisms are race conscious but do not lead to different treatment based on a classification that tells each student he or she is to be defined by race, so it is unlikely any of them would demand strict scrutiny to be found permissible. ...

* * *

This Nation has a moral and ethical obligation to fulfill its historic commitment to creating an integrated society that ensures equal opportunity for all of its children. A compelling interest exists in avoiding racial isolation, an interest that a school district, in its discretion and expertise, may choose to pursue. Likewise, a district may consider it a compelling interest to achieve a diverse student population. Race may be one component of that diversity, but other demographic factors, plus special talents and needs, should also be considered. What the government is not permitted to do, absent a showing of necessity not made here, is to classify every student on the basis of race and to assign each of them to schools based on that classification. Crude measures of this sort threaten to reduce children to racial chits valued and traded according to one school's supply and another's demand.

That statement, to be sure, invites this response: A sense of stigma may already become the fate of those separated out by circumstances beyond their immediate control. But to this the replication must be: Even so, measures other than differential treatment based on racial typing of individuals first must be exhausted.

The decision today should not prevent school districts from continuing the important work of bringing together students of different racial, ethnic, and economic backgrounds. Due to a variety of factors—some influenced by government, some not—neighborhoods in our communities do not reflect the diversity of our Nation as a whole. Those entrusted with directing our public schools can bring to bear the creativity of experts, parents, administrators, and other concerned citizens to find a way to achieve the compelling interests they face without resorting to widespread governmental allocation of benefits and burdens on the basis of racial classifications.

With this explanation I concur in the judgment of the Court.

Justice STEVENS, dissenting.

While I join Justice BREYER's eloquent and unanswerable dissent in its entirety, it is appropriate to add these words.

There is a cruel irony in THE CHIEF JUSTICE's reliance on our decision in *Brown v. Board of Education,* 349 U.S. 294, 75 S.Ct. 753, 99 L.Ed. 1083 1955). The first sentence in the concluding paragraph of his opinion states: "Before *Brown,* schoolchildren were told where they could and could not go to school based on the color of their skin." This sentence reminds me of Anatole France's observation: "[T]he majestic equality of the la[w], ... forbid[s] rich and poor alike to sleep under the bridges, to beg in the streets, and to steal their bread." THE CHIEF JUSTICE fails to note that it was only black schoolchildren who were so ordered; indeed, the history books do not tell stories of white children struggling to attend black schools. In this and other ways, THE CHIEF JUSTICE rewrites the history of one of this Court's most important decisions.

THE CHIEF JUSTICE rejects the conclusion that the racial classifications at issue here should be viewed differently than others, because they do not impose burdens on one race alone and do not stigmatize or exclude. ...

The Court has changed significantly since it decided *School Comm. of Boston* in 1968. It was then more faithful to *Brown* and more respectful of our precedent than it is today. It is my firm conviction that no Member of the Court that I joined in 1975 would have agreed with today's decision. [Chief Justice Burger, Justices Brennan, Stewart, White, Marshall, Blackmun, Powell, and Rehnquist were on the Court in 1975.]

Justice BREYER, with whom Justice STEVENS, Justice SOUTER, and Justice GINSBURG join, dissenting.

These cases consider the longstanding efforts of two local school boards to integrate their public schools. The school board plans before us resemble many others adopted in the last 50 years by primary and secondary schools throughout the Nation. All of those plans represent local efforts to bring about the kind of racially integrated education that *Brown v. Board of Education,* 347 U.S. 483, 74 S.Ct. 686, 98 L.Ed. 873 (1954), long ago promised—efforts that this Court has repeatedly required, permitted, and encouraged local authorities to undertake. This Court has recognized that the public interests at stake in such cases are "compelling." We have approved of "narrowly tailored" plans that are no less race conscious than the plans before us. And we have understood that the Constitution *permits* local communities to adopt desegregation plans even where it does not *require* them to do so.

The plurality pays inadequate attention to this law, to past opinions' rationales, their language, and the contexts in which they arise. As a result, it reverses course and reaches the wrong conclusion. In doing so, it distorts precedent, it misapplies the relevant constitutional principles, it announces legal rules that will obstruct efforts by state and local governments to deal effectively with the growing resegregation of public schools, it threatens to substitute for present calm a disruptive round of race-related litigation, and it undermines *Brown*'s promise of integrated primary and secondary education that local communities have sought to make a reality. This cannot be justified in the name of the Equal Protection Clause. ...

Until today, this Court understood the Constitution as affording the people, acting through their elected representatives, freedom to select the use of "race-conscious" criteria from among their available options. Today, however, the Court restricts (and some Members would eliminate) that leeway. I fear the consequences of doing so for the law, for the schools, for the democratic process, and for America's efforts to create, out of its diversity, one Nation.

VI

Conclusions

To show that the school assignment plans here meet the requirements of the Constitution, I have written at exceptional length. But that length is necessary. I cannot refer to the history of the plans in these cases to justify the use of race-conscious criteria without describing that history in full. I cannot rely upon *Swann*'s statement that the use of race-conscious limits is permissible without showing, rather than simply asserting, that the statement represents a constitutional principle firmly rooted in federal and state law. Nor can I explain my disagreement with the Court's holding and the plurality's opinion without offering a detailed account of the arguments they propound and the consequences they risk.

Thus, the opinion's reasoning is long. But its conclusion is short: The plans before us satisfy the requirements of the Equal Protection Clause. And it is the plurality's opinion, not this dissent, that "fails to ground the result it would reach in law."

Four basic considerations have led me to this view. *First,* the histories of Louisville and Seattle reveal complex circumstances and a long tradition of conscientious efforts by local school boards to resist racial segregation in public schools. ... *Second,* since this Court's decision in *Brown,* the law has consistently and unequivocally approved of both voluntary and compulsory race-conscious measures to combat segregated schools. ... *Third,* the plans before us, subjected to rigorous judicial review, are supported by compelling state interests and are narrowly tailored to accomplish those goals. ... *Fourth,* the plurality's approach risks serious harm to the law and for the Nation. ...

Indeed, the consequences of the approach the Court takes today are serious. Yesterday, the plans under review were lawful. Today, they are not. Yesterday, the citizens of this Nation could look for guidance to this Court's unanimous pronouncements concerning desegregation. Today, they cannot. Yesterday, school boards had available to them a full range of means to combat segregated schools. Today, they do not.

The Court's decision undermines other basic institutional principles as well. What has happened to *stare decisis?* The history of the plans before us, their educational importance, their highly limited use of race—all these and more—make clear that the compelling interest here is stronger than in *Grutter.* The plans here are more narrowly tailored than the law school admissions program there at issue. Hence, applying *Grutter*'s strict test, their lawfulness follows *a fortiori.* To hold to the contrary is to transform that test from "strict" to "fatal in fact"—the very opposite of what *Grutter* said. And what has happened to *Swann?* To *McDaniel?* To *Crawford?* To *Harris?* To *School Committee of Boston?* To *Seattle School Dist. No. 1?* After decades of vibrant life, they would all, under the plurality's logic, be written out of the law. ...

* * *

Finally, what of the hope and promise of *Brown?* For much of this Nation's history, the races remained divided. It was not long ago that people of different races drank from separate fountains, rode on separate buses, and studied in separate schools. In this Court's finest hour, *Brown v. Board of Education* challenged this history and helped to change it. For *Brown* held out a promise. It was a promise embodied in three Amendments designed to make citizens of slaves. It was the promise of true racial equality—not as a matter of fine words on paper, but as a matter of everyday life in the Nation's cities and schools. It was about the nature of a democracy that must work for all Americans. It sought one law, one Nation, one people, not simply as a matter of legal principle but in terms of how we actually live.

Not everyone welcomed this Court's decision in *Brown*. Three years after that decision was handed down, the Governor of Arkansas ordered state militia to block the doors of a white schoolhouse so that black children could not enter. The President of the United States dispatched the 101st Airborne Division to Little Rock, Arkansas, and federal troops were needed to enforce a desegregation decree. See *Cooper v. Aaron,* 358 U.S. 1, 78 S.Ct. 1401, 3 L.Ed.2d 5 (1958). Today, almost 50 years later, attitudes toward race in this Nation have changed dramatically. Many parents, white and black alike, want their children to attend schools with children of different races. Indeed, the very school districts that once spurned integration now strive for it. The long history of their efforts reveals the complexities and difficulties they have faced. And in light of those challenges, they have asked us not to take from their hands the instruments they have used to rid their schools of racial segregation, instruments that they believe are needed to overcome the problems of cities divided by race and poverty. The plurality would decline their modest request.

The plurality is wrong to do so. The last half century has witnessed great strides toward racial equality, but we have not yet realized the promise of *Brown*. To invalidate the plans under review is to threaten the promise of *Brown*. The plurality's position, I fear, would break that promise. This is a decision that the Court and the Nation will come to regret.

I must dissent.

Notes and Questions

1. *How did they vote?* Make a list of the Justices who wrote separate opinions in these cases. What do they say about affirmative action? About racial discrimination? About *Brown v. Board of Education*?
2. *Who is persuasive?* Which Justice(s) present the most persuasive interpretation of *Brown*? Which Justice(s) provide less persuasive interpretations?
3. Brown's *meaning.* Does this decision convince you that the *Brown* opinion should or could have elaborated on the right announced in a way that would have deterred the battles over affirmative action?
4. Brown *today.* Are these decisions consistent or inconsistent with *Brown* and its progeny? Should the Court have issued essentially *Brown III*, with a more fulsome explanation of the metes and bounds of the right announced in *Brown I*?
5. You learned in Chapter 5 that the Indian Child Welfare Act establishes a preference that Native American children be placed with Native American families whenever they are adopted. Individuals and states challenged the law on numerous grounds. Opponents of the law argued the law is an impermissible racial classification, while supporters explained the law is based on a political classification of Native American tribes. The oral argument in *Haaland v. Brackeen* is available at https://www.oyez.org/cases/2022/21-376. Do you think this law is racial discrimination, or is it an appropriate use of Congress's power to regulate commerce with the Indian tribes?

9. Enforcing *Brown* in the Schools—What Result?

You have seen the many ways that the Justices on the Court have disagreed about racial equality and the way the law protects it.

Those disagreements were present in the school cases when the Justices disagreed about how the courts should review attempts to desegregate the schools. In *Swann v. Charlotte-Mecklenburg Board of Education*, 402 U.S. 1 (1971), the Court addressed the role of the lower courts in reviewing desegregation plans. It identified four central questions about those plans.

"The central issue in this case is that of student assignment, and there are essentially four problem areas:

1. to what extent racial balance or racial quotas may be used as an implement in a remedial order to correct a previously segregated system;
2. whether every all-Negro and all-white school must be eliminated as an indispensable part of a remedial process of desegregation;
3. what the limits are, if any, on the rearrangement of school districts and attendance zones, as a remedial measure; and
4. what the limits are, if any, on the use of transportation facilities to correct state-enforced racial school segregation." *Id.* at 22.

The Court concluded on those issues that "1) remedial plans were to be judged by their effectiveness, and the use of mathematical ratios or quotas were legitimate 'starting points' for solutions; 2) predominantly or exclusively black schools required close scrutiny by courts; 3) noncontiguous attendance zones, as interim corrective measures, were within the courts' remedial powers; and 4) no rigid guidelines could be established concerning busing of students to particular schools." *Swann v. Charlotte-Mecklenburg Board of Education. Oyez,* www.oyez.org/cases/1970/281. Accessed 11 May. 2022.

Three years later, in *Milliken v. Bradley,* 418 U.S. 717 (1974), the Court issued a narrower rule, reversing a district court's desegregation ruling. Because of the pervasive segregation in Detroit, the lower court had required "consolidation of 54 independent school districts historically administered as separate units into a vast new super school district." *Id.* at 743. A majority of the Supreme Court concluded that the court should not have included the districts outside Detroit in its analysis.

"The record before us, voluminous as it is, contains evidence of *de jure* segregated conditions only in the Detroit schools; indeed, that was the theory on which the litigation was initially based, and on which the District Court took evidence. With no showing of significant violation by the 53 outlying school districts and no evidence of any interdistrict violation or effect, the court went beyond the original theory of the case as framed by the pleadings and mandated a metropolitan area remedy. To approve the remedy ordered by the court would impose on the outlying districts, not shown to have committed any constitutional violation, a wholly impermissible remedy based on a standard not hinted at in *Brown I* and *II* or any holding of this Court." *Id.* at 745.

The dissenters argued that the majority "cripples the ability of the judiciary" to undertake its task, leaving "very real practical limits on the extent to which racially identifiable schools can be eliminated within the school district." *Id.* at 764.

In 1991, the Court then ruled that a lower court could end a desegregation plan once the plan was "in compliance with the commands of the Equal Protection Clause of the Fourteenth Amendment, and that it was unlikely that the school board would return to its former ways." *Board of Education of Oklahoma City Public Schools v. Powell*, 498 U.S. 237, 247 (1991). The dissent argued that the majority had concluded "13 years of desegregation was enough," and that one-race schools might reemerge under the majority's plan. *Id.* at 251. They thought the decree's purposes had not yet been achieved.

Which of these cases, whether the majorities or the dissents, are consistent with *Brown I* or *Brown II*? How would these cases be affected by *Parents Involved?* What is the legacy of *Brown* for the courts' authority to desegregate the public schools? What is the status of a one-race school?

As you saw in Chapter 6, when you read *Shelby County v. Holder* and the other voting rights cases, race has played a key role in the voting cases. Do these cases make you reconsider your position on voting rights and the role that racial discrimination plays in it?

C. Gender Equality and Equal Protection

A proposed Equal Rights Amendment (ERA) says: "Equality of rights under the law shall not be denied or abridged by the United States or by any state on account of sex. The Congress shall have the power to enforce, by appropriate legislation, the provisions of this article." What difference would it make to the Constitution if it included an Equal Rights Amendment? How would it affect how the Court interprets gender discrimination?

The ERA was voted on by the states but has not become law. How does the Court protect against gender discrimination in the following cases? Would the cases change if the ERA were added to the Constitution?

As you read, think about this: How much of a commitment did the Nineteenth Amendment make to women's equality? The Nineteenth Amendment says, "The right of citizens of the United States to vote shall not be denied or abridged by the United States or by any State on account of sex. Congress shall have power to enforce this article by appropriate legislation." Is the Nineteenth Amendment sufficient by itself for women's equality?

1. The Journey to the Equal Protection Clause's Protection of Women

In the following case, the plurality made a strong statement against gender discrimination. What did they argue? Why did Justice Powell prefer to wait until the ERA was part of the Constitution? Can you tell from the oral argument, https://www.oyez.org/cases/1972/71-1694, what the Justices' different perspectives on gender discrimination were? Pay close attention to then-attorney Ruth Bader Ginsburg, who participated in the oral argument. Ginsburg, of course, later became a Justice on the Supreme Court and wrote an opinion below, *United States v. Virginia.* Summarize the strengths and weaknesses of Ginsburg's oral argument. How does her argument compare to that of the other lawyers?

Frontiero v. Richardson
SUPREME COURT OF THE UNITED STATES, 1973
411 U.S. 677, 93 S.Ct. 1764

Attorneys and Law Firms

Joseph J. Levin, Jr., Montgomery, Ala., for appellants.

Ruth B. Ginsburg, New York City, for American Civil Liberties Union, amicus curiae, by special leave of Court.

Samuel Huntington, Washington, D.C., for appellees.

Mr. Justice BRENNAN announced the judgment of the Court in an opinion in which Mr. Justice DOUGLAS, Mr. Justice WHITE, and Mr. Justice MARSHALL join.

The question before us concerns the right of a female member of the uniformed services to claim her spouse as a 'dependent' for the purposes of obtaining increased quarters allowances and medical and dental benefits on an equal footing with male members. Under these statutes, a serviceman may claim his wife as a 'dependent' without regard to whether she is in fact dependent upon him for any part of her support. A servicewoman, on the other hand, may not claim her husband as a 'dependent' under these programs unless he is in fact dependent upon her for over one-half of his support. Thus, the question for decision is whether this difference in treatment constitutes an unconstitutional discrimination against servicewomen in violation of the Due Process Clause of the Fifth Amendment. ...

I

... Appellant Sharron Frontiero, a lieutenant in the United States Air Force, sought increased quarters allowances, and housing and medical benefits for her husband, appellant Joseph Frontiero, on the ground that he was her 'dependent.' Although such benefits would automatically have been granted with respect to the wife of a male member of the uniformed services, appellant's application was denied because she failed to demonstrate that her husband was dependent on her for more than one-half of his support. ...

II

At the outset, appellants contend that classifications based upon sex, like classifications based upon race, alienage, and national origin, are inherently suspect and must therefore be subjected to close judicial scrutiny. We agree and, indeed, find at least implicit support for such an approach in our unanimous decision only last Term in Reed v. Reed, 404 U.S. 71, 92 S.Ct. 251, 30 L.Ed.2d 225 (1971).

In Reed, the Court considered the constitutionality of an Idaho statute providing that, when two individuals are otherwise equally entitled to appointment as administrator of an estate, the male applicant must be preferred to the female. Appellant, the mother of the deceased, and appellee, the father, filed competing petitions for appointment as administrator of their son's estate. Since the parties, as parents of the deceased, were members of the same entitlement class the statutory preference was invoked and the father's petition was therefore granted. Appellant claimed that this statute, by giving a mandatory preference to males over females without regard to their individual qualifications, violated the Equal Protection Clause of the Fourteenth Amendment.

The Court noted that the Idaho statute 'provides that different treatment be accorded to the applicants on the basis of their sex; it thus establishes a classification subject to scrutiny under the Equal Protection Clause.' Under 'traditional' equal protection analysis, a legislative classification must be sustained unless it is 'patently arbitrary' and bears no rational relationship to a legitimate governmental interest.

In an effort to meet this standard, appellee contended that the statutory scheme was a reasonable measure designed to reduce the workload on probate courts by eliminating one class of contests. Moreover, appellee argued that the mandatory preference for male applicants was in itself reasonable since 'men (are) as a rule more conversant with business affairs than ... women.' Indeed, appellee maintained that 'it is a matter of common knowledge, that women still are not engaged in politics, the professions, business or industry to the extent that men are.' ...

Despite these contentions, however, the Court held the statutory preference for male applicants unconstitutional. In reaching this result, the Court implicitly rejected appellee's apparently rational explanation of the statutory scheme, and concluded that, by ignoring the individual qualifications of particular applicants, the challenged statute provide 'dissimilar treatment for men and women who are ... similarly situated.' The Court therefore held that, even though the State's interest in achieving administrative efficiency 'is not without some legitimacy,' '(t)o give a mandatory preference to members of either sex over members of the other, merely to accomplish the elimination of hearings on the merits, is to make the very kind of arbitrary legislative choice forbidden by the (Constitution). ...' This departure from 'traditional' rational-basis analysis with respect to sex-based classifications is clearly justified.

There can be no doubt that our Nation has had a long and unfortunate history of sex discrimination. Traditionally, such discrimination was rationalized by an attitude of 'romantic paternalism' which, in practical effect, put women, not on a pedestal, but in a cage. Indeed, this paternalistic attitude became so firmly rooted in our national consciousness that, 100 years ago, a distinguished Member of this Court was able to proclaim:

> 'Man is, or should be, women's protector and defender. The natural and proper timidity and delicacy which belongs to the female sex evidently unfits it for many of the occupations of civil life. The constitution of the family organization, which is founded in the divine ordinance, as well as in the nature of things, indicates the domestic sphere as that which properly belongs to the domain and functions of womanhood. The harmony, not to say identity, of interests and views which belong, or should belong, to the family institution is repugnant to the idea of a woman adopting a distinct and independent career from that of her husband. ... '... The paramount destiny and mission of woman are to fulfil the noble and benign offices of wife and mother. This is the law of the Creator.'

Bradwell v. State of Illinois, 16 Wall. 130, 141, 21 L.Ed.2d 442 (1873) (Bradley, J., concurring).

As a result of notions such as these, our statute books gradually became laden with gross, stereotyped distinctions between the sexes and, indeed, throughout much of the 19th century the position of women in our society was, in many respects, comparable to that of blacks under the pre-Civil War slave codes. Neither slaves nor women could hold office, serve on juries, or bring suit in their own names, and married women traditionally were denied the legal capacity to hold or convey property or to serve as legal guardians of their own children. And although blacks were guaranteed the right to vote in 1870, women were denied even that right—which is itself 'preservative of other basic civil and political rights'—until adoption of the Nineteenth Amendment half a century later.

It is true, of course, that the position of women in America has improved markedly in recent decades. Nevertheless, it can hardly be doubted that, in part because of the high visibility of the sex characteristic, women still face pervasive, although at times more subtle, discrimination in our educational institutions, in the job market and, perhaps most conspicuously, in the political arena.

Moreover, since sex, like race and national origin, is an immutable characteristic determined solely by the accident of birth, the imposition of special disabilities upon the members of a particular sex because of their sex would seem to violate 'the basic concept of our system that legal burdens should bear some relationship to individual responsibility. ...' And what differentiates sex from such non-suspect statuses as intelligence or physical disability, and aligns it with the recognized suspect criteria, is that the sex characteristic frequently bears no relation to ability to perform or contribute to society. As a result, statutory distinctions between the sexes often have the effect of invidiously relegating the entire class of females to inferior legal status without regard to the actual capabilities of its individual members.

We might also note that, over the past decade, Congress has itself manifested an increasing sensitivity to sex-based classifications. In Tit. VII of the Civil Rights Act of 1964, for example, Congress expressly declared that no employer, labor union, or other organization subject to the provisions of the Act shall discriminate against any individual on the basis of 'race, color, religion, sex, or national origin.' Similarly, the Equal Pay Act of 1963 provides that no employer covered by the Act 'shall discriminate ... between employees on the basis of sex.' And s 1 of the Equal Rights Amendment, passed by Congress on March 22, 1972, and submitted to the legislatures of the States for ratification, declares that '(e)quality of rights under the law shall not be denied or abridged by the United States or by any State on account of sex.' Thus, Congress itself has concluded that classifications based upon sex are inherently invidious, and this conclusion of a coequal branch of Government is not without significance to the question presently under consideration.

With these considerations in mind, we can only conclude that classifications based upon sex, like classifications based upon race, alienage, or national origin, are inherently suspect, and must therefore be subjected to strict judicial scrutiny. Applying the analysis mandated by that stricter standard of review, it is clear that the statutory scheme now before us is constitutionally invalid.

III

... In any case, our prior decisions make clear that, although efficacious administration of governmental programs is not without some importance, 'the Constitution recognizes higher values than speed and efficiency.' And when we enter the realm of 'strict judicial scrutiny,' there can be no doubt that 'administrative convenience' is not a shibboleth, the mere recitation of which dictates constitutionality. On the contrary, any statutory scheme which draws a sharp line between the sexes, Solely for the purpose of achieving administrative convenience, necessarily commands 'dissimilar treatment for men and women who are ... similarly situated,' and therefore involves the 'very kind of arbitrary legislative choice forbidden by the (Constitution). ...' Reed v. Reed, 404 U.S., at 77, 76, 92 S.Ct., at 254. We therefore conclude that, by according differential treatment to male and female members of the uniformed services for the sole purpose of achieving administrative convenience, the challenged statutes violate the Due Process Clause of the Fifth Amendment insofar as they require a female member to prove the dependency of her husband.

Mr. Justice STEWART concurs in the judgment, agreeing that the statutes before us work an invidious discrimination in violation of the Constitution. Reed v. Reed, 404 U.S. 71, 92 S.Ct. 251, 30 L.Ed.2d 225.

Mr. Justice REHNQUIST dissents [preferring to rely on the district court's decision].

Mr. Justice POWELL, with whom THE CHIEF JUSTICE and Mr. Justice BLACKMUN join, concurring in the judgment.

I agree that the challenged statutes constitute an unconstitutional discrimination against servicewomen in violation of the Due Process Clause of the Fifth Amendment, but I cannot join the opinion of Mr. Justice BRENNAN, which would hold that all classifications based upon sex, 'like classifications based upon race, alienage, and national origin,' are 'inherently suspect and must therefore be subjected to close judicial scrutiny.' ...

There is another, and I find compelling, reason for deferring a general categorizing of sex classifications as invoking the strictest test of judicial scrutiny. The Equal Rights Amendment, which if adopted will resolve the substance of this precise question, has been approved by the Congress and submitted for ratification by the States. If this Amendment is duly adopted, it will represent the will of the people accomplished in the manner prescribed by the Constitution. By acting prematurely and unnecessarily, as I view it, the Court has assumed a decisional responsibility at the very time when state legislatures, functioning within the traditional democractic process, are debating the proposed Amendment. It seems to me that this reaching out to pre-empt by judicial action a major political decision which is currently in process of resolution does not reflect appropriate respect for duly prescribed legislative processes. ...

Notes and Questions

1. *Justice Reed.* What is the significance of the *Reed* case, on its own, and in this Court's opinion? What do you think of this video about Justice Ginsburg's work on *Reed?* See KTVB, *Reed v. Reed*, Sept. 20, 2020, at https://www.youtube.com/watch?v=nWDUWctS4Qk&list=PLsFE_Nvl6h_braQ_NxoD1jg8oDdM_l8uI&index=17.
2. *DP or EP?* Why did the *Frontiero* Court talk about the Due Process Clause instead of the Equal Protection Clause?
3. *What should the standard be?* What test did the plurality choose for gender discrimination? How does it compare to the test for racial discrimination?

4. *Where is the ERA?* What would have happened if the Court had waited for the ERA before addressing the Fourteenth Amendment's treatment of gender discrimination? Would that have been a good idea? How would it have worked? What would the cases look like if all the Justices had agreed to wait for the ERA? How much work could *Reed* have done by itself?
5. *Bradwell.* The Court quoted from the case of Myra Bradwell, an Illinois woman who applied for a license to practice law, but was denied. She invoked the Fourteenth Amendment but lost. The Court ruled that practicing law was not a privilege or immunity under the Fourteenth Amendment. *Bradwell v. The State*, 83 U.S. 130 (1873). The Court stated that man and woman were in different spheres, and that women are wives and mothers according to the "law of the Creator." What did it take to move the law away from that approach to women's rights?

2. The Test for Gender and Equal Protection

There is a significant difference between the reasoning of *Frontiero* and the following case, *Craig v. Boren*. What changed? The composition of the Court or something else? Is the newer decision a plurality or a majority? Does that make a difference? Can you tell from the oral argument, https://www.oyez.org/cases/1976/75-628, that *Craig* would be a 7–2 opinion? Why does Justice Rehnquist dissent here as he did in *Frontiero*? Do they believe there is gender discrimination in the United States? Does it matter to these cases if the plaintiff is a man or a woman?

Craig v. Boren
SUPREME COURT OF THE UNITED STATES, 1976
429 U.S. 190, 97 S.Ct. 451

BRENNAN, J., delivered the opinion of the Court, in which WHITE, MARSHALL, POWELL, and STEVENS, JJ., joined, and in all but Part II-D of which BLACKMUN, J., joined. POWELL, J., and STEVENS, J., filed concurring opinions. BLACKMUN, J., filed a statement concurring in part. STEWART, J., filed an opinion concurring in the judgment. BURGER, C.J., and REHNQUIST, J., filed dissenting opinions.

Mr. Justice BRENNAN delivered the opinion of the Court.

The interaction of two sections of an Oklahoma statute prohibits the sale of "nonintoxicating" 3.2% beer to males under the age of 21 and to females under the age of 18. The question to be decided is whether such a gender-based differential constitutes a denial to males 18–20 years of age of the equal protection of the laws in violation of the Fourteenth Amendment. ...

We turn then to the question whether, under Reed, the difference between males and females with respect to the purchase of 3.2% beer warrants the differential in age drawn by the Oklahoma statute. We conclude that it does not. ...

We accept for purposes of discussion the District Court's identification of the objective underlying [the statutes] as the enhancement of traffic safety. Clearly, the protection of public health and safety represents an important function of state and local governments. However, appellees' statistics in our view cannot support the conclusion that the gender-based distinction closely serves to achieve that objective and therefore the distinction cannot under Reed withstand equal protection challenge. We hold, therefore, that under Reed, Oklahoma's 3.2% beer statute invidiously discriminates against males 18–20 years of age. ...

Mr. Justice POWELL, concurring.

... It seems to me that the statistics offered by appellees and relied upon by the District Court do tend generally to support the view that young men drive more, possibly are inclined to drink more, and for various reasons are involved in more accidents than young women. Even so, I am not persuaded that these facts and the inferences fairly drawn from them justify this classification based on a three-year age differential between the sexes, and especially one that it so easily circumvented as to be virtually meaningless. Putting it differently, this gender-based classification does not bear a fair and substantial relation to the object of the legislation.

Mr. Justice STEVENS, concurring.

There is only one Equal Protection Clause. It requires every State to govern impartially. It does not direct the courts to apply one standard of review in some cases and a different standard in other cases. Whatever criticism may be leveled at a judicial opinion implying that there are at least three such standards applies with the same force to a double standard.

I am inclined to believe that what has become known as the two-tiered analysis of equal protection claims does not describe a completely logical method of deciding cases, but rather is a method the Court has employed to explain decisions that actually apply a single standard in a reasonably consistent fashion. I also suspect that a careful explanation of the reasons motivating particular decisions may contribute more to an identification of that standard than an attempt to articulate it in all-encompassing terms. It may therefore be appropriate for me to state the principal reasons which persuaded me to join the Court's opinion. ...

The question then is whether the traffic safety justification put forward by the State is sufficient to make an otherwise offensive classification acceptable.

The classification is not totally irrational. For the evidence does indicate that there are more males than females in this age bracket who drive and also more who drink. Nevertheless, there are several reasons why I regard the justification as unacceptable. It is difficult to believe that the statute was actually intended to cope with the problem of traffic safety, since it has only a minimal effect on access to a not very intoxicating beverage and does not prohibit its consumption. Moreover, the empirical data submitted by the State accentuate the unfairness of treating all 18–21-year-old males as inferior to their female counterparts. The legislation imposes a restraint on 100% of the males in the class allegedly because about 2% of them have probably violated one or more laws relating to the consumption of alcoholic beverages.[7] It is unlikely that this law will have a significant deterrent effect either on that 2% or on the law-abiding 98%. But even assuming some such slight benefit, it does not seem to me that an insult to all of the young men of the State can be justified by visiting the sins of the 2% on the 98%.

Mr. Justice STEWART, concurring in the judgment.

... The disparity created by these Oklahoma statutes amounts to total irrationality. For the statistics upon which the State now relies, whatever their other shortcomings, wholly fail to prove or even suggest that 3.2% beer is somehow more deleterious when it comes into the hands of a male aged 18–20 than of a female of like age. The disparate statutory treatment of the sexes here, without even a colorably valid justification or explanation, thus amounts to invidious discrimination. See Reed v. Reed.

Mr. Chief Justice BURGER, dissenting.

... Though today's decision does not go so far as to make gender-based classifications "suspect," it makes gender a disfavored classification. Without an independent constitutional basis supporting the right asserted or disfavoring the classification adopted, I can justify no substantive constitutional protection other than the normal protection afforded by the Equal Protection Clause. ...

Mr. Justice REHNQUIST, dissenting.

The Court's disposition of this case is objectionable on two grounds. First is its conclusion that men challenging a gender-based statute which treats them less favorably than women may invoke a more stringent standard of judicial review than pertains to most other types of classifications. Second is the Court's enunciation of this standard, without citation to any source, as being that "classifications by gender must serve important governmental objectives and must be substantially related to achievement of those objectives." Ante at 457 (emphasis added). The only redeeming feature of the Court's opinion, to my mind, is that it apparently signals a retreat by those who joined the plurality opinion in Frontiero v. Richardson, 411 U.S. 677, 93 S.Ct. 1764, 36 L.Ed.2d 583 (1973), from their view that sex is a "suspect" classification for purposes of equal protection analysis. I think the Oklahoma statute challenged here need pass only the "rational basis" equal protection analysis expounded in cases such as McGowan v. Maryland, 366 U.S. 420, 81 S.Ct. 1101, 6 L.Ed.2d 393 (1961), and Williamson v. Lee Optical Co., 348 U.S. 483, 75 S.Ct. 461, 99 L.Ed. 563 (1955), and I believe that it is constitutional under that analysis. ...

It is true that a number of our opinions contain broadly phrased dicta implying that the same test should be applied to all classifications based on sex, whether affecting females or males. E. g., Frontiero v. Richardson, supra, 411 U.S., at 688, 93 S.Ct., at 1771; Reed v. Reed, 404 U.S. 71, 76, 92 S.Ct. 251, 254, 30 L.Ed.2d 225 (1971). However, before today, no decision of this Court has applied an elevated level of scrutiny to invalidate a statutory discrimination harmful to males, except where the statute impaired an important personal interest protected by the Constitution. There being no such interest here, and there being no plausible argument that this is a discrimination against females, the Court's reliance on our previous sex-discrimination cases is ill-founded. It treats gender classification as a talisman which without regard to the rights involved or the persons affected calls into effect a heavier burden of judicial review.

The Court's conclusion that a law which treats males less favorably than females "must serve important governmental objectives and must be substantially related to achievement of those objectives" apparently comes out of thin air. ...

The Oklahoma Legislature could have believed that 18–20-year-old males drive substantially more, and tend more often to be intoxicated than their female counterparts; that they prefer beer and admit to drinking and driving at a higher rate than females; and that they suffer traffic injuries out of proportion to the part they make up of the population. Under the appropriate rational-basis test for equal protection, it is neither irrational nor arbitrary to bar them from making purchases of 3.2% beer, which purchases might in many cases be made by a young man who immediately returns to his vehicle with the beverage in his possession. The record does not give any good indication of the true proportion of males in the age group who drink and drive (except that it is no doubt greater than the 2% who are arrested), but whatever it may be I cannot see that the mere purchase right involved could conceivably raise a due process question. There being no violation of either equal protection or due process, the statute should accordingly be upheld.

Notes and Questions

1. *Which one?* Which Justice's opinion did you find most persuasive in this case? Why?
2. *Justice Powell.* Why did Justice Powell concur in this opinion?
3. *Justice Stevens.* Justice Stevens was famous for his repeated argument that there is only one Equal Protection Clause and not different tiers of scrutiny. What is his test for the one Equal Protection Clause? Would you think of replacing all the equal protection law you have studied with Justice Stevens's one test?

3. Single-Sex Schools

Justice Ruth Bader Ginsburg, who litigated the early women's rights cases, wrote the following opinion in *United States v. Virginia.* Does she use the same tests as the earlier two cases, or does she change the law in any way? By the time this case is decided, there are two women on the Court, Justices Sandra Day O'Connor and Ruth Bader Ginsburg. Are there questions in the oral argument, https://www.oyez.org/cases/1995/94-1941, that show they have a different perspective on the question than the other Justices do? Or are the Justices' perspectives all the same? Can you tell from the argument that Justice Scalia will be the lone dissenter in the case? How would you expect Chief Justice Rehnquist to vote in this case, given his dissents in the earlier cases you have read?

United States v. Virginia

SUPREME COURT OF THE UNITED STATES, 1996
518 U.S. 515, 116 S.Ct. 2264

GINSBURG, J., delivered the opinion of the Court, in which STEVENS, O'CONNOR, KENNEDY, SOUTER, AND BREYER, JJ., JOINED. REHNQUIST, C.J., FILED AN OPINION CONCURRING IN THE JUDGMENT. SCALIA, J., FILED A DISSENTING OPINION. THOMAS, J., TOOK NO PART IN THE CONSIDERATION OR DECISION OF THE CASE.

Virginia's public institutions of higher learning include an incomparable military college, Virginia Military Institute (VMI). The United States maintains that the Constitution's equal protection guarantee precludes Virginia from reserving exclusively to men the unique educational opportunities VMI affords. We agree.

I

Founded in 1839, VMI is today the sole single-sex school among Virginia's 15 public institutions of higher learning. VMI's distinctive mission is to produce "citizen-soldiers," men prepared for leadership in civilian life and in military service. VMI pursues this mission through pervasive training of a kind not available anywhere else in Virginia. Assigning prime place to character development, VMI uses an "adversative method" modeled on English public schools and once characteristic of military instruction. VMI constantly endeavors to instill physical and mental discipline in its cadets and impart to them a strong moral code. The school's graduates leave VMI with heightened comprehension of their capacity to deal with duress and stress, and a large sense of accomplishment for completing the hazardous course.

VMI has notably succeeded in its mission to produce leaders; among its alumni are military generals, Members of Congress, and business executives. The school's alumni overwhelmingly perceive that their VMI training helped them to realize their personal goals. VMI's endowment reflects the loyalty of its graduates; VMI has the largest per-student endowment of all public undergraduate institutions in the Nation.

Neither the goal of producing citizen-soldiers nor VMI's implementing methodology is inherently unsuitable to women. And the school's impressive record in producing leaders has made admission desirable to some women. Nevertheless, Virginia has elected to preserve exclusively for men the advantages and opportunities a VMI education affords.

II

... In 1990, prompted by a complaint filed with the Attorney General by a female high-school student seeking admission to VMI, the United States sued the Commonwealth of Virginia and VMI, alleging that VMI's exclusively male admission policy violated the Equal Protection Clause of the Fourteenth Amendment. ...

In response to the Fourth Circuit's ruling, Virginia proposed a parallel program for women: Virginia Women's Institute for Leadership (VWIL). The 4-year, state-sponsored undergraduate program would be located at Mary Baldwin College, a private liberal arts school for women, and would be open, initially, to about 25 to 30 students. Although VWIL would share VMI's mission—to produce "citizen-soldiers"—the VWIL program would differ, as does Mary Baldwin College, from VMI in academic offerings, methods of education, and financial resources. ...

Training its attention on methods of instruction appropriate for "most women," the Task Force determined that a military model would be "wholly inappropriate" for VWIL. ...

III

The cross-petitions in this suit present two ultimate issues. First, does Virginia's exclusion of women from the educational opportunities provided by VMI—extraordinary opportunities for military training and civilian leadership development—deny to women "capable of all of the individual activities required of VMI cadets," the equal protection of the laws guaranteed by the Fourteenth Amendment? Second, if VMI's "unique" situation,—as Virginia's sole single-sex public institution of higher education—offends the Constitution's equal protection principle, what is the remedial requirement?

IV

We note, once again, the core instruction of this Court's pathmarking decisions in *J.E.B. v. Alabama ex rel. T.*

B., 511 U.S. 127, 136–137, and n. 6, 114 S.Ct. 1419, 1425–1426, and n. 6, 128 L.Ed.2d 89 (1994), and *Mississippi Univ. for Women,* 458 U.S., at 724, 102 S.Ct., at 3336 (internal quotation marks omitted): Parties who seek to defend gender-based government action must demonstrate an "exceedingly persuasive justification" for that action ...

Measuring the record in this case against the review standard just described, we conclude that Virginia has shown no "exceedingly persuasive justification" for excluding all women from the citizen-soldier training afforded by VMI. We therefore affirm the Fourth Circuit's initial judgment, which held that Virginia had violated the Fourteenth Amendment's Equal Protection Clause. Because the remedy proffered by Virginia—the Mary Baldwin VWIL program—does not cure the constitutional violation, *i.e.,* it does not provide equal opportunity, we reverse the Fourth Circuit's final judgment in this case.

V

... In sum, we find no persuasive evidence in this record that VMI's male-only admission policy "is in furtherance of a state policy of 'diversity.'" No such policy, the Fourth Circuit observed, can be discerned from the movement of all other public colleges and universities in Virginia away from single-sex education. That court also questioned "how one institution with autonomy, but with no authority over any other state institution, can give effect to a state policy of diversity among institutions." A purpose genuinely to advance an array of educational options, as the Court of Appeals recognized, is not served by VMI's historic and constant plan—a plan to "affor[d] a unique educational benefit only to males." However "liberally" this plan serves the Commonwealth's sons, it makes no provision whatever for her daughters. That is not *equal* protection.

Surely that goal is great enough to accommodate women, who today count as citizens in our American democracy equal in stature to men. Just as surely, the Commonwealth's great goal is not substantially advanced by women's categorical exclusion, in total disregard of their individual merit, from the Commonwealth's premier "citizen-soldier" corps. Virginia, in sum, "has fallen far short of establishing the 'exceedingly persuasive justification,'" *Mississippi Univ. for Women,* 458 U.S., at 731, 102 S.Ct., at 3340, that must be the solid base for any gender-defined classification.

VI

... In contrast to the generalizations about women on which Virginia rests, we note again these dispositive realities: VMI's "implementing methodology" is not "inherently unsuitable to women," 976 F.2d, at 899; "some women ... do well under [the] adversative model," "some women, at least, would want to attend [VMI] if they had the opportunity," "some women are capable of all of the individual activities required of VMI cadets," and "can meet the physical standards [VMI] now impose[s] on men." It is on behalf of these women that the United States has instituted this suit, and it is for them that a remedy must be crafted,[19] a remedy that will end their exclusion from a state-supplied educational opportunity for which they are fit, a decree that will "bar like discrimination in the future."

In myriad respects other than military training, VWIL does not qualify as VMI's equal. VWIL's student body, faculty, course offerings, and facilities hardly match VMI's. Nor can the VWIL graduate anticipate the benefits associated with VMI's 157-year history, the school's prestige, and its influential alumni network.

VII

... A prime part of the history of our Constitution, historian Richard Morris recounted, is the story of the extension of constitutional rights and protections to people once ignored or excluded. VMI's story continued as our comprehension of "We the People" expanded. There is no reason to believe that the admission of women capable of all the activities required of VMI cadets would destroy the Institute rather than enhance its capacity to serve the "more perfect Union."

Chief Justice REHNQUIST, concurring in the judgment.

...

I

Two decades ago in *Craig v. Boren,* 429 U.S. 190, 197, 97 S.Ct. 451, 456–457, 50 L.Ed.2d 397 (1976), we announced that "[t]o withstand constitutional challenge, ... classifications by gender must serve important governmental objectives and must be substantially related to achievement of those objectives." We have adhered to that standard of scrutiny ever since. While the majority adheres to this test today, it also says that the Commonwealth must demonstrate an "'exceedingly persuasive justification'" to support a gender-based classification. It is unfortunate that the Court thereby introduces an element of uncertainty respecting the appropriate test. ...

In the end, the women's institution Virginia proposes, VWIL, fails as a remedy, because it is distinctly inferior to the existing men's institution and will continue to be for the foreseeable future. VWIL simply is not, in any sense, the institution that VMI is. In particular, VWIL is a program appended to a private college, not a self-standing institution; and VWIL is substantially underfunded as compared to VMI. I therefore ultimately agree with the Court that Virginia has not provided an adequate remedy.

Justice SCALIA, dissenting.

Today the Court shuts down an institution that has served the people of the Commonwealth of Virginia with pride and distinction for over a century and a half. To achieve that desired result, it rejects (contrary to our established practice) the factual findings of two courts below, sweeps aside the precedents of this Court, and ignores the history of our people. As to facts: It explicitly rejects the finding that there exist "gender-based developmental differences" supporting Virginia's restriction of the "adversative" method to only a men's institution, and the finding that the all-male composition of the Virginia Military Institute (VMI) is essential to that institution's character. As to precedent: It drastically revises our established standards for reviewing sex-based classifications. And as to history: It counts for nothing the long tradition, enduring down to the present, of men's military colleges supported by both States and the Federal Government. ...

III

With this explanation of how the Court has succeeded in making its analysis seem orthodox—and indeed, if intimations are to be believed, even overly generous to VMI—I now proceed to describe how the analysis should have been conducted. The question to be answered, I repeat, is whether the exclusion of women from VMI is "substantially related to an important governmental objective."

It is beyond question that Virginia has an important state interest in providing effective college education for its citizens. That single-sex instruction is an approach substantially related to that interest should be evident enough from the long and continuing history in this country of men's and women's colleges. But beyond that, as the Court of Appeals here stated: "That single-gender education at the college level is beneficial to both sexes is a *fact established in this case*." ...

There can be no serious dispute that, as the District Court found, single-sex education and a distinctive educational method "represent legitimate contributions to diversity in the Virginia higher education system." *Ibid.* As a theoretical matter, Virginia's educational interest would have been *best* served (insofar as the two factors we have mentioned are concerned) by six different types of public colleges—an all-men's, an all-women's, and a coeducational college run in the "adversative method," and an all-men's, an all-women's, and a coeducational college run in the "traditional method." But as a practical matter, of course, Virginia's financial resources, like any State's, are not limitless, and the Commonwealth must select among the available options. Virginia thus has decided to fund, in addition to some 14 coeducational 4-year colleges, one college that is run as an all-male school on the adversative model: the Virginia Military Institute. ... In these circumstances, Virginia's election to fund one public all-male institution and one on the adversative model—and to concentrate its resources in a single entity that serves both these interests in diversity—is substantially related to the Commonwealth's important educational interests.

Notes and Questions

1. *What is the test?* Explain the Ginsburg test, with its reference to an "exceedingly persuasive justification." Is that test different from the earlier gender rights cases or the same?
2. *Why a concurrence?* Why did Rehnquist concur here and not dissent as he did in the earlier opinions? What does he think about Justice Ginsburg's test?
3. *Why a dissent?* Why did Scalia dissent? Is there a constitutional need for public single-sex schools?

4. *The results.* Two women graduated from VMI in 1999. First Women Graduate from VMI, APNews, May 15, 1999, https://apnews.com/article/80b0f5d4f2d83f523a01237feca0a59e. After Justice Ginsburg's death in 2020, other women VMI graduates said she had "changed this place for the better." Another graduate said at the time the decision came down, "I'm going to VMI. Because I'm just as powerful and capable and smart as any man in this classroom." Heather Graf, Virginia Military Institute's Female Cadets and Graduates Reflect on RBG's Legacy, ABC7 News, Sept. 21, 2020, at https://wjla.com/news/local/virginia-military-institutes-female-cadets-graduates-reflect-on-rbgs-legacy. In 2021, a woman graduate became the school's top military commander. She succeeded the school's first Black leader. A *Washington Post* story describes the difficult situations women often face at VMI. Ian Shapira, Derision, misogyny, sexual assault: VMI women face attacks on campus and online: Women at Virginia Military Institute describe an atmosphere of hostility and an expectation of backlash from male cadets if they report being groped or raped, *Washington Post*, July 12, 2021, https://www.washingtonpost.com/education/2021/07/12/vmi-women-sex-assault-misogyny/. What do these stories tell you about the Equal Protection Clause?
5. *Video.* What do you think of Justice Ginsburg's comments on *VMI?* See WSLS 10, Justice Ginsburg talks about decision to open VMI to women, Feb. 1, 2017, at https://www.youtube.com/watch?v=qt8fYNSqrDc&list=PLsFE_Nvl6h_braQ_NxoD1jg8oDdM_l8uI&index=20.

D. LGBTQ Equality

We've already read that the Fourteenth Amendment prohibits racial and gender discrimination. We've asked if gender rights would enjoy more protection if the Constitution included an Equal Rights Amendment.

Now we turn to what the Constitution says about sexual orientation discrimination. Note the trajectory of the right from 1986 on and the explanations in the cases for why it isn't and why it is protected. What level of scrutiny should the Court employ in analyzing it? The strictest scrutiny? Intermediate scrutiny? Rational basis scrutiny? Justice Stevens's one-level Equal Protection Clause scrutiny?

1. Does Equal Protection Protect LGBTQ Equality?

The Court's teaching on homosexuality has changed over the years. In 1986, in *Bowers v. Hardwick*, 478 U.S. 186 (1986), the Court ruled in a decision invoking tradition and the Bible that there was no constitutional protection for acts of homosexual sodomy, and, therefore, the states could outlaw such practices. Following are the votes in *Bowers*:

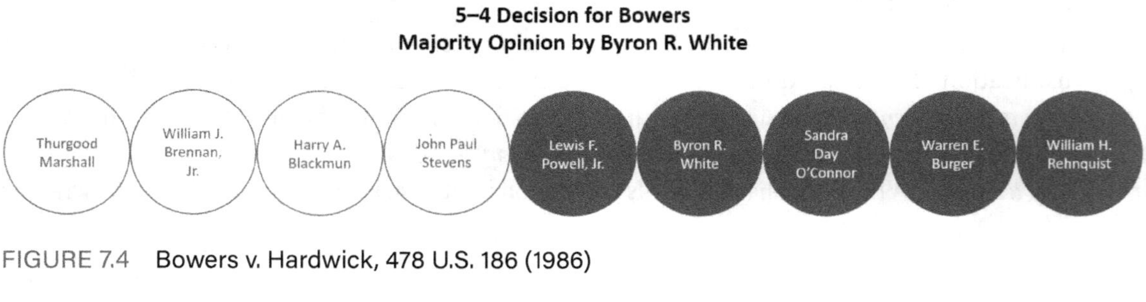

FIGURE 7.4 Bowers v. Hardwick, 478 U.S. 186 (1986)

The following case, *Romer v. Evans*, takes a different tack a mere ten years later. Here is the vote in *Romer*:

6–3 Decision
Majority Opinion by Anthony M. Kennedy

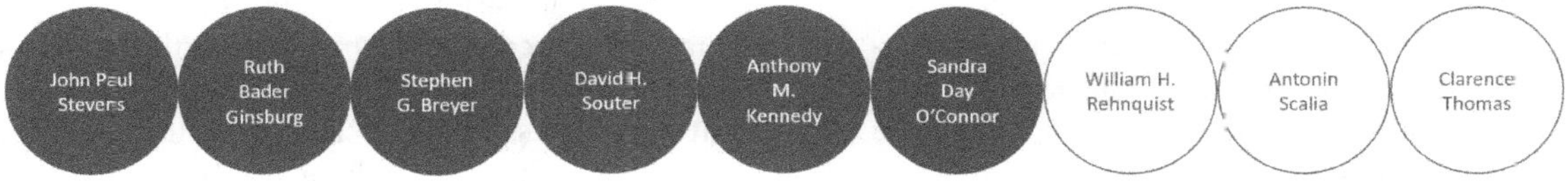

FIGURE 7.5 Romer v. Evans, 517 US 620 (1996)

Justice Anthony Kennedy wrote all of the Court's gay rights decisions until he retired. In 1996, he started with *Romer v. Evans*, a Colorado case about a state constitutional amendment that limited LGBTQ rights. Despite the infamous ruling in *Bowers*, he said the state amendment violated Equal Protection. You can read the oral argument at https://www.oyez.org/cases/1995/94-1039. Can you tell the Justices' attitudes toward gay rights in their questions in this case? Why do you think Justice O'Connor joined Justice Kennedy's opinion but not his overruling of *Bowers*?

Can you figure out now how the Court moved from *Bowers* to this invalidation of an anti-LGBTQ state amendment to a constitutional right to same-sex marriage in so few years?

Romer v. Evans

SUPREME COURT OF THE UNITED STATES, 1996
517 U.S. 620, 116 S.Ct. 1620

KENNEDY, J., delivered the opinion of the Court, in which STEVENS, O'CONNOR, SOUTER, GINSBURG, and BREYER, JJ., joined. SCALIA, J., filed a dissenting opinion, in which REHNQUIST, C.J., and THOMAS, J., joined.

One century ago, the first Justice Harlan admonished this Court that the Constitution "neither knows nor tolerates classes among citizens." *Plessy v. Ferguson,* 163 U.S. 537, 559, 16 S.Ct. 1138, 1146, 41 L.Ed. 256 (1896) (dissenting opinion). Unheeded then, those words now are understood to state a commitment to the law's neutrality where the rights of persons are at stake. The Equal Protection Clause enforces this principle and today requires us to hold invalid a provision of Colorado's Constitution.

I

The enactment challenged in this case is an amendment to the Constitution of the State of Colorado, adopted in a 1992 statewide referendum. The parties and the state courts refer to it as "Amendment 2," its designation when submitted to the voters. The impetus for the amendment and the contentious campaign that preceded its adoption came in large part from ordinances that had been passed in various Colorado municipalities. For example, the cities of Aspen and Boulder and the city and County of Denver each had enacted ordinances which banned discrimination in many transactions and activities, including housing, employment, education, public accommodations, and health and welfare services. What gave rise to the statewide controversy was the protection the ordinances afforded to persons discriminated against by reason of their sexual orientation. Amendment 2 repeals these ordinances to the extent they prohibit discrimination on the basis of "homosexual, lesbian or bisexual orientation, conduct, practices or relationships."

Yet Amendment 2, in explicit terms, does more than repeal or rescind these provisions. It prohibits all legislative, executive or judicial action at any level of state or local government designed to protect the named class, a class we shall refer to as homosexual persons or gays and lesbians. The amendment reads:

> "No Protected Status Based on Homosexual, Lesbian or Bisexual Orientation. Neither the State of Colorado, through any of its branches or departments, nor any of its agencies, political subdivisions, municipalities or school districts, shall enact, adopt or enforce any statute, regulation, ordinance or policy whereby homosexual, lesbian or bisexual orientation, conduct, practices or relationships shall constitute or otherwise be the basis of or entitle any person or class of persons to have or claim any minority status, quota preferences, protected status or claim of discrimination. This Section of the Constitution shall be in all respects self-executing." ...

II

The State's principal argument in defense of Amendment 2 is that it puts gays and lesbians in the same position as all other persons. So, the State says, the measure does no more than deny homosexuals special rights. This reading of the amendment's language is implausible. We rely not upon our own interpretation of the amendment but upon the authoritative construction of Colorado's Supreme Court. ...

> "The 'ultimate effect' of Amendment 2 is to prohibit any governmental entity from adopting similar, or more protective statutes, regulations, ordinances, or policies in the future unless the state constitution is first amended to permit such measures." ...

Amendment 2 bars homosexuals from securing protection against the injuries that these public-accommodations laws address. That in itself is a severe consequence, but there is more. Amendment 2, in addition, nullifies specific legal protections for this targeted class in all transactions in housing, sale of real estate, insurance, health and welfare services, private education, and employment.

Not confined to the private sphere, Amendment 2 also operates to repeal and forbid all laws or policies providing specific protection for gays or lesbians from discrimination by every level of Colorado government. ...

III

The Fourteenth Amendment's promise that no person shall be denied the equal protection of the laws must coexist with the practical necessity that most legislation classifies for one purpose or another, with resulting disadvantage to various groups or persons. We have attempted to reconcile the principle with the reality by stating that, if a law neither burdens a fundamental right nor targets a suspect class, we will uphold the legislative classification so long as it bears a rational relation to some legitimate end.

Amendment 2 fails, indeed defies, even this conventional inquiry. First, the amendment has the peculiar property of imposing a broad and undifferentiated disability on a single named group, an exceptional and, as we shall explain, invalid form of legislation. Second, its sheer breadth is so discontinuous with the reasons offered for it that the amendment seems inexplicable by anything but animus toward the class it affects; it lacks a rational relationship to legitimate state interests. ...

It is not within our constitutional tradition to enact laws of this sort. Central both to the idea of the rule of law and to our own Constitution's guarantee of equal protection is the principle that government and each of its parts remain open on impartial terms to all who seek its assistance. "'Equal protection of the laws is not achieved through indiscriminate imposition of inequalities.'" ...

We must conclude that Amendment 2 classifies homosexuals not to further a proper legislative end but to make them unequal to everyone else. This Colorado cannot do. A State cannot so deem a class of persons a stranger to its laws. Amendment 2 violates the Equal Protection Clause, and the judgment of the Supreme Court of Colorado is affirmed.

Justice SCALIA, with whom THE CHIEF JUSTICE and Justice THOMAS join, dissenting.

The Court has mistaken a Kulturkampf for a fit of spite. The constitutional amendment before us here is not the manifestation of a "'bare ... desire to harm'" homosexuals, *ante,* at 1628, but is rather a modest attempt by seemingly tolerant Coloradans to preserve traditional sexual mores against the efforts of a politically powerful minority to revise those mores through use of the laws. That objective, and the means chosen to achieve it, are not only unimpeachable under any constitutional doctrine hitherto pronounced (hence the opinion's heavy reliance upon principles of righteousness rather than judicial holdings); they have been specifically approved by the Congress of the United States and by this Court.

In holding that homosexuality cannot be singled out for disfavorable treatment, the Court contradicts a decision, unchallenged here, pronounced only 10 years ago, see *Bowers v. Hardwick,* 478 U.S. 186, 106 S.Ct. 2841, 92 L.Ed.2d 140 (1986), and places the prestige of this institution behind the proposition that opposition to homosexuality is as reprehensible as racial or religious bias. Whether it is or not is *precisely* the cultural debate that gave rise to the Colorado constitutional amendment (and to the preferential laws against which the amendment was directed). Since the Constitution of the United States says nothing about this subject, it is left to be resolved by normal democratic means, including the democratic adoption of provisions in state constitutions. This Court has no business imposing upon all Americans the resolution favored by the elite class from which the Members of this institution are selected, pronouncing that "animosity" toward homosexuality, is evil. I vigorously dissent. ...

III

... But though Coloradans are, as I say, *entitled* to be hostile toward homosexual conduct, the fact is that the degree of hostility reflected by Amendment 2 is the smallest conceivable. ...

* * *

Today's opinion has no foundation in American constitutional law, and barely pretends to. The people of Colorado have adopted an entirely reasonable provision which does not even disfavor homosexuals in any substantive sense, but merely denies them preferential treatment. Amendment 2 is designed to prevent piecemeal deterioration of the sexual morality favored by a majority of Coloradans, and is not only an appropriate means to that legitimate end, but a means that Americans have employed before. Striking it down is an act, not of judicial judgment, but of political will. I dissent.

Notes and Questions

1. *Scope of the Equal Protection Clause.* What does the Equal Protection Clause protect? What does the majority say it protects in this case? How is the clause applied in this case? Why does the dissent disagree with the majority's analysis?
2. *What level of review?* The Court could have written that homosexuals are a discrete and insular minority that has long faced discrimination, and, therefore, any legislation about them was subject to strict scrutiny. Why did the Court not add gays and lesbians as a *suspect class* subject to strict scrutiny under the Equal Protection Clause's precedents? In other words, why didn't the Court treat LGBTQ equal protection analysis the same as racial equal protection analysis?
3. *The dissent.* What do you think about Justice Scalia's opening line: "The Court has mistaken a Kulturkampf for a fit of spite." What does that mean? Is the dissent correct that if *Bowers* is the law, then Amendment 2 must be constitutional?

2. The Constitution Protects Same-Sex Relations

In 2003, seven years after *Romer* was decided and seventeen years post-*Bowers*, the Court overruled *Bowers* in the following case, *Lawrence v. Texas.* The oral argument is at https://www.oyez.org/cases/2002/02-102.

Justice Kennedy wrote this opinion as well. He was joined by Justice Stevens, who dissented in *Bowers.* Justice O'Connor, who was also part of the majority in *Bowers,* joined Justice Kennedy's opinion, but she did not accept that *Bowers* should be overruled. Why? Chief Justice Rehnquist, who was part of the majority of *Bowers,* dissented in this case.

What do you learn from the oral argument about whether *Bowers* should have been overruled? Can you tell which Justices support its overruling and which do not? Are the justifications for overruling consistent with the reasoning of *Casey*, which addresses whether *Roe* should have been overruled? Note that the Justices in the following case disagree about using the Due Process Clause or the Equal Protection Clause as the basis for the judgment. What are the ramifications of choosing one clause or another?

Lawrence v. Texas

SUPREME COURT OF THE UNITED STATES, 2003
539 U.S. 558, 123 S.Ct. 2472

KENNEDY, J., delivered the opinion of the Court, in which STEVENS, SOUTER, GINSBURG, and BREYER, JJ., joined. O'CONNOR, J., filed an opinion concurring in the judgment. SCALIA, J., filed a dissenting opinion, in which REHNQUIST, C.J., and THOMAS, J., joined. THOMAS, J., filed a dissenting opinion.

Liberty protects the person from unwarranted government intrusions into a dwelling or other private places. In our tradition the State is not omnipresent in the home. And there are other spheres of our lives and existence, outside the home, where the State should not be a dominant presence. Freedom extends beyond spatial bounds. Liberty presumes an autonomy of self that includes freedom of thought, belief, expression, and certain intimate conduct. The instant case involves liberty of the person both in its spatial and in its more transcendent dimensions.

I

The question before the Court is the validity of a Texas statute making it a crime for two persons of the same sex to engage in certain intimate sexual conduct.

In Houston, Texas, officers of the Harris County Police Department were dispatched to a private residence in response to a reported weapons disturbance. They entered an apartment where one of the petitioners, John Geddes Lawrence, resided. The right of the police to enter does not seem to have been questioned. The officers observed Lawrence and another man, Tyron Garner, engaging in a sexual act. The two petitioners were arrested, held in custody overnight, and charged and convicted before a Justice of the Peace. ...

We granted certiorari, 537 U.S. 1044, 123 S.Ct. 661, 154 L.Ed.2d 514 (2002), to consider three questions:

1. Whether petitioners' criminal convictions under the Texas 'Homosexual Conduct' law—which criminalizes sexual intimacy by same-sex couples, but not identical behavior by different-sex couples—violate the Fourteenth Amendment guarantee of equal protection of the laws.
2. Whether petitioners' criminal convictions for adult consensual sexual intimacy in the home violate their vital interests in liberty and privacy protected by the Due Process Clause of the Fourteenth Amendment.
3. Whether *Bowers v. Hardwick, supra,* should be overruled. ...

II

... In summary, the historical grounds relied upon in *Bowers* are more complex than the majority opinion and the concurring opinion by Chief Justice Burger indicate. Their historical premises are not without doubt and, at the very least, are overstated. ...

In our own constitutional system the deficiencies in *Bowers* became even more apparent in the years following its announcement. The 25 States with laws prohibiting the relevant conduct referenced in the *Bowers* decision are reduced now to 13, of which 4 enforce their laws only against homosexual conduct. In those States where sodomy is still proscribed, whether for same-sex or heterosexual conduct, there is a pattern of nonenforcement with respect to consenting adults acting in private. The State of Texas admitted in 1994 that as of that date it had not prosecuted anyone under those circumstances. ...

Equality of treatment and the due process right to demand respect for conduct protected by the substantive guarantee of liberty are linked in important respects, and a decision on the latter point advances both interests. If protected conduct is made criminal and the law which does so remains unexamined for its substantive validity, its stigma might remain even if it were not enforceable as drawn for equal protection reasons. When homosexual conduct is made criminal by the law of the State, that declaration in and of itself is an invitation to subject homosexual persons to discrimination both in the public and in the private spheres. The central holding of *Bowers* has been brought in question by this case, and it should be addressed. Its continuance as precedent demeans the lives of homosexual persons. ...

The foundations of *Bowers* have sustained serious erosion from our recent decisions in *Casey* and *Romer*. ...

Bowers was not correct when it was decided, and it is not correct today. It ought not to remain binding precedent. *Bowers v. Hardwick* should be and now is overruled.

The present case does not involve minors. It does not involve persons who might be injured or coerced or who are situated in relationships where consent might not easily be refused. It does not involve public conduct or prostitution. It does not involve whether the government must give formal recognition to any relationship that homosexual persons seek to enter. The case does involve two adults who, with full and mutual consent from each other, engaged in sexual practices common to a homosexual lifestyle. The petitioners are entitled to respect for their private lives. The State cannot demean their existence or control their destiny by making their private sexual conduct a crime. Their right to liberty under the Due Process Clause gives them the full right to engage in their conduct without intervention of the government. "It is a promise of the Constitution that there is a realm of personal liberty which the government may not enter." *Casey, supra,* at 847, 112 S.Ct. 2791. The Texas statute furthers no legitimate state interest which can justify its intrusion into the personal and private life of the individual. ...

Justice O'CONNOR, concurring in the judgment.

... I joined *Bowers,* and do not join the Court in overruling it. Nevertheless, I agree with the Court that Texas' statute banning same-sex sodomy is unconstitutional. Rather than relying on the substantive component of the Fourteenth Amendment's Due Process Clause, as the Court does, I base my conclusion on the Fourteenth Amendment's Equal Protection Clause. ...

The statute at issue here makes sodomy a crime only if a person "engages in deviate sexual intercourse with another individual of the same sex." Sodomy between opposite-sex partners, however, is not a crime in Texas. That is, Texas treats the same conduct differently based solely on the participants. Those harmed by this law are people who have a same-sex sexual orientation and thus are more likely to engage in behavior prohibited by § 21.06.

The Texas statute makes homosexuals unequal in the eyes of the law by making particular conduct—and only that conduct—subject to criminal sanction. It appears that prosecutions under Texas' sodomy law are rare. This case shows, however, that prosecutions under § 21.06 *do* occur. And while the penalty imposed on petitioners in this case was relatively minor, the consequences of conviction are not. It appears that petitioners' convictions, if upheld, would disqualify them from or restrict their ability to engage in a variety of professions, including medicine, athletic training, and interior design. Indeed, were petitioners to move to one of four States, their convictions would require them to register as sex offenders to local law enforcement. ...

The only question in front of the Court in *Bowers* was whether the substantive component of the Due Process Clause protected a right to engage in homosexual sodomy. *Bowers* did not hold that moral disapproval of a group is a rational basis under the Equal Protection Clause to criminalize homosexual sodomy when heterosexual sodomy is not punished.

This case raises a different issue than *Bowers:* whether, under the Equal Protection Clause, moral disapproval is a legitimate state interest to justify by itself a statute that bans homosexual sodomy, but not heterosexual sodomy. It is not. Moral disapproval of this group, like a bare desire to harm the group, is an interest that is insufficient to satisfy rational basis review under the Equal Protection Clause. Indeed, we have never held that moral disapproval, without any other asserted state interest, is a sufficient rationale under the Equal Protection Clause to justify a law that discriminates among groups of persons. ...

Whether a sodomy law that is neutral both in effect and application would violate the substantive component of the Due Process Clause is an issue that need not be decided today. I am confident, however, that so long as the Equal Protection Clause requires a sodomy law to apply equally to the private consensual conduct of homosexuals and heterosexuals alike, such a law would not long stand in our democratic society. ...

That this law as applied to private, consensual conduct is unconstitutional under the Equal Protection Clause does not mean that other laws distinguishing between heterosexuals and homosexuals would similarly fail under rational basis review. Texas cannot assert any legitimate state interest here, such as national security or preserving the traditional institution of marriage. Unlike the moral disapproval of same-sex relations—the asserted state interest in this case—other reasons exist to promote the institution of marriage beyond mere moral disapproval of an excluded group. ...

Justice SCALIA, with whom THE CHIEF JUSTICE and Justice THOMAS join, dissenting.

...

I

... What a massive disruption of the current social order, therefore, the overruling of *Bowers* entails. Not so the overruling of *Roe,* which would simply have restored the regime that existed for centuries before 1973, in which the permissibility of, and restrictions upon, abortion were determined legislatively State by State. *Casey,* however, chose to base its *stare decisis* determination on a different "sort" of reliance. "[P]eople," it said, "have organized intimate relationships and made choices that define their views of themselves and their places in society, in reliance on the availability of abortion in the event that contraception should fail." This falsely assumes that the consequence of overruling *Roe* would have been to make abortion unlawful. It would not; it would merely have *permitted* the States to do so. Many States would unquestionably have declined to prohibit abortion, and others would not have prohibited it within six months (after which the most significant reliance interests would have expired). Even for persons in States other than these, the choice would not have been between abortion and childbirth, but between abortion nearby and abortion in a neighboring State.

To tell the truth, it does not surprise me, and should surprise no one, that the Court has chosen today to revise the standards of *stare decisis* set forth in *Casey.* It has thereby exposed *Casey's* extraordinary deference to precedent for the result-oriented expedient that it is. ...

IV

I turn now to the ground on which the Court squarely rests its holding: the contention that there is no rational basis for the law here under attack. This proposition is so out of accord with our jurisprudence—indeed, with the jurisprudence of *any* society we know—that it requires little discussion.

The Texas statute undeniably seeks to further the belief of its citizens that certain forms of sexual behavior are "immoral and unacceptable," *Bowers, supra,* at 196, 106 S.Ct. 2841—the same interest furthered by criminal laws against fornication, bigamy, adultery, adult incest, bestiality, and obscenity. *Bowers* held that this *was* a legitimate state interest. The Court today reaches the opposite conclusion. The Texas statute, it says, "furthers *no legitimate state interest* which can justify its intrusion into the personal and private life of the individual." The Court embraces instead Justice STEVENS' declaration in his *Bowers* dissent, that "'the fact that the governing majority in a State has traditionally viewed a particular practice as immoral is not a sufficient reason for upholding a law prohibiting the practice.'" This effectively decrees the end of all morals legislation. If, as the Court asserts, the promotion of majoritarian sexual morality is not even a *legitimate* state interest, none of the above-mentioned laws can survive rational-basis review.

V

Finally, I turn to petitioners' equal-protection challenge, which no Member of the Court save Justice O'CONNOR, embraces: On its face § 21.06(a) applies equally to all persons. Men and women, heterosexuals and homosexuals, are all subject to its prohibition of deviate sexual intercourse with someone of the same sex. To be sure, § 21.06 does distinguish between the sexes insofar as concerns the partner with whom the sexual acts are performed: men can violate the law only with other men, and women only with other women. But this cannot itself be a denial of equal protection, since it is precisely the same distinction regarding partner that is drawn in state laws prohibiting marriage with someone of the same sex while permitting marriage with someone of the opposite sex. ...

Justice O'CONNOR simply decrees application of "a more searching form of rational basis review" to the Texas statute. The cases she cites do not recognize such a standard, and reach their conclusions only after finding, as required by conventional rational-basis analysis, that no conceivable legitimate state interest supports the classification at issue. Nor does Justice O'CONNOR explain precisely what her "more searching form" of rational-basis review consists of. It must at least mean, however, that laws exhibiting "a desire to harm a politically unpopular group," are invalid *even though* there may be a conceivable rational basis to support them.

This reasoning leaves on pretty shaky grounds state laws limiting marriage to opposite-sex couples. Justice O'CONNOR seeks to preserve them by the conclusory statement that "preserving the traditional institution of marriage" is a legitimate state interest. But "preserving the traditional institution of marriage" is just a kinder way of describing the State's *moral disapproval* of same-sex couples. Texas's interest in § 21.06 could be recast in similarly euphemistic terms: "preserving the traditional sexual mores of our society." In the jurisprudence Justice O'CONNOR has seemingly created, judges can validate laws by characterizing them as "preserving the traditions of society" (good); or invalidate them by characterizing them as "expressing moral disapproval" (bad).

* * *

Today's opinion is the product of a Court, which is the product of a law-profession culture, that has largely signed on to the so-called homosexual agenda, by which I mean the agenda promoted by some homosexual activists directed at eliminating the moral opprobrium that has traditionally attached to homosexual conduct. ...

The matters appropriate for this Court's resolution are only three: Texas's prohibition of sodomy neither infringes a "fundamental right" (which the Court does not dispute), nor is unsupported by a rational relation to what the Constitution considers a legitimate state interest, nor denies the equal protection of the laws. I dissent.

Justice THOMAS, dissenting.

I join Justice SCALIA's dissenting opinion. I write separately to note that the law before the Court today "is ... uncommonly silly." *Griswold v. Connecticut*, 381 U.S. 479, 527, 85 S.Ct. 1678, 14 L.Ed.2d 510 (1965) (Stewart, J., dissenting). If I were a member of the Texas Legislature, I would vote to repeal it. Punishing someone for expressing his sexual preference through noncommercial consensual conduct with another adult does not appear to be a worthy way to expend valuable law enforcement resources.

Notwithstanding this, I recognize that as a Member of this Court I am not empowered to help petitioners and others similarly situated. My duty, rather, is to "decide cases 'agreeably to the Constitution and laws of the United States.'" And, just like Justice Stewart, I "can find [neither in the Bill of Rights nor any other part of the Constitution a] general right of privacy," or as the Court terms it today, the "liberty of the person both in its spatial and more transcendent dimensions."

Notes and Questions

1. *Time to overrule?* Why did Justice Kennedy overrule *Bowers*? Why did he find a due process right involved in this case?
2. *How did Justice O'Connor vote?* Why did Justice O'Connor refuse to overrule *Bowers*? Why did she nonetheless join the majority? Why did she talk about the Equal Protection Clause when Justice Kennedy wrote about the Due Process Clause?
3. *Justice Scalia.* Why did Justice Scalia dissent? Did he offer good reasons as to why *Bowers* should remain valid?
4. *Justice Thomas.* Justice Thomas references Justice Stewart's dissent in *Griswold* and talks about the law challenged in *Lawrence* being "uncommonly silly." Do you agree with Thomas's description of the duties of Members of the Court?
5. *Kennedy.* Why did Justice Kennedy argue that the "foundations of *Bowers* have sustained serious erosion from our recent decisions in *Casey* and *Romer*"? What do those two cases have

to do with *Bowers* or *Lawrence*? What does Justice Scalia think about the Court's decisions in *Casey* and *Romer*?

6. *What does marriage have to do with it?* Why are the Justices talking so much about marriage?
7. In *United States v. Windsor*, 570 U.S. 744 (2013), the Court ruled that the federal Defense of Marriage Act was unconstitutional under the Fifth Amendment. Recall that the Fifth Amendment was ruled to have an equal protection component in the District of Columbia schools that were litigated when *Brown v. Board of Education* was. Edith Windsor was unable to collect federal tax benefits when her spouse Thea Clara Spyer died. President Obama and the Attorney General announced that they would not defend a statute that said marriage must be between a man and a woman. Do you know why? Can you figure out who were the five and who were the four Justices in 2013?

3. The Constitution Protects Same-Sex Marriage

The Court identified a constitutional right to same-sex marriage in the next case, *Obergefell v. Hodges*. As you read this case, keep in mind *Loving*, the interracial marriage case, which we read above. Recall that the *Loving* decision was unanimous. *Obergefell*, however, was a 5–4 opinion. The lengthy oral argument, at https://www.oyez.org/cases/2014/14-556, demonstrates that the Justices were split on rights with respect to homosexuality, morality, and religious viewpoints. While you listen to the oral argument, consider who presents the best argument for same-sex marriage and who presents the best argument against it.

And, of course, it is another opinion by Justice Kennedy!

Obergefell v. Hodges

SUPREME COURT OF THE UNITED STATES, 2015

576 U.S. ___, 135 S.Ct. 2584

KENNEDY, J., delivered the opinion of the Court, in which GINSBURG, BREYER, SOTOMAYOR, and KAGAN, JJ., joined. ROBERTS, C.J., filed a dissenting opinion, in which SCALIA and THOMAS, JJ., joined. SCALIA, J., filed a dissenting opinion, in which THOMAS, J., joined. THOMAS, J., filed a dissenting opinion, in which SCALIA, J., joined. ALITO, J., filed a dissenting opinion, in which SCALIA and THOMAS, JJ., joined.

The Constitution promises liberty to all within its reach, a liberty that includes certain specific rights that allow persons, within a lawful realm, to define and express their identity. The petitioners in these cases seek to find that liberty by marrying someone of the same sex and having their marriages deemed lawful on the same terms and conditions as marriages between persons of the opposite sex.

I

These cases come from Michigan, Kentucky, Ohio, and Tennessee, States that define marriage as a union between one man and one woman. The petitioners are 14 same-sex couples and two men whose same-sex partners are deceased. ...

II

... This Court first gave detailed consideration to the legal status of homosexuals in *Bowers v. Hardwick*, 478 U.S. 186, 106 S.Ct. 2841, 92 L.Ed.2d 140 (1986). There it upheld the constitutionality of a Georgia law deemed to criminalize certain homosexual acts. Ten years later, in *Romer v. Evans*, 517 U.S. 620, 116 S.Ct. 1620, 134 L.Ed.2d 855 (1996), the Court invalidated an amendment to Colorado's Constitution that sought to foreclose any branch or political subdivision of the State from protecting persons against discrimination based on sexual orientation. Then, in 2003, the Court overruled *Bowers,* holding that laws making same-sex intimacy a crime "demea[n] the lives of homosexual persons." *Lawrence v. Texas,* 539 U.S. 558, 575, 123 S.Ct. 2472, 156 L.Ed.2d 508. ...

III

Under the Due Process Clause of the Fourteenth Amendment, no State shall "deprive any person of life, liberty, or property, without due process of law." The fundamental liberties protected by this Clause include most of the rights enumerated in the Bill of Rights. In addition these liberties extend to certain personal choices central to individual dignity and autonomy, including intimate choices that define personal identity and beliefs.

The identification and protection of fundamental rights is an enduring part of the judicial duty to interpret the Constitution. That responsibility, however, "has not been reduced to any formula." Rather, it requires courts to exercise reasoned judgment in identifying interests of the person so fundamental that the State must accord them its respect. That process is guided by many of the same considerations relevant to analysis of other constitutional provisions that set forth broad principles rather than specific requirements. History and tradition guide and discipline this inquiry but do not set its outer boundaries. See *Lawrence, supra,* at 572, 123 S.Ct. 2472. That method respects our history and learns from it without allowing the past alone to rule the present.

The nature of injustice is that we may not always see it in our own times. The generations that wrote and ratified the Bill of Rights and the Fourteenth Amendment did not presume to know the extent of freedom in all of its dimensions, and so they entrusted to future generations a charter protecting the right of all persons to enjoy liberty as we learn its meaning. When new insight reveals discord between the Constitution's central protections and a received legal stricture, a claim to liberty must be addressed.

Applying these established tenets, the Court has long held the right to marry is protected by the Constitution. In *Loving v. Virginia,* 388 U.S. 1, 12, 87 S.Ct. 1817, 18 L.Ed.2d 1010 (1967), which invalidated bans on interracial unions, a unanimous Court held marriage is "one of the vital personal rights essential to the orderly pursuit of happiness by free men." ...

This analysis compels the conclusion that same-sex couples may exercise the right to marry. The four principles and traditions to be discussed demonstrate that the reasons marriage is fundamental under the Constitution apply with equal force to same-sex couples.

A first premise of the Court's relevant precedents is that the right to personal choice regarding marriage is inherent in the concept of individual autonomy. ... A second principle in this Court's jurisprudence is that the right to marry is fundamental because it supports a two-person union unlike any other in its importance to the committed individuals. ... A third basis for protecting the right to marry is that it safeguards children and families and thus draws meaning from related rights of childrearing, procreation, and education. ... Fourth and finally, this Court's cases and the Nation's traditions make clear that marriage is a keystone of our social order. ...

The right to marry is fundamental as a matter of history and tradition, but rights come not from ancient sources alone. They rise, too, from a better informed understanding of how constitutional imperatives define a liberty that remains urgent in our own era. Many who deem same-sex marriage to be wrong reach that conclusion based on decent and honorable religious or philosophical premises, and neither they nor their beliefs are disparaged here. But when that sincere, personal opposition becomes enacted law and public policy, the necessary consequence is to put the imprimatur of the State itself on an exclusion that soon demeans or stigmatizes those whose own liberty is then denied. Under the Constitution, same-sex couples seek in marriage the same legal treatment as opposite-sex couples, and it would disparage their choices and diminish their personhood to deny them this right.

The right of same-sex couples to marry that is part of the liberty promised by the Fourteenth Amendment is derived, too, from that Amendment's guarantee of the equal protection of the laws. The Due Process Clause and the Equal Protection Clause are connected in a profound way, though they set forth independent principles. Rights implicit in liberty and rights secured by equal protection may rest on different precepts and are not always co-extensive, yet in some instances each may be instructive as to the meaning and reach of the other. In any particular case one Clause may be thought to capture the essence of the right in a more accurate and comprehensive way, even as the two Clauses may converge in the identification and definition of the right. This interrelation of the two principles furthers our understanding of what freedom is and must become.

The Court's cases touching upon the right to marry reflect this dynamic. In *Loving* the Court invalidated a prohibition on interracial marriage under both the Equal Protection Clause and the Due Process Clause. ...

In *Lawrence* the Court acknowledged the interlocking nature of these constitutional safeguards in the context of the legal treatment of gays and lesbians. Although *Lawrence* elaborated its holding under the Due Process Clause, it acknowledged, and sought to remedy, the continuing inequality that resulted from laws making intimacy in the lives of gays and lesbians a crime against the State. *Lawrence* therefore drew upon principles of liberty and equality to define and protect the rights of gays and lesbians, holding the State "cannot demean their existence or control their destiny by making their private sexual conduct a crime."

This dynamic also applies to same-sex marriage. It is now clear that the challenged laws burden the liberty of same-sex couples, and it must be further acknowledged that they abridge central precepts of equality. Here the marriage laws enforced by the respondents are in essence unequal: same-sex couples are denied all the benefits afforded to opposite-sex couples and are barred from exercising a fundamental right. Especially against a long history of disapproval of their relationships, this denial to same-sex couples of the right to marry works a grave and continuing harm. The imposition of this disability on gays and lesbians serves to disrespect and subordinate them. And the Equal Protection Clause, like the Due Process Clause, prohibits this unjustified infringement of the fundamental right to marry.

These considerations lead to the conclusion that the right to marry is a fundamental right inherent in the liberty of the person, and under the Due Process and Equal Protection Clauses of the Fourteenth Amendment couples of the same-sex may not be deprived of that right and that liberty. The Court now holds that same-sex couples may exercise the fundamental right to marry. No longer may this liberty be denied to them. ...

V

These cases also present the question whether the Constitution requires States to recognize same-sex marriages validly performed out of State. As made clear by the case of Obergefell and Arthur, and by that of DeKoe and Kostura, the recognition bans inflict substantial and continuing harm on same-sex couples. ...

Being married in one State but having that valid marriage denied in another is one of "the most perplexing and distressing complication[s]" in the law of domestic relations. Leaving the current state of affairs in place would maintain and promote instability and uncertainty. For some couples, even an ordinary drive into a neighboring State to visit family or friends risks causing severe hardship in the event of a spouse's hospitalization while across state lines. In light of the fact that many States already allow same-sex marriage—and hundreds of thousands of these marriages already have occurred—the disruption caused by the recognition bans is significant and ever-growing.

* * *

No union is more profound than marriage, for it embodies the highest ideals of love, fidelity, devotion, sacrifice, and family. In forming a marital union, two people become something greater than once they were. As some of the petitioners in these cases demonstrate, marriage embodies a love that may endure even past death. It would misunderstand these men and women to say they disrespect the idea of marriage. Their plea is that they do respect it, respect it so deeply that they seek to find its fulfillment for themselves. Their hope is not to be condemned to live in loneliness, excluded from one of civilization's oldest institutions. They ask for equal dignity in the eyes of the law. The Constitution grants them that right.

Chief Justice ROBERTS, with whom Justice SCALIA and Justice THOMAS join, dissenting.

... But this Court is not a legislature. Whether same-sex marriage is a good idea should be of no concern to us. Under the Constitution, judges have power to say what the law is, not what it should be. The people who ratified the Constitution authorized courts to exercise "neither force nor will but merely judgment." The Federalist No. 78, p. 465 (C. Rossiter ed. 1961) (A. Hamilton) (capitalization altered).

Although the policy arguments for extending marriage to same-sex couples may be compelling, the legal arguments for requiring such an extension are not. The fundamental right to marry does not include a right to make a State change its definition of marriage. And a State's decision to maintain the meaning of marriage that has persisted in every culture throughout human history can hardly be called irrational. In short, our Constitution does not enact any one theory of marriage. The people of a State are free to expand marriage to include same-sex couples, or to retain the historic definition.

Today, however, the Court takes the extraordinary step of ordering every State to license and recognize same-sex marriage. Many people will rejoice at this decision, and I begrudge none their celebration. But for those who believe in a government of laws, not of men, the majority's approach is deeply disheartening. Supporters of same-sex marriage have achieved considerable success persuading their fellow citizens—through the democratic process—to adopt their view. That ends today. Five lawyers have closed the debate and enacted their own vision of marriage as a matter of constitutional law. Stealing this issue from the people will for many cast a cloud over same-sex marriage, making a dramatic social change that much more difficult to accept.

The majority's decision is an act of will, not legal judgment. ...

Understand well what this dissent is about: It is not about whether, in my judgment, the institution of marriage should be changed to include same-sex couples. It is instead about whether, in our democratic republic, that decision should rest with the people acting through their elected representatives, or with five lawyers who happen to hold commissions authorizing them to resolve legal disputes according to law. The Constitution leaves no doubt about the answer. ...

It is striking how much of the majority's reasoning would apply with equal force to the claim of a fundamental right to plural marriage. If "[t]here is dignity in the bond between two men or two women who seek to marry and in their autonomy to make such profound choices," why would there be any less dignity in the bond between three people who, in exercising their autonomy, seek to make the profound choice to marry? If a same-sex couple has the constitutional right to marry because their children would otherwise "suffer the stigma of knowing their families are somehow lesser," why wouldn't the same reasoning apply to a family of three or more persons raising children? If not having the opportunity to marry "serves to disrespect and subordinate" gay and lesbian couples, why wouldn't the same "imposition of this disability," serve to disrespect and subordinate people who find fulfillment in polyamorous relationships? ...

If you are among the many Americans—of whatever sexual orientation—who favor expanding same-sex marriage, by all means celebrate today's decision. Celebrate the achievement of a desired goal. Celebrate the opportunity for a new expression of commitment to a partner. Celebrate the availability of new benefits. But do not celebrate the Constitution. It had nothing to do with it.

Justice SCALIA, with whom Justice THOMAS joins, dissenting.

I join THE CHIEF JUSTICE's opinion in full. I write separately to call attention to this Court's threat to American democracy. ...

So it is not of special importance to me what the law says about marriage. It is of overwhelming importance, however, who it is that rules me. Today's decree says that my Ruler, and the Ruler of 320 million Americans coast-to-coast, is a majority of the nine lawyers on the Supreme Court. The opinion in these cases is the furthest extension in fact—and the furthest extension one can even imagine—of the Court's claimed power to create "liberties" that the Constitution and its Amendments neglect to mention. This practice of constitutional revision by an unelected committee of nine, always accompanied (as it is today) by extravagant praise of liberty, robs the People of the most important liberty they asserted in the Declaration of Independence and won in the Revolution of 1776: the freedom to govern themselves. ...

II

But what really astounds is the hubris reflected in today's judicial Putsch. The five Justices who compose today's majority are entirely comfortable concluding that every State violated the Constitution for all of the 135 years between the Fourteenth Amendment's ratification and Massachusetts' permitting of same-sex marriages in 2003. They have discovered in the Fourteenth Amendment a "fundamental right" overlooked by every person alive at the time of ratification, and almost everyone else in the time since. They see what lesser legal minds—minds like Thomas Cooley, John Marshall Harlan, Oliver Wendell Holmes, Jr., Learned Hand, Louis Brandeis, William Howard Taft,

Benjamin Cardozo, Hugo Black, Felix Frankfurter, Robert Jackson, and Henry Friendly—could not. They are certain that the People ratified the Fourteenth Amendment to bestow on them the power to remove questions from the democratic process when that is called for by their "reasoned judgment." These Justices *know* that limiting marriage to one man and one woman is contrary to reason; they *know* that an institution as old as government itself, and accepted by every nation in history until 15 years ago, cannot possibly be supported by anything other than ignorance or bigotry. And they are willing to say that any citizen who does not agree with that, who adheres to what was, until 15 years ago, the unanimous judgment of all generations and all societies, stands against the Constitution. ...

Justice THOMAS, with whom Justice SCALIA joins, dissenting.

The Court's decision today is at odds not only with the Constitution, but with the principles upon which our Nation was built. Since well before 1787, liberty has been understood as freedom from government action, not entitlement to government benefits. The Framers created our Constitution to preserve that understanding of liberty. Yet the majority invokes our Constitution in the name of a "liberty" that the Framers would not have recognized, to the detriment of the liberty they sought to protect. Along the way, it rejects the idea—captured in our Declaration of Independence—that human dignity is innate and suggests instead that it comes from the Government. This distortion of our Constitution not only ignores the text, it inverts the relationship between the individual and the state in our Republic. I cannot agree with it. ...

I have elsewhere explained the dangerous fiction of treating the Due Process Clause as a font of substantive rights. *McDonald v. Chicago,* 561 U.S. 742, 811–812, 130 S.Ct. 3020, 177 L.Ed.2d 894 (2010) (THOMAS, J., concurring in part and concurring in judgment). It distorts the constitutional text, which guarantees only whatever "process" is "due" before a person is deprived of life, liberty, and property. U.S. Const., Amdt. 14, § 1. Worse, it invites judges to do exactly what the majority has done here—"'roa[m] at large in the constitutional field' guided only by their personal views" as to the "'fundamental rights'" protected by that document.

By straying from the text of the Constitution, substantive due process exalts judges at the expense of the People from whom they derive their authority. ...

Our Constitution—like the Declaration of Independence before it—was predicated on a simple truth: One's liberty, not to mention one's dignity, was something to be shielded from—not provided by—the State. Today's decision casts that truth aside. In its haste to reach a desired result, the majority misapplies a clause focused on "due process" to afford substantive rights, disregards the most plausible understanding of the "liberty" protected by that clause, and distorts the principles on which this Nation was founded. Its decision will have inestimable consequences for our Constitution and our society. I respectfully dissent.

Justice ALITO, with whom Justice SCALIA and Justice THOMAS join, dissenting.

Until the federal courts intervened, the American people were engaged in a debate about whether their States should recognize same-sex marriage. The question in these cases, however, is not what States *should* do about same-sex marriage but whether the Constitution answers that question for them. It does not. The Constitution leaves that question to be decided by the people of each State. ...

III

Today's decision usurps the constitutional right of the people to decide whether to keep or alter the traditional understanding of marriage. The decision will also have other important consequences.

It will be used to vilify Americans who are unwilling to assent to the new orthodoxy. In the course of its opinion, the majority compares traditional marriage laws to laws that denied equal treatment for African-Americans and women. The implications of this analogy will be exploited by those who are determined to stamp out every vestige of dissent. ...

Today's decision shows that decades of attempts to restrain this Court's abuse of its authority have failed. A lesson that some will take from today's decision is that preaching about the proper method of interpreting the Constitution or the virtues of judicial self-restraint and humility cannot compete with the temptation to achieve what is viewed as a noble end by any practicable means. I do not doubt that my colleagues in the majority sincerely see in the Constitution a vision of liberty that happens to coincide with their own. But this sincerity is cause for concern, not comfort. What it evidences is the deep and perhaps irremediable corruption of our legal culture's conception of constitutional interpretation.

Most Americans—understandably—will cheer or lament today's decision because of their views on the issue of same-sex marriage. But all Americans, whatever their thinking on that issue, should worry about what the majority's claim of power portends.

Notes and Questions

1. *Two different constitutional bases.* Why is same-sex marriage an issue of both equal protection and due process? What do those clauses separately contribute to the analysis?
2. *Federal right or state power?* Do you agree that the Fourteenth Amendment gives the Court power to declare that same-sex marriage is protected by the Constitution? Or do you agree with the dissenters, who say that the Constitution gives such a power to the states, not the Court, to decide what marriage should be? What is the role of the Ninth Amendment in such discussions?
3. *Compare to* Loving. Why was *Loving* unanimous and this opinion 5–4?
4. *Inevitable?* Was *Obergefell* the inevitable result of *Lawrence*?
5. *Polygamy.* Is Chief Justice Roberts correct that once same-sex marriage is constitutional, polygamy must be, too? What is the difference between same-sex marriage and polygamy? Polygamy is illegal in every state. Should those laws be held unconstitutional on the reasoning of this case?
6. *Justice Alito and the rights of religious opponents to same-sex marriage.* Do you agree with Justice Alito that the result of this case will be unfair to opponents of same-sex marriage? What rights do they have that Justice Alito worries about?
7. *Privacy rights and substantive due process.* Why is Justice Thomas so opposed to rights to privacy founded in substantive due process?
8. *Statutory rights protecting against LGBTQ discrimination.* In *Bostock v. Clayton County, Georgia*, 140 S.Ct. 1731 (2020), the Court was asked to interpret whether Title VII, the Civil Rights Act of 1964—which bans discrimination on the basis of race, color, religion, sex, or national origin—protects LGBTQ from discrimination. Justice Gorsuch's opinion, joined by Roberts, Ginsburg, Breyer, Sotomayor, and Kagan, ruled that the term "sex" in Title VII includes homosexual and transgender discrimination. In Gorsuch's words, "it is impossible to discriminate against a person for being homosexual or transgender without discriminating against that individual based on sex." The dissenters, Alito, Thomas, and Kavanaugh, thought the majority had misread the statute, which banned sex discrimination, not sexual orientation discrimination.
9. Will *Obergefell* be overruled, as Justice Thomas has suggested it should be? What would happen if the Court overruled *Obergefell*? Does Congress's Respect for Marriage Act protect same-sex marriage if *Obergefell* is overruled? What do you think of the Senate vote upholding same-sex marriage rights? See https://www.washingtonpost.com/politics/interactive/2022/senator-vote-count-respect-for-marriage-act/?itid=lk_inline_manual_3.

A Look Ahead

In the next chapter, we cover what other rights the Fourteenth Amendment protects, looking at the privileges or immunities section of the amendment, the economic rights that the Constitution protects, the right to privacy, which supports contraception and abortion rights, and the right to die.

Credits

Fig. 7.1: Adapted from: Oyez, "How the Justices Voted in Loving," https://www.oyez.org/cases/1966/395. Copyright © 2022 by Oyez, Inc.

Fig. 7.2: Adapted from: Oyez, "How the Justices Violed in Grutter," https://www.oyez.org/cases/2002/02-241. Copyright © 2022 by Oyez, Inc.

Fig. 7.3: Adapted from: Oyez, "How the Justices Voted in Gratz," https://www.oyez.org/cases/2002/02-516. Copyright © 2022 by Oyez, Inc.

Fig. 7.4: Adapted from: Oyez, "How the Justices Voted in Bowers," https://www.oyez.org/cases/1985/85-140. Copyright © 2022 by Oyez, Inc.

Fig. 7.5: Adapted from: Oyez, "How the Justices Voted in Romer," https://www.oyez.org/cases/1995/94-1039. Copyright © 2022 by Oyez, Inc.

Eight

What Other Rights Does the Fourteenth Amendment Protect?

Introduction

In Chapter 6, you learned about the role of slavery in the history of the Constitution and the Thirteenth, Fourteenth, and Fifteenth Amendments, which are the Reconstruction amendments following the end of the Civil War. The Fourteenth Amendment has garnered more of the Court's attention in opinions than either the Thirteenth or the Fifteenth. In Chapter 7, you saw that the Fourteenth Amendment has been interpreted to prohibit racial, gender, and sexual orientation discrimination.

Remember the text of Section 1 of the Fourteenth Amendment: "All persons born or naturalized in the United States, and subject to the jurisdiction thereof, are **citizens** of the United States and of the state wherein they reside. No state shall make or enforce any law which shall abridge the **privileges or immunities** of citizens of the United States; nor shall any state deprive any person of life, liberty, or property, without **due process of law**; nor deny to any person within its jurisdiction the **equal protection** of the laws."

In this chapter, we look at what rights the Fourteenth Amendment protects. We start with the Privileges or Immunities Clause of the Fourteenth Amendment and compare it to the Privileges and Immunities Clause of Article IV. Can you figure out the differences and similarities between those two clauses? Do you think the Court should or will expand the meaning of either of these clauses in the future? Should privileges or immunities be the clause that incorporates the Bill of Rights?

Then, we ask if the Fourteenth Amendment grants any special protection to economic rights, e.g., the freedom for employers and employees to contract. We look at the Court's *Lochner v. New York* case and then, examine the Court's later choice to apply rational basis scrutiny to economic regulations. Then, we ask if the Court's punitive damages jurisprudence is the modern version of *Lochner*.

Finally, we ask if the amendment protects the right to contraception, abortion, and the right to die. Is it due process or equal protection that protects these rights? The abortion cases have focused on the Court's treatment of its precedents and when and whether they should be overruled. Does the Due Process Clause of the amendment protect abortion, or is it unprotected because it is not listed in the Constitution? What is the constitutional root of contraception or of the right to die? Privacy or liberty?

A. Privileges or/and Immunities? 14th Amendment and Article IV

There are two similar sections of the Constitution that employ the words "privileges" and "immunities." In the main body of the Constitution, Article IV, Section 2, says: "The citizens of each state shall be entitled to all privileges and immunities of citizens in the several states." The Fourteenth Amendment states, "No state shall make or enforce any law which shall abridge the privileges or immunities of citizens of the United States." Why, if there was already an Article IV protection of privileges and immunities, did the Fourteenth Amendment add a second reference? Do you know the difference between the citizen of a state and a citizen of the United States? Can someone be both at the same time?

One of the reasons there is not a lot of law about P or I is the *Slaughter-House Cases*, excerpted below. Would you have written the opinion the way it was written? Why or why not? Did the Court bring privileges or immunities back to life in *Saenz?*

1. Amendment XIV: *Slaughter-House Cases* to *Saenz*

a. Slaughter-House Cases

Look at the Justices who decided the Slaughter-House cases in 1872. https://www.oyez.org/cases/1850-1900/83us36.

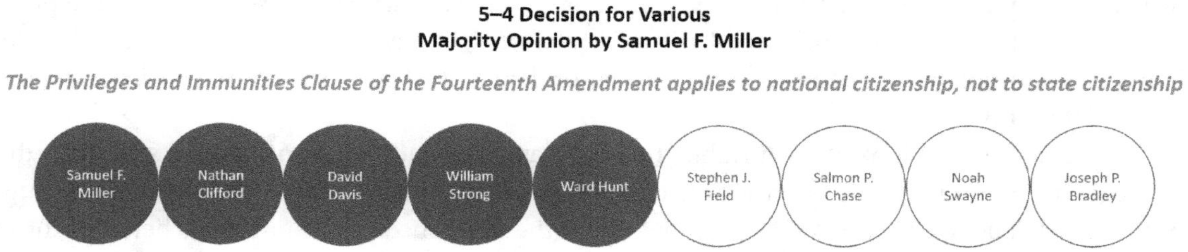

FIGURE 8.1 Slaughter-House Cases, 83 US 36 (1873)

This case notoriously undermined the meaning of the Privileges or Immunities Clause in the Fourteenth Amendment, leading the Court to rarely rely on it until *Saenz v. Roe* was decided in 1999. Do you agree with what the Court says about privileges or immunities? Why or why not?

Slaughter-House Cases

SUPREME COURT OF THE UNITED STATES, 1872

83 U.S. 36, 21 L.Ed. 394

Mr. Justice MILLER, now, April 14th, 1873, delivered the opinion of the court.

These cases are brought here by writs of error to the Supreme Court of the State of Louisiana. They arise out of the efforts of the butchers of New Orleans to resist the Crescent City Live-Stock Landing and Slaughter-House Company in the exercise of certain powers conferred by the charter which created it, and which was granted by the legislature of that State.

The cases named on a preceding page, with others which have been brought here and dismissed by agreement, were all decided by the Supreme Court of Louisiana in favor of the Slaughter-House Company, as we shall hereafter call it for the sake of brevity, and these writs are brought to reverse those decisions.

The records were filed in this court in 1870, and were argued before it as length on a motion made by plaintiffs in error for an order in the nature of an injunction or supersedeas, pending the action of the court on the merits. The opinion on that motion is reported in 10 Wallace, 273. ...

The records show that the plaintiffs in error relied upon, and asserted throughout the entire course of the litigation in the State courts, that the grant of privileges in the charter of defendant, which they were contesting, was a violation of the most important provisions of the thirteenth and fourteenth articles of amendment of the Constitution of the United States. The jurisdiction and the duty of this court to review the judgment of the State court on those questions is clear and is imperative.

The statute thus assailed as unconstitutional was passed March 8th, 1869, and is entitled 'An act to protect the health of the city of New Orleans, to locate the stock-landings and slaughter-houses, and to incorporate the Crescent City Live-Stock Landing and Slaughter-House Company.'

The first section forbids the landing or slaughtering of animals whose flesh is intended for food, within the city of New Orleans and other parishes and boundaries named and defined, or the keeping or establishing any slaughter-houses or *abattoirs* within those limits except by the corporation thereby created, which is also limited to certain places afterwards mentioned. Suitable penalties are enacted for violations of this prohibition.

The second section designates the corporators, gives the name to the corporation, and confers on it the usual corporate powers.

The third and fourth sections authorize the company to establish and erect within certain territorial limits, therein defined, one or more stock-yards, stock-landings, and slaughter-houses, and imposes upon it the duty of erecting, on or before the first day of June, 1869, one grand slaughter-house of sufficient capacity for slaughtering five hundred animals per day.

It declares that the company, after it shall have prepared all the necessary buildings, yards, and other conveniences for that purpose, shall have the sole and exclusive privilege of conducting and carrying on the live-stock landing and slaughter-house business within the limits and privilege granted by the act, and that all such animals shall be landed at the stock-landings and slaughtered at the slaughter-houses of the company, and nowhere else. Penalties are enacted for infractions of this provision, and prices fixed for the maximum charges of the company for each steamboat and for each animal landed.

Section five orders the closing up of all other stock-landings and slaughter-houses after the first day of June, in the parishes of Orleans, Jefferson, and St. Bernard, and makes it the duty of the company to permit any person to slaughter animals in their slaughter-houses under a heavy penalty for each refusal. Another section fixes a limit to the charges to be made by the company for each animal so slaughtered in their building, and another provides for an inspection of all animals intended to be so slaughtered, by an officer appointed by the governor of the State for that purpose. ...

Unless, therefore, it can be maintained that the exclusive privilege granted by this charter to the corporation, is beyond the power of the legislature of Louisiana, there can be no just exception to the validity of the statute. And in this respect we are not able to see that these privileges are especially odious or objectionable. The duty imposed as a consideration for the privilege is well defined, and its enforcement well guarded. The prices or charges to be made by the company are limited by the statute, and we are not advised that they are on the whole exorbitant or unjust.

The proposition is, therefore, reduced to these terms: Can any exclusive privileges be granted to any of its citizens, or to a corporation, by the legislature of a State? ...

It may, therefore, be considered as established, that the authority of the legislature of Louisiana to pass the present statute is ample, unless some restraint in the exercise of that power be found in the constitution of that State or in the amendments to the Constitution of the United States, adopted since the date of the decisions we have already cited.

If any such restraint is supposed to exist in the constitution of the State, the Supreme Court of Louisiana having necessarily passed on that question, it would not be open to review in this court.

The plaintiffs in error accepting this issue, allege that the statute is a violation of the Constitution of the United States in these several particulars:

> That it creates an involuntary servitude forbidden by the thirteenth article of amendment;
>
> That it abridges the privileges and immunities of citizens of the United States;
>
> That it denies to the plaintiffs the equal protection of the laws; and,
>
> That it deprives them of their property without due process of law; contrary to the provisions of the first section of the fourteenth article of amendment. ...
>
> It is quite clear, then, that there is a citizenship of the United States, and a citizenship of a State, which are distinct from each other, and which depend upon different characteristics or circumstances in the individual.

We think this distinction and its explicit recognition in this amendment of great weight in this argument, because the next paragraph of this same section, which is the one mainly relied on by the plaintiffs in error, speaks only of privileges and immunities of citizens of the United States, and does not speak of those of citizens of the several States. The argument, however, in favor of the plaintiffs rests wholly on the assumption that the citizenship is the same, and the privileges and immunities guaranteed by the clause are the same.

The language is, 'No State shall make or enforce any law which shall abridge the privileges or immunities of citizens of *the United States*.' It is a little remarkable, if this clause was intended as a protection to the citizen of a State against the legislative power of his own State, that the word citizen of the State should be left out when it is so carefully used, and used in contradistinction to citizens of the United States, in the very sentence which precedes it. It is too clear for argument that the change in phraseology was adopted understandingly and with a purpose.

Of the privileges and immunities of the citizen of the United States, and of the privileges and immunities of the citizen of the State, and what they respectively are, we will presently consider; but we wish to state here that it is only the former which are placed by this clause under the protection of the Federal Constitution, and that the latter, whatever they may be, are not intended to have any additional protection by this paragraph of the amendment.

If, then, there is a difference between the privileges and immunities belonging to a citizen of the United States as such, and those belonging to the citizen of the State as such the latter must rest for their security and protection where they have heretofore rested; for they are not embraced by this paragraph of the amendment. ...

In the Constitution of the United States, which superseded the Articles of Confederation, the corresponding provision is found in section two of the fourth article, in the following words: 'The citizens of each State shall be entitled to all the privileges and immunities of citizens of the several States.'

There can be but little question that the purpose of both these provisions is the same, and that the privileges and immunities intended are the same in each. In the article of the Confederation we have some of these specifically mentioned, and enough perhaps to give some general idea of the class of civil rights meant by the phrase.

Fortunately we are not without judicial construction of this clause of the Constitution. The first and the leading case on the subject is that of *Corfield* v. *Coryell*, decided by Mr. Justice Washington in the Circuit Court for the District of Pennsylvania in 1823.

'The inquiry,' he says, 'is, what are the privileges and immunities of citizens of the several States? We feel no hesitation in confining these expressions to those privileges and immunities which are *fundamental;* which belong of right to the citizens of all free governments, and which have at all times been enjoyed by citizens of the several States which compose this Union, from the time of their becoming free, independent, and sovereign. What these fundamental principles are, it would be more tedious than difficult to enumerate. They may all, however, be comprehended under the following general heads: protection by the government, with the right to acquire and possess property of every kind, and to pursue and obtain happiness and safety, subject, nevertheless, to such restraints as the government may prescribe for the general good of the whole.'

This definition of the privileges and immunities of citizens of the States is adopted in the main by this court in the recent case of *Ward* v. *The State of Maryland*, while it declines to undertake an authoritative definition beyond what was necessary to that decision. The description, when taken to include others not named, but which are of the same general character, embraces nearly every civil right for the establishment and protection of which organized government is instituted. They are, in the language of Judge Washington, those rights which the fundamental. Throughout his opinion, they are spoken of as rights belonging to the individual as a citizen of a State. They are so spoken of in the constitutional provision which he was construing. And they have always been held to be the class of rights which the State governments were created to establish and secure. ...

Was it the purpose of the fourteenth amendment, by the simple declaration that no State should make or enforce any law which shall abridge the privileges and immunities of *citizens of the United States,* to transfer the security and protection of all the civil rights which we have mentioned, from the States to the Federal government? And where it is declared that Congress shall have the power to enforce that article, was it intended to bring within the power of Congress the entire domain of civil rights heretofore belonging exclusively to the States? ...

Having shown that the privileges and immunities relied on in the argument are those which belong to citizens of the States as such, and that they are left to the State governments for security and protection, and not by this article placed under the special care of the Federal government, we may hold ourselves excused from defining the privileges and immunities of citizens of the United States which no State can abridge, until some case involving those privileges may make it necessary to do so. ...

But it is useless to pursue this branch of the inquiry, since we are of opinion that the rights claimed by these plaintiffs in error, if they have any existence, are not privileges and immunities of citizens of the United States within the meaning of the clause of the fourteenth amendment under consideration. ...

Mr. Justice FIELD, dissenting:

... The act of Louisiana presents the naked case, unaccompanied by any public considerations, where a right to pursue a lawful and necessary calling, previously enjoyed by every citizen, and in connection with which a thousand persons were daily employed, is taken away and vested exclusively for twenty-five years, for an extensive district and a large population, in a single corporation, or its exercise is for that period restricted to the establishments of the corporation, and there allowed only upon onerous conditions. ...

The question presented is, therefore, one of the gravest importance, not merely to the parties here, but to the whole country. It is nothing less than the question whether the recent amendments to the Federal Constitution protect the citizens of the United States against the deprivation of their common rights by State legislation. In my judgment the fourteenth amendment does afford such protection, and was so intended by the Congress which framed and the States which adopted it. ...

It is not necessary, however, as I have said, to rest my objections to the act in question upon the terms and meaning of the thirteenth amendment. The provisions of the fourteenth amendment, which is properly a supplement to the thirteenth, cover, in my judgment, the case before us, and inhibit any legislation which confers special and exclusive privileges like these under consideration. The amendment was adopted to obviate objections which had been raised and pressed with great force to the validity of the Civil Rights Act, and to place the common rights of American citizens under the protection of the National government. ...

The amendment was adopted to obviate objections which had been raised and pressed with great force to the validity of the Civil Rights Act, and to place the common rights of American citizens under the protection of the National government. ...

The privileges and immunities designated are those *which of right belong to the citizens of all free governments.* Clearly among these must be placed the right to pursue a lawful employment in a lawful manner, without other restraint than such as equally affects all persons. In the discussions in Congress upon the passage of the Civil Rights Act repeated reference was made to this language of Mr. Justice Washington. It was cited by Senator Trumbull with the observation that it enumerated the very rights belonging to a citizen of the United States set forth in the first section of the act, and with the statement that all persons born in the United States, being declared by the act citizens of the United States, would thenceforth be entitled to the rights of citizens, and that these were the great fundamental rights set forth in the act; and that they were set forth 'as appertaining to every freeman.' ...

In all these cases there is a recognition of the equality of right among citizens in the pursuit of the ordinary avocations of life, and a declaration that all grants of exclusive privileges, in contravention of this equality, are against common right, and void. ...

Mr. Justice BRADLEY, also dissenting:

... I think sufficient has been said to show that citizenship is not an empty name, but that, in this country at least, it has connected with it certain incidental rights, privileges, and immunities of the greatest importance. And to say that these rights and immunities attach only to State citizenship, and not to citizenship of the United States, appears to me to evince a very narrow and insufficient estimate of constitutional history and the rights of men, not to say the rights of the American people. ...

Now, here is a clear prohibition on the States against making or enforcing any law which shall abridge the privileges or immunities of citizens of the United States.

If my views are correct with regard to what are the privileges and immunities of citizens, it follows conclusively that any law which establishes a sheer monopoly, depriving a large class of citizens of the privilege of pursuing a lawful employment, does abridge the privileges of those citizens. ...

Mr. Justice SWAYNE, dissenting:

... The construction adopted by the majority of my brethren is, in my judgment, much too narrow. It defeats, by a limitation not anticipated, the intent of those by whom the instrument was framed and of those by whom it was adopted. To the extent of that limitation it turns, as it were, what was meant for bread into a stone. By the Constitution, as it stood before the war, ample protection was given against oppression by the Union, but little was given against wrong and oppression by the States. That want was intended to be supplied by this amendment. Against the former this court has been called upon more than once to interpose. Authority of the same amplitude was intended to be conferred as to the latter. But this arm of our jurisdiction is, in these cases, stricken down by the judgment just given. Nowhere, than in this court, ought the will of the nation, as thus expressed, to be more liberally construed or more cordially executed. This determination of the majority seems to me to lie far in the other direction. ...

Notes and Questions

1. *What do these terms mean*? Can you tell what "privileges" and "immunities" are from this opinion? What is contained on the list of privileges and immunities?
2. *Why do the dissenters have a different understanding of this section of the Fourteenth Amendment?*
3. *How would you read "privileges or immunities" today?*

b. Saenz*—127 Years Later*

What do you learn about privileges or immunities in the oral argument for the following case, *Saenz,* https://www.oyez.org/cases/1998/98-97? Pay attention to whether the lawyers and Justices talk about the right to travel and whether it is constitutionally protected. Why would the Court be talking about privileges or immunities after so many years?

Saenz v. Roe

SUPREME COURT OF THE UNITED STATES, 1999

526 U.S. 489, 119 S.Ct. 1518

STEVENS, J., delivered the opinion of the Court, in which O'CONNOR, SCALIA, KENNEDY, SOUTER, GINSBURG, and BREYER, JJ., joined. REHNQUIST, C. J., filed a dissenting opinion, in which THOMAS, J., joined. THOMAS, J., filed a dissenting opinion, in which REHNQUIST, C. J., joined.

In 1992, California enacted a statute limiting the maximum welfare benefits available to newly arrived residents. The scheme limits the amount payable to a family that has resided in the State for less than 12 months to the amount payable by the State of the family's prior residence. The questions presented by this case are whether the 1992 statute was constitutional when it was enacted and, if not, whether an amendment to the Social Security Act enacted by Congress in 1996 affects that determination. ...

III

The word "travel" is not found in the text of the Constitution. Yet the "constitutional right to travel from one State to another" is firmly embedded in our jurisprudence. ...

IV

The "right to travel" discussed in our cases embraces at least three different components. It protects the right of a citizen of one State to enter and to leave another State, the right to be treated as a welcome visitor rather than an unfriendly alien when temporarily present in the second State, and, for those travelers who elect to become permanent residents, the right to be treated like other citizens of that State.

It was the right to go from one place to another, including the right to cross state borders while en route, that was vindicated in *Edwards v. California,* 314 U.S. 160, 62 S.Ct. 164, 86 L.Ed. 119 (1941), which invalidated a state law that impeded the free interstate passage of the indigent. We reaffirmed that right in *United States v. Guest,* 383 U.S. 745, 86 S.Ct. 1170, 16 L.Ed.2d 239 (1966), which afforded protection to the "'right to travel freely to and from the State of Georgia and to use highway facilities and other instrumentalities of interstate commerce within the State of Georgia.'" *Id.,* at 757, 86 S.Ct. 1170. Given that § 11450.03 imposed no obstacle to respondents' entry into California, we think the State is correct when it argues that the statute does not directly impair the exercise of the right to free interstate movement. For the purposes of this case, therefore, we need not identify the source of that particular right in the text of the Constitution. The right of "free ingress and regress to and from" neighboring States, which was expressly mentioned in the text of the Articles of Confederation, may simply have been "conceived from the beginning to be a necessary concomitant of the stronger Union the Constitution created." *Id.,* at 758, 86 S.Ct. 1170.

The second component of the right to travel is, however, expressly protected by the text of the Constitution. The first sentence of Article IV, § 2, provides:

> "The Citizens of each State shall be entitled to all Privileges and Immunities of Citizens in the several States."

Thus, by virtue of a person's state citizenship, a citizen of one State who travels in other States, intending to return home at the end of his journey, is entitled to enjoy the "Privileges and Immunities of Citizens in the several States" that he visits. This provision removes "from the citizens of each State the disabilities of alienage in the other States." *Paul v. Virginia,* 8 Wall. 168, 180, 19 L.Ed. 357 (1868) ("[W]ithout some provision ... removing from the citizens of each State the disabilities of alienage in the other States, and giving them equality of privilege with citizens of those States, the Republic would have constituted little more than a league of States; it would not have constituted the Union which now exists"). It provides important protections for nonresidents who enter a State whether to obtain employment, *Hicklin v. Orbeck,* 437 U.S. 518, 98 S.Ct. 2482, 57 L.Ed.2d 397 (1978), to procure medical services, *Doe v. Bolton,* 410 U.S. 179, 200, 93 S.Ct. 739, 35 L.Ed.2d 201 (1973), or even to engage in commercial shrimp fishing, *Toomer v. Witsell,* 334 U.S. 385, 68 S.Ct. 1156, 92 L.Ed. 1460 (1948). Those protections are not "absolute," but the Clause "does bar discrimination against citizens of other States where there is no substantial reason for the discrimination beyond the mere fact that they are citizens of other States." *Id.,* at 396, 68 S.Ct. 1156. There may be a substantial reason for requiring the nonresident to pay more than the resident for a hunting license, see *Baldwin v. Fish and Game Comm'n of Mont.,* 436 U.S. 371, 390–391, 98 S.Ct. 1852, 56 L.Ed.2d 354 (1978), or to enroll in the state university, see *Vlandis v. Kline,* 412 U.S. 441, 445, 93 S.Ct. 2230, 37 L.Ed.2d 63 (1973), but our cases have not identified any acceptable reason for qualifying the protection afforded by the Clause for "the 'citizen of State A who ventures into State B' to settle there and establish a home." *Zobel,* 457 U.S., at 74, 102 S.Ct. 2309 (O'CONNOR, J., concurring in judgment). Permissible justifications for discrimination between residents and nonresidents are simply inapplicable to a nonresident's exercise of the right to move into another State and become a resident of that State.

What is at issue in this case, then, is this third aspect of the right to travel—the right of the newly arrived citizen to the same privileges and immunities enjoyed by other citizens of the same State. That right is protected not only by the new arrival's status as a state citizen, but also by her status as a citizen of the United States. That additional source of protection is plainly identified in the opening words of the Fourteenth Amendment:

> "All persons born or naturalized in the United States, and subject to the jurisdiction thereof, are citizens of the United States and of the State wherein they reside. No State shall make or enforce any law which shall abridge the privileges or immunities of citizens of the United States; ... ."

Despite fundamentally differing views concerning the coverage of the Privileges or Immunities Clause of the Fourteenth Amendment, most notably expressed in the majority and dissenting opinions in the *Slaughter–House Cases,* 16 Wall. 36, 21 L.Ed. 394 (1872), it has always been common ground that this Clause protects the third component of the right to travel. Writing for the majority in the *Slaughter–House Cases,* Justice Miller explained that one of the privileges conferred by this Clause "is that a citizen of the United States can, of his own volition, become a citizen of any State of the Union by a *bonâ fide* residence therein, with the same rights as other citizens of that State." ...

V

... But since the right to travel embraces the citizen's right to be treated equally in her new State of residence, the discriminatory classification is itself a penalty.

It is undisputed that respondents and the members of the class that they represent are citizens of California and that their need for welfare benefits is unrelated to the length of time that they have resided in California. We thus have no occasion to consider what weight might be given to a citizen's length of residence if the bona fides of her claim to state citizenship were questioned. Moreover, because whatever benefits they receive will be consumed while they remain in California, there is no danger that recognition of their claim will encourage citizens of other States to establish residency for just long enough to acquire some readily portable benefit, such as a divorce or a college education, that will be enjoyed after they return to their original domicile. See, *e.g., Sosna v. Iowa,* 419 U.S. 393, 95 S.Ct. 553, 42 L.Ed.2d 532 (1975); *Vlandis v. Kline,* 412 U.S. 441, 93 S.Ct. 2230, 37 L.Ed.2d 63 (1973).

The classifications challenged in this case—and there are many—are defined entirely by (a) the period of residency in California and (b) the location of the prior residences of the disfavored class members. The favored class of beneficiaries includes all eligible California citizens who have resided there for at least one year, plus those new arrivals who last resided in another country or in a State that provides benefits at least as generous as California's. Thus, within the broad category of citizens who resided in California for less than a year, there are many who are treated like lifetime residents. And within the broad subcategory of new arrivals who are treated less favorably, there are many smaller classes whose benefit levels are determined by the law of the States from whence they came. To justify § 11450.03, California must therefore explain not only why it is sound fiscal policy to discriminate against those who have been citizens for less than a year, but also why it is permissible to apply such a variety of rules within that class. ...

In short, the State's legitimate interest in saving money provides no justification for its decision to discriminate among equally eligible citizens.

VI

The question that remains is whether congressional approval of durational residency requirements in the 1996 amendment to the Social Security Act somehow resuscitates the constitutionality of § 11450.03. That question is readily answered, for we have consistently held that Congress may not authorize the States to violate the Fourteenth Amendment. Moreover, the protection afforded to the citizen by the Citizenship Clause of that Amendment is a limitation on the powers of the National Government as well as the States. ...

Chief Justice REHNQUIST, with whom Justice THOMAS joins, dissenting.

The Court today breathes new life into the previously dormant Privileges or Immunities Clause of the Fourteenth Amendment—a Clause relied upon by this

Court in only one other decision, *Colgate v. Harvey,* 296 U.S. 404, 56 S.Ct. 252, 80 L.Ed. 299 (1935), overruled five years later by *Madden v. Kentucky,* 309 U.S. 83, 60 S.Ct. 406, 84 L.Ed. 590 (1940). It uses this Clause to strike down what I believe is a reasonable measure falling under the head of a "good-faith residency requirement." Because I do not think any provision of the Constitution—and surely not a provision relied upon for only the second time since its enactment 130 years ago—requires this result, I dissent. ...

I therefore believe that the durational residence requirement challenged here is a permissible exercise of the State's power to "assur[e] that services provided for its residents are enjoyed only by residents." *Martinez,* 461 U.S., at 328, 103 S.Ct. 1838. The 1-year period established in § 11450.03 is the same period this Court approved in *Starns* and *Sosna.* The requirement does not deprive welfare recipients of all benefits; indeed, the limitation has no effect whatsoever on a recipient's ability to enjoy the full 5-year period of welfare eligibility; to enjoy the full range of employment, training, and accompanying supportive services; or to take full advantage of health care benefits under Medicaid. This waiting period does not preclude new residents from all cash payments, but merely limits them to what they received in their prior State of residence. Moreover, as the Court recognizes, any pinch resulting from this limitation during the 1-year period is mitigated by other programs such as homeless assistance and an increase in food stamp allowance. The 1-year period thus permissibly balances the new resident's needs for subsistence with the State's need to ensure the bona fides of their claim to residence.

Finally, Congress' express approval in 42 U.S.C. § 604(c) of durational residence requirements for welfare recipients like the one established by California only goes to show the reasonableness of a law like § 11450.03. ...

Justice THOMAS, with whom THE CHIEF JUSTICE joins, dissenting.

I join THE CHIEF JUSTICE's dissent. I write separately to address the majority's conclusion that California has violated "the right of the newly arrived citizen to the same privileges and immunities enjoyed by other citizens of the same State." In my view, the majority attributes a meaning to the Privileges or Immunities Clause that likely was unintended when the Fourteenth Amendment was enacted and ratified.

...

Nevertheless, their [Members of the 39th Congress] repeated references to the *Corfield* decision, combined with what appears to be the historical understanding of the Clause's operative terms, supports the inference that, at the time the Fourteenth Amendment was adopted, people understood that "privileges or immunities of citizens" were fundamental rights, rather than every public benefit established by positive law. Accordingly, the majority's conclusion—that a State violates the Privileges or Immunities Clause when it "discriminates" against citizens who have been domiciled in the State for less than a year in the distribution of welfare benefits—appears contrary to the original understanding and is dubious at best.

As THE CHIEF JUSTICE points out, it comes as quite a surprise that the majority relies on the Privileges or Immunities Clause at all in this case. That is because, as I have explained the *Slaughter-House Cases* sapped the Clause of any meaning. Although the majority appears to breathe new life into the Clause today, it fails to address its historical underpinnings or its place in our constitutional jurisprudence. Because I believe that the demise of the Privileges or Immunities Clause has contributed in no small part to the current disarray of our Fourteenth Amendment jurisprudence, I would be open to reevaluating its meaning in an appropriate case. Before invoking the Clause, however, we should endeavor to understand what the Framers of the Fourteenth Amendment thought that it meant. We should also consider whether the Clause should displace, rather than augment, portions of our equal protection and substantive due process jurisprudence. The majority's failure to consider these important questions raises the specter that the Privileges or Immunities Clause will become yet another convenient tool for inventing new rights, limited solely by the "predilections of those who happen at the time to be Members of this Court." *Moore v. East Cleveland,* 431 U.S. 494, 502, 97 S.Ct. 1932, 52 L.Ed.2d 531 (1977).

I respectfully dissent.

Notes and Questions

1. *The right to travel.* Is there really a right to travel in the Constitution? Where does Justice Stevens find it?
2. *The purpose of invoking privileges or immunities?* Why does Stevens invoke privileges or immunities in this decision?
3. *The opposition.* Why do Rehnquist and Thomas oppose using Privileges or Immunities Clause?
4. *Incorporation.* In other chapters, we have learned that Justice Thomas and Justice Black relied on the Privileges or Immunities Clause as the source of applying the Bill of Rights to the states. Why does Thomas use it for incorporation so much? What is the difference between this case and one deciding incorporation?

2. Article IV Privileges and Immunities: *Piper*

The next case takes us to the Privileges and Immunities Clause of Article IV. The Court states that it is intended to create a "national economic union." Can you tell from the oral argument in this case, https://www.oyez.org/cases/1984/83-1466, what the privileges and immunities of state citizenship are that must be accorded to all? Do the questions lead you to believe that the vote would be so lopsided (8–1)? Does Justice Rehnquist, in his dissent, indicate that he disagrees with all the other Justices?

Supreme Court of New Hampshire v. Piper

SUPREME COURT OF THE UNITED STATES, 1985

470 U.S. 274, 105 S.Ct. 1272

Justice POWELL delivered the opinion of the Court in which BURGER, C.J., and BRENNAN, MARSHALL, BLACKMUN, STEVENS, and O'CONNOR, JJ., joined. WHITE, J., filed an opinion concurring in the result, REHNQUIST, J., filed a dissenting opinion.

The Rules of the Supreme Court of New Hampshire limit bar admission to state residents. We here consider whether this restriction violates the Privileges and Immunities Clause of the United States Constitution, Art. IV, § 2. ...

II

A

Article IV, § 2, of the Constitution provides that the "Citizens of each State shall be entitled to all Privileges and Immunities of Citizens in the several States." This Clause was intended to "fuse into one Nation a collection of independent, sovereign States." *Toomer v. Witsell,* 334 U.S. 385, 395, 68 S.Ct. 1156, 1162, 92 L.Ed. 1460 (1948). Recognizing this purpose, we have held that it is "[o]nly with respect to those 'privileges' and 'immunities' bearing on the vitality of the Nation as a single entity" that a State must accord residents and nonresidents equal treatment. *Baldwin v. Montana Fish & Game Comm'n, supra,* at 383, 98 S.Ct., at 1860. In *Baldwin,* for example, we concluded that a State may charge a nonresident more than it charges a resident for the same elk-hunting license. Because elk hunting is "recreation" rather than a "means of a livelihood," we found that the right to a hunting license was not "fundamental" to the promotion of interstate harmony. 436 U.S., at 388, 98 S.Ct., at 1863.

Derived, like the Commerce Clause, from the fourth of the Articles of Confederation, the Privileges and Immunities Clause was intended to create a national economic union. It is therefore not surprising that this Court repeatedly has found that "one of the privileges which the Clause guarantees to citizens of State A is that of doing business in State B on terms of substantial equality with the citizens of that State." *Toomer v. Witsell, supra,* 334 U.S., at 396, 68 S.Ct., at 1162. In *Ward v. Maryland,* 12 Wall. 418, 20 L.Ed. 449 (1871), the Court invalidated a statute under which nonresidents were required to pay $300 per year for a license to trade in goods not manufactured in Maryland, while resident traders paid a fee varying from $12 to $150. Similarly, in *Toomer, supra,* the Court held that nonresident fishermen could not be required to pay a license fee of $2,500 for each shrimp boat owned when residents were charged only $25 per boat. Finally, in *Hicklin v. Orbeck*, 437 U.S. 518, 98 S.Ct. 2482, 57 L.Ed.2d 397 (1978), we found violative of the Privileges and Immunities Clause a statute containing a resident hiring preference for all employment related to the development of the State's oil and gas resources.

There is nothing in *Ward, Toomer,* or *Hicklin* suggesting that the practice of law should not be viewed as a "privilege" under Art. IV, § 2. ...

III

The conclusion that Rule 42 deprives nonresidents of a protected privilege does not end our inquiry. The Court has stated that "[l]ike many other constitutional provisions, the privileges and immunities clause is not an absolute." *Toomer v. Witsell,* 334 U.S., at 396, 68 S.Ct., at 1162; see *United Building & Construction Trades Council v. Mayor & Council of Camden,* 465 U.S. 208, 222, 104 S.Ct. 1020, 1029, 79 L.Ed.2d 249 (1984). The Clause does not preclude discrimination against nonresidents where (i) there is a substantial reason for the difference in treatment; and (ii) the discrimination practiced against nonresidents bears a substantial relationship to the State's objective. In deciding whether the discrimination bears a close or substantial relationship to the State's objective, the Court has considered the availability of less restrictive means.

The Supreme Court of New Hampshire offers several justifications for its refusal to admit nonresidents to the bar. It asserts that nonresident members would be less likely (i) to become, and remain, familiar with local rules and procedures; (ii) to behave ethically; (iii) to be available for court proceedings; and (iv) to do *pro bono* and other volunteer work in the State. We find that none of these reasons meets the test of "substantiality," and that the means chosen do not bear the necessary relationship to the State's objectives. ...

In summary, appellant neither advances a "substantial reason" for its discrimination against nonresident applicants to the bar, nor demonstrates that the discrimination practiced bears a close relationship to its proffered objectives. ...

Justice WHITE, concurring in the result.

... I do not, and the Court itself need not, reach out to decide the facial validity of the New Hampshire residency requirement. I would postpone to another day such questions as whether the State may constitutionally condition membership in the New Hampshire Bar upon maintaining an office for the practice of law in the State of New Hampshire.

I concur in the judgment invalidating the New Hampshire residency requirement as applied to appellee Piper.

Justice REHNQUIST, dissenting.

... The reason that the practice of law should be treated differently is that law is one occupation that does not readily translate across state lines. ...

The Court admits that even in the ordinary course of litigation a trial judge will want trial lawyers to be available on short notice; the uncertainties of managing a trial docket are such that lawyers rarely are given a single date on which a trial will begin; they may be required to "stand by"—or whatever the local terminology is—for days at a time, and then be expected to be ready in a matter of hours, with witnesses, when the case in front of them suddenly settles. A State reasonably can decide that a trial court should not have added to its present scheduling difficulties the uncertainties and added delays fostered by counsel who might reside 1,000 miles from New Hampshire. If there is any single problem with state legal systems that this Court might consider "substantial," it is the problem of delay in litigation—a subject that has been profusely explored in the literature over the past several years. Surely the State has a substantial interest in taking steps to minimize this problem.

Thus, I think that New Hampshire had more than enough "substantial reasons" to conclude that its lawyers should also be its residents. I would hold that the Rule of the New Hampshire Supreme Court does not violate the Privileges and Immunities Clause of Art. IV.

Notes and Questions

1. *The big picture.* What is the big picture that the Court is painting here of our "national economic union"? How does this decision influence who can be an attorney and how? Should the Court be making such determinations?

2. *The differences among the Justices.* How do the Justices disagree about privileges and immunities in this opinion? Which one do you find most persuasive?
3. *The Court applies privileges and immunities to protect out-of-staters from discrimination based on their constitutional rights or their important economic activities. Doe v. Bolton*, 410 U.S. 179 (1973), said states could not prohibit out-of-staters from receiving abortions in their state. In contrast, the Court found no fundamental right was involved in a Virginia law that allowed state citizens, but not noncitizens, access to public records. *McBurney v. Young*, 569 U.S. 221 (2013). The Court declared unconstitutional a law that charged in-state residents $25.27 and out-of-state residents $2,500 for a commercial shipping boat. *Toomer v. Witsell*, 334 U.S. 385 (1948). The Court also rejected a challenge to a Montana law that charged out-of-state hunters much more than in-state hunters because hunting was not a constitutional right or an important economic activity. *Baldwin v. Fish and Game Commission of Montana*, 436 U.S. 371 (1978). Do you know what privileges and immunities are protected in your state?

B. Economic Rights Under the Fourteenth Amendment

1. *Lochner v. New York* and the Constitutional Right to Contract

We have seen the many ways that the Fourteenth Amendment has been used to outlaw discrimination—racial, national origin, gender, and sexual orientation discrimination. But does the amendment also protect economic rights? This has been an important question in the history of the Court because of the Court's 1905 decision, *Lochner*, which ruled that the Fourteenth Amendment prevented the State of New York from regulating the working hours of bakers. The Court said this was prohibited by a "freedom of contract" of employers and employees. The case was later rejected, with opinions like *Williamson v. Lee Optical* calling for a rational basis level of scrutiny for economic legislation instead of strict scrutiny. The strict scrutiny accorded to economic rights in *Lochner* meant that the Court was in the position of second-guessing the judgment of lawmakers on the governance of business and the emerging rights of workers. The Court found itself ill-suited for those determinations, and, as part of a larger movement, wherein the Court was increasingly deferential to lawmakers on matters of procedure, like statutes of limitations, and economics, the doctrine became a dead letter—until recently.

We see again in these cases that the Equal Protection Clause usually looks at what the level of classification is and then assigns the appropriate level of scrutiny, depending on the right.

Part of the statute reviewed in *Lochner v. New York* is the following:

> § 110, *Hours of labor in bakeries and confectionery establishments.*—No employee shall be required or permitted to work in a biscuit, bread, or cake bakery or confectionery establishment more than sixty hours in any one week, or more than ten hours in any one day, unless for the purpose of making a shorter work day on the last day of the week; nor more hours in any one week than will make an average of ten hours per day for the number of days during such week in which such employee shall work.

Do you think it violates the Fourteenth Amendment?

Lochner v. New York

SUPREME COURT OF THE UNITED STATES, 1905

198 U.S. 45, 25 S.Ct. 539

Mr. Justice PECKHAM delivered the opinion of the court [joined by Justices FULLER, BREWER, BROWN and McKENNA].

The indictment, it will be seen, charges that the plaintiff in error violated the 110th section of article 8, chapter 415, of the Laws of 1897, known as the labor law of the state of New York, in that he wrongfully and unlawfully required and permitted an employee working for him to work more than sixty hours in one week.

The statute necessarily interferes with the right of contract between the employer and employees, concerning the number of hours in which the latter may labor in the bakery of the employer. The general right to make a contract in relation to his business is part of the liberty of the individual protected by the 14th Amendment of the Federal Constitution. *Allgeyer* v. *Louisiana*, 165 U.S. 578, 41 L. ed. 832, 17 Sup. Ct. Rep. 427. Under that provision no state can deprive any person of life, liberty, or property without due process of law. The right to purchase or to sell labor is part of the liberty protected by this amendment, unless there are circumstances which exclude the right. There are, however, certain powers, existing in the sovereignty of each state in the Union, somewhat vaguely termed police powers, the exact description and limitation of which have not been attempted by the courts. Those powers, broadly stated, and without, at present, any attempt at a more specific limitation, relate to the safety, health, morals, and general welfare of the public. Both property and liberty are held on such reasonable conditions as may be imposed by the governing power of the state in the exercise of those powers, and with such conditions the 14th Amendment was not designed to interfere.

The state, therefore, has power to prevent the individual from making certain kinds of contracts, and in regard to them the Federal Constitution offers no protection. If the contract be one which the state, in the legitimate exercise of its police power, has the right to prohibit, it is not prevented from prohibiting it by the 14th Amendment. Contracts in violation of a statute, either of the Federal or state government, or a contract to let one's property for immoral purposes, or to do any other unlawful act, could obtain no protection from the Federal Constitution, as coming under the liberty of person or of free contract. Therefore, when the state, by its legislature, in the assumed exercise of its police powers, has passed an act which seriously limits the right to labor or the right of contract in regard to their means of livelihood between persons who are *sui juris* (both employer and employee), it becomes of great importance to determine which shall prevail,—the right of the individual to labor for such time as he may choose, or the right of the state to prevent the individual from laboring, or from entering into any contract to labor, beyond a certain time prescribed by the state. ...

But the question would still remain: Is it within the police power of the state? and that question must be answered by the court.

The question whether this act is valid as a labor law, pure and simple, may be dismissed in a few words. There is no reasonable ground for interfering with the liberty of person or the right of free contract, by determining the hours of labor, in the occupation of a baker. There is no contention that bakers as a class are not equal in intelligence and capacity to men in other trades or manual occupations, or that they are not able to assert their rights and care for themselves without the protecting arm of the state, interfering with their independence of judgment and of action. They are in no sense wards of the state. Viewed in the light of a purely labor law, with no reference whatever to the question of health, we think that a law like the one before us involves neither the safety, the morals, nor the welfare, of the public, and that the interest of the public is not in the slightest degree affected by such an act. The law must be upheld, if at all, as a law pertaining to the health of the individual engaged in the occupation of a baker. It does not affect any other portion of the public than those who are engaged in that occupation. Clean and wholesome bread does not depend upon whether the baker works but ten hours per day or only sixty hours a week. The limitation of the hours of labor does not come within the police power on that ground.

It is a question of which of two powers or rights shall prevail,—the power of the state to legislate or the right of the individual to liberty of person and freedom of contract. The mere assertion that the subject relates, though but in a remote degree, to the public health, does not necessarily render the enactment valid. The act must have a more direct relation, as a means to an end, and the end itself must be appropriate and legitimate, before an act can be held to be valid which interferes with the general right of an individual to be free in his person and in his power to contract in relation to his own labor. ...

We think the limit of the police power has been reached and passed in this case. There is, in our judgment, no reasonable foundation for holding this to be necessary or appropriate as a health law to safeguard the public health, or the health of the individuals who are following the trade of a baker. If this statute be valid, and if, therefore, a proper case is made out in which to deny the right of an individual, *sui juris*, as employer or employee, to make contracts for the labor of the latter under the protection of the provisions of the Federal Constitution, there would seem to be no length to which legislation of this nature might not go. The case differs widely, as we have already stated, from the expressions of this court in regard to laws of this nature, as stated in *Holden* v. *Hardy*, 169 U.S. 366, 42 L. ed. 780, 18 Sup. Ct. Rep. 383, and *Jacobson* v. *Massachusetts*, 197 U.S. 11, 25 Sup. Ct. Rep. 358, 49 L. ed.——. ...

It is also urged, pursuing the same line of argument, that it is to the interest of the state that its population should be strong and robust, and therefore any legislation which may be said to tend to make people healthy must be valid as health laws, enacted under the police power. If this be a valid argument and a justification for this kind of legislation, it follows that the protection of the Federal Constitution from undue interference with liberty of person and freedom of contract is visionary, wherever the law is sought to be justified as a valid exercise of the police power. Scarcely any law but might find shelter under such assumptions, and conduct, properly so called, as well as contract, would come under the restrictive sway of the legislature. Not only the hours of employees, but the hours of employers, could be regulated, and doctors, lawyers, scientists, all professional men, as well as athletes and artisans, could be forbidden to fatigue their brains and bodies by prolonged hours of exercise, lest the fighting strength of the state be impaired. We mention these extreme cases because the contention is extreme. We do not believe in the soundness of the views which uphold this law. On the contrary, we think that such a law as this, although passed in the assumed exercise of the police power, and as relating to the public health, or the health of the employees named, is not within that power, and is invalid. The act is not, within any fair meaning of the term, a health law, but is an illegal interference with the rights of individuals, both employers and employees, to make contracts regarding labor upon such terms as they may think best, or which they may agree upon with the other parties to such contracts. Statutes of the nature of that under review, limiting the hours in which grown and intelligent men may labor to earn their living, are mere meddlesome interferences with the rights of the individual, and they are not asved from condemnation by the claim that they are passed in the exercise of the police power and upon the subject of the health of the individual whose rights are interfered with, unless there be some fair ground, reasonable in and of itself, to say that there is material danger to the public health, or to the health of the employees, if the hours of labor are not curtailed. If this be not clearly the case, the individuals whose rights are thus made the subject of legislative interference are under the protection of the Federal Constitution regarding their liberty of contract as well as of person; and the legislature of the state has no power to limit their right as proposed in this statute. ...

It is manifest to us that the limitation of the hours of labor as provided for in this section of the statute under which the indictment was found, and the plaintiff in error convicted, has no such direct relation to, and no such substantial effect upon, the health of the employee, as to justify us in regarding the section as really a health law. It seems to us that the real object and purpose were simply to regulate the hours of labor between the master and his employees (all being men, *Sui juris*), in a private business, not dangerous in any degree to morals, or in any real and substantial degree to the health of the employees. Under such circumstances the freedom of master and employee to contract with each other in relation to their employment, and in defining the same, cannot be prohibited or interfered with, without violating the Federal Constitution. ...

Mr. Justice HOLMES dissenting:

... This case is decided upon an economic theory which a large part of the country does not entertain. If it were a question whether I agreed with that theory, I should desire to study it further and long before making up my mind. But I do not conceive that to be my duty, because I strongly believe that my agreement or disagreement has nothing to do with the right of a majority to embody their opinions in law. It is settled by various decisions of this court that state constitutions and state laws may regulate life in many ways which we as legislators might think as injudicious, or if you like as tyrannical, as this, and which, equally with this, interfere with the liberty to contract.... The 14th Amendment does not enact Mr. Herbert Spencer's Social Statics. The other day we sustained the Massachusetts vaccination law. *Jacobson* v. *Massachusetts*, 197 U.S. 11, 25 Sup. Ct. Rep. 358, 49 L. ed. ___.... But a Constitution is not intended to embody a particular economic theory, whether of paternalism and the organic relation of the citizen to the state or of *laissez faire*. It is made for people of fundamentally differing views, and the accident of our finding certain opinions natural and familiar, or novel, and even shocking, ought not to conclude our judgment upon the question whether statutes embodying them conflict with the Constitution of the United States.

Mr. Justice HARLAN (with whom Mr. Justice WHITE and Mr. Justice DAY concurred) dissenting:

... Professor Hirt in his treatise on the 'Diseases of the Workers' has said: 'The labor of the bakers is among the hardest and most laborious imaginable, because it has to be performed under conditions injurious to the health of those engaged in it. It is hard, very hard, work, not only because it requires a great deal of physical exertion in an overheated workshop and during unreasonably long hours, but more so because of the erratic demands of the public, compelling the baker to perform the greater part of his work at night, thus depriving him of an opportunity to enjoy the necessary rest and sleep,—a fact which is highly injurious to his health.' ...

I take leave to say that the New York statute, in the particulars here involved, cannot be held to be in conflict with the 14th Amendment, without enlarging the scope of the amendment far beyond its original purpose, and without bringing under the supervision of this court matters which have been supposed to belong exclusively to the legislative departments of the several states when exerting their conceded power to guard the health and safety of their citizens by such regulations as they in their wisdom deem best. Health laws of every description constitute, said Chief Justice Marshall, a part of that mass of legislation which 'embraces everything within the territory of a state, not surrendered to the general government; all which can be most advantageously exercised by the states themselves.' *Gibbons* v. *Ogden*, 9 Wheat. 1, 203, 6 L. ed. 23, 71. A decision that the New York statute is void under the 14th Amendment will, in my opinion, involve consequences of a far-reaching and mischievous character; for such a decision would seriously cripple the inherent power of the states to care for the lives, health, and wellbeing of their citizens. Those are matters which can be best controlled by the states. The preservation of the just powers of the states is quite as vital as the preservation of the powers of the general government. ...

Notes and Questions

1. *Regulating the health of bakers.* What does Justice Peckham, writing for the majority, say about the relationship of this law to the health of bakers? What kind of legislation does he think the state could pass regarding bakers if not this one?
2. *The free market.* Does Justice Peckham's opinion best protect the free market? Does he intend to?
3. *Jacobson.* The Justices refer frequently to *Jacobson* in which the Court allowed states to require vaccinations. What does that case have to do with this one? Do you think *Jacobson* might be overruled by the current Court?
4. *Justice Holmes.* Justice Holmes is well known for his dissents. What do you think of the excerpts of this one? Do you know what Mr. Herbert Spencer's Social Statics is?
5. *A treatise on bakers' health.* For what purposes did Justice Harlan cite a treatise on bakers' health?
6. *Who gets to regulate?* Harlan says this opinion would expand the Fourteenth Amendment and cites *Gibbons*, the early Commerce Clause case that you read in Chapter 2. Do you agree that the opinion crippled the power of the states? How much power should the states have, as opposed to the courts, on these issues?

2. The Court Rejects *Lochner* in *Williamson v. Lee Optical*

The next case is famous for reducing the level of scrutiny in economic cases dramatically. As you read, compare the *Lochner* approach to this approach.

Williamson v. Lee Optical of Oklahoma, Inc.

SUPREME COURT OF THE UNITED STATES, 1955

348 U.S. 483, 75 S.Ct. 461

Mr. Justice DOUGLAS delivered the [unanimous] decision of the Court, [with Justices WARREN, BLACK, REED, FRANKFURTER, BURTON, CLARK and MINTON].

... The District Court held unconstitutional portions of three sections of the Act. First, it held invalid under the Due Process Clause of the Fourteenth Amendment the portions of s 2 which make it unlawful for any person not a licensed optometrist or ophthalmologist to fit lenses to a face or to duplicate or replace into frames lenses or other optical appliances, except upon written prescriptive authority of an Oklahoma licensed ophthalmologist or optometrist.

An ophthalmologist is a duly licensed physician who specializes in the care of the eyes. An optometrist examines eyes for refractive error, recognizes (but does not treat) diseases of the eye, and fills prescriptions for eyeglasses. The optician is an artisan qualified to grind lenses, fill prescriptions, and fit frames.

The effect of s 2 is to forbid the optician from fitting or duplicating lenses without a prescription from an ophthalmologist or optometrist. In practical effect, it means that no optician can fit old glasses into new frames or supply a lens, whether it be a new lens or one to duplicate a lost or broken lens, without a prescription. ...

The Oklahoma law may exact a needless, wasteful requirement in many cases. But it is for the legislature, not the courts, to balance the advantages and disadvantages of the new requirement. It appears that in many cases the optician can easily supply the new frames or new lenses without reference to the old written prescription. It also appears that many written prescriptions contain no directive data in regard to fitting spectacles to the face. But in some cases the directions contained in the prescription are essential, if the glasses are to be fitted so as to correct the particular defects of vision or alleviate the eye condition. The legislature might have concluded that the frequency of occasions when a prescription is necessary was sufficient to justify this regulation of the fitting of eyeglasses. Likewise, when it is necessary to duplicate a lens, a written prescription may or may not be necessary. But the legislature might have concluded that one was needed often enough to require one in every case. Or the legislature may have concluded that eye examinations were so critical, not only for correction of vision but also for detection of latent ailments or diseases, that every change in frames and every duplication of a lens should be accompanied by a prescription from a medical expert. To be sure, the present law does not require a new examination of the eyes every time the frames are changed or the lenses duplicated. For if the old prescription is on file with the optician, he can go ahead and make the new fitting or duplicate the lenses. But the law need not be in every respect logically consistent with its aims to be constitutional. It is enough that there is an evil at hand for correction, and that it might be thought that the particular legislative measure was a rational way to correct it.

The day is gone when this Court uses the Due Process Clause of the Fourteenth Amendment to strike down state laws, regulatory of business and industrial conditions, because they may be unwise, improvident, or out of harmony with a particular school of thought. ...

Secondly, the District Court held that it violated the Equal Protection Clause of the Fourteenth Amendment to subject opticians to this regulatory system and to exempt, as s 3 of the Act does, all sellers of ready-to-wear glasses. The problem of legislative classification is a perennial one, admitting of no doctrinaire definition. Evils in the same field may be of different dimensions and proportions, requiring different remedies. Or so the legislature may think. Or the reform may take one step at a time, addressing itself to the phase of the problem which seems most acute to the legislative mind. The legislature may select one phase of one field and apply a remedy there, neglecting the others. The prohibition of the Equal Protection Clause goes no further than the invidious discrimination. We cannot say that

that point has been reached here. For all this record shows, the ready-to-wear branch of this business may not loom large in Oklahoma or may present problems of regulation distinct from the other branch.

Third, the District Court held unconstitutional, as violative of the Due Process Clause of the Fourteenth Amendment, that portion of s 3 which makes it unlawful 'to solicit the sale of * * * frames, mountings * * * or any other optical appliances.' ... We see no constitutional reason why a State may not treat all who deal with the human eye as members of a profession who should use no merchandising methods for obtaining customers. ...

Notes and Questions

1. *The test.* Why does the Court say, "The day is gone when this Court uses the Due Process Clause of the Fourteenth Amendment to strike down state laws, regulatory of business and industrial conditions, because they may be unwise, improvident, or out of harmony with a particular school of thought"?
2. *Two clauses at play.* What are the Due Process Clause arguments and the Equal Protection Clause arguments about the Oklahoma law? How did the Court determine what the outcome of those arguments was?
3. *Permitting incremental lawmaking.* Many commentators have noted that the Court upheld the legislature deciding issues "one step at a time." In other words, legislatures are not required to solve a problem all at once in a single law. Is there any other language in the opinion that shows the Court's deference to legislation?
4. *Williamson vs. Lochner.* How would you compare this case to *Lochner*?

3. Intellectual Disability Receives Rational Basis Review

In 2010, President Barack Obama signed legislation requiring that the federal government not use the terms "mental retardation" and "mentally retarded" but instead should replace them with "intellectual disability" and "individual with an intellectual disability." Michelle Diament, Obama Signs Bill Replacing 'Mental Retardation' With 'Intellectual Disability,' Oct. 5, 2010, https://www.disabilityscoop.com/2010/10/05/obama-signs-rosas-law/10547/. The following case from 1985 uses "mental retardation" and "mentally retarded" repeatedly in discussing what level of scrutiny is applicable under the Equal Protection Clause.

What do you learn about "mental retardation" and the "mentally retarded" in *Cleburne*'s oral argument, available at https://www.oyez.org/cases/1984/84-468? If you read this opinion carefully, you will see that the Justices disagree about how to analyze an Equal Protection problem. Which Justice does the best job of explaining how the Equal Protection Clause should work? Is there an opinion you would favor most on what Equal Protection means?

City of Cleburne, Texas v. Cleburne Living Center, Inc.

SUPREME COURT OF THE UNITED STATES, 1985

473 U.S. 432, 105 S.Ct. 3249

Justice WHITE delivered the opinion of the Court, in which BURGER, C.J., and POWELL, REHNQUIST, STEVENS, and O'CONNOR, JJ., joined. STEVENS, J., filed a concurring opinion, in which BURGER, C.J., joined. MARSHALL, J., filed an opinion concurring in the judgment in part and dissenting in part, in which BRENNAN and BLACKMUN, JJ., joined.

A Texas city denied a special use permit for the operation of a group home for the mentally retarded, acting pursuant to a municipal zoning ordinance requiring permits for such homes. The Court of Appeals for the Fifth Circuit held that mental retardation is a "quasi-suspect" classification and that the ordinance violated the Equal Protection Clause because it did not substantially further an important governmental purpose. We hold that a lesser standard of scrutiny is appropriate, but conclude that under that standard the ordinance is invalid as applied in this case. ...

The Equal Protection Clause of the Fourteenth Amendment commands that no State shall "deny to any person within its jurisdiction the equal protection of the laws," which is essentially a direction that all persons similarly situated should be treated alike. Section 5 of the Amendment empowers Congress to enforce this mandate, but absent controlling congressional direction, the courts have themselves devised standards for determining the validity of state legislation or other official action that is challenged as denying equal protection. The general rule is that legislation is presumed to be valid and will be sustained if the classification drawn by the statute is rationally related to a legitimate state interest. When social or economic legislation is at issue, the Equal Protection Clause allows the States wide latitude, and the Constitution presumes that even improvident decisions will eventually be rectified by the democratic processes.

The general rule gives way, however, when a statute classifies by race, alienage, or national origin. ... Legislative classifications based on gender also call for a heightened standard of review. ...

We have declined, however, to extend heightened review to differential treatment based on age:

> "While the treatment of the aged in this Nation has not been wholly free of discrimination, such persons, unlike, say, those who have been discriminated against on the basis of race or national origin, have not experienced a 'history of purposeful unequal treatment' or been subjected to unique disabilities on the basis of stereotyped characteristics not truly indicative of their abilities." *Massachusetts Board of Retirement v. Murgia,* 427 U.S. 307, 313, 96 S.Ct. 2562, 2567, 49 L.Ed.2d 520 (1976).

The lesson of *Murgia* is that where individuals in the group affected by a law have distinguishing characteristics relevant to interests the State has the authority to implement, the courts have been very reluctant, as they should be in our federal system and with our respect for the separation of powers, to closely scrutinize legislative choices as to whether, how, and to what extent those interests should be pursued. In such cases, the Equal Protection Clause requires only a rational means to serve a legitimate end.

III

Against this background, we conclude for several reasons that the Court of Appeals erred in holding mental retardation a quasi-suspect classification calling for a more exacting standard of judicial review than is normally accorded economic and social legislation. First, it is undeniable, and it is not argued otherwise here, that those who are mentally retarded have a reduced ability to cope with and function in the everyday world. Nor are they all cut from the same pattern: as the testimony in this record indicates, they range from those whose disability is not immediately evident to those who must be constantly cared for.[1] They are thus different, immutably so, in relevant respects, and the States' interest in dealing with and providing for them is plainly a legitimate one. How this large and diversified group is to be treated under the law is a difficult and often a technical matter, very much a task for legislators guided by qualified professionals and not by the perhaps ill-informed opinions of the judiciary. Heightened scrutiny inevitably involves substantive judgments about legislative decisions, and we doubt that the predicate for such judicial oversight is present where the classification deals with mental retardation.

Second, the distinctive legislative response, both national and state, to the plight of those who are mentally retarded demonstrates not only that they have unique problems, but also that the lawmakers have been addressing their difficulties in a manner that belies a continuing antipathy or prejudice and a

1. Mentally retarded individuals fall into four distinct categories. The vast majority-approximately 89%-are classified as "mildly" retarded, meaning that their IQ is between 50 and 70. Approximately 6% are "moderately" retarded, with IQs between 35 and 50. The remaining two categories are "severe" (IQs of 20 to 35) and "profound" (IQs below 20). These last two categories together account for about 5% of the mentally retarded population. App. 39 (testimony of Dr. Philip Roos).

corresponding need for more intrusive oversight by the judiciary. Thus, the Federal Government has not only outlawed discrimination against the mentally retarded in federally funded programs, see § 504 of the Rehabilitation Act of 1973, 29 U.S.C. § 794, but it has also provided the retarded with the right to receive "appropriate treatment, services, and habilitation" in a setting that is "least restrictive of [their] personal liberty." Developmental Disabilities Assistance and Bill of Rights Act, 42 U.S.C. §§ 6010(1), (2). In addition, the Government has conditioned federal education funds on a State's assurance that retarded children will enjoy an education that, "to the maximum extent appropriate," is integrated with that of nonmentally retarded children. Education of the Handicapped Act, 20 U.S.C. § 1412(5)(B). The Government has also facilitated the hiring of the mentally retarded into the federal civil service by exempting them from the requirement of competitive examination. See 5 CFR § 213.3102(t) (1984). The State of Texas has similarly enacted legislation that acknowledges the special status of the mentally retarded by conferring certain rights upon them, such as "the right to live in the least restrictive setting appropriate to [their] individual needs and abilities," including "the right to live ... in a group home." Mentally Retarded Persons Act of 1977, Tex.Rev.Civ. Stat.Ann., Art. 5547-300, § 7 (Vernon Supp.1985).

Such legislation thus singling out the retarded for special treatment reflects the real and undeniable differences between the retarded and others. ...

Third, the legislative response, which could hardly have occurred and survived without public support, negates any claim that the mentally retarded are politically powerless in the sense that they have no ability to attract the attention of the lawmakers. ...

Fourth, if the large and amorphous class of the mentally retarded were deemed quasi-suspect for the reasons given by the Court of Appeals, it would be difficult to find a principled way to distinguish a variety of other groups who have perhaps immutable disabilities setting them off from others, who cannot themselves mandate the desired legislative responses, and who can claim some degree of prejudice from at least part of the public at large. One need mention in this respect only the aging, the disabled, the mentally ill, and the infirm. We are reluctant to set out on that course, and we decline to do so. ...

Our refusal to recognize the retarded as a quasi-suspect class does not leave them entirely unprotected from invidious discrimination. To withstand equal protection review, legislation that distinguishes between the mentally retarded and others must be rationally related to a legitimate governmental purpose. ...

May the city require the permit for this facility when other care and multiple-dwelling facilities are freely permitted? ...

Because in our view the record does not reveal any rational basis for believing that the Featherston home would pose any special threat to the city's legitimate interests, we affirm the judgment below insofar as it holds the ordinance invalid as applied in this case. ...

The short of it is that requiring the permit in this case appears to us to rest on an irrational prejudice against the mentally retarded, including those who would occupy the Featherston facility and who would live under the closely supervised and highly regulated conditions expressly provided for by state and federal law.

The judgment of the Court of Appeals is affirmed insofar as it invalidates the zoning ordinance as applied to the Featherston home.

Justice STEVENS, with whom THE CHIEF JUSTICE joins, concurring.

The Court of Appeals disposed of this case as if a critical question to be decided were which of three clearly defined standards of equal protection review should be applied to a legislative classification discriminating against the mentally retarded.[2] In fact, our cases have not delineated three-or even one or two-such well-defined standards. Rather, our cases reflect a continuum of judgmental responses to differing classifications which have been explained in opinions by terms ranging from "strict scrutiny" at one extreme to "rational basis" at the other. I have never been persuaded that these so-called "standards" adequately explain the decisional process. Cases involving classifications based on alienage, illegal residency, illegitimacy, gender, age, or-as in this case-mental retardation, do not fit well into sharply defined classifications. ...

In my own approach to these cases, I have always asked myself whether I could find a "rational basis" for the classification at issue. The term "rational," of course, includes a requirement that an impartial lawmaker

2. The three standards-"rationally related to a legitimate state interest," "somewhat heightened review," and "strict scrutiny" are briefly described *ante*.

could logically believe that the classification would serve a legitimate public purpose that transcends the harm to the members of the disadvantaged class. Thus, the word "rational"—for me at least—includes elements of legitimacy and neutrality that must always characterize the performance of the sovereign's duty to govern impartially.

The rational-basis test, properly understood, adequately explains why a law that deprives a person of the right to vote because his skin has a different pigmentation than that of other voters violates the Equal Protection Clause. It would be utterly irrational to limit the franchise on the basis of height or weight; it is equally invalid to limit it on the basis of skin color. None of these attributes has any bearing at all on the citizen's willingness or ability to exercise that civil right. We do not need to apply a special standard, or to apply "strict scrutiny," or even "heightened scrutiny," to decide such cases.

In every equal protection case, we have to ask certain basic questions. What class is harmed by the legislation, and has it been subjected to a "tradition of disfavor" by our laws? What is the public purpose that is being served by the law? What is the characteristic of the disadvantaged class that justifies the disparate treatment? In most cases the answer to these questions will tell us whether the statute has a "rational basis." ...

The discrimination against the mentally retarded that is at issue in this case is the city's decision to require an annual special use permit before property in an apartment house district may be used as a group home for persons who are mildly retarded. The record convinces me that this permit was required because of the irrational fears of neighboring property owners, rather than for the protection of the mentally retarded persons who would reside in respondent's home.

Although the city argued in the Court of Appeals that legitimate interests of the neighbors justified the restriction, the court unambiguously rejected that argument. In this Court, the city has argued that the discrimination was really motivated by a desire to protect the mentally retarded from the hazards presented by the neighborhood. Zoning ordinances are not usually justified on any such basis, and in this case, for the reasons explained by the Court, I find that justification wholly unconvincing. I cannot believe that a rational member of this disadvantaged class could ever approve of the discriminatory application of the city's ordinance in this case.

Justice MARSHALL, with whom Justice BRENNAN and Justice BLACKMUN join, concurring in the judgment in part and dissenting in part.

... Yet Cleburne's ordinance surely would be valid under the traditional rational-basis test applicable to economic and commercial regulation. In my view, it is important to articulate, as the Court does not, the facts and principles that justify subjecting this zoning ordinance to the searching review-the heightened scrutiny-that actually leads to its invalidation. Moreover, in invalidating Cleburne's exclusion of the "feebleminded" only as applied to respondents, rather than on its face, the Court radically departs from our equal protection precedents. Because I dissent from this novel and truncated remedy, and because I cannot accept the Court's disclaimer that no "more exacting standard" than ordinary rational-basis review is being applied, I write separately. ...

But however labeled, the rational basis test invoked today is most assuredly not the rational-basis test of *Williamson v. Lee Optical of Oklahoma, Inc.*, 348 U.S. 483, 75 S.Ct. 461, 99 L.Ed. 563 (1955), and their progeny. ...

I share the Court's criticisms of the overly broad lines that Cleburne's zoning ordinance has drawn. But if the ordinance is to be invalidated for its imprecise classifications, it must be pursuant to more powerful scrutiny than the minimal rational-basis test used to review classifications affecting only economic and commercial matters. ...

The suggestion that the traditional rational-basis test allows this sort of searching inquiry creates precedent for this Court and lower courts to subject economic and commercial classifications to similar and searching "ordinary" rational-basis review-a small and regrettable step back toward the days of *Lochner v. New York*, 198 U.S. 45, 25 S.Ct. 539, 49 L.Ed. 937 (1905). Moreover, by failing to articulate the factors that justify today's "second order" rational-basis review, the Court provides no principled foundation for determining when more searching inquiry is to be invoked. ...

In light of the importance of the interest at stake and the history of discrimination the retarded have suffered, the Equal Protection Clause requires us to do more than review the distinctions drawn by Cleburne's zoning ordinance as if they appeared in a taxing statute or in economic or commercial legislation. The searching scrutiny I would give to restrictions on the ability of the retarded to establish community group homes leads me to conclude that Cleburne's vague generalizations for classifying the "feeble-minded" with drug addicts, alcoholics, and the insane, and excluding them where the elderly, the ill, the boarder, and the transient are allowed, are not substantial or important enough to overcome the suspicion that the ordinance rests on impermissible assumptions or outmoded and perhaps invidious stereotypes. ...

As the history of discrimination against the retarded and its continuing legacy amply attest, the mentally retarded have been, and in some areas may still be, the targets of action the Equal Protection Clause condemns. With respect to a liberty so valued as the right to establish a home in the community, and so likely to be denied on the basis of irrational fears and outright hostility, heightened scrutiny is surely appropriate.

IV

In light of the scrutiny that should be applied here, Cleburne's ordinance sweeps too broadly to dispel the suspicion that it rests on a bare desire to treat the retarded as outsiders, pariahs who do not belong in the community. The Court, while disclaiming that special scrutiny is necessary or warranted, reaches the same conclusion. Rather than striking the ordinance down, however, the Court invalidates it merely as applied to respondents. I must dissent from the novel proposition that "the preferred course of adjudication" is to leave standing a legislative Act resting on "irrational prejudice" thereby forcing individuals in the group discriminated against to continue to run the Act's gauntlet.

The Court appears to act out of a belief that the ordinance might be "rational" as applied to some subgroup of the retarded under some circumstances, such as those utterly without the capacity to live in a community, and that the ordinance should not be invalidated *in toto* if it is capable of ever being validly applied. But the issue is not "whether the city may never insist on a special use permit for the mentally retarded in an R-3 zone." The issue is whether the city may require a permit pursuant to a blunderbuss ordinance drafted many years ago to exclude all the "feeble-minded," or whether the city must enact a new ordinance carefully tailored to the exclusion of some well-defined subgroup of retarded people in circumstances in which exclusion might reasonably further legitimate city purposes. ...

V

The Court's opinion approaches the task of principled equal protection adjudication in what I view as precisely the wrong way. The formal label under which an equal protection claim is reviewed is less important than careful identification of the interest at stake and the extent to which society recognizes the classification as an invidious one. Yet in focusing obsessively on the appropriate label to give its standard of review, the Court fails to identify the interests at stake or to articulate the principle that classifications based on mental retardation must be carefully examined to assure they do not rest on impermissible assumptions or false stereotypes regarding individual ability and need. No guidance is thereby given as to when the Court's freewheeling, and potentially dangerous, "rational-basis standard" is to be employed, nor is attention directed to the invidiousness of grouping all retarded individuals together. Moreover, the Court's narrow, as-applied remedy fails to deal adequately with the overbroad presumption that lies at the heart of this case. Rather than leaving future retarded individuals to run the gauntlet of this overbroad presumption, I would affirm the judgment of the Court of Appeals in its entirety and would strike down on its face the provision at issue. I therefore concur in the judgment in part and dissent in part.

Notes and Questions

1. *Level of scrutiny for the mentally disabled?* Why do you think the Fifth Circuit ruled that the mentally disabled were a suspect class? Why did the majority reject that conclusion? Why did Justice Marshall reject the majority's standard that rational basis review should apply? Is the majority's rational basis review the same as Justice Stevens's perspective on equal protection? How would you distinguish White's, Stevens's, and Marshall's opinions from one another?
2. *Level of scrutiny for age discrimination?* What has the Court said about the appropriate level of scrutiny for the aged? Why?

3. *Justice Marshall.* Why is Justice Marshall unhappy with the as-applied nature of the majority's ruling?
4. *Your EP map.* Write out your analysis of how the Equal Protection Clause should work.

4. Punitive Damages and Due Process

In one sense, *Lochner* has by now been rejected by the Supreme Court for its Fourteenth Amendment analysis of economic regulations. Yet, more recently, the Court has taken a number of punitive damages cases, concluding that the Fourteenth Amendment's Due Process Clause sets limits on what punitive damages a state court can confer in civil tort lawsuits.

In *BMW of North America, Inc., v. Gore,* 517 U.S. 559, 116 S.Ct. 1589 (1996), Justice Stevens wrote an opinion about an Alabama case in which Dr. Ira Gore, Jr., discovered that his car had been repainted before he bought it. Gore sued BMW for $4,000 actual damages and $4 million punitive damages to punish BMW for its failure to disclose the state of the car. The jury awarded him those damages. The Alabama court reduced the punitive damages to $2 million, and the case went to the Supreme Court.

The Court ruled those damages were "grossly excessive" under the Due Process Clause. Stevens wrote that:

> Three guideposts, each of which indicates that BMW did not receive adequate notice of the magnitude of the sanction that Alabama might impose for adhering to the nondisclosure policy adopted in 1983, lead us to the conclusion that the $2 million award against BMW is grossly excessive: the degree of reprehensibility of the nondisclosure; the disparity between the harm or potential harm suffered by Dr. Gore and his punitive damages award; and the difference between this remedy and the civil penalties authorized or imposed in comparable cases. *Id.* at 574–75.

In the second guidepost, Stevens wrote about the ratio between the actual and punitive damages, arguing that the damages must bear a "reasonable relationship" to one another. In this case, the fact that the punitive were 500 times the actual damages was too high. Stevens was joined by Justices O'Connor, Kennedy, Souter, and Breyer. In concurrence Justice Breyer, joined by O'Connor and Souter, concluded the "severe lack of proportionality between the size of the award and the underlying punitive damages objectives shows that the award falls into the category of 'gross excessiveness' set forth in this Court's prior cases." *Id.* at 596.

In dissent, Justices Scalia and Thomas concluded that "the Court's activities in this area are an unjustified incursion into the province of state governments." *Id.* at 598. The Court's guideposts "provide no real guidance at all." *Id.* at 605. In another dissent, Justice Ginsburg and Chief Justice Rehnquist warned that the Court "unnecessarily and unwisely ventures into territory traditionally within the States' domain, and does so in the face of reform measures recently adopted or currently under consideration in legislative arenas." *Id.* at 607.

Which argument is a better interpretation of the Fourteenth Amendment's Due Process Clause? The majority's or the dissent's?

In an automobile insurance case, the Court ruled that $145 million punitive damages were too high for a case with $1 million compensatory damages. The Court employed the *Gore* test. The Court also ruled that State Farm could not be penalized for conduct outside Utah where the claim arose. The Court refused to set a specific rule for the ratio of punitive to compensatory damages but did note that "few awards exceeding a single-digit ratio" between punitive and compensatory would be acceptable. *State Farm Mutual Automobile Insurance Co. v. Campbell*, 538 U.S. 408 (2003).

Then, in a smoking case, the Court rejected a $79.5 million punitive damages award on an $800,000 compensatory verdict. The Court said that punitives could not be used to award damages in the names of nonparties to the case. *Philip Morris, USA v. Williams*, 549 U.S. 306 (2007).

In an admiralty law case about an oil spill, the Court said there could not be more than a 1:1 ratio between the compensatory and punitive damages. The jury in that case had awarded $507 million compensatory and $2.5 billion punitive damages. *Exxon Shipping Co. v. Baker*, 554 U.S. 471 (2008).

Recently, the Court denied certiorari, however, in a cancer case against Johnson and Johnson where the 22 plaintiffs claimed the company's products had caused their ovarian cancer. The jury awarded $25 million in compensatory damages to each individual, to total $550 million. They then added punitive damages, with Johnson and Johnson held to $3.15 billion and an associated company to $990 million. *Ingham v. Johnson & Johnson*, 608 S.W.3d 663, 680 (Mo. Ct. App. 2020), reh'g and/or transfer denied (July 28, 2020), transfer denied (Nov. 3, 2020), certiorari denied, 141 S. Ct. 2716, 210 L. Ed. 2d 879 (2021). Would the 1:1 ratio be a good rule for all the cases? These cases are trying to figure out what the limit is! Is it numerical or a percentage? How do the Justices choose such limits? What guides them? What would you do if you were a trial judge in a case with punitive damages?

C. The Right to Privacy as Due Process

The Court has identified a "right to privacy" that covers rights to contraception, abortion, consensual sex between adults, suicide, assisted suicide, and physician-assisted suicide. Look through your whole Constitution. Is a "right of privacy" identified there? Is reproductive liberty identified there? Is a right to die protected anywhere? How do you assess the constitutional arguments of the Justices in the following cases? Each case is faced with two distinct questions: what is the source of the right in the Constitution? And what is the scope of the right? What is the relationship between the legislative power and the judicial power in these cases?

1. Contraception

Historically, many states had laws that banned any sale or use of contraceptives. Why did they have such laws? Does the oral argument answer the question about which element of the Constitution was implicated by a contraceptive ban? Were the bans unconstitutional for heterosexual married couples only? See https://www.oyez.org/cases/1964/496. Does the oral argument say anything about the Ninth Amendment?

Do you prefer the Fourteenth or the Ninth Amendment as the basis for the right in the following case? Does it have to be an either or decision? Who is Griswold, and why does she have standing to bring this case?

Griswold v. Connecticut
SUPREME COURT OF THE UNITED STATES, 1965
381 U.S. 479, 85 S.Ct. 1678

Mr. Justice DOUGLAS delivered the opinion of the Court. [DOUGLAS was joined by Chief Justice WARREN, and CLARK, HARLAN, BRENNAN, WHITE and GOLDBERG. Justices BLACK and STEWART dissented.]

Appellant Griswold is Executive Director of the Planned Parenthood League of Connecticut. Appellant Buxton is a licensed physician and a professor at the Yale Medical School who served as Medical Director for the League at its Center in New Haven—a center open and operating from November 1 to November 10, 1961, when appellants were arrested.

They gave information, instruction, and medical advice to *married persons* as to the means of preventing conception. They examined the wife and prescribed the best contraceptive device or material for her use. Fees were usually charged, although some couples were serviced free.

The statutes whose constitutionality is involved in this appeal are ss 53—32 and 54—196 of the General Statutes of Connecticut (1958 rev.). The former provides:

> 'Any person who uses any drug, medicinal article or instrument for the purpose of preventing conception shall be fined not less than fifty dollars or imprisoned not less than sixty days nor more than one year or be both fined and imprisoned.'

Section 54—196 provides:

> 'Any person who assists, abets, counsels, causes, hires or commands another to commit any offense may be prosecuted and punished as if he were the principal offender.'

The appellants were found guilty as accessories and fined $100 each, against the claim that the accessory statute as so applied violated the Fourteenth Amendment. ...

The foregoing cases suggest that specific guarantees in the Bill of Rights have penumbras, formed by emanations from those guarantees that help give them life and substance. See Poe v. Ullman, 367 U.S. 497, 516—522, 81 S.Ct. 1752, 6 L.Ed.2d 989 (dissenting opinion). Various guarantees create zones of privacy. The right of association contained in the penumbra of the First Amendment is one, as we have seen. The Third Amendment in its prohibition against the quartering of soldiers 'in any house' in time of peace without the consent of the owner is another facet of that privacy. The Fourth Amendment explicitly affirms the 'right of the people to be secure in their persons, houses, papers, and effects, against unreasonable searches and seizures.' The Fifth Amendment in its Self-Incrimination Clause enables the citizen to create a zone of privacy which government may not force him to surrender to his detriment. The Ninth Amendment provides: 'The enumeration in the Constitution, of certain rights, shall not be construed to deny or disparage others retained by the people.'

The Fourth and Fifth Amendments were described in Boyd v. United States, 116 U.S. 616, 630, 6 S.Ct. 524, 532, 29 L.Ed. 746, as protection against all governmental invasions 'of the sanctity of a man's home and the privacies of life.'* We recently referred in Mapp v. Ohio, 367 U.S. 643, 656, 81 S.Ct. 1684, 1692, 6 L.Ed.2d 1081, to the Fourth Amendment as creating a 'right to privacy, no less important than any other right carefully and particularly reserved to the people.'

We have had many controversies over these penumbral rights of 'privacy and repose.' These cases bear witness that the right of privacy which presses for recognition here is a legitimate one.

The present case, then, concerns a relationship lying within the zone of privacy created by several fundamental constitutional guarantees. And it concerns a law which, in forbidding the use of contraceptives rather than regulating their manufacture or sale, seeks to achieve its goals by means having a maximum destructive impact upon that relationship. Such a law cannot stand in light of the familiar principle, so often applied by this Court, that a 'governmental purpose to control or prevent activities constitutionally subject to state regulation may not be achieved by means which sweep unnecessarily broadly and thereby invade the area of protected freedoms.' NAACP v. Alabama, 377 U.S. 288, 307, 84 S.Ct. 1302, 1314, 12 L.Ed.2d 325. Would we allow the police to search the sacred precincts of marital bedrooms for telltale signs of the use of contraceptives? The very idea is repulsive to the notions of privacy surrounding the marriage relationship.

We deal with a right of privacy older than the Bill of Rights—older than our political parties, older than our school system. Marriage is a coming together for better or for worse, hopefully enduring, and intimate to the degree of being sacred. It is an association that promotes a way of life, not causes; a harmony in living, not political faiths; a bilateral loyalty, not commercial or social projects. Yet it is an association for as noble a purpose as any involved in our prior decisions.

Reversed.

Mr. Justice GOLDBERG, whom THE CHIEF JUSTICE and Mr. Justice BRENNAN join, concurring.

... My conclusion that the concept of liberty is not so restricted and that it embraces the right of marital privacy though that right is not mentioned explicitly in the Constitution is supported both by numerous decisions of this Court, referred to in the Court's opinion, and by the language and history of the Ninth Amendment. In reaching the conclusion that the right of marital privacy is protected, as being within the protected penumbra of specific guarantees of the Bill of Rights, the Court refers to the Ninth Amendment. I add these words to emphasize the relevance of that Amendment to the Court's holding. ...

The language and history of the Ninth Amendment reveal that the Framers of the Constitution believed that there are additional fundamental rights, protected from governmental infringement, which exist alongside those fundamental rights specifically mentioned in the first eight constitutional amendments. ...

While this Court has had little occasion to interpret the Ninth Amendment, '(i)t cannot be presumed that any clause in the constitution is intended to be without effect.' Marbury v. Madison, 1 Cranch 137, 174, 2 L.Ed. 60. In interpreting the Constitution, 'real effect should be given to all the words it uses.' The Ninth Amendment to the Constitution may be regarded by some as a recent discovery and may be forgotten by others, but since 1791 it has been a basic part of the Constitution which we are sworn to uphold. To hold that a right so basic and fundamental and so deep-rooted in our society as the right of privacy in marriage may be infringed because that right is not guaranteed in so many words by the first eight amendments to the Constitution is to ignore the Ninth Amendment and to give it no effect whatsoever. Moreover, a judicial construction that this fundamental right is not protected by the Constitution because it is not mentioned in explicit terms by one of the first eight amendments or elsewhere in the Constitution would violate the Ninth Amendment, which specifically states that '(t)he enumeration in the Constitution, of certain rights shall not be construed to deny or disparage others retained by the people.' ...

In sum, I believe that the right of privacy in the marital relation is fundamental and basic—a personal right 'retained by the people' within the meaning of the Ninth Amendment. Connecticut cannot constitutionally abridge this fundamental right, which is protected by the Fourteenth Amendment from infringement by the States. I agree with the Court that petitioners' convictions must therefore be reversed.

Mr. Justice HARLAN, concurring in the judgment.

I fully agree with the judgment of reversal, but find myself unable to join the Court's opinion. The reason is that it seems to me to evince an approach to this case very much like that taken by my Brothers BLACK and STEWART in dissent, namely: the Due Process Clause of the Fourteenth Amendment does not touch this Connecticut statute unless the enactment is found to violate some right assured by the letter or penumbra of the Bill of Rights. ...

In my view, the proper constitutional inquiry in this case is whether this Connecticut statute infringes the Due Process Clause of the Fourteenth Amendment because the enactment violates basic values 'implicit in the concept of ordered liberty.' For reasons stated at length in my dissenting opinion in Poe v. Ullman, I believe that it does. While the relevant inquiry may be aided by resort to one or more of the provisions of the Bill of Rights, it is not dependent on them or any of their radiations. The Due Process Clause of the Fourteenth Amendment stands, in my opinion, on its own bottom. ...

Mr. Justice WHITE, concurring in the judgment.

... In these circumstances one is rather hard pressed to explain how the ban on use by married persons in any way prevents use of such devices by persons engaging in illicit sexual relations and thereby contributes to the State's policy against such relationships. Neither the state courts nor the State before the bar of this Court has tendered such an explanation. It is purely fanciful to believe that the broad proscription on use facilitates discovery of use by persons engaging in a prohibited relationship or for some other reason makes such use more unlikely and thus can be supported by any sort of administrative consideration. ...

Mr. Justice BLACK, with whom Mr. Justice STEWART joins, dissenting.

... I get nowhere in this case by talk about a constitutional 'right or privacy' as an emanation from one or more constitutional provisions. I like my privacy as well as the next one, but I am nevertheless compelled to admit that government has a right to invade it unless prohibited by some specific constitutional provision. For these reasons I cannot agree with the Court's judgment and the reasons it gives for holding this Connecticut law unconstitutional. ...

I think that if properly construed neither the Due Process Clause nor the Ninth Amendment, nor both together, could under any circumstances be a proper basis for invalidating the Connecticut law. I discuss the due process and Ninth Amendment arguments together because on analysis they turn out to be the same thing—merely using different words to claim for this Court and the federal judiciary power to invalidate any legislative act which the judges find irrational, unreasonable or offensive. ...

I do not believe that we are granted power by the Due Process Clause or any other constitutional provision or provisions to measure constitutionality by our belief that legislation is arbitrary, capricious or unreasonable, or accomplishes no justifiable purpose, or is offensive to our own notions of 'civilized standards of conduct.' Such an appraisal of the wisdom of legislation is an attribute of the power to make laws, not of the power to interpret them. The use by federal courts of such a formula or doctrine or whatnot to veto federal or state laws simply takes away from Congress and States the power to make laws based on their own judgment of fairness and wisdom and transfers that power to this Court for ultimate determination—a power which was specifically denied to federal courts by the convention that framed the Constitution. ...

I repeat so as not to be misunderstood that this Court does have power, which it should exercise, to hold laws unconstitutional where they are forbidden by the Federal Constitution. My point is that there is no provision of the Constitution which either expressly or impliedly vests power in this Court to sit as a supervisory agency over acts of duly constituted legislative bodies and set aside their laws because of the Court's belief that the legislative policies adopted are unreasonable, unwise, arbitrary, capricious or irrational. The adoption of such a loose, flexible, uncontrolled standard for holding laws unconstitutional, if ever it is finally achieved, will amount to a great unconstitutional shift of power to the courts which I believe and am constrained to say will be bad for the courts and worse for the country. Subjecting federal and state laws to such an unrestrained and unrestrainable judicial control as to the wisdom of legislative enactments would, I fear, jeopardize the separation of governmental powers that the Framers set up and at the same time threaten to take away much of the power of States to govern themselves which the Constitution plainly intended them to have. ...

Mr. Justice STEWART, whom Mr. Justice BLACK joins, dissenting.

Since 1879 Connecticut has had on its books a law which forbids the use of contraceptives by anyone. I think this is an uncommonly silly law. As a practical matter, the law is obviously unenforceable, except in the oblique context of the present case. As a philosophical matter, I believe the use of contraceptives in the relationship of marriage should be left to personal and private choice, based upon each individual's moral, ethical, and religious beliefs. As a matter of social policy, I think professional counsel about methods of birth control should be available to all, so that each individual's choice can be meaningfully made. But we are not asked in this case to say whether we think this law is unwise, or even asinine. We are asked to hold that it violates the United States Constitution. And that I cannot do. ...

What provision of the Constitution, then, does make this state law invalid? The Court says it is the right of privacy 'created by several fundamental constitutional guarantees.' With all deference, I can find no such general right of privacy in the Bill of Rights, in any other part of the Constitution, or in any case ever before decided by this Court.

At the oral argument in this case we were told that the Connecticut law does not 'conform to current community standards.' But it is not the function of this Court to decide cases on the basis of community standards. We are here to decide cases 'agreeably to the Constitution and laws of the United States.' It is the essence of judicial duty to subordinate our own personal views, our own ideas of what legislation is wise and what is not. If, as I should surely hope, the law before us does not reflect the standards of the people of Connecticut, the people of Connecticut can freely exercise their true Ninth and Tenth Amendment rights to persuade their elected representatives to repeal it. That is the constitutional way to take this law off the books.

Notes and Questions

1. *The doctor or the woman?* Note that this case was brought by the doctor prescribing the contraception, not the couple seeking it. This is a common theme in the contraception and abortion cases where the right is discussed in the context of a doctor's involvement and medical judgment. Do you agree that a doctor should be able to challenge a law banning contraception in addition to the couple seeking it? Does *Griswold* mean that couples only have a right in this opinion to medically-prescribed contraception?
2. *Singles, too. Eisenstadt v. Baird*, 405 U.S. 438 (1972) expanded the right that *Griswold* found for married couples to individuals.
3. *Video.* Watch a video about *Griswold* at United 4 Social Change, *Griswold v. Connecticut* (1965), Mar. 18, 2021, at https://www.youtube.com/watch?v=-5keiBzhG-E.
4. *Abortion.* What is the relationship between laws against contraception and laws against abortion? Does *Griswold*'s holding and reasoning suggest that the Constitution protects a right to abortion just as it protects a right to contraception? What is the best source of that right in the Constitution?

2. Abortion

a. Roe *Establishes the Right*

There are two oral arguments for you to read in the first abortion case, *Roe v. Wade,* available at https://www.oyez.org/cases/1971/70-18. How persuasive are the lawyers on whether the Constitution does or does not hold a right to abortion? Can you tell from the argument whether the Justices are having any trouble figuring out whether abortion is protected by the Constitution?

Why do you think *Roe* was recently overruled? Was *Roe* wrong the day it was decided? If *Roe* were overruled, how would access to abortion be regulated, by whom, and where?

Roe v. Wade

SUPREME COURT OF THE UNITED STATES, 1973

410 U.S. 113, 93 S.Ct. 705

Mr. Justice BLACKMUN delivered the opinion of the Court.

... The Texas statutes under attack here are typical of those that have been in effect in many States for approximately a century. The Georgia statutes, in contrast, have a modern cast and are a legislative product that, to an extent at least, obviously reflects the influences of recent attitudinal change, of advancing medical knowledge and techniques, and of new thinking about an old issue.

We forthwith acknowledge our awareness of the sensitive and emotional nature of the abortion controversy, of the vigorous opposing views, even among physicians, and of the deep and seemingly absolute convictions that the subject inspires. One's philosophy, one's experiences, one's exposure to the raw edges of human existence, one's religious training, one's attitudes toward life and family and their values, and the moral standards one establishes and seeks to observe, are all likely to influence and to color one's thinking and conclusions about abortion.

In addition, population growth, pollution, poverty, and racial overtones tend to complicate and not to simplify the problem. ...

I

The Texas statutes that concern us here are Arts. 1191-1194 and 1196 of the State's Penal Code, Vernon's Ann.P.C. These make it a crime to 'procure an abortion,' as therein defined, or to attempt one, except with respect to 'an abortion procured or attempted by medical advice for the purpose of saving the life of the mother.' Similar statutes are in existence in a majority of the States. ...

II

Jane Roe,[3] a single woman who was residing in Dallas County, Texas, instituted this federal action in March 1970 against the District Attorney of the county. She sought a declaratory judgment that the Texas criminal abortion statutes were unconstitutional on their face, and an injunction restraining the defendant from enforcing the statutes. ...

V

The principal thrust of appellant's attack on the Texas statutes is that they improperly invade a right, said to be possessed by the pregnant woman, to choose to terminate her pregnancy. Appellant would discover this right in the concept of personal 'liberty' embodied in the Fourteenth Amendment's Due Process Clause; or in personal marital, familial, and sexual privacy said to be protected by the Bill of Rights or its penumbras, see Griswold v. Connecticut, 381 U.S. 479, 85 S.Ct. 1678, 14 L.Ed.2d 510 (1965); Eisenstadt v. Baird, 405 U.S. 438 (1972); id., at 460, 92 S.Ct. 1029, at 1042, 31 L.Ed.2d 349 (White, J., concurring in result); or among those rights reserved to the people by the Ninth Amendment, Griswold v. Connecticut, 381 U.S., at 486, 85 S.Ct., at 1682 (Goldberg, J., concurring). Before addressing this claim, we feel it desirable briefly to survey, in several aspects, the history of abortion, for such insight as that history may afford us, and then to examine the state purposes and interests behind the criminal abortion laws.

VI

... It is thus apparent that at common law, at the time of the adoption of our Constitution, and throughout the major portion of the 19th century, abortion was viewed with less disfavor than under most American statutes currently in effect. Phrasing it another way, a woman enjoyed a substantially broader right to terminate a pregnancy than she does in most States today. At least with respect to the early stage of pregnancy, and very possibly without such a limitation, the opportunity to make this choice was present in this country well into the 19th century. Even later, the law continued for some time to treat less punitively an abortion procured in early pregnancy.

VIII

... This right of privacy, whether it be founded in the Fourteenth Amendment's concept of personal liberty and restrictions upon state action, as we feel it is, or, as the District Court determined, in the Ninth Amendment's reservation of rights to the people, is broad enough to encompass a woman's decision whether or not to terminate her pregnancy. The detriment that the State would impose upon the pregnant woman by denying this choice altogether is apparent. Specific and direct harm medically diagnosable even in early pregnancy may be involved. Maternity, or additional offspring, may force upon the woman a distressful life and future. Psychological harm may be imminent. Mental and physical health may be taxed by child care. There is also the distress, for all concerned, associated with the unwanted child, and there is the problem of bringing a child into a family already unable, psychologically and otherwise, to care for it. In other cases, as in this one, the additional difficulties and continuing stigma of unwed motherhood may be involved. All these are factors the woman and her responsible physician necessarily will consider in consultation.

On the basis of elements such as these, appellant and some amici argue that the woman's right is absolute

3. The name is a pseudonym.

and that she is entitled to terminate her pregnancy at whatever time, in whatever way, and for whatever reason she alone chooses. With this we do not agree. Appellant's arguments that Texas either has no valid interest at all in regulating the abortion decision, or no interest strong enough to support any limitation upon the woman's sole determination, are unpersuasive. The Court's decisions recognizing a right of privacy also acknowledge that some state regulation in areas protected by that right is appropriate. As noted above, a State may properly assert important interests in safeguarding health, in maintaining medical standards, and in protecting potential life. At some point in pregnancy, these respective interests become sufficiently compelling to sustain regulation of the factors that govern the abortion decision. The privacy right involved, therefore, cannot be said to be absolute. In fact, it is not clear to us that the claim asserted by some amici that one has an unlimited right to do with one's body as one pleases bears a close relationship to the right of privacy previously articulated in the Court's decisions. The Court has refused to recognize an unlimited right of this kind in the past. Jacobson v. Massachusetts, 197 U.S. 11, 25 S.Ct. 358, 49 L.Ed. 643 (1905) (vaccination); Buck v. Bell, 274 U.S. 200, 47 S.Ct. 584, 71 L.Ed. 1000 (1927) (sterilization).

We, therefore, conclude that the right of personal privacy includes the abortion decision, but that this right is not unqualified and must be considered against important state interests in regulation. ...

IX

... The appellee and certain amici argue that the fetus is a 'person' within the language and meaning of the Fourteenth Amendment. ... All this, together with our observation, supra, that throughout the major portion of the 19th century prevailing legal abortion practices were far freer than they are today, persuades us that the word 'person,' as used in the Fourteenth Amendment, does not include the unborn. ...

X

In view of all this, we do not agree that, by adopting one theory of life, Texas may override the rights of the pregnant woman that are at stake. We repeat, however, that the State does have an important and legitimate interest in preserving and protecting the health of the pregnant woman, whether she be a resident of the State or a non-resident who seeks medical consultation and treatment there, and that it has still another important and legitimate interest in protecting the potentiality of human life. These interests are separate and distinct. Each grows in substantiality as the woman approaches term and, at a point during pregnancy, each becomes 'compelling.'

With respect to the State's important and legitimate interest in the health of the mother, the 'compelling' point, in the light of present medical knowledge, is at approximately the end of the first trimester. This is so because of the now-established medical fact, referred to above, that until the end of the first trimester mortality in abortion may be less than mortality in normal childbirth. It follows that, from and after this point, a State may regulate the abortion procedure to the extent that the regulation reasonably relates to the preservation and protection of maternal health. Examples of permissible state regulation in this area are requirements as to the qualifications of the person who is to perform the abortion; as to the licensure of that person; as to the facility in which the procedure is to be performed, that is, whether it must be a hospital or may be a clinic or some other place of less-than-hospital status; as to the licensing of the facility; and the like.

This means, on the other hand, that, for the period of pregnancy prior to this 'compelling' point, the attending physician, in consultation with his patient, is free to determine, without regulation by the State, that, in his medical judgment, the patient's pregnancy should be terminated. If that decision is reached, the judgment may be effectuated by an abortion free of interference by the State.

With respect to the State's important and legitimate interest in potential life, the 'compelling' point is at viability. This is so because the fetus then presumably has the capability of meaningful life outside the mother's womb. State regulation protective of fetal life after viability thus has both logical and biological justifications. If the State is interested in protecting fetal life after viability, it may go so far as to proscribe abortion during that period, except when it is necessary to preserve the life or health of the mother.

Measured against these standards, Art. 1196 of the Texas Penal Code, in restricting legal abortions to those 'procured or attempted by medical advice for the purpose of saving the life of the mother,' sweeps too broadly. The statute makes no distinction between abortions performed early in pregnancy and those performed later, and it limits to a single reason, 'saving' the mother's life, the legal justification for the procedure. The statute, therefore, cannot survive the constitutional attack made upon it here. ...

XI

To summarize and to repeat:

1. A state criminal abortion statute of the current Texas type, that excepts from criminality only a life-saving procedure on behalf of the mother, without regard to pregnancy stage and without recognition of the other interests involved, is violative of the Due Process Clause of the Fourteenth Amendment.
   (a) For the stage prior to approximately the end of the first trimester, the abortion decision and its effectuation must be left to the medical judgment of the pregnant woman's attending physician.
   (b) For the stage subsequent to approximately the end of the first trimester, the State, in promoting its interest in the health of the mother, may, if it chooses, regulate the abortion procedure in ways that are reasonably related to maternal health.
   (c) For the stage subsequent to viability, the State in promoting its interest in the potentiality of human life may, if it chooses, regulate, and even proscribe, abortion except where it is necessary, in appropriate medical judgment, for the preservation of the life or health of the mother. ...

Mr. Justice STEWART, concurring.

... Clearly, therefore, the Court today is correct in holding that the right asserted by Jane Roe is embraced within the personal liberty protected by the Due Process Clause of the Fourteenth Amendment. ...

Mr. Justice REHNQUIST, dissenting.

II

... If the Court means by the term 'privacy' no more than that the claim of a person to be free from unwanted state regulation of consensual transactions may be a form of 'liberty' protected by the Fourteenth Amendment, there is no doubt that similar claims have been upheld in our earlier decisions on the basis of that liberty. I agree with the statement of Mr. Justice STEWART in his concurring opinion that the 'liberty,' against deprivation of which without due process the Fourteenth Amendment protects, embraces more than the rights found in the Bill of Rights. But that liberty is not guaranteed absolutely against deprivation, only against deprivation without due process of law. The test traditionally applied in the area of social and economic legislation is whether or not a law such as that challenged has a rational relation to a valid state objective. Williamson v. Lee Optical Inc., 348 U.S. 483, 491, 75 S.Ct. 461, 466, 99 L.Ed. 563 (1955). The Due Process Clause of the Fourteenth Amendment undoubtedly does place a limit, albeit a broad one, on legislative power to enact laws such as this. If the Texas statute were to prohibit an abortion even where the mother's life is in jeopardy, I have little doubt that such a statute would lack a rational relation to a valid state objective under the test stated in Williamson, supra. But the Court's sweeping invalidation of any restrictions on abortion during the first trimester is impossible to justify under that standard, and the conscious weighing of competing factors that the Court's opinion apparently substitutes for the established test is far more appropriate to a legislative judgment than to a judicial one. ...

To reach its result, the Court necessarily has had to find within the Scope of the Fourteenth Amendment a right that was apparently completely unknown to the drafters of the Amendment. ...

Notes and Questions

1. *What is the right?* A woman holds a right to obtain an abortion in *Roe.* What are the parameters of this right? Can she obtain it without consulting a doctor? When is her right most robust, and when is it least strong?
2. *Trimesters.* Why did Justice Blackmun choose the trimester approach to pregnancy? What is a trimester? Why is it relevant to the analysis of state laws? Does the trimester system provide a stable framework for assessing the constitutionality of state laws? Why or why not?

3. *Dissent.* Why did Justice Rehnquist dissent? How do you analyze the privacy argument of the majority and the dissent?

b. *Roe Is Reaffirmed and Reinterpreted in* Casey

Roe was controversial enough that many have called for its overruling during the succeeding decades. After the *Webster v, Reproductive Health Services* decision in 1989, challenges to *Roe* poured into the Court. During the 1989 Term, there were several cases the Court had taken on the subject, but they settled before the Court could hear them. Then people wondered if the Court might overrule it during the presidential election year 1992. Do you think the outcome of the case would have affected the election? Look at the long list of Justices and opinions at the beginning of the next case, *Casey*. As you read this case, make a chart of which Justices joined which opinion so you can keep track. Why did Justices O'Connor, Kennedy, and Souter vote together? How do you make sense of a case like this with so many views and theories expressed? How much of the question about overruling is part of the oral argument in this case, *Planned Parenthood of Pennsylvania v. Casey*, available at https://www.oyez.org/cases/1991/91-744?

Casey affirmed *Roe* and yet changed it. Justice Blackmun would have stayed with his *Roe* perspective. An important element of a Supreme Court decision is what guidance is provided for the lower courts to decide the issue in future. What is the test in *Casey* that the lower federal courts would be required to follow? Can you explain it?

Planned Parenthood of Southeastern Pennsylvania v. Casey
SUPREME COURT OF THE UNITED STATES, 1992
505 U.S. 833, 112 S.Ct. 2791

O'CONNOR, KENNEDY, and SOUTER, JJ., announced the judgment of the Court and delivered the opinion of the Court with respect to Parts I, II, III, V–A, V–C, and VI, in which BLACKMUN and STEVENS, JJ., joined, an opinion with respect to Part V–E, in which STEVENS, J., joined, and an opinion with respect to Parts IV, V–B, and V–D. STEVENS, J., filed an opinion concurring in part and dissenting in part. BLACKMUN, J., filed an opinion concurring in part, concurring in the judgment in part, and dissenting in part. REHNQUIST, C.J., filed an opinion concurring in the judgment in part and dissenting in part, in which WHITE, SCALIA, and THOMAS, JJ., joined. SCALIA, J., filed an opinion concurring in the judgment in part and dissenting in part, in which REHNQUIST, C.J., and WHITE and THOMAS, JJ., joined.

I

Liberty finds no refuge in a jurisprudence of doubt. Yet 19 years after our holding that the Constitution protects a woman's right to terminate her pregnancy in its early stages, *Roe v. Wade,* 410 U.S. 113, 93 S.Ct. 705, 35 L.Ed.2d 147 (1973), that definition of liberty is still questioned. Joining the respondents as *amicus curiae,* the United States, as it has done in five other cases in the last decade, again asks us to overrule *Roe.*

At issue in these cases are five provisions of the Pennsylvania Abortion Control Act of 1982, as amended in 1988 and 1989. The Act requires that a woman seeking an abortion give her informed consent prior to the abortion procedure, and specifies that she be provided with certain information at least 24 hours before the abortion is performed. § 3205. For a minor to obtain an abortion, the Act requires the informed consent of one of her parents, but provides for a judicial bypass option if the minor does not wish to or cannot obtain a parent's consent. § 3206. Another provision of the Act requires that, unless certain exceptions apply, a married woman seeking an abortion must sign a statement indicating that she has notified her husband of her intended abortion. § 3209. The Act exempts compliance with these three requirements in the event of a "medical emergency," which is defined in § 3203 of the Act. See §§ 3203, 3205(a), 3206(a), 3209(c). In addition to the above provisions regulating the performance of abortions, the Act imposes certain reporting requirements on facilities that provide abortion services. §§ 3207(b), 3214(a), 3214(f). ...

IIIA

... So in this case we may enquire whether *Roe*'s central rule has been found unworkable; whether the rule's limitation on state power could be removed without serious inequity to those who have relied upon it or significant damage to the stability of the society governed by it; whether the law's growth in the intervening years has left *Roe*'s central rule a doctrinal anachronism discounted by society; and whether *Roe*'s premises of fact have so far changed in the ensuing two decades as to render its central holding somehow irrelevant or unjustifiable in dealing with the issue it addressed.

1

Although *Roe* has engendered opposition, it has in no sense proven "unworkable," representing as it does a simple limitation beyond which a state law is unenforceable. While *Roe* has, of course, required judicial assessment of state laws affecting the exercise of the choice guaranteed against government infringement, and although the need for such review will remain as a consequence of today's decision, the required determinations fall within judicial competence.

2

The inquiry into reliance counts the cost of a rule's repudiation as it would fall on those who have relied reasonably on the rule's continued application. ... for two decades of economic and social developments, people have organized intimate relationships and made choices that define their views of themselves and their places in society, in reliance on the availability of abortion in the event that contraception should fail. The ability of women to participate equally in the economic and social life of the Nation has been facilitated by their ability to control their reproductive lives. The Constitution serves human values, and while the effect of reliance on *Roe* cannot be exactly measured, neither can the certain cost of overruling *Roe* for people who have ordered their thinking and living around that case be dismissed.

3

No evolution of legal principle has left *Roe*'s doctrinal footings weaker than they were in 1973. No development of constitutional law since the case was decided has implicitly or explicitly left *Roe* behind as a mere survivor of obsolete constitutional thinking. ...

4

... The soundness or unsoundness of that constitutional judgment in no sense turns on whether viability occurs at approximately 28 weeks, as was usual at the time of *Roe,* at 23 to 24 weeks, as it sometimes does today, or at some moment even slightly earlier in pregnancy, as it may if fetal respiratory capacity can somehow be enhanced in the future. Whenever it may occur, the attainment of viability may continue to serve as the critical fact, just as it has done since *Roe* was decided; which is to say that no change in *Roe*'s factual underpinning has left its central holding obsolete, and none supports an argument for overruling it.

5

The sum of the precedential enquiry to this point shows *Roe*'s underpinnings unweakened in any way affecting its central holding. While it has engendered disapproval, it has not been unworkable. ...

IV

From what we have said so far it follows that it is a constitutional liberty of the woman to have some freedom to terminate her pregnancy. We conclude that the basic decision in *Roe* was based on a constitutional analysis which we cannot now repudiate. The woman's liberty is not so unlimited, however, that from the outset the State cannot show its concern for the life of the unborn, and at a later point in fetal development the State's interest in life has sufficient force so that the right of the woman to terminate the pregnancy can be restricted.

That brings us, of course, to the point where much criticism has been directed at *Roe,* a criticism that always inheres when the Court draws a specific rule from what in the Constitution is but a general standard. We conclude, however, that the urgent claims of the woman to retain the ultimate control over her destiny and her body, claims implicit in the meaning of liberty, require us to perform that function. Liberty must not be extinguished for want of a line that is clear. And it falls to us to give some real substance to the woman's liberty to determine whether to carry her pregnancy to full term.

We conclude the line should be drawn at viability, so that before that time the woman has a right to choose to terminate her pregnancy. We adhere to this principle for two reasons. First, as we have said, is the doctrine of *stare decisis*. Any judicial act of line-drawing may seem somewhat arbitrary, but *Roe* was a reasoned statement, elaborated with great care. We have twice reaffirmed it in the face of great opposition. Although we must overrule those parts of *Thornburgh* and *Akron I* which, in our view, are inconsistent with *Roe*'s statement that the State has a legitimate interest in promoting the life or potential life of the unborn, the central premise of those cases represents an unbroken commitment by this Court to the essential holding of *Roe*. It is that premise which we reaffirm today.

The second reason is that the concept of viability, as we noted in *Roe*, is the time at which there is a realistic possibility of maintaining and nourishing a life outside the womb, so that the independent existence of the second life can in reason and all fairness be the object of state protection that now overrides the rights of the woman. Consistent with other constitutional norms, legislatures may draw lines which appear arbitrary without the necessity of offering a justification. But courts may not. We must justify the lines we draw. And there is no line other than viability which is more workable. To be sure, as we have said, there may be some medical developments that affect the precise point of viability, but this is an imprecision within tolerable limits given that the medical community and all those who must apply its discoveries will continue to explore the matter. The viability line also has, as a practical matter, an element of fairness. In some broad sense it might be said that a woman who fails to act before viability has consented to the State's intervention on behalf of the developing child.

The woman's right to terminate her pregnancy before viability is the most central principle of *Roe v. Wade*. It is a rule of law and a component of liberty we cannot renounce.

On the other side of the equation is the interest of the State in the protection of potential life. The *Roe* Court recognized the State's "important and legitimate interest in protecting the potentiality of human life." The weight to be given this state interest, not the strength of the woman's interest, was the difficult question faced in *Roe*. We do not need to say whether each of us, had we been Members of the Court when the valuation of the state interest came before it as an original matter, would have concluded, as the *Roe* Court did, that its weight is insufficient to justify a ban on abortions prior to viability even when it is subject to certain exceptions. The matter is not before us in the first instance, and coming as it does after nearly 20 years of litigation in *Roe*'s wake we are satisfied that the immediate question is not the soundness of *Roe*'s resolution of the issue, but the precedential force that must be accorded to its holding. And we have concluded that the essential holding of *Roe* should be reaffirmed.

Yet it must be remembered that *Roe v. Wade* speaks with clarity in establishing not only the woman's liberty but also the State's "important and legitimate interest in potential life." That portion of the decision in *Roe* has been given too little acknowledgment and implementation by the Court in its subsequent cases. Those cases decided that any regulation touching upon the abortion decision must survive strict scrutiny, to be sustained only if drawn in narrow terms to further a compelling state interest. Not all of the cases decided under that formulation can be reconciled with the holding in *Roe* itself that the State has legitimate interests in the health of the woman and in protecting the potential life within her. In resolving this tension, we choose to rely upon *Roe*, as against the later cases.

Roe established a trimester framework to govern abortion regulations. Under this elaborate but rigid construct, almost no regulation at all is permitted during the first trimester of pregnancy; regulations designed to protect the woman's health, but not to further the State's interest in potential life, are permitted during the second trimester; and during the third trimester, when the fetus is viable, prohibitions are permitted provided the life or health of the mother is not at stake. Most of our cases since *Roe* have involved the application of rules derived from the trimester framework.

The trimester framework no doubt was erected to ensure that the woman's right to choose not become so subordinate to the State's interest in promoting fetal life that her choice exists in theory but not in fact. We do not agree, however, that the trimester approach is necessary to accomplish this objective. A framework of this rigidity was unnecessary and in its later interpretation sometimes contradicted the State's permissible exercise of its powers.

Though the woman has a right to choose to terminate or continue her pregnancy before viability, it does not at all follow that the State is prohibited from taking steps to ensure that this choice is thoughtful and informed. Even in the earliest stages of pregnancy, the State may enact rules and regulations designed to encourage her to know that there are philosophic and social arguments of great weight that can be brought to bear in favor of continuing the pregnancy to full term and that there are procedures and institutions to allow adoption of unwanted children as well as a certain degree of state assistance if the mother chooses to raise the child herself. "'[T]he Constitution does not forbid a State or city, pursuant to democratic processes, from expressing a preference for normal childbirth.'" It follows that States are free to enact laws to provide a reasonable framework for a woman to make a decision that has such profound and lasting meaning. This, too, we find consistent with *Roe*'s central premises, and indeed the inevitable consequence of our holding that the State has an interest in protecting the life of the unborn.

We reject the trimester framework, which we do not consider to be part of the essential holding of *Roe*. See *Webster v. Reproductive Health Services*, 492 U.S., at 518, 109 S.Ct., at 3056–3057 (opinion of REHNQUIST, C.J.); *id.*, at 529, 109 S.Ct., at 3063 (O'CONNOR, J., concurring in part and concurring in judgment) (describing the trimester framework as "problematic"). Measures aimed at ensuring that a woman's choice contemplates the consequences for the fetus do not necessarily interfere with the right recognized in *Roe*, although those measures have been found to be inconsistent with the rigid trimester framework announced in that case. A logical reading of the central holding in *Roe* itself, and a necessary reconciliation of the liberty of the woman and the interest of the State in promoting prenatal life, require, in our view, that we abandon the trimester framework as a rigid prohibition on all previability regulation aimed at the protection of fetal life. The trimester framework suffers from these basic flaws: in its formulation it misconceives the nature of the pregnant woman's interest; and in practice it undervalues the State's interest in potential life, as recognized in *Roe*. ...

The very notion that the State has a substantial interest in potential life leads to the conclusion that not all regulations must be deemed unwarranted. Not all burdens on the right to decide whether to terminate a pregnancy will be undue. In our view, the undue burden standard is the appropriate means of reconciling the State's interest with the woman's constitutionally protected liberty. ...

A finding of an undue burden is a shorthand for the conclusion that a state regulation has the purpose or effect of placing a substantial obstacle in the path of a woman seeking an abortion of a nonviable fetus. A statute with this purpose is invalid because the means chosen by the State to further the interest in potential life must be calculated to inform the woman's free choice, not hinder it. And a statute which, while furthering the interest in potential life or some other valid state interest, has the effect of placing a substantial obstacle in the path of a woman's choice cannot be considered a permissible means of serving its legitimate ends. To the extent that the opinions of the Court or of individual Justices use the undue burden standard in a manner that is inconsistent with this analysis, we set out what in our view should be the controlling standard. ...

Our adoption of the undue burden analysis does not disturb the central holding of *Roe v. Wade*, and we reaffirm that holding. Regardless of whether exceptions are made for particular circumstances, a State may not prohibit any woman from making the ultimate decision to terminate her pregnancy before viability. ...

VA

... the medical emergency definition imposes no undue burden on a woman's abortion right. ...

VB

... To the extent *Akron I* and *Thornburgh* find a constitutional violation when the government requires, as it does here, the giving of truthful, nonmisleading information about the nature of the procedure, the attendant health risks and those of childbirth, and the "probable gestational age" of the fetus, those cases go too far, are inconsistent with *Roe*'s acknowledgment of an important interest in potential life, and are overruled. ...

If the information the State requires to be made available to the woman is truthful and not misleading, the requirement may be permissible.

We also see no reason why the State may not require doctors to inform a woman seeking an abortion of the availability of materials relating to the consequences to the fetus, even when those consequences have no direct relation to her health. ...

We are left with the argument that the various aspects of the informed consent requirement are unconstitutional because they place barriers in the way of abortion on demand. Even the broadest reading of *Roe,* however, has not suggested that there is a constitutional right to abortion on demand. Rather, the right protected by *Roe* is a right to decide to terminate a pregnancy free of undue interference by the State. Because the informed consent requirement facilitates the wise exercise of that right, it cannot be classified as an interference with the right *Roe* protects. The informed consent requirement is not an undue burden on that right.

VC

Section 3209 of Pennsylvania's abortion law provides, except in cases of medical emergency, that no physician shall perform an abortion on a married woman without receiving a signed statement from the woman that she has notified her spouse that she is about to undergo an abortion. The woman has the option of providing an alternative signed statement certifying that her husband is not the man who impregnated her; that her husband could not be located; that the pregnancy is the result of spousal sexual assault which she has reported; or that the woman believes that notifying her husband will cause him or someone else to inflict bodily injury upon her. A physician who performs an abortion on a married woman without receiving the appropriate signed statement will have his or her license revoked, and is liable to the husband for damages. ...

The spousal notification requirement is thus likely to prevent a significant number of women from obtaining an abortion. It does not merely make abortions a little more difficult or expensive to obtain; for many women, it will impose a substantial obstacle. We must not blind ourselves to the fact that the significant number of women who fear for their safety and the safety of their children are likely to be deterred from procuring an abortion as surely as if the Commonwealth had outlawed abortion in all cases. ...

Section 3209 embodies a view of marriage consonant with the common-law status of married women but repugnant to our present understanding of marriage and of the nature of the rights secured by the Constitution. Women do not lose their constitutionally protected liberty when they marry. The Constitution protects all individuals, male or female, married or unmarried, from the abuse of governmental power, even where that power is employed for the supposed benefit of a member of the individual's family. These considerations confirm our conclusion that § 3209 is invalid.

VD

We next consider the parental consent provision. ... We have been over most of this ground before. Our cases establish, and we reaffirm today, that a State may require a minor seeking an abortion to obtain the consent of a parent or guardian, provided that there is an adequate judicial bypass procedure. ...

VE

For each abortion performed, a report must be filed identifying: the physician (and the second physician where required); the facility; the referring physician or agency; the woman's age; the number of prior pregnancies and prior abortions she has had; gestational age; the type of abortion procedure; the date of the abortion; whether there were any pre-existing medical conditions which would complicate pregnancy; medical complications with the abortion; where applicable, the basis for the determination that the abortion was medically necessary; the weight of the aborted fetus; and whether the woman was married, and if so, whether notice was provided or the basis for the failure to give notice. Every abortion facility must also file quarterly reports showing the number of abortions performed broken down by trimester. In all events, the identity of each woman who has had an abortion remains confidential. ...

We think that under this standard, all the provisions at issue here, except that relating to spousal notice, are constitutional. ...

Subsection (12) of the reporting provision requires the reporting of, among other things, a married woman's "reason for failure to provide notice" to her husband. § 3214(a)(12). This provision in effect requires women, as a condition of obtaining an abortion, to provide the Commonwealth with the precise information we have already recognized that many women have pressing reasons not to reveal. Like the spousal notice requirement itself, this provision places an undue burden on a woman's choice, and must be invalidated for that reason. ...

Justice STEVENS, concurring in part and dissenting in part.

...

II

... In my opinion, the principles established in this long line of cases and the wisdom reflected in Justice Powell's opinion for the Court in *Akron* (and followed by the Court just six years ago in *Thornburgh*) should govern our decision today. Under these principles, Pa.Cons.Stat. §§ 3205(a)(2)(i)–(iii) (1990) of the Pennsylvania statute are unconstitutional. Those sections require a physician or counselor to provide the woman with a range of materials clearly designed to persuade her to choose not to undergo the abortion. While the Commonwealth is free, pursuant to § 3208 of the Pennsylvania law, to produce and disseminate such material, the Commonwealth may not inject such information into the woman's deliberations just as she is weighing such an important choice.

Under this same analysis, §§ 3205(a)(1)(i) and (iii) of the Pennsylvania statute are constitutional. Those sections, which require the physician to inform a woman of the nature and risks of the abortion procedure and the medical risks of carrying to term, are neutral requirements comparable to those imposed in other medical procedures. Those sections indicate no effort by the Commonwealth to influence the woman's choice in any way. If anything, such requirements *enhance,* rather than skew, the woman's decisionmaking.

III

The 24-hour waiting period required by §§ 3205(a)(1)–(2) of the Pennsylvania statute raises even more serious concerns. Such a requirement arguably furthers the Commonwealth's interests in two ways, neither of which is constitutionally permissible. ...

Part of the constitutional liberty to choose is the equal dignity to which each of us is entitled. A woman who decides to terminate her pregnancy is entitled to the same respect as a woman who decides to carry the fetus to term. The mandatory waiting period denies women that equal respect. ...

IV

... The 24-hour delay requirement fails both parts of this test. The findings of the District Court establish the severity of the burden that the 24-hour delay imposes on many pregnant women. Yet even in those cases in which the delay is not especially onerous, it is, in my opinion, "undue" because there is no evidence that such a delay serves a useful and legitimate purpose. As indicated above, there is no legitimate reason to require a woman who has agonized over her decision to leave the clinic or hospital and return again another day. While a general requirement that a physician notify her patients about the risks of a proposed medical procedure is appropriate, a rigid requirement that all patients wait 24 hours or (what is true in practice) much longer to evaluate the significance of information that is either common knowledge or irrelevant is an irrational and, therefore, "undue" burden. ...

Justice BLACKMUN, concurring in part, concurring in the judgment in part, and dissenting in part.

... I do not underestimate the significance of today's joint opinion. Yet I remain steadfast in my belief that the right to reproductive choice is entitled to the full protection afforded by this Court before *Webster.* And I fear for the darkness as four Justices anxiously await the single vote necessary to extinguish the light.

I

Make no mistake, the joint opinion of Justices O'CONNOR, KENNEDY, and SOUTER is an act of personal courage and constitutional principle. In contrast to previous decisions in which Justices O'CONNOR and KENNEDY postponed reconsideration of *Roe v. Wade,* 410 U.S. 113, 93 S.Ct. 705, 35 L.Ed.2d 147 (1973), the authors of the joint opinion today join Justice STEVENS and me in concluding that "the essential holding of *Roe v. Wade* should be retained and once again reaffirmed." In brief, five Members of this Court today recognize that "the Constitution protects a woman's right to terminate her pregnancy in its early stages." ...

Lastly, while I believe that the joint opinion errs in failing to invalidate the other regulations, I am pleased that the joint opinion has not ruled out the possibility that these regulations may be shown to impose an unconstitutional burden. The joint opinion makes clear that its specific holdings are based on the insufficiency of the record before it. I am confident that in the future evidence will be produced to show that "in a large fraction of the cases in which [these regulations are] relevant, [they] will operate as a substantial obstacle to a woman's choice to undergo an abortion."

II

Today, no less than yesterday, the Constitution and decisions of this Court require that a State's abortion restrictions be subjected to the strictest of judicial scrutiny. Our precedents and the joint opinion's principles require us to subject all non-*de-minimis* abortion regulations to strict scrutiny. Under this standard, the Pennsylvania statute's provisions requiring content-based counseling, a 24-hour delay, informed parental consent, and reporting of abortion-related information must be invalidated. ...

In sum, *Roe*'s requirement of strict scrutiny as implemented through a trimester framework should not be disturbed. No other approach has gained a majority, and no other is more protective of the woman's fundamental right. Lastly, no other approach properly accommodates the woman's constitutional right with the State's legitimate interests.

C

Application of the strict scrutiny standard results in the invalidation of all the challenged provisions. Indeed, as this Court has invalidated virtually identical provisions in prior cases, *stare decisis* requires that we again strike them down. ...

IV

In one sense, the Court's approach is worlds apart from that of THE CHIEF JUSTICE and Justice SCALIA. And yet, in another sense, the distance between the two approaches is short—the distance is but a single vote.

I am 83 years old. I cannot remain on this Court forever, and when I do step down, the confirmation process for my successor well may focus on the issue before us today. That, I regret, may be exactly where the choice between the two worlds will be made.

Chief Justice REHNQUIST, with whom Justice WHITE, Justice SCALIA, and Justice THOMAS join, concurring in the judgment in part and dissenting in part.

The joint opinion, following its newly minted variation on *stare decisis,* retains the outer shell of *Roe v. Wade,* but beats a wholesale retreat from the substance of that case. We believe that *Roe* was wrongly decided, and that it can and should be overruled consistently with our traditional approach to *stare decisis* in constitutional cases. We would adopt the approach of the plurality in *Webster v. Reproductive Health Services,* 492 U.S. 490, 109 S.Ct. 3040, 106 L.Ed.2d 410 (1989), and uphold the challenged provisions of the Pennsylvania statute in their entirety. ...

We think, therefore, both in view of this history and of our decided cases dealing with substantive liberty under the Due Process Clause, that the Court was mistaken in *Roe* when it classified a woman's decision to terminate her pregnancy as a "fundamental right" that could be abridged only in a manner which withstood "strict scrutiny." In so concluding, we repeat the observation made in *Bowers v. Hardwick,* 478 U.S. 186, 106 S.Ct. 2841, 92 L.Ed.2d 140 (1986):

> "Nor are we inclined to take a more expansive view of our authority to discover new fundamental rights imbedded in the Due Process Clause. The Court is most vulnerable and comes nearest to illegitimacy when it deals with judge-made constitutional law having little or no cognizable roots in the language or design of the Constitution."

We believe that the sort of constitutionally imposed abortion code of the type illustrated by our decisions following *Roe* is inconsistent "with the notion of a Constitution cast in general terms, as ours is, and usually speaking in general principles, as ours does." *Webster v. Reproductive Health Services,* 492 U.S., at 518, 109 S.Ct., at 3056–3057 (plurality opinion). The Court in *Roe* reached too far when it analogized the right to abort a fetus to the rights involved in *Pierce, Meyer, Loving,* and *Griswold,* and thereby deemed the right to abortion fundamental. ...

The end result of the joint opinion's paeans of praise for legitimacy is the enunciation of a brand new standard for evaluating state regulation of a woman's right to abortion—the "undue burden" standard. As indicated above, *Roe v. Wade* adopted a "fundamental right" standard under which state regulations could survive only if they met the requirement of "strict scrutiny." While we disagree with that standard, it at least had a recognized basis in constitutional law at the time *Roe* was decided. The same cannot be said for the "undue burden" standard, which is created largely out of whole cloth by the authors of the joint opinion. It is a standard which even today does not command the support of a majority of this Court. And it will not, we believe, result in the sort of "simple limitation," easily applied, which the joint opinion anticipates. In sum, it is a standard which is not built to last. ...

For the reasons stated, we therefore would hold that each of the challenged provisions of the Pennsylvania statute is consistent with the Constitution. It bears emphasis that our conclusion in this regard does not carry with it any necessary approval of these regulations. Our task is, as always, to decide only whether the challenged provisions of a law comport with the United States Constitution. If, as we believe, these do, their wisdom as a matter of public policy is for the people of Pennsylvania to decide.

Justice SCALIA, with whom THE CHIEF JUSTICE, Justice WHITE, and Justice THOMAS join, concurring in the judgment in part and dissenting in part.

My views on this matter are unchanged from those I set forth in my separate opinions in *Webster v. Reproductive Health Services,* 492 U.S. 490, 532, 109 S.Ct. 3040, 3064, 106 L.Ed.2d 410 (1989) (opinion concurring in part and concurring in judgment), and *Ohio v. Akron Center for Reproductive Health,* 497 U.S. 502, 520, 110 S.Ct. 2972, 2984, 111 L.Ed.2d 405 (1990) (*Akron II*) (concurring opinion). The States may, if they wish, permit abortion on demand, but the Constitution does not *require* them to do so. The permissibility of abortion, and the limitations upon it, are to be resolved like most important questions in our democracy: by citizens trying to persuade one another and then voting. As the Court acknowledges, "where reasonable people disagree the government can adopt one position or the other." ...

I will not swell the United States Reports with repetition of what I have said before; and applying the rational basis test, I would uphold the Pennsylvania statute in its entirety. I must, however, respond to a few of the more outrageous arguments in today's opinion, which it is beyond human nature to leave unanswered. I shall discuss each of them under a quotation from the Court's opinion to which they pertain. ...

There is a poignant aspect to today's opinion. Its length, and what might be called its epic tone, suggest that its authors believe they are bringing to an end a troublesome era in the history of our Nation and of our Court. "It is the dimension" of authority, they say, to "cal[l] the contending sides of national controversy to end their national division by accepting a common mandate rooted in the Constitution."

There comes vividly to mind a portrait by Emanuel Leutze that hangs in the Harvard Law School: Roger Brooke Taney, painted in 1859, the 82d year of his life, the 24th of his Chief Justiceship, the second after his opinion in *Dred Scott.* He is all in black, sitting in a shadowed red armchair, left hand resting upon a pad of paper in his lap, right hand hanging limply, almost lifelessly, beside the inner arm of the chair. He sits facing the viewer and staring straight out. There seems to be on his face, and in his deep-set eyes, an expression of profound sadness and disillusionment. Perhaps he always looked that way, even when dwelling upon the happiest of thoughts. But those of us who know how the lustre of his great Chief Justiceship came to be eclipsed by *Dred Scott* cannot help believing that he had that case—its already apparent consequences for the Court and its soon-to-be-played-out consequences for the Nation—burning on his mind. I expect that two years earlier he, too, had thought himself "call[ing] the contending sides of national controversy to end their national division by accepting a common mandate rooted in the Constitution."

It is no more realistic for us in this litigation, than it was for him in that, to think that an issue of the sort they both involved—an issue involving life and death, freedom and subjugation—can be "speedily and finally settled" by the Supreme Court, as President James Buchanan in his inaugural address said the issue of slavery in the territories would be. Quite to the contrary, by foreclosing all democratic outlet for the deep passions this issue arouses, by banishing the issue from the political forum that gives all participants, even the losers, the satisfaction of a fair hearing and an honest fight, by continuing the imposition of a rigid national rule instead of allowing for regional differences, the Court merely prolongs and intensifies the anguish.

We should get out of this area, where we have no right to be, and where we do neither ourselves nor the country any good by remaining.

Notes and Questions

1. *The new standard.* What is the new test of a woman's constitutional right to obtain an abortion? Why is the trimester framework rejected? How are lower courts supposed to apply the new standard?
2. *Who persuades you?* When you look at your chart of all these arguments, which Justice(s) persuade you the most? Why or why not?
3. *A chart of the cases.* The following chart of Justices' votes in abortion cases provides some insight into the evolution of a woman's right to obtain an abortion from the pre-*Roe Griswold* case until 2022. What do these votes tell you about the development of this right and the role of the Justices in deciding the scope of its constitutionality? The author of the majority opinion is written in caps. Does the description of the cases explain why *Akron* and *Thornburgh* were overruled in *Casey*? Does it explain why *Roe* and *Casey* were overruled in *Dobbs*?

c. Chart of the Privacy Rights Abortion Cases, Starting with Griswold

Griswold v. Connecticut (1965)

Holding: Finding a constitutional right to privacy for a married couple to obtain contraception from a doctor.

Majority: DOUGLAS, joined by C. J. Warren, Clark, Brennan, Goldberg

Concurrence(s): GOLDBERG, joined by C. J. Warren, Brennan

Concurrence(s) in the Judgment: HARLAN

WHITE

Dissent(s): BLACK, joined by Stewart

STEWART, joined by Black

Roe v. Wade (1973)

Holding: Finding a woman's constitutional right to obtain an abortion with the advice of a doctor, which varies during the course of the pregnancy according to each trimester.

Majority: BLACKMUN, joined by C. J. Burger, Douglas, Brennan, Stewart, Marshall, Blackmun, Powell

Concurrence(s): BURGER

DOUGLAS

STEWART

Dissent(s): WHITE, joined by Rehnquist

REHNQUIST

Maher v. Roe (1977)

Holding: Restrictions on Medicaid benefits for abortions do not violate the right to an abortion because discouraging abortions does not amount to direct interference with a constitutionally guaranteed right. Additionally, disparities in abortion access based on financial need alone pass scrutiny under the Equal Protection Clause.

Majority: POWELL, joined by C. J. Burger, Stewart, White, Rehnquist, Stevens

Concurrence(s): C. J. BURGER

Dissent(s): BRENNAN, joined by Marshall, Blackmun

MARSHALL

BLACKMUN, joined by Brennan, Marshall

Harris v. McRae (1980)

Holding: Denying any substantive due process right to funding of an abortion. Constitutional protected activity does not necessitate government funding in pursuit of that activity.

Majority: STEWART, joined by C. J. Burger, White, Powell, Rehnquist

Concurrence(s): WHITE

Dissent(s): BRENNAN, joined by Marshall, Blackmun

MARSHALL

BLACKMUN

STEVENS

Akron v. Akron Center for Reproductive Health (1983)

Holding: Striking down requirements that post-first trimester abortions be performed in a hospital; some parental consent requirements for minors; detailed informed consent provisions, including information on the development of the fetus, physical and emotional consequences of abortion, agencies for adoption, as well as a 24-hour waiting period as violations of a woman's right to privacy and constitutionally guaranteed right to an abortion.

Majority: POWELL, joined by C. J. Burger, Brennan, Marshall, Blackmun, Stevens

Dissent: O'CONNOR, joined by White, Rehnquist

Thornburgh v. American College of Obstetricians and Gynecologists (1986)

Holding: Striking down the "informed consent," printed material, waiting period, record-keeping, reporting, and second physician requirements as intrusions on the privacy of both a woman and her physician.

Majority: BLACKMUN, joined by Brennan, Marshall, Powell, Stevens

Concurrence(s): STEVENS

Dissent: C. J. BURGER

WHITE, joined by Rehnquist

O'CONNOR, joined by Rehnquist

Webster v. Reproductive Health Services (1989)

Holding: Concluding the Due Process Clause does not necessitate government aid in obtaining one's constitutionally guaranteed right to an abortion. Upholding viability tests based on the state's interest in protecting potentially viable life.

Majority: C. J. REHNQUIST (part II-C), unanimously; joined by White, O'Connor, Scalia, Kennedy (parts I, II-A, II-B)

Plurality: C. J. REHNQUIST (parts II-D, III), joined by White, Kennedy

Concurrence(s): O'CONNOR

SCALIA

Partial Concur/Dissent(s): BLACKMUN, joined by Marshall, Brennan

STEVENS

	I	II-A	II-B	II-C	II-D	III
REHNQUIST	✔	✔	✔	✔	✔	✔
White	✔	✔	✔	✔	✔	✔
O'Connor	✔	✔	✔	✔		
Scalia	✔	✔	✔	✔		
Kennedy	✔	✔	✔	✔	✔	✔
Blackmun				✔		
Marshall				✔		
Brennan				✔		
Stevens				✔		

This is a chart of the votes in *Webster.*

Hodgson v. Minnesota (1990)

Holding: Provisions requiring a girl under the age of 18 to notify both parents before obtaining an abortion fails to meet the rationality standard of scrutiny and is unconstitutional. The same requirement coupled with a judicial bypass option allowing an underage patient to obtain an abortion without consulting both or either parent is constitutional.

Majority: STEVENS (parts I, II, IV, VII), joined by Brennan, Marshall, Blackmun, O'Connor

Concurrence(s): STEVENS (part III), joined by Brennan

STEVENS (parts V, VI), joined by O'Connor

O'CONNOR

Partial Concur/Dissent(s): MARSHALL, joined by Brennan, Blackmun

SCALIA

KENNEDY, joined by C. J. Rehnquist, White, Scalia

Dissent(s): STEVENS (Part VIII)

	I	II	III	IV	V	VI	VII	VIII
STEVENS	✔	✔	✔	✔	✔	✔	✔	
Brennan	✔	✔	✔	✔			✔	
Marshall	✔	✔		✔			✔	
Blackmun	✔	✔		✔			✔	
O'Connor	✔	✔		✔	✔	✔	✔	✔
Scalia								✔
Kennedy								✔
White								✔
Rehnquist								✔

This is a chart of the votes in *Hodgson*.

Rust v. Sullivan (1991)

Holding: Restrictions on using federal funding for providing abortions, despite those same funds being used for family planning, to be consistent with the First and Fifth Amendment rights of healthcare providers and their patients.

Majority: C. J. REHNQUIST, joined by White, Scalia, Kennedy, Souter

Dissent(s): BLACKMUN, joined by Marshall, Stevens, O'Connor

STEVENS

O'CONNOR

Planned Parenthood of Southeastern Pennsylvania v. Casey (1992)

Holding: Reaffirming Roe and establishing an "undue burden" test to determine whether a statute violates a patient's right to an abortion. Under the undue burden test, only the requirement that a married patient notify her husband of an abortion failed and was struck down.

Majority: O'CONNOR, KENNEDY, SOUTER, (parts I, II, III, V-A, V-C, VI) joined by Blackmun, Stevens

Pluralities: O'CONNOR, KENNEDY, SOUTER (part V-E), joined by Stevens

O'CONNOR, KENNEDY, SOUTER (parts IV, V-B, V-D)

Partial Concur/Dissent(s): STEVENS

BLACKMUN

C. J. REHNQUIST, joined by White, Scalia, Thomas

SCALIA, joined by C. J. Rehnquist, White, Thomas

	I	II	III	IV	V-A	V-B	V-C	V-D	V-E	VI
Scalia										
Rehnquist										
White										
Thomas										
O'Connor	✔	✔	✔	✔	✔	✔	✔	✔	✔	✔
Kennedy	✔	✔	✔	✔	✔	✔	✔	✔	✔	✔
Souter	✔	✔	✔	✔	✔	✔	✔	✔	✔	✔
Blackmun	✔	✔	✔		✔		✔			✔
Stevens	✔	✔	✔		✔		✔		✔	✔

This is a chart of the votes in *Casey*.

Stenberg v. Carhart (2000)

Holding: Finding that partial birth abortions place an undue burden on a patient's right to an abortion and to make decisions concerning their healthcare.

Majority: BREYER, joined by Stevens, O'Connor, Souter, Ginsburg

Concurrence(s): STEVENS, joined by Ginsburg

O'CONNOR

GINSBURG, joined by Stevens

Dissent(s): C. J. REHNQUIST

SCALIA

KENNEDY, joined by C. J. Rehnquist

THOMAS, joined by C. J. Rehnquist, Scalia

Gonzales v. Carhart (2007)

Holding: Finding that a federal law banning partial birth abortions does NOT place an undue burden on a patient's right to an abortion. Qualifying Stenberg without overturning it due to the federal law being less vague and ambiguous than the state law in question in Stenberg.

Majority: KENNEDY, joined by C. J. Roberts, Scalia, Thomas, Alito

Concurrence(s): THOMAS, joined by Scalia

Dissent(s): GINSBURG, joined by Stevens, Souter, Breyer

Whole Woman's Health v. Hellerstedt (2016)

Holding: Abortion regulations that do not sufficiently serve their stated government interest unconstitutionally impose an undue burden on patients seeking abortions.

Majority: BREYER, joined by Kennedy, Ginsburg, Sotomayor, Kagan

Concurrence(s): GINSBURG

Dissent(s): THOMAS

ALITO, joined by C. J. Roberts, Thomas

June Medical Services v. Russo (2020)

Holding: Reaffirming *Whole Woman's Health v. Hellerstedt* and striking down a similar law.

Plurality: BREYER, joined by Ginsburg, Sotomayor, Kagan

Concurrence(s) in the Judgment: C. J. ROBERTS

Dissent(s): THOMAS

ALITO, joined by Gorsuch, Thomas (in part), Kavanaugh (in part)

GORSUCH

KAVANAUGH

d. Whole Woman's Health *and* June Medical Services

Look at the last two cases on the list. They address very similar claims. *Whole Woman's Health* involved a challenge to two Texas laws by an abortion provider. One provision required doctors performing abortions to have admitting privileges at a hospital within 30 miles of where the abortion was performed. Another regulation required that abortion clinics meet the same standards as ambulatory surgical centers for their building requirements. The Court voted 5–3 in favor of the abortion provider, holding the two provisions unconstitutional. Breyer wrote the majority opinion, joined by Kennedy, Ginsburg, Sotomayor, and Kagan. The three dissenters, who would have upheld both provisions, were Roberts, Thomas, and Alito.

The Court then took up *June Medical Services* where the Louisiana admitting privileges law was almost identical to Texas's unconstitutional one. This case also raised an issue of third-party standing, meaning that the abortion providers could not bring a lawsuit on behalf of women getting an abortion because their interests were different. The majority concluded that argument was waived, but the dissenters embraced it. How would you describe who has standing in abortion cases based on what you learned about standing earlier in this book?

Breyer also wrote the majority opinion in *June Medical*, joined in the opinion by Ginsburg, Sotomayor, and Kagan, and by Roberts in the judgment. Alito, Thomas, Gorsuch, and Kavanaugh dissented. Breyer concluded that the law's substantial obstacle put an undue burden on the right to abortion. Breyer also said that the Court should weigh the benefits of any abortion statute against its burdens in deciding whether there was an obstacle.

Roberts—surprisingly—concurred even though he had dissented in *Whole Woman's Health*. He emphasized stare decisis, saying that everyone must respect the Court's precedents. Roberts challenged Breyer's balancing test, saying it was not part of the legacy of *Casey*.

The dissents also rejected the majority's balancing test. They argued that doctors should have more opportunity to get admitting privileges at the hospitals. And they favored the third party standing argument.

After Justice Ruth Bader Ginsburg died, Justice Amy Coney Barrett replaced her on the Court.

e. Overruling Roe *and* Casey

The Court came very close to overruling *Roe* in the 1989 Term when there were three cases accepted that squarely posed the question. Justice O'Connor's vote was needed to make it happen. She had resisted in *Webster* the year before much to Justice Scalia's consternation.

Mississippi banned abortions after fifteen weeks. Texas banned abortions after six weeks. Both laws went to the Supreme Court. Listen to the oral argument in *Dobbs*, at https://www.oyez.org/cases/2021/19-1392. Can you tell from the argument that *Roe* will be overruled? See *Dobbs v. Jackson Women's Health,* 141 S.Ct. 2619 (2021); *Whole Woman's Health v. Jackson,* 142 S.Ct. 522 (2021). The Court allowed the Texas law to proceed. A draft of an Alito decision overruling *Roe* and *Casey* was released to Politico in May 2022. See Politico Staff, Read Justice Alito's initial draft abortion opinion which would overturn *Roe v. Wade*, Politico, May 2, 2022, at https://www.politico.com/news/2022/05/02/read-justice-alito-initial-abortion-opinion-overturn-roe-v-wade-pdf-00029504. How does the draft compare to the Court's final opinion, provided below?

Dobbs v. Jackson Women's Health Organization (2022)

Holding: Overruling *Roe* and *Casey*, leaving states to regulate abortion

Majority: ALITO, joined by Thomas, Gorsuch, Kavanaugh, Barrett

Concurrence in the Judgment: C. J. ROBERTS

Concurrence: THOMAS, KAVANAUGH

Dissent(s): BREYER, SOTOMAYOR, KAGAN (writing together)

How do you analyze the Court's overruling of *Roe* and *Casey*?

Dobbs v. Jackson Women's Health Organization

SUPREME COURT OF THE UNITED STATES, 2022

597 U.S. ___, 142 S.Ct. 2228

ALITO, J., delivered the opinion of the Court, in which THOMAS, GORSUCH, KAVANAUGH, and BARRETT, JJ., joined. THOMAS, J., and KAVANAUGH, J., filed concurring opinions. ROBERTS, C. J., filed an opinion concurring in the judgment. BREYER, SOTOMAYOR, and KAGAN, JJ., filed a dissenting opinion.

Abortion presents a profound moral issue on which Americans hold sharply conflicting views.

Some believe fervently that a human person comes into being at conception and that abortion ends an innocent life. Others feel just as strongly that any regulation of abortion invades a woman's right to control her own body and prevents women from achieving full equality. Still others in a third group think that abortion should be allowed under some but not all circumstances, and those within this group hold a variety of views about the particular restrictions that should be imposed. ...

We hold that *Roe* and *Casey* must be overruled. The Constitution makes no reference to abortion, and no such right is implicitly protected by any constitutional provision, including the one on which the defenders of *Roe* and *Casey* now chiefly rely—the Due Process Clause of the Fourteenth Amendment. That provision has been held to guarantee some rights that are not mentioned in the Constitution, but any such right must be "deeply rooted in this Nation's history and tradition" and "implicit in the concept of ordered liberty." *Glucksberg.*

The right to abortion does not fall within this category. Until the latter part of the 20th century, such a right was entirely unknown in American law. Indeed, when the Fourteenth Amendment was adopted, three quarters of the States made abortion a crime at all stages of pregnancy. The abortion right is also critically different from any other right that this Court has held to fall within the Fourteenth Amendment's protection of "liberty." *Roe's* defenders characterize the abortion right as similar to the rights recognized in past decisions involving matters such as intimate sexual relations, contraception, and marriage, but abortion is fundamentally different, as both *Roe* and *Casey* acknowledged, because it destroys what those decisions called "fetal life" and what the law now before us describes as an "unborn human being."

Stare decisis, the doctrine on which *Casey*'s controlling opinion was based, does not compel unending adherence to abuse of judicial authority. *Roe* was egregiously wrong from the start. Its reasoning was exceptionally weak, and the decision has had damaging consequences. And far from bringing about a national settlement of the abortion issue, *Roe* and *Casey* have enflamed debate and deepened division.

It is time to heed the Constitution and return the issue of abortion to the people's elected representatives. "The permissibility of abortion, and the limitations, upon it, are to be resolved like most important questions in our democracy: by citizens trying to persuade one another and then voting." *Casey* (Scalia, J., concurring in judgment in part and dissenting in part). That is what the Constitution and the rule of law demand. ...

I ...

II

We begin by considering the critical question whether the Constitution, properly understood, confers a right to obtain an abortion. Skipping over that question, the controlling opinion in *Casey* reaffirmed *Roe's* "central holding" based solely on the doctrine of *stare decisis*, but as we will explain, proper application of *stare decisis* required an assessment of the strength of the grounds on which *Roe* was based.

We therefore turn to the question that the *Casey* plurality did not consider, and we address that question in three steps. First, we explain the standard that our cases have used in determining whether the Fourteenth Amendment's reference to "liberty" protects a particular right. Second, we examine whether the right at issue in this case is rooted in our Nation's history and tradition and whether it is an essential component of what we have described as "ordered liberty." Finally, we consider whether a right to obtain an abortion is part of a broader entrenched right that is supported by other precedents.

A

Constitutional analysis must begin with "the language of the instrument," which offers a "fixed standard" for ascertaining what our founding document means, 1 J. Story, Commentaries on the Constitution of the United States § 399, p. 383 (1833). The Constitution makes no express reference to a right to obtain an abortion, and therefore those who claim that it protects such a right must show that the right is somehow implicit in the constitutional text ...

[Opinion rejects arguments that abortion is grounded in the First, Fourth, Fifth, Ninth, and Fourteenth Amendments, adding that it is not rooted in the Equal Protection Clause either.]

The underlying theory on which this argument rests—that the Fourteenth Amendment's Due Process Clause provides substantive, as well as procedural, protection for "liberty"—has long been controversial. But our decisions have held that the Due Process Clause protects two categories of substantive rights.

The first consists of rights guaranteed by the first eight Amendments. ... The second category—which is the one in question here—comprises a select list of fundamental rights that are not mentioned anywhere in the Constitution. ...

Timbs and *McDonald* concerned the question whether the Fourteenth Amendment protects rights that are expressly set out in the Bill of Rights, and it would be anomalous if similar historical support were not required when a putative right is not mentioned anywhere in the Constitution. Thus, in *Glucksberg*, which held that the Due Process Clause does not confer a right to assisted suicide, the Court surveyed more than 700 years of Anglo-American common law tradition and made clear that a fundamental right must be "objectively, deeply rooted in this Nation's history and tradition."

Historical inquiries of this nature are essential whenever we are asked to recognize a new component of the "liberty" protected by the Due Process Clause because the term "liberty" alone provides little guidance. ...

In interpreting what is meant by the Fourteenth Amendment's reference to "liberty," we must guard against the natural human tendency to confuse what that Amendment protects with our own ardent views about the liberty that Americans should enjoy. That is why the Court has long been "reluctant" to recognize rights that are not mentioned in the Constitution. ...

On occasion, when the Court has ignored the "[a]ppropriate limits" imposed by "'respect for the teachings of history,'" it has fallen into the freewheeling judicial policymaking that characterized discredited decisions such as *Lochner v. New York*. The Court must not fall prey to such an unprincipled approach. Instead, guided by the history and tradition that map the essential components of our Nation's concept of ordered liberty, we must ask what the *Fourteenth Amendment* means by the term "liberty." When we engage in that inquiry in the present case, the clear answer is that the Fourteenth Amendment does not protect the right to an abortion.

B

Until the latter part of the 20th century, there was no support in American law for a constitutional right to obtain an abortion. No state constitutional provision had recognized such a right. Until a few years before *Roe* was handed down, no federal or state court had recognized such a right. Nor had any scholarly treatise of which we are aware. And although law review articles are not reticent about advocating new rights, the earliest article proposing a constitutional right to abortion that has come to our attention was published only a few years before *Roe*.

Not only was there no support for such a constitutional right until shortly before *Roe*, but abortion had long been a *crime* in every single State. At common law, abortion was criminal in at least some stages of pregnancy and was regarded as unlawful and could have very serious consequences at all stages. American law followed the common law until a wave of statutory restrictions in the 1800s expanded criminal liability for abortions. By the time of the adoption of the Fourteenth Amendment, three-quarters of the States had made abortion a crime at any stage of pregnancy, and the remaining States would soon follow.

Roe either ignored or misstated this history, and *Casey* declined to reconsider *Roe's* faulty historical analysis. It is therefore important to set the record straight.

a

... Although a pre-quickening abortion was not itself considered homicide, it does not follow that abortion was *permissible* at common law—much less that abortion was a legal *right*. ...

That the common law did not condone even pre-quickening abortions is confirmed by what one might call a proto-felony-murder rule. Hale and Blackstone explained a way in which a pre-quickening abortion could rise to the level of a homicide. Hale wrote that if a physician gave a woman "with child" a "potion" to cause an abortion, and the woman died, it was "murder" because the potion was given "*unlawfully* to destroy her child within her." 1 Hale 429–430 (emphasis added). As Blackstone explained, to be "murder" a killing had to be done with "malice aforethought, ... either express or implied." 4 Blackstone 198 (emphasis deleted). In the case of an abortionist, Blackstone wrote, "the law will imply [malice]" for the same reason that it would imply malice if a person who intended to kill one person accidentally killed a different person. ...

Notably, Blackstone, like Hale, did not state that this proto-felony-murder rule required that the woman be "with quick child"—only that she be "with child." ...

In sum, although common-law authorities differed on the severity of punishment for abortions committed at different points in pregnancy, none endorsed the practice. Moreover, we are aware of no common-law case or authority, and the parties have not pointed to any, that remotely suggests a positive *right* to procure an abortion at any stage of pregnancy. ...

b ...

c

The original ground for drawing a distinction between pre- and post-quickening abortions is not entirely clear, but some have attributed the rule to the difficulty of proving that a pre-quickening fetus was alive. At that time, there were no scientific methods for detecting pregnancy in its early stages,[31] and thus, as one court put it in 1872: "[U]ntil the period of quickening there is no *evidence* of life; and whatever may be said of the feotus, the law has fixed upon this period of gestation as the time when the child is endowed with life" because "foetal movements are the first clearly marked and well defined *evidences of life*."

The Solicitor General offers a different explanation of the basis for the quickening rule, namely, that before quickening the common law did not regard a fetus "as having a 'separate and independent existence.'" But the case on which the Solicitor General relies for this proposition also suggested that the criminal law's quickening rule was out of step with the treatment of prenatal life in other areas of law, noting that "to many purposes, in reference to civil rights, an infant *in ventre sa mere* is regarded as a person in being."

At any rate, the original ground for the quickening rule is of little importance for present purposes because the rule was abandoned in the 19th century. ...

In this country during the 19th century, the vast majority of the States enacted statutes criminalizing abortion at all stages of pregnancy. By 1868, the year when the Fourteenth Amendment was ratified, three-quarters of the States, 28 out of 37, had enacted statutes making abortion a crime even if it was performed before quickening. Of the nine States that had not yet criminalized abortion at all stages, all but one did so by 1910.

The trend in the Territories that would become the last 13 States was similar: All of them criminalized abortion at all stages of pregnancy between 1850 (the Kingdom of Hawaii) and 1919 (New Mexico). By the end of the 1950s, according to the *Roe* Court's own count, statutes in all but four States and the District of Columbia prohibited abortion "however and whenever performed, unless done to save or preserve the life of the mother."

This overwhelming consensus endured until the day *Roe* was decided. At that time, also by the *Roe* Court's own count, a substantial majority—30 States—still prohibited abortion at all stages except to save the life of the mother. And though *Roe* discerned a "trend toward liberalization" in about "one-third of the States," those States still criminalized some abortions and regulated them more stringently than *Roe* would allow. In short, the "Court's opinion in *Roe* itself convincingly refutes the notion that the abortion liberty is deeply rooted in the history or tradition of our people."

d

The inescapable conclusion is that a right to abortion is not deeply rooted in the Nation's history and traditions. On the contrary, an unbroken tradition of prohibiting abortion on pain of criminal punishment persisted from the earliest days of the common law until 1973. The Court in *Roe* could have said of abortion exactly what *Glucksberg* said of assisted suicide: "Attitudes toward [abortion] have changed since Bracton, but our laws have consistently condemned, and continue to prohibit, [that practice]."

... Instead of following these authorities, *Roe* relied largely on two articles by a pro-abortion advocate who claimed that Coke had intentionally misstated the common law because of his strong anti-abortion views. These articles have been discredited, and it has come to light that even members of Jane Roe's legal team did not regard them as serious scholarship. An internal memorandum characterized this author's work as donning "the guise of impartial scholarship while advancing the proper ideological goals."[39] Continued reliance on such scholarship is unsupportable. ...

According to [amicus] account, which is based almost entirely on statements made by one prominent proponent of the statutes, important motives for the laws were the fear that Catholic immigrants were having more babies than Protestants and that the availability of abortion was leading White Protestant women to "shir[k their] maternal duties."

Resort to this argument is a testament to the lack of any real historical support for the right that *Roe* and *Casey* recognized. This Court has long disfavored arguments based on alleged legislative motives. The Court has recognized that inquiries into legislative motives "are a hazardous matter." Even when an argument about legislative motive is backed by statements made by legislators who voted for a law, we have been reluctant to attribute those motives to the legislative body as a whole. "What motivates one legislator to make a speech about a statute is not necessarily what motivates scores of others to enact it."

... Are we to believe that the hundreds of lawmakers whose votes were needed to enact [laws outlawing abortion] were motivated by hostility to Catholics and women?

There is ample evidence that the passage of these laws was instead spurred by a sincere belief that abortion kills a human being. ...

One may disagree with this belief (and our decision is not based on any view about when a State should regard prenatal life as having rights or legally cognizable interests), but even *Roe* and *Casey* did not question the good faith of abortion opponents. And we see no reason to discount the significance of the state laws in question based on these *amici*'s suggestions about legislative motive.

C

Instead of seriously pressing the argument that the abortion right itself has deep roots, supporters of *Roe* and *Casey* contend that the abortion right is an integral part of a broader entrenched right. *Roe* termed this a right to privacy and *Casey* described it as the freedom to make "intimate and personal" choices that are "central to personal dignity and autonomy." ...

What sharply distinguishes the abortion right from the rights recognized in the cases on which *Roe* and *Casey* rely is something that both those decisions acknowledged: Abortion destroys what those decisions call "potential life" and what the law at issue in this case regards as the life of an "unborn human being." None of the other decisions cited by *Roe* and *Casey* involved the critical moral question posed by abortion. They are therefore inapposite. They do not support the right to obtain an abortion, and by the same token, our conclusion that the Constitution does not confer such a right does not undermine them in any way.

... Americans who believe that abortion should be restricted press countervailing arguments about modern developments. They note that attitudes about the pregnancy of unmarried women have changed drastically; that federal and state laws ban discrimination on the basis of pregnancy; that leave for pregnancy and childbirth are now guaranteed by law in many cases; that the costs of medical care associated with pregnancy are covered by insurance or government assistance; that States have increasingly adopted "safe haven" laws, which generally allow women to drop off babies anonymously; and that a woman who puts her newborn up for adoption today has little reason to fear that the baby will not find a suitable home. They also claim that many people now have a new appreciation of fetal life and that when prospective parents who want to have a child view a sonogram, they typically have no doubt that what they see is their daughter or son.

Both sides make important policy arguments, but supporters of *Roe* and *Casey* must show that this Court has the authority to weigh those arguments and decide how abortion may be regulated in the States. They have failed to make that showing, and we thus return the power to weigh those arguments to the people and their elected representatives.

D

The dissent is very candid that it cannot show that a constitutional right to abortion has any foundation, let alone a "'deeply rooted'" one, "'in this Nation's history and tradition.'" The dissent does not identify *any* pre-*Roe* authority that supports such a right—no state constitutional provision or statute, no federal or state judicial precedent, not even a scholarly treatise. Nor does the dissent dispute the fact that abortion was illegal at common law at least after quickening; that the 19th century saw a trend toward criminalization of pre-quickening abortions; that by 1868, a supermajority of States (at least 26 of 37) had enacted statutes criminalizing abortion at all stages of pregnancy; that by the late 1950s at least 46 States prohibited abortion "however and whenever performed" except if necessary to save "the life of the mother,"; and that when

Roe was decided in 1973 similar statutes were still in effect in 30 States.

The dissent's failure to engage with this long tradition is devastating to its position. We have held that the "established method of substantive-due-process analysis" requires that an unenumerated right be "'deeply rooted in this Nation's history and tradition'" before it can be recognized as a component of the "liberty" protected in the Due Process Clause. But despite the dissent's professed fidelity to *stare decisis*, it fails to seriously engage with that important precedent—which it cannot possibly satisfy. ...

... The dissent cannot establish that a right to abortion has *ever* been part of this Nation's tradition.

The most striking feature of the dissent is the absence of any serious discussion of the legitimacy of the States' interest in protecting fetal life. ...

Our opinion is not based on any view about if and when prenatal life is entitled to any of the rights enjoyed after birth. The dissent, by contrast, would impose on the people a particular theory about when the rights of personhood begin. According to the dissent, the Constitution *requires* the States to regard a fetus as lacking even the most basic human right—to live—at least until an arbitrary point in a pregnancy has passed. Nothing in the Constitution or in our Nation's legal traditions authorizes the Court to adopt that "'theory of life.'" ...

III

We next consider whether the doctrine of *stare decisis* counsels continued acceptance of *Roe* and *Casey*. ...

Some of our most important constitutional decisions have overruled prior precedents. We mention three. In *Brown v. Board of Education,* the Court repudiated the "separate but equal" doctrine, which had allowed States to maintain racially segregated schools and other facilities. In so doing, the Court overruled the infamous decision in *Plessy v. Ferguson,* along with six other Supreme Court precedents that had applied the separate-but-equal rule.

In *West Coast Hotel v. Parrish,* the Court overruled *Adkins v. Children's Hospital,* which had held that a law setting minimum wages for women violated the "liberty" protected by the Fifth Amendment's Due Process Clause. *West Coast Hotel* signaled the demise of an entire line of important precedents that had protected an individual liberty right against state and federal health and welfare legislation. [See, e.g., *Lochner*].

Finally, in *West Virginia Bd. of Ed. v. Barnette,* after the lapse of only three years, the Court overruled *Minersville School Dist. v. Gobitis,* and held that public school students could not be compelled to salute the flag in violation of their sincere beliefs. *Barnette* stands out because nothing had changed during the intervening period other than the Court's belated recognition that its earlier decision had been seriously wrong. ...

No Justice of this Court has ever argued that the Court should never overrule a constitutional decision, but overruling a precedent is a serious matter. It is not a step that should be taken lightly. ...

In this case, five factors weigh strongly in favor of overruling *Roe* and *Casey*: the nature of their error, the quality of their reasoning, the "workability" of the rules they imposed on the country, their disruptive effect on other areas of the law, and the absence of concrete reliance.

A

The nature of the Court's error. ...

Roe was on a collision course with the Constitution from the day it was decided, *Casey* perpetuated its errors, and those errors do not concern some arcane corner of the law of little importance to the American people. Rather, wielding nothing but "raw judicial power," the Court usurped the power to address a question of profound moral and social importance that the Constitution unequivocally leaves for the people. ... Together, *Roe* and *Casey* represent an error that cannot be allowed to stand. ...

B

The quality of the reasoning. ... [*Roe*] was more than just wrong. It stood on exceptionally weak grounds. ...

a

The weaknesses in *Roe*'s reasoning are well-known. Without any grounding in the constitutional text, history, or precedent, it imposed on the entire country a detailed set of rules much like those that one might expect to find in a statute or regulation. ...

This elaborate scheme was the Court's own brainchild. Neither party advocated the trimester framework; nor did either party or any *amicus* argue that "viability" should mark the point at which the scope of the abortion right and a State's regulatory authority should be substantially transformed. ...

b

... When it came to the most important historical fact—how the States regulated abortion when the Fourteenth Amendment was adopted—the Court said almost nothing. ...

Roe's failure even to note the overwhelming consensus of state laws in effect in 1868 is striking, and what it said about the common law was simply wrong. Relying on two discredited articles by an abortion advocate, the Court erroneously suggested—contrary to Bracton, Coke, Hale, Blackstone, and a wealth of other authority—that the common law had probably never really treated post-quickening abortion as a crime. ...

When the Court summarized the basis for the scheme it imposed on the country, it asserted that its rules were "consistent with" the following: (1) "the relative weights of the respective interests involved," (2) "the lessons and examples of medical and legal history," (3) "the lenity of the common law," and (4) "the demands of the profound problems of the present day." Put aside the second and third factors, which were based on the Court's flawed account of history, and what remains are precisely the sort of considerations that legislative bodies often take into account when they draw lines that accommodate competing interests. The scheme *Roe* produced *looked* like legislation, and the Court provided the sort of explanation that might be expected from a legislative body.

c

... An even more glaring deficiency [with *Roe*] was *Roe*'s failure to justify the critical distinction it drew between pre-and post-viability abortions. Here is the Court's entire explanation:

> "With respect to the State's important and legitimate interest in potential life, the 'compelling' point is at viability. This is so because the fetus then presumably has the capability of meaningful life outside the womb."

As Professor Laurence Tribe has written, "[c]learly, this mistakes 'a definition for a syllogism.'" Tribe 4 (quoting Ely 924). The definition of a "viable" fetus is one that is capable of surviving outside the womb, but why is this the point at which the State's interest becomes compelling? If, as *Roe* held, a State's interest in protecting prenatal life is compelling "after viability," why isn't that interest "equally compelling before viability"? *Roe* did not say, and no explanation is apparent.

... But even if one takes the view that "personhood" begins when a certain attribute or combination of attributes is acquired, it is very hard to see why viability should mark the point where "personhood" begins.

... And if viability is meant to mark a line having universal moral significance, can it be that a fetus that is viable in a big city in the United States has a privileged moral status not enjoyed by an identical fetus in a remote area of a poor country?

In addition, as the Court once explained, viability is not really a hard-and-fast line. A physician determining a particular fetus's odds of surviving outside the womb must consider "a number of variables," including "gestational age," "fetal weight," a woman's "general health and nutrition," the "quality of the available medical facilities," and other factors. It is thus "only with difficulty" that a physician can estimate the "probability" of a particular fetus's survival. And even if each fetus's probability of survival could be ascertained with certainty, settling on a "probabilit[y] of survival" that should count as "viability" is another matter. Is a fetus viable with a 10 percent chance of survival? 25 percent? 50 percent? Can such a judgment be made by a State? And can a State specify a gestational age limit that applies in all cases? Or must these difficult questions be left entirely to the individual "attending physician on the particular facts of the case before him"?

The viability line, which *Casey* termed *Roe*'s central rule, makes no sense, and it is telling that other countries almost uniformly eschew such a line. The Court thus asserted raw judicial power to impose, as a matter of constitutional law, a uniform viability rule that allowed the States less freedom to regulate abortion than the majority of western democracies enjoy. ...

d ...

C

Workability. ... *Casey's* "undue burden" test has scored poorly on the workability scale.

The difficulty of applying *Casey*'s new rules surfaced in that very case. The controlling opinion found that Pennsylvania's 24-hour waiting period requirement and its informed-consent provision did not impose "undue burden[sbut Justice Stevens, applying the same test, reached the opposite result. That did not bode well, and then-Chief Justice Rehnquist aptly observed that "the undue burden standard presents nothing more workable than the trimester framework."

The ambiguity of the "undue burden" test also produced disagreement in later cases. In *Whole Woman's Health*, the Court adopted the cost-benefit interpretation of the test, stating that "[t]he rule announced in *Casey* ... requires that courts consider the burdens a law imposes on abortion access *together with the benefits those laws confer*." But five years later, a majority of the Justices rejected that interpretation. See *June Medical*. But THE CHIEF JUSTICE—who cast the deciding vote—argued that "[n]othing about *Casey* suggested that a weighing of costs and benefits of an abortion regulation was a job for the courts." And the four Justices in dissent rejected the plurality's interpretation of *Casey*.

This Court's experience applying *Casey* has confirmed Chief Justice Rehnquist's prescient diagnosis that the undue-burden standard was "not built to last."

... *Casey*'s undue burden test has proved to be unworkable. "Plucked from nowhere," it "seems calculated to perpetuate give-it-a-try litigation" before judges assigned an unwieldy and inappropriate task. Continued adherence to that standard would undermine, not advance, the "evenhanded, predictable, and consistent development of legal principles."

D

Effect on other areas of law. ...

The Court's abortion cases have diluted the strict standard for facial constitutional challenges. They have ignored the Court's third-party standing doctrine. They have disregarded standard *res judicata* principles. They have flouted the ordinary rules on the severability of unconstitutional provisions, as well as the rule that statutes should be read where possible to avoid unconstitutionality. And they have distorted First Amendment doctrines. ...

E

Reliance interests. ...

Our decision returns the issue of abortion to those legislative bodies, and it allows women on both sides of the abortion issue to seek to affect the legislative process by influencing public opinion, lobbying legislators, voting, and running for office. Women are not without electoral or political power. It is noteworthy that the percentage of women who register to vote and cast ballots is consistently higher than the percentage of men who do so. In the last election in November 2020, women, who make up around 51.5 percent of the population of Mississippi, constituted 55.5 percent of the voters who cast ballots.

Unable to show concrete reliance on *Roe* and *Casey* themselves, the Solicitor General suggests that overruling those decisions would "threaten the Court's precedents holding that the Due Process Clause protects other rights." [citing *Obergefell, Lawrence, Griswold.*] That is not correct for reasons we have already discussed. As even the *Casey* plurality recognized, "[a]bortion is a unique act" because it terminates "life or potential life." And to ensure that our decision is not misunderstood or mischaracterized, we emphasize that our decision concerns the constitutional right to abortion and no other right. Nothing in this opinion should be understood to cast doubt on precedents that do not concern abortion.

IV

... We do not pretend to know how our political system or society will respond to today's decision overruling *Roe* and *Casey*. And even if we could foresee what will happen, we would have no authority to let that knowledge influence our decision. We can only do our job, which is to interpret the law, apply longstanding principles of *stare decisis*, and decide this case accordingly.

We therefore hold that the Constitution does not confer a right to abortion. *Roe* and *Casey* must be overruled, and the authority to regulate abortion must be returned to the people and their elected representatives. ...

V

A

Finally, the dissent suggests that our decision calls into question *Griswold*, *Eisenstadt*, *Lawrence*, and *Obergefell*. But we have stated unequivocally that "[n]othing in this opinion should be understood to cast doubt on precedents that do not concern abortion." We have also explained why that is so: rights regarding contraception and same-sex relationships are inherently different from the right to abortion because the latter (as we have stressed) uniquely involves what *Roe* and *Casey* termed "potential life." Therefore, a right to abortion cannot be justified by a purported analogy to the rights recognized in those other cases or by "appeals to a broader right to autonomy." It is hard to see how we could be clearer. Moreover, even putting aside that these cases are distinguishable, there is a further point that the dissent ignores: Each precedent is subject to its own *stare decisis* analysis, and the factors that our doctrine instructs us to consider like reliance and workability are different for these cases than for our abortion jurisprudence.

B

We now turn to the concurrence in the judgment, which reproves us for deciding whether *Roe* and *Casey* should be retained or overruled. That opinion (which for convenience we will call simply "the concurrence") recommends a "more measured course," which it defends based on what it claims is "a straightforward *stare decisis* analysis." ...

... For all these reasons, *stare decisis* cannot justify the new "reasonable opportunity" rule propounded by the concurrence. If that rule is to become the law of the land, it must stand on its own, but the concurrence makes no attempt to show that this rule represents a correct interpretation of the Constitution. The concurrence does not claim that the right to a reasonable opportunity to obtain an abortion is "'deeply rooted in this Nation's history and tradition'" and "'implicit in the concept of ordered liberty.'" *Glucksberg*. Nor does it propound any other theory that could show that the Constitution supports its new rule. And if the Constitution protects a woman's right to obtain an abortion, the opinion does not explain why that right should end after the point at which all "reasonable" women will have decided whether to seek an abortion. While the concurrence is moved by a desire for judicial minimalism, "we cannot embrace a narrow ground of decision simply because it is narrow; it must also be right." For the reasons that we have explained, the concurrence's approach is not.

The concurrence would "leave for another day whether to reject any right to an abortion at all," but "another day" would not be long in coming. Some States have set deadlines for obtaining an abortion that are shorter than Mississippi's. If we held only that Mississippi's 15-week rule is constitutional, we would soon be called upon to pass on the constitutionality of a panoply of laws with shorter deadlines or no deadline at all. The "measured course" charted by the concurrence would be fraught with turmoil until the Court answered the question that the concurrence seeks to defer. ...

In sum, the concurrence's quest for a middle way would only put off the day when we would be forced to confront the question we now decide. The turmoil wrought by *Roe* and *Casey* would be prolonged. It is far better—for this Court and the country—to face up to the real issue without further delay.

VI

We must now decide what standard will govern if state abortion regulations undergo constitutional challenge and whether the law before us satisfies the appropriate standard.

A

Under our precedents, rational-basis review is the appropriate standard for such challenges. ...

A law regulating abortion, like other health and welfare laws, is entitled to a "strong presumption of validity." It must be sustained if there is a rational basis on which the legislature could have thought that it would serve legitimate state interests. ...

B

These legitimate interests justify Mississippi's Gestational Age Act. Except "in a medical emergency or in the case of a severe fetal abnormality," the statute prohibits abortion "if the probable gestational age of the unborn human being has been determined to be greater than fifteen (15) weeks." The Mississippi Legislature's findings recount the stages of "human prenatal development" and assert the State's interest in "protecting the life of the unborn." The legislature also found that abortions performed after 15 weeks typically use the dilation and evacuation procedure, and the legislature found the use of this procedure "for nontherapeutic or elective reasons [to be] a barbaric practice, dangerous for the maternal patient, and demeaning to the medical profession." These legitimate interests provide a rational basis for the Gestational Age Act, and it follows that respondents' constitutional challenge must fail.

VII

We end this opinion where we began. Abortion presents a profound moral question. The Constitution does not prohibit the citizens of each State from regulating or prohibiting abortion. *Roe* and *Casey* arrogated that authority. We now overrule those decisions and return that authority to the people and their elected representatives.

The judgment of the Fifth Circuit is reversed, and the case is remanded for further proceedings consistent with this opinion.

It is so ordered.

Justice THOMAS, concurring.

I join the opinion of the Court because it correctly holds that there is no constitutional right to abortion.

...

... in future cases, we should reconsider all of this Court's substantive due process precedents, including *Griswold*, *Lawrence*, and *Obergefell*. ...

... Now today, the Court rightly overrules *Roe* and *Casey*—two of this Court's "most notoriously incorrect" substantive due process decisions, after more than 63 million abortions have been performed, see National Right to Life Committee, Abortion Statistics (Jan. 2022), https://www.nrlc.org/uploads/factsheets/FS01AbortionintheUS.pdf. The harm caused by this Court's forays into substantive due process remains immeasurable.

* * *

Because the Court properly applies our substantive due process precedents to reject the fabrication of a constitutional right to abortion, and because this case does not present the opportunity to reject substantive due process entirely, I join the Court's opinion. But, in future cases, we should "follow the text of the Constitution, which sets forth certain substantive rights that cannot be taken away, and adds, beyond that, a right to due process when life, liberty, or property is to be taken away." Substantive due process conflicts with that textual command and has harmed our country in many ways. Accordingly, we should eliminate it from our jurisprudence at the earliest opportunity.

Justice KAVANAUGH, concurring. ...

I

...

The issue before this Court, however, is not the policy or morality of abortion. The issue before this Court is what the Constitution says about abortion. The Constitution does not take sides on the issue of abortion. The text of the Constitution does not refer to or encompass abortion. To be sure, this Court has held that the Constitution protects unenumerated rights that are deeply rooted in this Nation's history and tradition, and implicit in the concept of ordered liberty. But a right to abortion is not deeply rooted in American history and tradition, as the Court today thoroughly explains.

On the question of abortion, the Constitution is therefore neither pro-life nor pro-choice. The Constitution is neutral and leaves the issue for the people and their elected representatives to resolve through the democratic process in the States or Congress—like the numerous other difficult questions of American social and economic policy that the Constitution does not address. ...

To be clear, then, the Court's decision today *does not outlaw* abortion throughout the United States. On the contrary, the Court's decision properly leaves the question of abortion for the people and their elected representatives in the democratic process. Through that democratic process, the people and their representatives may decide to allow or limit abortion. ...

The Constitution does not grant the nine unelected Members of this Court the unilateral authority to rewrite the Constitution to create new rights and liberties based on our own moral or policy views. As Justice Rehnquist stated, this Court has not "been granted a roving commission, either by the Founding Fathers or by the framers of the Fourteenth Amendment, to strike down laws that are based upon notions of policy or morality suddenly found unacceptable by a majority of this Court." ...

II ...

III

After today's decision, the nine Members of this Court will no longer decide the basic legality of pre-viability abortion for all 330 million Americans. But the parties' arguments have raised other related questions, and I address some of them here.

First is the question of how this decision will affect other precedents involving issues such as contraception and marriage—in particular, the decisions in *Griswold, Eisenstadt, Loving,* and I emphasize what the Court today states: Overruling *Roe* does *not* mean the overruling of those precedents, and does *not* threaten or cast doubt on those precedents.

Second, as I see it, some of the other abortion-related legal questions raised by today's decision are not especially difficult as a constitutional matter. For example, may a State bar a resident of that State from traveling to another State to obtain an abortion? In my view, the answer is no based on the constitutional right to interstate travel. May a State retroactively impose liability or punishment for an abortion that occurred before today's decision takes effect? In my view, the answer is no based on the Due Process Clause or the *Ex Post Facto* Clause. ...

Chief Justice ROBERTS, concurring in the judgment.

We granted certiorari to decide one question: "Whether all pre-viability prohibitions on elective abortions are unconstitutional." ...

... I would take a more measured course. I agree with the Court that the viability line established by *Roe* and *Casey* should be discarded under a straightforward *stare decisis* analysis. That line never made any sense. Our abortion precedents describe the right at issue as a woman's right to choose to terminate her pregnancy. That right should therefore extend far enough to ensure a reasonable opportunity to choose, but need not extend any further—certainly not all the way to viability. Mississippi's law allows a woman three months to obtain an abortion, well beyond the point at which it is considered "late" to discover a pregnancy. I see no sound basis for questioning the adequacy of that opportunity.

But that is all I would say, out of adherence to a simple yet fundamental principle of judicial restraint: If it is not necessary to decide more to dispose of a case, then it is necessary *not* to decide more. Perhaps we are not always perfect in following that command, and certainly there are cases that warrant an exception. But this is not one of them. Surely we should adhere closely to principles of judicial restraint here, where the broader path the Court chooses entails repudiating a constitutional right we have not only previously recognized, but also expressly reaffirmed applying the doctrine of *stare decisis*. The Court's opinion is thoughtful and thorough, but those virtues cannot compensate for the fact that its dramatic and consequential ruling is unnecessary to decide the case before us.

I

... In short, the viability rule was created outside the ordinary course of litigation, is and always has been completely unreasoned, and fails to take account of state interests since recognized as legitimate. It is indeed "telling that other countries almost uniformly eschew" a viability line. Only a handful of countries, among them China and North Korea, permit elective abortions after twenty weeks; the rest have coalesced around a 12-week line. See The World's Abortion Laws, Center for Reproductive Rights (Feb. 23, 2021) (online source archived at www.supremecourt.gov) (Canada, China, Iceland, Guinea-Bissau, the Netherlands, North Korea, Singapore, and Vietnam permit elective abortions after twenty weeks). The Court rightly rejects the arbitrary viability rule today.

II

...

Here, there is a clear path to deciding this case correctly without overruling *Roe* all the way down to the studs: recognize that the viability line must be discarded, as the majority rightly does, and leave for another day whether to reject any right to an abortion at all. ...

... Given all this, it is no surprise that the vast majority of abortions happen in the first trimester. Presumably most of the remainder would also take place earlier if later abortions were not a legal option. Ample evidence thus suggests that a 15-week ban provides sufficient time, absent rare circumstances, for a woman "to decide for herself" whether to terminate her pregnancy.

III

...

The Court's decision to overrule *Roe* and *Casey* is a serious jolt to the legal system—regardless of how you view those cases. A narrower decision rejecting the misguided viability line would be markedly less unsettling, and nothing more is needed to decide this case.

...

The Court says we should consider whether to overrule *Roe* and *Casey* now, because if we delay we would be forced to consider the issue again in short order. There would be "turmoil" until we did so, according to the Court, because of existing state laws with "shorter deadlines or no deadline at all." But under the narrower approach proposed here, state laws outlawing abortion altogether would still violate binding precedent. And to the extent States have laws that set the cutoff date earlier than fifteen weeks, any litigation over that timeframe would proceed free of the distorting effect that the viability rule has had on our constitutional debate. The same could be true, for that matter, with respect to legislative consideration in the States. We would then be free to exercise our discretion in deciding whether and when to take up the issue, from a more informed perspective.

* * *

Both the Court's opinion and the dissent display a relentless freedom from doubt on the legal issue that I cannot share. I am not sure, for example, that a ban on terminating a pregnancy from the moment of conception must be treated the same under the Constitution as a ban after fifteen weeks. A thoughtful Member of this Court [Justice Frankfurter] once counseled that the difficulty of a question "admonishes us to observe the wise limitations on our function and to confine ourselves to deciding only what is necessary to the disposition of the immediate case." I would decide the question we granted review to answer—whether the previously recognized abortion right bars all abortion restrictions prior to viability, such that a ban on abortions after fifteen weeks of pregnancy is necessarily unlawful. The answer to that question is no, and there is no need to go further to decide this case.

I therefore concur only in the judgment.

Justice BREYER, Justice SOTOMAYOR, and Justice KAGAN, dissenting.

...

Roe and *Casey* well understood the difficulty and divisiveness of the abortion issue. The Court knew that Americans hold profoundly different views about the "moral[ity]" of "terminating a pregnancy, even in its earliest stage." And the Court recognized that "the State has legitimate interests from the outset of the pregnancy in protecting" the "life of the fetus that may become a child." So the Court struck a balance, as it often does when values and goals compete. It held that the State could prohibit abortions after fetal viability, so long as the ban contained exceptions to safeguard a woman's life or health. It held that even before viability, the State could regulate the abortion procedure in multiple and meaningful ways. But until the viability line was crossed, the Court held, a State could not impose a "substantial obstacle" on a woman's "right to elect the procedure" as she (not the government) thought proper, in light of all the circumstances and complexities of her own life.

Today, the Court discards that balance. It says that from the very moment of fertilization, a woman has no rights to speak of. A State can force her to bring a pregnancy to term, even at the steepest personal and familial costs. An abortion restriction, the majority holds, is permissible whenever rational, the lowest level of scrutiny known to the law. And because, as the Court has often stated, protecting fetal life is rational, States will feel free to enact all manner of restrictions. The Mississippi law at issue here bars abortions after the 15th week of pregnancy. Under the majority's ruling, though, another State's law could do so after ten weeks, or five or three or one—or, again, from the moment of fertilization. States have already passed such laws, in anticipation of today's ruling. More will follow. Some States have enacted laws extending to all forms of abortion procedure, including taking medication in one's own home. They have passed laws without any exceptions for when the woman is the victim of rape or incest. Under those laws, a woman will have to bear her rapist's child or a young girl her father's—no matter if doing so will destroy her life. So too, after today's ruling, some States may compel women to carry to term a fetus with severe physical anomalies—for example, one afflicted with Tay-Sachs disease, sure to die within a few years of birth. States may even argue that a prohibition on abortion need make no provision for protecting a woman from risk of death or physical harm. Across a vast array of circumstances, a State will be able to impose its moral choice on a woman and coerce her to give birth to a child.

Enforcement of all these draconian restrictions will also be left largely to the States' devices. A State can of course impose criminal penalties on abortion providers, including lengthy prison sentences. But some States will not stop there. Perhaps, in the wake of today's decision, a state law will criminalize the woman's conduct too, incarcerating or fining her for daring to seek or obtain an abortion. And as Texas has recently shown, a State can turn neighbor against neighbor, enlisting fellow citizens in the effort to root out anyone who tries to get an abortion, or to assist another in doing so.

The majority tries to hide the geographically expansive effects of its holding. Today's decision, the majority says, permits "each State" to address abortion as it pleases. That is cold comfort, of course, for the poor woman who cannot get the money to fly to a distant State for a procedure. Above all others, women lacking financial resources will suffer from today's decision. In any event, interstate restrictions will also soon be in the offing. After this decision, some States may block women from traveling out of State to obtain abortions, or even from receiving abortion medications from out of State. Some may criminalize efforts, including the provision of information or funding, to help women gain access to other States' abortion services. Most threatening of all, no language in today's decision stops the Federal Government from prohibiting abortions nationwide, once again from the moment of conception and without exceptions for rape or incest. If that happens, "the views of [an individual State's] citizens" will not matter. The challenge for a woman will be to finance a trip not to "New York [or] California" but to Toronto.

Whatever the exact scope of the coming laws, one result of today's decision is certain: the curtailment of women's rights, and of their status as free and equal citizens. Yesterday, the Constitution guaranteed that a woman confronted with an unplanned pregnancy could (within reasonable limits) make her own decision about whether to bear a child, with all the life-transforming consequences that act involves. And in thus safeguarding each woman's reproductive freedom, the Constitution also protected "[t]he ability of women to participate equally in [this Nation's] economic and social life." But no longer. As of today, this Court holds, a State can always force a woman to give birth, prohibiting even the earliest abortions. A State can thus transform what, when freely undertaken, is a wonder into what, when forced, may be a nightmare. Some women, especially women of means, will find ways around the State's assertion of power. Others—those without money or childcare or the ability to take time off from work—will not be so fortunate. Maybe they will try an unsafe method of abortion, and come to physical harm, or even die. Maybe they will undergo pregnancy and have a child, but at significant personal or familial cost. At the least, they will incur the cost of losing control of their lives. The Constitution will, today's majority holds, provide no shield, despite its guarantees of liberty and equality for all.

And no one should be confident that this majority is done with its work. The right *Roe* and *Casey* recognized does not stand alone. To the contrary, the Court has linked it for decades to other settled freedoms involving bodily integrity, familial relationships, and procreation. Most obviously, the right to terminate a pregnancy arose straight out of the right to purchase and use contraception. See *Griswold, Eisenstadt.* In turn, those rights led, more recently, to rights of same-sex intimacy and marriage. See *Lawrence, Obergefell.* They are all part of the same constitutional fabric, protecting autonomous decisionmaking over the most personal of life decisions. The majority (or to be more accurate, most of it) is eager to tell us today that nothing it does "cast[s] doubt on precedents that do not concern abortion." But how could that be? The lone rationale for what the majority does today is that the right to elect an abortion is not "deeply rooted in history": Not until *Roe*, the majority argues, did people think abortion fell within the Constitution's guarantee of liberty. The same could be said, though, of most of the rights the majority claims it is not tampering with. The majority could write just as long an opinion showing, for example, that until the mid-20th century, "there was no support in American law for a constitutional right to obtain [contraceptives]." So one of two things must be true. Either the majority does not really believe in its own reasoning. Or if it does, all rights that have no history stretching back to the mid-19th century are insecure. Either the mass of the majority's opinion is hypocrisy, or additional constitutional rights are under threat. It is one or the other.

... The Court departs from its obligation to faithfully and impartially apply the law. We dissent.

I

... We believe in a Constitution that puts some issues off limits to majority rule. Even in the face of public opposition, we uphold the right of individuals—yes, including women—to make their own choices and chart their own futures. Or at least, we did once.

A

...

We make one initial point about this analysis in light of the majority's insistence that *Roe* and *Casey*, and we in defending them, are dismissive of a "State's interest in protecting prenatal life." Nothing could get those decisions more wrong. As just described, *Roe* and *Casey* invoked powerful state interests in that protection, operative at every stage of the pregnancy and overriding the woman's liberty after viability. The strength of those state interests is exactly why the Court allowed greater restrictions on the abortion right than on other rights deriving from the Fourteenth Amendment. But what *Roe* and *Casey* also recognized—which today's majority does not—is that a woman's freedom and equality are likewise involved. That fact—the presence of countervailing interests—is what made the abortion question hard, and what necessitated balancing. The majority scoffs at that idea, castigating us for "repeatedly prais[ing] the 'balance'" the two cases arrived at (with the word "balance" in scare quotes). To the majority "balance" is a dirty word, as moderation is a foreign concept. The majority would allow States to ban abortion from conception onward because it does not think forced childbirth at all implicates a woman's rights to equality and freedom. Today's Court, that is, does not think there is anything of constitutional significance attached to a woman's control of her body and the path of her life. *Roe* and *Casey* thought that one-sided view misguided. In some sense, that is the difference in a nutshell between our precedents and the majority opinion. The constitutional regime we have lived in for the last 50 years recognized competing interests, and sought a balance between them. The constitutional regime we enter today erases the woman's interest and recognizes only the State's (or the Federal Government's).

B

...

The majority's core legal postulate, then, is that we in the 21st century must read the Fourteenth Amendment just as its ratifiers did. And that is indeed what the majority emphasizes over and over again. If the ratifiers did not understand something as central to freedom, then neither can we. Or said more particularly: If those people did not understand reproductive rights as part of the guarantee of liberty conferred in the Fourteenth Amendment, then those rights do not exist.

As an initial matter, note a mistake in the just preceding sentence. We referred there to the "people" who ratified the Fourteenth Amendment: What rights did those "people" have in their heads at the time? But, of course, "people" did not ratify the Fourteenth Amendment. Men did. So it is perhaps not so surprising that the ratifiers were not perfectly attuned to the importance of reproductive rights for women's liberty, or for their capacity to participate as equal members of our Nation. Indeed, the ratifiers—both in 1868 and when the original Constitution was approved in 1788—did not understand women as full members of the community embraced by the phrase "We the People." In 1868, the first wave of American feminists were explicitly told—of course by men—that it was not their time to seek constitutional protections. (Women would not get even the vote for another half-century.) To be sure, most women in 1868 also had a foreshortened view of their rights: If most men could not then imagine giving women control over their bodies, most women could not imagine having that kind of autonomy. But that takes away nothing from the core point. Those responsible for the original Constitution, including the Fourteenth Amendment, did not perceive women as equals, and did not recognize women's rights. When the majority says that we must read our foundational charter as viewed at the time of ratification (except that we may also check it against the Dark Ages), it consigns women to second-class citizenship.

...

And eliminating that right, we need to say before further describing our precedents, is not taking a "neutral" position, as Justice KAVANAUGH tries to argue. His idea is that neutrality lies in giving the abortion issue to the States, where some can go one way and some another. But would he say that the Court is being "scrupulously neutral" if it allowed New York and California to ban all the guns they want? If the Court allowed some States to use unanimous juries and others not? If the Court told the States: Decide for yourselves whether to put restrictions on church attendance? We could go on—and in fact we will. Suppose Justice KAVANAUGH were to say (in line with the majority opinion) that the rights we just listed are more textually or historically grounded than the right to choose. What, then, of the right to contraception or same-sex marriage? Would it be "scrupulously neutral" for the Court to eliminate those rights too? The point of all these examples is that when it comes to rights, the Court does not act "neutrally" when it leaves everything up to the States. Rather, the Court acts neutrally when it protects the right against all comers. And to apply that point to the case here: When the Court decimates a right women have held for 50 years, the Court is not being "scrupulously neutral." It is instead taking sides: against women who wish to exercise the right, and for States (like Mississippi) that want to bar them from doing so. Justice KAVANAUGH cannot obscure that point by appropriating the rhetoric of even-handedness. His position just is what it is: A brook-no-compromise refusal to recognize a woman's right to choose, from the first day of a pregnancy. And that position, as we will now show, cannot be squared with this Court's longstanding view that women indeed have rights (whatever the state of the world in 1868) to make the most personal and consequential decisions about their bodies and their lives.

Casey similarly recognized the need to extend the constitutional sphere of liberty to a previously excluded group. The Court then understood, as the majority today does not, that the men who ratified the Fourteenth Amendment and wrote the state laws of the time did not view women as full and equal citizens. A woman then, *Casey* wrote, "had no legal existence separate from her husband." Women were seen only "as the center of home and family life," without "full and independent legal status under the Constitution." But that could not be true any longer: The State could not now insist on the historically dominant "vision of the woman's role." And equal citizenship, *Casey* realized, was inescapably connected to reproductive rights. "The ability of women to participate equally" in the "life of the Nation"—in all its economic, social, political, and legal aspects—"has been facilitated by their ability to control their reproductive lives." Without the ability to decide whether and when to have children, women could not—in the way men took for granted—determine how they would live their lives, and how they would contribute to the society around them. ...

The first problem with the majority's account comes from Justice THOMAS's concurrence—which makes clear he is not with the program. In saying that nothing in today's opinion casts doubt on non-abortion precedents, Justice THOMAS explains, he means only that they are not at issue in this very case. But he lets us know what he wants to do when they are. "[I]n future cases," he says, "we should reconsider all of this Court's substantive due process precedents, including *Griswold*, *Lawrence*, and *Obergefell*." And when we reconsider them? Then "we have a duty" to "overrul[e] these demonstrably erroneous decisions." So at least one Justice is planning to use the ticket of today's decision again and again and again.

Even placing the concurrence to the side, the assurance in today's opinion still does not work. Or at least that is so if the majority is serious about its sole reason for overturning *Roe* and *Casey*: the legal status of abortion in the 19th century. Except in the places quoted above, the state interest in protecting fetal life plays no part in the majority's analysis. To the contrary, the majority takes pride in not expressing a view "about the status of the fetus." The majority's departure from *Roe* and *Casey* rests instead—and only—on whether a woman's decision to end a pregnancy involves any Fourteenth Amendment liberty interest (against which *Roe* and *Casey* balanced the state interest in preserving fetal life). According to the majority, no liberty interest is present—because (and only because) the law offered no protection to the woman's choice in the 19th century. But here is the rub. The law also did not then (and would not for ages) protect a wealth of other things. It did not protect the rights recognized in *Lawrence* and *Obergefell* to same-sex intimacy and marriage. It did not protect the right recognized in *Loving* to marry across racial lines. It did not protect the right recognized in *Griswold* to contraceptive use. For that matter, it did not protect the right recognized in *Skinner*, not to be sterilized without consent. So if the majority is right in its legal analysis, all those decisions were wrong, and all those matters properly belong to the States too—whatever the particular state interests involved. And if that is true, it is impossible to understand (as a matter of logic and principle) how the majority can say that its opinion today does not threaten—does not even "undermine"—any number of other constitutional rights.

... If the majority is serious about its historical approach, then *Griswold* and its progeny are in the line of fire too. Or if it is not serious, then ... what *is* the basis of today's decision? If we had to guess, we suspect the prospects of this Court approving bans on contraception are low. But once again, the future significance of today's opinion will be decided in the future. At the least, today's opinion will fuel the fight to get contraception, and any other issues with a moral dimension, out of the Fourteenth Amendment and into state legislatures.

Anyway, today's decision, taken on its own, is catastrophic enough. As a matter of constitutional method, the majority's commitment to replicate in 2022 every view about the meaning of liberty held in 1868 has precious little to recommend it. Our law in this constitutional sphere, as in most, has for decades upon decades proceeded differently. It has considered fundamental constitutional principles, the whole course of the Nation's history and traditions, and the step-by-step evolution of the Court's precedents. It is disciplined but not static. It relies on accumulated judgments, not just the sentiments of one long-ago generation of men (who themselves believed, and drafted the Constitution to reflect, that the world progresses). And by doing so, it includes those excluded from that olden conversation, rather than perpetuating its bounds.

As a matter of constitutional substance, the majority's opinion has all the flaws its method would suggest. Because laws in 1868 deprived women of any control over their bodies, the majority approves States doing so today. Because those laws prevented women from charting the course of their own lives, the majority says States can do the same again. Because in 1868, the government could tell a pregnant woman—even in the first days of her pregnancy—that she could do nothing but bear a child, it can once more impose that command. Today's decision strips women of agency over what even the majority agrees is a contested and contestable moral issue. It forces her to carry out the State's will, whatever the circumstances and whatever the harm it will wreak on her and her family. In the Fourteenth Amendment's terms, it takes away her liberty. Even before we get to *stare decisis*, we dissent.

II

... To repeat: The point of a right is to shield individual actions and decisions "from the vicissitudes of political controversy, to place them beyond the reach of majorities and officials and to establish them as legal principles to be applied by the courts." However divisive, a right is not at the people's mercy.

... The majority has overruled *Roe* and *Casey* for one and only one reason: because it has always despised them, and now it has the votes to discard them. The majority thereby substitutes a rule by judges for the rule of law.

A

... This Court will surely face critical questions about how that test applies. Must a state law allow abortions when necessary to protect a woman's life and health? And if so, exactly when? How much risk to a woman's life can a State force her to incur, before the Fourteenth Amendment's protection of life kicks in? Suppose a patient with pulmonary hypertension has a 30-to-50 percent risk of dying with ongoing pregnancy; is that enough? And short of death, how much illness or injury can the State require her to accept, consistent with the Amendment's protection of liberty and equality? Further, the Court may face questions about the application of abortion regulations to medical care most people view as quite different from abortion. What about the morning-after pill? IUDs? In vitro fertilization? And how about the use of dilation and evacuation or medication for miscarriage management?

Finally, the majority's ruling today invites a host of questions about interstate conflicts. Can a State bar women from traveling to another State to obtain an abortion? Can a State prohibit advertising out-of-state abortions or helping women get to out-of-state providers? Can a State interfere with the mailing of drugs used for medication abortions? The Constitution protects travel and speech and interstate commerce, so today's ruling will give rise to a host of new constitutional questions. Far from removing the Court from the abortion issue, the majority puts the Court at the center of the coming "interjurisdictional abortion wars."

...

B

...

... In sum, the majority can point to neither legal nor factual developments in support of its decision. Nothing that has happened in this country or the world in recent decades undermines the core insight of *Roe* and *Casey*. It continues to be true that, within the constraints those decisions established, a woman, not the government, should choose whether she will bear the burdens of pregnancy, childbirth, and parenting.

... *Roe* and *Casey* continue to reflect, not diverge from, broad trends in American society. It is, of course, true that many Americans, including many women, opposed those decisions when issued and do so now as well. Yet the fact remains: *Roe* and *Casey* were the product of a profound and ongoing change in women's roles in the latter part of the 20th century. Only a dozen years before *Roe*, the Court described women as "the center of home and family life," with "special responsibilities" that precluded their full legal status under the Constitution. *Hoyt v. Florida*. By 1973, when the Court decided *Roe*, fundamental social change was underway regarding the place of women—and the law had begun to follow. See *Reed v. Reed*. By 1992, when the Court decided *Casey*, the traditional view of a woman's role as only a wife and mother was "no longer consistent with our understanding of the family, the individual, or the Constitution." Under that charter, *Casey* understood, women must take their place as full and equal citizens. And for that to happen, women must have control over their reproductive decisions. Nothing since *Casey*—no changed law, no changed fact—has undermined that promise.

C

... Today the majority refuses to face the facts. "The most striking feature of the [majority] is the absence of any serious discussion" of how its ruling will affect women. By characterizing *Casey*'s reliance arguments as "generalized assertions about the national psyche," it reveals how little it knows or cares about women's lives or about the suffering its decision will cause.

In *Casey*, the Court observed that for two decades individuals "have organized intimate relationships and made" significant life choices "in reliance on the availability of abortion in the event that contraception should fail." Over another 30 years, that reliance has solidified. For half a century now, in *Casey*'s words, "[t]he ability of women to participate equally in the economic and social life of the Nation has been facilitated by their ability to control their reproductive lives." Indeed, all women now of childbearing age have grown up expecting that they would be able to avail themselves of *Roe*'s and *Casey*'s protections.

The disruption of overturning *Roe* and *Casey* will therefore be profound. Abortion is a common medical procedure and a familiar experience in women's lives. About 18 percent of pregnancies in this country end in abortion, and about one quarter of American women will have an abortion before the age of 45. Those numbers reflect the predictable and life-changing effects of carrying a pregnancy, giving birth, and becoming a parent. As *Casey* understood, people today rely on their ability to control and time pregnancies when making countless life decisions: where to live, whether and how to invest in education or careers, how to allocate financial resources, and how to approach intimate and family relationships. Women may count on abortion access for when contraception fails. They may count on abortion access for when contraception cannot be used, for example, if they were raped. They may count on abortion for when something changes in the midst of a pregnancy, whether it involves family or financial circumstances, unanticipated medical complications, or heartbreaking fetal diagnoses. Taking away the right to abortion, as the majority does today, destroys all those individual plans and expectations. In so doing, it diminishes women's opportunities to participate fully and equally in the Nation's political, social, and economic life.

The majority's response to these obvious points exists far from the reality American women actually live. The majority proclaims that "'reproductive planning could take virtually immediate account of any sudden restoration of state authority to ban abortions.'" The facts are: 45 percent of pregnancies in the United States are unplanned. Even the most effective contraceptives fail, and effective contraceptives are not universally accessible. Not all sexual activity is consensual and not all contraceptive choices are made by the party who risks pregnancy. The Mississippi law at issue here, for example, has no exception for rape or incest, even for underage women. Finally, the majority ignores, as explained above, that some women decide to have an abortion because their circumstances change during a pregnancy. Human bodies care little for hopes and plans. Events can occur after conception, from unexpected medical risks to changes in family circumstances, which profoundly alter what it means to carry a pregnancy to term. In all these situations, women have expected that they will get to decide, perhaps in consultation with their families or doctors but free from state interference, whether to continue a pregnancy. For those who will now have to undergo that pregnancy, the loss of *Roe* and *Casey* could be disastrous.

That is especially so for women without money. ... In States that bar abortion, women of means will still be able to travel to obtain the services they need. It is women who cannot afford to do so who will suffer most. These are the women most likely to seek abortion care in the first place. Women living below the federal poverty line experience unintended pregnancies at rates five times higher than higher income women do, and nearly half of women who seek abortion care live in households below the poverty line. Even with *Roe*'s protection, these women face immense obstacles to raising the money needed to obtain abortion care early in their pregnancy. After today, in States where legal abortions are not available, they will lose any ability to obtain safe, legal abortion care. They will not have the money to make the trip necessary; or to obtain childcare for that time; or to take time off work. Many will endure the costs and risks of pregnancy and giving birth against their wishes. Others will turn in desperation to illegal and unsafe abortions. They may lose not just their freedom, but their lives.

...

The Court's failure to perceive the whole swath of expectations *Roe* and *Casey* created reflects an impoverished view of reliance. According to the majority, a reliance interest must be "very concrete," like those involving "property" or "contract." While many of this Court's cases addressing reliance have been in the "commercial context," none holds that interests must be analogous to commercial ones to warrant *stare decisis* protection. This unprecedented assertion is, at bottom, a radical claim to power. By disclaiming any need to consider broad swaths of individuals' interests, the Court arrogates to itself the authority to overrule established legal principles without even acknowledging the costs of its decisions for the individuals who live under the law, costs that this Court's *stare decisis* doctrine instructs us to privilege when deciding whether to change course.

... Closing our eyes to the suffering today's decision will impose will not make that suffering disappear. ...

... Rescinding an individual right in its entirety and conferring it on the State, an action the Court takes today for the first time in history, affects all who have relied on our constitutional system of government and its structure of individual liberties protected from state oversight. *Roe* and *Casey* have of course aroused controversy and provoked disagreement. But the right those decisions conferred and reaffirmed is part of society's understanding of constitutional law and of how the Court has defined the liberty and equality that women are entitled to claim.

After today, young women will come of age with fewer rights than their mothers and grandmothers had. The majority accomplishes that result without so much as considering how women have relied on the right to choose or what it means to take that right away. The majority's refusal even to consider the life-altering consequences of reversing *Roe* and *Casey* is a stunning indictment of its decision.

D

... Justice Jackson once called a decision he dissented from a "loaded weapon," ready to hand for improper uses. *Korematsu*. We fear that today's decision, departing from *stare decisis* for no legitimate reason, is its own loaded weapon. Weakening *stare decisis* threatens to upend bedrock legal doctrines, far beyond any single decision. Weakening *stare decisis* creates profound legal instability. And as *Casey* recognized, weakening *stare decisis* in a hotly contested case like this one calls into question this Court's commitment to legal principle. It makes the Court appear not restrained but aggressive, not modest but grasping. In all those ways, today's decision takes aim, we fear, at the rule of law.

III

"Power, not reason, is the new currency of this Court's decisionmaking." *Payne* (Marshall, J., dissenting). *Roe* has stood for fifty years. *Casey*, a precedent about precedent specifically confirming *Roe*, has stood for thirty. And the doctrine of *stare decisis*—a critical element of the rule of law—stands foursquare behind their continued existence. The right those decisions established and preserved is embedded in our constitutional law, both originating in and leading to other rights protecting bodily integrity, personal autonomy, and family relationships. The abortion right is also embedded in the lives of women—shaping their expectations, influencing their choices about relationships and work, supporting (as all reproductive rights do) their social and economic equality. Since the right's recognition (and affirmation), nothing has changed to support what the majority does today. Neither law nor facts nor attitudes have provided any new reasons to reach a different result than *Roe* and *Casey* did. All that has changed is this Court.

...

Earlier this Term, this Court signaled that Mississippi's stratagem would succeed. Texas was one of the fistful of States to have recently banned abortions after six weeks of pregnancy. It added to that "flagrantly unconstitutional" restriction an unprecedented scheme to "evade judicial scrutiny." *Whole Woman's Health* v. *Jackson*, (SOTOMAYOR, J., dissenting). And five Justices acceded to that cynical maneuver. They let Texas defy this Court's constitutional rulings, nullifying *Roe* and *Casey* ahead of schedule in the Nation's second largest State.

And now the other shoe drops, courtesy of that same five-person majority. (We believe that THE CHIEF JUSTICE's opinion is wrong too, but no one should think that there is not a large difference between upholding a 15-week ban on the grounds he does and allowing States to prohibit abortion from the time of conception.) Now a new and bare majority of this Court—acting at practically the first moment possible—overrules *Roe* and *Casey*. It converts a series of dissenting opinions expressing antipathy toward *Roe* and *Casey* into a decision greenlighting even total abortion bans. It eliminates a 50-year-old constitutional right that safeguards women's freedom and equal station. It breaches a core rule-of-law principle, designed to promote constancy in the law. In doing all of that, it places in jeopardy other rights, from contraception to same-sex intimacy and marriage. And finally, it undermines the Court's legitimacy.

...

... Quoting Justice Stewart, *Casey* explained that to do so—to reverse prior law "upon a ground no firmer than a change in [the Court's] membership"—would invite the view that "this institution is little different from the two political branches of the Government." No view, *Casey* thought, could do "more lasting injury to this Court and to the system of law which it is our abiding mission to serve." For overruling *Roe*, *Casey* concluded, the Court would pay a "terrible price."

The Justices who wrote those words—O'Connor, Kennedy, and Souter—they were judges of wisdom. They would not have won any contests for the kind of ideological purity some court watchers want Justices to deliver. But if there were awards for Justices who left this Court better than they found it? And who for that reason left this country better? And the rule of law stronger? Sign those Justices up.

They knew that "the legitimacy of the Court [is] earned over time." They also would have recognized that it can be destroyed much more quickly. They worked hard to avert that outcome in *Casey*. The American public, they thought, should never conclude that its constitutional protections hung by a thread—that a new majority, adhering to a new "doctrinal school," could "by dint of numbers" alone expunge their rights. It is hard—no, it is impossible—to conclude that anything else has happened here. One of us once said that "[i]t is not often in the law that so few have so quickly changed so much." S. Breyer, Breaking the Promise of *Brown*: The Resegregation of America's Schools 30 (2022). For all of us, in our time on this Court, that has never been more true than today. In overruling *Roe* and *Casey*, this Court betrays its guiding principles.

With sorrow—for this Court, but more, for the many millions of American women who have today lost a fundamental constitutional protection—we dissent.

Notes and Questions

1. *Why overrule* Roe? Why did the majority overrule *Roe* and *Casey*? What are the specific arguments that the majority used for overruling?
2. *Why not?* Why did the dissenters reject overruling *Roe*? Is it because they agree with it on all counts?
3. *Who* has the better argument on overruling, the majority or the dissent?
4. *The life of the mother.* What do each of the opinions say about the death of the mother as an exception to an abortion ban? Does the mother have a right to life under the 14th Amendment?
5. *Chief Justice Roberts* concurred in the judgment only. He thought the Court should uphold Mississippi's law while not overturning the whole abortion precedent, and said whatever the right is, it "should therefore extend far enough to ensure a reasonable opportunity to choose,

but need not extend any further—certainly not all the way to viability." Do you agree with him? Do you think he found a satisfactory middle ground for resolving the case?

6. *Justice Thomas.* Do you think Justice Thomas would overrule *Lawrence, Obergefell,* and *Griswold*? Why or why not? What are his problems with those cases? Do you think he would overrule *Loving v. Virginia,* the interracial marriage case? Do you think the current Court would overrule all these opinions in future cases?
7. *Potential life.* Is abortion different from contraception and LGBTQ sexual relations and marriage because only abortion involves a "potential life"? The majority and concurrences draw this line. Are you persuaded?
8. *Justice Kavanaugh.* Justice Kavanaugh states, "After today's decision, the nine Members of this Court will no longer decide the basic legality of pre-viability abortion for all 330 million Americans." Why does he say that the majority's decision only covers pre-viability abortions? What about post-viability abortions, particularly when the life of the mother is at risk? What do you think about his opining issues that are not yet decided, such as the right to travel and retroactive application of criminalization of an abortion?
9. *Stare decisis.* Should the abortion cases have been upheld because of stare decisis, as the dissent suggests, or does stare decisis support the majority's view that it was correct to overrule them, because they were wrongly decided cases?
10. *Rational basis.* Why did the majority choose a rational basis test for state laws regarding abortion? What laws could be upheld on a rational basis? Are there any abortion cases that would fail rational basis scrutiny? What test do the dissenters use instead of rational basis?
11. *State Laws.* What do you expect states to do about abortion rights, now that they have the power to set the limits they wish? What can you learn from Guttmacher's map of abortion law in the states, available at https://www.guttmacher.org/news-release/2022/abortion-after-roe-new-comprehensive-map-tracks-abortion-policies-and-statistics? What is your state's law on abortion? Do you agree with it? How do you react when you hear 26 states have banned or will ban abortion?
12. *Fourteenth Amendment.* Do you agree with the majority that abortion should be judged according to the principles of the time the amendment was added to the Constitution, or with the dissent that such a perspective completely ignores women's rights as the majority, because women were not persons at the time of the framing? The majority quickly rejected any argument that women's abortion rights were protected by the Equal Protection Clause. Why?
13. *Lochner.* Is *Roe* now a *Lochner* case, permanently dismissed for its constitutional errors?

3. The Right to Die

A different question from the preceding contraception and abortion cases is whether the right to die is protected by the Fourteenth Amendment. Is the right to die a privacy interest? A liberty interest? Is there a constitutionally protected right to refuse medical treatment? Is there a constitutionally protected right to refuse nutrition and hydration? Is a right to suicide, assisted suicide, euthanasia, or physician-assisted suicide in the Constitution?

a. Right to Refuse Medical Treatment

In *Cruzan v. Director, Missouri Department of Health*, 497 U.S. 261, 110 S.Ct. 2841 (1988), Nancy Cruzan was badly injured in a severe car accident from which she did not recover. She was in a permanent vegetative state. Her parents asked permission to discontinue her nutrition and hydration. The Court ruled that Missouri could place a clear and convincing evidence standard on proving that incompetent patients would refuse treatment. Chief Justice Rehnquist wrote the opinion, joined by White, O'Connor, Scalia, and Kennedy. Justices Brennan, Marshall, Blackmun, and Stevens dissented. Rehnquist wrote that the "principle that a competent person has a constitutionally protected liberty interest in refusing unwanted medical treatment may be inferred from our prior decisions." Although the Court "assume[d] that the United States Constitution would grant a competent person a constitutionally protected right to refuse lifesaving hydration and nutrition," Missouri was allowed to maintain a tough evidentiary standard, the clear and convincing evidence standard, because of its desire to protect and preserve life. Note that Rehnquist, a dissenter in *Roe*, identified the right of competent persons as a liberty interest, not a privacy interest.

Justice O'Connor's concurrence suggested that people appoint durable powers of attorney, or proxies, in advance, to make their medical judgments for them if they cannot. Justice Scalia's concurrence said courts have no business using their jurisprudence in this field because the Constitution has nothing to say about it. Suicide rights, he wrote, are not "known to the nine Justices of this Court any better than they are known to nine people picked at random from the Kansas City telephone directory."

Justice Brennan dissented that Cruzan had a "fundamental right to be free of unwanted artificial nutrition and hydration, which right is not outweighed by any interests of the State," and that Missouri had burdened that right. She had a right to "die with dignity." Justice Stevens dissented that the state must focus on Cruzan's best interests, and that the Court's decision "interferes with constitutional interests of the highest order" because it protected the state and not the dying individual.

Consider everything that you have learned about the protections of the Fourteenth Amendment. What does the amendment protect for competent patients? For patients who are incompetent? Why do you reach your conclusion? Is one Justice's argument more persuasive than another's? Do you have an alternative argument to suggest?

b. Right to Physician-Assisted Suicide

Nine years later, the Court faced an argument that laws against assisted suicide violated the Constitution. We've talked numerous times about the Due Process and Equal Protection Clauses of the Fourteenth Amendment. *Both* arguments were made in the right to die cases. Those invoking due process argued there was a constitutional right to die. Equal protection argued that patients were allowed to refuse lifesaving treatment but could not get assisted suicide. That was a different, unequal treatment that the clause did not justify.

The patients lost both their due process and their equal protection arguments. In *Washington v. Glucksberg*, 521 U.S. 702, 117 S.Ct. 2258 (1997), a unanimous Court held that Washington's assisted suicide ban did not violate the Fourteenth Amendment's Due Process Clause. The Court recognized the long history of assisted suicide laws, meaning that history and tradition supported Washington's statute. "[O]ur laws have consistently condemned, and continue to prohibit, assisting suicide." Voters had supported those statutes. Constitutional liberty did not support a right to die, and assisted suicide is different from the refusal of medical treatment.

Justice O'Connor concurred that patients had the ability to have their pain treated while dying. Justice Stevens concurred, noting that dying patients have a liberty interest in the manner of their death. Justice Breyer concurred that he would rather talk about a "right to die with dignity" than a right to physician-assisted suicide and noted that the law did not force patients to undergo pain as Justice O'Connor had noted.

The Court cited *Glucksberg* frequently in *Dobbs.* Can you figure out why?

In *Vacco v. Quill*, 521 U.S. 793, 117 S.Ct. 2293 (1997), the Court rejected an equal protection challenge. The challengers said it violated equal protection to allow some patients to refuse lifesaving treatment while others could not choose suicide. The Court rejected that argument. The Court endorsed the distinction between assisting suicide and lifesaving treatment.

Oregon was the first state to pass assisted suicide legislation. What standards would you want in place when a person decides to commit suicide? Draft a physician-assisted suicide law that appropriately respects the rights of all involved persons. Ten states and the District of Columbia now have assisted suicide laws. Is your state one of them? See States with Legal Physician-Assisted Suicide, ProCon.org, at https://euthanasia.procon.org/states-with-legal-physician-assisted-suicide/. Do the states on this website have laws that match the one you recommended? What does the Constitution say about states that pass assisted-suicide laws? Are there any constitutional limits on those laws?

A Look Ahead

The last two chapters covered the Fourteenth Amendment's rights cases. We now turn to the First Amendment. First, we will cover the protection of speech; assembly; and petition and then, the Religion Clauses.

Credit

Fig. 8.1: Adapted from: Oyez, "How the Justices Voted in the Slaughter-House Cases," https://www.oyez.org/cases/1850-1900/83us36. Copyright © 2022 by Oyez, Inc.

Nine

The First Amendment: Rights to Speech, Assembly, and Petition

Introduction

The First Amendment to the U.S. Constitution states, "Congress shall make no law respecting an establishment of religion, or prohibiting the free exercise thereof; or abridging the freedom of speech, or of the press; or the right of the people peaceably to assemble, and to petition the government for a redress of grievances." As you can see from the language, it contains several categories related to religion, speech, press, assembly, and petitioning the government. In this chapter, we will address the Free Speech Clause, the Right to Assembly Clause, and the Freedom of Petition Clause. The next chapter will cover the Religion Clauses.

We start with the right to freedom of speech. The Court has decided numerous cases explaining what speech is protected and when and how it is protected. It is worthwhile to review the levels of scrutiny chart in Chapter 6 before reading the cases in this chapter.

A. Free Speech

1. Right to Criticize the Government and Others

a. Speech Critical of the Government

The following case involves a man who was berating the government in a public space in front of a crowd with mixed reactions to his views. Can you figure out why the First Amendment protects the right to criticize the government? Why would that right be so important in the U.S. Constitution? Is there speech that people can be arrested for? What would that kind of speech look like? When does it violate the Constitution to punish people for their speech? Why did six Justices in the following 1951 case uphold the man's arrest? Why were there three dissenters? What does this case tell you about the types of speech that are highly valued by the First Amendment?

Feiner v. New York
SUPREME COURT OF THE UNITED STATES, 1951
340 U.S. 315, 71 S.Ct. 303

Mr. Chief Justice VINSON delivered the opinion of the Court.

Petitioner was convicted of the offense of disorderly conduct, a misdemeanor under the New York penal laws, in the Court of Special Sessions of the City of Syracuse and was sentenced to thirty days in the county penitentiary. …

On the evening of March 8, 1949, petitioner Irving Feiner was addressing an open-air meeting at the corner of South McBride and Harrison Streets in the City of Syracuse. At approximately 6:30 p.m., the police received a telephone complaint concerning the meeting, and two officers were detailed to investigate. One of these officers went to the scene immediately, the other arriving some twelve minutes later. They found a crowd of about seventy-five or eighty people, both Negro and white, filling the sidewalk and spreading out into the street. Petitioner, standing on a large wooden box on the sidewalk, was addressing the crowd through a loud-speaker system attached to an automobile. Although the purpose of his speech was to urge his listeners to attend a meeting to be held that night in the Syracuse Hotel, in its course he was making derogatory remarks concerning President Truman, the American Legion, the Mayor of Syracuse, and other local political officials. …

Because of the feeling that existed in the crowd both for and against the speaker, the officers finally 'stepped in to prevent it from resulting in a fight.' One of the officers approached the petitioner, not for the purpose of arresting him, but to get him to break up the crowd. He asked petitioner to get down off the box, but the latter refused to accede to his request and continued talking. The officer waited for a minute and then demanded that he cease talking. Although the officer had thus twice requested petitioner to stop over the course of several minutes, petitioner not only ignored him but continued talking. During all this time, the crowd was pressing closer around petitioner and the officer. Finally, the officer told petitioner he was under arrest and ordered him to get down from the box, reaching up to grab him. Petitioner stepped down, announcing over the microphone that 'the law has arrived, and I suppose they will take over now.' In all, the officer had asked petitioner to get down off the box three times over a space of four or five minutes. Petitioner had been speaking for over a half hour. …

We are well aware that the ordinary murmurings and objections of a hostile audience cannot be allowed to silence a speaker, and are also mindful of the possible danger of giving overzealous police officials complete discretion to break up otherwise lawful public meetings. But we are not faced here with such a situation. It is one thing to say that the police cannot be used as an instrument for the suppression of unpopular views, and another to say that, when as here the speaker passes the bounds of argument or persuasion and undertakes incitement to riot, they are powerless to prevent a breach of the peace. Nor in this case can we condemn the considered judgment of three New York courts approving the means which the police, faced with a crisis, used in the exercise of their power and duty to preserve peace and order. The findings of the state courts as to the existing situation and the imminence of greater disorder coupled with petitioner's deliberate defiance of the police officers convince us that we should not reverse this conviction in the name of free speech.

Mr. Justice FRANKFURTER concurs in the result.

Here, Feiner forced pedestrians to walk in the street by collecting a crowd on the public sidewalk, he attracted additional attention by using sound amplifiers, he indulged in name-calling, he told part of his audience that it should rise up in arms. In the crowd of 75 to 80 persons, there was angry muttering and pushing. Under these circumstances, and in order to prevent a disturbance of the peace, an officer asked Feiner to stop speaking. When he had twice ignored the request, Feiner was arrested. The trial judge concluded that 'the officers were fully justified in feeling that a situation was developing which could very, very easily result in a serious disorder.' His view was sustained by an intermediate appellate court and by a unanimous decision of the New York Court of Appeals. The estimate of a particular local situation thus comes here with the momentum of the weightiest judicial authority of New York.

It is true that breach-of-peace statutes, like most tools of government, may be misused. Enforcement of these statutes calls for public tolerance and intelligent police administration. These, in the long run, must give substance to whatever this Court may say about free speech. But the possibility of misuse is not alone a sufficient reason to deny New York the power here asserted or so limit it by constitutional construction as to deny its practical exercise.

Mr. Justice BLACK, dissenting.

The record before us convinces me that petitioner, a young college student, has been sentenced to the penitentiary for the unpopular views he expressed on matters of public interest while lawfully making a street-corner speech in Syracuse, New York. Today's decision, however, indicates that we must blind ourselves to this fact because the trial judge fully accepted the testimony of the prosecution witnesses on all important points. Many times in the past this Court has said that despite findings below, we will examine the evidence for ourselves to ascertain whether federally protected rights have been denied; otherwise review here would fail of its purpose in safeguarding constitutional guarantees. Even a partial abandonment of this rule marks a dark day for civil liberties in our Nation.

But still more has been lost today. Even accepting every 'finding of fact' below, I think this conviction makes a mockery of the free speech guarantees of the First and Fourteenth Amendments. ...

In my judgment, today's holding means that as a practical matter, minority speakers can be silenced in any city. Hereafter, despite the First and Fourteenth Amendments, the policeman's club can take heavy toll of a current administration's public critics. Criticism of public officials will be too dangerous for all but the most courageous.

Mr. Justice DOUGLAS, with whom Mr. Justice MINTON concurs, dissenting.

... A speaker may not, of course, incite a riot any more than he may incite a breach of the peace by the use of 'fighting words'. See Chaplinsky v. State of New Hampshire, 315 U.S. 568, 62 S.Ct. 766, 86 L.Ed. 1031. But this record shows no such extremes. It shows an unsympathetic audience and the threat of one man to haul the speaker from the stage. It is against that kind of threat that speakers need police protection. If they do not receive it and instead the police throw their weight on the side of those who would break up the meetings, the police become the new censors of speech. Police censorship has all the vices of the censorship from city halls which we have repeatedy struck down. ...

Notes and Questions

1. *The relevant facts.* What did the speaker say in this case? What did the police do? How do the facts influence the Court's analysis of the outcome? Do you agree with the Court's assessment of the facts?
2. *Drawing the line.* The Court did not accord absolute protection to this speech but rather assessed the right against the government's interest in peace and order. Chief Justice Vinson says "findings of the state courts as to the existing situation and the imminence of greater disorder coupled with petitioner's deliberate defiance of the police officers" meant the conviction could be upheld. Given the facts of the case, do you agree with where the Court drew the line?
3. *Justice Frankfurter.* Why did Justice Frankfurter write a concurrence? What analysis does he offer that is different from the majority?
4. *Justice Black.* Justice Black had a very strict view of the First Amendment, believing that "no law" means no law. Does that point come across in his dissent in this case? Do you agree with his conclusion that minority speakers may now be silenced legally?
5. *Justice Douglas.* Justice Douglas refers to a famous case, *Chaplinsky*, which is often cited in free speech cases because it states that the government may suppress "fighting words." Do you agree with him that there were no fighting words in this case? What does he mean by censorship?

b. Religious Speech

The following case, *Cantwell v. Connecticut,* was decided before *Feiner* and addresses a different type of speech—religious speech. Again, this is a case about speech that criticizes, but in this case, it is criticism of the Catholic Church by Jehovah's Witnesses. The Court frequently relies on *Cantwell* in its free speech cases. Can you explain why it is important? Unlike *Feiner, Cantwell* was unanimous. Why do you think all the Justices on the Court agreed that Cantwell's harsh speech was protected by the First Amendment? The author is Justice Owen Roberts, not the current Chief Justice John Roberts. You can find a list of all the Justices of the Court at https://www.supremecourt.gov/about/members_text.aspx.

Cantwell v. Connecticut
SUPREME COURT OF THE UNITED STATES, 1940
310 U.S. 206, 60 S.Ct. 900

Mr. Justice ROBERTS, delivered the opinion of the Court. [He was joined by Justices HUGHES, McREYNOLDS, STONE, BLACK, REED, FRANKFURTER, DOUGLAS and MURPHY.]

... On the day of their arrest the appellants were engaged in going singly from house to house on Cassius Street in New Haven. They were individually equipped with a bag containing books and pamphlets on religious subjects, a portable phonograph and a set of records, each of which, when played, introduced, and was a description of, one of the books. Each appellant asked the person who responded to his call for permission to play one of the records. If permission was granted he asked the person to buy the book described and, upon refusal, he solicited such contribution towards the publication of the pamphlets as the listener was willing to make. If a contribution was received a pamphlet was delivered upon condition that it would be read.

Cassius Street is in a thickly populated neighborhood, where about ninety per cent of the residents are Roman Catholics. A phonograph record, describing a book entitled 'Enemies', included an attack on the Catholic religion. None of the persons interviewed were members of Jehovah's Witnesses. ...

Cantwell's conduct, in the view of the court below, considered apart from the effect of his communication upon his hearers, did not amount to a breach of the peace. One may, however, be guilty of the offense if he commit acts or make statements likely to provoke violence and disturbance of good order, even though no such eventuality be intended. Decisions to this effect are many, but examination discloses that, in practically all, the provocative language which was held to amount to a breach of the peace consisted of profane, indecent, or abusive remarks directed to the person of the hearer. Resort to epithets or personal abuse is not in any proper sense communication of information or opinion safeguarded by the Constitution, and its punishment as a criminal act would raise no question under that instrument.

We find in the instant case no assault or threatening of bodily harm, no truculent bearing, no intentional discourtesy, no personal abuse. On the contrary, we find only an effort to persuade a willing listener to buy a book or to contribute money in the interest of what Cantwell, however misguided others may think him, conceived to be true religion.

In the realm of religious faith, and in that of political belief, sharp differences arise. In both fields the tenets of one man may seem the rankest error to his neighbor. To persuade others to his own point of view, the pleader, as we know, at times, resorts to exaggeration, to vilification of men who have been, or are, prominent in church or state, and even to false statement. But the people of this nation have ordained in the light of history, that, in spite of the probability of excesses and abuses, these liberties are, in the long view, essential to enlightened opinion and right conduct on the part of the citizens of a democracy. ...

Although the contents of the record not unnaturally aroused animosity, we think that, in the absence of a statute narrowly drawn to define and punish specific conduct as constituting a clear and present danger to a substantial interest of the State, the petitioner's communication, considered in the light of the constitutional guarantees, raised no such clear and present menace to public peace and order as to render him liable to conviction of the common law offense in question.

Notes and Questions

1. *Clear and present danger.* Note that Justice Roberts uses the language "clear and present danger to a substantial interest of the State" in his analysis. This is a standard that has been invoked in a number of free speech cases involving the threat of speech transforming into action as you will see in the *Brandenburg* decision later in the chapter. What would be such a clear and present danger? Why is the state allowed to punish clear and present dangers but not other speech?
2. *The facts.* What do you think of the Court's summary of the facts of this case: "We find in the instant case no assault or threatening of bodily harm, no truculent bearing, no intentional discourtesy, no personal abuse. On the contrary, we find only an effort to persuade a willing listener to buy a book or to contribute money in the interest of what Cantwell, however misguided others may think him, conceived to be true religion."
3. *Religion and speech.* What role does religion play in this speech case?

c. Symbolic Speech

The next case involves symbolic speech where an action communicates a message. Of course, not every action is protected by the Free Speech Clause. Is burning a flag speech? How do you know? Does a state law banning desecration of the United States flag violate the First Amendment? Is this a hard question or an easy one? Why did the Court rule 5–4 in the following case that laws prohibiting flag burning violate the First Amendment? Listen to the oral argument in the case, available at https://www.oyez.org/cases/1988/88-155. Do some Justices support the freedom of speech more than others? How did the Justices describe flag burning? As good protected speech or as something else? What is your opinion on which lawyer did a better job? Is burning a flag a criticism of government?

Can you figure out why the Justices voted as follows?

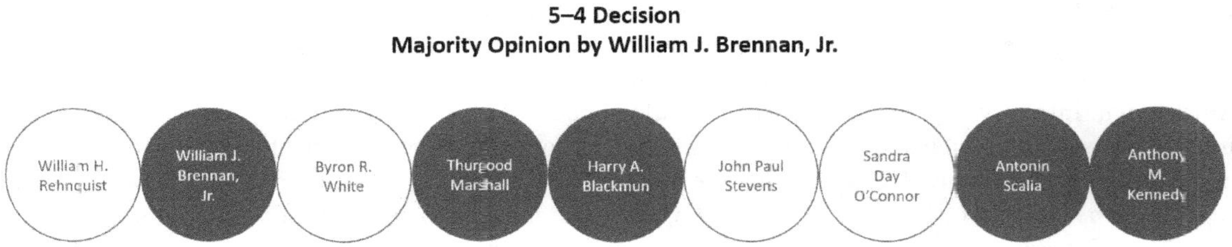

FIGURE 9.1 Texas v. Johnson, 491 US 397 (1989)

Texas v. Johnson
SUPREME COURT OF THE UNITED STATES, 1989
491 U.S. 397, 109 S.Ct. 2533

BRENNAN, J., delivered the opinion of the Court, in which MARSHALL, BLACKMUN, SCALIA, and KENNEDY, JJ., joined. KENNEDY, J., filed a concurring opinion. REHNQUIST, C.J., filed a dissenting opinion, in which WHITE and O'CONNOR, JJ., joined. STEVENS, J., filed a dissenting opinion.

After publicly burning an American flag as a means of political protest, Gregory Lee Johnson was convicted of desecrating a flag in violation of Texas law. This case presents the question whether his conviction is consistent with the First Amendment. We hold that it is not. ...

Johnson was convicted of flag desecration for burning the flag rather than for uttering insulting words. This fact somewhat complicates our consideration of his conviction under the First Amendment. We must first determine whether Johnson's burning of the flag constituted expressive conduct, permitting him to invoke the First Amendment in challenging his conviction. If his conduct was expressive, we next decide whether the State's regulation is related to the suppression of free expression. If the State's regulation is not related to expression, then the less stringent standard we announced in *United States v. O'Brien* for regulations of noncommunicative conduct controls. See *O'Brien, supra,* at 377, 88 S.Ct., at 1679. If it is, then we are outside of *O'Brien*'s test, and we must ask whether this interest justifies Johnson's conviction under a more demanding standard. A third possibility is that the State's asserted interest is simply not implicated on these facts, and in that event the interest drops out of the picture.

The First Amendment literally forbids the abridgment only of "speech," but we have long recognized that its protection does not end at the spoken or written word. While we have rejected "the view that an apparently limitless variety of conduct can be labeled 'speech' whenever the person engaging in the conduct intends thereby to express an idea," we have acknowledged that conduct may be "sufficiently imbued with elements of communication to fall within the scope of the First and Fourteenth Amendments."

In deciding whether particular conduct possesses sufficient communicative elements to bring the First Amendment into play, we have asked whether "[a]n intent to convey a particularized message was present, and [whether] the likelihood was great that the message would be understood by those who viewed it." ...

Especially pertinent to this case are our decisions recognizing the communicative nature of conduct relating to flags. Attaching a peace sign to the flag, *Spence, supra,* at 409–410, 94 S.Ct., at 2729–30; refusing to salute the flag, *Barnette,* 319 U.S., at 632, 63 S.Ct., at 1182; and displaying a red flag, *Stromberg v. California,* 283 U.S. 359, 368–369, 51 S.Ct. 532, 535–36, 75 L.Ed. 1117 (1931), we have held, all may find shelter under the First Amendment. ...

Johnson burned an American flag as part—indeed, as the culmination—of a political demonstration that coincided with the convening of the Republican Party and its renomination of Ronald Reagan for President. The expressive, overtly political nature of this conduct was both intentional and overwhelmingly apparent. At his trial, Johnson explained his reasons for burning the flag as follows: "The American Flag was burned as Ronald Reagan was being renominated as President. And a more powerful statement of symbolic speech, whether you agree with it or not, couldn't have been made at that time. It's quite a just position [juxtaposition]. We had new patriotism and no patriotism." In these circumstances, Johnson's burning of the flag was conduct "sufficiently imbued with elements of communication," to implicate the First Amendment.

The government generally has a freer hand in restricting expressive conduct than it has in restricting the written or spoken word. See *O'Brien,* 391 U.S. at 376–377, 88 S.Ct., at 1678–1679. ...

In order to decide whether *O'Brien*'s test applies here, therefore, we must decide whether Texas has asserted an interest in support of Johnson's conviction that is unrelated to the suppression of expression. If we find that an interest asserted by the State is simply not implicated on the facts before us, we need not ask whether *O'Brien*'s test applies. The State offers two separate interests to justify this conviction: preventing breaches of the peace and preserving the flag as a symbol of nationhood and national unity. We hold that the first interest is not implicated on this record and that the second is related to the suppression of expression.

Texas claims that its interest in preventing breaches of the peace justifies Johnson's conviction for flag desecration. However, no disturbance of the peace actually occurred or threatened to occur because of Johnson's burning of the flag. ...

The State also asserts an interest in preserving the flag as a symbol of nationhood and national unity. In *Spence,* we acknowledged that the government's interest in preserving the flag's special symbolic value "is directly related to expression in the context of activity" such as affixing a peace symbol to a flag. We are equally persuaded that this interest is related to expression in the case of Johnson's burning of the flag. ...

In short, nothing in our precedents suggests that a State may foster its own view of the flag by prohibiting expressive conduct relating to it. To bring its argument outside our precedents, Texas attempts to convince us that even if its interest in preserving the flag's symbolic role does not allow it to prohibit words or some expressive conduct critical of the flag, it does permit it to forbid the outright destruction of the flag. The State's argument cannot depend here on the distinction between written or spoken words and nonverbal conduct. That distinction, we have shown, is of no moment where the nonverbal conduct is expressive, as it is here, and where the regulation of that conduct is related to expression, as it is here. In addition, both *Barnette* and *Spence* involved expressive conduct, not only verbal communication, and both found that conduct protected. ...

We are fortified in today's conclusion by our conviction that forbidding criminal punishment for conduct such as Johnson's will not endanger the special role played by our flag or the feelings it inspires. To paraphrase Justice Holmes, we submit that nobody can suppose that this one gesture of an unknown man will change our Nation's attitude towards its flag. See *Abrams v. United States,* 250 U.S. 616, 628, 40 S.Ct. 17, 21, 63 L.Ed. 1173 (1919) (Holmes, J., dissenting). Indeed, Texas' argument that the burning of an American flag "'is an act having a high likelihood to cause a breach of the peace,'" Brief for Petitioner 31, quoting *Sutherland v. DeWulf,* 323 F.Supp. 740, 745 (SD Ill.1971) (citation omitted), and its statute's implicit assumption that physical mistreatment of the flag will lead to "serious offense," tend to confirm that the flag's special role is not in danger; if it were, no one would riot or take offense because a flag had been burned.

We are tempted to say, in fact, that the flag's deservedly cherished place in our community will be strengthened, not weakened, by our holding today. Our decision is a reaffirmation of the principles of freedom and inclusiveness that the flag best reflects, and of the conviction that our toleration of criticism such as Johnson's is a sign and source of our strength. Indeed, one of the proudest images of our flag, the one immortalized in our own national anthem, is of the bombardment it survived at Fort McHenry. It is the Nation's resilience, not its rigidity, that Texas sees reflected in the flag—and it is that resilience that we reassert today.

The way to preserve the flag's special role is not to punish those who feel differently about these matters. It is to persuade them that they are wrong. ...

Johnson was convicted for engaging in expressive conduct. The State's interest in preventing breaches of the peace does not support his conviction because Johnson's conduct did not threaten to disturb the peace. Nor does the State's interest in preserving the flag as a symbol of nationhood and national unity justify his criminal conviction for engaging in political expression.

Justice KENNEDY, concurring.

I write not to qualify the words Justice BRENNAN chooses so well, for he says with power all that is necessary to explain our ruling. I join his opinion without reservation, but with a keen sense that this case, like others before us from time to time, exacts its personal toll. This prompts me to add to our pages these few remarks. ...

With all respect to those views, I do not believe the Constitution gives us the right to rule as the dissenting Members of the Court urge, however painful this judgment is to announce. Though symbols often are what we ourselves make of them, the flag is constant in expressing beliefs Americans share, beliefs in law and peace and that freedom which sustains the human spirit. The case here today forces recognition of the costs to which those beliefs commit us. It is poignant but fundamental that the flag protects those who hold it in contempt. ...

Chief Justice REHNQUIST, with whom Justice WHITE and Justice O'CONNOR join, dissenting.

In holding this Texas statute unconstitutional, the Court ignores Justice Holmes' familiar aphorism that "a page of history is worth a volume of logic." *New York Trust Co. v. Eisner,* 256 U.S. 345, 349, 41 S.Ct. 506, 507, 65 L.Ed. 963 (1921). For more than 200 years, the American flag has occupied a unique position as the symbol of our Nation, a uniqueness that justifies a governmental prohibition against flag burning in the way respondent Johnson did here. ...

No other American symbol has been as universally honored as the flag. In 1931, Congress declared "The Star-Spangled Banner" to be our national anthem. In 1949, Congress declared June 14th to be Flag Day. In 1987, John Philip Sousa's "The Stars and Stripes Forever" was designated as the national march. Congress has also established "The Pledge of Allegiance to the Flag" and the manner of its deliverance. The flag has appeared as the principal symbol on approximately 33 United States postal stamps and in the design of at least 43 more, more times than any other symbol. ...

The American flag, then, throughout more than 200 years of our history, has come to be the visible symbol embodying our Nation. It does not represent the views of any particular political party, and it does not represent any particular political philosophy. The flag is not simply another "idea" or "point of view" competing for recognition in the marketplace of ideas. Millions and millions of Americans regard it with an almost mystical reverence regardless of what sort of social, political, or philosophical beliefs they may have. I cannot agree that the First Amendment invalidates the Act of Congress, and the laws of 48 of the 50 States, which make criminal the public burning of the flag. ...

But the Court today will have none of this. The uniquely deep awe and respect for our flag felt by virtually all of us are bundled off under the rubric of "designated symbols," that the First Amendment prohibits the government from "establishing." But the government has not "established" this feeling; 200 years of history have done that. The government is simply recognizing as a fact the profound regard for the American flag created by that history when it enacts statutes prohibiting the disrespectful public burning of the flag.

The Court concludes its opinion with a regrettably patronizing civics lecture, presumably addressed to the Members of both Houses of Congress, the members of the 48 state legislatures that enacted prohibitions against flag burning, and the troops fighting under that flag in Vietnam who objected to its being burned: "The way to preserve the flag's special role is not to punish those who feel differently about these matters. It is to persuade them that they are wrong." The Court's role as the final expositor of the Constitution is well established, but its role as a Platonic guardian admonishing those responsible to public opinion as if they were truant school-children has no similar place in our system of government. ...

Justice STEVENS, dissenting.

... The Court is therefore quite wrong in blandly asserting that respondent "was prosecuted for his expression of dissatisfaction with the policies of this country, expression situated at the core of our First Amendment values." Respondent was prosecuted because of the method he chose to express his dissatisfaction with those policies. Had he chosen to spray-paint—or perhaps convey with a motion picture projector—his message of dissatisfaction on the facade of the Lincoln Memorial, there would be no question about the power of the Government to prohibit his means of expression. The prohibition would be supported by the legitimate interest in preserving the quality of an important national asset. Though the asset at stake in this case is intangible, given its unique value, the same interest supports a prohibition on the desecration of the American flag.

The ideas of liberty and equality have been an irresistible force in motivating leaders like Patrick Henry, Susan B. Anthony, and Abraham Lincoln, schoolteachers like Nathan Hale and Booker T. Washington, the Philippine Scouts who fought at Bataan, and the soldiers who scaled the bluff at Omaha Beach. If those ideas are worth fighting for—and our history demonstrates that they are—it cannot be true that the flag that uniquely symbolizes their power is not itself worthy of protection from unnecessary desecration.

I respectfully dissent.

Notes and Questions

1. *Speech vs. action.* Why does Justice Brennan conclude burning a flag is speech and not pure action? Why is it speech critical of the government of the United States? Why does Justice Brennan think the speech is protected by the First Amendment?
2. *The scope of the right.* What do you think of Justice Brennan's statement, "The State offers two separate interests to justify this conviction: preventing breaches of the peace and preserving the flag as a symbol of nationhood and national unity. We hold that the first interest is not implicated on this record and that the second is related to the suppression of expression"? He is not envisioning an absolute right to burn a flag, which is a quintessential way to express criticism of the government. Why?
3. *Justice Kennedy.* Why did Justice Kennedy concur even though he agreed completely with Justice Brennan's opinion?

4. *History vs. logic.* Justice Rehnquist invokes Justice Holmes's statement that "a page of history is worth a volume of logic." What is the argument of history about this case? What is the conclusion of logic? What sense do you make of Rehnquist's history that "For more than 200 years, the American flag has occupied a unique position as the symbol of our Nation, a uniqueness that justifies a governmental prohibition against flag burning in the way respondent Johnson did here." Is the state justified in prohibiting flag burning because of that history?
5. *Justice Stevens.* What do you make of Justice Stevens's dissent that "it cannot be true that the flag that uniquely symbolizes their power is not itself worthy of protection from unnecessary desecration." Do you agree or disagree with him?
6. *Most and least persuasive?* Which Justice's opinion did you like the most? The least?

We have learned that the Court has distinguished what is speech and how much protection it is accorded in certain circumstances. In the next section, we examine whether hate speech should be protected by the First Amendment.

2. Hate or Offensive Speech

a. Government Regulation of Hate Speech

In the following case, teenagers burned a cross on a Black family's lawn. Police prosecuted them under a hate speech law that penalized displaying symbols that "arouse anger, alarm or resentment in others on the basis of race, color, creed, religion or gender." The Court unanimously ruled that the statute was unconstitutional. Is that surprising, given how negative it is to burn a cross on a family's lawn? Is burning a cross like burning a flag and, therefore, protected speech?

Read the oral argument at https://www.oyez.org/cases/1991/90-7675. Can you tell from the argument that the opinion will be unanimous? Did the city's lawyer give you any reasons to think the city should win? Why did Justice Blackmun talk so much to the city's lawyer about the City of St. Paul? Do you think this video, Quimbee, *R.A.V. v. City of St. Paul*, Sept. 21, 2000, at https://www.youtube.com/watch?v=elaio3D0cXY, captures the meaning of the case?

R.A.V. v. City of St. Paul, Minnesota
SUPREME COURT OF THE UNITED STATES, 1992
505 U.S. 377, 112 S.Ct. 2538

SCALIA, J., delivered the opinion of the Court, in which REHNQUIST, C.J., and KENNEDY, SOUTER, and THOMAS, JJ., joined. WHITE, J., filed an opinion concurring in the judgment, in which BLACKMUN and O'CONNOR, JJ., joined, and in which STEVENS, J., joined except as to Part I–A. BLACKMUN, J., filed an opinion concurring in the judgment. STEVENS, J., filed an opinion concurring in the judgment, in Part I of which WHITE and BLACKMUN, JJ., joined.

In the predawn hours of June 21, 1990, petitioner and several other teenagers allegedly assembled a crudely made cross by taping together broken chair legs. They then allegedly burned the cross inside the fenced yard of a black family that lived across the street from the house where petitioner was staying. Although this conduct could have been punished under any of a number of laws, one of the two provisions under which respondent city of St. Paul chose to charge petitioner (then a juvenile) was the St. Paul Bias–Motivated

Crime Ordinance, St. Paul, Minn., Legis.Code § 292.02 (1990), which provides:

> "Whoever places on public or private property a symbol, object, appellation, characterization or graffiti, including, but not limited to, a burning cross or Nazi swastika, which one knows or has reasonable grounds to know arouses anger, alarm or resentment in others on the basis of race, color, creed, religion or gender commits disorderly conduct and shall be guilty of a misdemeanor."

Petitioner moved to dismiss this count on the ground that the St. Paul ordinance was substantially overbroad and impermissibly content based and therefore facially invalid under the First Amendment. ...

I

... The First Amendment generally prevents government from proscribing speech, see, *e.g., Cantwell v. Connecticut,* 310 U.S. 296, 309–311, 60 S.Ct. 900, 905–906, 84 L.Ed. 1213 (1940), or even expressive conduct, see, *e.g., Texas v. Johnson,* 491 U.S. 397, 406, 109 S.Ct. 2533, 2540, 105 L.Ed.2d 342 (1989), because of disapproval of the ideas expressed. Content-based regulations are presumptively invalid. *Simon & Schuster, Inc. v. Members of N.Y. State Crime Victims Bd.,* 502 U.S. 105, 115, 112 S.Ct. 501, 508, 116 L.Ed.2d 476 (1991) *id.,* at 124, 112 S.Ct., at 512–513 (KENNEDY, J., concurring in judgment); *Consolidated Edison Co. of N.Y. v. Public Serv. Comm'n of N.Y.,* 447 U.S. 530, 536, 100 S.Ct. 2326, 2332–2333, 65 L.Ed.2d 319 (1980); *Police Dept. of Chicago v. Mosley,* 408 U.S. 92, 95, 92 S.Ct. 2286, 2289–2290, 33 L.Ed.2d 212 (1972). From 1791 to the present, however, our society, like other free but civilized societies, has permitted restrictions upon the content of speech in a few limited areas, which are "of such slight social value as a step to truth that any benefit that may be derived from them is clearly outweighed by the social interest in order and morality." *Chaplinsky, supra,* 315 U.S., at 572, 62 S.Ct. at 762. We have recognized that "the freedom of speech" referred to by the First Amendment does not include a freedom to disregard these traditional limitations. See, *e.g., Roth v. United States,* 354 U.S. 476, 77 S.Ct. 1304, 1 L.Ed.2d 1498 (1957) (obscenity); *Beauharnais v. Illinois,* 343 U.S. 250, 72 S.Ct. 725, 96 L.Ed. 919 (1952) (defamation); *Chaplinsky v. New Hampshire, supra* ("'fighting' words"); see generally *Simon & Schuster, supra,* 502 U.S., at 124, 112 S.Ct., at 513–514 (KENNEDY, J., concurring in judgment). Our decisions since the 1960's have narrowed the scope of the traditional categorical exceptions for defamation, see *New York Times Co. v. Sullivan,* 376 U.S. 254, 84 S.Ct. 710, 11 L.Ed.2d 686 (1964); *Gertz v. Robert Welch, Inc.,* 418 U.S. 323, 94 S.Ct. 2997, 41 L.Ed.2d 789 (1974); see generally *Milkovich v. Lorain Journal Co.,* 497 U.S. 1, 13–17, 110 S.Ct. 2695, 2702–2705, 111 L.Ed.2d 1 (1990), and for obscenity, see *Miller v. California,* 413 U.S. 15, 93 S.Ct. 2607, 37 L.Ed.2d 419 (1973), but a limited categorical approach has remained an important part of our First Amendment jurisprudence.

We have sometimes said that these categories of expression are "not within the area of constitutionally protected speech," or that the "protection of the First Amendment does not extend" to them. Such statements must be taken in context, however, and are no more literally true than is the occasionally repeated shorthand characterizing obscenity "as not being speech at all." What they mean is that these areas of speech can, consistently with the First Amendment, be regulated *because of their constitutionally proscribable content* (obscenity, defamation, etc.)—not that they are categories of speech entirely invisible to the Constitution, so that they may be made the vehicles for content discrimination unrelated to their distinctively proscribable content. Thus, the government may proscribe libel; but it may not make the further content discrimination of proscribing *only* libel critical of the government. We recently acknowledged this distinction in *Ferber,* 458 U.S., at 763, 102 S.Ct., at 3357–3358, where, in upholding New York's child pornography law, we expressly recognized that there was no "question here of censoring a particular literary theme. ..." See also *id.,* at 775, 102 S.Ct., at 3364 (O'CONNOR, J., concurring) ("As drafted, New York's statute does not attempt to suppress the communication of particular ideas").

Our cases surely do not establish the proposition that the First Amendment imposes no obstacle whatsoever to regulation of particular instances of such proscribable expression, so that the government "may regulate [them] freely." ...

The concurrences describe us as setting forth a new First Amendment principle that prohibition of constitutionally proscribable speech cannot be "underinclusiv[e]," *post,* at 2553 (WHITE, J., concurring in judgment)—a First Amendment "absolutism" whereby "[w]ithin a particular 'proscribable' category of expression, ... a government must either proscribe *all* speech or no speech at all," *post,* at 2562 (STEVENS, J., concurring in judgment). That easy target is of the concurrences' own invention. In our view, the First Amendment imposes not an "underinclusiveness" limitation but a "content discrimination" limitation upon a State's prohibition of proscribable speech. There is no problem whatever, for example, with a State's prohibiting obscenity (and other forms of proscribable expression) only in certain media or markets, for although that prohibition would be "underinclusive," it would not discriminate on the basis of content.

Even the prohibition against content discrimination that we assert the First Amendment requires is not absolute. It applies differently in the context of proscribable speech than in the area of fully protected speech. The rationale of the general prohibition, after all, is that content discrimination "raises the specter that the Government may effectively drive certain ideas or viewpoints from the marketplace." But content discrimination among various instances of a class of proscribable speech often does not pose this threat. ...

II

Applying these principles to the St. Paul ordinance, we conclude that, even as narrowly construed by the Minnesota Supreme Court, the ordinance is facially unconstitutional. Although the phrase in the ordinance, "arouses anger, alarm or resentment in others," has been limited by the Minnesota Supreme Court's construction to reach only those symbols or displays that amount to "fighting words," the remaining, unmodified terms make clear that the ordinance applies only to "fighting words" that insult, or provoke violence, "on the basis of race, color, creed, religion or gender." Displays containing abusive invective, no matter how vicious or severe, are permissible unless they are addressed to one of the specified disfavored topics. Those who wish to use "fighting words" in connection with other ideas—to express hostility, for example, on the basis of political affiliation, union membership, or homosexuality—are not covered. The First Amendment does not permit St. Paul to impose special prohibitions on those speakers who express views on disfavored subjects.

In its practical operation, moreover, the ordinance goes even beyond mere content discrimination, to actual viewpoint discrimination. Displays containing some words—odious racial epithets, for example—would be prohibited to proponents of all views. But "fighting words" that do not themselves invoke race, color, creed, religion, or gender—aspersions upon a person's mother, for example—would seemingly be usable *ad libitum* in the placards of those arguing *in favor* of racial, color, etc., tolerance and equality, but could not be used by those speakers' opponents. One could hold up a sign saying, for example, that all "anti-Catholic bigots" are misbegotten; but not that all "papists" are, for that would insult and provoke violence "on the basis of religion." St. Paul has no such authority to license one side of a debate to fight freestyle, while requiring the other to follow Marquis of Queensberry rules.

What we have here, it must be emphasized, is not a prohibition of fighting words that are directed at certain persons or groups (which would be *facially* valid if it met the requirements of the Equal Protection Clause); but rather, a prohibition of fighting words that contain (as the Minnesota Supreme Court repeatedly emphasized) messages of "bias-motivated" hatred and in particular, as applied to this case, messages "based on virulent notions of racial supremacy." One must wholeheartedly agree with the Minnesota Supreme Court that "[i]t is the responsibility, even the obligation, of diverse communities to confront such notions in whatever form they appear," but the manner of that confrontation cannot consist of selective limitations upon speech. St. Paul's brief asserts that a general "fighting words" law would not meet the city's needs because only a content-specific measure can communicate to minority groups that the "group hatred" aspect of such speech "is not condoned by the majority." The point of the First Amendment is that majority preferences must be expressed in some fashion other than silencing speech on the basis of its content. ...

The content-based discrimination reflected in the St. Paul ordinance comes within neither any of the specific exceptions to the First Amendment prohibition we discussed earlier nor a more general exception for content discrimination that does not threaten censorship of ideas. It assuredly does not fall within the exception for content discrimination based on the very reasons why the particular class of speech at issue (here, fighting words) is proscribable. As explained earlier, the reason why fighting words are categorically excluded from the protection of the First Amendment is not that their content communicates any particular idea, but that their content embodies a particularly intolerable (and socially unnecessary) *mode* of expressing *whatever* idea the speaker wishes to convey. St. Paul has not singled out an especially offensive mode of expression—it has not, for example, selected for prohibition only those fighting words that communicate ideas in a threatening (as opposed to a merely obnoxious) manner. Rather, it has proscribed fighting words of whatever manner that communicate messages of racial, gender, or religious intolerance. Selectivity of this sort creates the possibility that the city is seeking to handicap the expression of particular ideas. That possibility would alone be enough to render the ordinance presumptively invalid, but St. Paul's comments and concessions in this case elevate the possibility to a certainty. ...

The dispositive question in this case, therefore, is whether content discrimination is reasonably necessary to achieve St. Paul's compelling interests; it plainly is not. An ordinance not limited to the favored topics, for example, would have precisely the same beneficial effect. In fact the only interest distinctively served by the content limitation is that of displaying the city council's special hostility towards the particular biases thus singled out. That is precisely what the First Amendment forbids. The politicians of St. Paul are entitled to express that hostility—but not through the means of imposing unique limitations upon speakers who (however benightedly) disagree.

Let there be no mistake about our belief that burning a cross in someone's front yard is reprehensible. But St. Paul has sufficient means at its disposal to prevent such behavior without adding the First Amendment to the fire. ...

Justice WHITE, with whom Justice BLACKMUN and Justice O'CONNOR join, and with whom Justice STEVENS joins except as to Part I–A, concurring in the judgment.

I agree with the majority that the judgment of the Minnesota Supreme Court should be reversed. However, our agreement ends there. ...

But in the present case, the majority casts aside long-established First Amendment doctrine without the benefit of briefing and adopts an untried theory. This is hardly a judicious way of proceeding, and the Court's reasoning in reaching its result is transparently wrong.

IA

... Today, however, the Court announces that earlier Courts did not mean their repeated statements that certain categories of expression are "not within the area of constitutionally protected speech." The present Court submits that such clear statements "must be taken in context" and are not "literally true." ...

In its decision today, the Court points to "[n]othing ... in this Court's precedents warrant[ing] disregard of this longstanding tradition." Nevertheless, the majority holds that the First Amendment protects those narrow categories of expression long held to be undeserving of First Amendment protection—at least to the extent that lawmakers may not regulate some fighting words more strictly than others because of their content. The Court announces that such content-based distinctions violate the First Amendment because "[t]he government may not regulate use based on hostility—or favoritism—towards the underlying message expressed." Should the government want to criminalize certain fighting words, the Court now requires it to criminalize all fighting words.

To borrow a phrase: "Such a simplistic, all-or-nothing-at-all approach to First Amendment protection is at odds with common sense and with our jurisprudence as well." It is inconsistent to hold that the government may proscribe an entire category of speech because the content of that speech is evil, *Ferber, supra,* 458 U.S., at 763–764, 102 S.Ct., at 3358–3359; but that the government may not treat a subset of that category differently without violating the First Amendment; the content of the subset is by definition worthless and undeserving of constitutional protection.

IB

In a second break with precedent, the Court refuses to sustain the ordinance even though it would survive under the strict scrutiny applicable to other protected expression. Assuming, *arguendo,* that the St. Paul ordinance is a content-based regulation of protected expression, it nevertheless would pass First Amendment review under settled law upon a showing that the regulation "'is necessary to serve a compelling state interest and is narrowly drawn to achieve that end.'" ...

As with its rejection of the Court's categorical analysis, the majority offers no reasoned basis for discarding our firmly established strict scrutiny analysis at this time.

IC

... As I see it, the Court's theory does not work and will do nothing more than confuse the law. Its selection of this case to rewrite First Amendment law is particularly inexplicable, because the whole problem could have been avoided by deciding this case under settled First Amendment principles.

II

Although I disagree with the Court's analysis, I do agree with its conclusion: The St. Paul ordinance is unconstitutional. However, I would decide the case on overbreadth grounds. ...

The mere fact that expressive activity causes hurt feelings, offense, or resentment does not render the expression unprotected.

In the First Amendment context, "[c]riminal statutes must be scrutinized with particular care; those that make unlawful a substantial amount of constitutionally protected conduct may be held facially invalid even if they also have legitimate application." The St. Paul antibias ordinance is such a law. Although the ordinance reaches conduct that is unprotected, it also makes criminal expressive conduct that causes only hurt feelings, offense, or resentment, and is protected by the First Amendment. The ordinance is therefore fatally overbroad and invalid on its face.

III

Today, the Court has disregarded two established principles of First Amendment law without providing a coherent replacement theory. Its decision is an arid, doctrinaire interpretation, driven by the frequently irresistible impulse of judges to tinker with the First Amendment. The decision is mischievous at best and will surely confuse the lower courts. I join the judgment, but not the folly of the opinion.

Justice BLACKMUN, concurring in the judgment.

... I see no First Amendment values that are compromised by a law that prohibits hoodlums from driving minorities out of their homes by burning crosses on their lawns, but I see great harm in preventing the people of Saint Paul from specifically punishing the race-based fighting words that so prejudice their community.

I concur in the judgment, however, because I agree with Justice WHITE that this particular ordinance reaches beyond fighting words to speech protected by the First Amendment.

Justice STEVENS, with whom Justice WHITE and Justice BLACKMUN join as to Part I, concurring in the judgment.

... Thus, while I agree that the St. Paul ordinance is unconstitutionally overbroad for the reasons stated in Part II of Justice WHITE's opinion, I write separately to suggest how the allure of absolute principles has skewed the analysis of both the majority and Justice WHITE's opinions.

I

... Drawing on broadly worded dicta, the Court establishes a near-absolute ban on content-based regulations of expression and holds that the First Amendment prohibits the regulation of fighting words by subject matter. Thus, while the Court rejects the "all-or-nothing-at-all" nature of the categorical approach, it promptly embraces an absolutism of its own: Within a particular "proscribable" category of expression, the Court holds, a government must either proscribe *all* speech or no speech at all. This aspect of the Court's ruling fundamentally misunderstands the role and constitutional status of content-based regulations on speech, conflicts with the very nature of First Amendment jurisprudence, and disrupts well-settled principles of First Amendment law. ...

Disregarding this vast body of case law, the Court today goes beyond even the overstatement in *Mosley* and applies the prohibition on content-based regulation to speech that the Court had until today considered wholly "unprotected" by the First Amendment—namely, fighting words. This new absolutism in the prohibition of content-based regulations severely contorts the fabric of settled First Amendment law. ...

In sum, the central premise of the Court's ruling—that "[c]ontent-based regulations are presumptively invalid"—has simplistic appeal, but lacks support in our First Amendment jurisprudence. To make matters worse, the Court today extends this overstated claim to reach categories of hitherto unprotected speech and, in doing so, wreaks havoc in an area of settled law. Finally, although the Court recognizes exceptions to its new principle, those exceptions undermine its very conclusion that the St. Paul ordinance is unconstitutional. Stated directly, the majority's position cannot withstand scrutiny.

II

Although I agree with much of Justice WHITE's analysis, I do not join Part I–A of his opinion because I have reservations about the "categorical approach" to the First Amendment. These concerns, which I have noted on other occasions, see, *e.g., New York v. Ferber,* 458 U.S. 747, 778, 102 S.Ct. 3348, 3365–3366, 73 L.Ed.2d 1113 (1982) (opinion concurring in judgment), lead me to find Justice WHITE's response to the Court's analysis unsatisfying. ...

This evolution, I believe, indicates that the categorical approach is unworkable and the quest for absolute categories of "protected" and "unprotected" speech ultimately futile. My analysis of the faults and limits of this approach persuades me that the categorical approach presented in Part I–A of Justice WHITE's opinion is not an adequate response to the novel "underbreadth" analysis the Court sets forth today.

III

As the foregoing suggests, I disagree with both the Court's and part of Justice WHITE's analysis of the constitutionality of the St. Paul ordinance. Unlike the Court, I do not believe that all content-based regulations are equally infirm and presumptively invalid; unlike Justice WHITE, I do not believe that fighting words are wholly unprotected by the First Amendment. To the contrary, I believe our decisions establish a more complex and subtle analysis, one that considers the content and context of the regulated speech, and the nature and scope of the restriction on speech. Applying this analysis and assuming, *arguendo,* (as the Court does) that the St. Paul ordinance is *not* overbroad, I conclude that such a selective, subject-matter regulation on proscribable speech is constitutional. ...

In sum, the St. Paul ordinance (as construed by the Court) regulates expressive activity that is wholly proscribable and does so not on the basis of viewpoint, but rather in recognition of the different harms caused by such activity. Taken together, these several considerations persuade me that the St. Paul ordinance is not an unconstitutional content-based regulation of speech. Thus, were the ordinance not overbroad, I would vote to uphold it.

Notes and Questions

1. *The tests.* There is a majority opinion and three concurrences. Draw a diagram showing which Justices joined which side. What are the different First Amendment tests that the Justices propose? Identify each one of them. Why do they favor the different tests?
2. *The majority's characterization of the act.* What does Justice Scalia, writing for the majority, say the cross burning is? Is it like flag burning? Is it speech or conduct or expressive conduct and what consequences attach to that decision?
3. *Hate speech.* What does this case say about regulating hate speech? Does the Court leave an opening to regulate it?

b. Offensive Trademarks

Does *RAV*'s analysis of a hate speech law help you decide the outcome in the *Matal* case? *Matal* involved a challenge to a clause of a trademark law, which prohibited trademarks that disparage members of a racial or ethnic group. The case involved a singing group named the Slants. Why would this Disparagement Clause violate the First Amendment? Read the oral argument, available at https://www.oyez.org/cases/2016/15-1293. Who does the best job explaining what the First Amendment protects? Does not protect? Does this video, US Law Essentials, *Matal v. Tam*: Free Speech and

Offensive Trademarks, Jul. 11, 2017, at https://www.youtube.com/watch?v=1zCqbJf6qOU, give you a good sense of the Court's holding in *Matal*? Why are the Slants protected?

Matal v. Tam

SUPREME COURT OF THE UNITED STATES, 2017

582 U.S. ___, 137 S.Ct. 1744

ALITO, J., announced the judgment of the Court and delivered the opinion of the Court with respect to Parts I, II, and III–A, in which ROBERTS, C.J., and KENNEDY, GINSBURG, BREYER, SOTOMAYOR, and KAGAN, JJ., joined, and in which THOMAS, J., joined except for Part II, and an opinion with respect to Parts III–B, III–C, and IV, in which ROBERTS, C.J., and THOMAS and BREYER, JJ., joined. KENNEDY, J., filed an opinion concurring in part and concurring in the judgment, in which GINSBURG, SOTOMAYOR, and KAGAN, JJ., joined. THOMAS, J., filed an opinion concurring in part and concurring in the judgment. GORSUCH, J., took no part in the consideration or decision of the case.

This case concerns a dance-rock band's application for federal trademark registration of the band's name, "The Slants." "Slants" is a derogatory term for persons of Asian descent, and members of the band are Asian–Americans. But the band members believe that by taking that slur as the name of their group, they will help to "reclaim" the term and drain its denigrating force.

The Patent and Trademark Office (PTO) denied the application based on a provision of federal law prohibiting the registration of trademarks that may "disparage ... or bring ... into contemp[t] or disrepute" any "persons, living or dead." We now hold that this provision violates the Free Speech Clause of the First Amendment. It offends a bedrock First Amendment principle: Speech may not be banned on the ground that it expresses ideas that offend. ...

II

Before reaching the question whether the disparagement clause violates the First Amendment, we consider Tam's argument that the clause does not reach marks that disparage racial or ethnic groups. The clause prohibits the registration of marks that disparage "persons," and Tam claims that the term "persons" "includes only natural and juristic persons," not "non-juristic entities such as racial and ethnic groups."

Tam never raised this argument before the PTO or the Federal Circuit, and we declined to grant certiorari on this question when Tam asked us to do so. Normally, that would be the end of the matter in this Court. ...

Even if resort to legislative history and early enforcement practice were appropriate, we would find Tam's arguments unconvincing. ...

III

Because the disparagement clause applies to marks that disparage the members of a racial or ethnic group, we must decide whether the clause violates the Free Speech Clause of the First Amendment. And at the outset, we must consider three arguments that would either eliminate any First Amendment protection or result in highly permissive rational-basis review. Specifically, the Government contends (1) that trademarks are government speech, not private speech, (2) that trademarks are a form of government subsidy, and (3) that the constitutionality of the disparagement clause should be tested under a new "government-program" doctrine. We address each of these arguments below.

A

... Trademarks are private, not government, speech.

B

... Cases like *Rust* and *Finley* are not instructive in analyzing the constitutionality of restrictions on speech imposed in connection with such services.

C

... [T]he disparagement clause cannot be saved by analyzing it as a type of government program in which some content- and speaker-based restrictions are permitted.

IV

Having concluded that the disparagement clause cannot be sustained under our government-speech or subsidy cases or under the Government's proposed "government-program" doctrine, we must confront a dispute between the parties on the question whether trademarks are commercial speech and are thus subject to the relaxed scrutiny outlined in *Central Hudson Gas & Elec. Corp. v. Public Serv. Comm'n of N. Y.,* 447 U.S. 557, 100 S.Ct. 2343, 65 L.Ed.2d 341 (1980). ...

We need not resolve this debate between the parties because the disparagement clause cannot withstand even *Central Hudson* review. Under *Central Hudson,* a restriction of speech must serve "a substantial interest," and it must be "narrowly drawn." This means, among other things, that "[t]he regulatory technique may extend only as far as the interest it serves." The disparagement clause fails this requirement.

It is claimed that the disparagement clause serves two interests. The first is phrased in a variety of ways in the briefs. Echoing language in one of the opinions below, the Government asserts an interest in preventing "'underrepresented groups'" from being "'bombarded with demeaning messages in commercial advertising.'" An *amicus* supporting the Government refers to "encouraging racial tolerance and protecting the privacy and welfare of individuals." But no matter how the point is phrased, its unmistakable thrust is this: The Government has an interest in preventing speech expressing ideas that offend. And, as we have explained, that idea strikes at the heart of the First Amendment. Speech that demeans on the basis of race, ethnicity, gender, religion, age, disability, or any other similar ground is hateful; but the proudest boast of our free speech jurisprudence is that we protect the freedom to express "the thought that we hate."

The second interest asserted is protecting the orderly flow of commerce. Commerce, we are told, is disrupted by trademarks that "involv[e] disparagement of race, gender, ethnicity, national origin, religion, sexual orientation, and similar demographic classification." Such trademarks are analogized to discriminatory conduct, which has been recognized to have an adverse effect on commerce.

A simple answer to this argument is that the disparagement clause is not "narrowly drawn" to drive out trademarks that support invidious discrimination. The clause reaches any trademark that disparages *any person, group, or institution.* It applies to trademarks like the following: "Down with racists," "Down with sexists," "Down with homophobes." It is not an anti-discrimination clause; it is a happy-talk clause. In this way, it goes much further than is necessary to serve the interest asserted.

The clause is far too broad in other ways as well. The clause protects every person living or dead as well as every institution. Is it conceivable that commerce would be disrupted by a trademark saying: "James Buchanan was a disastrous president" or "Slavery is an evil institution"?

There is also a deeper problem with the argument that commercial speech may be cleansed of any expression likely to cause offense. The commercial market is well stocked with merchandise that disparages prominent figures and groups, and the line between commercial and non-commercial speech is not always clear, as this case illustrates. If affixing the commercial label permits the suppression of any speech that may lead to political or social "volatility," free speech would be endangered.

* * *

For these reasons, we hold that the disparagement clause violates the Free Speech Clause of the First Amendment. The judgment of the Federal Circuit is affirmed.

Justice KENNEDY, with whom Justice GINSBURG, Justice SOTOMAYOR, and Justice KAGAN join, concurring in part and concurring in the judgment.

... As the Court is correct to hold, § 1052(a) constitutes viewpoint discrimination—a form of speech suppression so potent that it must be subject to rigorous constitutional scrutiny. The Government's action and the statute on which it is based cannot survive this scrutiny.

The Court is correct in its judgment, and I join Parts I, II, and III–A of its opinion. This separate writing explains in greater detail why the First Amendment's protections against viewpoint discrimination apply to the trademark here. It submits further that the viewpoint discrimination rationale renders unnecessary any extended treatment of other questions raised by the parties. ...

The danger of viewpoint discrimination is that the government is attempting to remove certain ideas or perspectives from a broader debate. That danger is all the greater if the ideas or perspectives are ones a particular audience might think offensive, at least at first hearing. An initial reaction may prompt further reflection, leading to a more reasoned, more tolerant position. ...

... [O]ur cases are clear that viewpoint discrimination is not permitted where, as here, the Government "expends funds to encourage a diversity of views from private speakers."

A law that can be directed against speech found offensive to some portion of the public can be turned against minority and dissenting views to the detriment of all. The First Amendment does not entrust that power to the government's benevolence. Instead, our reliance must be on the substantial safeguards of free and open discussion in a democratic society.

For these reasons, I join the Court's opinion in part and concur in the judgment.

Justice THOMAS, concurring in part and concurring in the judgment.

I join the opinion of Justice ALITO, except for Part II. Respondent failed to present his statutory argument either to the Patent and Trademark Office or to the Court of Appeals, and we declined respondent's invitation to grant certiorari on this question. I see no reason to address this legal question in the first instance.

I also write separately because "I continue to believe that when the government seeks to restrict truthful speech in order to suppress the ideas it conveys, strict scrutiny is appropriate, whether or not the speech in question may be characterized as 'commercial.'" *Lorillard Tobacco Co. v. Reilly,* 533 U.S. 525, 572, 121 S.Ct. 2404, 150 L.Ed.2d 532 (2001) (THOMAS, J., concurring in part and concurring in judgment); see also, *e.g., 44 Liquormart, Inc. v. Rhode Island,* 517 U.S. 484, 518, 116 S.Ct. 1495, 134 L.Ed.2d 711 (1996) (same). I nonetheless join Part IV of Justice ALITO's opinion because it correctly concludes that the disparagement clause, is unconstitutional even under the less stringent test announced in *Central Hudson Gas & Elec. Corp. v. Public Serv. Comm'n of N. Y.,* 447 U.S. 557, 100 S.Ct. 2343, 65 L.Ed.2d 341 (1980).

Notes and Questions

1. *The test.* What is Justice Alito's test for the First Amendment's Free Speech Clause in this case? Where does he add clarity? Where does he confuse you?
2. *Fractured Court in this case.* Why do you think that are there so many concurrences and so many joinders in different parts of Alito's opinion?
3. *Justice Kennedy.* Why did Justice Kennedy concur?
4. *Justice Thomas.* Why did Justice Thomas concur?
5. *Draft opinion.* If you were to write a simpler version of this opinion, how would you write it? Practice a draft opinion.
6. *The bottom line on hate speech.* In light of the last several cases, what is the Court's doctrine on hate speech?

3. Content-Based vs. Content-Neutral Regulations

The Court has repeatedly distinguished between "content-based" and "content-neutral" laws in the First Amendment context. In *RAV*, for example, the Court said that the law was content-based and concluded it was unconstitutional. Can you tell from that case why content-based regulations of speech are likely to violate the First Amendment?

a. Municipal Sign Codes

Reed v. Town of Gilbert is a case about a law governing signs in Gilbert, Arizona, that restricted the size, number, duration, and location of temporary directional signs. The lower courts found the sign code constitutional, but the Supreme Court ruled unanimously that it was an unconstitutional content-based restriction.

Can you tell from reading the oral argument, https://www.oyez.org/cases/2014/13-502, what a content-based restriction is? How would you be able to identify one? Can you come up with an example of a content-based and a content-neutral statute?

Reed v. Town of Gilbert
SUPREME COURT OF THE UNITED STATES, 2015
576 U.S. 155, 135 S.Ct. 2218

THOMAS, J., delivered the opinion of the Court, in which ROBERTS, C.J., and SCALIA, KENNEDY, ALITO, and SOTOMAYOR, JJ., joined. ALITO, J., filed a concurring opinion, in which KENNEDY and SOTOMAYOR, JJ., joined. BREYER, J., filed an opinion concurring in the judgment. KAGAN, J., filed an opinion concurring in the judgment, in which GINSBURG and BREYER, JJ., joined.

The town of Gilbert, Arizona (or Town), has adopted a comprehensive code governing the manner in which people may display outdoor signs. The Sign Code identifies various categories of signs based on the type of information they convey, then subjects each category to different restrictions. One of the categories is "Temporary Directional Signs Relating to a Qualifying Event," loosely defined as signs directing the public to a meeting of a nonprofit group. The Code imposes more stringent restrictions on these signs than it does on signs conveying other messages. We hold that these provisions are content-based regulations of speech that cannot survive strict scrutiny.

I

A

The Sign Code prohibits the display of outdoor signs anywhere within the Town without a permit, but it then exempts 23 categories of signs from that requirement. These exemptions include everything from bazaar signs to flying banners. Three categories of exempt signs are particularly relevant here.

The first is "Ideological Sign[s]." This category includes any "sign communicating a message or ideas for noncommercial purposes that is not a Construction Sign, Directional Sign, Temporary Directional Sign Relating to a Qualifying Event, Political Sign, Garage Sale Sign, or a sign owned or required by a governmental agency." ... The second category is "Political Sign[s]." This includes any "temporary sign designed to influence the outcome of an election called by a public body." ... The third category is "Temporary Directional Signs Relating to a Qualifying Event." ...

B

Petitioners Good News Community Church (Church) and its pastor, Clyde Reed, wish to advertise the time and location of their Sunday church services. The Church is a small, cash-strapped entity that owns no building, so it holds its services at elementary schools or other locations in or near the Town. In order to inform the public about its services, which are held in a variety of different locations, the Church began placing 15 to 20 temporary signs around the Town, frequently in the public right-of-way abutting the street. The signs typically displayed the Church's name, along with the time and location of the upcoming service. Church members would post the signs early in the day on Saturday and then remove them around midday on Sunday. The display of these signs requires little money and manpower, and thus has proved to be an economical and effective way for the Church to let the community know where its services are being held each week.

This practice caught the attention of the Town's Sign Code compliance manager, who twice cited the Church for violating the Code. ...

II

A

The First Amendment, applicable to the States through the Fourteenth Amendment, prohibits the enactment of laws "abridging the freedom of speech." U.S. Const., Amdt. 1. Under that Clause, a government, including a municipal government vested with state authority, "has no power to restrict expression because of its message, its ideas, its subject matter, or its content." Content-based laws—those that target speech based on its communicative content—are presumptively unconstitutional and may be justified only if the government proves that they are narrowly tailored to serve compelling state interests.

Government regulation of speech is content based if a law applies to particular speech because of the topic discussed or the idea or message expressed. This commonsense meaning of the phrase "content based" requires a court to consider whether a regulation of speech "on its face" draws distinctions based on the message a speaker conveys. Some facial distinctions based on a message are obvious, defining regulated speech by particular subject matter, and others are more subtle, defining regulated speech by its function or purpose. Both are distinctions drawn based on the message a speaker conveys, and, therefore, are subject to strict scrutiny.

Our precedents have also recognized a separate and additional category of laws that, though facially content neutral, will be considered content-based regulations of speech: laws that cannot be "'justified without reference to the content of the regulated speech,'" or that were adopted by the government "because of disagreement with the message [the speech] conveys," Those laws, like those that are content based on their face, must also satisfy strict scrutiny.

B

The Town's Sign Code is content based on its face. It defines "Temporary Directional Signs" on the basis of whether a sign conveys the message of directing the public to church or some other "qualifying event." It defines "Political Signs" on the basis of whether a sign's message is "designed to influence the outcome of an election." And it defines "Ideological Signs" on the basis of whether a sign "communicat[es] a message or ideas" that do not fit within the Code's other categories. It then subjects each of these categories to different restrictions.

The restrictions in the Sign Code that apply to any given sign thus depend entirely on the communicative content of the sign. If a sign informs its reader of the time and place a book club will discuss John Locke's Two Treatises of Government, that sign will be treated differently from a sign expressing the view that one should vote for one of Locke's followers in an upcoming election, and both signs will be treated differently from a sign expressing an ideological view rooted in Locke's theory of government. More to the point, the Church's signs inviting people to attend its worship services are treated differently from signs conveying other types of ideas. On its face, the Sign Code is a content-based regulation of speech. We thus have no need to consider the government's justifications or purposes for enacting the Code to determine whether it is subject to strict scrutiny. ...

III

Because the Town's Sign Code imposes content-based restrictions on speech, those provisions can stand only if they survive strict scrutiny, "'which requires the Government to prove that the restriction furthers a compelling interest and is narrowly tailored to achieve that interest,'" Thus, it is the Town's burden to demonstrate that the Code's differentiation between temporary directional signs and other types of signs, such as political signs and ideological signs, furthers a compelling governmental interest and is narrowly tailored to that end.

The Town cannot do so. It has offered only two governmental interests in support of the distinctions the Sign Code draws: preserving the Town's aesthetic appeal and traffic safety. Assuming for the sake of argument that those are compelling governmental interests, the Code's distinctions fail as hopelessly underinclusive.

Starting with the preservation of aesthetics, temporary directional signs are "no greater an eyesore," than ideological or political ones. Yet the Code allows unlimited proliferation of larger ideological signs while strictly limiting the number, size, and duration of smaller directional ones. The Town cannot claim that placing strict limits on temporary directional signs is necessary to beautify the Town while at the same time allowing unlimited numbers of other types of signs that create the same problem.

The Town similarly has not shown that limiting temporary directional signs is necessary to eliminate threats to traffic safety, but that limiting other types of signs is not. The Town has offered no reason to believe that directional signs pose a greater threat to safety than do ideological or political signs. If anything, a sharply worded ideological sign seems more likely to distract a driver than a sign directing the public to a nearby church meeting.

In light of this underinclusiveness, the Town has not met its burden to prove that its Sign Code is narrowly tailored to further a compelling government interest. Because a "'law cannot be regarded as protecting an interest of the highest order, and thus as justifying a restriction on truthful speech, when it leaves appreciable damage to that supposedly vital interest unprohibited,'" the Sign Code fails strict scrutiny.

IV

... A sign ordinance narrowly tailored to the challenges of protecting the safety of pedestrians, drivers, and passengers—such as warning signs marking hazards on private property, signs directing traffic, or street numbers associated with private houses—well might survive strict scrutiny. The signs at issue in this case, including political and ideological signs and signs for events, are far removed from those purposes. As discussed above, they are facially content based and are neither justified by traditional safety concerns nor narrowly tailored.

Justice ALITO, with whom Justice KENNEDY and Justice SOTOMAYOR join, concurring.

I join the opinion of the Court but add a few words of further explanation.

As the Court shows, the regulations at issue in this case are replete with content-based distinctions, and as a result they must satisfy strict scrutiny. ... This does not mean, however, that municipalities are powerless to enact and enforce reasonable sign regulations. I will not attempt to provide anything like a comprehensive list, but here are some rules that would not be content based:

Rules regulating the size of signs. These rules may distinguish among signs based on any content-neutral criteria, including any relevant criteria listed below.

Rules regulating the locations in which signs may be placed. These rules may distinguish between free-standing signs and those attached to buildings.

Rules distinguishing between lighted and unlighted signs.

Rules distinguishing between signs with fixed messages and electronic signs with messages that change.

Rules that distinguish between the placement of signs on private and public property.

Rules distinguishing between the placement of signs on commercial and residential property.

Rules distinguishing between on-premises and off-premises signs.

Rules restricting the total number of signs allowed per mile of roadway.

Rules imposing time restrictions on signs advertising a one-time event. Rules of this nature do not discriminate based on topic or subject and are akin to rules restricting the times within which oral speech or music is allowed. ...

Justice BREYER, concurring in the judgment.

I join Justice KAGAN's separate opinion. Like Justice KAGAN I believe that categories alone cannot satisfactorily resolve the legal problem before us. The First Amendment requires greater judicial sensitivity both to the Amendment's expressive objectives and to the public's legitimate need for regulation than a simple recitation of categories, such as "content discrimination" and "strict scrutiny," would permit. In my view, the category "content discrimination" is better considered in many contexts, including here, as a rule of thumb, rather than as an automatic "strict scrutiny" trigger, leading to almost certain legal condemnation. ...

But content discrimination, while helping courts to identify unconstitutional suppression of expression, cannot and should not *always* trigger strict scrutiny. ...

The better approach is to generally treat content discrimination as a strong reason weighing against the constitutionality of a rule where a traditional public forum, or where viewpoint discrimination, is threatened, but elsewhere treat it as a rule of thumb, finding it a helpful, but not determinative legal tool, in an appropriate case, to determine the strength of a justification. I would use content discrimination as a supplement to a more basic analysis, which, tracking most of our First Amendment cases, asks whether the regulation at issue works harm to First Amendment interests that is disproportionate in light of the relevant regulatory objectives. Answering this question requires examining the seriousness of the harm to speech, the importance of the countervailing objectives, the extent to which the law will achieve those objectives, and whether there are other, less restrictive ways of doing so. Admittedly, this approach does not have the simplicity of a mechanical use of categories. But it does permit the government to regulate speech in numerous instances where the voters have authorized the government to regulate and where courts should hesitate to substitute judicial judgment for that of administrators.

Here, regulation of signage along the roadside, for purposes of safety and beautification is at issue. There is no traditional public forum nor do I find any general effort to censor a particular viewpoint. Consequently, the specific regulation at issue does not warrant "strict scrutiny." Nonetheless, for the reasons that Justice KAGAN sets forth, I believe that the Town of Gilbert's regulatory rules violate the First Amendment. I consequently concur in the Court's judgment only.

Justice KAGAN, with whom Justice GINSBURG and Justice BREYER join, concurring in the judgment.

... In *City of Ladue v. Gilleo,* 512 U.S. 43, 114 S.Ct. 2038, 129 L.Ed.2d 36 (1994), the Court assumed *arguendo* that a sign ordinance's exceptions for address signs, safety signs, and for-sale signs in residential areas did not trigger strict scrutiny. We did not need to, and so did not, decide the level-of-scrutiny question because the law's breadth made it unconstitutional under any standard.

The majority could easily have taken *Ladue*'s tack here. The Town of Gilbert's defense of its sign ordinance—most notably, the law's distinctions between directional signs and others—does not pass strict scrutiny, or intermediate scrutiny, or even the laugh test. The Town, for example, provides no reason at all for prohibiting more than four directional signs on a property while placing no limits on the number of other types of signs. Similarly, the Town offers no coherent justification for restricting the size of directional signs to 6 square feet while allowing other signs to reach 20 square feet. The best the Town could come up with at oral argument was that directional signs "need to be smaller because they need to guide travelers along a route." Why exactly a smaller sign better helps travelers get to where they are going is left a mystery. The absence of any sensible basis for these and other distinctions dooms the Town's ordinance under even the intermediate scrutiny that the Court typically applies to "time, place, or manner" speech regulations. Accordingly, there is no need to decide in this case whether strict scrutiny applies to every sign ordinance in every town across this country containing a subject-matter exemption.

I suspect this Court and others will regret the majority's insistence today on answering that question in the affirmative. As the years go by, courts will discover that thousands of towns have such ordinances, many of them "entirely reasonable." And as the challenges to them mount, courts will have to invalidate one after the other. (This Court may soon find itself a veritable Supreme Board of Sign Review.) And courts will strike down those democratically enacted local laws even though no one—certainly not the majority—has ever explained why the vindication of First Amendment values requires that result. Because I see no reason why such an easy case calls for us to cast a constitutional pall on reasonable regulations quite unlike the law before us, I concur only in the judgment.

Notes and Questions

1. *Defining "content-based."* Does Justice Thomas, writing for the majority, provide a good explanation of what a content-based law is? What is it?
2. *The type of speech.* Do you think that Justice Thomas's opinion is influenced by the fact that the speech is religious? Why or why not?
3. *Application of strict scrutiny.* Do you agree with Thomas that the Sign Code is content-based regulation that should be subjected to strict scrutiny? Justice Kagan would not select a level of scrutiny in this case. Why?
4. *The list.* What is the point of Justice Alito's list of sign regulations that are not content-based? Do you agree his list is not content-based? Why?
5. *The implications.* Will this opinion really turn the Court into a Supreme Board of Sign Review? Why or why not? What advice would you give a town drafting sign laws about how to draft one without violating the First Amendment? Draft a constitutional sign law.
6. *Justice Kagan.* Why does Justice Kagan think Gilbert's law fails the laugh test?

7. Artist Lorie Smith is a website designer who designs wedding websites in the State of Colorado. Colorado has the Colorado Anti-Discrimination Act (CADA), which prohibits LGBTQ discrimination. Smith refuses to create same-sex wedding websites because she opposes same-sex marriage for religious reasons. The Supreme Court is hearing her argument that CADA violates her free speech rights. Colorado argues that its public accommodations laws govern all businesses. What arguments will each side make? The oral arguments are available on Oyez's *303 Creative LLC v. Elenis* website, https://www.oyez.org/cases/2022/21-476. How do you think the Court will rule in this case, for Smith or for Colorado? Why do you think that? Is it obvious from their questions how the Justices will rule?

b. Digitized Signs as Speech

The Supreme Court granted certiorari on a digital sign case from Austin, Texas, where the city only permits digitized signs on premises. Austin did not allow off-premises digitized signs. This case raises the question of what level of scrutiny to apply to a sign law and what standard *Reed* established. Listen to the oral argument at https://www.oyez.org/cases/2021/20-1029. Can you predict the result from the oral argument? Who provides the most persuasive pathway to decide this case? Does Justice Alito's list from *Reed* prove useful?

City of Austin, Texas v. Reagan National Advertising of Austin, LLC

SUPREME COURT OF THE UNITED STATES, 2022

142 S.Ct. 1464, 212 L.Ed.2d 418

SOTOMAYOR, J., delivered the opinion of the Court, in which ROBERTS, C. J., and BREYER, KAGAN, and KAVANAUGH, JJ., joined. BREYER, J., filed a concurring opinion. ALITO, J., filed an opinion concurring in the judgment in part and dissenting in part. THOMAS, J., filed a dissenting opinion, in which GORSUCH and BARRETT, JJ., joined.

Like thousands of jurisdictions around the country, the City of Austin, Texas (City), regulates signs that advertise things that are not located on the same premises as the sign, as well as signs that direct people to offsite locations. These are known as off-premises signs, and they include, most notably, billboards. The question presented is whether, under this Court's precedents interpreting the Free Speech Clause of the First Amendment, the City's regulation is subject to strict scrutiny. We hold that it is not.

I

A

... The City of Austin is one such municipality. The City distinguishes between on-premises and off-premises signs in its sign code, and specially regulates the latter, in order to "protect the aesthetic value of the city and to protect public safety."

During the time period relevant to this dispute, the City's sign code defined the term "off-premise sign" to mean "a sign advertising a business, person, activity, goods, products, or services not located on the site where the sign is installed, or that directs persons to any location not on that site." This definition was materially analogous to the one used in the federal Highway Beautification Act and many other state and local codes referenced above. The code prohibited the construction of any new off-premises signs, but allowed existing off-premises signs to remain as grandfathered "non-conforming signs." An owner of a grandfathered off-premises sign could "continue or maintain [it] at its existing location" and could change the "face of the sign," but could not "increase the degree of the existing nonconformity," "change the method or technology used to convey a message," or "increase the illumination of the sign." By contrast, the code permitted the digitization of on-premises signs. § 25–10–102(6) (permitting "electronically controlled changeable-copy sign[s]").

B

Respondents, Reagan National Advertising of Austin, LLC (Reagan), and Lamar Advantage Outdoor Company, L. P. (Lamar), are outdoor-advertising companies that own billboards in Austin. In April and June of 2017, Reagan sought permits from the City to digitize some of its off-premises billboards. The City denied the applications. ...

II

A regulation of speech is facially content based under the First Amendment if it "target[s] speech based on its communicative content"—that is, if it "applies to particular speech because of the topic discussed or the idea or message expressed." *Reed*, 576 U.S. at 163, 135 S.Ct. 2218. The Court of Appeals interpreted *Reed* to mean that if "[a] reader must ask: who is the speaker and what is the speaker saying" to apply a regulation, then the regulation is automatically content based. This rule, which holds that a regulation cannot be content neutral if it requires reading the sign at issue, is too extreme an interpretation of this Court's precedent. Unlike the regulations at issue in *Reed*, the City's off-premises distinction requires an examination of speech only in service of drawing neutral, location-based lines. It is agnostic as to content. Thus, absent a content-based purpose or justification, the City's distinction is content neutral and does not warrant the application of strict scrutiny.

A

...

In this case, enforcing the City's challenged sign code provisions requires reading a billboard to determine whether it directs readers to the property on which it stands or to some other, offsite location. Unlike the sign code at issue in *Reed*, however, the City's provisions at issue here do not single out any topic or subject matter for differential treatment. A sign's substantive message itself is irrelevant to the application of the provisions; there are no content-discriminatory classifications for political messages, ideological messages, or directional messages concerning specific events, including those sponsored by religious and nonprofit organizations. Rather, the City's provisions distinguish based on location: A given sign is treated differently based solely on whether it is located on the same premises as the thing being discussed or not. The message on the sign matters only to the extent that it informs the sign's relative location. The on-/off-premises distinction is therefore similar to ordinary time, place, or manner restrictions. *Reed* does not require the application of strict scrutiny to this kind of location-based regulation. Cf. *Frisby v. Schultz*, 487 U.S. 474, 482, 108 S.Ct. 2495, 101 L.Ed.2d 420 (1988) (sustaining an ordinance that prohibited "only picketing focused on, and taking place in front of, a particular residence" as content neutral).

B

...

Underlying these cases and others is a rejection of the view that *any* examination of speech or expression inherently triggers heightened First Amendment concern. Rather, it is regulations that discriminate based on "the topic discussed or the idea or message expressed" that are content based. *Reed*, 576 U.S. at 171, 135 S.Ct. 2218. The sign code provisions challenged here do not discriminate on those bases.

C

...

The argument stretches *Reed*'s "function or purpose" language too far. The principle the *Reed* Court articulated is more straightforward. While overt subject-matter discrimination is facially content based (for example, "'Ideological Sign[s],'" defined as those "'communicating a message or ideas for noncommercial purposes'"), so, too, are subtler forms of discrimination that achieve identical results based on function or purpose (for example, "'Political Sign[s],'" defined as those "'designed to influence the outcome of an election'"). *Id.*, at 159, 160, 163–164, 135 S.Ct. 2218 (alterations in original). In other words, a regulation of speech cannot escape classification as facially content based simply by swapping an obvious subject-matter distinction for a "function or purpose" proxy that achieves the same result. That does not mean that any classification that considers function or purpose is *always* content based. Such a reading of "function or purpose" would contravene numerous precedents, including many of those discussed above. *Reed* did not purport to cast doubt on these cases.

Nor did *Reed* cast doubt on the Nation's history of regulating off-premises signs. Off-premises billboards of the sort that predominate today were not present in the founding era, but as large outdoor advertisements proliferated in the 1800s, regulation followed. As early as 1932, the Court had already approved a location-based differential for advertising signs. See *Packer Corp.*, 285 U.S. at 107, 110, 52 S.Ct. 273. Thereafter, for the last 50-plus years, federal, state, and local jurisdictions have repeatedly relied upon on-/off-premises distinctions to address the distinct safety and esthetic challenges posed by billboards and other methods of outdoor advertising. See *supra*, at ____. The unbroken tradition of on-/off-premises distinctions counsels against the adoption of Reagan's novel rule. See *Williams-Yulee v. Florida Bar*, 575 U.S. 433, 446, 135 S.Ct. 1656, 191 L.Ed.2d 570 (2015) (recognizing "history and tradition of regulation" as relevant when considering the scope of the First Amendment).

D

...

III

This Court's determination that the City's ordinance is facially content neutral does not end the First Amendment inquiry. If there is evidence that an impermissible purpose or justification underpins a facially content-neutral restriction, for instance, that restriction may be content based. See *Reed*, 576 U.S. at 164, 135 S.Ct. 2218. Moreover, to survive intermediate scrutiny, a restriction on speech or expression must be "'narrowly tailored to serve a significant governmental interest.'" *Ward v. Rock Against Racism*, 491 U.S. 781, 791, 109 S.Ct. 2746, 105 L.Ed.2d 661 (1989).

The parties dispute whether the City can satisfy these requirements. This Court, however, is "a court of final review and not first view," and it does not "[o]rdinarily ... decide in the first instance issues not decided below." *Zivotofsky v. Clinton*, 566 U.S. 189, 201, 132 S.Ct. 1421, 182 L.Ed.2d 423 (2012) (internal quotation marks omitted). "In particular, when we reverse on a threshold question, we typically remand for resolution of any claims the lower courts' error prevented them from addressing." *Ibid.* Because the Court of Appeals did not address these issues, the Court leaves them for remand and expresses no view on the matters.

Justice BREYER, concurring

Reed v. Town of Gilbert, 576 U.S. 155, 135 S.Ct. 2218, 192 L.Ed.2d 236 (2015), is binding precedent here. Given that precedent, I join the majority's opinion. I write separately because I continue to believe that the Court's reasoning in *Reed* was wrong. ... Here, I would conclude that the City of Austin's (City's) regulation of off-premises signs works no such disproportionate harm. I therefore agree with the majority's conclusion that strict scrutiny and its attendant presumption of unconstitutionality are unwarranted. The majority reaches this conclusion by applying *Reed's* formal framework, as *stare decisis* requires. I would add that *Reed's* strict formalism can sometimes disserve the very First Amendment interests it was designed to protect. ...

If *Reed* is taken as setting forth a formal rule that courts must strictly scrutinize regulations simply because they refer to particular content, we have good reason to fear the consequences of that decision. One possibility is that courts will strike down "'entirely reasonable'" regulations that reflect the will of the people. *Reed*, 576 U.S. at 171, 135 S.Ct. 2218; *e.g., Barr*, 591 U.S., at ____, 140 S.Ct., at 2361-2362 (striking down the Telephone Consumer Protection Act's exception allowing robocalls that collect government debt); *IMDB.com v. Becerra*, 962 F.3d 1111, 1125–1127 (CA9 2020) (striking down a California law prohibiting certain websites from publishing the birthdates of entertainment professionals). If so, the Court's content-based line-drawing will "substitut[e] judicial for democratic decisionmaking" and threaten the ability of the people to translate their ideas into policy. *Sorrell*, 564 U.S. at 603, 131 S.Ct. 2653 (BREYER, J., dissenting). ...

... I would reject *Reed's* approach, which too rigidly ties content discrimination to strict scrutiny (and, consequently, to "almost certain legal condemnation"). *Id.*, at 176, 135 S.Ct. 2218. Instead, I would treat content discrimination as a rule of thumb to be applied with what Justice KAGAN has called "a dose of common sense." *Id.*, at 183, 135 S.Ct. 2218 (opinion concurring in judgment). Where content-based regulations are at issue, I would ask a more basic First Amendment question: Does "the regulation at issue wor[k] harm to First Amendment interests that is disproportionate in light of the relevant regulatory objectives"? *Id.*, at 179, 135 S.Ct. 2218 (opinion of BREYER, J.). I believe we should answer that question by examining "the seriousness of the harm to speech, the importance of the countervailing objectives, the extent to which the law will achieve those objectives, and whether there are other, less restrictive ways of doing so." ...

I wish only to illustrate why I believe a strong presumption of unlawfulness is out of place here. ...

... The City's regulation here appears to work at most a limited, niche-like harm to First Amendment interests. Respondents own a number of grandfathered off-premises signs. They can use those signs to communicate whatever messages they choose. They complain only that they cannot digitize the signs, which would allow them to display several messages in rapid succession. Perhaps digitization would enable them to make more effective use of their billboard space. But their inability to maximize the use of their space in this way is unlikely to meaningfully interfere with their participation in the "marketplace of ideas."

At the same time, the City has asserted a legitimate interest in maintaining the regulation. As I have said, the public has an interest in ensuring traffic safety and preserving an esthetically pleasing environment, *supra* this page, and the City here has reasonably explained how its regulation of off-premises signs in general, and digitization in particular, serves those interests. *Amici* tell us that billboards, especially digital ones, can distract drivers and cause accidents. They add that on-premises signs are less likely to cause accidents. The City further says that billboards cause more visual clutter than on-premises signs because the latter are "typically 'small in size' and integrated into the premises."

I would leave for the courts below to weigh these harms and interests, and any alternatives, in the first instance, without a strong presumption of unconstitutionality.

Justice ALITO, concurring in the judgment in part and dissenting in part.

I agree with the majority that we must reverse the decision of the Court of Appeals holding that the provisions of the Austin City Code regulating on- and off-premises signs are facially unconstitutional. The Court of Appeals reasoned that those provisions impose content-based restrictions and that they cannot satisfy strict scrutiny, but the Court of Appeals did not apply the tests that must be met before a law is held to be facially unconstitutional. "Normally, a plaintiff bringing a facial challenge must 'establish that no set of circumstances exists under which the [law] would be valid,' or show that the law lacks 'a plainly legitimate sweep.'" A somewhat less demanding test applies when a law affects freedom of speech. Under our First Amendment "overbreadth" doctrine, a law restricting speech is unconstitutional "if a substantial number of its applications are unconstitutional, judged in relation to the statute's plainly legitimate sweep."

In this case, the Court of Appeals did not apply either of those tests, and it is doubtful that they can be met. Many (and possibly the great majority) of the situations in which the relevant provisions may apply involve commercial speech, and under our precedents, regulations of commercial speech are analyzed differently. ...

Because the Court of Appeals erred in holding that the code provisions are facially unconstitutional, I agree that we should reverse that decision. On remand, the lower courts should determine whether those provisions are unconstitutional as applied to each of the billboards at issue.

Today's decision, however, goes further and holds flatly that "[t]he sign code provisions challenged here do not discriminate" on the basis of "'the topic discussed or the idea or message expressed,'" and that categorical statement is incorrect. The provisions defining on- and off-premises signs clearly discriminate on those grounds, and at least as applied in some situations, strict scrutiny should be required. ...

... Consider what this definition would mean as applied to signs posted in the front window of a commercial establishment, say, a little coffee shop. If the owner put up a sign advertising a new coffee drink, the sign would be classified as on-premises, but suppose the owner instead mounted a sign in the same location saying: "Contribute to X's legal defense fund" or "Free COVID tests available at Y pharmacy" or "Attend City Council meeting to speak up about Z." All those signs would appear to fall within the definition of an off-premises sign and would thus be disallowed. See also *post*, at 3–4 (THOMAS, J., dissenting). Providing disparate treatment for the sign about a new drink and the signs about social and political matters constitutes discrimination on the basis of topic or subject matter.

... For these reasons, I would simply hold that the provisions at issue are not facially unconstitutional, and I would refrain from making any broader pronouncements.

Justice THOMAS, with whom Justice GORSUCH and Justice BARRETT join, dissenting.

In *Reed v. Town of Gilbert*, 576 U.S. 155 (2015), we held that a speech regulation is content based—and thus presumptively invalid—if it "draws distinctions based on the message a speaker conveys. Here, the city of Austin imposes special restrictions on "off-premise[s] sign[s]," defined as signs that "advertis[e] a business, person, activity, goods, products, or services not located on the site where the sign is installed, or that direc[t] persons to any location not on that site." Under *Reed*, Austin's off-premises restriction is content based. It discriminates against certain signs based on the message they convey—*e.g.*, whether they promote an on- or off-site event, activity, or service.... the majority's reasoning is reminiscent of this Court's erroneous decision in *Hill v. Colorado*, 530 U.S. 703 (2000), which upheld a blatantly content-based prohibition on "counseling" near abortion clinics on the ground that it discriminated against "an extremely broad category of communications." Because I would adhere to *Reed* rather than echo *Hill*'s long-discredited approach, I respectfully dissent....

Under *Reed*'s approach for identifying content-based regulations, Austin's off-premises sign restriction is content based. As relevant to this suit, Austin's sign code imposes stringent restrictions on a category of "off-premise[s] sign[s]." The code defines "off-premise[s] sign[s]" as those "advertising a business, person, activity, goods, products, or services not located on the site where the sign is installed," or as signs "direct[ing] persons to any location not on that site." This broad definition sweeps in a wide swath of signs, from 14- by 48-foot billboards to 24- by 18-inch yard signs. The sign code prohibits new off-premises signs and makes it difficult (or impossible) to change existing off-premises signs, including by digitizing them.

Like the town of Gilbert in *Reed*, Austin has identified a "categor[y] of signs based on the type of information they convey, [and] then subject[ed that] category to different restrictions." A sign that conveys a message about off-premises activities is restricted, while one that conveys a message about on-premises activities is not. And, per *Reed*, it does not matter that Austin's code "defin[es] regulated speech by its function or purpose"—*i.e.*, advertising or directing passersby elsewhere. Again, all that matters is that the regulation "draws distinctions based on" a sign's "communicative content," which the off-premises restriction plainly does.

This conclusion is not undermined because the off-premises sign restriction depends in part on a content-neutral element: the location of the sign. Much like in *Reed*, that an Austin official applying the sign code must know *where* the sign is does not negate the fact that he also must know *what* the sign says. Take, for instance, a sign outside a Catholic bookstore. If the sign says, "Visit the Holy Land," it is likely an off-premises sign because it conveys a message directing people elsewhere (unless the name of the bookstore is "Holy Land Books"). But if the sign instead says, "Buy More Books," it is likely a permissible on-premises sign (unless the sign also contains the address of another bookstore across town). Finally, suppose the sign says, "Go to Confession." After examining the sign's message, an official would need to inquire whether a priest ever hears confessions at that location. If one does, the sign could convey a permissible "on-premises" message. If not, the sign conveys an impermissible off-premises message. Because enforcing the sign code in any of these instances "requires [Austin] officials to determine whether a sign" conveys a particular message, the sign code is content based under *Reed*.

In sum, the off-premises rule is content based and thus invalid unless Austin can satisfy strict scrutiny. Because Austin has offered nothing to make that showing, the Court of Appeals did not err in holding that the off-premises rule violates the First Amendment....

Despite asserting that the Court of Appeals' analysis under *Reed* would "contravene numerous precedents," the majority identifies no decision of this Court supporting the idea that a speech restriction is not content based so long as it regulates a sufficiently broad or non-substantive category of communicative content. In fact, there is only one case that could possibly validate the majority's aberrant analysis: *Hill v. Colorado*. That *Hill* is the majority's only support underscores the danger that today's decision poses to the First Amendment.

Hill involved a law that prohibited persons outside abortion clinics from knowingly approaching within eight feet of another person without consent "for the purpose of ... engaging in oral protest, education, or counseling." *Hill* concluded, implausibly, that this regulation was content neutral.

The majority's reasoning in this case is just as implausible. The majority asserts that the off-premises rule is not content based because it does not target a sufficiently "specific" or "substantive" category of communications. *Hill* correspondingly held that restrictions on "protest, education, or counseling" were not content-based classifications because they cover "an extremely broad category of communications." The majority also tries to disguise its redefinition of content neutrality by characterizing Austin's rule as a "neutral, location-based" restriction. So too did *Hill* try to conceal its doctrinal innovation by characterizing the buffer-zone law as a neutral "place restriction." Finally, the majority finds it immaterial that Austin's rule can be enforced only by "reading a [sign] to determine whether it" contains an off-premises message. *Hill* likewise found it irrelevant that "the content of the oral statements" would need to "be examined to determine whether" the prohibition applied.

The parallel between the majority's opinion and *Hill* should be discomforting given that *Hill* represented "an unprecedented departure" from this Court's First Amendment jurisprudence. *Id.*, at 772, 120 S.Ct. 2480 (KENNEDY, J., dissenting). ...

Because *Reed* provided a clear and neutral rule that protected the freedom of speech from governmental caprice and viewpoint discrimination, I would adhere to that precedent rather than risk resuscitating *Hill*. I respectfully dissent.

Notes and Questions

1. *Content-based or neutral*? What is a content-based regulation? What is a content-neutral regulation? Can you tell the difference between them? Why did the Fifth Circuit say the statute was content-based? Why did Sotomayor say it was content-neutral? Why did the dissenters say it was content-based?
2. *Justice Breyer*. Why did Justice Breyer concur? How much of the majority's opinion does he agree with?
3. *Justice Alito*. Why did Justice Alito write a concurrence in part and a dissent in part? What analysis does he offer that is consistent with the majority? What analysis does he offer that is different from the majority?
4. *The Catholic bookstore*. Go through Justice Thomas's analysis of the Catholic bookstore. Does this hypothetical prove to you that the Austin regulation is content-based? Why do Justice Thomas and the majority disagree about content-based and content-neutral?
5. *Abortion*. Why does Justice Thomas say this case is just like the abortion protest case, *Hill*?
6. *The board of sign review*? Does this case show that *Reed* was correct that the Court would turn into a Court for sign review? Which Justice provides the best reading of *Reed* in this case?
7. *Strict scrutiny*. When does the Court apply strict scrutiny in a speech case?

c. Attorney Discipline

Here is another arena where the First Amendment plays a role: attorney discipline. Are you surprised by that? As you go through law school, you will learn that lawyers can be disciplined for their misconduct. You should never procrastinate on your client's work! In the following case, *Williams-Yulee v. Florida Bar*, Florida had a law that judicial candidates could not personally solicit campaign funds. An attorney was found guilty of doing so. In a 5–4 decision, the Court ruled that the solicitation law did not violate the First Amendment.

Listen to the oral argument, https://www.oyez.org/cases/2014/13-1499, to determine what the law had to do with the First Amendment. Can you predict from the Justices' questions what they think about the First Amendment? Why it applies here? What test they would apply? Do you prefer the animals' version of the argument, PuppyJusticeAnimated, *Williams-Yulee v. the Florida Bar*, Jan. 20, 2015, at https://www.youtube.com/watch?v=3woZgUwNVmg?

Williams-Yulee v. Florida Bar
SUPREME COURT OF THE UNITED STATES, 2015
575 U.S. 433, 135 S.Ct. 1656

ROBERTS, C.J., delivered the opinion of the Court, except as to Part II. BREYER, SOTOMAYOR, and KAGAN, JJ., joined that opinion in full, and GINSBURG, J., joined except as to Part II. BREYER, J., filed a concurring opinion. GINSBURG, J., filed an opinion concurring in part and concurring in the judgment, in which BREYER, J., joined as to Part II. SCALIA, J., filed a dissenting opinion, in which THOMAS, J., joined. KENNEDY, J., and ALITO, J., filed dissenting opinions.

Our Founders vested authority to appoint federal judges in the President, with the advice and consent of the Senate, and entrusted those judges to hold their offices during good behavior. The Constitution permits States to make a different choice, and most of them have done so. In 39 States, voters elect trial or appellate judges at the polls. In an effort to preserve public confidence in the integrity of their judiciaries, many of those States prohibit judges and judicial candidates from personally soliciting funds for their campaigns. We must decide whether the First Amendment permits such restrictions on speech.

We hold that it does. Judges are not politicians, even when they come to the bench by way of the ballot. And a State's decision to elect its judiciary does not compel it to treat judicial candidates like campaigners for political office. A State may assure its people that judges will apply the law without fear or favor—and without having personally asked anyone for money. We affirm the judgment of the Florida Supreme Court.

IB

... Lanell Williams-Yulee, who refers to herself as Yulee, has practiced law in Florida since 1991. In September 2009, she decided to run for a seat on the county court for Hillsborough County, a jurisdiction of about 1.3 million people that includes the city of Tampa. Shortly after filing paperwork to enter the race, Yulee drafted a letter announcing her candidacy. The letter described her experience and desire to "bring fresh ideas and positive solutions to the Judicial bench." App. to Pet. for Cert. 31a. The letter then stated:

> "An early contribution of $25, $50, $100, $250, or $500, made payable to 'Lanell Williams-Yulee Campaign for County Judge', will help raise the initial funds needed to launch the campaign and get our message out to the public. I ask for your support [i]n meeting the primary election fund raiser goals. Thank you in advance for your support."

Yulee signed the letter and mailed it to local voters. She also posted the letter on her campaign Web site.

Yulee's bid for the bench did not unfold as she had hoped. She lost the primary to the incumbent judge. Then the Florida Bar filed a complaint against her. As relevant here, the Bar charged her with violating Rule 4-8.2(b) of the Rules Regulating the Florida Bar. That Rule requires judicial candidates to comply with applicable provisions of Florida's Code of Judicial Conduct, including the ban on personal solicitation of campaign funds in Canon 7C(1).

Yulee admitted that she had signed and sent the fundraising letter. But she argued that the Bar could not discipline her for that conduct because the First Amendment protects a judicial candidate's right to solicit campaign funds in an election. ...

II

... In sum, we hold today what we assumed in *White:* A State may restrict the speech of a judicial candidate only if the restriction is narrowly tailored to serve a compelling interest.

III

... Here, Canon 7C(1) advances the State's compelling interest in preserving public confidence in the integrity of the judiciary, and it does so through means narrowly tailored to avoid unnecessarily abridging speech. This is therefore one of the rare cases in which a speech restriction withstands strict scrutiny. ...

The principal dissent observes that bans on judicial candidate solicitation lack a lengthy historical pedigree. We do not dispute that fact, but it has no relevance here. As the precedent cited by the principal dissent demonstrates, a history and tradition of regulation are important factors in determining whether to recognize "new categories of unprotected speech." But nobody argues that solicitation of campaign funds by judicial candidates is a category of unprotected speech. As explained above, the First Amendment fully applies to Yulee's speech. The question is instead whether that Amendment permits the particular regulation of speech at issue here. ...

Yulee acknowledges the State's compelling interest in judicial integrity. She argues, however, that the Canon's failure to restrict other speech equally damaging to judicial integrity and its appearance undercuts the Bar's position. In particular, she notes that Canon 7C(1) allows a judge's campaign committee to solicit money, which arguably reduces public confidence in the integrity of the judiciary just as much as a judge's personal solicitation. Yulee also points out that Florida permits judicial candidates to write thank you notes to campaign donors, which ensures that candidates know who contributes and who does not. ...

Viewed in light of these principles, Canon 7C(1) raises no fatal underinclusivity concerns. The solicitation ban aims squarely at the conduct most likely to undermine public confidence in the integrity of the judiciary: personal requests for money by judges and judicial candidates. The Canon applies evenhandedly to all judges and judicial candidates, regardless of their viewpoint or chosen means of solicitation. And unlike some laws that we have found impermissibly underinclusive, Canon 7C(1) is not riddled with exceptions. Indeed, the Canon contains zero exceptions to its ban on personal solicitation. ...

Taken to its logical conclusion, the position advanced by Yulee and the principal dissent is that Florida may ban the solicitation of funds by judicial candidates only if the State bans *all* solicitation of funds in judicial elections. The First Amendment does not put a State to that all-or-nothing choice. We will not punish Florida for leaving open more, rather than fewer, avenues of expression, especially when there is no indication that the selective restriction of speech reflects a pretextual motive. ...

By any measure, Canon 7C(1) restricts a narrow slice of speech. A reader of Justice KENNEDY's dissent could be forgiven for concluding that the Court has just upheld a latter-day version of the Alien and Sedition Acts, approving "state censorship" that "locks the First Amendment out," imposes a "gag" on candidates, and inflicts "dead weight" on a "silenced" public debate. But in reality, Canon 7C(1) leaves judicial candidates free to discuss any issue with any person at any time. Candidates can write letters, give speeches, and put up billboards. They can contact potential supporters in person, on the phone, or online. They can promote their campaigns on radio, television, or other media. They cannot say, "Please give me money." They can, however, direct their campaign committees to do so. Whatever else may be said of the Canon, it is surely not a "wildly disproportionate restriction upon speech." (SCALIA, J., dissenting). ...

* * *

The desirability of judicial elections is a question that has sparked disagreement for more than 200 years. Hamilton believed that appointing judges to positions with life tenure constituted "the best expedient which can be devised in any government to secure a steady, upright, and impartial administration of the laws." The Federalist No. 78, at 465. Jefferson thought that making judges "dependent on none but themselves" ran counter to the principle of "a government founded on the public will." 12 The Works of Thomas Jefferson 5 (P. Ford ed. 1905). The federal courts reflect the view of Hamilton; most States have sided with Jefferson. Both methods have given our Nation jurists of wisdom and rectitude who have devoted themselves to maintaining "the public's respect ... and a reserve of public goodwill, without becoming subservient to public opinion." Rehnquist, Judicial Independence, 38 U. Rich. L.Rev. 579, 596 (2004).

It is not our place to resolve this enduring debate. Our limited task is to apply the Constitution to the question presented in this case. Judicial candidates have a First Amendment right to speak in support of their campaigns. States have a compelling interest in preserving public confidence in their judiciaries. When the State adopts a narrowly tailored restriction like the one at issue here, those principles do not conflict. A State's decision to elect judges does not compel it to compromise public confidence in their integrity.

Justice BREYER, concurring.

As I have previously said, I view this Court's doctrine referring to tiers of scrutiny as guidelines informing our approach to the case at hand, not tests to be mechanically applied. On that understanding, I join the Court's opinion.

Justice GINSBURG, with whom Justice BREYER joins as to Part II, concurring in part and concurring in the judgment.

I

I join the Court's opinion save for Part II. As explained in my dissenting opinion in *Republican Party of*

Minnesota v. White, 536 U.S. 765, 803, 122 S.Ct. 2528, 153 L.Ed.2d 694 (2002), I would not apply exacting scrutiny to a State's endeavor sensibly to "differentiate elections for political offices ... , from elections designed to select those whose office it is to administer justice without respect to persons."

II

I write separately to reiterate the substantial latitude, in my view, States should possess to enact campaign-finance rules geared to judicial elections. ...

The Court's recent campaign-finance decisions, trained on political actors, should not hold sway for judicial elections. ...

States may therefore impose different campaign-finance rules for judicial elections than for political elections. Experience illustrates why States may wish to do so. When the political campaign-finance apparatus is applied to judicial elections, the distinction of judges from politicians dims. Donors, who gain audience and influence through contributions to political campaigns, anticipate that investment in campaigns for judicial office will yield similar returns. Elected judges understand this dynamic. As Ohio Supreme Court Justice Paul Pfeifer put it: "Whether they succeed or not," campaign contributors "mean to be buying a vote." Liptak & Roberts, Campaign Cash Mirrors a High Court's Rulings, N.Y. Times, Oct. 1, 2006, pp. A1, A22 (internal quotation marks omitted). ...

Justice SCALIA, with whom Justice THOMAS joins, dissenting.

An ethics canon adopted by the Florida Supreme Court bans a candidate in a judicial election from asking anyone, under any circumstances, for a contribution to his campaign. Faithful application of our precedents would have made short work of this wildly disproportionate restriction upon speech. Intent upon upholding the Canon, however, the Court flattens one settled First Amendment principle after another. ...

Because Canon 7C(1) restricts fully protected speech on the basis of content, it presumptively violates the First Amendment. We may uphold it only if the State meets its burden of showing that the Canon survives strict scrutiny—that is to say, only if it shows that the Canon is narrowly tailored to serve a compelling interest. I do not for a moment question the Court's conclusion that States have different compelling interests when regulating judicial elections than when regulating political ones. Unlike a legislator, a judge must be impartial—without bias for or against any party or attorney who comes before him. I accept for the sake of argument that States have a compelling interest in ensuring that its judges are *seen* to be impartial. I will likewise assume that a judicial candidate's request to a litigant or attorney presents a danger of coercion that a political candidate's request to a constituent does not. But Canon 7C(1) does not narrowly target concerns about impartiality or its appearance; it applies even when the person asked for a financial contribution has no chance of ever appearing in the candidate's court. And Florida does not invoke concerns about coercion, presumably because the Canon bans solicitations regardless of whether their object is a lawyer, litigant, or other person vulnerable to judicial pressure. So Canon 7C(1) fails exacting scrutiny and infringes the First Amendment. This case should have been just that straightforward. ...

This is not strict scrutiny; it is sleight of hand. ...

Neither the Court nor the State identifies the slightest evidence that banning requests for contributions will substantially improve public trust in judges. Nor does common sense make this happy forecast obvious. The concept of judicial integrity "dates back at least eight centuries," and judicial elections in America date back more than two centuries,—but rules against personal solicitations date back only to 1972. The peaceful coexistence of judicial elections and personal solicitations for most of our history calls into doubt any claim that allowing personal solicitations would imperil public faith in judges. Many States allow judicial candidates to ask for contributions even today, but nobody suggests that public confidence in judges fares worse in these jurisdictions than elsewhere. And in any event, if candidates' appeals for money are "'characteristically intertwined'" with discussion of qualifications and views on public issues, how can the Court be so sure that the public will regard them as improprieties rather than as legitimate instances of campaigning? In the final analysis, Florida comes nowhere near making the convincing demonstration required by our cases that the speech restriction in this case substantially advances its objective. ...

* * *

This Court has not been shy to enforce the First Amendment in recent Terms—even in cases that do not involve election speech. It has accorded robust protection to depictions of animal torture, sale of violent video games to children, and lies about having won military medals. See *United States v. Stevens,* 559 U.S. 460, 130 S.Ct. 1577, 176 L.Ed.2d 435 (2010); *Entertainment Merchants,* 564 U.S. ____, 131 S.Ct. 2729, 180 L.Ed.2d 708; *Alvarez,* 567 U.S. ____, 132 S.Ct. 2537, 183 L.Ed.2d 574. Who would have thought that the same Court would today exert such heroic efforts to save so plain an abridgement of the freedom of speech? It is no great mystery what is going on here. The judges of this Court, like the judges of the Supreme Court of Florida who promulgated Canon 7C(1), evidently consider the preservation of public respect for the courts a policy objective of the highest order. So it is—but so too are preventing animal torture, protecting the innocence of children, and honoring valiant soldiers. The Court did not relax the Constitution's guarantee of freedom of speech when legislatures pursued those goals; it should not relax the guarantee when the Supreme Court of Florida pursues this one. The First Amendment is not abridged for the benefit of the Brotherhood of the Robe.

Justice KENNEDY, dissenting.

The dissenting opinion by Justice SCALIA gives a full and complete explanation of the reasons why the Court's opinion contradicts settled First Amendment principles. This separate dissent is written to underscore the irony in the Court's having concluded that the very First Amendment protections judges must enforce should be lessened when a judicial candidate's own speech is at issue. It is written to underscore, too, the irony in the Court's having weakened the rigors of the First Amendment in a case concerning elections, a paradigmatic forum for speech and a process intended to protect freedom in so many other manifestations. ...

With all due respect for the Court, it seems fair and necessary to say its decision rests on two premises, neither one correct. One premise is that in certain elections—here an election to choose the best qualified judge—the public lacks the necessary judgment to make an informed choice. Instead, the State must protect voters by altering the usual dynamics of free speech. The other premise is that since judges should be accorded special respect and dignity, their election can be subject to certain content-based rules that would be unacceptable in other elections. In my respectful view neither premise can justify the speech restriction at issue here. Although States have a compelling interest in seeking to ensure the appearance and the reality of an impartial judiciary, it does not follow that the State may alter basic First Amendment principles in pursuing that goal. ...

In addition to narrowing the First Amendment's reach, there is another flaw in the Court's analysis. That is its error in the application of strict scrutiny. The Court's evisceration of that judicial standard now risks long-term harm to what was once the Court's own preferred First Amendment test. As Justice SCALIA well explains, the state law at issue fails strict scrutiny for any number of reasons. The candidate who is not wealthy or well connected cannot ask even a close friend or relative for a bit of financial help, despite the lack of any increased risk of partiality and despite the fact that disclosure laws might be enacted to make the solicitation and support public. This law comes nowhere close to being narrowly tailored. And by saying that it survives that vital First Amendment requirement, the Court now writes what is literally a casebook guide to eviscerating strict scrutiny any time the Court encounters speech it dislikes. On these premises, and for the reasons explained in more detail by Justice SCALIA, it is necessary for me to file this respectful dissent.

Justice ALITO, dissenting.

... Florida has a compelling interest in making sure that its courts decide cases impartially and in accordance with the law and that its citizens have no good reason to lack confidence that its courts are performing their proper role. But the Florida rule is not narrowly tailored to serve that interest.

Indeed, this rule is about as narrowly tailored as a burlap bag. It applies to all solicitations made in the name of a candidate for judicial office—including, as was the case here, a mass mailing. It even applies to an ad in a newspaper. It applies to requests for contributions in any amount, and it applies even if the person solicited is not a lawyer, has never had any interest at stake in any case in the court in question, and has no prospect of ever having any interest at stake in any litigation in that court. If this rule can be characterized as narrowly tailored, then narrow tailoring has no meaning, and strict scrutiny, which is essential to the protection of free speech, is seriously impaired. ...

Notes and Questions

1. *Applying strict scrutiny.* The Justices agree in this case on the level of scrutiny to be applied: strict, but they apply it with opposite results. Which element of strict scrutiny—the compelling interest element or the tailoring requirement—leads each of the dissents to conclude the campaign finance law for judges fails strict scrutiny?
2. *Justice Breyer's concurrence.* What is Justice Breyer's message to the other Justices in his concurrence? Do you agree with him?
3. *Justice Ginsburg draws a distinction.* What is the point of Justice Ginsburg's concurrence?
4. *Three dissents.* Why are there three different dissents? How do each of the dissents explain their rejection of the majority's reasoning?
5. *So many opinions.* Why are there so many opinions in this case? What do you think the Court's ruling should have been? One of the Justice's opinions or one of your own writing? How would you write the opinion?

d. The Role of "Secondary Effects" in Analyzing Speech Protections

The following case is about adult theaters. Should they be protected by the First Amendment? Or do they present speech that the First Amendment does not protect? How could you tell the difference between one and the other? Read through the oral argument at https://www.oyez.org/cases/1985/84-1360. Can you figure out what the Justices thought about adult theaters? Did you anticipate that Justices Brennan and Marshall would dissent? Does this description of the opinion, Ronald Steiner, *City of Renton v. Playtime Theatres, Inc.* (1986), at https://www.mtsu.edu/first-amendment/article/22/city-of-renton-v-playtime-theatres-inc, help you understand it? Do you understand what the Court means by secondary effects?

City of Renton v. Playtime Theaters, Inc.

SUPREME COURT OF THE UNITED STATES, 1986

475 U.S. 41, 106 S.Ct. 925

REHNQUIST, J., delivered the opinion of the Court, in which BURGER, C.J., and WHITE, POWELL, STEVENS, and O'CONNOR, JJ., joined. BLACKMUN, J., concurred in the result. BRENNAN, J., filed a dissenting opinion, in which MARSHALL, J., joined.

This case involves a constitutional challenge to a zoning ordinance, enacted by appellant city of Renton, Washington, that prohibits adult motion picture theaters from locating within 1,000 feet of any residential zone, single- or multiple-family dwelling, church, park, or school. Appellees, Playtime Theatres, Inc., and Sea-First Properties, Inc., filed an action in the United States District Court for the Western District of Washington seeking a declaratory judgment that the Renton ordinance violated the First and Fourteenth Amendments and a permanent injunction against its enforcement. ...

In our view, the resolution of this case is largely dictated by our decision in *Young v. American Mini Theatres, Inc., supra.* There, although five Members of the Court did not agree on a single rationale for the decision, we held that the city of Detroit's zoning ordinance, which prohibited locating an adult theater within 1,000 feet of any two other "regulated uses" or within 500 feet of any residential zone, did not violate the First and Fourteenth Amendments. The Renton ordinance, like the one in *American Mini Theatres,* does not ban adult theaters altogether, but merely provides that such theaters may not be located within 1,000 feet of any residential zone, single- or multiple-family dwelling, church, park, or school. The ordinance is therefore properly analyzed as a form of time, place, and manner regulation.

Describing the ordinance as a time, place, and manner regulation is, of course, only the first step in our inquiry. This Court has long held that regulations enacted for the purpose of restraining speech on the basis of its content presumptively violate the First Amendment. On the other hand, so-called "content-neutral" time, place, and manner regulations are acceptable so long as they are designed to serve a substantial governmental interest and do not unreasonably limit alternative avenues of communication.

At first glance, the Renton ordinance, like the ordinance in *American Mini Theatres,* does not appear to fit neatly into either the "content-based" or the "content-neutral" category. To be sure, the ordinance treats theaters that specialize in adult films differently from other kinds of theaters. Nevertheless, as the District Court concluded, the Renton ordinance is aimed not at the *content* of the films shown at "adult motion picture theatres," but rather at the *secondary effects* of such theaters on the surrounding community. The District Court found that the City Council's "*predominate* concerns" were with the secondary effects of adult theaters, and not with the content of adult films themselves. ...

The District Court's finding as to "predominate" intent, left undisturbed by the Court of Appeals, is more than adequate to establish that the city's pursuit of its zoning interests here was unrelated to the suppression of free expression. The ordinance by its terms is designed to prevent crime, protect the city's retail trade, maintain property values, and generally "protec[t] and preserv[e] the quality of [the city's] neighborhoods, commercial districts, and the quality of urban life," not to suppress the expression of unpopular views. See App. To Juris. Statement 90a. As Justice POWELL observed in *American Mini Theatres,* "[i]f [the city] had been concerned with restricting the message purveyed by adult theaters, it would have tried to close them or restrict their number rather than circumscribe their choice as to location."

In short, the Renton ordinance is completely consistent with our definition of "content-neutral" speech regulations as those that "are *justified* without reference to the content of the regulated speech." The ordinance does not contravene the fundamental principle that underlies our concern about "content-based" speech regulations: that "government may not grant the use of a forum to people whose views it finds acceptable, but deny use to those wishing to express less favored or more controversial views."

It was with this understanding in mind that, in *American Mini Theatres,* a majority of this Court decided that, at least with respect to businesses that purvey sexually explicit materials, zoning ordinances designed to combat the undesirable secondary effects of such businesses are to be reviewed under the standards applicable to "content-neutral" time, place, and manner regulations. Justice STEVENS, writing for the plurality, concluded that the city of Detroit was entitled to draw a distinction between adult theaters and other kinds of theaters "without violating the government's paramount obligation of neutrality in its regulation of protected communication," noting that "[i]t is th[e] secondary effect which these zoning ordinances attempt to avoid, not the dissemination of 'offensive' speech." ...

The appropriate inquiry in this case, then, is whether the Renton ordinance is designed to serve a substantial governmental interest and allows for reasonable alternative avenues of communication. It is clear that the ordinance meets such a standard. As a majority of this Court recognized in *American Mini Theatres,* a city's "interest in attempting to preserve the quality of urban life is one that must be accorded high respect." ...

In sum, we find that the Renton ordinance represents a valid governmental response to the "admittedly serious problems" created by adult theaters. Renton has not used "the power to zone as a pretext for suppressing expression," but rather has sought to make some areas available for adult theaters and their patrons, while at the same time preserving the quality of life in the community at large by preventing those theaters from locating in other areas. This, after all, is the essence of zoning. Here, as in *American Mini Theatres,* the city has enacted a zoning ordinance that meets these goals while also satisfying the dictates of the First Amendment.

Justice BRENNAN, with whom Justice MARSHALL joins, dissenting.

Renton's zoning ordinance selectively imposes limitations on the location of a movie theater based exclusively on the content of the films shown there.

The constitutionality of the ordinance is therefore not correctly analyzed under standards applied to content-neutral time, place, and manner restrictions. But even assuming that the ordinance may fairly be characterized as content neutral, it is plainly unconstitutional under the standards established by the decisions of this Court. Although the Court's analysis is limited to cases involving "businesses that purvey sexually explicit materials," and thus does not affect our holdings in cases involving state regulation of other kinds of speech, I dissent. ...

The fact that adult movie theaters may cause harmful "secondary" land-use effects may arguably give Renton a compelling reason to regulate such establishments; it does not mean, however, that such regulations are content neutral. Because the ordinance imposes special restrictions on certain kinds of speech on the basis of *content*, I cannot simply accept, as the Court does, Renton's claim that the ordinance was not designed to suppress the content of adult movies. ...

In this case, the city has not justified treating adult movie theaters differently from other adult entertainment businesses. The ordinance's underinclusiveness is cogent evidence that it was aimed at the *content* of the films shown in adult movie theaters. ...

In sum, the circumstances here strongly suggest that the ordinance was designed to suppress expression, even that constitutionally protected, and thus was not to be analyzed as a content-neutral time, place, and manner restriction. The Court allows Renton to conceal its illicit motives, however, by reliance on the fact that other communities adopted similar restrictions. The Court's approach largely immunizes such measures from judicial scrutiny, since a municipality can readily find other municipal ordinances to rely upon, thus always retrospectively justifying special zoning regulations for adult theaters.[7] Rather than speculate about Renton's motives for adopting such measures, our cases require the conclusion that the ordinance, like any other content-based restriction on speech, is constitutional "only if the [city] can show that [it] is a precisely drawn means of serving a compelling [governmental] interest." Only this strict approach can insure that cities will not use their zoning powers as a pretext for suppressing constitutionally protected expression. ...

However, respondents do not ask Renton to guarantee low-price sites for their businesses, but seek only a reasonable opportunity to operate adult theaters in the city. By denying them this opportunity, Renton can effectively ban a form of protected speech from its borders. The ordinance "greatly restrict[s] access to ... lawful speech," *American Mini Theatres, supra,* 427 U.S., at 71, n. 35, 96 S.Ct., at 2453, n. 35 (plurality opinion), and is plainly unconstitutional.

Notes and Questions

1. *Content-based vs. content-neutral.* Why did the Court conclude that this case is governed by *Young?* What did the Court say about whether this was a content-based or content-neutral regulation? Did its analysis of content-based and content-neutral make sense to you? Do you agree with the majority decision's result?
2. *Secondary effects. Renton* is famous for the secondary effects test. As the Court stated it, the "Renton ordinance is aimed not at the *content* of the films shown at 'adult motion picture theatres,' but rather at the *secondary effects* of such theaters on the surrounding community." That concern for secondary effects made the law constitutional. What do you think of secondary effects as a test for First Amendment jurisprudence? Does the focus on secondary effects mean the law is content-neutral?
3. *The dissent.* Justice Brennan's dissent says the ordinance is content-based and not content-neutral. Why does he conclude that? Do the two opinions give you a better understanding of what content-based and content-neutral mean? What does "secondary effects" add to that analysis? Do you agree with the dissent that the ordinance restricts too much speech?

4. Incitement, Defamation, and Commercial Speech

The cases in this chapter have been teaching you about the types of speech the First Amendment protects, how much protection each type is accorded, and what level of scrutiny governs a particular type of speech in a particular context. Can you bring any order to these cases? In this section, we look at other kinds of speech, including violent speech, defamatory publications, and commercial speech, to identify levels of protection for these categories and the relevant level of scrutiny.

a. The Role of Incitement to Lawless Action in Free Speech Analysis

Brandenburg is an often-cited 1969 case about an Ohio law that made it illegal to advocate crime and other unlawful conduct and to congregate to teach about criminality. The unanimous eight-Justice Court, in a *per curiam* opinion, ruled for the speaker, Brandenburg, a Ku Klux Klan leader, and not for Ohio, concluding that the law was unconstitutional. Can you tell from the oral argument, https://www.oyez.org/cases/1968/492, why the Justices agreed on that? Is there anything in the argument that captures what they were concerned about? What Justice does the best job of explaining what the First Amendment protects? The case was about a Ku Klux Klan rally. How is that treated in the argument? Does this video, Center for Civil Education, *Brandenburg v. Ohio*, May 14, 2021, at https://www.youtube.com/watch?v=G8aULrPI4Y8, teach you about *Brandenburg's* role in Court history? Does this video, Quimbee, *Brandenburg v. Ohio* Case Brief Summary, Sept. 16, 2020, at https://www.youtube.com/watch?v=RgwKzgA_koc, explain the Court's holding?

Brandenburg v. Ohio
SUPREME COURT OF THE UNITED STATES, 1969
395 U.S. 444, 89 S.Ct. 1827

PER CURIAM.

The appellant, a leader of a Ku Klux Klan group, was convicted under the Ohio Criminal Syndicalism statute for 'advocat(ing) * * * the duty, necessity, or propriety of crime, sabotage, violence, or unlawful methods of terrorism as a means of accomplishing industrial or political reform' and for 'voluntarily assembl(ing) with any society, group, or assemblage of persons formed to teach or advocate the doctrines of criminal syndicalism.' Ohio Rev. Code Ann. s 2923.13. He was fined $1,000 and sentenced to one to 10 years' imprisonment. ...

The record shows that a man, identified at trial as the appellant, telephoned an announcer-reporter on the staff of a Cincinnati television station and invited him to come to a Ku Klux Klan 'rally' to be held at a farm in Hamilton County. With the cooperation of the organizers, the reporter and a cameraman attended the meeting and filmed the events. Portions of the films were later broadcast on the local station and on a national network.

The prosecution's case rested on the films and on testimony identifying the appellant as the person who communicated with the reporter and who spoke at the rally. The State also introduced into evidence several articles appearing in the film, including a pistol, a rifle, a shotgun, ammunition, a Bible, and a red hood worn by the speaker in the films.

One film showed 12 hooded figures, some of whom carried firearms. They were gathered around a large wooden cross, which they burned. No one was present other than the participants and the newsmen who made the film. Most of the words uttered during the scene were incomprehensible when the film was projected, but scattered phrases could be understood that were derogatory of Negroes and, in one instance, of Jews. Another scene on the same film showed the appellant, in Klan regalia, making a speech. The speech, in full, was as follows:

> 'This is an organizers' meeting. We have had quite a few members here today which

> are—we have hundreds, hundreds of members throughout the State of Ohio. I can quote from a newspaper clipping from the Columbus, Ohio Dispatch, five weeks ago Sunday morning. The Klan has more members in the State of Ohio than does any other organization. We're not a revengent organization, but if our President, our Congress, our Supreme Court, continues to suppress the white, Caucasian race, it's possible that there might have to be some revengeance taken.
>
> 'We are marching on Congress July the Fourth, four hundred thousand strong. From there we are dividing into two groups, one group to march on St. Augustine, Florida, the other group to march into Mississippi. Thank you.'

The second film showed six hooded figures one of whom, later identified as the appellant, repeated a speech very similar to that recorded on the first film. The reference to the possibility of 'revengeance' was omitted, and one sentence was added: 'Personally, I believe the nigger should be returned to Africa, the Jew returned to Israel.' Though some of the figures in the films carried weapons, the speaker did not. ...

These later decisions [including *Dennis*] have fashioned the principle that the constitutional guarantees of free speech and free press do not permit a State to forbid or proscribe advocacy of the use of force or of law violation except where such advocacy is directed to inciting or producing imminent lawless action and is likely to incite or produce such action. ...

Measured by this test, Ohio's Criminal Syndicalism Act cannot be sustained. The Act punishes persons who 'advocate or teach the duty, necessity, or propriety' of violence 'as a means of accomplishing industrial or political reform'; or who publish or circulate or display any book or paper containing such advocacy; or who 'justify' the commission of violent acts 'with intent to exemplify, spread or advocate the propriety of the doctrines of criminal syndicalism'; or who 'voluntarily assemble' with a group formed 'to teach or advocate the doctrines of criminal syndicalism.' Neither the indictment nor the trial judge's instructions to the jury in any way refined the statute's bald definition of the crime in terms of mere advocacy not distinguished from incitement to imminent lawless action.

Accordingly, we are here confronted with a statute which, by its own words and as applied, purports to punish mere advocacy and to forbid, on pain of criminal punishment, assembly with others merely to advocate the described type of action. Such a statute falls within the condemnation of the First and Fourteenth Amendments. The contrary teaching of Whitney v. California, supra, cannot be supported, and that decision is therefore overruled.

Mr. Justice BLACK, concurring.

I agree with the views expressed by Mr. Justice DOUGLAS in his concurring opinion in this case that the 'clear and present danger' doctrine should have no place in the interpretation of the First Amendment. I join the Court's opinion, which, as I understand it, simply cites Dennis v. United States, 341 U.S. 494, 71 S.Ct. 857, 95 L.Ed. 1137 (1951), but does not indicate any agreement on the Court's part with the 'clear and present danger' doctrine on which Dennis purported to rely.

Mr. Justice DOUGLAS, concurring.

... The 'clear and present danger' test was adumbrated by Mr. Justice Holmes in a case arising during World War I— ... Schenck v. United States, 249 U.S. 47, 52, 39 S.Ct. 247, 249, 63 L.Ed. 470. ...

> 'The question in every case is whether the words used are used in such circumstances and are of such a nature as to create a clear and present danger that they will bring about the substantive evils that Congress has a right to prevent. It is a question of proximity and degree.' ...

Though I doubt if the 'clear and present danger' test is congenial to the First Amendment in time of a declared war, I am certain it is not reconcilable with the First Amendment in days of peace. ...

Judge Learned Hand, who wrote for the Court of Appeals in affirming the judgment in Dennis, coined the 'not improbable' test, United States v. Dennis, 2 Cir., 183 F.2d 201, 214, which this Court adopted and which Judge Hand preferred over the 'clear and present danger' test. Indeed, in his book, The Bill of Rights 59 (1958), in referring to Holmes' creation of the 'clear and present danger' test, he said, 'I cannot help thinking that for once Homer nodded.'

My own view is quite different. I see no place in the regime of the First Amendment for any 'clear and present danger' test, whether strict and tight as some would make it, or free-wheeling as the Court in Dennis rephrased it.

When one reads the opinions closely and sees when and how the 'clear and present danger' test has been applied, great misgivings are aroused. First, the threats were often loud but always puny and made serious only by judges so wedded to the status quo that critical analysis made them nervous. Second, the test was so twisted and perverted in Dennis as to make the trial of those teachers of Marxism an all-out political trial which was part and parcel of the cold war that has eroded substantial parts of the First Amendment. ...

The example usually given by those who would punish speech is the case of one who falsely shouts fire in a crowded theatre.

This is, however, a classic case where speech is brigaded with action. They are indeed inseparable and a prosecution can be launched for the overt acts actually caused. Apart from rare instances of that kind, speech is, I think, immune from prosecution.

Notes and Questions

1. *How to treat speech advocating for illegal ends.* What do you think of the *Brandenburg* test: the "principle that the constitutional guarantees of free speech and free press do not permit a State to forbid or proscribe advocacy of the use of force or of law violation except where such advocacy is directed to inciting or producing imminent lawless action and is likely to incite or produce such action"? List other First Amendment tests that you have read about in this chapter.
2. *Defining the type of danger.* Does "clear and present danger" mean violence or is it broader and applicable to illegal acts that are not violent?
3. *No level of scrutiny.* This case was decided before the modern Court's levels of scrutiny were in place. How would you apply a level of scrutiny in a "clear and present danger" case?
4. *Justice Black.* Why does Justice Black oppose the clear and present danger test? How is it different from the majority's test?
5. *Justice Douglas.* What does Justice Douglas say about the clear and present danger test?
6. *The predecessor case. Brandenburg* overruled *Whitney v. California*, 274 U.S. 357 (1927). In that case, the Court unanimously upheld Charlotte Whitney's conviction under California's Criminal Syndicalism Act for organizing a protest group that advocated the unlawful use of violence. The Court held the state could punish those who abuse their freedom of speech by uttering words "inimical to the public welfare, tending to incite crime, disturb the peace or endanger the foundations of organized government and threaten its overthrow." In that case, Justice Brandeis, joined by Justice Holmes, wrote a concurrence advocating a "clear and present danger" test. Why was *Whitney* overruled in *Brandenburg?*
7. *Drawing the line between prosecutable speech and that which is not.* When should speech be immune from prosecution? When should it be prosecutable? What is your reaction to the rule of this case?

b. Regulating Defamation as a Violation of Free Speech

New York Times v. Sullivan is a very famous case about a libel action brought against the *New York Times* by Alabama officials whose names appeared in an ad in the paper. It has set the standard for media lawsuits ever since it was decided in 1964. In this case, you should focus on how a plaintiff can win—or lose—a defamation case. You may have studied defamation in tort law. Why is it affected by the First Amendment?

There are two oral arguments in *New York Times*, held on consecutive days in 1964, https://www.oyez.org/cases/1963/39. Can you tell from the oral arguments why state defamation law is governed by the First Amendment? The ad described in the opinion was included in the Appendix to the opinion and is included below. What can you tell about its constitutionality by studying the ad today?

New York Times Co. v. Sullivan
SUPREME COURT OF THE UNITED STATES, 1964
376 U.S. 254, 84 S.Ct. 710

Mr. Justice BRENNAN delivered the opinion of the Court. [He was joined by Justices WARREN, CLARK, HARLAN, STEWART, and WHITE.]

We are required in this case to determine for the first time the extent to which the constitutional protections for speech and press limit a State's power to award damages in a libel action brought by a public official against critics of his official conduct.

Respondent L. B. Sullivan is one of the three elected Commissioners of the City of Montgomery, Alabama. He testified that he was 'Commissioner of Public Affairs and the duties are supervision of the Police Department, Fire Department, Department of Cemetery and Department of Scales.' He brought this civil libel action against the four individual petitioners, who are Negroes and Alabama clergymen, and against petitioner the New York Times Company, a New York corporation which publishes the New York Times, a daily newspaper. A jury in the Circuit Court of Montgomery County awarded him damages of $500,000, the full amount claimed, against all the petitioners, and the Supreme Court of Alabama affirmed.

Respondent's complaint alleged that he had been libeled by statements in a full-page advertisement that was carried in the New York Times on March 29, 1960. Entitled 'Heed Their Rising Voices,' the advertisement began by stating that 'As the whole world knows by now, thousands of Southern Negro students are engaged in widespread non-violent demonstrations in positive affirmation of the right to live in human dignity as guaranteed by the U.S. Constitution and the Bill of Rights.' It went on to charge that 'in their efforts to uphold these guarantees, they are being met by an unprecedented wave of terror by those who would deny and negate that document which the whole world looks upon as setting the pattern for modern freedom. * * *' Succeeding paragraphs purported to illustrate the 'wave of terror' by describing certain alleged events. The text concluded with an appeal for funds for three purposes: support of the student movement, 'the struggle for the right-to-vote,' and the legal defense of Dr. Martin Luther King, Jr., leader of the movement, against a perjury indictment then pending in Montgomery. ...

Of the 10 paragraphs of text in the advertisement, the third and a portion of the sixth were the basis of respondent's claim of libel. They read as follows:

Third paragraph:

> 'In Montgomery, Alabama, after students sang 'My Country, 'Tis of Thee' on the State Capitol steps, their leaders were expelled from school, and truckloads of police armed with shotguns and tear-gas ringed the Alabama State College Campus. When the entire student body protested to state authorities by refusing to re-register, their dining hall was padlocked in an attempt to starve them into submission.'

Sixth paragraph:

> 'Again and again the Southern violators have answered Dr. King's peaceful protests with intimidation and violence. They have bombed his home almost killing his wife and child. They have assaulted his person. They have arrested him seven times—for 'speeding,' 'loitering' and similar 'offenses.' And now they have charged him with 'perjury'—a felony under which they could imprison him for ten years. * * *' ...

It is uncontroverted that some of the statements contained in the two paragraphs were not accurate descriptions of events which occurred in Montgomery. ...

III

We hold today that the Constitution delimits a State's power to award damages for libel in actions brought by public officials against critics of their official conduct. Since this is such an action, the rule requiring proof of actual malice is applicable. While Alabama law apparently requires proof of actual malice for an award of punitive damages, where general damages are concerned malice is 'presumed.' Such a presumption is inconsistent with the federal rule. 'The power to create presumptions is not a means of escape from constitutional restrictions.' Since the trial judge did not instruct the jury to differentiate between general and punitive damages, it may be that the verdict was wholly an award of one or the other. But it is impossible to know, in view of the general verdict returned. Because of this uncertainty, the judgment must be reversed and the case remanded.

Since respondent may seek a new trial, we deem that considerations of effective judicial administration require us to review the evidence in the present record to determine whether it could constitutionally support a judgment for respondent. This Court's duty is not limited to the elaboration of constitutional principles; we must also in proper cases review the evidence to make certain that those principles have been constitutionally applied. This is such a case, particularly since the question is one of alleged trespass across 'the line between speech unconditionally guaranteed and speech which may legitimately be regulated.' In cases where that line must be drawn, the rule is that we 'examine for ourselves the statements in issue and the circumstances under which they were made to see * * * whether they are of a character which the principles of the First Amendment, as adopted by the Due Process Clause of the Fourteenth Amendment, protect.' We must 'make an independent examination of the whole record,' so as to assure ourselves that the judgment does not constitute a forbidden intrusion on the field of free expression.

Applying these standards, we consider that the proof presented to show actual malice lacks the convincing clarity which the constitutional standard demands, and hence that it would not constitutionally sustain the judgment for respondent under the proper rule of law. The case of the individual petitioners requires little discussion. Even assuming that they could constitutionally be found to have authorized the use of their names on the advertisement, there was no evidence whatever that they were aware of any erroneous statements or were in any way reckless in that regard. The judgment against them is thus without constitutional support.

As to the Times, we similarly conclude that the facts do not support a finding of actual malice. The statement by the Times' Secretary that, apart from the padlocking allegation, he thought the advertisement was 'substantially correct,' affords no constitutional warrant for the Alabama Supreme Court's conclusion that it was a 'cavalier ignoring of the falsity of the advertisement (from which), the jury could not have but been impressed with the bad faith of The Times, and its maliciousness inferable therefrom.' The statement does not indicate malice at the time of the publication; even if the advertisement was not 'substantially correct'—although respondent's own proofs tend to show that it was—that opinion was at least a reasonable one, and there was no evidence to impeach the witness' good faith in holding it. The Times' failure to retract upon respondent's demand, although it later retracted upon the demand of Governor Patterson, is likewise not adequate evidence of malice for constitutional purposes. Whether or not a failure to retract may ever constitute such evidence, there are two reasons why it does not here. First, the letter written by the Times reflected a reasonable doubt on its part as to whether the advertisement could reasonably be taken to refer to respondent at all. Second, it was not a final refusal, since it asked for an explanation on this point—a request that respondent chose to ignore. Nor does the retraction upon the demand of the Governor supply the necessary proof. It may be doubted that a failure to retract which is not itself evidence of malice can retroactively become such by virtue of a retraction subsequently made to another party. But in any event that did not happen here, since the explanation given by the Times' Secretary for the distinction drawn between respondent and the Governor was a reasonable one, the good faith of which was not impeached. ...

We think the evidence against the Times supports at most a finding of negligence in failing to discover the misstatements, and is constitutionally insufficient to show the recklessness that is required for a finding of actual malice.

Mr. Justice BLACK, with whom Mr. Justice DOUGLAS joins (concurring).

I concur in reversing this half-million-dollar judgment against the New York Times Company and the four individual defendants. I base my vote to reverse on the belief that the First and Fourteenth Amendments not merely 'delimit' a State's power to award damages to 'public officials against critics of their official conduct' but completely prohibit a State from exercising such a power. The Court goes on to hold that a State can subject such critics to damages if 'actual malice' can be proved against them. 'Malice,' even as defined by the Court, is an elusive, abstract concept, hard to prove and hard to disprove. The requirement that malice be proved provides at best an evanescent protection for the right critically to discuss public affairs and certainly does not measure up to the sturdy safeguard embodied in the First Amendment. Unlike the Court, therefore, I vote to reverse exclusively on the ground that the Times and the individual defendants had an absolute, unconditional constitutional right to publish in the Times advertisement their criticisms of the Montgomery agencies and officials. ...

We would, I think, more faithfully interpret the First Amendment by holding that at the very least it leaves the people and the press free to criticize officials and discuss public affairs with impunity. ...

Mr. Justice GOLDBERG, with whom Mr. Justice DOUGLAS joins (concurring in the result).

... In my view, the First and Fourteenth Amendments to the Constitution afford to the citizen and to the press an absolute, unconditional privilege to criticize official conduct despite the harm which may flow from excesses and abuses.

For these reasons, I strongly believe that the Constitution accords citizens and press an unconditional freedom to criticize official conduct. It necessarily follows that in a case such as this, where all agree that the allegedly defamatory statements related to official conduct, the judgments for libel cannot constitutionally be sustained.

Notes and Questions

1. *Actual malice.* What is actual malice? How could a plaintiff prove actual malice in court? Why did Justice Brennan choose actual malice as the legal standard here? Imagine that a private person brought this lawsuit and not public officials. Should they be accorded the same standard? What if the publication were online, reaching millions of viewers. Does "actual malice" as a standard make more or less sense on those facts? When could a plaintiff win under *New York Times*? When would they lose?
2. *Justice Black's absolute approach.* Why did Justice Black think the *Times* "had an absolute, unconditional constitutional right to publish in the Times advertisement their criticisms of the Montgomery agencies and officials"? Should the press be free to criticize the government "with impunity"? How is that different from Brennan's test? Which do you prefer?
3. *Justice Goldberg's absolute approach.* Do you agree with Justice Goldberg that citizens and the press have "an absolute, unconditional privilege to criticize official conduct"? Is there a distinction between Justices Black's and Goldberg's absolute protection theories?
4. *What is the purpose of the* Times's *opinions of the actual malice standard?* In 2019, Justice Clarence Thomas called for *Times* to be overruled as it had no basis in the Constitution. Thomas thought the states should enjoy more freedom to allow libel suits to proceed. Thomas wrote a concurrence to an opinion denying certiorari in *McKee v. Cosby*, 139 S. Ct. 675 (2019). The lower courts had ruled that Kathrine McKee had become a public figure with her rape accusations against Bill Cosby, and she could not make the demanding showing that *New York Times* required. Thomas said *Times* was "policy-driven decisions masquerading as constitutional law." *McKee v. Cosby*, 139 S. Ct. 675, 676 (2019). Thomas, always focused on the original meaning of

The New York Times.

NEW YORK, TUESDAY, MARCH 29, 1960.

"*The growing movement of peaceful mass demonstrations by Negroes is something new in the South, something understandable. . . . Let Congress heed their rising voices, for they will be heard.*"

—New York Times editorial
Saturday, March 19, 1960

Heed Their Rising Voices

As the whole world knows by now, thousands of Southern Negro students are engaged in widespread non-violent demonstrations in positive affirmation of the right to live in human dignity as guaranteed by the U. S. Constitution and the Bill of Rights. In their efforts to uphold these guarantees, they are being met by an unprecedented wave of terror by those who would deny and negate that document which the whole world looks upon as setting the pattern for modern freedom. . . .

In Orangeburg, South Carolina, when 400 students peacefully sought to buy doughnuts and coffee at lunch counters in the business district, they were forcibly ejected, tear-gassed, soaked to the skin in freezing weather with fire hoses, arrested en masse and herded into an open barbed-wire stockade to stand for hours in the bitter cold.

In Montgomery, Alabama, after students sang "My Country, 'Tis of Thee" on the State Capitol steps, their leaders were expelled from school, and truck-loads of police armed with shotguns and tear-gas ringed the Alabama State College Campus. When the entire student body protested to state authorities by refusing to re-register, their dining hall was padlocked in an attempt to starve them into submission.

In Tallahassee, Atlanta, Nashville, Savannah, Greensboro, Memphis, Richmond, Charlotte, and a host of other cities in the South, young American teenagers, in face of the entire weight of official state apparatus and police power, have boldly stepped forth as protagonists of democracy. Their courage and amazing restraint have inspired millions and given a new dignity to the cause of freedom.

Small wonder that the Southern violators of the Constitution fear this new, non-violent brand of freedom fighter . . . even as they fear the upswelling right-to-vote movement. Small wonder that they are determined to destroy the one man who, more than any other, symbolizes the new spirit now sweeping the South—the Rev. Dr. Martin Luther King, Jr., world-famous leader of the Montgomery Bus Protest. For it is his doctrine of non-violence which has inspired and guided the students in their widening wave of sit-ins; and it this same Dr. King who founded and is president of the Southern Christian Leadership Conference—the organization which is spearheading the surging right-to-vote movement. Under Dr. King's direction the Leadership Conference conducts Student Workshops and Seminars in the philosophy and technique of non-violent resistance.

Again and again the Southern violators have answered Dr. King's peaceful protests with intimidation and violence. They have bombed his home almost killing his wife and child. They have assaulted his person. They have arrested him seven times—for "speeding," "loitering" and similar "offenses." And now they have charged him with "perjury"—a *felony* under which they could imprison him for *ten years*. Obviously, their real purpose is to remove him physically as the leader to whom the students and millions of others—look for guidance and support, and thereby to intimidate *all* leaders who may rise in the South. Their strategy is to behead this affirmative movement, and thus to demoralize Negro Americans and weaken their will to struggle. The defense of Martin Luther King, spiritual leader of the student sit-in movement, clearly, therefore, is an integral part of the total struggle for freedom in the South.

Decent-minded Americans cannot help but applaud the creative daring of the students and the quiet heroism of Dr. King. But this is one of those moments in the stormy history of Freedom when men and women of good will must do more than applaud the rising-to-glory of others. The America whose good name hangs in the balance before a watchful world, the America whose heritage of Liberty these Southern Upholders of the Constitution are defending, is *our* America as well as theirs . . .

We must heed their rising voices—yes—but we must add our own.

We must extend ourselves above and beyond moral support and render the material help so urgently needed by those who are taking the risks, facing jail, and even death in a glorious re-affirmation of our Constitution and its Bill of Rights.

We urge you to join hands with our fellow Americans in the South by supporting, with your dollars, this Combined Appeal for all three needs—the defense of Martin Luther King—the support of the embattled students—and the struggle for the right-to-vote.

Your Help Is Urgently Needed . . . NOW!!

Stella Adler
Raymond Pace Alexander
Shelly Appleton
Harry Van Arsdale
Harry Belafonte
Julie Belafonte
Dr. Algernon Black
Marc Blitztein
William Bowe
William Branch
Marlon Brando
Mrs. Ralph Bunche
Diahann Carroll
Dr. Alan Knight Chalmers
Joseph Cohen
Richard Coe
Nat King Cole
Cheryl Crawford
Dorothy Dandridge
Ossie Davis
Sammy Davis, Jr.
Ruby Dee
Harry Duffy
Scotty Eckford
Dr. Philip Elliott
Dr. Harry Emerson Fosdick
Anthony Franciosa
Mathew Guinan
Lorraine Hansbury
Rev. Donald Harrington
Nat Hentoff
James Hicks
Mary Hinkson
Van Heflin
Langston Hughes
Morris Iushewitz
Mahalia Jackson
Paul Jennings
Mordecai Johnson
John Killens
Eartha Kitt
Rabbi Edward Klein
Hope Lange
John Lewis
Viveca Lindfors
David Livingston
William Michaelson
Carl Murphy
Don Murray
John Murray
A. J. Muste
Frederick O'Neal
Peter Ottley
L. Joseph Overton
Albert P. Palmer
Clarence Pickett
Shad Polier
Sidney Poitier
Michael Potoker
A. Philip Randolph
John Raitt
Elmer Rice
Cleveland Robinson
Jackie Robinson
Mrs. Eleanor Roosevelt
Bayard Rustin
Robert Ryan
Maureen Stapleton
Frank Silvera
Louis Simon
Hope Stevens
David Sullivan
Julius Sum
George Tabori
Rev. Gardner C. Taylor
Norman Thomas
Kenneth Tynan
Charles White
Shelley Winters
Max Youngstein

We in the south who are struggling daily for dignity and freedom warmly endorse this appeal

Rev. Ralph D. Abernathy (Montgomery, Ala.)
Rev. Fred L. Shuttlesworth (Birmingham, Ala.)
Rev. Kelley Miller Smith (Nashville, Tenn.)
Rev. W. A. Dennis (Chattanooga, Tenn.)
Rev. C. K. Steele (Tallahassee, Fla.)
Rev. Matthew D. McCollom (Orangeburg, S. C.)
Rev. William Holmes Borders (Atlanta, Ga.)
Rev. Douglas Moore (Durham, N. C.)
Rev. Wyatt Tee Walker (Petersburg, Va.)
Rev. Walter L. Hamilton (Norfolk, Va.)
I. S. Levy (Columbia, S. C.)
Rev. Martin Luther King, Sr. (Atlanta, Ga.)
Rev. Henry C. Bunton (Memphis, Tenn.)
Rev. S. S. Seay, Sr. (Montgomery, Ala.)
Rev. Samuel W. Williams (Atlanta, Ga.)
Rev. A. L. Davis (New Orleans, La.)
Mrs. Katie E. Whickham (New Orleans, La.)
Rev. W. H. Hall (Hattiesburg, Miss.)
Rev. J. E. Lowery (Mobile, Ala.)
Rev. T. J. Jemison (Baton Rouge, La.)

COMMITTEE TO DEFEND MARTIN LUTHER KING AND THE STRUGGLE FOR FREEDOM IN THE SOUTH
312 West 125th Street, New York 27, N. Y. UNiversity 6-1700

Chairmen: A. Philip Randolph, Dr. Gardner C. Taylor; *Chairmen of Cultural Division:* Harry Belafonte, Sidney Poitier; *Treasurer:* Nat King Cole; *Executive Director:* Bayard Rustin; *Chairmen of Church Division:* Father George B. Ford, Rev. Harry Emerson Fosdick, Rev. Thomas Kilgore, Jr., Rabbi Edward E. Klein; *Chairmen of Labor Division:* Morris Iushewitz, Cleveland Robinson

Please mail this coupon TODAY!

Committee To Defend Martin Luther King
and
The Struggle For Freedom In The South
312 West 125th Street, New York 27, N. Y.
UNiversity 6-1700

I am enclosing my contribution of $_____ for the work of the Committee.

Name _____ (PLEASE PRINT)
Address _____
City _____ Zone _____ State _____

☐ I want to help ☐ Please send further information

Please make checks payable to:
Committee To Defend Martin Luther King

FIGURE 9.2 New York Times front page, March 29, 1960.

the Constitution, thought it would allow the lawsuits as in the past public figures did not have to meet heightened scrutiny. "In short, there appears to be little historical evidence suggesting that the *New York Times* actual-malice rule flows from the original understanding of the First or Fourteenth Amendment." Thomas later said "surely this Court should not remove a woman's right to defend her reputation in court simply because she accuses a powerful man of rape." Would you overrule the use of "actual malice" or alter its application depending on the facts? Would it make sense to say that it cannot be applied in sexual abuse and assault cases?

5. *The New York Times test in the context of the expansion of means of communication.* On a different cert. denial, Justice Gorsuch joined Thomas in questioning *Times*. Gorsuch noted that the media today are very different from 1964. Speaking of the actual malice standard, he wrote, "But if that justification had force in a world with comparatively few platforms for speech, it's less obvious what force it has in a world in which everyone carries a soapbox in their hands." *Berisha v. Lawson*, 141 S. Ct. 2424, 2427–28 (2021). "But given the momentous changes in the Nation's media landscape since 1964, I cannot help but think the Court would profit from returning its attention, whether in this case or another, to a field so vital to the 'safe deposit' of our liberties." *Id.* at 2430. Do you think *Times* should be overruled because of the proliferation of means of communication? Would you replace it with a different standard?

c. Sexual Images of Children

In our earlier cases, we talked about some kinds of speech that do not enjoy First Amendment protection. Do you remember what those areas of speech were? What about fighting words? Defamation? Obscenity? What protection does hate speech enjoy?

How much First Amendment protection do you think child pornography, also known as child sex abuse materials, should enjoy? None? Some, but less than fighting words? More than fighting words? Does thinking about child pornography give you a better idea of what speech deserves First Amendment protection?

The opening line of the oral argument in *Ferber*, https://www.oyez.org/cases/1981/81-55, is: "The issue in this case is whether New York can make it a crime to disseminate materials, for example, a movie, which show a 12-year-old child actually having sex with an animal or an adult without requiring that the entire movie be obscene." What do you think the answer to that question is? Which lawyer did a better job arguing about child pornography, the one arguing for the speaker or the one arguing for the state?

Amici are friends of the Court, who argue on behalf of one side or another to support the parties' arguments in a case. Who would be good amici on each side in this case?

New York v. Ferber
SUPREME COURT OF THE UNITED STATES, 1982
458 U.S. 747, 102 S.Ct. 3348

Justice WHITE delivered the opinion of the Court. [He was joined by Justices BURGER, POWELL, REHNQUIST, and O'CONNOR.]

At issue in this case is the constitutionality of a New York criminal statute which prohibits persons from knowingly promoting sexual performances by children under the age of 16 by distributing material which depicts such performances. ...

This case arose when Paul Ferber, the proprietor of a Manhattan bookstore specializing in sexually oriented products, sold two films to an undercover police officer. The films are devoted almost exclusively to depicting young boys masturbating. Ferber was indicted on two counts of violating § 263.10 and two counts of violating § 263.15, the two New York laws controlling dissemination of child pornography. After a jury trial, Ferber was acquitted of the two counts of promoting an obscene sexual performance, but found guilty of the two counts under § 263.15, which did not require proof that the films were obscene. ...

This case, however, constitutes our first examination of a statute directed at and limited to depictions of sexual activity involving children. We believe our inquiry should begin with the question of whether a State has somewhat more freedom in proscribing works which portray sexual acts or lewd exhibitions of genitalia by children. ...

In *Miller v. California*, a majority of the Court agreed that a "state offense must also be limited to works which, taken as a whole, appeal to the prurient interest in sex, which portray sexual conduct in a patently offensive way, and which, taken as a whole, do not have serious literary, artistic, political, or scientific value." Over the past decade, we have adhered to the guidelines expressed in *Miller*, which subsequently has been followed in the regulatory schemes of most States.

The *Miller* standard, like its predecessors, was an accommodation between the State's interests in protecting the "sensibilities of unwilling recipients" from exposure to pornographic material and the dangers of censorship inherent in unabashedly content-based laws. Like obscenity statutes, laws directed at the dissemination of child pornography run the risk of suppressing protected expression by allowing the hand of the censor to become unduly heavy. For the following reasons, however, we are persuaded that the States are entitled to greater leeway in the regulation of pornographic depictions of children.

First. It is evident beyond the need for elaboration that a State's interest in "safeguarding the physical and psychological well-being of a minor" is "compelling." ...

Second. The distribution of photographs and films depicting sexual activity by juveniles is intrinsically related to the sexual abuse of children in at least two ways. First, the materials produced are a permanent record of the children's participation and the harm to the child is exacerbated by their circulation. Second, the distribution network for child pornography must be closed if the production of material which requires the sexual exploitation of children is to be effectively controlled. ...

The *Miller* standard, like all general definitions of what may be banned as obscene, does not reflect the State's particular and more compelling interest in prosecuting those who promote the sexual exploitation of children. We therefore cannot conclude that the *Miller* standard is a satisfactory solution to the child pornography problem. ...

Third. The advertising and selling of child pornography provide an economic motive for and are thus an integral part of the production of such materials, an activity illegal throughout the Nation. ...

Fourth. The value of permitting live performances and photographic reproductions of children engaged in lewd sexual conduct is exceedingly modest, if not *de minimis*. We consider it unlikely that visual depictions of children performing sexual acts or lewdly exhibiting their genitals would often constitute an important and necessary part of a literary performance or scientific or educational work. ...

Fifth. Recognizing and classifying child pornography as a category of material outside the protection of the First Amendment is not, incompatible with our earlier decisions. ...

There are, of course, limits on the category of child pornography which, like obscenity, is unprotected by the First Amendment. As with all legislation in this sensitive area, the conduct to be prohibited must be adequately defined by the applicable state law, as written or authoritatively construed. Here the nature of the harm to be combated requires that the state offense be limited to works that *visually* depict sexual conduct by children below a specified age. The category of "sexual conduct" proscribed must also be suitably limited and described.

The test for child pornography is separate from the obscenity standard enunciated in *Miller*, but may be compared to it for the purpose of clarity. The *Miller* formulation is adjusted in the following respects: A trier of fact need not find that the material appeals to the prurient interest of the average person; it is not required that sexual conduct portrayed be done so in a patently offensive manner; and the material at issue need not be considered as a whole. We note that the distribution of descriptions or other depictions of sexual conduct, not otherwise obscene, which do not involve live performance or photographic or other visual reproduction of live performances, retains First Amendment protection. As with obscenity laws, criminal responsibility may not be imposed without some element of scienter on the part of the defendant. ...

[W]e hold that § 263.15 is not substantially overbroad. We consider this the paradigmatic case of a state statute whose legitimate reach dwarfs its arguably impermissible applications. New York, as we have held, may constitutionally prohibit dissemination of material specified in § 263.15. While the reach of the statute is directed at the hard core of child pornography, the Court of Appeals was understandably concerned that some protected expression, ranging from medical textbooks to pictorials in the National Geographic would fall prey to the statute. How often, if ever, it may be necessary to employ children to engage in conduct clearly within the reach of § 263.15 in order to produce educational, medical, or artistic works cannot be known with certainty. Yet we seriously doubt, and it has not been suggested, that these arguably impermissible applications of the statute amount to more than a tiny fraction of the materials within the statute's reach. Nor will we assume that the New York courts will widen the possibly invalid reach of the statute by giving an expansive construction to the proscription on "lewd exhibition[s] of the genitals." Under these circumstances, § 263.15 is "not substantially overbroad and ... whatever overbreadth may exist should be cured through case-by-case analysis of the fact situations to which its sanctions, assertedly, may not be applied." ...

Justice O'CONNOR, concurring.

Although I join the Court's opinion, I write separately to stress that the Court does not hold that New York must except "material with serious literary, scientific, or educational value," from its statute. The Court merely holds that, even if the First Amendment shelters such material, New York's current statute is not sufficiently overbroad to support respondent's facial attack. The compelling interests identified in today's opinion, see *ante*, at 3354–3358, suggest that the Constitution might in fact permit New York to ban knowing distribution of works depicting minors engaged in explicit sexual conduct, regardless of the social value of the depictions. For example, a 12-year-old child photographed while masturbating surely suffers the same psychological harm whether the community labels the photograph "edifying" or "tasteless." The audience's appreciation of the depiction is simply irrelevant to New York's asserted interest in protecting children from psychological, emotional, and mental harm. ...

On the other hand, it is quite possible that New York's statute is overbroad because it bans depictions that do not actually threaten the harms identified by the Court. For example, clinical pictures of adolescent sexuality, such as those that might appear in medical textbooks, might not involve the type of sexual exploitation and abuse targeted by New York's statute. Nor might such depictions feed the poisonous "kiddie porn" market that New York and other States have attempted to regulate. Similarly, pictures of children engaged in rites widely approved by their cultures, such as those that might appear in issues of the National Geographic, might not trigger the compelling interests identified by the Court. It is not necessary to address these possibilities further today, however, because this potential overbreadth is not sufficiently substantial to warrant facial invalidation of New York's statute.

Justice BRENNAN, with whom Justice MARSHALL joins, concurring in the judgment.

... In short, it is inconceivable how a depiction of a child that is itself a serious contribution to the world of art or literature or science can be deemed "material outside the protection of the First Amendment."

I, of course, adhere to my view that, in the absence of exposure, or particular harm, to juveniles or unconsenting adults, the State lacks power to suppress sexually oriented materials. ...

Justice STEVENS, concurring in the judgment.

... A hypothetical example will illustrate my concern. Assume that the operator of a New York motion picture theater specializing in the exhibition of foreign feature films is offered a full-length movie containing one scene that is plainly lewd if viewed in isolation but that nevertheless is part of a serious work of art. If the child actor resided abroad, New York's interest in protecting its young from sexual exploitation would be far less compelling than in the case before us. The federal interest in free expression would, however, be just as strong as if an adult actor had been used. There are at least three different ways to deal with the statute's potential application to that sort of case.

First, at one extreme and as the Court appears to hold, the First Amendment inquiry might be limited to determining whether the offensive scene, viewed in isolation, is lewd. ...

Second, at the other extreme and as the New York Court of Appeals correctly perceived, the application of this Court's cases requiring that an obscenity determination be based on the artistic value of a production taken as a whole would afford the exhibitor constitutional protection and result in a holding that the statute is invalid because of its overbreadth. ...

Third, as an intermediate position, I would refuse to apply overbreadth analysis for reasons unrelated to any prediction concerning the relative number of protected communications that the statute may prohibit. Specifically, I would postpone decision of my hypothetical case until it actually arises. ...

Notes and Questions

1. *The type of speech.* Is child pornography protected speech? Should sexual depictions of children enjoy any First Amendment protection?
2. *The* Miller *case.* The Court focused on *Miller*, its case about pornography's protection under the First Amendment. Why is that case relevant here? Why is this case different? How did the Court distinguish *Miller?* Why are states "entitled to greater leeway in the regulation of pornographic depictions of children" than adults?
3. *Overbreadth.* Why are the Justices disagreeing about overbreadth? What do they say about the Amendment's protection of artistic presentations of child sexuality?
4. *The concurrences.* Why did O'Connor, Brennan, and Stevens concur? What do their concurrences add to the analysis?
5. *Regulation of the Internet and online child sexual exploitation.* In 1997, the Supreme Court invalidated the Communications Decency Act and, along the way, created a category of protected speech involving adults viewing sexual images of children. *Reno v. ACLU,* 521 U.S. 844 (1997). How do you square *Ferber* with that reasoning?

d. Commercial Speech

There is a huge swath of speech we have not yet covered, namely advertisements. How do they fit into the First Amendment? Do they enjoy First Amendment protection? Why or why not? Virginia had laws saying pharmacists could not advertise the prices of their prescription drugs. Can you tell from the oral argument, https://www.oyez.org/cases/1975/74-895, what the arguments for and against First Amendment protection are? Justice Rehnquist was the lone dissenter in the case. Can you tell why from his questions during the oral argument?

Virginia State Board of Pharmacy v. Virginia Citizens Consumer Council, Inc.

SUPREME COURT OF THE UNITED STATES, 1976

425 U.S. 748, 96 S.Ct. 1817

Mr. Justice BLACKMUN delivered the opinion of the Court [joined by BURGER, BRENNAN, STEWART, WHITE, MARSHALL, and POWELL].

The plaintiff-appellees in this case attack, as violative of the First and Fourteenth Amendments, that portion of s 54-524.35 of Va.Code Ann. (1974), which provides that a pharmacist licensed in Virginia is guilty of unprofessional conduct if he "(3) publishes, advertises or promotes, directly or indirectly, in any manner whatsoever, any amount, price, fee, premium, discount, rebate or credit terms ... for any drugs which may be dispensed only by prescription." ...

Here, in contrast, the question whether there is a First Amendment exception for "commercial speech" is squarely before us. Our pharmacist does not wish to editorialize on any subject, cultural, philosophical, or political. He does not wish to report any particularly newsworthy fact, or to make generalized observations even about commercial matters. The "idea" he wishes to communicate is simply this: "I will sell you the X prescription drug at the Y price." Our question, then, is whether this communication is wholly outside the protection of the First Amendment. ...

V

We begin with several propositions that already are settled or beyond serious dispute. It is clear, for example, that speech does not lose its First Amendment protection because money is spent to project it, as in a paid advertisement of one form or another. Speech likewise is protected even though it is carried in a form that is "sold" for profit, and even though it may involve a solicitation to purchase or otherwise pay or contribute money.

If there is a kind of commercial speech that lacks all First Amendment protection, therefore, it must be distinguished by its content. Yet the speech whose content deprives it of protection cannot simply be speech on a commercial subject. No one would contend that our pharmacist may be prevented from being heard on the subject of whether, in general, pharmaceutical prices should be regulated, or their advertisement forbidden. Nor can it be dispositive that a commercial advertisement is noneditorial, and merely reports a fact. Purely factual matter of public interest may claim protection.

Our question is whether speech which does "no more than propose a commercial transaction," is so removed from any "exposition of ideas," and from "'truth, science, morality, and arts in general, in its diffusion of liberal sentiments on the administration of Government,'" that it lacks all protection. Our answer is that it is not. ...

Generalizing, society also may have a strong interest in the free flow of commercial information. Even an individual advertisement, though entirely "commercial," may be of general public interest. The facts of decided cases furnish illustrations: advertisements stating that referral services for legal abortions are available, Bigelow v. Virginia, supra; that a manufacturer of artificial furs promotes his product as an alternative to the extinction by his competitors of fur-bearing mammals, see Fur Information & Fashion Council, Inc. v. E. F. Timme & Son, 364 F.Supp. 16 (S.D.N.Y.1973); and that a domestic producer advertises his product as an alternative to imports that tend to deprive American residents of their jobs, cf. Chicago Joint Board v. Chicago Tribune Co., 435 F.2d 470 (C.A.7 1970), cert. denied, 402 U.S. 973, 91 S.Ct. 1662, 29 L.Ed.2d 138 (1971). Obviously, not all commercial messages contain the same or even a very great public interest element. There are few to which such an element, however, could not be added. Our pharmacist, for example, could cast himself as a commentator on store-to-store disparities in drug prices, giving his own and those of a competitor as proof. We see little point in requiring him to do so, and little difference if he does not.

Moreover, there is another consideration that suggests that no line between publicly "interesting" or "important" commercial advertising and the opposite kind could ever be drawn. Advertising, however tasteless and excessive it sometimes may seem, is nonetheless dissemination of information as to who is producing and selling what product, for what reason, and at what price. So long as we preserve a predominantly free enterprise economy, the allocation of our resources in large measure will be made through numerous private economic decisions. It is a matter of public interest that those decisions, in the aggregate, be intelligent and well informed. To this end, the free flow of commercial information is indispensable. And if it is indispensable to the proper allocation of resources in a free enterprise system, it is also indispensable to the formation of intelligent opinions as to how that system ought to be regulated or altered. Therefore, even if the First Amendment were thought to be primarily an instrument to enlighten public decisionmaking in a democracy, we could not say that the free flow of information does not serve that goal. ...

There is, of course, an alternative to this highly paternalistic approach. That alternative is to assume that this information is not in itself harmful, that people will perceive their own best interests if only they are well enough informed, and that the best means to that end is to open the channels of communication rather than to close them. If they are truly open, nothing prevents the "professional" pharmacist from marketing his own assertedly superior product, and contrasting it with that of the low-cost, high-volume prescription drug retailer. But the choice among these alternative approaches is not ours to make or the Virginia General Assembly's. It is precisely this kind of choice, between the dangers of suppressing information, and the dangers of its misuse if it is freely available, that the First Amendment makes for us. Virginia is free to require whatever professional standards it wishes of its pharmacists; it may subsidize them or protect them from competition in other ways. But it may not do so by keeping the public in ignorance of the entirely lawful terms that competing pharmacists are offering. In this sense, the justifications Virginia has offered for suppressing the flow of prescription drug price information, far from persuading us that the flow is not protected by the First Amendment, have reinforced our view that it is. We so hold.

VI

In concluding that commercial speech, like other varieties, is protected, we of course do not hold that it can never be regulated in any way. Some forms of commercial speech regulation are surely permissible. We mention a few only to make clear that they are not before us and therefore are not foreclosed by this case.

There is no claim, for example, that the prohibition on prescription drug price advertising is a mere time, place, and manner restriction. ...

Nor is there any claim that prescription drug price advertisements are forbidden because they are false or misleading in any way. Untruthful speech, commercial or otherwise, has never been protected for its own sake. Obviously, much commercial speech is not provably false, or even wholly false, but only deceptive or misleading. We foresee no obstacle to a State's dealing effectively with this problem. The First Amendment, as we construe it today, does not prohibit the State from insuring that the stream of commercial information flow cleanly as well as freely.

Also, there is no claim that the transactions proposed in the forbidden advertisements are themselves illegal in any way.

What is at issue is whether a State may completely suppress the dissemination of concededly truthful information about entirely lawful activity, fearful of that information's effect upon its disseminators and its recipients. Reserving other questions,[1] we conclude that the answer to this one is in the negative.

Mr. Chief Justice BURGER, concurring.

... I doubt that we know enough about evaluating the quality of medical and legal services to know which claims of superiority are "misleading" and which are justifiable. Nor am I sure that even advertising the price of certain professional services is not inherently misleading, since what the professional must do will vary greatly in individual cases. It is important to note that the Court wisely leaves these issues to another day.

Mr. Justice STEWART, concurring.

... But since it is a cardinal principle of the First Amendment that "government has no power to restrict expression because of its message, its ideas, its subject matter, or its content,"[2] the Court's decision calls into immediate question the constitutional legitimacy of every state and federal law regulating false or deceptive advertising. I write separately to explain why I think today's decision does not preclude such governmental regulation. ...

Mr. Justice REHNQUIST, dissenting.

The logical consequences of the Court's decision in this case, a decision which elevates commercial intercourse between a seller hawking his wares and a buyer seeking to strike a bargain to the same plane as has been previously reserved for the free marketplace of ideas, are far reaching indeed. Under the Court's opinion the way will be open not only for dissemination of price information but for active promotion of prescription drugs, liquor, cigarettes, and other products the use of which it has previously been thought desirable to discourage. Now, however, such promotion is protected by the First Amendment so long as it is not misleading or does not promote an illegal product or enterprise. In coming to this conclusion, the Court has

1. We stress that we have considered in this case the regulation of commercial advertising by pharmacists. Although we express no opinion as to other professions, the distinctions, historical and functional, between professions, may require consideration of quite different factors. Physicians and lawyers, for example, do not dispense standardized products; they render professional Services of almost infinite variety and nature, with the consequent enhanced possibility for confusion and deception if they were to undertake certain kinds of advertising.

overruled a legislative determination that such advertising should not be allowed and has done so on behalf of a consumer group which is not directly disadvantaged by the statute in question. This effort to reach a result which the Court obviously considers desirable is a troublesome one, for two reasons. It extends standing to raise First Amendment claims beyond the previous decisions of this Court. It also extends the protection of that Amendment to purely commercial endeavors which its most vigorous champions on this Court had thought to be beyond its pale. ...

Here the rights of the appellees seem to me to be marginal at best. There is no ideological content to the information which they seek and it is freely available to them they may even publish it if they so desire. The only persons directly affected by this statute are not parties to this lawsuit. On the other hand, the societal interest against the promotion of drug use for every ill, real or imaginary, seems to me extremely strong. I do not believe that the First Amendment mandates the Court's "open door policy" toward such commercial advertising.

Notes and Questions

1. *The level of protection.* Why do advertisements enjoy some First Amendment protection? How much protection do they enjoy?
2. *Commercial speech.* What is commercial speech? How is it different from other speech? How much constitutional protection does Blackmun give to it?
3. *The concurrences.* Why did Stewart and Burger concur? What did their concurrences add to the analysis?
4. *The dissent.* Why did Justice Rehnquist dissent? What does he say about commercial speech? Why is he so opposed to Justice Blackmun's opinion?

B. Freedom of Assembly and Petition

The next case, *Edwards v. South Carolina,* states that the prosecution of a group of Black students violated "their constitutionally protected rights of free speech, free assembly, and freedom to petition for redress of their grievances." We have been talking about free speech. What do free assembly and freedom to petition for redress of their grievances protect? Why are they important enough to be mentioned in the First Amendment?

Review the *South Carolina* oral argument, available at https://www.oyez.org/cases/1962/86. Who does the best job explaining what the First Amendment protects? What it does not protect? Can you tell from the argument that Justice Clark will be the sole dissenter in the case? Are his questions different from those of the other Justices?

Edwards v. South Carolina

SUPREME COURT OF THE UNITED STATES, 1963

372 U.S. 229, 83 S.Ct. 680

Mr. Justice STEWART delivered the opinion of the Court [joined by WARREN, BLACK, DOUGLAS, HARLAN, BRENNAN, WHITE and GOLDBERG]

The petitioners, 187 in number, were convicted in a magistrate's court in Columbia, South Carolina, of the common law crime of breach of the peace. ...

Late in the morning of March 2, 1961, the petitioners, high school and college students of the Negro race, met at the Zion Baptist Church in Columbia. From there, at about noon, they walked in separate groups of about 15 to the South Carolina State House grounds, an area of two city blocks open to the general public.

Their purpose was 'to submit a protest to the citizens of South Carolina, along with the Legislative Bodies of South Carolina, our feelings and our dissatisfaction with the present condition of discriminatory actions against Negroes, in general, and to let them know that we were dissatisfied and that we would like for the laws which prohibited Negro privileges in this State to be removed.' ...

Police protection at the scene was at all times sufficient to meet any foreseeable possibility of disorder.

In the situation and under the circumstances thus described, the police authorities advised the petitioners that they would be arrested if they did not disperse within 15 minutes. Instead of dispersing, the petitioners engaged in what the City Manager described as 'boisterous,' 'loud,' and 'flamboyant' conduct, which, as his later testimony made clear, consisted of listening to a 'religious harangue' by one of their leaders, and loudly singing 'The Star Spangled Banner' and other patriotic and religious songs, while stamping their feet and clapping their hands. After 15 minutes had passed, the police arrested the petitioners and marched them off to jail. ...

And it is clear to us that in arresting, convicting, and punishing the petitioners under the circumstances disclosed by this record, South Carolina infringed the petitioners' constitutionally protected rights of free speech, free assembly, and freedom to petition for redress of their grievances.

It has long been established that these First Amendment freedoms are protected by the Fourteenth Amendment from invasion by the States. The circumstances in this case reflect an exercise of these basic constitutional rights in their most pristine and classic form. The petitioners felt aggrieved by laws of South Carolina which allegedly 'prohibited Negro privileges in this State.' They peaceably assembled at the site of the State Government[10] and there peaceably expressed their grievances 'to the citizens of South Carolina, along with the Legislative Bodies of South Carolina.' Not until they were told by police officials that they must disperse on pain of arrest did they do more. Even then, they but sang patriotic and religious songs after one of their leaders had delivered a 'religious harangue.' There was no violence or threat of violence on their part, or on the part of any member of the crowd watching them. Police protection was 'ample.'

This, therefore, was a far cry from the situation in Feiner v. New York, 340 U.S. 315, 71 S.Ct. 303, 95 L.Ed. 295, where two policemen were faced with a crowd which was 'pushing, shoving and milling around,' id., at 317, 71 S.Ct. at 305, where at least one member of the crowd 'threatened violence if the police did not act,' id., at 317, 71 S.Ct. at 305, where 'the crowd was pressing closer around petitioner and the officer,' id., at 318, 71 S.Ct. at 305, and where 'the speaker passes the bounds of argument or persuasion and undertakes incitement to riot.' Id., at 321, 71 S.Ct. at 306. And the record is barren of any evidence of 'fighting words.' See Chaplinsky v. New Hampshire, 315 U.S. 568, 62 S.Ct. 766, 86 L.Ed. 1031. ...

These petitioners were convicted of an offense so generalized as to be, in the words of the South Carolina Supreme Court, 'not susceptible of exact definition.' And they were convicted upon evidence which showed no more than that the opinions which they were peaceably expressing were sufficiently opposed to the views of the majority of the community to attract a crowd and necessitate police protection. ...

As Chief Justice Hughes wrote in Stromberg v. California, 'The maintenance of the opportunity for free political discussion to the end that government may be responsive to the will of the people and that changes may be obtained by lawful means, an opportunity essential to the security of the Republic, is a fundamental principle of our constitutional system. A statute which upon its face, and as authoritatively construed, is so vague and indefinite as to permit the punishment of the fair use of this opportunity is repugnant to the guaranty of liberty contained in the Fourteenth Amendment. * * *'

For these reasons we conclude that these criminal convictions cannot stand.

Mr. Justice CLARK, dissenting.

The convictions of the petitioners, Negro high school and college students, for breach of the peace under South Carolina law are accepted by the Court 'as binding upon us to that extent' but are held violative of 'petitioners' constitutionally protected rights of free speech, free assembly, and freedom to petition for redress of their grievances.' Petitioners, of course, had a right to peaceable assembly, to espouse their cause and to petition, but in my view the manner in which they exercised those rights was by no means the passive demonstration which this Court relates; rather, as the City Manager of Columbia testified, 'a dangerous situation was really building up' which South

Carolina's courts expressly found had created 'an actual interference with traffic and an imminently threatened disturbance of the peace of the community.' Since the Court does not attack the state courts' findings and accepts the convictions as 'binding' to the extent that the petitioners' conduct constituted a breach of the peace, it is difficult for me to understand its understatement of the facts and reversal of the convictions. ...

The gravity of the danger here surely needs no furthre explication. The imminence of that danger has been emphasized at every stage of this proceeding, from the complaints charging that the demonstrations 'tended directly to immediate violence' to the State Supreme Court's affirmance on the authority of Feiner, supra. This record, then, shows no steps backward from a standard of 'clear and present danger.' But to say that the police may not intervene until the riot has occurred is like keeping out the doctor until the patient dies. ...

I would affirm the convictions.

Notes and Questions

1. *The law being challenged by the students.* Why is breach of the peace a crime?
2. *The different clauses.* What facts of this case implicate free assembly and freedom to petition for redress of their grievance? How are those freedoms different from free speech?
3. *The fact differences from* Feiner. Do you agree that the facts in this case are a "far cry" from *Feiner*? Why are the cases different? What facts distinguish *Feiner* from *Edwards?* Why does this case cite *Chaplinsky*?
4. *The dissenter.* Why did Justice Clark dissent? Why is he the only dissenter? Do you agree with him that "to say that the police may not intervene until the riot has occurred is like keeping out the doctor until the patient dies"? Why, unlike the majority, did he think the situation was dangerous enough to allow restricting the petitioners?

A Look Ahead

In this chapter, we looked at some sections of the First Amendment, namely its rights to speech, assembly, and petition. We move to another section of the First Amendment in the next chapter. We consider the Religion Clauses—the Free Exercise Clause and the Establishment Clause—of the First Amendment.

Credits

Fig. 9.1: Adapted from: Oyez, "How the Justices Voted in Texas," https://www.oyez.org/cases/1988/88-155. Copyright © 2022 by Oyez, Inc.

IMG 9.1: New York Times, "Heed Their Rising Voices," https://commons.wikimedia.org/wiki/File:Heed_Their_Rising_Voices.jpg, 1960.

Ten

The First Amendment's Two Religion Clauses

Introduction

The First Amendment has two religion clauses: "Congress shall make no law ... respecting an establishment of religion, or prohibiting the free exercise thereof."

The Court has repeatedly interpreted each clause separately but often interprets one clause in the context of considering the relationship between them. The Court has separated religion cases into three categories: the right to believe, which is absolute; the right to religious speech, which is highly protected; and the right to conduct, which is less protected due to the impact of conduct on others.

We will first discuss the free exercise of religion and then turn to establishment. As you read these cases, ask yourself just how much free exercise the Constitution protects. Are individuals free to do anything they believe is right? Should there be any limits on the exercise of religion?

The Establishment Clause prohibits a government based on religion. When would we have that? How can we avoid it?

Does your religion affect your answers to these questions?

As you read through the chapter, please consider what is your favorite case in this chapter? Why?

The first case, *Reynolds v. United States*, interprets the Free Exercise Clause and was decided in 1878. It set an early precedent on the meaning of "free exercise." If the case were reargued today, would it be a religious freedom case? Or a sexual freedom case?

A. The Free Exercise of Religion

1. The First Case

The Supreme Court's first free exercise case involved a Congressional ban on polygamy in the Utah Territory. For context, every state outlawed polygamy as well. Does the Congressional law target certain religious believers or regulate all those who practice polygamy?

Reynolds v. United States
SUPREME COURT OF THE UNITED STATES, 1878
98 U.S. 145, 8 Otto 145, 25 L.Ed. 244

MR. CHIEF JUSTICE WAITE delivered the opinion of the court. [He was joined by Justices CLIFFORD, SWAYNE, MILLER, STRONG, BRADLEY, HUNT, and HARLAN.]

...

Should the accused have been acquitted if he married the second time, because he believed it to be his religious duty? ...

5. On the trial, the plaintiff in error, the accused, proved that at the time of his alleged second marriage he was, and for many years before had been, a member of the Church of Jesus Christ of Latter-Day Saints, commonly called the Mormon Church, and a believer in its doctrines; that it was an accepted doctrine of that church "that it was the duty of male members of said church, circumstances permitting, to practise polygamy; ... that this duty was enjoined by different books which the members of said church believed to be of divine origin, and among others the Holy Bible, and also that the members of the church believed that the practice of polygamy was directly enjoined upon the male members thereof by the Almighty God, in a revelation to Joseph Smith, the founder and prophet of said church; that the failing or refusing to practise polygamy by such male members of said church, when circumstances would admit, would be punished, and that the penalty for such failure and refusal would be damnation in the life to come." He also proved "that he had received permission from the recognized authorities in said church to enter into polygamous marriage; ... that Daniel H. Wells, one having authority in said church to perform the marriage ceremony, married the said defendant on or about the time the crime is alleged to have been committed, to some woman by the name of Schofield, and that such marriage ceremony was performed under and pursuant to the doctrines of said church."

Upon this proof he asked the court to instruct the jury that if they found from the evidence that he "was married as charged—if he was married—in pursuance of and in conformity with what he believed at the time to be a religious duty, that the verdict must be 'not guilty.'" This request was refused, and the court did charge "that there must have been a criminal intent, but that if the defendant, under the influence of a religious belief that it was right,—under an inspiration, if you please, that it was right,—deliberately married a second time, having a first wife living, the want of consciousness of evil intent—the want of understanding on his part that he was committing a crime—did not excuse him; but the law inexorably in such case implies the criminal intent."

Upon this charge and refusal to charge the question is raised, whether religious belief can be accepted as a justification of an overt act made criminal by the law of the land. The inquiry is not as to the power of Congress to prescribe criminal laws for the Territories, but as to the guilt of one who knowingly violates a law which has been properly enacted, if he entertains a religious belief that the law is wrong.

Congress cannot pass a law for the government of the Territories which shall prohibit the free exercise of religion. The first amendment to the Constitution expressly forbids such legislation. Religious freedom is guaranteed everywhere throughout the United States, so far as congressional interference is concerned. The question to be determined is, whether the law now under consideration comes within this prohibition.

The word "religion" is not defined in the Constitution. We must go elsewhere, therefore, to ascertain its meaning, and nowhere more appropriately, we think, than to the history of the times in the midst of which the provision was adopted. The precise point of the inquiry is, what is the religious freedom which has been guaranteed.

Before the adoption of the Constitution, attempts were made in some of the colonies and States to legislate not only in respect to the establishment of religion, but in respect to its doctrines and precepts as well. The people were taxed, against their will, for the support of religion, and sometimes for the support of particular sects to whose tenets they could not and did not subscribe. Punishments were prescribed for a failure to attend upon public worship, and sometimes for entertaining heretical opinions. The controversy upon this general subject was animated in many of the States, but seemed at last to culminate in Virginia. In 1784, the House of Delegates of that State having under consideration "a bill establishing provision for teachers of the Christian religion," postponed it until the next session, and directed that the bill should be published and distributed, and that the people be requested "to signify their opinion respecting the adoption of such a bill at the next session of assembly."

This brought out a determined opposition. Amongst others, Mr. Madison prepared a "Memorial and Remonstrance," which was widely circulated and signed, and in which he demonstrated "that religion, or the duty we owe the Creator," was not within the cognizance of civil government. [ ] At the next session the proposed bill was not only defeated, but another, "for establishing religious freedom," drafted by Mr. Jefferson, was passed. [ ] In the preamble of this act [ ] religious freedom is defined; and after a recital "that to suffer the civil magistrate to intrude his powers into the field of opinion, and to restrain the profession or propagation of principles on supposition of their ill tendency, is a dangerous fallacy which at once destroys all religious liberty," it is declared "that it is time enough for the rightful purposes of civil government for its officers to interfere when principles break out into overt acts against peace and good order." In these two sentences is found the true distinction between what properly belongs to the church and what to the State.

In a little more than a year after the passage of this statute the convention met which prepared the Constitution of the United States. Of this convention Mr. Jefferson was not a member, he being then absent as minister to France. As soon as he saw the draft of the Constitution proposed for adoption, he, in a letter to a friend, expressed his disappointment at the absence of an express declaration insuring the freedom of religion, [ ] but was willing to accept it as it was, trusting that the good sense and honest intentions of the people would bring about the necessary alterations. [ ] Five of the States, while adopting the Constitution, proposed amendments. Three—New Hampshire, New York, and Virginia—included in one form or another a declaration of religious freedom in the changes they desired to have made, as did also North Carolina, where the convention at first declined to ratify the Constitution until the proposed amendments were acted upon. Accordingly, at the first session of the first Congress the amendment now under consideration was proposed with others by Mr. Madison. It met the views of the advocates of religious freedom, and was adopted. Mr. Jefferson afterwards, in reply to an address to him by a committee of the Danbury Baptist Association [ ], took occasion to say: "Believing with you that religion is a matter which lies solely between man and his god; that he owes account to none other for his faith or his worship; that the legislative powers of the government reach actions only, and not opinions,—I contemplate with sovereign reverence that act of the whole American people which declared that their legislature should 'make no law respecting an establishment of religion or prohibiting the free exercise thereof,' thus building a wall of separation between church and State. Adhering to this expression of the supreme will of the nation in behalf of the rights of conscience, I shall see with sincere satisfaction the progress of those sentiments which tend to restore man to all his natural rights, convinced he has no natural right in opposition to his social duties." Coming as this does from an acknowledged leader of the advocates of the measure, it may be accepted almost as an authoritative declaration of the scope and effect of the amendment thus secured. Congress was deprived of all legislative power over mere opinion, but was left free to reach actions which were in violation of social duties or subversive of good order.

Polygamy has always been odious among the northern and western nations of Europe, and, until the establishment of the Mormon Church, was almost exclusively a feature of the life of Asiatic and of African people. At common law, the second marriage was always void [ ], and from the earliest history of England polygamy has been treated as an offence against society. After the establishment of the ecclesiastical courts, and until the time of James I., it was punished through the instrumentality of those tribunals, not merely because ecclesiastical rights had been violated, but because upon the separation of the ecclesiastical courts from the civil the ecclesiastical were supposed to be the most appropriate for the trial of matrimonial causes and offences against the rights of marriage, just as they were for testamentary causes and the settlement of the estate of Deceased persons.

By the statute of 1 James I. (c. 11), the offence, if committed in England or Wales, was made punishable in the civil courts, and the penalty was death. As this statute was limited in its operation to England

and Wales, it was at a very early period re-enacted, generally with some modifications, in all the colonies. In connection with the case we are now considering, it is a significant fact that on the 8th of December, 1788, after the passage of the act establishing religious freedom, and after the convention of Virginia had recommended as an amendment to the Constitution of the United States the declaration in a bill of rights that "all men have an equal, natural, and unalienable right to the free exercise of religion, according to the dictates of conscience," the legislature of that State substantially enacted the statute of James I., death penalty included, because, as recited in the preamble, "it hath been doubted whether bigamy or poligamy be punishable by the laws of this Commonwealth." [ ] From that day to this we think it may safely be said there never has been a time in any State of the Union when polygamy has not been an offence against society, cognizable by the civil courts and punishable with more or less severity. In the face of all this evidence, it is impossible to believe that the constitutional guaranty of religious freedom was intended to prohibit legislation in respect to this most important feature of social life. Marriage, while from its very nature a sacred obligation, is nevertheless, in most civilized nations, a civil contract, and usually regulated by law. Upon it society may be said to be built, and out of its fruits spring social relations and social obligations and duties, with which government is necessarily required to deal. ... An exceptional colony of polygamists under an exceptional leadership may sometimes exist for a time without appearing to disturb the social condition of the people who surround it; but there cannot be a doubt that, unless restricted by some form of constitution, it is within the legitimate scope of the power of every civil government to determine whether polygamy or monogamy shall be the law of social life under its dominion.

In our opinion, the statute immediately under consideration is within the legislative power of Congress. It is constitutional and valid as prescribing a rule of action for all those residing in the Territories, and in places over which the United States have exclusive control. This being so, the only question which remains is, whether those who make polygamy a part of their religion are excepted from the operation of the statute. If they are, then those who do not make polygamy a part of their religious belief may be found guilty and punished, while those who do, must be acquitted and go free. This would be introducing a new element into criminal law. Laws are made for the government of actions, and while they cannot interfere with mere religious belief and opinions, they may with practices. Suppose one believed that human sacrifices were a necessary part of religious worship, would it be seriously contended that the civil government under which he lived could not interfere to prevent a sacrifice? Or if a wife religiously believed it was her duty to burn herself upon the funeral pile of her dead husband, would it be beyond the power of the civil government to prevent her carrying her belief into practice?

So here, as a law of the organization of society under the exclusive dominion of the United States, it is provided that plural marriages shall not be allowed. Can a man excuse his practices to the contrary because of his religious belief? To permit this would be to make the professed doctrines of religious belief superior to the law of the land, and in effect to permit every citizen to become a law unto himself. Government could exist only in name under such circumstances. ...

Notes and Questions

1. *Marriage and the public good.* What is the harm in having a person operate as a law unto themselves?
2. *The facts about polygamy.* Due to the Case and Controversy Clause, every case the Court decides is based on a factual basis, not the law in a vacuum. The Court states that polygamy has long been condemned due to the "patriarchy principle." Do you think that polygamy should be legal today? On what factual bases do you derive that conclusion? Some Mormons held onto polygamy and are now known as the Fundamentalist Latter Day Saints (FLDS). Their practices have followed the math of polygamy—the birth rate of males and females is roughly equal. In order to achieve a culture where one man has many wives, two dynamics follow: (1) the men must draw from increasingly younger females to keep adding wives and (2) the group must

remove some younger men. The FLDS has employed both dynamics as have other religious groups that practice polygamy.

3. *Comparing the marriage cases.* Compare and contrast the marriage rights cases you read in earlier chapters, e.g., *Loving* and *Obergefell* to *Reynolds*. How do the cases stack up against each other? Could you use those cases to argue polygamy should be constitutionally protected today?

2. Strict Scrutiny

The following case is a well-known religious freedom case, where Adell Sherbert was fired because she refused to work on her Sabbath, which was Saturday. The state denied her unemployment compensation benefits for "work misconduct" for refusing to work on her Sabbath. The Court ruled that the state had violated the First Amendment. Does her lawyer do a good job in the oral argument, which is available at https://www.oyez.org/cases/1962/526? Do you agree with the Court's conclusion or the dissent? How does this First Amendment ruling differ from *Reynolds*?

Sherbert v. Verner

SUPREME COURT OF THE UNITED STATES, 1963

374 U.S. 398, 83 S.Ct. 1790

MR. JUSTICE BRENNAN delivered the opinion of the Court. [He was joined by Justices WARREN, BLACK, DOUGLAS, CLARK and GOLDBERG.]

Appellant, a member of the Seventh-Day Adventist Church, was discharged by her South Carolina employer because she would not work on Saturday, the Sabbath Day of her faith. When she was unable to obtain other employment because from conscientious scruples she would not take Saturday work, she filed a claim for unemployment compensation benefits under the South Carolina Unemployment Compensation Act. That law provides that, to be eligible for benefits, a claimant must be "able to work and * * * is available for work"; and, further, that a claimant is ineligible for benefits "if * * * he has failed, without good cause * * * to accept available suitable work when offered him by the employment office or the employer * * *." The appellee Employment Security Commission, in administrative proceedings under the statute, found that appellant's restriction upon her availability for Saturday work brought her within the provision disqualifying for benefits insured workers who fail, without good cause, to accept "suitable work when offered * * * by the employment office or the employer * * *." ... [T]he South Carolina Supreme Court rejected appellant's contention that, as applied to her, the disqualifying provisions of the South Carolina statute abridged her right to the free exercise of her religion secured under the Free Exercise Clause of the First Amendment through the Fourteenth Amendment. The State Supreme Court held specifically that appellant's ineligibility infringed no constitutional liberties because such a construction of the statute "places no restriction upon the appellant's freedom of religion nor does it in any way prevent her in the exercise of her right and freedom to observe her religious beliefs in accordance with the dictates of her conscience." ... We reverse the judgment of the South Carolina Supreme Court and remand for further proceedings not inconsistent with this opinion. ...

II

We turn first to the question whether the disqualification for benefits imposes any burden on the free exercise of appellant's religion. We think it is clear that it does. In a sense the consequences of such a disqualification to religious principles and practices may be only an indirect result of welfare legislation within the State's general competence to enact; it is true that no criminal sanctions directly compel appellant to work a six-day week. But this is only the beginning, not the end, of our inquiry. For "if the purpose or effect of a law is to impede the observance of one or all religions or is to discriminate invidiously between religions, that law is constitutionally invalid even though the burden may be characterized as being only indirect." Here not only is it apparent that appellant's declared ineligibility for benefits derives solely from the practice of her religion, but the pressure upon her to forego that practice is unmistakable. The ruling forces her to choose between following the precepts of her religion and forfeiting benefits, on the one hand, and abandoning one of the precepts of her religion in order to accept work, on the other hand. Governmental imposition of such a choice puts the same kind of burden upon the free exercise of religion as would a fine imposed against appellant for her Saturday worship.

Nor may the South Carolina court's construction of the statute be saved from constitutional infirmity on the ground that unemployment compensation benefits are not appellant's "right" but merely a "privilege." It is too late in the day to doubt that the liberties of religion and expression may be infringed by the denial of or placing of conditions upon a benefit or privilege. ... Likewise, to condition the availability of benefits upon this appellant's willingness to violate a cardinal principle of her religious faith effectively penalizes the free exercise of her constitutional liberties.

Significantly South Carolina expressly saves the Sunday worshipper from having to make the kind of choice which we here hold infringes the Sabbatarian's religious liberty. When in times of "national emergency" the textile plants are authorized by the State Commissioner of Labor to operate on Sunday, "no employee shall be required to work on Sunday * * * who is conscientiously opposed to Sunday work; and if any employee should refuse to work on Sunday on account of conscientious * * * objections he or she shall not jeopardize his or her seniority by such refusal or be discriminated against in any other manner." S.C. Code, § 64–4. No question of the disqualification of a Sunday worshipper for benefits is likely to arise, since we cannot suppose that an employer will discharge him in violation of this statute. The unconstitutionality of the disqualification of the Sabbatarian is thus compounded by the religious discrimination which South Carolina's general statutory scheme necessarily effects.

III

We must next consider whether some compelling state interest enforced in the eligibility provisions of the South Carolina statute justifies the substantial infringement of appellant's First Amendment right. It is basic that no showing merely of a rational relationship to some colorable state interest would suffice; in this highly sensitive constitutional area, "only the gravest abuses, endangering paramount interests, give occasion for permissible limitation." No such abuse or danger has been advanced in the present case. The appellees suggest no more than a possibility that the filing of fraudulent claims by unscrupulous claimants feigning religious objections to Saturday work might not only dilute the unemployment compensation fund but also hinder the scheduling by employers of necessary Saturday work. But that possibility is not apposite here because no such objection appears to have been made before the South Carolina Supreme Court, and we are unwilling to assess the importance of an asserted state interest without the views of the state court. Nor, if the contention had been made below, would the record appear to sustain it; there is no proof whatever to warrant such fears of malingering or deceit as those which the respondents now advance. Even if consideration of such evidence is not foreclosed by the prohibition against judicial inquiry into the truth or falsity of religious beliefs, United States v. Ballard, 322 U.S. 78, 64 S.Ct. 882, 88 L.Ed. 1148—a question as to which we intimate no view since it is not before us—it is highly doubtful whether such evidence would be sufficient to warrant a substantial infringement of religious liberties. For even if the possibility of spurious claims did threaten to dilute the fund and disrupt the scheduling of work, it would plainly be incumbent upon the appellees to demonstrate that no alternative forms of regulation would combat such abuses without infringing First Amendment rights. ...

IV

... Our holding today is only that South Carolina may not constitutionally apply the eligibility provisions so as to constrain a worker to abandon his religious convictions respecting the day of rest. This holding but reaffirms a principle that we announced a decade and a half ago, namely that no State may "exclude individual Catholics, Lutherans, Mohammedans, Baptists, Jews, Methodists, Non-believers, Presbyterians, or the members of any other faith, *because of their faith, or lack of it*, from receiving the benefits of public welfare legislation."

Reversed and remanded.

MR. JUSTICE HARLAN, whom MR. JUSTICE WHITE joins, dissenting.

... [T]he implications of the present decision are far more troublesome than its apparently narrow dimensions would indicate at first glance. The meaning of today's holding is that the State must furnish unemployment benefits to one who is unavailable for work if the unavailability stems from the exercise of religious convictions. The State, in other words, must *single out* for financial assistance those whose behavior is religiously motivated, even though it denies such assistance to others whose identical behavior (in this case, inability to work on Saturdays) is not religiously motivated.

It has been suggested that such singling out of religious conduct for special treatment may violate the constitutional limitations on state action. My own view, however, is that at least under the circumstances of this case it would be a permissible accommodation of religion for the State, if it *chose* to do so, to create an exception to its eligibility requirements for persons like the appellant. The constitutional obligation of "neutrality" is not so narrow a channel that the slightest deviation from an absolutely straight course leads to condemnation. There are too many instances in which no such course can be charted, too many areas in which the pervasive activities of the State justify some special provision for religion to prevent it from being submerged by an all-embracing secularism. The State violates its obligation of neutrality when, for example, it mandates a daily religious exercise in its public schools, with all the attendant pressures on the school children that such an exercise entails. But there is, I believe, enough flexibility in the Constitution to permit a legislative judgment accommodating an unemployment compensation law to the exercise of religious beliefs such as appellant's.

For very much the same reasons, however, I cannot subscribe to the conclusion that the State is constitutionally *compelled* to carve out an exception to its general rule of eligibility in the present case. Those situations in which the Constitution may require special treatment on account of religion are, in my view, few and far between, and this view is amply supported by the course of constitutional litigation in this area. Such compulsion in the present case is particularly inappropriate in light of the indirect, remote, and insubstantial effect of the decision below on the exercise of appellant's religion and in light of the direct financial assistance to religion that today's decision requires.

For these reasons I respectfully dissent from the opinion and judgment of the Court.

Notes and Questions

1. *The tests.* What is the test that Justice Brennan's opinion for the majority used to determine whether *Sherbert*'s religious rights had been violated? What test does Justice Harlan suggest? Is either reasoning consistent with the *Reynolds* test? How?
2. *What level of scrutiny for religion and religious conduct?* As explained in earlier chapters, the Court eventually adopted a matrix for decisions, based on whether the government must prove a compelling, important, or rational interest. Should burdens on religion imposed by law always get strict scrutiny? Does *Sherbert* adopt the ordinary strict scrutiny tailoring requirement, narrowly tailored, or does it adopt the most extreme tailoring requirement, the least restrictive means.
3. *The First Amendment.* The First Amendment was not actually the "first" in James Madison's draft list of amendments. Yet, arguments are made that religion is special because it's in the first. Should it receive special treatment? Why or why not?

3. Neutral Laws of General Applicability

Does the following case adhere to the rule of *Reynolds* as Justice Scalia's opinion for the majority argues? The oral argument is at https://www.oyez.org/cases/1989/88-1213. Can you tell from the argument what persuaded a majority of the Court to join this opinion?

Employment Div., Dept. of Human Resources of Oregon v. Smith

SUPREME COURT OF THE UNITED STATES, 1990

494 U.S. 872, 110 S.Ct. 1595

JUSTICE SCALIA delivered the opinion of the Court, in which REHNQUIST, C.J., and WHITE, STEVENS and KENNEDY, joined.

This case requires us to decide whether the Free Exercise Clause of the First Amendment permits the State of Oregon to include religiously inspired peyote use within the reach of its general criminal prohibition on use of that drug, and thus permits the State to deny unemployment benefits to persons dismissed from their jobs because of such religiously inspired use.

I

Oregon law prohibits the knowing or intentional possession of a "controlled substance" unless the substance has been prescribed by a medical practitioner. The law defines "controlled substance" as a drug classified in Schedules I through V of the Federal Controlled Substances Act, as modified by the State Board of Pharmacy. Persons who violate this provision by possessing a controlled substance listed on Schedule I are "guilty of a Class B felony." As compiled by the State Board of Pharmacy under its statutory authority, Schedule I contains the drug peyote, a hallucinogen derived from the plant *Lophophora williamsii Lemaire.*

Respondents Alfred Smith and Galen Black (hereinafter respondents) were fired from their jobs with a private drug rehabilitation organization because they ingested peyote for sacramental purposes at a ceremony of the Native American Church, of which both are members. When respondents applied to petitioner Employment Division (hereinafter petitioner) for unemployment compensation, they were determined to be ineligible for benefits because they had been discharged for work-related "misconduct."

... Citing our decision[] in *Sherbert*, the [Oregon Supreme] court concluded that respondents were entitled to payment of unemployment benefits. ...

II

Respondents' claim for relief rests on our decisions in *Sherbert v. Verner, supra, [and other unemployment compensation cases],* in which we held that a State could not condition the availability of unemployment insurance on an individual's willingness to forgo conduct required by his religion. As we observed in *Smith I,* however, the conduct at issue in those cases was not prohibited by law. ...

A

The Free Exercise Clause of the First Amendment, which has been made applicable to the States by incorporation into the Fourteenth Amendment, provides that "Congress shall make no law respecting an establishment of religion, or *prohibiting the free exercise thereof.* ..." U.S. Const., Amdt. 1 (emphasis added.) The free exercise of religion means, first and foremost, the right to believe and profess whatever religious doctrine one desires. Thus, the First Amendment obviously excludes all "governmental regulation of religious *beliefs* as such." The government may not compel affirmation of religious belief, punish the expression of religious doctrines it believes to be false, impose special disabilities on the basis of religious views or religious status, or lend its power to one or the other side in controversies over religious authority or dogma.

But the "exercise of religion" often involves not only belief and profession but the performance of (or abstention from) physical acts: assembling with others for a worship service, participating in sacramental use of bread and wine, proselytizing, abstaining from certain foods or certain modes of transportation. It would be true, we think (though no case of ours has involved the point), that a State would be "prohibiting the free exercise [of religion]" if it sought to ban such acts or abstentions only when they are engaged in for religious reasons, or only because of the religious belief that they display. It would doubtless be unconstitutional, for example, to ban the casting of "statues that are to be used for worship purposes," or to prohibit bowing down before a golden calf.

Respondents in the present case, however, seek to carry the meaning of "prohibiting the free exercise [of religion]" one large step further. They contend that their religious motivation for using peyote places them beyond the reach of a criminal law that is not specifically directed at their religious practice, and that is concededly constitutional as applied to those who use the drug for other reasons. They assert, in other words, that "prohibiting the free exercise [of religion]" includes requiring any individual to observe a generally applicable law that requires (or forbids) the performance of an act that his religious belief forbids (or requires). As a textual matter, we do not think the words must be given that meaning. It is no more necessary to regard the collection of a general tax, for example, as "prohibiting the free exercise [of religion]" by those citizens who believe support of organized government to be sinful, than it is to regard the same tax as "abridging the freedom ... of the press" of those publishing companies that must pay the tax as a condition of staying in business. It is a permissible reading of the text, in the one case as in the other, to say that if prohibiting the exercise of religion (or burdening the activity of printing) is not the object of the tax but merely the incidental effect of a generally applicable and otherwise valid provision, the First Amendment has not been offended.

Our decisions reveal that the latter reading is the correct one. We have never held that an individual's religious beliefs excuse him from compliance with an otherwise valid law prohibiting conduct that the State is free to regulate. On the contrary, the record of more than a century of our free exercise jurisprudence contradicts that proposition. As described succinctly by Justice Frankfurter in *Gobitis*, "Conscientious scruples have not, in the course of the long struggle for religious toleration, relieved the individual from obedience to a general law not aimed at the promotion or restriction of religious beliefs. The mere possession of religious convictions which contradict the relevant concerns of a political society does not relieve the citizen from the discharge of political responsibilities." We first had occasion to assert that principle in *Reynolds*, where we rejected the claim that criminal laws against polygamy could not be constitutionally applied to those whose religion commanded the practice. ...

Subsequent decisions have consistently held that the right of free exercise does not relieve an individual of the obligation to comply with a "valid and neutral law of general applicability on the ground that the law proscribes (or prescribes) conduct that his religion prescribes (or proscribes)." ...

The only decisions in which we have held that the First Amendment bars application of a neutral, generally applicable law to religiously motivated action have involved not the Free Exercise Clause alone, but the Free Exercise Clause in conjunction with other constitutional protections, such as freedom of speech and of the press, see *Cantwell v. Connecticut* (invalidating a licensing system for religious and charitable solicitations under which the administrator had discretion to deny a license to any cause he deemed nonreligious; *Murdock v. Pennsylvania* (invalidating a flat tax on solicitation as applied to the dissemination of religious ideas); or the right of parents, acknowledged in *Pierce*, to direct the education of their children, see *Wisconsin v. Yoder* (invalidating compulsory school-attendance laws as applied to Amish parents who refused on religious grounds to send their children to school). Some of our cases prohibiting compelled expression, decided exclusively upon free speech grounds, have also involved freedom of religion, cf. *Wooley v. Maynard* (invalidating compelled display of a license plate slogan that offended individual religious beliefs); *Barnette* (invalidating compulsory flag salute statute challenged by religious objectors). And it is easy to envision a case in which a challenge on freedom of association grounds would likewise be reinforced by Free Exercise Clause concerns. Cf. *Roberts v. Jaycees* ("An individual's freedom to speak, to worship, and to petition the government for the redress of grievances could not be vigorously protected from interference by the State [if] a correlative freedom to engage in group effort toward those ends were not also guaranteed").

The present case does not present such a hybrid situation, but a free exercise claim unconnected with any communicative activity or parental right. Respondents urge us to hold, quite simply, that when otherwise prohibitable conduct is accompanied by religious convictions, not only the convictions but the conduct itself must be free from governmental regulation. We have never held that, and decline to do so now. There being no contention that Oregon's drug law represents an attempt to regulate religious beliefs, the communication of religious beliefs, or the raising of one's children in those beliefs, the rule to which we have adhered ever since *Reynolds* plainly controls. …

B

Respondents argue that even though exemption from generally applicable criminal laws need not automatically be extended to religiously motivated actors, at least the claim for a religious exemption must be evaluated under the balancing test set forth in *Sherbert v. Verner*. … We have never invalidated any governmental action on the basis of the *Sherbert* test except the denial of unemployment compensation. Although we have sometimes purported to apply the *Sherbert* test in contexts other than that, we have always found the test satisfied, [see *United States v. Lee*; *Gillette v. United States*]. In recent years we have abstained from applying the *Sherbert* test (outside the unemployment compensation field) at all. …

Even if we were inclined to breathe into *Sherbert* some life beyond the unemployment compensation field, we would not apply it to require exemptions from a generally applicable criminal law. …

We conclude today that the sounder approach, and the approach in accord with the vast majority of our precedents, is to hold the test inapplicable to such challenges. … To make an individual's obligation to obey such a law contingent upon the law's coincidence with his religious beliefs, except where the State's interest is "compelling"—permitting him, by virtue of his beliefs, "to become a law unto himself," *Reynolds v. United States*, 98 U.S., at 167—contradicts both constitutional tradition and common sense.

The "compelling government interest" requirement seems benign, because it is familiar from other fields. But using it as the standard that must be met before the government may accord different treatment on the basis of race, [ ], or before the government may regulate the content of speech is not remotely comparable to using it for the purpose asserted here. What it produces in those other fields—equality of treatment and an unrestricted flow of contending speech—are constitutional norms; what it would produce here—a private right to ignore generally applicable laws—is a constitutional anomaly. …

It is therefore not surprising that a number of States have made an exception to their drug laws for sacramental peyote use. But to say that a nondiscriminatory religious-practice exemption is permitted, or even that it is desirable, is not to say that it is constitutionally required, and that the appropriate occasions for its creation can be discerned by the courts. It may fairly be said that leaving accommodation to the political process will place at a relative disadvantage those religious practices that are not widely engaged in; but that unavoidable consequence of democratic government must be preferred to a system in which each conscience is a law unto itself or in which judges weigh the social importance of all laws against the centrality of all religious beliefs. …

The decision of the Oregon Supreme Court is accordingly reversed.

JUSTICE O'CONNOR, concurring in the judgment.

Although I agree with the result the Court reaches in this case, I cannot join its opinion. In my view, today's holding dramatically departs from well-settled First Amendment jurisprudence, appears unnecessary to resolve the question presented, and is incompatible with our Nation's fundamental commitment to individual religious liberty. …

II

B

Respondents, of course, do not contend that their conduct is automatically immune from all governmental regulation simply because it is motivated by their sincere religious beliefs. … Rather, respondents invoke our traditional compelling interest test to argue that the Free Exercise Clause requires the State to grant them a limited exemption from its general criminal prohibition against the possession of peyote. The Court today, however, denies them even the opportunity to make that argument, concluding that "the sounder approach, and the approach in accord with the vast majority of our precedents, is to hold the [compelling interest] test inapplicable to" challenges to general criminal prohibitions.

In my view, however, the essence of a free exercise claim is relief from a burden imposed by government on religious practices or beliefs, whether the burden is imposed directly through laws that prohibit or compel specific religious practices, or indirectly through laws that, in effect, make abandonment of one's own religion or conformity to the religious beliefs of others the price of an equal place in the civil community.... A State that makes criminal an individual's religiously motivated conduct burdens that individual's free exercise of religion in the severest manner possible, for it "results in the choice to the individual of either abandoning his religious principle or facing criminal prosecution." I would have thought it beyond argument that such laws implicate free exercise concerns.

Indeed, we have never distinguished between cases in which a State conditions receipt of a benefit on conduct prohibited by religious beliefs and cases in which a State affirmatively prohibits such conduct....

Once it has been shown that a government regulation or criminal prohibition burdens the free exercise of religion, we have consistently asked the government to demonstrate that unbending application of its regulation to the religious objector "is essential to accomplish an overriding governmental interest," or represents "the least restrictive means of achieving some compelling state interest." To me, the sounder approach—the approach more consistent with our role as judges to decide each case on its individual merits—is to apply this test in each case to determine whether the burden on the specific plaintiffs before us is constitutionally significant and whether the particular criminal interest asserted by the State before us is compelling. Even if, as an empirical matter, a government's criminal laws might usually serve a compelling interest in health, safety, or public order, the First Amendment at least requires a case-by-case determination of the question, sensitive to the facts of each particular claim. Given the range of conduct that a State might legitimately make criminal, we cannot assume, merely because a law carries criminal sanctions and is generally applicable, that the First Amendment *never* requires the State to grant a limited exemption for religiously motivated conduct....

There is nothing talismanic about neutral laws of general applicability or general criminal prohibitions, for laws neutral toward religion can coerce a person to violate his religious conscience or intrude upon his religious duties just as effectively as laws aimed at religion. Although the Court suggests that the compelling interest test, as applied to generally applicable laws, would result in a "constitutional anomaly," the First Amendment unequivocally makes freedom of religion, like freedom from race discrimination and freedom of speech, a "constitutional nor[m]," not an "anomaly." [ ] ... The Court's parade of horribles not only fails as a reason for discarding the compelling interest test, it instead demonstrates just the opposite: that courts have been quite capable of applying our free exercise jurisprudence to strike sensible balances between religious liberty and competing state interests.

Finally, the Court today suggests that the disfavoring of minority religions is an "unavoidable consequence" under our system of government and that accommodation of such religions must be left to the political process. In my view, however, the First Amendment was enacted precisely to protect the rights of those whose religious practices are not shared by the majority and may be viewed with hostility. The history of our free exercise doctrine amply demonstrates the harsh impact majoritarian rule has had on unpopular or emerging religious groups such as the Jehovah's Witnesses and the Amish.... The compelling interest test reflects the First Amendment's mandate of preserving religious liberty to the fullest extent possible in a pluralistic society. For the Court to deem this command a "luxury" is to denigrate "[t]he very purpose of a Bill of Rights."

[Justice O'Connor then upheld the denial of an exemption because Oregon had met the compelling state interest test with its overriding interest in preventing the physical harm caused by controlled substances. Justices Blackmun, Brennan and Marshall concurred with O'Connor's identification of the compelling state interest test; they, however, believed the state had not met its burden because there was no evidence that religious peyote use harmed people.]

JUSTICE BLACKMUN, with whom JUSTICE BRENNAN and JUSTICE MARSHALL join, dissenting.

This Court over the years painstakingly has developed a consistent and exacting standard to test the constitutionality of a state statute that burdens the free exercise of religion. Such a statute may stand only if the law in general, and the State's refusal to allow a religious exemption in particular, are justified by a compelling interest that cannot be served by less restrictive means.

Until today, I thought this was a settled and inviolate principle of this Court's First Amendment jurisprudence....

I

... The carefully circumscribed ritual context in which respondents used peyote is far removed from the irresponsible and unrestricted recreational use of unlawful drugs.[1] The Native American Church's internal restrictions on, and supervision of, its members' use of peyote substantially obviate the State's health and safety concerns.

II

... Respondents believe, and their sincerity has *never* been at issue, that the peyote plant embodies their deity, and eating it is an act of worship and communion. Without peyote, they could not enact the essential ritual of their religion. ...

If Oregon can constitutionally prosecute them for this act of worship, they, like the Amish, may be "forced to migrate to some other and more tolerant region." This potentially devastating impact must be viewed in light of the federal policy—reached in reaction to many years of religious persecution and intolerance—of protecting the religious freedom of Native Americans. [ ] ...

Notes and Questions

1. *The tests.* What test does the majority identify as the test for the First Amendment's Free Exercise Clause? Justice O'Connor? Justice Brennan? How do those tests relate to *Reynolds* and *Sherbert?* How do those tests differ from one another? Which test do you prefer for the First Amendment? Do you understand why the Justices have chosen different tests?
2. *Defending Smith.* We think *Smith* was well-reasoned even though some have argued it should be overruled. You will see in the *Fulton* case, below, that it is still good law. Why should you agree or disagree with us?
3. *RFRA.* In response to *Smith*, Congress passed the Religious Freedom Restoration Act, RFRA, which was intended to deliver to religious litigants what *Smith* did not: strict scrutiny for neutral and generally applicable laws that burden religion. According to the statute, "Government may substantially burden a person's exercise of religion only if it demonstrates that application of the burden to the person (1) is in furtherance of a compelling governmental interest and (2) is the least restrictive means of furthering that compelling governmental interest." 42 U.S.C. 2000bb-1. The Court ruled in *City of Boerne v. Flores,* 521 U.S. 507 (1997) that Congress did not have the power to apply RFRA to all the state governments because it was so far removed from the actual constitutional standard announced in *Smith.* In other words, the Court itself ruled that RFRA is not a "restoration" of their prior tests but rather a wholly new standard so extreme that it was unconstitutional to force the standard on every state law. RFRA was re-enacted in 2000 to apply to federal law.
4. *RFRA and the Affordable Care Act.* As explained earlier, the ACA is federal legislation about health care. It required employers to allow their employees to be insured for birth control. Religious businesses challenged the law's requirement that they provide contraceptive insurance to their employees. In *Burwell v. Hobby Lobby Stores,* 573 U.S. 682 (2014), the Court ruled 5–4 that the employers passed the RFRA test and were not required to provide contraceptive insurance for the contraceptives they rejected for religious reasons. Justice Alito wrote the majority opinion, arguing that Congress intended for RFRA to apply to corporations. This meant that nonprofit

1. In this respect, respondents' use of peyote seems closely analogous to the sacramental use of wine by the Roman Catholic Church. During Prohibition, the Federal Government exempted such use of wine from its general ban on possession and use of alcohol. However, compelling the Government's then general interest in prohibiting the use of alcohol may have been, it could not plausibly have asserted an interest sufficiently compelling to outweigh Catholics' right to take communion.

religious organizations and for-profit organizations had the same exemption rights under RFRA. Justice Ginsburg dissented, arguing that under *Smith* free exercise was not violated by the contraceptive mandate. Justice Ginsburg also thought that this exemption violated the rights of women seeking contraception.

Is it correct that the Free Exercise Clause does not allow an exemption from the contraceptive mandate but RFRA does? Is that a reason to praise RFRA or to reject it?

4. *Smith* Is Still the Law

Those who had been attempting to persuade the Court to reverse the reasoning of the vast majority of its cases demanded that Congress do so. Their disappointment in the Court's clear ruling led religious leaders and lobbyists to go to Congress to obtain what the Court would not. Congress did so with the passage of the federal RFRA, which was followed by roughly half of the states adopting their version of a RFRA. Those supporting the reasoning of RFRA that believers should not be burdened by the law hoped that *Smith* would be overruled in the following case, *Fulton v. Philadelphia.* Can you tell from the oral argument, https://www.oyez.org/cases/2020/19-123, that the City of Philadelphia would lose *unanimously* in the following opinion? Does this case tell you gays and lesbians have no rights to bring against religious institutions? Does the Free Exercise Clause protect a right to discriminate? Why does Philadelphia lose this case?

Fulton v. City of Philadelphia

SUPREME COURT OF THE UNITED STATES, 2021

593 U.S. ___; 141 S.Ct. 1868

ROBERTS, C. J., delivered the opinion of the Court, in which BREYER, SOTOMAYOR, KAGAN, KAVANAUGH, and BARRETT, JJ., joined. BARRETT, J., filed a concurring opinion, in which KAVANAUGH, J., joined, and in which BREYER, J., joined as to all but the first paragraph. ALITO, J., filed an opinion concurring in the judgment, in which THOMAS and GORSUCH, JJ., joined. GORSUCH, J., filed an opinion concurring in the judgment, in which THOMAS and ALITO, JJ., joined.

Chief Justice ROBERTS delivered the opinion of the Court.

Catholic Social Services is a foster care agency in Philadelphia. The City stopped referring children to CSS upon discovering that the agency would not certify same-sex couples to be foster parents due to its religious beliefs about marriage. The City will renew its foster care contract with CSS only if the agency agrees to certify same-sex couples. The question presented is whether the actions of Philadelphia violate the First Amendment.

I

... The religious views of CSS inform its work in this system. CSS believes that "marriage is a sacred bond between a man and a woman." Because the agency understands the certification of prospective foster families to be an endorsement of their relationships, it will not certify unmarried couples—regardless of their sexual orientation—or same-sex married couples. CSS does not object to certifying gay or lesbian individuals as single foster parents or to placing gay and lesbian children. No same-sex couple has ever sought certification from CSS. If one did, CSS would direct the couple to one of the more than 20 other agencies in the City, all of which currently certify same-sex couples. For over 50 years, CSS successfully contracted with the City to provide foster care services while holding to these beliefs. ...

The City stated that it would not enter a full foster care contract with CSS in the future unless the agency agreed to certify same-sex couples. ...

II

A

The Free Exercise Clause of the First Amendment, applicable to the States under the Fourteenth Amendment, provides that "Congress shall make no law ... prohibiting the free exercise" of religion. As an initial matter, it is plain that the City's actions have burdened CSS's religious exercise by putting it to the choice of curtailing its mission or approving relationships inconsistent with its beliefs. The City disagrees. In its view, certification reflects only that foster parents satisfy the statutory criteria, not that the agency endorses their relationships. But CSS believes that certification is tantamount to endorsement. And "religious beliefs need not be acceptable, logical, consistent, or comprehensible to others in order to merit First Amendment protection." *Thomas v. Review Bd. of Ind. Employment Security Div.*, 450 U.S. 707, 714, 101 S.Ct. 1425, 67 L.Ed.2d 624 (1981). Our task is to decide whether the burden the City has placed on the religious exercise of CSS is constitutionally permissible.

Smith held that laws incidentally burdening religion are ordinarily not subject to strict scrutiny under the Free Exercise Clause so long as they are neutral and generally applicable. CSS urges us to overrule *Smith*, and the concurrences in the judgment argue in favor of doing so, see (opinion of ALITO, J.); *post*, (opinion of GORSUCH, J.). But we need not revisit that decision here. This case falls outside *Smith* because the City has burdened the religious exercise of CSS through policies that do not meet the requirement of being neutral and generally applicable. See *Church of Lukumi Babalu Aye, Inc. v. Hialeah*, 508 U.S. 520, 531–532, 113 S.Ct. 2217, 124 L.Ed.2d 472 (1993).

Government fails to act neutrally when it proceeds in a manner intolerant of religious beliefs or restricts practices because of their religious nature. See *Masterpiece Cakeshop, Ltd. v. Colorado Civil Rights Comm'n*, 584 U.S. ____, __________, 138 S.Ct. 1719, 1730–1732, 201 L.Ed.2d 35 (2018); *Lukumi*, 508 U.S. at 533, 113 S.Ct. 2217. CSS points to evidence in the record that it believes demonstrates that the City has transgressed this neutrality standard, but we find it more straightforward to resolve this case under the rubric of general applicability.

A law is not generally applicable if it "invite[s]" the government to consider the particular reasons for a person's conduct by providing "'a mechanism for individualized exemptions.'" ...

Smith later explained that the unemployment benefits law in *Sherbert* was not generally applicable because the "good cause" standard permitted the government to grant exemptions based on the circumstances underlying each application. *Smith* went on to hold that "where the State has in place a system of individual exemptions, it may not refuse to extend that system to cases of 'religious hardship' without compelling reason." 494 U.S. at 884, 110 S.Ct. 1595 (quoting *Roy*, 476 U.S. at 708, 106 S.Ct. 2147); see also *Lukumi*, 508 U.S. at 537, 113 S.Ct. 2217 (same).

A law also lacks general applicability if it prohibits religious conduct while permitting secular conduct that undermines the government's asserted interests in a similar way. In *Church of Lukumi Babalu Aye, Inc. v. Hialeah*, for instance, the City of Hialeah adopted several ordinances prohibiting animal sacrifice, a practice of the Santeria faith. The City claimed that the ordinances were necessary in part to protect public health, which was "threatened by the disposal of animal carcasses in open public places." But the ordinances did not regulate hunters' disposal of their kills or improper garbage disposal by restaurants, both of which posed a similar hazard. The Court concluded that this and other forms of underinclusiveness meant that the ordinances were not generally applicable.

B

The City initially argued that CSS's practice violated section 3.21 of its standard foster care contract. We conclude, however, that this provision is not generally applicable as required by *Smith*. The current version of section 3.21 specifies in pertinent part:

> "**Rejection of Referral**. Provider shall not reject a child or family including, but not limited to, ... prospective foster or adoptive parents, for Services based upon ... their ... sexual orientation ... unless an exception is granted by the Commissioner or the Commissioner's designee, in his/her sole discretion."

This provision requires an agency to provide "Services," defined as "the work to be performed under this

Contract," to prospective foster parents regardless of their sexual orientation.

Like the good cause provision in *Sherbert*, section 3.21 incorporates a system of individual exemptions, made available in this case at the "sole discretion" of the Commissioner. The City has made clear that the Commissioner "has no intention of granting an exception" to CSS. But the City "may not refuse to extend that [exemption] system to cases of 'religious hardship' without compelling reason." ...

No matter the level of deference we extend to the City, the inclusion of a formal system of entirely discretionary exceptions in section 3.21 renders the contractual non-discrimination requirement not generally applicable. ...

Applying that "fundamental" rule here, an exception from section 3.21 also must govern the prohibition in section 15.1, lest the City's reservation of the authority to grant such an exception be a nullity. As a result, the contract as a whole contains no generally applicable non-discrimination requirement.

Finally, the City and intervenor-respondents contend that the availability of exceptions under section 3.21 is irrelevant because the Commissioner has never granted one. That misapprehends the issue. The creation of a formal mechanism for granting exceptions renders a policy not generally applicable, regardless whether any exceptions have been given, because it "invite[s]" the government to decide which reasons for not complying with the policy are worthy of solicitude, *Smith*, 494 U.S. at 884, 110 S.Ct. 1595—here, at the Commissioner's "sole discretion."

The concurrence objects that no party raised these arguments in this Court. (opinion of GORSUCH, J.). But CSS, supported by the United States, contended that the City's "made-for-CSS Section 3.21 permits discretionary 'exception[s]' from the requirement 'not [to] reject a child or family' based upon 'their ... sexual orientation,'" which "alone triggers strict scrutiny." The concurrence favors the City's reading of section 3.21, but we find CSS's position more persuasive.

C

In addition to relying on the contract, the City argues that CSS's refusal to certify same-sex couples constitutes an "Unlawful Public Accommodations Practice[ ]" in violation of the FairPractices Ordinance. ... We conclude that it does not because foster care agencies do not act as public accommodations in performing certifications. ...

III

The contractual non-discrimination requirement imposes a burden on CSS's religious exercise and does not qualify as generally applicable. The concurrence protests that the "Court granted certiorari to decide whether to overrule [*Smith*]," and chides the Court for seeking to "sidestep the question." But the Court also granted review to decide whether Philadelphia's actions were permissible under our precedents. CSS has demonstrated that the City's actions are subject to "the most rigorous of scrutiny" under those precedents. *Lukumi*, 508 U.S. at 546, 113 S.Ct. 2217. Because the City's actions are therefore examined under the strictest scrutiny regardless of *Smith*, we have no occasion to reconsider that decision here. ...

The City asserts that its non-discrimination policies serve three compelling interests: maximizing the number of foster parents, protecting the City from liability, and ensuring equal treatment of prospective foster parents and foster children. ...

Once properly narrowed, the City's asserted interests are insufficient. Maximizing the number of foster families and minimizing liability are important goals, but the City fails to show that granting CSS an exception will put those goals at risk. If anything, including CSS in the program seems likely to increase, not reduce, the number of available foster parents. As for liability, the City offers only speculation that it might be sued over CSS's certification practices. Such speculation is insufficient to satisfy strict scrutiny, particularly because the authority to certify foster families is delegated to agencies by the State, not the City.

That leaves the interest of the City in the equal treatment of prospective foster parents and foster children. We do not doubt that this interest is a weighty one, for "[o]ur society has come to the recognition that gay persons and gay couples cannot be treated as social outcasts or as inferior in dignity and worth." *Masterpiece Cakeshop*, 584 U.S., at ____, 138 S.Ct., at 1727. On the facts of this case, however, this interest cannot justify denying CSS an exception for its religious exercise. The creation of a system of exceptions under the contract undermines the City's contention that its non-discrimination policies can brook no departures. See *Lukumi*, 508 U.S. at 546–547, 113 S.Ct. 2217. The City offers no compelling reason why it has a particular interest in denying an exception to CSS while making them available to others. ...

Justice BARRETT, with whom Justice KAVANAUGH joins, and with whom Justice BREYER joins as to all but the first paragraph, concurring.

In *Employment Div., Dept. of Human Resources of Ore. v. Smith*, 494 U.S. 872, 110 S.Ct. 1595, 108 L.Ed.2d 876 (1990), this Court held that a neutral and generally applicable law typically does not violate the Free Exercise Clause—no matter how severely that law burdens religious exercise. Petitioners, their *amici*, scholars, and Justices of this Court have made serious arguments that *Smith* ought to be overruled. While history looms large in this debate, I find the historical record more silent than supportive on the question whether the founding generation understood the First Amendment to require religious exemptions from generally applicable laws in at least some circumstances. In my view, the textual and structural arguments against *Smith* are more compelling. As a matter of text and structure, it is difficult to see why the Free Exercise Clause—lone among the First Amendment freedoms—offers nothing more than protection from discrimination.

Yet what should replace *Smith*? ...

We need not wrestle with these questions in this case, though, because the same standard applies regardless whether *Smith* stays or goes. A longstanding tenet of our free exercise jurisprudence—one that both pre-dates and survives *Smith*—is that a law burdening religious exercise must satisfy strict scrutiny if it gives government officials discretion to grant individualized exemptions. As the Court's opinion today explains, the government contract at issue provides for individualized exemptions from its nondiscrimination rule, thus triggering strict scrutiny. And all nine Justices agree that the City cannot satisfy strict scrutiny. I therefore see no reason to decide in this case whether *Smith* should be overruled, much less what should replace it. I join the Court's opinion in full.

Justice ALITO, with whom Justice THOMAS and Justice GORSUCH join, concurring in the judgment.

This case presents an important constitutional question that urgently calls out for review: whether this Court's governing interpretation of a bedrock constitutional right, the right to the free exercise of religion, is fundamentally wrong and should be corrected.

In *Employment Div., Dept. of Human Resources of Ore. v. Smith*, 494 U.S. 872, 110 S.Ct. 1595, 108 L.Ed.2d 876 (1990), the Court abruptly pushed aside nearly 30 years of precedent and held that the First Amendment's Free Exercise Clause tolerates any rule that categorically prohibits or commands specified conduct so long as it does not target religious practice. Even if a rule serves no important purpose and has a devastating effect on religious freedom, the Constitution, according to *Smith*, provides no protection. This severe holding is ripe for reexamination.

I

... One of the questions that we accepted for review is "[w]hether *Employment Division v. Smith* should be revisited." We should confront that question.

Regrettably, the Court declines to do so. Instead, it reverses based on what appears to be a superfluous (and likely to be short-lived) feature of the City's standard annual contract with foster care agencies. *Smith*'s holding about categorical rules does not apply if a rule permits individualized exemptions, and the majority seizes on the presence in the City's standard contract of language giving a City official the power to grant exemptions. The City tells us that it has never granted such an exemption and has no intention of handing one to CSS, but the majority reverses the decision below because the contract supposedly confers that never-used power.

This decision might as well be written on the dissolving paper sold in magic shops. The City has been adamant about pressuring CSS to give in, and if the City wants to get around today's decision, it can simply eliminate the never-used exemption power. If it does that, then, voilà, today's decision will vanish—and the parties will be back where they started. The City will claim that it is protected by *Smith*; CSS will argue that *Smith* should be overruled; the lower courts, bound by *Smith*, will reject that argument; and CSS will file a new petition in this Court challenging *Smith*. What is the point of going around in this circle? ...

IV

... In sum, based on the text of the Free Exercise Clause and evidence about the original understanding of the free-exercise right, the case for *Smith* fails to overcome the more natural reading of the text. Indeed, the case against *Smith* is very convincing.

VD

Subsequent developments. Developments since *Smith* provide additional reasons for changing course. The *Smith* majority thought that adherence to *Sherbert* would invite "anarchy," 494 U.S. at 888, 110 S.Ct. 1595, but experience has shown that this fear was not well founded. Both RFRA and RLUIPA impose essentially the same requirements as *Sherbert*, and we have observed that the courts are well "up to the task" of applying that test.

Another significant development is the subsequent profusion of studies on the original meaning of the Free Exercise Clause. When *Smith* was decided, the available scholarship was thin, and the Court received no briefing on the subject. Since then, scholars have explored the subject in great depth.

* * *

Multiple factors strongly favor overruling *Smith*. Are there countervailing factors?

E

None is apparent. Reliance is often the strongest factor favoring the retention of a challenged precedent, but no strong reliance interests are cited in any of the numerous briefs urging us to preserve *Smith*. Indeed, the term is rarely even mentioned.

All that the City has to say on the subject is that overruling *Smith* would cause "substantial regulatory ... disruption" by displacing RFRA, RLUIPA, and related state laws. How would overruling *Smith* disrupt the operation of laws that were enacted to abrogate *Smith*? ...

* * *

Smith was wrongly decided. As long as it remains on the books, it threatens a fundamental freedom. And while precedent should not lightly be cast aside, the Court's error in *Smith* should now be corrected.

VI

If *Smith* is overruled, what legal standard should be applied in this case? The answer that comes most readily to mind is the standard that *Smith* replaced: A law that imposes a substantial burden on religious exercise can be sustained only if it is narrowly tailored to serve a compelling government interest.

Whether this test should be rephrased or supplemented with specific rules is a question that need not be resolved here because Philadelphia's ouster of CSS from foster care work simply does not further any interest that can properly be protected in this case. As noted, CSS's policy has not hindered any same-sex couples from becoming foster parents, and there is no threat that it will do so in the future.

CSS's policy has only one effect: It expresses the idea that same-sex couples should not be foster parents because only a man and a woman should marry. Many people today find this idea not only objectionable but hurtful. Nevertheless, protecting against this form of harm is not an interest that can justify the abridgment of First Amendment rights. ...

Suppressing speech—or religious practice—simply because it expresses an idea that some find hurtful is a zero-sum game. While CSS's ideas about marriage are likely to be objectionable to same-sex couples, lumping those who hold traditional beliefs about marriage together with racial bigots is insulting to those who retain such beliefs. In *Obergefell v. Hodges*, 576 U.S. 644, 135 S.Ct. 2584, 192 L.Ed.2d 609 (2015), the majority made a commitment. It refused to equate traditional beliefs about marriage, which it termed "decent and honorable," *id.*, at 672, 135 S.Ct. 2584, with racism, which is neither. And it promised that "religions, and those who adhere to religious doctrines, may continue to advocate with utmost, sincere conviction that, by divine precepts, same-sex marriage should not be condoned." *Id.*, at 679, 135 S.Ct. 2584. An open society can keep that promise while still respecting the "dignity," "worth," and fundamental equality of all members of the community. *Masterpiece Cakeshop*, 584 U.S., at ____, 138 S.Ct., at 1727.

* * *

... For all these reasons, I would overrule *Smith* and reverse the decision below. Philadelphia's exclusion of CSS from foster care work violates the Free Exercise Clause, and CSS is therefore entitled to an injunction barring Philadelphia from taking such action.

After receiving more than 2,500 pages of briefing and after more than a half-year of post-argument cogitation, the Court has emitted a wisp of a decision that leaves religious liberty in a confused and vulnerable state. Those who count on this Court to stand up for the First Amendment have every right to be disappointed—as am I.

Justice GORSUCH, with whom Justice THOMAS and Justice ALITO join, concurring in the judgment.

... Given all the maneuvering, it's hard not to wonder if the majority is so anxious to say nothing about *Smith*'s fate that it is willing to say pretty much anything about municipal law and the parties' briefs. One way or another, the majority seems determined to declare there is no "need" or "reason" to revisit *Smith* today.

But tell that to CSS. Its litigation has already lasted years—and today's (ir)resolution promises more of the same. Had we followed the path Justice ALITO outlines—holding that the City's rules cannot avoid strict scrutiny even if they qualify as neutral and generally applicable—this case would end today. Instead, the majority's course guarantees that this litigation is only getting started. As the final arbiter of state law, the Pennsylvania Supreme Court can effectively overrule the majority's reading of the Commonwealth's public accommodations law. The City can revise its FPO to make even plainer still that its law does encompass foster services. Or with a flick of a pen, municipal lawyers may rewrite the City's contract to close the § 3.21 loophole.

Once any of that happens, CSS will find itself back where it started. The City has made clear that it will never tolerate CSS carrying out its foster-care mission in accordance with its sincerely held religious beliefs. To the City, it makes no difference that CSS has not denied service to a single same-sex couple; that dozens of other foster agencies stand willing to serve same-sex couples; or that CSS is committed to help any inquiring same-sex couples find those other agencies. The City has expressed its determination to put CSS to a choice: Give up your sincerely held religious beliefs or give up serving foster children and families. If CSS is unwilling to provide foster-care services to same-sex couples, the City prefers that CSS provide no foster-care services at all. This litigation thus promises to slog on for years to come, consuming time and resources in court that could be better spent serving children. And throughout it all, the opacity of the majority's professed endorsement of CSS's arguments ensures the parties will be forced to devote resources to the unenviable task of debating what it *even means*.

Nor will CSS bear the costs of the Court's indecision alone. Individuals and groups across the country will pay the price—in dollars, in time, and in continued uncertainty about their religious liberties. Consider Jack Phillips, the baker whose religious beliefs prevented him from creating custom cakes to celebrate same-sex weddings. See *Masterpiece Cakeshop, Ltd. v. Colorado Civil Rights Comm'n*, 584 U.S. ____, 138 S.Ct. 1719, 201 L.Ed.2d 35 (2018). After being forced to litigate all the way to the Supreme Court, we ruled for him on narrow grounds similar to those the majority invokes today. Because certain government officials responsible for deciding Mr. Phillips's compliance with a local public accommodations law uttered statements exhibiting hostility to his religion, the Court held, those officials failed to act "neutrally" under *Smith*. See 584 U.S., at ____, 138 S.Ct., at 1730–1732. But with *Smith* still on the books, all that victory assured Mr. Phillips was a new round of litigation—with officials now presumably more careful about admitting their motives. See Associated Press, Lakewood Baker Jack Phillips Sued for Refusing Gender Transition Cake (Mar. 22, 2021), https://denver.cbslocal.com/2021/03/22/jack-phillips-masterpiece-cakeshop-lakewood-transgender/. A nine-year odyssey thus barrels on. No doubt, too, those who cannot afford such endless litigation under *Smith*'s regime have been and will continue to be forced to forfeit religious freedom that the Constitution protects.

The costs of today's indecision fall on lower courts too. As recent cases involving COVID–19 regulations highlight, judges across the country continue to struggle to understand and apply *Smith*'s test even thirty years after it was announced. In the last nine months alone, this Court has had to intervene at least half a dozen times to clarify how *Smith* works. See, *e.g., Tandon, ante,* at p. 1874; *Roman Catholic Diocese of Brooklyn v. Cuomo*, 592 U.S. ____, 141 S.Ct. 63, 208 L.Ed.2d 206 (2020) (*per curiam*); *High Plains Harvest Church v. Polis*, 592 U.S ____, 141 S.Ct. 527, 208 L.Ed.2d 503 (2020). To be sure, this Court began to resolve at least some of the confusion surrounding *Smith*'s application in *Tandon*. But *Tandon* treated the symptoms, not the underlying ailment. We owe it to the parties, to religious believers, and to our colleagues on the lower courts to cure the problem this Court created. ...

What possible benefit does the majority see in its studious indecision about *Smith* when the costs are so many? The particular appeal before us arises at the intersection of public accommodations laws and the First Amendment; it involves same-sex couples and the Catholic Church. Perhaps our colleagues believe today's circuitous path will at least steer the Court around the controversial subject matter and avoid "picking a side." But refusing to give CSS the benefit of what we know to be the correct interpretation of the Constitution *is* picking a side. *Smith* committed a constitutional error. Only we can fix it. Dodging the question today guarantees it will recur tomorrow. These cases will keep coming until the Court musters the fortitude to supply an answer. Respectfully, it should have done so today.

Notes and Questions

1. *The Free Exercise Clause test.* How did the different Justices treat *Smith* in this case? What did Chief Justice Roberts conclude about it? Why? How does he use *Smith* to reach his conclusion in this case? Do you agree with people who said Roberts's reasoning was confusing?
2. *Justice Barrett.* What did Justice Barrett think about the future of the Free Exercise Clause cases?
3. *Justice Alito.* What did Justice Alito conclude in his concurrence? Why did he concur in the judgment?
4. *Justice Gorsuch.* Why did Justice Gorsuch concur?
5. *Interpreting* Smith. Did the Court interpret *Smith* correctly? If you had to write the next opinion defining free exercise, what test would you use?
6. *LGBTQ rights.* With respect to LGBTQ rights, what is your reaction to this case? What does the result tell you about the Court and the future of LGBTQ rights?
7. In *Masterpiece Cakeshop, Ltd. v. Colorado Civil Rights Commission*, 138 S.Ct. 1719 (2018), Colorado ruled that Jack Phillips, the owner of Masterpiece Cakeshop, had violated its anti-discrimination laws by refusing to bake a cake for a same-sex couple. The Supreme Court ruled for the baker, in an opinion written by Justice Kennedy. The Court concluded the Colorado Civil Rights Commission had violated the Free Exercise Clause by saying very negative things about religion, instead of being neutral toward religion. The Commission was seen as hostile toward religion and thus not fair. How does this case compare to *Fulton* and *Smith*?
8. *The pandemic and free exercise.* The COVID cases involving the Free Exercise Clause have been dealt with through the Court's so-called "shadow docket" where the Court does not hear oral arguments but still makes relevant decisions.
9. a. In a 5–4 vote in *South Bay United Pentecostal Church v. Newsom*, 590 U.S. ___ (2020), the Supreme Court upheld California's COVID-19 law restricting religious rituals. State law limited attendance to 25% of building capacity or 100 attendees. Justices Ginsburg, Breyer, Kagan, and Sotomayor were joined by a concurrence from Chief Justice Roberts, who wrote that the law did not violate the First Amendment: "Similar or more severe restrictions apply to comparable secular gatherings, including lectures, concerts, movie showings, spectator sports, and theatrical performances, where large groups of people gather in close proximity for extended periods of time. And the Order exempts or treats more leniently only dissimilar activities, such as operating grocery stores, banks, and laundromats, in which people neither congregate in large groups nor remain in close proximity for extended periods."

   The key to the decision was that churches were being treated similarly to other similar gatherings. Medical science has determined that COVID is caused by droplets spewed into the air by individuals, and one of the most likely places to catch COVID was where individuals were close together and singing. Do you agree that similar uses were treated similarly? The dissent concluded that the California law singled out religion for worse treatment than other uses. What do you think? The dissent concluded the state had not shown a reason for discriminating against churches. They asked the questions, "Assuming all of the same precautions are taken, why can someone safely walk down a grocery store aisle but not a pew? And why can someone safely interact with a brave deliverywoman but not with a stoic minister?"

b. In another 5–4 vote, the Court summarily upheld Nevada's COVID policy, which allowed only 50 people to attend religious services. The majority did not write an opinion. There are dissents by Alito, Gorsuch, and Kavanaugh. *Calvary Chapel Dayton Valley v. Sisolak*, 591 U.S. ___ (2020).

10. a. The new Court, with Justice Amy Coney Barrett replacing Justice Ruth Bader Ginsburg, ruled in favor of the New York churches' and synagogues' challenges to Gov. Cuomo's COVID restrictions. The religious organizations faced 10- and 25-person restrictions on their gatherings during the red zone period, the worst time for COVID. Even though the red zone was not present when the Court heard the case, they ruled for the religions. The opinion granting injunctive relief (even though the facts on the ground had changed) was a per curiam decision. Justices Gorsuch and Kavanaugh wrote concurrences. Chief Justice Roberts dissented. Justice Breyer dissented with Sotomayor and Kagan. Justice Sotomayor dissented, joined by Justice Kagan. *Roman Catholic Diocese of Brooklyn, New York v. Cuomo*, https://www.oyez.org/cases/2020/20A87.

b. In a 6–3 decision in February 2021, the Court ruled that California must open the churches that had been closed for indoor worship due to COVID-19. Importantly, the Court did allow the state's bans on singing and chanting to continue. The state can still hold the churches to 25% of capacity attendance. Justices Gorsuch and Thomas would have given the churches freedom in all these areas. Alito joined those two but would have given the state 30 days before the injunction against it could take effect. In her first opinion for the Court, Justice Barrett, joined by Kavanaugh, argued that the churches had not yet shown that the singing and chanting bans were too strong but that they could litigate that in the future. Chief Justice Roberts deferred to the state's wishes on singing and chanting and size of attendance but ruled that there should not be deference to the closing of the churches. Justice Kagan dissented, joined by Breyer and Sotomayor, concluding that science had been abandoned in favor of judicial edict. *Harvest Rock Church v. Newsom*, https://www.becketlaw.org/case/harvest-rock-church-v-newsom/.

c. In April 2021, the Court reversed a Ninth Circuit ruling and concluded in *Tandon v. Newsom* that California could not restrict at-home religious exercise due to COVID. The per curiam decision was for Justices Thomas, Alito, Gorsuch, Kavanaugh, and Barrett. Chief Justice Roberts would not have granted the injunction against the state's practices. Justice Kagan dissented, joined by Breyer and Sotomayor. *Tandon v. Newsom*, 593 U.S. ___, 141 S.Ct. 1294 (2021). Justice Kagan dissents, "California limits religious gatherings in homes to three households. If the State also limits all secular gatherings in homes to three households, it has complied with the First Amendment." Why would the majority disagree with that?

What does the following chart of the Court's shadow docket cases tell you?

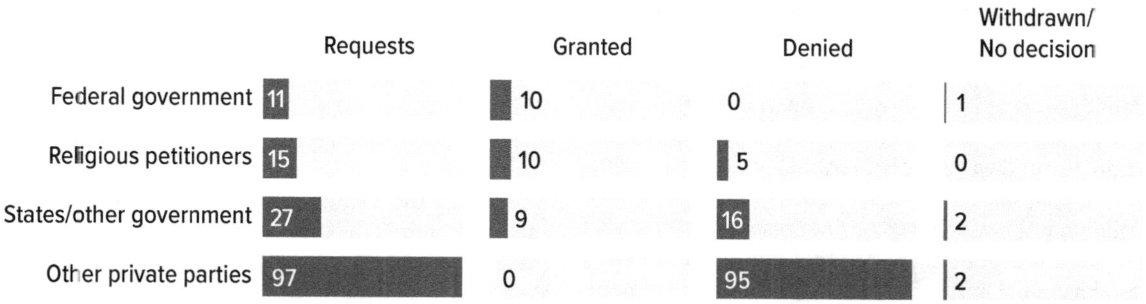

FIGURE 10.1 U.S. Supreme Court's "shadow docket" in action.

What do all these cases tell you about the state of free exercise law? What will happen next?

B. The Establishment Clause

1. The *Lemon* Test

You have learned what the Free Exercise Clause protects. What does the Establishment Clause prohibit? The following case, *Lemon v. Kurtzman*, is a well-known Establishment Clause case that identifies three factors to determine whether there is a violation of the Establishment Clause. Later courts and scholars turned the open-ended factors into a so-called "test." Can you tell from the oral argument, at https://www.oyez.org/cases/1970/89, what the three factors are? Are they identified in the argument? How did the Court choose these three factors as guidelines for the Establishment Clause? Warning: some Justices in later cases criticize *Lemon*. Can you tell why they object?

The Establishment Clause cases often talk about what the government can and cannot fund. Does *Lemon* clarify for you what rules the Court will follow?

Lemon v. Kurtzman

SUPREME COURT OF THE UNITED STATES, 1971
403 U.S. 602, 91 S.Ct. 2015

MR. CHIEF JUSTICE BURGER delivered the opinion of the Court. [He was joined by Justices BLACK, DOUGLAS, HARLAN II, STEWART, MARSHALL and BLACKMUN.]

These two appeals raise questions as to Pennsylvania and Rhode Island statutes providing state aid to church-related elementary and secondary schools. ... Pennsylvania has adopted a statutory program that provides financial support to nonpublic elementary and secondary schools by way of reimbursement for the cost of teachers' salaries, textbooks, and instructional materials in specified secular subjects. Rhode Island has adopted a statute under which the State pays directly to teachers in nonpublic elementary schools a supplement of 15% of their annual salary. Under each statute state aid has been given to church-related educational institutions. We hold that both statutes are unconstitutional. ...

II

... The language of the Religion Clauses of the First Amendment is at best opaque, particularly when compared with other portions of the Amendment. Its authors did not simply prohibit the establishment of a state church or a state religion, an area history shows they regarded as very important and fraught with great dangers. Instead they commanded that there should be "no law *respecting* an establishment of religion." A law may be one "respecting" the forbidden objective while falling short of its total realization. A law "respecting" the proscribed result, that is, the establishment of religion, is not always easily identifiable as one violative of the Clause. A given law might not *establish* a state religion but nevertheless be one "respecting" that end in the sense of being a step that could lead to such establishment and hence offend the First Amendment.

In the absence of precisely stated constitutional prohibitions, we must draw lines with reference to the three main evils against which the Establishment Clause was intended to afford protection: "sponsorship, financial support, and active involvement of the sovereign in religious activity."

Every analysis in this area must begin with consideration of the cumulative criteria developed by the Court over many years. Three such tests may be gleaned from our cases. First, the statute must have a secular legislative purpose; second, its principal or primary effect must be one that neither advances nor inhibits religion, finally, the statute must not foster "an excessive government entanglement with religion." ...

[The Court concluded that the acts had a secular purpose (to "enhance the quality of the secular education in all schools") and did not decide the primary effect prong, because] "the cumulative impact of the entire relationship arising under the statutes in each State involves excessive entanglement between government and religion."

III

... The State must be certain, given the Religion Clauses, that subsidized teachers do not inculcate religion—indeed the State here has undertaken to do so. To ensure that no trespass occurs, the State has therefore carefully conditioned its aid with pervasive restrictions. An eligible recipient must teach only those courses that are offered in the public schools and use only those texts and materials that are found in the public schools. In addition the teacher must not engage in teaching any course in religion.

A comprehensive, discriminating, and continuing state surveillance will inevitably be required to ensure that these restrictions are obeyed and the First Amendment otherwise respected. Unlike a book, a teacher cannot be inspected once so as to determine the extent and intent of his or her personal beliefs and subjective acceptance of the limitations imposed by the First Amendment. These prophylactic contacts will involve excessive and enduring entanglement between state and church. ...

IV

A broader base of entanglement of yet a different character is presented by the divisive political potential of these state programs. In a community where such a large number of pupils are served by church-related schools, it can be assumed that state assistance will entail considerable political activity. Partisans of parochial schools, understandably concerned with rising costs and sincerely dedicated to both the religious and secular educational missions of their schools, will inevitably champion this cause and promote political action to achieve their goals. Those who oppose state aid, whether for constitutional, religious, or fiscal reasons, will inevitably respond and employ all of the usual political campaign techniques to prevail. Candidates will be forced to declare and voters to choose. It would be unrealistic to ignore the fact that many people confronted with issues of this kind will find their votes aligned with their faith.

Ordinarily political debate and division, however vigorous or even partisan, are normal and healthy manifestations of our democratic system of government, but political division along religious lines was one of the principal evils against which the First Amendment was intended to protect. The potential divisiveness of such conflict is a threat to the normal political process. To have States or communities divide on the issues presented by state aid to parochial schools would tend to confuse and obscure other issues of great urgency. We have an expanding array of vexing issues, local and national, domestic and international, to debate and divide on. It conflicts with our whole history and tradition to permit questions of the Religion Clauses to assume such importance in our legislatures and in our elections that they could divert attention from the myriad issues and problems that confront every level of government. The highways of church and state relationships are not likely to be one-way streets, and the Constitution's authors sought to protect religious worship from the pervasive power of government. The history of many countries attests to the hazards of religion's intruding into the political arena or of political power intruding into the legitimate and free exercise of religious belief. ...

V

... Finally, nothing we have said can be construed to disparage the role of church-related elementary and secondary schools in our national life. Their contribution has been and is enormous. Nor do we ignore their economic plight in a period of rising costs and expanding need. Taxpayers generally have been spared vast sums by the maintenance of these educational institutions by religious organizations, largely by the gifts of faithful adherents.

The merit and benefits of these schools, however, are not the issue before us in these cases. The sole question is whether state aid to these schools can be squared with the dictates of the Religion Clauses. Under our system the choice has been made that government is to be entirely excluded from the area of religious instruction and churches excluded from the affairs of government. The Constitution decrees that religion must be a private matter for the individual, the family, and the institutions of private choice, and that while some involvement and entanglement are inevitable, lines must be drawn. ...

Notes and Questions

1. *The three factors.* What are the three factors identified by the Court to consider in establishment cases? Why did some Justices embrace them while others objected? Does this opinion tell you how to resolve any questions of funding for religious schools?
2. *Funding.* What funding can a religious school receive from the government, and what would be banned under *Lemon*?

2. Government Prayer

The Establishment Clause also relates to government prayer. Should the government ever be allowed to lead others in prayer and make it a prerequisite to involvement in government functions like town meetings? Do you agree with the majority or the dissent in the following case? Can you tell from the oral argument, https://www.oyez.org/cases/2013/12-696, what prayers can and cannot be said at town meetings? What are the limitations on government prayer after this case was decided?

Town of Greece, New York v. Galloway

SUPREME COURT OF THE UNITED STATES, 2014

134 S.Ct. 1811, 82 USLW 4334

JUSTICE KENNEDY delivered the opinion of the Court, except as to Part II-B. THE CHIEF JUSTICE and JUSTICE ALITO join this opinion in full. JUSTICE SCALIA and JUSTICE THOMAS join this opinion except as to Part II–B.

The Court must decide whether the town of Greece, New York, imposes an impermissible establishment of religion by opening its monthly board meetings with a prayer. It must be concluded, consistent with the Court's opinion in *Marsh v. Chambers* that no violation of the Constitution has been shown.

I

Greece, a town with a population of 94,000, is in upstate New York. For some years, it began its monthly town board meetings with a moment of silence. In 1999, the newly elected town supervisor, John Auberger, decided to replicate the prayer practice he had found meaningful while serving in the county legislature. Following the roll call and recitation of the Pledge of Allegiance, Auberger would invite a local clergyman to the front of the room to deliver an invocation. After the prayer, Auberger would thank the minister for serving as the board's "chaplain for the month" and present him with a commemorative plaque. The prayer was intended to place town board members in a solemn and deliberative frame of mind, invoke divine guidance in town affairs, and follow a tradition practiced by Congress and dozens of state legislatures.

The town followed an informal method for selecting prayer givers, all of whom were unpaid volunteers. A town employee would call the congregations listed in a local directory until she found a minister available for that month's meeting. The town eventually compiled a list of willing "board chaplains" who had accepted invitations and agreed to return in the future. The town at no point excluded or denied an opportunity to a would-be prayer giver. Its leaders maintained that a minister or layperson of any persuasion, including an atheist, could give the invocation. But nearly all of the congregations in town were Christian; and from 1999 to 2007, all of the participating ministers were too.

Greece neither reviewed the prayers in advance of the meetings nor provided guidance as to their tone or content, in the belief that exercising any degree of control over the prayers would infringe both the free exercise and speech rights of the ministers. The town instead left the guest clergy free to compose their own devotions. The resulting prayers often sounded both civic and religious themes. Typical were invocations that asked the divinity to abide at the meeting and bestow blessings on the community:

> "Lord we ask you to send your spirit of servanthood upon all of us gathered here this evening to do your work for the benefit of all in our community. We ask you to bless our elected and appointed officials so they may deliberate with wisdom and act with courage. Bless the members of our community who come here to speak before the board so they may state their cause with honesty and humility. ... Lord we ask you to bless us all, that everything we do here tonight will move you to welcome us one day into your kingdom as good and faithful servants. We ask this in the name of our brother Jesus. Amen."

Some of the ministers spoke in a distinctly Christian idiom; and a minority invoked religious holidays, scripture, or doctrine, as in the following prayer:

> "Lord, God of all creation, we give you thanks and praise for your presence and action in the world. We look with anticipation to the celebration of Holy Week and Easter. It is in the solemn events of next week that we find the very heart and center of our Christian faith. We acknowledge the saving sacrifice of Jesus Christ on the cross. We draw strength, vitality, and confidence from his resurrection at Easter. ... We pray for peace in the world, an end to terrorism, violence, conflict, and war. We pray for stability, democracy, and good government in those countries in which our armed forces are now serving, especially in Iraq and Afghanistan. ... Praise and glory be yours, O Lord, now and forever more. Amen."

Respondents Susan Galloway and Linda Stephens attended town board meetings to speak about issues of local concern, and they objected that the prayers violated their religious or philosophical views. At one meeting, Galloway admonished board members that she found the prayers "offensive," "intolerable," and an affront to a "diverse community." After respondents complained that Christian themes pervaded the prayers, to the exclusion of citizens who did not share those beliefs, the town invited a Jewish layman and the chairman of the local Baha'i temple to deliver prayers. A Wiccan priestess who had read press reports about the prayer controversy requested, and was granted, an opportunity to give the invocation. ...

II

In *Marsh v. Chambers*, the Court found no First Amendment violation in the Nebraska Legislature's practice of opening its sessions with a prayer delivered by a chaplain paid from state funds. The decision concluded that legislative prayer, while religious in nature, has long been understood as compatible with the Establishment Clause. As practiced by Congress since the framing of the Constitution, legislative prayer lends gravity to public business, reminds lawmakers to transcend petty differences in pursuit of a higher purpose, and expresses a common aspiration to a just and peaceful society. ...

A

... An insistence on nonsectarian or ecumenical prayer as a single, fixed standard is not consistent with the tradition of legislative prayer outlined in the Court's cases. ...

To hold that invocations must be nonsectarian would force the legislatures that sponsor prayers and the courts that are asked to decide these cases to act as supervisors and censors of religious speech, a rule that would involve government in religious matters to a far greater degree than is the case under the town's current practice of neither editing or approving prayers in advance nor criticizing their content after the fact. It would be but a few steps removed from that prohibition for legislatures to require chaplains to redact the religious content from their message in order to make it acceptable for the public sphere. Government may not mandate a civic religion that stifles any but the most generic reference to the sacred any more than it may prescribe a religious orthodoxy.

Respondents argue, in effect, that legislative prayer may be addressed only to a generic God. The law and the Court could not draw this line for each specific prayer or seek to require ministers to set aside their nuanced and deeply personal beliefs for vague and artificial ones. There is doubt, in any event, that consensus might be reached as to what qualifies as generic or nonsectarian. Honorifics like "Lord of Lords" or "King of Kings" might strike a Christian audience as ecumenical, yet these titles may have no place in the vocabulary of other faith traditions. The difficulty, indeed the futility, of sifting sectarian from nonsectarian speech is illustrated by a letter that a lawyer for the respondents sent the town in the early stages of this litigation. The letter opined that references to "Father, God, Lord God, and the Almighty" would be acceptable in public prayer, but that references to "Jesus Christ, the Holy Spirit, and the Holy Trinity" would not. Perhaps the writer believed the former grouping would be acceptable to monotheists. Yet even seemingly general references to God or the Father might alienate nonbelievers or polytheists. ...

In rejecting the suggestion that legislative prayer must be nonsectarian, the Court does not imply that no constraints remain on its content. The relevant constraint derives from its place at the opening of legislative sessions, where it is meant to lend gravity to the occasion and reflect values long part of the Nation's heritage. Prayer that is solemn and respectful in tone, that invites lawmakers to reflect upon shared ideals and common ends before they embark on the fractious business of governing, serves that legitimate function. If the course and practice over time shows that the invocations denigrate nonbelievers or religious minorities, threaten damnation, or preach conversion, many present may consider the prayer to fall short of the desire to elevate the purpose of the occasion and to unite lawmakers in their common effort. That circumstance would present a different case than the one presently before the Court.

The tradition reflected in *Marsh* permits chaplains to ask their own God for blessings of peace, justice, and freedom that find appreciation among people of all faiths. That a prayer is given in the name of Jesus, Allah, or Jehovah, or that it makes passing reference to religious doctrines, does not remove it from that tradition. These religious themes provide particular means to universal ends. Prayer that reflects beliefs specific to only some creeds can still serve to solemnize the occasion, so long as the practice over time is not "exploited to proselytize or advance any one, or to disparage any other, faith or belief."

...

Finally, the Court disagrees with the view taken by the Court of Appeals that the town of Greece contravened the Establishment Clause by inviting a predominantly Christian set of ministers to lead the prayer. The town made reasonable efforts to identify all of the congregations located within its borders and represented that it would welcome a prayer by any minister or layman who wished to give one. That nearly all of the congregations in town turned out to be Christian does not reflect an aversion or bias on the part of town leaders against minority faiths. So long as the town maintains a policy of nondiscrimination, the Constitution does not require it to search beyond its borders for non-Christian prayer givers in an effort to achieve religious balancing. The quest to promote "a 'diversity' of religious views" would require the town "to make wholly inappropriate judgments about the number of religions [it] should sponsor and the relative frequency with which it should sponsor each," a form of government entanglement with religion that is far more troublesome than the current approach.

B

... It is an elemental First Amendment principle that government may not coerce its citizens "to support or participate in any religion or its exercise." ...

Nothing in the record indicates that town leaders allocated benefits and burdens based on participation in the prayer, or that citizens were received differently depending on whether they joined the invocation or quietly declined. In no instance did town leaders signal disfavor toward nonparticipants or suggest that their stature in the community was in any way diminished. A practice that classified citizens based on their religious views would violate the Constitution, but that is not the case before this Court.

In their declarations in the trial court, respondents stated that the prayers gave them offense and made them feel excluded and disrespected. Offense, however, does not equate to coercion. ...

The inclusion of a brief, ceremonial prayer as part of a larger exercise in civic recognition suggests that its purpose and effect are to acknowledge religious leaders and the institutions they represent rather than to exclude or coerce nonbelievers.

JUSTICE ALITO, with whom JUSTICE SCALIA joins, concurring.

...

I

... [S]ince the principal dissent accuses the Court of being blind to the facts of this case, I recount facts that I find particularly salient. ...

For the first four years of the practice, a clerical employee in the office would randomly call religious organizations listed in the Greece "Community Guide," a local directory published by the Greece Chamber of Commerce, until she was able to find somebody willing to give the invocation. This employee eventually began keeping a list of individuals who had agreed to give the invocation, and when a second clerical employee took over the task of finding prayer-givers, the first employee gave that list to the second. The second employee then randomly called organizations on that list—and possibly others in the Community Guide—until she found someone who agreed to provide the prayer.

Apparently, all the houses of worship listed in the local Community Guide were Christian churches. That is unsurprising given the small number of non-Christians in the area. ...

II

I turn now to the narrow aspect of the principal dissent, and what we find here is that the principal dissent's objection, in the end, is really quite niggling. ...

B

If, as the principal dissent appears to concede, such a rotating system would obviate any constitutional problems, then despite all its high rhetoric, the principal dissent's quarrel with the town of Greece really boils down to this: The town's clerical employees did a bad job in compiling the list of potential guest chaplains. For that is really the only difference between what the town did and what the principal dissent is willing to accept. ...

The informal, imprecise way in which the town lined up guest chaplains is typical of the way in which many things are done in small and medium-sized units of local government. In such places, the members of the governing body almost always have day jobs that occupy much of their time. The town almost never has a legal office and instead relies for legal advice on a local attorney whose practice is likely to center on such things as land-use regulation, contracts, and torts. When a municipality like the town of Greece seeks in good faith to emulate the congressional practice on which our holding in *Marsh* was largely based, that municipality should not be held to have violated the Constitution simply because its method of recruiting guest chaplains lacks the demographic exactitude that might be regarded as optimal. ...

IV

... There can be little doubt that the decision in *Marsh* reflected the original understanding of the First Amendment. It is virtually inconceivable that the First Congress, having appointed chaplains whose responsibilities prominently included the delivery of prayers at the beginning of each daily session, thought that this practice was inconsistent with the Establishment Clause. ...

V

This brings me to my final point. I am troubled by the message that some readers may take from the principal dissent's rhetoric and its highly imaginative hypotheticals. ... I am concerned that at least some readers will take these hypotheticals as a warning that this is where today's decision leads—to a country in which religious minorities are denied the equal benefits of citizenship.

Nothing could be further from the truth. All that the Court does today is to allow a town to follow a practice that we have previously held is permissible for Congress and state legislatures. In seeming to suggest otherwise, the principal dissent goes far astray.

JUSTICE THOMAS, with whom JUSTICE SCALIA joins as to Part II, concurring in part and concurring in the judgment.

...

II

Even if the Establishment Clause were properly incorporated against the States, the municipal prayers at issue in this case bear no resemblance to the coercive state establishments that existed at the founding. "The coercion that was a hallmark of historical establishments of religion was coercion of religious orthodoxy and of financial support *by force of law and threat of penalty*." In a typical case, attendance at the established church was mandatory, and taxes were levied to generate church revenue. Dissenting ministers were barred from preaching, and political participation was limited to members of the established church. ... They exercised government power in order to exact financial support of the church, compel religious observance, or control religious doctrine. ...

Thus, to the extent coercion is relevant to the Establishment Clause analysis, it is actual legal coercion that counts—not the "subtle coercive pressures" allegedly felt by respondents in this case. The majority properly concludes that "[o]ffense ... does not equate to coercion," since "[a]dults often encounter speech they find disagreeable[,] and an Establishment Clause violation is not made out any time a person experiences a sense of affront from the expression of contrary religious views in a legislative forum." I would simply add, in light of the foregoing history of the Establishment Clause, that "[p]eer pressure, unpleasant as it may be, is not coercion" either.

JUSTICE BREYER, dissenting.

As we all recognize, this is a "fact-sensitive" case. ... I also here emphasize several factors that I believe underlie the conclusion that, on the particular facts of this case, the town's prayer practice violated the Establishment Clause.

First, Greece is a predominantly Christian town, but it is not exclusively so. A map of the town's houses of worship introduced in the District Court shows many Christian churches within the town's limits. It also shows a Buddhist temple within the town and several Jewish synagogues just outside its borders, in the adjacent city of Rochester, New York. Yet during the more than 120 monthly meetings at which prayers were delivered during the record period (from 1999 to 2010), only four prayers were delivered by non-Christians. And all of these occurred in 2008, shortly after the plaintiffs began complaining about the town's Christian prayer practice and nearly a decade after that practice had commenced. ...

Second, the town made no significant effort to inform the area's non-Christian houses of worship about the possibility of delivering an opening prayer. ... Third, in this context, the fact that nearly all of the prayers given reflected a single denomination takes on significance. That significance would have been the same had all the prayers been Jewish, or Hindu, or Buddhist, or of any other denomination. The significance is that, in a context where religious minorities exist and where more could easily have been done to include their participation, the town chose to do nothing. ... Fourth, the fact that the board meeting audience included citizens with business to conduct also contributes to the importance of making more of an effort to include members of other denominations. ... Fifth, neither does the Constitution forbid efforts to explain to those who give the prayers the nature of the occasion and the audience. ...

JUSTICE KAGAN, with whom JUSTICE GINSBURG, JUSTICE BREYER, and JUSTICE SOTOMAYOR join, dissenting.

For centuries now, people have come to this country from every corner of the world to share in the blessing of religious freedom. Our Constitution promises that they may worship in their own way, without fear of penalty or danger, and that in itself is a momentous offering. Yet our Constitution makes a commitment still more remarkable—that however those individuals worship, they will count as full and equal American citizens. A Christian, a Jew, a Muslim (and so forth)—each stands in the same relationship with her country, with her state and local communities, and with every level and body of government. So that when each person performs the duties or seeks the benefits of citizenship, she does so not as an adherent to one or another religion, but simply as an American.

I respectfully dissent from the Court's opinion because I think the Town of Greece's prayer practices violate that norm of religious equality—the breathtakingly generous constitutional idea that our public institutions belong no less to the Buddhist or Hindu than to the Methodist or Episcopalian. I do not contend that principle translates here into a bright separationist line. To the contrary, I agree with the Court's decision in *Marsh* upholding the Nebraska Legislature's tradition of beginning each session with a chaplain's prayer. And I believe that pluralism and inclusion in a town hall can satisfy the constitutional requirement of neutrality; such a forum need not become a religion-free zone. But still, the Town of Greece should lose this case. The practice at issue here differs from the one sustained in *Marsh* because Greece's town meetings involve participation by ordinary citizens, and the invocations given—directly to those citizens—were predominantly sectarian in content. Still more, Greece's Board did nothing to recognize religious diversity: In arranging for clergy members to open each meeting, the Town never sought (except briefly when this suit was filed) to involve, accommodate, or in any way reach out to adherents of non-Christian religions. So month in and month out for over a decade, prayers steeped in only one faith, addressed toward members of the public, commenced meetings to discuss local affairs and distribute government benefits. In my view, that practice does not square with the First Amendment's promise that every citizen, irrespective of her religion, owns an equal share in her government.

I

To begin to see what has gone wrong in the Town of Greece, consider several hypothetical scenarios in which sectarian prayer—taken straight from this case's record—infuses governmental activities:

- You are a party in a case going to trial; let's say you have filed suit against the government for violating one of your legal rights. The judge bangs his gavel to call the court to order, asks a minister to come to the front of the room, and instructs the 10 or so individuals present to rise for an opening prayer. The clergyman faces those in attendance and says: "Lord, God of all creation. ... We acknowledge the saving sacrifice of Jesus Christ on the cross. We draw strength ... from his resurrection at Easter. Jesus Christ, who took away the sins of the world, destroyed our death, through his dying and in his rising, he has restored our life. Blessed are you, who has raised up the Lord Jesus, you who will raise us, in our turn, and put us by His side. ... Amen." The judge then asks your lawyer to begin the trial.
- It's election day, and you head over to your local polling place to vote. As you and others wait to give your names and receive your ballots, an election official asks everyone there to join him in prayer. He says: "We pray this [day] for the guidance of the Holy Spirit as [we vote]. ... Let's just say the Our Father together. 'Our Father, who art in Heaven, hallowed be thy name; thy Kingdom come, thy will be done, on earth as it is in Heaven. ...'" And after he concludes, he makes the sign of the cross, and appears to wait expectantly for you and the other prospective voters to do so too.
- You are an immigrant attending a naturalization ceremony to finally become a citizen. The presiding official tells you and your fellow applicants that before administering the oath of allegiance, he would like a minister to pray for you and with you. The pastor steps to the front of the room, asks everyone to bow their heads, and recites: "[F]ather, son, and Holy Spirit—it is with a due sense of reverence and awe that we come before you [today] seeking your blessing. ... You are ... a wise God, oh Lord, ... as evidenced even in the plan of redemption that is fulfilled in Jesus Christ. We ask that you would give freely and abundantly wisdom to one and to all ... in the name of the Lord and Savior Jesus Christ, who lives with you and the Holy Spirit, one God for ever and ever. Amen."

I would hold that the government officials responsible for the above practices—that is, for prayer repeatedly invoking a single religion's beliefs in these settings—crossed a constitutional line. ... One glaring problem is that the government in all these hypotheticals has aligned itself with, and placed its imprimatur on, a particular religious creed. "The clearest command of the Establishment Clause," this Court has held, "is that one religious denomination cannot be officially preferred over another." ... By authorizing and overseeing prayers associated with a single religion—to the exclusion of all others—the government officials in my hypothetical cases (whether federal, state, or local does not matter) have violated that foundational principle. They have embarked on a course of religious favoritism anathema to the First Amendment.

And making matters still worse: They have done so in a place where individuals come to interact with, and participate in, the institutions and processes of their government. ...

II

C

... And the guideposts for addressing that inquiry include the principles of religious neutrality I discussed earlier. The government (whether federal, state, or local) may not favor, or align itself with, any particular creed. And that is nowhere more true than when officials and citizens come face to face in their shared institutions of governance. In performing civic functions and seeking civic benefits, each person of this nation must experience a government that belongs to one and all, irrespective of belief. And for its part, each government must ensure that its participatory processes will not classify those citizens by faith, or make relevant their religious differences. ...

None of this means that Greece's town hall must be religion- or prayer-free. "[W]e are a religious people," *Marsh* observed, and prayer draws some warrant from tradition in a town hall, as well as in Congress or a state legislature. What the circumstances here demand is the recognition that we are a pluralistic people too. When citizens of all faiths come to speak to each other and their elected representatives in a legislative session, the government must take especial care to ensure that the prayers they hear will seek to include, rather than serve to divide. No more is required—but that much is crucial—to treat every citizen, of whatever religion, as an equal participant in her government. ...

And contrary to the majority's (and Justice ALITO's) view, that is not difficult to do. If the Town Board had let its chaplains know that they should speak in nonsectarian terms, common to diverse religious groups, then no one would have valid grounds for complaint. ... Or if the Board preferred, it might have invited clergy of many faiths to serve as chaplains, as the majority notes that Congress does. When one month a clergy member refers to Jesus, and the next to Allah or Jehovah—as the majority hopefully though counterfactually suggests happened here, the government does not identify itself with one religion or align itself with that faith's citizens, and the effect of even sectarian prayer is transformed. ...

Notes and Questions

1. *Dangerous prayer?* What are the dangers that could flow from government-sponsored prayer? Why would some government-sponsored prayers be constitutional while some are not? What does *Lemon* say about such prayer?
2. *The hypotheticals.* How do you assess Justice Kagan's hypotheticals? Are they situations that make you uncomfortable? Comfortable? Do you agree with her statement of them? Or with Justice Alito's challenge to their significance?
3. *Chart the decision.* Make a chart that includes each Justice's reasoning about the Establishment Clause and the prayer in *Town of Greece*. Can this chart tell you where the Justices agree and where they disagree about the Establishment Clause?

Following is a case about a praying public school football coach. He won the decision, 6–3. Why? What facts of the case are most interesting to you?

Note *Lemon* is essentially overruled, but the majority does not use the word "overrule" to describe its action regarding *Lemon*. After 51 years, the majority rejects *Lemon* in the following opinion. Justice Sotomayor in dissent says much more clearly that *Lemon* has been overruled. The author of the majority opinion, Justice Gorsuch, is also dismissive of the endorsement test. And he says in this case there was no coercion. How does this case relate to the earlier religion cases you have read? Is it a new approach to the Religion Clauses, as Sotomayor suggests?

Kennedy v. Bremerton School District

SUPREME COURT OF THE UNITED STATES, 2022

597 U.S. ___, 142 S.Ct. 2407

GORSUCH, J., delivered the opinion of the Court, in which ROBERTS, C. J., and THOMAS, ALITO, and BARRETT, JJ., joined, and in which KAVANAUGH, J., joined, except as to Part III–B. THOMAS, J., and ALITO, J., filed concurring opinions. SOTOMAYOR, J., filed a dissenting opinion, in which BREYER and KAGAN, JJ., joined.

Joseph Kennedy lost his job as a high school football coach because he knelt at midfield after games to offer a quiet prayer of thanks. Mr. Kennedy prayed during a period when school employees were free to speak with a friend, call for a reservation at a restaurant, check email, or attend to other personal matters. He offered his prayers quietly while his students were otherwise occupied. Still, the Bremerton School District disciplined him anyway. It did so because it thought anything less could lead a reasonable observer to conclude (mistakenly) that it endorsed Mr. Kennedy's religious beliefs. That reasoning was misguided. Both the Free Exercise and Free Speech Clauses of the First Amendment protect expressions like Mr. Kennedy's. Nor does a proper understanding of the Amendment's Establishment Clause require the government to single out private religious speech for special disfavor. The Constitution and the best of our traditions counsel mutual respect and tolerance, not censorship and suppression, for religious and nonreligious views alike. ...

III

Now before us, Mr. Kennedy renews his argument that the District's conduct violated both the Free Exercise and Free Speech Clauses of the First Amendment. These Clauses work in tandem. Where the Free Exercise Clause protects religious exercises, whether communicative or not, the Free Speech Clause provides overlapping protection for expressive religious activities. That the First Amendment doubly protects religious speech is no accident. It is a natural outgrowth of the framers' distrust of government attempts to regulate religion and suppress dissent. See, *e.g.*, A Memorial and Remonstrance Against Religious Assessments, in Selected Writings of James Madison 21, 25 (R. Ketcham ed. 2006). "[I]n Anglo-American history, ... government suppression of speech has so commonly been directed *precisely* at religious speech that a free-speech clause without religion would be Hamlet without the prince." ...

A

... That Mr. Kennedy has discharged his burdens is effectively undisputed. No one questions that he seeks to engage in a sincerely motivated religious exercise. The exercise in question involves, as Mr. Kennedy has put it, giving "thanks through prayer" briefly and by himself "on the playing field" at the conclusion of each game he coaches. Mr. Kennedy has indicated repeatedly that he is willing to "wai[t] until the game is over and the players have left the field" to "wal[k] to mid-field to say [his] short, private, personal prayer." The contested exercise before us does not involve leading prayers with the team or before any other captive audience. Mr. Kennedy's "religious beliefs do not require [him] to lead any prayer ... involving students." At the District's request, he voluntarily discontinued the school tradition of locker-room prayers and his postgame religious talks to students. The District disciplined him *only* for his decision to persist in praying quietly without his players after three games in October 2015.

... Nor does anyone question that, in forbidding Mr. Kennedy's brief prayer, the District failed to act pursuant to a neutral and generally applicable rule. ...

... In this case, the District's challenged policies were neither neutral nor generally applicable. By its own admission, the District sought to restrict Mr. Kennedy's actions at least in part because of their religious character ...

B

When it comes to Mr. Kennedy's free speech claim, our precedents remind us that the First Amendment's protections extend to "teachers and students," neither of whom "shed their constitutional rights to freedom of speech or expression at the schoolhouse gate." Of course, none of this means the speech rights of public school employees are so boundless that they may deliver any message to anyone anytime they wish. In addition to being private citizens, teachers and coaches are also government employees paid in part to speak on the government's behalf and convey its intended messages.

... Applying these lessons here, it seems clear to us that Mr. Kennedy has demonstrated that his speech was private speech, not government speech. When Mr. Kennedy uttered the three prayers that resulted in his suspension, he was not engaged in speech "ordinarily within the scope" of his duties as a coach. He did not speak pursuant to government policy. He was not seeking to convey a government-created message. He was not instructing players, discussing strategy, encouraging better on-field performance, or engaged in any other speech the District paid him to produce as a coach. Simply put: Mr. Kennedy's prayers did not "ow[e their] existence" to Mr. Kennedy's responsibilities as a public employee.

The timing and circumstances of Mr. Kennedy's prayers confirm the point. During the postgame period when these prayers occurred, coaches were free to attend briefly to personal matters—everything from checking sports scores on their phones to greeting friends and family in the stands. We find it unlikely that Mr. Kennedy was fulfilling a responsibility imposed by his employment by praying during a period in which the District has acknowledged that its coaching staff was free to engage in all manner of private speech. That Mr. Kennedy offered his prayers when students were engaged in other activities like singing the school fight song further suggests that those prayers were not delivered as an address to the team, but instead in his capacity as a private citizen. Nor is it dispositive that Mr. Kennedy's prayers took place "within the office" environment—here, on the field of play. Instead, what matters is whether Mr. Kennedy offered his prayers while acting within the scope of his duties as a coach. And taken together, both the substance of Mr. Kennedy's speech and the circumstances surrounding it point to the conclusion that he did not.

IV

... Ultimately, however, it does not matter which [Free Speech or Free Exercise] standard we apply. The District cannot sustain its burden under any of them.

A

... To defend its approach, the District relied on *Lemon* and its progeny. In upholding the District's actions, the Ninth Circuit followed the same course. And, to be sure, in *Lemon* this Court attempted a "grand unified theory" for assessing Establishment Clause claims. That approach called for an examination of a law's purposes, effects, and potential for entanglement with religion. In time, the approach also came to involve estimations about whether a "reasonable observer" would consider the government's challenged action an "endorsement" of religion.

What the District and the Ninth Circuit overlooked, however, is that the "shortcomings" associated with this "ambitiou[s]," abstract, and ahistorical approach to the Establishment Clause became so "apparent" that this Court long ago abandoned *Lemon* and its endorsement test offshoot. The Court has explained that these tests "invited chaos" in lower courts, led to "differing results" in materially identical cases, and created a "minefield" for legislators. This Court has since made plain, too, that the Establishment Clause does not include anything like a "modified heckler's veto, in which ... religious activity can be proscribed" based on "'perceptions'" or "'discomfort.'" An Establishment Clause violation does not automatically follow whenever a public school or other government entity "fail[s] to censor" private religious speech. Nor does the Clause "compel the government to purge from the public sphere" anything an objective observer could reasonably infer endorses or "partakes of the religious." In fact, just this Term the Court unanimously rejected a city's attempt to censor religious speech based on *Lemon* and the endorsement test. See *Shurtleff*, 596 U.S., at ___–___ (slip op., at 1–2); *id*., at ___ (Alito, J., concurring in judgment) (slip op., at 1); *id*., at ___, ___–___ (opinion of Gorsuch, J.) (slip op., at 1, 4–5).

... In place of *Lemon* and the endorsement test, this Court has instructed that the Establishment Clause must be interpreted by "'reference to historical practices and understandings.'" ...

B

... And, the District says, coercing worship amounts to an Establishment Clause violation on anyone's account of the Clause's original meaning.

As it turns out, however, there is a pretty obvious reason why the Ninth Circuit did not adopt this theory in proceedings below: The evidence cannot sustain it. To be sure, this Court has long held that government may not, consistent with a historically sensitive understanding of the Establishment Clause, "make a religious observance compulsory." Government "may not coerce anyone to attend church," nor may it force citizens to engage in "a formal religious exercise." No doubt, too, coercion along these lines was among the foremost hallmarks of religious establishments the framers sought to prohibit when they adopted the First Amendment. Members of this Court have sometimes disagreed on what exactly qualifies as impermissible coercion in light of the original meaning of the Establishment Clause. But in this case Mr. Kennedy's private religious exercise did not come close to crossing any line one might imagine separating protected private expression from impermissible government coercion. ...

... But learning how to tolerate speech or prayer of all kinds is "part of learning how to live in a pluralistic society," a trait of character essential to "a tolerant citizenry." This Court has long recognized as well that "secondary school students are mature enough ... to understand that a school does not endorse," let alone coerce them to participate in, "speech that it merely permits on a nondiscriminatory basis." Of course, some will take offense to certain forms of speech or prayer they are sure to encounter in a society where those activities enjoy such robust constitutional protection. But "[o]ffense ... does not equate to coercion."

... Meanwhile, this case looks very different from those in which this Court has found prayer involving public school students to be problematically coercive. In *Lee*, this Court held that school officials violated the Establishment Clause by "including [a] clerical membe[r]" who publicly recited prayers "as part of [an] official school graduation ceremony" because the school had "in every practical sense compelled attendance and participation in" a "religious exercise." In *Santa Fe Independent School Dist.* v. *Doe*, the Court held that a school district violated the Establishment Clause by broadcasting a prayer "over the public address system" before each football game. The Court observed that, while students generally were not required to attend games, attendance *was* required for "cheerleaders, members of the band, and, of course, the team members themselves." None of that is true here. The prayers for which Mr. Kennedy was disciplined were not publicly broadcast or recited to a captive audience. Students were not required or expected to participate. And, in fact, none of Mr. Kennedy's students did participate in any of the three October 2015 prayers that resulted in Mr. Kennedy's discipline.

C

In the end, the District's case hinges on the need to generate conflict between an individual's rights under the Free Exercise and Free Speech Clauses and its own Establishment Clause duties—and then develop some explanation why one of these Clauses in the First Amendment should "'trum[p]'" the other two. But the project falters badly. Not only does the District fail to offer a sound reason to prefer one constitutional guarantee over another. It cannot even show that they are at odds. In truth, there is no conflict between the constitutional commands before us. There is only the "mere shadow" of a conflict, a false choice premised on a misconstruction of the Establishment Clause. And in no world may a government entity's concerns about phantom constitutional violations justify actual violations of an individual's First Amendment rights.

V

Respect for religious expressions is indispensable to life in a free and diverse Republic—whether those expressions take place in a sanctuary or on a field, and whether they manifest through the spoken word or a bowed head. Here, a government entity sought to punish an individual for engaging in a brief, quiet, personal religious observance doubly protected by the Free Exercise and Free Speech Clauses of the First Amendment. And the only meaningful justification the government offered for its reprisal rested on a mistaken view that it had a duty to ferret out and suppress religious observances even as it allows comparable secular speech. The Constitution neither mandates nor tolerates that kind of discrimination. Mr. Kennedy is entitled to summary judgment on his First Amendment claims. The judgment of the Court of Appeals is Reversed.

Justice THOMAS, concurring.

I join the Court's opinion because it correctly holds that Bremerton School District violated Joseph Kennedy's First Amendment rights. I write separately to emphasize that the Court's opinion does not resolve two issues related to Kennedy's free-exercise claim.

First, the Court refrains from deciding whether or how public employees' rights under the Free Exercise Clause may or may not be different from those enjoyed by the general public. ...

Second, the Court also does not decide what burden a government employer must shoulder to justify restricting an employee's religious expression because the District had no constitutional basis for reprimanding Kennedy under any possibly applicable standard of scrutiny.

Justice ALITO, concurring.

The expression at issue in this case is unlike that in any of our prior cases involving the free-speech rights of public employees. Petitioner's expression occurred while at work but during a time when a brief lull in his duties apparently gave him a few free moments to engage in private activities. When he engaged in this expression, he acted in a purely private capacity. The Court does not decide what standard applies to such expression under the Free Speech Clause but holds only that retaliation for this expression cannot be justified based on any of the standards discussed. On that understanding, I join the opinion in full.

Justice SOTOMAYOR, with whom Justice BREYER and Justice KAGAN join, dissenting.

This case is about whether a public school must permit a school official to kneel, bow his head, and say a prayer at the center of a school event. The Constitution does not authorize, let alone require, public schools to embrace this conduct. Since *Engel v. Vitale,* this Court consistently has recognized that school officials leading prayer is constitutionally impermissible. Official-led prayer strikes at the core of our constitutional protections for the religious liberty of students and their parents, as embodied in both the Establishment Clause and the Free Exercise Clause of the First Amendment.

The Court now charts a different path, yet again paying almost exclusive attention to the Free Exercise Clause's protection for individual religious exercise while giving short shrift to the Establishment Clause's prohibition on state establishment of religion. To the degree the Court portrays petitioner Joseph Kennedy's prayers as private and quiet, it misconstrues the facts. The record reveals that Kennedy had a longstanding practice of conducting demonstrative prayers on the 50-yard line of the football field. Kennedy consistently invited others to join his prayers and for years led student athletes in prayer at the same time and location. The Court ignores this history. The Court also ignores the severe disruption to school events caused by Kennedy's conduct, viewing it as irrelevant because the Bremerton School District (District) stated that it was suspending Kennedy to avoid it being viewed as endorsing religion. Under the Court's analysis, presumably this would be a different case if the District had cited Kennedy's repeated disruptions of school programming and violations of school policy regarding public access to the field as grounds for suspending him. As the District did not articulate those grounds, the Court assesses only the District's Establishment Clause concerns. It errs by assessing them divorced from the context and history of Kennedy's prayer practice.

Today's decision goes beyond merely misreading the record. The Court overrules *Lemon v. Kurtzman,* and calls into question decades of subsequent precedents that it deems "offshoot[s]" of that decision. In the process, the Court rejects longstanding concerns surrounding government endorsement of religion and replaces the standard for reviewing such questions with a new "history and tradition" test. In addition, while the Court reaffirms that the Establishment Clause prohibits the government from coercing participation in religious exercise, it applies a nearly toothless version of the coercion analysis, failing to acknowledge the unique pressures faced by students when participating in school-sponsored activities. This decision does a disservice to schools and the young citizens they serve, as well as to our Nation's longstanding commitment to the separation of church and state. I respectfully dissent. …

II

Properly understood, this case is not about the limits on an individual's ability to engage in private prayer at work. This case is about whether a school district is required to allow one of its employees to incorporate a public, communicative display of the employee's personal religious beliefs into a school event, where that display is recognizable as part of a longstanding practice of the employee ministering religion to students as the public watched. A school district is not required to permit such conduct; in fact, the Establishment Clause prohibits it from doing so.

A

… Given the twin Establishment Clause concerns of endorsement and coercion, it is unsurprising that the Court has consistently held integrating prayer into public school activities to be unconstitutional, including when student participation is not a formal requirement or prayer is silent. The Court also has held that incorporating a nondenominational general benediction into a graduation ceremony is unconstitutional. Finally, this Court has held that including prayers in student football games is unconstitutional, even when delivered by students rather than staff and even when students themselves initiated the prayer.

B

Under these precedents, the Establishment Clause violation at hand is clear ...

... Finally, Kennedy stresses that he never formally required students to join him in his prayers. But existing precedents do not require coercion to be explicit, particularly when children are involved. To the contrary, this Court's Establishment Clause jurisprudence establishes that "'the government may no more use social pressure to enforce orthodoxy than it may use more direct means.'" Thus, the Court has held that the Establishment Clause "will not permit" a school "'to exact religious conformity from a student as the price' of joining her classmates at a varsity football game." To uphold a coach's integration of prayer into the ceremony of a football game, in the context of an established history of the coach inviting student involvement in prayer, is to exact precisely this price from students.

C

... Here, the District's directive prohibiting Kennedy's demonstrative speech at the 50-yard line was narrowly tailored to avoid an Establishment Clause violation. The District's suspension of Kennedy followed a long history. The last three games proved that Kennedy did not intend to pray silently, but to thrust the District into incorporating a religious ceremony into its events, as he invited others to join his prayer and anticipated in his communications with the District that students would want to join as well. Notably, the District repeatedly sought to work with Kennedy to develop an accommodation to permit him to engage in religious exercise during or after his game-related responsibilities. Kennedy, however, ultimately refused to respond to the District's suggestions and declined to communicate with the District, except through media appearances. Because the District's valid Establishment Clause concerns satisfy strict scrutiny, Kennedy's free exercise claim fails as well.

III

Despite the overwhelming precedents establishing that school officials leading prayer violates the Establishment Clause, the Court today holds that Kennedy's midfield prayer practice did not violate the Establishment Clause. This decision rests on an erroneous understanding of the Religion Clauses. It also disregards the balance this Court's cases strike among the rights conferred by the Clauses. The Court relies on an assortment of pluralities, concurrences, and dissents by Members of the current majority to effect fundamental changes in this Court's Religion Clauses jurisprudence, all the while proclaiming that nothing has changed at all.

B

... In short, the endorsement inquiry dictated by precedent is a measured, practical, and administrable one, designed to account for the competing interests present within any given community.

Despite all of this authority, the Court claims that it "long ago abandoned" both the "endorsement test" and this Court's decision in *Lemon*. The Court chiefly cites the plurality opinion in *American Legion v. American Humanist Assn.*, 588 U.S. ___ (2019) to support this contention. That plurality opinion, to be sure, criticized *Lemon*'s effort at establishing a "grand unified theory of the Establishment Clause" as poorly suited to the broad "array" of diverse establishment claims. All the Court in *American Legion* ultimately held, however, was that application of the *Lemon* test to "longstanding monuments, symbols, and practices" was ill-advised for reasons specific to those contexts. The only categorical rejection of *Lemon* in *American Legion* appeared in separate writings. See Kavanaugh, Thomas, and Gorsuch.

The Court now goes much further, overruling *Lemon* entirely and in all contexts. It is wrong to do so. *Lemon* summarized "the cumulative criteria developed by the Court over many years" of experience "draw[ing] lines" as to when government engagement with religion violated the Establishment Clause. *Lemon* properly concluded that precedent generally directed consideration of whether the government action had a "secular legislative purpose," whether its "principal or primary effect must be one that neither advances nor inhibits religion," and whether in practice it "foster[s] 'an excessive government entanglement with religion.'" It is true "that rigid application of the *Lemon* test does not solve every Establishment Clause problem," but that does not mean that the test has no value.

To put it plainly, the purposes and effects of a government action matter in evaluating whether that action violates the Establishment Clause, as numerous precedents beyond *Lemon* instruct in the particular context of public schools. Neither the critiques of *Lemon* as setting out a dispositive test for all seasons nor the fact that the Court has not referred to *Lemon* in all situations support this Court's decision to dismiss that precedent entirely, particularly in the school context.

C

Upon overruling one "grand unified theory," the Court introduces another: It holds that courts must interpret whether an Establishment Clause violation has occurred mainly "by 'reference to historical practices and understandings.'" Here again, the Court professes that nothing has changed. In fact, while the Court has long referred to historical practice as one element of the analysis in specific Establishment Clause cases, the Court has never announced this as a general test or exclusive focus.

The Court reserves any meaningful explanation of its history-and-tradition test for another day, content for now to disguise it as established law and move on. It should not escape notice, however, that the effects of the majority's new rule could be profound. The problems with elevating history and tradition over purpose and precedent are well documented. See *Dobbs*, 597 U.S., at ___ (Breyer, Sotomayor, and Kagan, JJ., dissenting) (slip op., at 16) (explaining that the Framers "defined rights in general terms to permit future evolution in their scope and meaning"); *New York State Rifle & Pistol Assn., Inc.* v. *Bruen*, 597 U.S. ___, ___–___ (2022) (Breyer, J., dissenting) (slip op., at 24–28) (explaining the pitfalls of a "near-exclusive reliance on history" and offering examples of when this Court has "misread" history in the past); *Brown v. Davenport*, 595 U.S. ___ (2022) (Kagan, J., dissenting) (noting the inaccuracies risked when courts "play amateur historian").

For now, it suffices to say that the Court's history-and-tradition test offers essentially no guidance for school administrators. If even judges and Justices, with full adversarial briefing and argument tailored to precise legal issues, regularly disagree (and err) in their amateur efforts at history, how are school administrators, faculty, and staff supposed to adapt? How will school administrators exercise their responsibilities to manage school curriculum and events when the Court appears to elevate individuals' rights to religious exercise above all else? Today's opinion provides little in the way of answers; the Court simply sets the stage for future legal changes that will inevitably follow the Court's choice today to upset longstanding rules.

D

Finally, the Court acknowledges that the Establishment Clause prohibits the government from coercing people to engage in religion practice, but its analysis of coercion misconstrues both the record and this Court's precedents.

... The question before the Court is not whether a coach taking a knee to pray on the field would constitute an Establishment Clause violation in any and all circumstances. It is whether permitting Kennedy to continue a demonstrative prayer practice at the center of the football field after years of inappropriately leading students in prayer in the same spot, at that same time, and in the same manner, which led students to feel compelled to join him, violates the Establishment Clause. It does.

Having disregarded this context, the Court finds Kennedy's three-game practice distinguishable from precedent because the prayers were "quie[t]" and the students were otherwise "occupied." The record contradicts this narrative. Even on the Court's myopic framing of the facts, at two of the three games on which the Court focuses, players witnessed student peers from the other team and other authority figures surrounding Kennedy and joining him in prayer. The coercive pressures inherent in such a situation are obvious. Moreover, Kennedy's actual demand to the District was that he give "verbal" prayers specifically at the midfield position where he traditionally led team prayers, and that students be allowed to join him "voluntarily" and pray. Notably, the Court today does not embrace this demand, but it nonetheless rejects the District's right to ensure that students were not pressured to pray.

To reiterate, the District did not argue, and neither court below held, that "*any* visible religious conduct by a teacher or coach should be deemed ... impermissibly coercive on students." Nor has anyone contended that a coach may never visibly pray on the field. The courts below simply recognized that Kennedy continued to initiate prayers visible to students, while still on duty during school events, under the exact same circumstances as his past practice of leading student prayer. It is unprecedented for the Court to hold that this conduct, taken as a whole, did not raise cognizable coercion concerns. Importantly, nothing in the Court's opinion should be read as calling into question that Kennedy's conduct may have raised other concerns regarding disruption of school events or misuse of school facilities that would have separately justified employment action against Kennedy.

* * *

The Free Exercise Clause and Establishment Clause are equally integral in protecting religious freedom in our society. The first serves as "a promise from our government," while the second erects a "backstop that disables our government from breaking it" and "start[ing] us down the path to the past, when [the right to free exercise] was routinely abridged."

Today, the Court once again weakens the backstop. It elevates one individual's interest in personal religious exercise, in the exact time and place of that individual's choosing, over society's interest in protecting the separation between church and state, eroding the protections for religious liberty for all. Today's decision is particularly misguided because it elevates the religious rights of a school official, who voluntarily accepted public employment and the limits that public employment entails, over those of his students, who are required to attend school and who this Court has long recognized are particularly vulnerable and deserving of protection. In doing so, the Court sets us further down a perilous path in forcing States to entangle themselves with religion, with all of our rights hanging in the balance. As much as the Court protests otherwise, today's decision is no victory for religious liberty. I respectfully dissent.

Justice Sotomayor's dissent included the following pictures:

FIGURE 10.2 J. Kennedy in a prayer circle (Oct. 16, 2015).

FIGURE 10.3 J. Kennedy standing in a group of kneeling players.

FIGURE 10.4 J. Kennedy in a prayer circle (Oct. 26, 2015).

Notes and Questions

1. *Pictures.* In a highly unusual move, Justice Sotomayor's dissent includes pictures of Coach Kennedy's religious practice to dispute the majority's account of the facts. What did you envision as you read the majority opinion?

2. *Lemon, endorsement, coercion.* These three tests have been traditional Establishment Clause tests. Apply them as you learned them in earlier cases (as distinct from this case) to the facts of this case. Does Coach Kennedy win or lose under them?
3. *As interpreted in this opinion.* What does Justice Gorsuch say about these three tests? How does he apply them in this case?
4. *As interpreted by the dissent.* What does Justice Sotomayor's dissent say about these three tests?
5. *Public or private?* Why did the lower courts conclude Kennedy was a public employee subject to the Establishment Clause? Why did Gorsuch conclude this was a private matter of free exercise and free speech?
6. *Establishment Clause.* What does the "historical practices and understandings" standard for the Establishment Clause mean?
7. *Facts.* Why do the Justices disagree about the facts of Kennedy's prayer, with the majority focusing on how private and solitary it is, and the dissent providing pictures showing it is public?
8. *Lemon.* Would you have overruled *Lemon*? Why or why not?
9. *Deleted*? Professor Griffin wrote a blog post about this case arguing that the six Justices had deleted the Establishment Clause from the Constitution. Do you agree with her? Why or why not?
10. *Future.* What implications does this opinion have for future religious conduct in the schools?
11. *What about Stare Decisis?* Note that during the same term, the Court also overruled *Roe v. Wade* in *Dobbs v. Jackson Women's Health Organization.* A major focus in the *Dobbs* decision was whether overruling *Roe* was consistent with stare decisis. Why doesn't the majority in *Kennedy* follow the same doctrinal analysis before overruling *Lemon*?

3. The Secular Cross

Can their statements about prayer in *Town of Greece* explain how the Justices would vote about the Bladensburg Cross, which is pictured here? Is this cross case consistent with the outcome of *Kennedy v. Bremerton*?

FIGURE 10.5 The Bladensburg Peace Cross. App. 887, Court Appendix.

American Legion v. American Humanist Association

SUPREME COURT OF THE UNITED STATES, 2019

588 U.S. ___, 139 S.Ct. 2067

ALITO J., announced the judgment of the Court and delivered the opinion of the Court with respect to Parts I, II–B, II–C, III, and IV, in which ROBERTS, C. J., and BREYER, KAGAN, and KAVANAUGH, JJ., joined, and an opinion with respect to Parts II–A and II–D, in which ROBERTS, C. J., and BREYER and KAVANAUGH, JJ., joined. BREYER J., filed a concurring opinion, in which KAGAN J., joined. KAVANAUGH, J., filed a concurring opinion. KAGAN, J., filed an opinion concurring in part. THOMAS, J., filed an opinion concurring in the judgment. GORSUCH, J., filed an opinion concurring in the judgment, in which THOMAS, J., joined. GINSBURG, J., filed a dissenting opinion, in which SOTOMAYOR, J., joined.

Since 1925, the Bladensburg Peace Cross (Cross) has stood as a tribute to 49 area soldiers who gave their lives in the First World War. Eighty-nine years after the dedication of the Cross, respondents filed this lawsuit, claiming that they are offended by the sight of the memorial on public land and that its presence there and the expenditure of public funds to maintain it violate the Establishment Clause of the First Amendment. To remedy this violation, they asked a federal court to order the relocation or demolition of the Cross or at least the removal of its arms. The Court of Appeals for the Fourth Circuit agreed that the memorial is unconstitutional and remanded for a determination of the proper remedy. We now reverse.

Although the cross has long been a preeminent Christian symbol, its use in the Bladensburg memorial has a special significance. After the First World War, the picture of row after row of plain white crosses marking the overseas graves of soldiers who had lost their lives in that horrible conflict was emblazoned on the minds of Americans at home, and the adoption of the cross as the Bladensburg memorial must be viewed in that historical context. For nearly a century, the Bladensburg Cross has expressed the community's grief at the loss of the young men who perished, its thanks for their sacrifice, and its dedication to the ideals for which they fought. It has become a prominent community landmark, and its removal or radical alteration at this date would be seen by many not as a neutral act but as the manifestation of "a hostility toward religion that has no place in our Establishment Clause traditions." And contrary to respondents' intimations, there is no evidence of discriminatory intent in the selection of the design of the memorial or the decision of a Maryland commission to maintain it. The Religion Clauses of the Constitution aim to foster a society in which people of all beliefs can live together harmoniously, and the presence of the Bladensburg Cross on the land where it has stood for so many years is fully consistent with that aim.

I

A

The cross came into widespread use as a symbol of Christianity by the fourth century, and it retains that meaning today. But there are many contexts in which the symbol has also taken on a secular meaning. Indeed, there are instances in which its message is now almost entirely secular.

...

C

... The District Court granted summary judgment for the Commission and the American Legion. The Cross, the District Court held, satisfies both the three-pronged test announced in *Lemon*, and the analysis applied by Justice BREYER in upholding the Ten Commandments monument. ... A divided panel of the Court of Appeals for the Fourth Circuit reversed. The majority relied primarily on the *Lemon* test but also took cognizance of Justice BREYER's [Ten Commandments] concurrence. While recognizing that the Commission acted for a secular purpose, the court held that the Bladensburg Cross failed *Lemon's* "effects" prong because a reasonable observer would view the Commission's ownership and maintenance of the monument as an endorsement of Christianity. ... Chief Judge Gregory dissented in relevant part, contending that the majority misapplied the "effects" test by failing to give adequate consideration to the Cross's "physical setting, history, and usage." ...

II A

... This pattern is a testament to the *Lemon* test's shortcomings. As Establishment Clause cases involving a great array of laws and practices came to the Court, it became more and more apparent that the *Lemon* test could not resolve them. It could not "explain the Establishment Clause's tolerance, for example, of the prayers that open legislative meetings, ... certain references to, and invocations of, the Deity in the public words of public officials; the public references to God on coins, decrees, and buildings; or the attention paid to the religious objectives of certain holidays, including Thanksgiving." The test has been harshly criticized by Members of this Court, lamented by lower court judges, and questioned by a diverse roster of scholars. ...

B

... These four considerations show that retaining established, religiously expressive monuments, symbols, and practices is quite different from erecting or adopting new ones. The passage of time gives rise to a strong presumption of constitutionality. ...

D

... In *Town of Greece,* which concerned prayer before a town council meeting, there was disagreement about the inclusiveness of the town's practice. ...

The practice begun by the First Congress stands out as an example of respect and tolerance for differing views, an honest endeavor to achieve inclusivity and nondiscrimination, and a recognition of the important role that religion plays in the lives of many Americans. Where categories of monuments, symbols, and practices with a longstanding history follow in that tradition, they are likewise constitutional.

III

Applying these principles, we conclude that the Bladensburg Cross does not violate the Establishment Clause.

As we have explained, the Bladensburg Cross carries special significance in commemorating World War I. Due in large part to the image of the simple wooden crosses that originally marked the graves of American soldiers killed in the war, the cross became a symbol of their sacrifice, and the design of the Bladensburg Cross must be understood in light of that background. That the cross originated as a Christian symbol and retains that meaning in many contexts does not change the fact that the symbol took on an added secular meaning when used in World War I memorials.

Not only did the Bladensburg Cross begin with this meaning, but with the passage of time, it has acquired historical importance. ...

IV

The cross is undoubtedly a Christian symbol, but that fact should not blind us to everything else that the Bladensburg Cross has come to represent. For some, that monument is a symbolic resting place for ancestors who never returned home. For others, it is a place for the community to gather and honor all veterans and their sacrifices for our Nation. For others still, it is a historical landmark. For many of these people, destroying or defacing the Cross that has stood undisturbed for nearly a century would not be neutral and would not further the ideals of respect and tolerance embodied in the First Amendment. For all these reasons, the Cross does not offend the Constitution. ...

Justice BREYER, with whom Justice KAGAN joins, concurring

... As I have previously explained, "where the Establishment Clause is at issue," the Court must "'distinguish between real threat and mere shadow.'" In light of all the circumstances here, I agree with the Court that the Peace Cross poses no real threat to the values that the Establishment Clause serves.

Justice KAVANAUGH, concurring

... The opinion identifies five relevant categories of Establishment Clause cases: (1) religious symbols on government property and religious speech at government events; (2) religious accommodations and exemptions from generally applicable laws; (3) government benefits and tax exemptions for religious organizations; (4) religious expression in public schools; and (5) regulation of private religious speech in public forums.

The *Lemon* test does not explain the Court's decisions in any of those five categories. ...

And the Court's decisions over the span of several decades demonstrate that the *Lemon* test is not good law and does not apply to Establishment Clause cases in any of the five categories.

On the contrary, each category of Establishment Clause cases has its own principles based on history, tradition, and precedent. And the cases together lead to an overarching set of principles: If the challenged government practice is not coercive *and* if it (i) is rooted in history and tradition; or (ii) treats religious people, organizations, speech, or activity equally to comparable secular people, organizations, speech, or activity; or (iii) represents a permissible legislative accommodation or exemption from a generally applicable law, then there ordinarily is no Establishment Clause violation. ...

The conclusion that the cross does not violate the Establishment Clause does not necessarily mean that those who object to it have no other recourse. The Court's ruling *allows* the State to maintain the cross on public land. The Court's ruling does not *require* the State to maintain the cross on public land. The Maryland Legislature could enact new laws requiring removal of the cross or transfer of the land. The Maryland Governor or other state or local executive officers may have authority to do so under current Maryland law. And if not, the legislature could enact new laws to authorize such executive action. The Maryland Constitution, as interpreted by the Maryland Court of Appeals, may speak to this question. And if not, the people of Maryland can amend the State Constitution.

Those alternative avenues of relief illustrate a fundamental feature of our constitutional structure: This Court is not the *only* guardian of individual rights in America. ...

Justice KAGAN, concurring in part.

... Although I agree that rigid application of the test does not solve every Establishment Clause problem, I think that test's focus on purposes and effects is crucial in evaluating government action in this sphere—as this very suit shows. Although I too "look[ ] to history for guidance," I prefer at least for now to do so case-by-case, rather than to sign on to any broader statements about history's role in Establishment Clause analysis. ... Here, as elsewhere, the opinion shows sensitivity to and respect for this Nation's pluralism, and the values of neutrality and inclusion that the First Amendment demands.

Justice THOMAS, concurring in the judgment.

The Establishment Clause states that "Congress shall make no law respecting an establishment of religion." The text and history of this Clause suggest that it should not be incorporated against the States. Even if the Clause expresses an individual right enforceable against the States, it is limited by its text to "law[s]" enacted by a legislature, so it is unclear whether the Bladensburg Cross would implicate any incorporated right. And even if it did, this religious display does not involve the type of actual legal coercion that was a hallmark of historical establishments of religion. Therefore, the Cross is clearly constitutional. ...

As to the long-discredited test set forth *Lemon* and reiterated in *County of Allegheny*, the plurality rightly rejects its relevance to claims, like this one, involving "religious references or imagery in public monuments, symbols, mottos, displays, and ceremonies." I agree with that aspect of its opinion. I would take the logical next step and overrule the *Lemon* test in all contexts. ...

Regrettably, I cannot join the Court's opinion because it does not adequately clarify the appropriate standard for Establishment Clause cases. Therefore, I concur only in the judgment.

Justice GORSUCH, with whom Justice THOMAS joins, concurring in the judgment.

The American Humanist Association wants a federal court to order the destruction of a 94 year-old war memorial because its members are offended. Today, the Court explains that the plaintiffs are not entitled to demand the destruction of longstanding monuments, and I find much of its opinion compelling. In my judgment, however, it follows from the Court's analysis that suits like this one should be dismissed for lack of standing. Accordingly, while I concur in the judgment to reverse and remand the court of appeals' decision, I would do so with additional instructions to dismiss the case. ...

Offended observer standing cannot be squared with this Court's longstanding teachings about the limits of Article III. Not even today's dissent seriously attempts to defend it. So at this point you might wonder: How *did* the lower courts in this case indulge the plaintiffs' "offended observer" theory of standing? And why have other lower courts done similarly in other cases?

The truth is, the fault lies here. Lower courts invented offended observer standing for Establishment Clause cases in the 1970s in response to this Court's decision in *Lemon*. ...

As today's plurality rightly indicates in Part II–A, however, *Lemon* was a misadventure. It sought a "grand unified theory" of the Establishment Clause but left us only a mess. ...

With *Lemon* now shelved, little excuse will remain for the anomaly of offended observer standing, and the gaping hole it tore in standing doctrine in the courts of appeals should now begin to close. Nor does this development mean colorable Establishment Clause violations will lack for proper plaintiffs. By way of example only, a public school student compelled to recite a prayer will still have standing to sue. So will persons denied public office because of their religious affiliations or lack of them. And so will those who are denied government benefits because they do not practice a favored religion or any at all. On top of all that, States remain free to supply other forms of relief consistent with their own laws and constitutions.

Abandoning offended observer standing will mean only a return to the usual demands of Article III, requiring a real controversy with real impact on real persons to make a federal case out of it. ...

Justice GINSBURG, with whom Justice SOTOMAYOR joins, dissenting.

... The Latin cross is the foremost symbol of the Christian faith, embodying the "central theological claim of Christianity: that the son of God died on the cross, that he rose from the dead, and that his death and resurrection offer the possibility of eternal life." Precisely because the cross symbolizes these sectarian beliefs, it is a common marker for the graves of Christian soldiers. For the same reason, using the cross as a war memorial does not transform it into a secular symbol, as the Courts of Appeals have uniformly recognized. Just as a Star of David is not suitable to honor Christians who died serving their country, so a cross is not suitable to honor those of other faiths who died defending their nation. Soldiers of all faiths "are united by their love of country, but they are not united by the cross."

By maintaining the Peace Cross on a public highway, the Commission elevates Christianity over other faiths, and religion over nonreligion. Memorializing the service of American soldiers is an "admirable and unquestionably secular" objective. But the Commission does not serve that objective by displaying a symbol that bears "a starkly sectarian message." ...

Every Court of Appeals to confront the question has held that "[m]aking a ... Latin cross a war memorial does not make the cross secular," it "makes the war memorial sectarian."

The Peace Cross is no exception. That was evident from the start. At the dedication ceremony, the keynote speaker analogized the sacrifice of the honored soldiers to that of Jesus Christ, calling the Peace Cross "symbolic of Calvary," where Jesus was crucified. Local reporters variously described the monument as "[a] mammoth cross, a likeness of the Cross of Calvary, as described in the Bible," "a monster [C]alvary cross,"; and "a huge sacrifice cross,". The character of the monument has not changed with the passage of time. ...

The cross was never perceived as an appropriate headstone or memorial for Jewish soldiers and others who did not adhere to Christianity. ...

In fact, the "most popular and enduring memorial of the [post-World War I] decade" was "[t]he mass-produced *Spirit of the American Doughboy* statue." That statue, depicting a U.S. infantryman, "met with widespread approval throughout American communities." Indeed, the first memorial to World War I erected in Prince George's County "depict[s] a doughboy." The Peace Cross, as Plaintiffs' expert historian observed, was an "aberration ... even in the era [in which] it was built and dedicated." ...

Recognizing that a Latin cross does not belong on a public highway or building does not mean the monument must be "torn down." In some instances, the violation may be cured by relocating the monument to private land or by transferring ownership of the land and monument to a private party. ...

"If the aim of the Establishment Clause is genuinely to uncouple government from church," the Clause does "not permit ... a display of th[e] character" of Bladensburg's Peace Cross.

Notes and Questions

1. *Categorizing.* Is the cross secular or religious in your view?
2. *The spectrum of symbols.* Is the cross or the doughboy the better symbol of World War I? Should the Court care, and how would it determine what makes a better symbol?

3. *Is offense enough for standing?* Is a feeling of offense enough to give a party standing in Establishment Clause cases, or do you agree that offense should no longer allow a party standing to challenge a case?
4. *Justice Thomas.* What do you think of Justice Thomas's argument that the Establishment Clause should not be applied to the states? Why would that be true? What would be the result if the Establishment Clause no longer applied to the states?
5. *A religious symbol for many religions?* Are Jews honored by a public memorial in the shape of a cross? What about Muslims, Buddhists, Hindus, or Atheists?
6. *Religious symbols displayed by the government.* Are the displays shown in Figure 10.6 constitutionally permitted?

FIGURE 10.6 Appendices to opinion of Blackmun, J., in Allegheny County v. ACLU, 492 US. US 573 (1989).

The Supreme Court ruled the top display was unconstitutional and the bottom one was constitutional in *County of Allegheny v. American Civil Liberties Union,* 492 U.S. 573 (1989). The first picture is of a crèche on the Grand Staircase of the Allegheny County Courthouse. The second is a Chanukah menorah next to a Christmas tree and a sign about liberty that was outside the City-County Building. The pictures are displayed at Appendix A and B of the Court's opinion.

The Supreme Court said the Ten Commandments monument shown in Figure 10.7 was constitutional in *Van Orden v. Perry,* 545 U.S. 677 (2005). The picture is from the Appendix to Justice Stevens's dissent.

What religious symbols should be used in public monuments, including monuments about wars? Search around the Internet for symbols you would like to use in a monument. Create a public monument, and explain why it is constitutional or unconstitutional.

4. What Funding Should Go to Religious Schools?

In *Trinity Lutheran Church of Colombia v. Comer,* 582 U.S. ___, 137 S.Ct. 2012 (2017), the Court revisited religious funding. By a 7–2 vote, the Supreme Court ruled for Trinity Lutheran, concluding that Missouri's Blaine Amendment violated the Free Exercise Clause. Blaine amendments were state constitutional amendments that barred funding to religious schools. A Blaine amendment had been proposed for the federal constitution but did not succeed. In *Trinity,* the opinion by Chief Justice Roberts simply stated that to deny state funding because an organization is religious violates free exercise, which is a continuation of the equality principle that you may have noticed emerging in the Religion Clause cases. One of his footnotes left open a possibility that some aid to religion remains unconstitutional. In a concurrence, Justices Thomas and Gorsuch offered a broader protection of religious freedom. They seemed unwilling to recognize any future restrictions on government funding of religion where the government was already funding secular uses. Dissenting Justices Sotomayor and Ginsburg argued that the justices had forgotten the meaning of the Establishment Clause, which prohibits state funding of religion. Many commentators thought *Trinity Lutheran* had done away with the separation of church and state. If you read the very first Establishment Clause case, *Everson v. Board of Education*, 330 U.S. 1 (1947), you might well think they had gone off track. In that case, the Court was asked to decide whether New Jersey could fund student school buses that took children to public and private (mostly Catholic) schools. The Court spent an enormous amount of the opinion stating that funds to religion from government are dangerous just as James Madison had said that "not one penny" should be paid by the government for religious education in his *Memorial and Remonstrance.*

FIGURE 10.7 A tablet displaying the Ten Commandments, located on the grounds of the Texas State Capitol in Austin, Texas.

Post-*Trinity*, the Court heard the following case about Montana's Blaine Amendment and funding for religious schools. Does separation of church and state survive these rulings? Can you tell from the Montana oral argument, https://www.oyez.org/cases/2019/18-1195, that Montana would lose the case? Does the oral argument tell you anything about separation of church and state? What does this decision bode for funding of public schools in comparison to religious schools?

Espinoza v. Montana Department of Revenue

SUPREME COURT OF THE UNITED STATES, 2020

591 U.S. ___, 140 S.Ct. 2246

ROBERTS, C. J., delivered the opinion of the Court, in which THOMAS, ALITO, GORSUCH, and KAVANAUGH, JJ., joined. THOMAS, J., filed a concurring opinion, in which GORSUCH, J., joined. ALITO, J., and GORSUCH, J., filed concurring opinions. GINSBURG, J., filed a dissenting opinion, in which KAGAN, J., joined. BREYER, J., filed a dissenting opinion, in which KAGAN, J., joined as to Part I. SOTOMAYOR, J., filed a dissenting opinion.

Chief Justice ROBERTS delivered the opinion of the Court.

The Montana Legislature established a program to provide tuition assistance to parents who send their children to private schools. The program grants a tax credit to anyone who donates to certain organizations that in turn award scholarships to selected students attending such schools. When petitioners sought to use the scholarships at a religious school, the Montana Supreme Court struck down the program. The Court relied on the "no-aid" provision of the State Constitution, which prohibits any aid to a school controlled by a "church, sect, or denomination." The question presented is whether the Free Exercise Clause of the

United States Constitution barred that application of the no-aid provision.

I

A

In 2015, the Montana Legislature sought "to provide parental and student choice in education" by enacting a scholarship program for students attending private schools. The program grants a tax credit of up to $150 to any taxpayer who donates to a participating "student scholarship organization." The scholarship organizations then use the donations to award scholarships to children for tuition at a private school.

So far only one scholarship organization, Big Sky Scholarships, has participated in the program. Big Sky focuses on providing scholarships to families who face financial hardship or have children with disabilities. Scholarship organizations like Big Sky must, among other requirements, maintain an application process for awarding the scholarships; use at least 90% of all donations on scholarship awards; and comply with state reporting and monitoring requirements.

A family whose child is awarded a scholarship under the program may use it at any "qualified education provider"—that is, any private school that meets certain accreditation, testing, and safety requirements. Virtually every private school in Montana qualifies. Upon receiving a scholarship, the family designates its school of choice, and the scholarship organization sends the scholarship funds directly to the school. Neither the scholarship organization nor its donors can restrict awards to particular types of schools.

The Montana Legislature allotted $3 million annually to fund the tax credits, beginning in 2016. If the annual allotment is exhausted, it increases by 10% the following year. The program is slated to expire in 2023.

The Montana Legislature also directed that the program be administered in accordance with Article X, section 6, of the Montana Constitution, which contains a "no-aid" provision barring government aid to sectarian schools. In full, that provision states:

> "**Aid prohibited to sectarian schools**. ... The legislature, counties, cities, towns, school districts, and public corporations shall not make any direct or indirect appropriation or payment from any public fund or monies, or any grant of lands or other property for any sectarian purpose or to aid any church, school, academy, seminary, college, university, or other literary or scientific institution, controlled in whole or in part by any church, sect, or denomination." Mont. Const., Art. X, § 6(1).

Shortly after the scholarship program was created, the Montana Department of Revenue promulgated "Rule 1," over the objection of the Montana Attorney General. That administrative rule prohibited families from using scholarships at religious schools. It did so by changing the definition of "qualified education provider" to exclude any school "owned or controlled in whole or in part by any church, religious sect, or denomination." The Department explained that the Rule was needed to reconcile the scholarship program with the no-aid provision of the Montana Constitution.

The Montana Attorney General disagreed. In a letter to the Department, he advised that the Montana Constitution did not require excluding religious schools from the program, and if it did, it would "very likely" violate the United States Constitution by discriminating against the schools and their students. The Attorney General is not representing the Department in this case.

B

This suit was brought by three mothers whose children attend Stillwater Christian School in northwestern Montana. Stillwater is a private Christian school that meets the statutory criteria for "qualified education providers." It serves students in prekindergarten through 12th grade, and petitioners chose the school in large part because it "teaches the same Christian values that [they] teach at home." The child of one petitioner has already received scholarships from Big Sky, and the other petitioners' children are eligible for scholarships and planned to apply. While in effect, however, Rule 1 blocked petitioners from using scholarship funds for tuition at Stillwater. To overcome that obstacle, petitioners sued the Department of Revenue in Montana state court. Petitioners claimed that Rule 1 conflicted with the statute that created the scholarship program and could not be justified on the ground that it was compelled by the Montana Constitution's no-aid provision. Petitioners further alleged that the Rule discriminated on the basis of their religious views and the religious nature of the school they had chosen for their children.

The trial court enjoined Rule 1, holding that it was based on a mistake of law. The court explained that the Rule was not required by the no-aid provision, because that provision prohibits only "appropriations" that aid religious schools, "not tax credits."

The injunctive relief freed Big Sky to award scholarships to students regardless of whether they attended a religious or secular school. For the school year beginning in fall 2017, Big Sky received 59 applications and ultimately awarded 44 scholarships of $500 each. The next year, Big Sky received 90 applications and awarded 54 scholarships of $500 each. Several families, most with incomes of $30,000 or less, used the scholarships to send their children to Stillwater Christian.

In December 2018, the Montana Supreme Court reversed the trial court. The Court first addressed the scholarship program unmodified by Rule 1, holding that the program aided religious schools in violation of the no-aid provision of the Montana Constitution. In the Court's view, the no-aid provision "broadly and strictly prohibits aid to sectarian schools." The scholarship program provided such aid by using tax credits to "subsidize tuition payments" at private schools that are "religiously affiliated" or "controlled in whole or in part by churches." In that way, the scholarship program flouted the State Constitution's "guarantee to all Montanans that their government will not use state funds to aid religious schools."

The Montana Supreme Court went on to hold that the violation of the no-aid provision required invalidating the entire scholarship program. The Court explained that the program provided "no mechanism" for preventing aid from flowing to religious schools, and therefore the scholarship program could not "under *any* circumstance" be construed as consistent with the no-aid provision. As a result, the tax credit is no longer available to support scholarships at either religious or secular private schools.

The Montana Supreme Court acknowledged that "an overly-broad" application of the no-aid provision "could implicate free exercise concerns" and that "there may be a case" where "prohibiting the aid would violate the Free Exercise Clause." But, the Court concluded, "this is not one of those cases."

Finally, the Court agreed with petitioners that the Department had exceeded its authority in promulgating Rule 1. The Court explained that the statute creating the scholarship program had broadly defined qualifying schools to include all private schools, including religious ones, and the Department lacked authority to "transform" that definition with an administrative rule. ...

II

A

... Most recently, *Trinity Lutheran* distilled these and other decisions to the same effect into the "unremarkable" conclusion that disqualifying otherwise eligible recipients from a public benefit "solely because of their religious character" imposes "a penalty on the free exercise of religion that triggers the most exacting scrutiny." In *Trinity Lutheran*, Missouri provided grants to help nonprofit organizations pay for playground resurfacing, but a state policy disqualified any organization "owned or controlled by a church, sect, or other religious entity." Because of that policy, an otherwise eligible church-owned preschool was denied a grant to resurface its playground. Missouri's policy discriminated against the Church "simply because of what it is—a church," and so the policy was subject to the "strictest scrutiny," which it failed. We acknowledged that the State had not "criminalized" the way in which the Church worshipped or "told the Church that it cannot subscribe to a certain view of the Gospel." But the State's discriminatory policy was "odious to our Constitution all the same."

Here too Montana's no-aid provision bars religious schools from public benefits solely because of the religious character of the schools. The provision also bars parents who wish to send their children to a religious school from those same benefits, again solely because of the religious character of the school. This is apparent from the plain text. The provision bars aid to any school "controlled in whole or in part by any church, sect, or denomination." The provision's title—"Aid prohibited to sectarian schools"—confirms that the provision singles out schools based on their religious character. And the Montana Supreme Court explained that the provision forbids aid to any school that is "sectarian," "religiously affiliated," or "controlled in whole or in part by churches." The provision plainly excludes schools from government aid solely because of religious status. ...

The Montana Constitution discriminates based on religious status just like the Missouri policy in *Trinity*

Lutheran, which excluded organizations "owned or controlled by a church, sect, or other religious entity." ...

Some Members of the Court, moreover, have questioned whether there is a meaningful distinction between discrimination based on use or conduct and that based on status. We acknowledge the point but need not examine it here. It is enough in this case to conclude that strict scrutiny applies under *Trinity Lutheran* because Montana's no-aid provision discriminates based on religious status.

B

Seeking to avoid *Trinity Lutheran*, the Department contends that this case is instead governed by *Locke v. Davey*, 540 U.S. 712 (2004). ... *Locke* differs from this case in two critical ways. First, *Locke* explained that Washington had "merely chosen not to fund a distinct category of instruction": the "essentially religious endeavor" of training a minister "to lead a congregation." Thus, Davey "was denied a scholarship because of what he proposed *to do*—use the funds to prepare for the ministry." Apart from that narrow restriction, Washington's program allowed scholarships to be used at "pervasively religious schools" that incorporated religious instruction throughout their classes. By contrast, Montana's Constitution does not zero in on any particular "essentially religious" course of instruction at a religious school. Rather, as we have explained, the no-aid provision bars all aid to a religious school "simply because of what it is," putting the school to a choice between being religious or receiving government benefits. At the same time, the provision puts families to a choice between sending their children to a religious school or receiving such benefits.

Second, *Locke* invoked a "historic and substantial" state interest in not funding the training of clergy, explaining that "opposition to ... funding 'to support church leaders' lay at the historic core of the Religion Clauses." But it is clear that there is no "historic and substantial" tradition against aiding such schools comparable to the tradition against state-supported clergy invoked by *Locke*. ...

D

... The Montana Supreme Court asserted that the no -aid provision serves Montana's interest in separating church and State "more fiercely" than the Federal Constitution. But "that interest cannot qualify as compelling" in the face of the infringement of free exercise here. A State's interest "in achieving greater separation of church and State than is already ensured under the Establishment Clause ... is limited by the Free Exercise Clause." ... A State need not subsidize private education. But once a State decides to do so, it cannot disqualify some private schools solely because they are religious.

III

... Because the elimination of the program flowed directly from the Montana Supreme Court's failure to follow the dictates of federal law, it cannot be defended as a neutral policy decision, or as resting on adequate and independent state law grounds. ...

Justice Thomas, with whom Justice Gorsuch joins, concurring.

The Court correctly concludes that Montana's no-aid provision expressly discriminates against religion in violation of the Free Exercise Clause. And it properly provides relief to Montana religious schools and the petitioners who wish to use Montana's scholarship program to send their children to such schools. I write separately to explain how this Court's interpretation of the Establishment Clause continues to hamper free exercise rights. Until we correct course on that interpretation, individuals will continue to face needless obstacles in their attempts to vindicate their religious freedom.

I

A

... Thus, the modern view, which presumes that States must remain both completely separate from and virtually silent on matters of religion to comply with the Establishment Clause, is fundamentally incorrect. Properly understood, the Establishment Clause does not prohibit States from favoring religion. They can legislate as they wish, subject only to the limitations in the State and Federal Constitutions.

B

... But the Court's wayward approach to the Establishment Clause also impacts its free exercise jurisprudence. Specifically, its overly expansive understanding of the former Clause has led to a correspondingly cramped interpretation of the latter.

Under this Court's current approach, state and local governments may rely on the Establishment Clause to justify policies that others wish to challenge as violations of the Free Exercise Clause. Once the government demonstrates that its policy is *required* for compliance with the Constitution, any claim that the policy infringes on free exercise cannot survive. ...

II

... So long as this hostility remains, fostered by our distorted understanding of the Establishment Clause, free exercise rights will continue to suffer. ...

Justice ALITO, concurring.

... As originally adopted, Montana's Constitution prohibited the state and local governments from "ever mak[ing,] directly or indirectly, any appropriation" for "any sectarian purpose" or "to aid in the support of any school ... controlled in whole or in part by any church, sect or denomination whatever." At the time, "it was an open secret that 'sectarian' was code for 'Catholic.'" ... The term was likewise used against Mormons and Jews. ...

Catholic and Jewish schools sprang up because the common schools were not neutral on matters of religion. "Faced with public schools that were culturally Protestant and with curriculum[s] and textbooks that were, consequently, rife with material that Catholics and Jews found offensive, many Catholics and Orthodox Jews created separate schools," and those "who could afford to do so sent their children to" those schools. ...

Thus, the no-aid provision's terms keep it "[t]ethered" to its original "bias," and it is not clear at all that the State "actually confront[ed]" the provision's "tawdry past in reenacting it." ...

Today's public schools are quite different from those envisioned by Horace Mann, but many parents of many different faiths still believe that their local schools inculcate a worldview that is antithetical to what they teach at home. Many have turned to religious schools, at considerable expense, or have undertaken the burden of homeschooling. The tax-credit program adopted by the Montana Legislature but overturned by the Montana Supreme Court provided necessary aid for parents who pay taxes to support the public schools but who disagree with the teaching there. The program helped parents of modest means do what more affluent parents can do: send their children to a school of their choice. The argument that the decision below treats everyone the same is reminiscent of Anatole France's sardonic remark that "'[t]he law, in its majestic equality, forbids the rich as well as the poor to sleep under bridges, to beg in the streets, and to steal bread.'"

Justice GORSUCH, concurring.

... I agree with all the Court says on these scores and join its opinion in full. I write separately only to address an additional point. ... I was not sure about characterizing the State's discrimination in *Trinity Lutheran* as focused only on religious status, and I am even less sure about characterizing the State's discrimination here that way. ...

So whether the Montana Constitution is better described as discriminating against religious status or use makes no difference: It is a violation of the right to free exercise either way, unless the State can show its law serves some compelling and narrowly tailored governmental interest, conditions absent here for reasons the Court thoroughly explains. ...

The right to *be* religious without the right to *do* religious things would hardly amount to a right at all. Effectively, the court told the state legislature and parents of Montana like Ms. Espinoza: You can have school choice, but if anyone dares to choose to send a child to an accredited religious school, the program will be shuttered. That condition on a public benefit discriminates against the free exercise of religion. Calling it discrimination on the basis of religious status or religious activity makes no difference: It is unconstitutional all the same.

Justice GINSBURG, with whom Justice KAGAN joins, dissenting.

... Instead, the Court decides a question that, in my view, this case does not present: "[W]hether excluding religious schools and affected families from [the scholarship] program was consistent with the Federal Constitution." The Court goes on to hold that the Montana Supreme Court's application of the no - aid provision violates the Free Exercise Clause because it "'condition[s] the availability of benefits upon a recipient's willingness to surrender [its] religiously impelled status.'" As I see it, the decision below—which maintained neutrality between sectarian and nonsectarian private schools—did no such thing. ...

A State may distinguish within a benefit program between secular and sectarian schools, or it may decline to fund all private schools. The Court agrees that the First Amendment permits the latter course.

Because that is the path the Montana Supreme Court took in this case, there was no reason for this Court to address the alternative. …

Nearing the end of its opinion, the Court writes: "A State need not subsidize private education. But once a State decides to do so, it cannot disqualify some private schools solely because they are religious." Because Montana's Supreme Court did not make such a decision—its judgment put all private school parents in the same boat—this Court had no occasion to address the matter. On that sole ground, and reaching no other issue, I dissent from the Court's judgment.

Justice BREYER, with whom Justice KAGAN joins as to Part I, dissenting.

… The majority barely acknowledges the play-in-the-joints doctrine here. It holds that the Free Exercise Clause forbids a State to draw any distinction between secular and religious uses of government aid to private schools that is not required by the Establishment Clause. The majority's approach and its conclusion in this case, I fear, risk the kind of entanglement and conflict that the Religion Clauses are intended to prevent. I consequently dissent.

I

…

C

… In my view, the program at issue here is strikingly similar to the program we upheld in *Locke* and importantly different from the program we found unconstitutional in *Trinity Lutheran*. Like the State of Washington in *Locke*, Montana has chosen not to fund (at a distance) "an essentially religious endeavor"—an education designed to "'induce religious faith.'" That kind of program simply cannot be likened to Missouri's decision to exclude a church school from applying for a grant to resurface its playground. …

It is true that Montana's no-aid provision broadly bars state aid to schools based on their religious affiliation. But this case does not involve a claim of status-based discrimination. The schools do not apply or compete for scholarships, they are not parties to this litigation, and no one here purports to represent their interests. We are instead faced with a suit by *parents* who assert that *their* free exercise rights are violated by the application of the no-aid provision to prevent them from *using* taxpayer-supported scholarships to attend the schools of their choosing. In other words, the problem, as in *Locke*, is what petitioners "'propos[e] *to do*—use the funds to'" obtain a religious education. … The majority next contends that there is no "'historic and substantial' tradition against aiding" religious schools "comparable to the tradition against state-supported clergy invoked by *Locke*." But the majority ignores the reasons for the founding era bans that we relied upon in *Locke*. …

I see no meaningful difference between the concerns that Madison and Jefferson raised and the concerns inevitably raised by taxpayer support for scholarships to religious schools. In both instances state funds are sought for those who would "instruc[t] such citizens, as from their circumstances and want of education, cannot otherwise attain such knowledge" in the tenets of religious faith. In both cases, that would compel taxpayers "to support the propagation of opinions" on matters of religion with which they may disagree, by teachers whom they have not chosen. And, in both cases, the allocation of state aid to such purposes threatens to "destroy that moderation and harmony which the forbearance of our laws to intermeddle with Religion, has produced among its several sects." …

If, for 250 years, we have drawn a line at forcing taxpayers to pay the salaries of those who teach their faith from the pulpit, I do not see how we can today require Montana to adopt a different view respecting those who teach it in the classroom.

II

… If making scholarships available to only secular nonpublic schools exerts "coercive" pressure on parents whose faith impels them to enroll their children in religious schools, then how is a State's decision to fund only secular *public* schools any less coercive? Under the majority's reasoning, the parents in both cases are put to a choice between their beliefs and a taxpayer-sponsored education.

Accepting the majority's distinction between public and nonpublic schools does little to address the uncertainty that its holding introduces. … Here, those purposes, along with the examples set by our decisions in *Locke* and *Trinity Lutheran*, lead me to believe that Montana's differential treatment of religious schools is constitutional. …

Justice SOTOMAYOR, dissenting.

… The Montana Supreme Court invalidated the program on state -law grounds, thereby foreclosing the as-applied challenge petitioners raise here. Indeed, nothing required the state court to uphold the program or the state legislature to maintain it. The Court nevertheless reframes the case and appears to ask whether a longstanding Montana constitutional provision is facially invalid under the Free Exercise Clause, even though petitioners disavowed bringing such a claim. But by resolving a constitutional question not presented, the Court fails to heed Article III principles older than the Religion Clause it expounds. ...

Because this decision further "slights both our precedents and our history" and "weakens this country's longstanding commitment to a separation of church and state beneficial to both," I respectfully dissent.

I

B

... Having held that petitioners may not be "exclu[ded] from the scholarship program" that no longer exists, the Court remands to the Montana Supreme Court for "further proceedings not inconsistent with this opinion." But it is hard to tell what this Court wishes the state court to do. There is no program from which petitioners are currently "exclu[ded]," so must the Montana Supreme Court order the State to recreate one? Has this Court just announced its authority to require a state court to order a state legislature to fund religious exercise, overruling centuries of contrary precedent and historical practice? ...

Today's ruling is perverse. Without any need or power to do so, the Court appears to require a State to reinstate a tax- credit program that the Constitution did not demand in the first place. We once recognized that "[w]hile the Free Exercise Clause clearly prohibits the use of state action to deny the rights of free exercise to anyone, it has never meant that a majority could use the machinery of the State to practice its beliefs." Today's Court, by contrast, rejects the Religion Clauses' balanced values in favor of a new theory of free exercise, and it does so only by setting aside well-established judicial constraints.

Notes and Questions

1. *The majority.* What was Chief Justice Roberts's reasoning for the majority in this case? Do you agree with them that the Montana rules violated religious freedom?
2. *The dissents.* What does Justice Sotomayor say in her dissent? Did the Court rule on an issue it did not need to rule on? Why does Justice Ginsburg also say the Court decided a question not necessary to the case?
3. *Justice Breyer.* What is the "play-in-the-joints" concept mentioned by Justice Breyer? What are the joints? What does Justice Breyer say about coercion and the Establishment Clause?
4. *Status vs. use.* What is the distinction between religious status and religious use, a point that Gorsuch makes here and in *Trinity Lutheran,* as well. Why does he think that difference is significant? Do you think it is?

5. Any Limits on Religious Funding?

At this point, James Madison's warning in his *Memorial and Remonstrance* that "not one penny" of taxpayer funds should go to religious education is no longer part of the calculation the Court makes in school funding cases. *Espinoza* deconstructed the concept to a great degree, but it still left open the possibility that the Establishment Clause would impose some limits. The Court next took the following case, which sets the stage for the possibility that there are no meaningful limits on religious school funding.

The case is *Carson as Next Friend of O.C. v. Makin*, 141 S. Ct. 2883 (2021). The petitioners are parents of religious school students who lost their case in the First Circuit. On their cert. petition, the question presented was:

> Does a state violate the Religion Clauses or Equal Protection Clause of the United States Constitution by prohibiting students participating in an otherwise generally available student-aid program from choosing to use their aid to attend schools that provide religious, or "sectarian," instruction?

The First Circuit upheld the state's school program, in a panel opinion joined by retired Justice David Souter. The parents appealed. You can read the oral argument on the case's website, https://www.oyez.org/cases/2021/20-1088. Are all the Justices' votes predictable from the questions they asked at the oral argument? Did any questions surprise you? Did any Justice sound likely to vote with the schools instead of the parents? Would you expect the Justices to disagree with Justice Souter?

The parents won this case. Is this the result you predicted? Which opinion do you find most persuasive? And which is the least? Does this case give us a new Establishment Clause analysis? What is left of the Establishment Clause?

Carson v. Makin

SUPREME COURT OF THE UNITED STATES, 2022

596 U.S. ___, 142 S.Ct. 1987

ROBERTS, C. J., delivered the opinion of the Court, in which THOMAS, ALITO, GORSUCH, KAVANAUGH, and BARRETT, JJ., joined. BREYER, J., filed a dissenting opinion, in which KAGAN, J., joined, and in which SOTOMAYOR, J., joined as to all but Part I–B. SOTOMAYOR, J., filed a dissenting opinion.

Maine has enacted a program of tuition assistance for parents who live in school districts that do not operate a secondary school of their own. Under the program, parents designate the secondary school they would like their child to attend—public or private—and the school district transmits payments to that school to help defray the costs of tuition. Most private schools are eligible to receive the payments, so long as they are "nonsectarian." The question presented is whether this restriction violates the Free Exercise Clause of the First Amendment.

I

A

Maine's Constitution provides that the State's legislature shall "require ... towns to support public schools ... [to] provide for the support and maintenance of public schools." ... Maine is the most rural State in the Union, and for many school districts the realities of remote geography and low population density make those commands difficult to heed. Indeed, of Maine's 260 school administrative units (SAUs), fewer than half operate a public secondary school of their own.

Maine has sought to deal with this problem in part by creating a program of tuition assistance for families that reside in such areas. ... Parents who wish to take advantage of this benefit first select the school they wish their child to attend. *Ibid.* If they select a private school that has been "approved" by the Maine Department of Education, the parents' SAU "shall pay the tuition" at the chosen school up to a specified maximum rate.

To be "approved" to receive these payments, a private school must meet certain basic requirements under Maine's compulsory education law. The school must either be "[c]urrently accredited by a New England association of schools and colleges" or separately "approv[ed] for attendance purposes" by the Department. Schools seeking approval from the Department must meet specified curricular requirements, such as using English as the language of instruction, offering a course in "Maine history, including the Constitution of Maine ... and Maine's cultural and ethnic heritage," and maintaining a student-teacher ratio of not more than 30 to 1.

The program imposes no geographic limitation: Parents may direct tuition payments to schools inside or outside the State, or even in foreign countries. In schools that qualify for the program because they are accredited, teachers need not be certified by the State, and Maine's curricular requirements do not apply, Single-sex schools are eligible. ...

Prior to 1981, parents could also direct the tuition assistance payments to religious schools. Indeed, in the 1979–1980 school year, over 200 Maine students opted to attend such schools through the tuition assistance program. In 1981, however, Maine imposed a new requirement that any school receiving tuition assistance payments must be "a nonsectarian school in accordance with the First Amendment of the United States Constitution. That provision was enacted in response to an opinion by the Maine attorney general taking the position that public funding of private religious schools violated the Establishment Clause of the First Amendment. We subsequently held, however, that a benefit program under which private citizens "direct government aid to religious schools wholly as a result of their own genuine and independent private choice" does not offend the Establishment Clause. *Zelman*. Following our decision in *Zelman,* the Maine Legislature considered a proposed bill to repeal the "nonsectarian" requirement, but rejected it. ...

B

... Petitioners David and Amy Carson reside in Glenburn, Maine. When this litigation commenced, the Carsons' daughter attended high school at Bangor Christian Schools (BCS), which was founded in 1970 as a ministry of Bangor Baptist Church. The Carsons sent their daughter to BCS because of the school's high academic standards and because the school's Christian worldview aligns with their sincerely held religious beliefs. Given that BCS is a "sectarian" school that cannot qualify for tuition assistance payments under Maine's program, the Carsons paid the tuition for their daughter to attend BCS themselves.

Petitioners Troy and Angela Nelson live in Palermo, Maine. When this litigation commenced, the Nelsons' daughter attended high school at Erskine Academy, a secular private school, and their son attended middle school at Temple Academy, a "sectarian" school affiliated with Centerpoint Community Church. The Nelsons sent their son to Temple Academy because they believed it offered him a high-quality education that aligned with their sincerely held religious beliefs. While they wished to send their daughter to Temple Academy too, they could not afford to pay the cost of the Academy's tuition for both of their children.

[Neither BCS nor Temple] is eligible to receive tuition payments under Maine's tuition assistance program. ...

II

A

The Free Exercise Clause of the First Amendment protects against "indirect coercion or penalties on the free exercise of religion, not just outright prohibitions." ...

We have recently applied these principles in the context of two state efforts to withhold otherwise available public benefits from religious organizations. ...

We deemed it "unremarkable in light of our prior decisions" to conclude that the Free Exercise Clause did not permit Missouri to "expressly discriminate[ ] against otherwise eligible recipients by disqualifying them from a public benefit solely because of their religious character." *Trinity Lutheran.* While it was true that Trinity Lutheran remained "free to continue operating as a church," it could enjoy that freedom only "at the cost of automatic and absolute exclusion from the benefits of a public program for which the Center [was] otherwise fully qualified." Such discrimination, we said, was "odious to our Constitution" and could not stand.

Two Terms ago, in *Espinoza*, we reached the same conclusion as to a Montana program that provided tax credits to donors who sponsored scholarships for private school tuition. ...

B

The "unremarkable" principles applied in *Trinity Lutheran* and *Espinoza* suffice to resolve this case. ...

Our recent decision in *Espinoza* applied these basic principles in the context of religious education that we consider today. ... While the wording of the Montana and Maine provisions is different, their effect is the same: to "disqualify some private schools" from funding "solely because they are religious." A law that operates in that manner, we held in *Espinoza*, must be subjected to "the strictest scrutiny."

To satisfy strict scrutiny, government action "must advance 'interests of the highest order' and must be narrowly tailored in pursuit of those interests." *Lukumi Babalu Aye*. "A law that targets religious conduct for distinctive treatment ... will survive strict scrutiny only in rare cases."

This is not one of them. As noted, a neutral benefit program in which public funds flow to religious organizations through the independent choices of private benefit recipients does not offend the Establishment Clause. *Zelman*. Maine's decision to continue excluding religious schools from its tuition assistance program after *Zelman* thus promotes stricter separation of church and state than the Federal Constitution requires.

But as we explained in both *Trinity Lutheran* and *Espinoza*, such an "interest in separating church and state 'more fiercely' than the Federal Constitution ... 'cannot qualify as compelling' in the face of the infringement of free exercise." Justice BREYER stresses the importance of "government neutrality" when it comes to religious matters, but there is nothing neutral about Maine's program. The State pays tuition for certain students at private schools—so long as the schools are not religious. That is discrimination against religion. A State's antiestablishment interest does not justify enactments that exclude some members of the community from an otherwise generally available public benefit because of their religious exercise.*

III

...

A

The First Circuit held that the "nonsectarian" requirement was constitutional because the benefit was properly viewed not as tuition assistance payments to be used at approved private schools, but instead as funding for the "rough equivalent of the public school education that Maine may permissibly require to be secular." ...

... The benefit is *tuition* at a public *or* private school, selected by the parent, with no suggestion that the "private school" must somehow provide a "public" education.

... the curriculum taught at participating private schools need not even resemble that taught in the Maine public schools. For example, Maine public schools must abide by certain "parameters for essential instruction in English language arts; mathematics; science and technology; social studies; career and education development; visual and performing arts; health, physical education and wellness; and world languages." But NEASC-accredited private schools are exempt from these requirements, and instead subject only to general "standards and indicators" governing the implementation of their own chosen curriculum.

Private schools approved by the Department (rather than accredited by NEASC) are likewise exempt from many of the State's curricular requirements, so long as fewer than 60% of their students receive tuition assistance from the State. For instance, such schools need not abide by Maine's "comprehensive, statewide system of learning results," including the "parameters for essential instruction" referenced above, and they need not administer the annual state assessments in English language arts, mathematics, and science.

There are other distinctions, too. Participating schools need not hire state-certified teachers. And the schools can be single-sex. In short, it is simply not the case that these schools, to be eligible for state funds, must offer an education that is equivalent—roughly or otherwise—to that available in the Maine public schools. ...

Indeed, were we to accept Maine's argument, our decision in *Espinoza* would be rendered essentially meaningless. By Maine's logic, Montana could have obtained the same result that we held violated the First Amendment simply by redefining its tax credit for sponsors of generally available scholarships as limited to "tuition payments for the rough equivalent of a Montana public education"—meaning a secular education. But our holding in *Espinoza* turned on the substance of free exercise protections, not on the presence or absence of magic words. That holding applies fully whether the prohibited discrimination is in an express provision like or in a party's reconceptualization of the public benefit. ...

The dissents are wrong to say that under our decision today Maine "*must*" fund religious education. Maine chose to allow some parents to direct state tuition payments to private schools; that decision was not "forced upon" it. The State retains a number of options: it could expand the reach of its public school system, increase the availability of transportation, provide some combination of tutoring, remote learning, and partial attendance, or even operate boarding schools of its own. As we held in *Espinoza*, a "State need not subsidize private education. But once a State decides to do so, it cannot disqualify some private schools solely because they are religious."

B

The Court of Appeals also attempted to distinguish this case from *Trinity Lutheran* and *Espinoza* on the ground that the funding restrictions in those cases were "solely status-based religious discrimination," while the challenged provision here "imposes a use-based restriction." Justice BREYER makes the same argument. ...

... In *Trinity Lutheran* and *Espinoza*, we held that the Free Exercise Clause forbids discrimination on the basis of religious status. But those decisions never suggested that use-based discrimination is any less offensive to the Free Exercise Clause. This case illustrates why. "[E]ducating young people in their faith, inculcating its teachings, and training them to live their faith are responsibilities that lie at the very core of the mission of a private religious school." *Morrissey-Berru; Hosanna-Tabor.*

Any attempt to give effect to such a distinction by scrutinizing whether and how a religious school pursues its educational mission would also raise serious concerns about state entanglement with religion and denominational favoritism. Indeed, Maine concedes that the Department barely engages in any such scrutiny when enforcing the "nonsectarian" requirement. That suggests that any status-use distinction lacks a meaningful application not only in theory, but in practice as well. In short, the prohibition on status-based discrimination under the Free Exercise Clause is not a permission to engage in use-based discrimination. ...

Our opinions in *Trinity Lutheran* and *Espinoza*, however, have already explained why *Locke* can be of no help to Maine here. Both precedents emphasized, as did *Locke* itself, that the funding in *Locke* was intended to be used "to prepare for the ministry."

As we explained at length in *Espinoza*, "it is clear that there is no 'historic and substantial' tradition against aiding [private religious] schools comparable to the tradition against state-supported clergy invoked by *Locke*. ...

* * *

Maine's "nonsectarian" requirement for its otherwise generally available tuition assistance payments violates the Free Exercise Clause of the First Amendment. Regardless of how the benefit and restriction are described, the program operates to identify and exclude otherwise eligible schools on the basis of their religious exercise. The judgment of the Court of Appeals is reversed, and the case is remanded for further proceedings consistent with this opinion.

It is so ordered.

Justice BREYER, with whom Justice KAGAN joins, and with whom Justice SOTOMAYOR joins except as to Part I–B, dissenting.

The First Amendment begins by forbidding the government from "mak[ing] [any] law respecting an establishment of religion." It next forbids them to make any law "prohibiting the free exercise thereof." The Court today pays almost no attention to the words in the first Clause while giving almost exclusive attention to the words in the second. The majority also fails to recognize the "'play in the joints'" between the two Clauses. That "play" gives States some degree of legislative leeway. It sometimes allows a State to further antiestablishment interests by withholding aid from religious institutions without violating the Constitution's protections for the free exercise of religion. In my view, Maine's nonsectarian requirement falls squarely within the scope of that constitutional leeway. I respectfully dissent.

I

A

... The Religion Clauses thus created a compromise in the form of religious freedom. They aspired to create a "benevolent neutrality"—one which would "permit religious exercise to exist without sponsorship and without interference." "[T]he basic purpose of these provisions" was "to insure that no religion be sponsored or favored, none commanded, and none inhibited." This religious freedom in effect meant that people "were entitled to worship God in their own way and to teach their children" in that way. We have historically interpreted the Religion Clauses with these basic principles in mind.

And in applying these Clauses, we have often said that "there is room for play in the joints" between them. ... This includes choosing not to fund certain religious activity where States have strong, establishment-related reasons for not doing so. And, States have freedom to make this choice even when the Establishment Clause does not itself prohibit the State from funding that activity. ...

B

I have previously discussed my views of the relationship between the Religion Clauses and how I believe these Clauses should be interpreted to advance their goal of avoiding religious strife. ...

This potential for religious strife is still with us. We are today a Nation with well over 100 different religious groups, from Free Will Baptist to African Methodist, Buddhist to Humanist. See Pew Research Center, America's Changing Religious Landscape 21 (May 12, 2015). ... As Thomas Jefferson, one of the leading drafters and proponents of those Clauses, wrote, "'to compel a man to furnish contributions of money for the propagation of opinions which he disbelieves, is sinful and tyrannical.'" And as James Madison, another drafter and proponent, said, compelled taxpayer sponsorship of religion "is itself a signal of persecution," which "will destroy that moderation and harmony which the forbearance of our laws to intermeddle with Religion, has produced amongst its several sects." ...

I have also previously explained why I believe that a "rigid, bright-line" approach to the Religion Clauses—an approach without any leeway or "play in the joints"—will too often work against the Clauses' underlying purposes. Not all state-funded programs that have religious restrictions carry the same risk of creating social division and conflict. In my view, that risk can best be understood by considering the particular benefit at issue, along with the reasons for the particular religious restriction at issue. ...

II

... We have previously found, as the majority points out, that "a neutral benefit program in which public funds flow to religious organizations through the independent choices of private benefit recipients does not offend the Establishment Clause." *Zelman*. We have thus concluded that a State *may*, consistent with the Establishment Clause, provide funding to religious schools through a general public funding program if the "government aid ... reach[es] religious institutions only by way of the deliberate choices of ... individual [aid] recipients."

But the key word is "may." We have never previously held what the Court holds today, namely, that a State *must* (not *may*) use state funds to pay for religious education as part of a tuition program designed to ensure the provision of free statewide public school education.

What happens once "may" becomes "must"? Does that transformation mean that a school district that pays for public schools must pay equivalent funds to parents who wish to send their children to religious schools? Does it mean that school districts that give vouchers for use at charter schools must pay equivalent funds to parents who wish to give their children a religious education? What other social benefits are there the State's provision of which means—under the majority's interpretation of the Free Exercise Clause—that the State must pay parents for the religious equivalent of the secular benefit provided? The concept of "play in the joints" means that courts need not, and should not, answer with "must" these questions that can more appropriately be answered with "may."

The majority also asserts that "[t]he 'unremarkable' principles applied in *Trinity Lutheran* and *Espinoza* suffice to resolve this case." Not so. The state-funded program at issue in *Trinity Lutheran* provided payment for resurfacing school playgrounds to make them safer for children. Any Establishment Clause concerns arising from providing money to religious schools for the creation of safer play yards are readily distinguishable from those raised by providing money to religious schools through the program at issue here—a tuition program designed to ensure that all children receive their constitutionally guaranteed right to a free public education. After all, cities and States normally pay for police forces, fire protection, paved streets, municipal transport, and hosts of other services that benefit churches as well as secular organizations. But paying the salary of a religious teacher as part of a public school tuition program is a different matter.

... Maine chooses not to fund only those schools that "'promot[e] the faith or belief system with which [the schools are] associated and/or presen[t] the [academic] material taught through the lens of this faith'"—*i.e.*, schools that will use public money for religious purposes. Maine thus excludes schools from its tuition program not because of the schools' religious character but because the schools will use the funds to teach and promote religious ideals.

... Here, again, Maine denies tuition money to schools not because of their religious affiliation, but because they will use state funds to promote religious views.

These distinctions are important. The very point of the Establishment Clause is to prevent the government from sponsoring religious activity itself, thereby favoring one religion over another or favoring religion over nonreligion. *Engel.* State funding of religious activity risks the very social conflict based upon religion that the Religion Clauses were designed to prevent. And, unlike the circumstances present in *Trinity Lutheran* and *Espinoza*, it is religious activity, not religious labels, that lies at the heart of this case.

III

A

... By contrast, public schools, including those in Maine, seek first and foremost to provide a primarily civic education. ...

Maine legislators who endorsed the State's nonsectarian requirement recognized these differences between public and religious education. They did not want Maine taxpayers to finance, through a tuition program designed to ensure the provision of free public education, schools that would use state money for teaching religious practices. ... Maine's nonsectarian requirement, they believed, furthered the State's antiestablishment interests in not promoting religion in its public school system; the requirement prevented public funds—funds allocated to ensure that all children receive their constitutional right to a free public education—from being given to schools that would use the funds to promote religion.

In the majority's view, the fact that private individuals, not Maine itself, choose to spend the State's money on religious education saves Maine's program from Establishment Clause condemnation. But that fact, as I have said, simply *permits* Maine to route funds to religious schools. It does not *require* Maine to spend its money in that way. That is because, as explained above, this Court has long followed a legal doctrine that gives States flexibility to navigate the tension between the two Religion Clauses. ...

Nothing in our Free Exercise Clause cases *compels* Maine to give tuition aid to private schools that will use the funds to provide a religious education. As explained above, this Court's decisions in *Trinity Lutheran* and *Espinoza* prohibit States from denying aid to religious schools solely because of a school's religious *status*—that is, its affiliation with or control by a religious organization. But we have never said that the Free Exercise Clause prohibits States from withholding funds because of the religious *use* to which the money will be put. To the contrary, we upheld in *Locke* a State's decision to deny public funding to a recipient "because of what he proposed *to do*" with the money, when what he proposed to do was to "use the funds to prepare for the ministry." Maine does not refuse to pay tuition at private schools because of religious status or affiliation. The State only denies funding to schools that will use the money to promote religious beliefs through a religiously integrated education—an education that, in Maine's view, is not a replacement for a civic-focused public education. See This makes Maine's decision to withhold public funds more akin to the state decision that we upheld in *Locke* and unlike the withholdings that we invalidated in *Trinity Lutheran* and *Espinoza*. ...

... Maine endeavors to provide children the religiously neutral education required in public school systems. And that, in significant part, reflects the State's antiestablishment interests in avoiding spending public money to support what is essentially religious activity. The Religion Clauses give Maine the ability, and flexibility, to make this choice.

B

In my view, Maine's nonsectarian requirement is also constitutional because it supports, rather than undermines, the Religion Clauses' goal of avoiding religious strife. ...

Maine legislators who endorsed the State's nonsectarian requirement understood this potential for social conflict. ... Legislators also recognized that these private schools make religiously based enrollment and hiring decisions. Bangor Christian and Temple Academy, for example, have admissions policies that allow them to deny enrollment to students based on gender, gender-identity, sexual orientation, and religion, and both schools require their teachers to be Born Again Christians. Legislators did not want Maine taxpayers to pay for these religiously based practices—practices not universally endorsed by all citizens of the State—for fear that doing so would cause a significant number of Maine citizens discomfort or displeasure. The nonsectarian requirement helped avoid this conflict—the precise kind of social conflict that the Religion Clauses themselves sought to avoid. ...

This is a situation ripe for conflict, as it forces Maine into the position of evaluating the adequacy or appropriateness of the schools' religiously inspired curriculum. Maine does not want this role. As one legislator explained, one of the reasons for the nonsectarian requirement was that "[g]overnment officials cannot, and should not, review the religious teachings of religious schools." Another legislator cautioned that the State would be unable to "reconcile" the curriculum of "private religious schools who teach religion in the classroom" with Maine "standards ... that do not include any sort of religion in them."

Nor do the schools want Maine in this role. Bangor Christian asserted that it would only consider accepting public funds if it "did not have to make any changes in how it operates." Temple Academy similarly stated that it would only accept state money if it had "in writing that the school would not have to alter its admissions standards, hiring standards, or curriculum." The nonsectarian requirement ensures that Maine is not pitted against private religious schools in these battles over curriculum or operations, thereby avoiding the social strife resulting from this state-versus-religion confrontation. By invalidating the nonsectarian requirement, the majority today subjects the State, the schools, and the people of Maine to social conflict of a kind that they, and the Religion Clauses, sought to prevent.

... There is no meaningful difference between a State's payment of the salary of a religious minister and the salary of someone who will teach the practice of religion to a person's children. At bottom, there is almost no area "as central to religious belief as the shaping, through primary education, of the next generation's minds and spirits. The Establishment Clause was intended to keep the State out of this area.

* * *

Maine wishes to provide children within the State with a secular, public education. This wish embodies, in significant part, the constitutional need to avoid spending public money to support what is essentially the teaching and practice of religion. That need is reinforced by the fact that we are today a Nation of more than 330 million people who ascribe to over 100 different religions. In that context, state neutrality with respect to religion is particularly important. The Religion Clauses give Maine the right to honor that neutrality by choosing not to fund religious schools as part of its public school tuition program. I believe the majority is wrong to hold the contrary. And with respect, I dissent.

Justice SOTOMAYOR, dissenting.

This Court continues to dismantle the wall of separation between church and state that the Framers fought to build. Justice BREYER explains why the Court's analysis falters on its own terms, and I join all but Part I–B of his dissent. I write separately to add three points.

First, this Court should not have started down this path five years ago. *Trinity.* ...

As Justice BREYER explains, this status-use distinction readily distinguishes this case from *Trinity Lutheran* and *Espinoza*. I warned in *Trinity Lutheran*, however, that the Court's analysis could "be manipulated to call for a similar fate for lines drawn on the basis of religious use." That fear has come to fruition: The Court now holds for the first time that "any status-use distinction" is immaterial in both "theory" and "practice." It reaches that conclusion by embracing arguments from prior separate writings and ignoring decades of precedent affording governments flexibility in navigating the tension between the Religion Clauses. As a result, in just a few years, the Court has upended constitutional doctrine, shifting from a rule that permits States to decline to fund religious organizations to one that requires States in many circumstances to subsidize religious indoctrination with taxpayer dollars.

Second, the consequences of the Court's rapid transformation of the Religion Clauses must not be understated. From a doctrinal perspective, the Court's failure to apply the play-in-the-joints principle here, leaves one to wonder what, if anything, is left of it. The Court's increasingly expansive view of the Free Exercise Clause risks swallowing the space between the Religion Clauses that once "permit[ted] religious exercise to exist without sponsorship and without interference."

From a practical perspective, today's decision directs the State of Maine (and, by extension, its taxpaying citizens) to subsidize institutions that undisputedly engage in religious instruction. In addition, while purporting to protect against discrimination of one kind, the Court requires Maine to fund what many of its citizens believe to be discrimination of other kinds. See (BREYER, J., dissenting) (summarizing Bangor Christian Schools' and Temple Academy's policies denying enrollment to students based on gender identity, sexual orientation, and religion). The upshot is that Maine must choose between giving subsidies to its residents or refraining from financing religious teaching and practices.

Finally, the Court's decision is especially perverse because the benefit at issue is the public education to which all of Maine's children are entitled under the State Constitution. ...

The Court's analysis does leave some options open to Maine. For example, under state law, school administrative units (SAUs) that cannot feasibly operate their own schools may contract directly with a public school in another SAU, or with an approved private school, to educate their students. I do not understand today's decision to mandate that SAUs contract directly with schools that teach religion, which would go beyond *Zelman's* private-choice doctrine and blatantly violate the Establishment Clause. Nonetheless, it is irrational for this Court to hold that the Free Exercise Clause bars Maine from giving money to parents to fund the only type of education the State may provide consistent with the Establishment Clause: a religiously neutral one. Nothing in the Constitution requires today's result.

* * *

What a difference five years makes. In 2017, I feared that the Court was "lead[ing] us ... to a place where separation of church and state is a constitutional slogan, not a constitutional commitment." *Trinity Lutheran* (dissenting opinion). Today, the Court leads us to a place where separation of church and state becomes a constitutional violation. If a State cannot offer subsidies to its citizens without being required to fund religious exercise, any State that values its historic antiestablishment interests more than this Court does will have to curtail the support it offers to its citizens. With growing concern for where this Court will lead us next, I respectfully dissent.

Notes and Questions

1. *1981.* Why did Maine change its law in 1981?
2. *"Unremarkable."* Why does Chief Justice Roberts say the *Trinity* and *Espinoza* principles are unremarkable? Does the dissent agree? What do you conclude about whether those two cases are remarkable or unremarkable? Did they change the Court's teaching about the religion clauses or not?
3. *Neutrality.* What do the Justices say about the need for a law to be neutral? Is the Maine law as written neutral? Is it neutral following Roberts's interpretation of it?
4. *Status or Use.* You saw in *Trinity Lutheran* and *Espinoza* that the Court's majority said it violated free exercise for the state to discriminate against religious status. Justice Gorsuch always insisted that religious use should also be protected against discrimination. Does Chief Justice Roberts adopt Gorsuch's analysis here? Why do the dissenters say that the earlier cases held that the government is allowed to discriminate against religious use, and that Maine should be allowed to here?
5. *Separation.* Does the Court still support the idea that the First Amendment protects the separation of church and state? What does the Court say free exercise protects? What does the Court say establishment prohibits? Do you agree with Justice Sotomayor that "the Court leads us to a place where separation of church and state becomes a constitutional violation"?
6. *Discrimination allowed.* What do you think of the dissent's argument that the majority allows government funds to go to schools that discriminate on the basis of sexual orientation, gender, and religion, and to schools that insist a teacher must be a Born Again Christian?
7. *The play in the joints.* What is the play in the joints between the Religion Clauses that Justice Breyer defends? Do you agree the majority does not support a reading of the clauses that allows for such play?

8. *Locke v. Davey.* Why does Justice Breyer think *Locke*, the clergy funding case, requires a victory for the schools in this case? Why does Chief Justice Roberts disagree with him?
9. *Justice Sotomayor.* Why does Justice Sotomayor refuse to join Part I–B of Breyer's opinion? Why did she write a separate dissent?
10. *The Children.* Do you agree with Professor Hamilton that children's civil rights are ignored in this decision because "the Court's thumb rests heavily on the parents' imposition of religion and not on the distinct rights and needs of the students"? How could the Court have protected children's civil rights? See Marci Hamilton, The Supreme Court Further Dismantles the Establishment Clause, Empowers Religious Parents to Obtain Taxpayer Funds for Sectarian Schools, and Ignores the Rights of the Children in *Carson v. Makin,* https://verdict.justia.com/2022/06/22/the-supreme-court-further-dismantles-the-establishment-clause-empowers-religious-parents-to-obtain-taxpayer-funds-for-sectarian-schools-and-ignores-the-rights-of-the-children-in-carson-v-makin.
11. *The Future.* What can Maine do now with its schools to obey the majority's conclusions?

Congratulations on Finishing Your Class!

Now you've made it through this chapter, which is your most favorite opinion and which would you like to see overruled? What do you think the Free Exercise Clause should protect? What do you think the Establishment Clause should prohibit? How does religious freedom fit with the other constitutional values that you studied in the rest of this book?

Credits

Fig. 10.1: Lawrence Hurley & Andrew Chung, "U.S. Supreme Court's 'Shadow Docket' in Action," https://www.reuters.com/legal/government/us-supreme-courts-shadow-docket-favored-religion-trump-2021-07-28. Copyright © 2021 by Reuters.
Fig. 10.2: "Photograph of J. Kennedy in prayer circle (Oct. 16, 2015), from 'Kennedy v. Bremerton School District'," https://www.supremecourt.gov/opinions/21pdf/21-418_i425.pdf, pp. 9, 2015.
Fig. 10.3: "Photograph of J. Kennedy standing in group of kneeling players, from 'Kennedy v. Bremerton School District'," https://www.supremecourt.gov/opinions/21pdf/21-418_i425.pdf, pp. 5, 2015.
Fig. 10.4: "Photograph of J. Kennedy in prayer circle (Oct. 26, 2015), from 'Kennedy v. Bremerton School District'," https://www.supremecourt.gov/opinions/21pdf/21-418_i425.pdf, pp. 10, 2015.
Fig. 10.5: Source: App. 887, Court Appendix.
Fig. 10.6: Source: Appendices to opinion of Blackumn, J., 492 U.S.
Fig. 10.7: Source: https://en.wikipedia.org/wiki/File:TenCommandmentsAustinStateCapitol.jpg.

www.ingramcontent.com/pod-product-compliance
Lightning Source LLC
LaVergne TN
LVHW080725110826
845252LV00062B/1220
* 9 7 8 1 7 9 3 5 5 4 7 3 4 *